THIRD EDITION

Teaching Sport Concepts and Skills

A Tactical Games Approach for Ages 7 to 18

Stephen A. Mitchell

Judith L. Oslin

Linda L. Griffin

Human Kinetics

Library of Congress Cataloging-in-Publication Data

Mitchell, Stephen A., 1959-
  Teaching sport concepts and skills : a tactical games approach for ages 7 to 18 / Stephen A. Mitchell, Judith L. Oslin, Linda L. Griffin. -- Third edition.
       pages cm
  Includes bibliographical references.
  1.Sports--Study and teaching. 2.Coaching (Athletics) I. Oslin, Judith L., 1950- II. Griffin, Linda L., 1954- III. Title.
  GV361.M65 2013
  796.07--dc23

                    2012031795

ISBN-10: 1-4504-1122-3 (print)
ISBN-13: 978-1-4504-1122-6 (print)

This book is a revised edition of the following books published by Human Kinetics, Inc.: *Teaching Sport Concepts and Skills, Second Edition,* published in 2005, and *Sport Foundations for Elementary Physical Education,* published in 2003.

The web addresses cited in this text were current as of November 2012, unless otherwise noted.

Acquisitions Editor: Scott Wikgren; **Developmental Editor:** Ragen E. Sanner; **Assistant Editor:** Anne Rumery; **Copyeditor:** Patsy Fortney; **Permissions Manager:** Dalene Reeder; **Graphic Designer:** Joe Buck; **Graphic Artist:** Tara Welsch; **Cover Designer:** Keith Blomberg; **DVD Face Designer:** Susan Rothermel Allen; **Photograph (cover):** © Human Kinetics; **Photographs (interior):** Photo on page 169 © Rob/fotolia.com; photos on pages 312, 326, 348 © PhotoDisc; photos on pages 364, 365, 367, 368, 369, 372, 375 © Tom McGrew/Hot Shots; all others © Human Kinetics, unless otherwise noted; **Art Manager:** Kelly Hendren; **Associate Art Manager:** Alan L. Wilborn; **Illustrations:** © Human Kinetics; **Printer:** United Graphics

The contents of this DVD are licensed for educational public performance for viewing by a traditional (live) audience, via closed circuit television, or via computerized local area networks within a single building or geographically unified campus. To request a license to broadcast these contents to a wider audience—for example, throughout a school district or state, or on a television station—please contact your sales representative (www.HumanKinetics.com/SalesRepresentatives).

Printed in the United States of America   10 9 8 7 6

The paper in this book is certified under a sustainable forestry program.

Human Kinetics
Website: www.HumanKinetics.com

United States: Human Kinetics
P.O. Box 5076
Champaign, IL 61825-5076
800-747-4457
e-mail: info@hkusa.com

Canada: Human Kinetics
475 Devonshire Road, Unit 100
Windsor, ON N8Y 2L5
800-465-7301 (in Canada only)
e-mail: info@hkcanada.com

Europe: Human Kinetics
107 Bradford Road
Stanningley
Leeds LS28 6AT, United Kingdom
+44 (0)113 255 5665
e-mail: hk@hkeurope.com

For information about Human Kinetics' coverage in other areas of the world,
please visit our website: www.HumanKinetics.com

To Katie and Matt, who both make me so proud

—Stephen A. Mitchell

To Connie for her unwavering love and support

—Judith L. Oslin

To the WPG, which includes family and neighborhood friends and their appreciation for playing the game

—Linda L. Griffin

Contents

Introduction   ix | Acknowledgments   xi

Part I   Tactical Games Teaching **1**

Chapter 1   **Tactical Games Explanation and Review**   **3**

Rationale for a Tactical Approach 4
Game Frameworks 5
Game Performance. 6
Levels of Tactical Complexity 6
Teaching Tactical Awareness and Skill Acquisition. 8
Implementing a Tactical Games Approach Using This Book 10
Summary. 10

Chapter 2   **Principles of Games Teaching and Learning**   **13**

Transfer of Tactical Knowledge in Games. 14
Implications for Curriculum Development 15
Teaching During Game Play 16
Summary. 18

Chapter 3   **Preparing Students for a Tactical Games Approach**   **19**

Training Students to Play Small-Sided Games 20
Teaching Appropriate Sport Behavior 21
Teaching Rules and Routines 22
Summary. 23

Chapter 4   **Getting Started With Tactical Games Teaching**   **25**

Conceptual Framework for Planning Tactical Teaching 25
Putting the Planning Framework Into Action 29
The Teacher and the Change Process 30
Implementing Practices 32
Summary. 35

Chapter 5   **Tactical Games Curriculum Model**   **37**

Assumptions Underpinning a Tactical Games Curriculum 38
Conceptual Framework. 38
Model-Based Instruction 39
Summary. 42

Chapter 6   **Assessing Outcomes**   **43**

Assessment Beliefs 43
Assessment Strategies 45
Assessing Learning Outcomes 47
Summary. 61

Part II — Lesson Plans for a Tactical Games Approach at the Elementary Level: Building Sport Foundations 63

Chapter 7 — Invasion Games at the Elementary Level — 65

Elementary Invasion Games Tactics 65
Levels of Elementary Invasion Game Complexity 66
Modifications for Elementary Invasion Games 67
Progressions for Teaching Elementary Invasion Games 69
Scope and Sequence 72
Level I 73
Level II 84
Level III 95
Teaching Cues for Invasion Game Skills 103
Summary 103

Chapter 8 — Net and Wall Games at the Elementary Level — 105

Elementary Net Games Tactics and Levels of Game Complexity 106
Modifications for Elementary Net and Wall Games 106
Progressions for Teaching Elementary Net and Wall Games 108
Level I 108
Level II 117
Level III 122
Summary 138

Chapter 9 — Striking and Fielding Games at the Elementary Level — 139

Elementary Striking and Fielding Games Tactics 140
Levels of Elementary Striking and Fielding Game Complexity 140
Modifications for Elementary Striking and Fielding Games 140
Progressions for Teaching Elementary Striking and Fielding Games 146
Level I 146
Level II 154
Level III 168
Level IV 180
Summary 196

Chapter 10 — Target Games at the Elementary Level — 197

Elementary Target Games Tactics and Levels of Game Complexity 198
Modifications for Elementary Target Games 198
Progressions for Teaching Elementary Target Games 199
Bowling as an Exemplar for Teaching Target Games 201
Target Games Lessons 201
Level I 202
Level II 210
Level III 215
Summary 219

Part III Lesson Plans for a Tactical Games Approach at the
Secondary Level: Developing Sport Performance. 221

Chapter 11 Soccer   **223**

Level I. 224
Level II. 235
Level III 243
Level IV 251
Level V. 263
Summary. 274

Chapter 12 Basketball   **275**

Level I. 276
Level II. 286
Level III 293
Level IV 301
Summary. 309

Chapter 13 Lacrosse   **311**

Level I. 312
Level II. 326
Level III 338
Level IV 348
Summary. 357

Chapter 14 Rugby   **359**

Level I. 361
Level II. 368
Level III 374
Summary. 380

Chapter 15 Flag Football   **381**

Level I. 382
Level II. 390
Summary. 399

Chapter 16 Volleyball   **401**

Volleyball Tactics. 402
Teaching Volleyball 404
Levels of Tactical Complexity 405
Level I. 406
Level II. 418
Level III 428
Level IV 441
Level V. 447
Summary. 454

Chapter 17 Badminton   455

Level I 456
Level II 463
Level III 469
Summary 474

Chapter 18 Tennis   475

Level I 477
Level II 488
Level III 497
Summary 503

Chapter 19 Softball   505

Level I 512
Level II 523
Level III 532
Level IV 537
Summary 544

Chapter 20 Cricket   545

Level I 549
Level II 566
Level III 583
Summary 598

Chapter 21 Golf   599

Safety 599
Instruction Tips 600
Tactical Reality Golf 600
Level I 603
Level II 613
Summary 624

Chapter 22 Bowling   625

Organization of Lanes and Equipment 625
Instruction Tips 626
Level I 628
Level II 634
Level III 640
Level IV 647
Summary 652

Final Thoughts   653 | References and Resources   655
About the Authors   658 | DVD-ROM User Instructions   660

Introduction

We are pleased to write this third edition of *Teaching Sport Concepts and Skills: A Tactical Games Approach for Ages 7 to 18*. We received many positive comments on each of the first two editions of the book, particularly from those of you who teach at the secondary level. In this edition we expand the focus of the book to incorporate tactical games teaching at the elementary level, by blending content from our elementary book *Sport Foundations for Elementary Physical Education: A Tactical Games Approach* with the more secondary-focused material to create a book that is a resource for all teachers (hence the slight change in the title to include *for Ages 7 to 18*). We hope this book achieves that goal and becomes a useful addition to the growing literature on tactical games teaching. Regardless of the level at which you teach, you may already have knowledge and experience of tactical games teaching, perhaps gained from reading and using ideas from the original books. Do not be concerned, however, if you do not.

In part I of the book we begin with a thorough review of tactical games teaching and build a sound conceptual understanding of the approach. We provide thoughts on how best to prepare students for learning games through a tactical approach and also address some important principles of games teaching and learning, including the idea of tactical transfer and the process of teaching within the game. Tactical transfer is the understanding of how to solve the common problems presented across situations in similar game types. We have always argued that learning to solve the problems presented by one game can facilitate an understanding of how to solve problems in other games. A sound conceptual understanding is important to your ability to implement a tactical games approach. Also in part I we have moved forward the chapters on implementation (chapter 4), curriculum planning (chapter 5), and assessing game learning and performance (chapter 6), the latter reflecting the importance attached to assessment in the current educational climate. Chapter 6 on assessment addresses psychomotor, cognitive, and affective assessments in terms of standards-based curricula and provides examples of assessment integrated into lessons.

In part II we describe how elementary physical education teachers can use a conceptual approach to games teaching, beginning at about the second grade (ages 7 and 8). Lesson plans are included for invasion, net and wall, striking and fielding games, and target games using content from *Sport Foundations for Elementary Physical Education: A Tactical Games Approach*. We hope part II creates an effective link to the more sport-specific chapters in part III.

We carefully reviewed the sport-specific chapters in part III. Because the quality of teacher questioning is very important in tactical games teaching, we have reviewed and, where necessary, revised the suggested questions to ensure that they are consistent with lesson goals and game conditions, and that they elicit student responses that identify the need for skill practice. Within Practice Task segments we made a stronger effort to address broader ranges of student ability by providing task extensions where appropriate to increase the challenge when the need arises. Lastly, in response to requests from our own students and from teachers with whom we work, we added a chapter on flag football.

This edition also includes a professionally produced DVD-ROM that shows some of the lessons in action at both the elementary and secondary levels. This tool shows you not only how to implement the theory behind the tactical games approach, but also how to teach others in either a teacher-coach preparation setting or a youth sport or school setting. The volleyball segments show complete question-and-answer sessions, highlighting an effective method for making sure students are processing the lesson properly. A simple menu of demonstrated games makes it easy to find what you wish to review for yourself or to show others. The DVD-ROM also houses reproducible worksheets and assessments that you can print out for use in your classroom or with students. The following icon within the text of a lesson identifies that lesson or game as being included on the DVD-ROM. The icon also appears with thumbnails of reproducibles that are available on the DVD-ROM.

Games teaching and learning is a substantial part of most physical education curricula, and games playing provides an exciting and interactive environment for learning in all domains. We hope this book challenges all who read it. If you have experience with tactical games teaching, we challenge you to take it to other areas of the curriculum, to maximize the potential of tactical transfer through effective curriculum design, and to assess learning outcomes across all domains. If the idea of tactical games teaching is new to you, we challenge you to think deeply, to question your current practice as it relates to games teaching, and to adopt this new, student-centered approach to teaching and learning.

Acknowledgments

We are truly grateful for all that we have learned from the opportunity to have three editions of a book. The publication of each edition keeps us growing as teachers, scholars, and colleagues. We have many people to acknowledge, including our families and colleagues who have encouraged us along the way, the teachers with whom we have worked in field-testing our ideas, the staff at Human Kinetics (especially Ragen, our patient developmental editor for the last two editions), and all those who are advocates of teaching tactical games. In particular, for this edition, we must acknowledge the contribution of Shawn Bates, the PE teacher at Longcoy Elementary School in Kent, and Rita Covin, the PE teacher at Nordonia Middle School in Macedonia. Together with their students, these model teachers have provided excellent examples (as shown on the DVD-ROM) of how to use a tactical games approach in elementary and secondary physical education.

Part I

Tactical Games Teaching

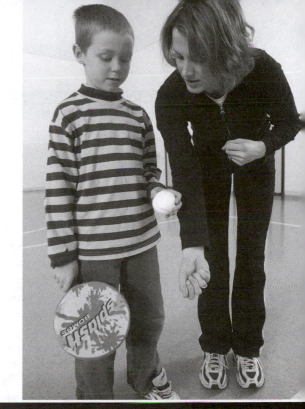

Chapter 1

Tactical Games Explanation and Review

About two-thirds of a typical physical education curriculum involves games teaching and learning. We believe that, given this emphasis, physical educators must try to teach games effectively. Many people, particularly fitness advocates, have viewed sports and games negatively, labeling them as elitist, overly competitive, and not conducive to developing health and fitness. This negativity perhaps stems from an emphasis on large-sided, zero-sum games in which the winners and losers are obvious, and active participation is minimal for many students. We believe that sports and games can be fun, educative, and challenging and can enhance health and self-esteem. Although games teaching should remain a valuable part of the physical education curriculum, we concede that the way games have traditionally been taught is problematic. This is the reason we wrote this book.

Many physical educators teach both the skills and tactics of games but have problems linking these com-ponents. For example, in units on basketball in which classes spend several days covering passing, dribbling, and shooting, skill development is not apparent during subsequent lessons on game play. Skills have usually been taught in isolation, out of their tactical context. The approach we outline in this book links tactics and skills by emphasizing the appropriate timing of skill practice and application within the tactical context of the game.

Tactical awareness, critical to game performance, is the ability to identify tactical problems that arise during a game and to respond appropriately. Responses might involve on-the-ball skills, such as passing and shooting, and off-the-ball movements, such as supporting and covering. For example, a tactical problem in soccer is for the team to maintain possession of the ball. Players maintain possession by selecting and executing passing, ball-control, and sup-port skills. In a tactical approach, students are placed in a game situation that emphasizes maintaining possession *before* they identify and practice solutions such as passing, ball control, and support. Another tactical problem in soccer is defending space. Players defend space by marking opponents, pressuring the player with the ball, covering for teammates, and clearing the ball from danger areas. The link between skills and tactics enables students to learn about a game and improve their performance, especially because game tactics provide the opportunity for applying game-related motor skills.

RATIONALE FOR A TACTICAL APPROACH

We believe that traditional games teaching in schools has done little to educate students about games playing. The tactical approach we advocate in this book promotes an interest in learning games, an understanding of game play, and the ability to play games.

Interest and Excitement

The traditional approach to games teaching is technical and focuses on teaching skills in answer to the question, how is this skill performed? For example, instruction in badminton often develops the techniques of service, the overhead clear, the drop shot, and the smash by concentrating on specific critical elements of these skills. Although this format might improve technique, it has been criticized for teaching skills before students can grasp their significance within the game. As a result, students lose the context of the skill, and games teaching becomes a series of textbook drills (Pigott 1982).

Drills often lead students to ask, "Why are we doing this?" or "When can we play a game?" For example, you might hear these questions during a volleyball lesson in which students must pass or set the ball against a wall. For many students, particularly those who are less skilled, the game that follows is characterized by aimless participation following a breakdown of techniques for passing and setting. This frustrates both students and teacher. It is possible that the only thing many children learn about games is that they cannot perform the necessary complex skills (Booth

1983). In addition, skilled students often perceive isolated drills as tedious and irrelevant to their performance during game play.

A tactical approach provides an exciting alternative through which students can learn to play games. Our research and the experience of others indicate that students find a tactical approach motivational and that teachers prefer it (Berkowitz 1996; Burrows 1986; Griffin, Oslin, and Mitchell 1995; Gubacs-Collins 2007; Hopper 2003; Mitchell, Griffin, and Oslin 1994). Another attractive feature of a tactical approach is its sequential nature, which eliminates redundancy in games teaching for both teacher and students.

Knowledge as Empowerment

Although skill execution is critical to game performance, deciding *what to do* in game situations is just as important. French and Thomas (1987) stated that "mistakes commonly observed in young children in various sports may stem from a lack of knowledge about what to do in the context of a given sport situation" (p. 17). Furthermore, Bunker and Thorpe (1986) proposed that the uniqueness of games lies in the decision-making processes that precede the use of appropriate techniques. Not understanding the game impairs the student's ability to identify the correct technique for a situation. Bunker and Thorpe (1986) also suggested that an increased understanding of games, achieved through teaching for tactical awareness, empowers children to easily and skillfully solve the problems each game situation poses.

The next time you teach a games lesson, observe the differences between the performances of students with high and low abilities. You will see more proficient skill execution by students with greater ability, but you will also notice better game-related decision making and skill selection in response to specific situations. Enhanced decisions reflect greater knowledge of the game, an observation supported by the research of McPherson (1994, 1995).

Transfer of Understanding and Performance

A tactical focus may help your students carry understanding from one game to another. Although some invasion games, such as rugby and flag football, have unique rules that set them slightly apart from others, most invasion games are tactically similar even though they require different skills. For example, tactical problems in soccer, field hockey, and basketball, all of which are invasion games, are similar. In our experience the best novice soccer players are those with experience of other invasion games, because they already understand the spatial aspects of soccer. We can make a similar case for net and wall games (e.g., badminton, tennis), striking and fielding games (e.g., softball, cricket), and target games (e.g., golf, bowling) (Werner and Almond 1990). These similarities enable us to group games according to their tactics. We define invasion games as those in which the goal is to invade an opponent's territory. Net and wall games involve propelling an object into space so an opponent is unable to make a return. In striking and fielding games, the goal is to strike an object, usually a ball, so that it eludes defenders. In target games, the performer propels an object, preferably with great accuracy, toward a target. We elaborate on the importance and implications of tactical transfer in chapter 2.

Physical educators have suggested that a tactical focus in games teaching suits both the elementary and secondary levels (Bunker and Thorpe 1982; Doolittle and Girard 1991; Mitchell, Oslin, and Griffin 2003). In this book we address how physical educators can use a tactical approach to enhance students' game performance at various developmental stages by identifying, sequencing, and teaching the tactical problems of games at successive stages of development. We offer frameworks for games, provide a broader definition of game performance, and identify levels of tactical complexity for each game.

GAME FRAMEWORKS

An initial concern for those wishing to teach games and sport tactically is developing frameworks for identifying and breaking down relevant tactical problems, a process originated by Spackman (1983). By selecting teaching materials from a framework, you ensure that your students become familiar with the game and that any skills you teach relate to the game context. Table 1.1 shows a framework that identifies tactical problems and the off-the-ball movements and on-the-ball skills necessary for solving these problems. The example uses soccer, which is taught at all developmental levels.

Table 1.1 Tactical Problems, Movements, and Skills in Soccer

Tactical problems	Off-the-ball movements	On-the-ball skills
SCORING (OFFENSE)		
Maintaining possession of the ball	• Dribbling for control • Supporting the ball carrier	• Passing—short and long • Control—feet, thigh, chest
Attacking the goal	Using a target player	Shooting, shielding, turning
Creating space in attack	• Crossover play • Overlapping run	• First-time passing • Crossover play • Overlapping run
Using space in attack	Timing runs to goal, shielding	• Width—dribbling, crossing, heading • Depth—shielding
PREVENTING SCORING (DEFENSE)		
Defending space	Marking, pressuring, preventing the turn, delaying, covering, making recovery runs	Clearing the ball
Defending the goal	Goalkeeping—positioning	Goalkeeping—receiving the ball, making saves, distributing (throwing and punting)
Winning the ball		Tackling—block, poke, slide
RESTARTING PLAY		
Throw-in—attacking and defending	Defensive marking at throw-ins	Executing a quick throw
Corner kick—attacking and defending	Defensive marking at corners	• Short corner kick • Near-post corner kick • Far-post corner kick
Free kick—attacking and defending	• Defending—marking at free kicks • Defending—setting a wall	Attacking—shooting from free kicks

Table 1.1 identifies the major tactical problems in scoring, preventing scoring, and restarting play. To score, a team must solve the progressively complex problems of maintaining possession of the ball, attacking the goal, creating space while attacking, and using that space effectively. Each tactical problem includes relevant off-the-ball movements and on-the-ball skills. For example, to maintain possession of the ball, players must support teammates who have the ball and must pass and control the ball over various distances. Although we have done this for you in many of this book's chapters, you could develop similar frameworks for other games by asking yourself two questions:

- What are the problems in scoring, preventing scoring, and restarting play?
- What off-the-ball movements and on-the-ball skills are necessary to solve these problems?

GAME PERFORMANCE

The two questions at the end of the previous section suggest that a tactical approach defines game performance as more than simply executing motor skills. Table 1.1 shows that movements made by players who do not have the ball are important and should be considered in games teaching. For example, a player who can pass the ball accurately is of limited value unless she has potential receivers who have moved to support her. Off-the-ball movements are often ignored in favor of on-the-ball skills, but you should teach these movements to maximize students' performance. We believe in this strongly because, in any game, players possess the ball, Frisbee, or puck only briefly during play. Consider 30 minutes of a soccer game played by teams of 6 players. Dividing 30 minutes by 10 outfield players (each team has a goalkeeper) demonstrates that each outfield player possesses the ball for an average of only three minutes! What are the outfield players doing the remainder of the time? They are moving to appropriate positions to attack or defend and deciding how to contribute to the game. Yet in physical education, we rarely teach these aspects of game performance.

This book provides a broad definition of game performance. Game play involves not only the execution of motor skills but also components such as the following:

- Making decisions
- Supporting teammates who have the ball
- Marking or guarding opponents

- Covering teammates
- Adjusting position as play unfolds
- Ensuring adequate court or field coverage by means of a base position

This expanded definition of game performance has implications for your goals, content, and assessment procedures. Expanded goals and content appear in each of the sport-specific chapters, and ideas for assessment are presented in chapter 6.

LEVELS OF TACTICAL COMPLEXITY

Having identified important tactical problems and their associated skills for a particular game, you must ensure that the tactical complexity of the game matches your students' development. We provide a way to do this in table 1.2, in which we identify levels of tactical complexity, again using soccer as an example. The table identifies at which level various skills should be introduced to students learning the game. For example, under Scoring in table 1.2, the first row identifies what skills students must learn to be able to maintain possession of the ball. At level I, students are introduced to dribbling and passing and controlling with their feet. These skills aren't repeated in subsequent levels in this row because the students will already know them, having been introduced to them in level I.

One thing to note immediately in table 1.2 is that not all tactical problems are addressed at all levels because this would not be developmentally appropriate. So you will notice some blank spaces in the table. Simply, some tactical problems are too complex for novice players to understand. For example, novice players might understand the need to maintain possession of the ball and to attack the goal because those are the basic requirements for scoring goals. But you notice that we do not suggest a focus on defending space for novices because this would negate the success they might otherwise have offensively, and offensive success is a key motivational aspect of games playing. Likewise, notice that we do not suggest an offensive focus on concepts such as using width and depth when attacking in the early levels, because it would be unrealistic to expect these players to understand these more advanced concepts; such an understanding comes from experience playing the game.

You might present the same tactical problem at successive stages of development. Consider the problem of defending space in soccer. We can reasonably expect novice players to appreciate that defense is needed to

Table 1.2 Levels of Tactical Complexity for Soccer

Tactical problems	Level I	Level II	Level III	Level IV	Level V
SCORING					
Maintaining possession of the ball	• Dribbling for control • Passing (short) • Control (with the feet)	Supporting the ball carrier		• Passing—long • Control—thigh, chest	
Attacking the goal	Shooting	• Shooting • Turning • Shielding	Using a target player		
Creating space in attack			First-time passing	Overlapping run	Crossover play
Using space in attack				Width—dribbling, crossing, heading	• Depth—shielding • Timing of runs to goal, shielding
PREVENTING SCORING					
Defending space		Marking, pressuring	Preventing the turn	Clearing the ball	Delaying, covering, making recovery runs
Defending the goal		• Goalkeeper positioning and receiving the ball • Distributing—throwing			• Goalkeeping—making saves • Distributing—punting
Winning the ball			Tackling—block, poke	Tackling—slide	
RESTARTING PLAY					
Throw-in—attacking and defending	Executing a quick throw	Defensive marking at throw-ins			
Corner kick—attacking and defending	Short corner kick	Defensive marking at corners	Near-post corner kick		Far-post corner kick
Free kick—attacking and defending			Attacking—shooting from free kicks		Defending—marking and setting a wall

prevent opponents from scoring. In its simplest form, defense involves marking, or guarding, an opponent to deny access to the ball. However, only as their tactical awareness develops do students appreciate the need for players to defend as a team by delaying the opponent's attacks and covering for teammates challenging for the ball. You may add to the complexity of game understanding as tactical awareness develops. That is, as students improve their tactical understanding, games should involve problems of increasing complexity. If you can identify levels of tactical complexity, planning developmentally appropriate content becomes a process of planning versions of the game for students at varying stages of awareness. The key question is, how tactically complex do I want the game to be? In contrast, the question you address in a technical approach is, what skills should I teach in my unit? Table 1.2 identifies possible levels of tactical complexity in soccer.

As indicated in table 1.2, level I skills include basic short passing, receiving, shooting, throwing the ball in, and using a short corner to restart when appropriate. Teaching longer passing to young students is inappropriate because it is unnecessary in small-sided games on small fields, and few students possess the necessary strength for longer passing. Thus you might revisit maintaining possession at a later level (perhaps level IV) by addressing long passing when your students can understand its value and can perform advanced skills.

Having introduced soccer in its most basic tactical form, at level II you can further develop student understanding and skill. You can show students that, by supporting the player with the ball, they increase the probability of their team's retaining possession. Developing an awareness of the need to defend space and the goal is also appropriate for level II students, because they will have begun considering ways of preventing opponents from scoring. Simple tactical problems at level II include denying space to opponents who are close to the ball or goal and positioning the goalkeeper to decrease the size of the goal to the smallest possible target. When students understand the need for these tactics, they can practice relevant movements such as marking (or guarding) and skills such as basic goalkeeping. Finally, revisiting basic starts and restarts allows the small-sided game to resemble the mature game but in modified form.

As indicated in table 1.2, you might teach more advanced tactical problems, such as creating and using space in attack, at a later stage. At level III students can progress to creating space as they attack the goal. At this time you might revisit the problem of defending space by introducing the concept of pressuring the player with the ball. You could also introduce the problem of winning the ball and teach simple tackling skills. The problem of winning the ball is confronted again at level IV with work on slide tackling. Level IV students might also address more advanced solutions for creating and using space. At level V, students should understand the problems presented by the game and employ more advanced tactics and skills in more mature, and perhaps larger-sided, game situations. In fact, at the high school level, you might encourage students to take on greater responsibility for solving tactical problems by requiring them to develop their own practices. The exact level at which students should explore a tactical problem and its associated skills depends on task complexity and student understanding and skill. We recommend that when working with novice players (levels I and II), you begin with essential tactical problems related to scoring and preventing scoring. As you address more complex solutions to tactical problems, the game will increasingly resemble its mature form.

Individualizing Instruction

As you know, within any class students vary in their levels of understanding and performance. To individualize instruction, you can present advanced performers with the more complex solutions to a specific tactical problem. For example, when you teach novice soccer players to maintain possession of the ball by accurate short passing and receiving, some students will progress faster than others. You may introduce more skillful students to the concept of support or to longer passing techniques to continue to challenge them. Similarly, novice softball players learning to defend space by fielding the ball and accurately throwing to first base progress at different rates. You could introduce students with higher abilities to the concept of defending the base or to the footwork involved in covering first base. In other words, you can increase the level of tactical complexity within the specific tactical problem being addressed. Doing so is sound developmental teaching.

TEACHING TACTICAL AWARENESS AND SKILL ACQUISITION

In this section we outline using a tactical approach to teach an individual game lesson. Notice the use of small-sided games to expose students to specific tactical problems and the importance of the teacher's questioning to provoke critical thinking and problem solving.

Tactical Model

A critical question we now address is, how do I teach for tactical awareness within the physical education lesson? Bunker and Thorpe (1982) suggested a six-stage model for games teaching, Teaching Games for Understanding, which has been very useful in guiding physical educators. To illustrate this approach, we consolidated the model into three stages, which we present in figure 1.1.

The outline in figure 1.1 suggests that teaching for tactical awareness should start with a game, or more precisely, a game modified to represent its advanced form and exaggerated to present students with tactical problems (Thorpe, Bunker, and Almond 1986). For example, a tactical problem in badminton is to set up the attack by creating space on the opponent's side of the net. You might begin with a half-court singles game because it represents the full-court game but is played on a narrower court. The narrowness exag-

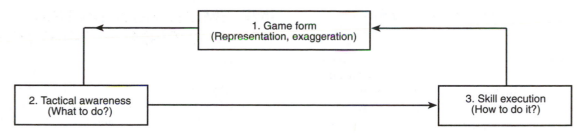

Figure 1.1   A tactical approach to games teaching.

gerates the need to play shots to the back and front of the court to create space.

Young or novice students will be unable to play the advanced form of most games because of limited tactical understanding and skill. The game form should relate to the level of student development. Consider the dimensions of playing areas, the numbers participating, and the equipment used when choosing a game form. If you establish a developmentally appropriate form, students' play can represent the advanced game. For example, small-sided volleyball games played in smaller areas with lighter balls and lower nets use the same principles, problems, and skills found in the full game.

Critical Conditions and Questions

Students gradually learn the rules of games through the conditions you apply. After the initial game, questions are necessary, and the quality of your questions is the key to fostering students' critical thinking and problem solving. First, ask about the goal of the activity, and then ask students what they must do to achieve that goal (i.e., what skills or movements they must use to be successful). Questioning why certain skills or movements are required might also be appropriate. Once students are aware of what they need to do and why, you can ask them how they should perform the necessary skills. These questions help students identify the aspects of technique that they ought to practice, thus leading to the practice phase of the lesson. The following example illustrates the process.

Establish an appropriate game form, such as 2 versus 2 (2v2) soccer in a restricted (20- by 20-yard) playing area with an objective of making a specific number of consecutive passes (such as four) before the ball is lost. (If you use the metric system in your measurements, you can use the same number of meters.) This objective forces students to confront what they must do to maintain possession. Appropriate teacher–student questioning might go as follows:

- Teacher: What was the goal of that game?
  Students: For each team to keep the ball for four passes.
- Teacher: What does your team have to do to keep the ball for four consecutive passes?
  Students: Pass the ball.
- Teacher: Yes, and what else?
  Students: We also have to receive passes.
- Teacher: OK, you have to be able to pass and receive the ball. How many teams managed to make four consecutive passes? (It is likely that only a few pairs made this target because passing is difficult in a 2v2 game.)
- Teacher: Well, perhaps some practice with passing and receiving would be a good idea then.

The quality of your questions is critical, and these questions should be an integral part of your planning. Literature on tactical games teaching, be it the original work of Bunker and Thorpe (1982), the Australian conception of *Game Sense* (Den Duyn 1997), or our own *Teaching Sport Concepts and Skills* (1997) and *Sport Foundations for Elementary Physical Education (2003),* has consistently emphasized the importance of asking quality questions. *Game Sense* provides good general advice on the types of questions you might ask students. These questions fall into three categories:

- Time: When is the best time to . . . ?
- Space: Where is or where can . . . ?

⬦ **TIP BOX**

It is essential when modifying or conditioning any game that you encourage students to think tactically. By changing the rules, you exaggerate playing conditions to ensure that players ask, what must I do to succeed in this situation?

- Risk: Which choice is safest and which is most risky?

We encourage you to develop questions that are meaningful to your students. You can never anticipate all the answers you might receive, even when questioning secondary students, so be prepared to probe and, if necessary, ask a forced-choice question (Do you think . . . ?) to focus responses. Questioning is not a teaching skill easily mastered, and it does not come naturally to everyone. At first it is acceptable to be plan dependent and to write questions on note cards if necessary. Note cards may seem mechanical, but with practice you will develop natural questioning skills for the varied situations of your students and gymnasium.

Continuing the previous example, through a developmentally appropriate game and through skillful questioning, students should begin to realize that accurate passing and swift ball control are essential. At this point formal practice of passing and receiving becomes appropriate. During this practice, you can describe how to perform the necessary skills and movements by using teaching cues related to the critical elements of each technique. Note that although passing and receiving have become the focus of the lesson, you didn't initially inform students of this focus. Rather, you led them to identify the lesson focus through a well-designed modified game and through skillful questioning. Many teachers new to a tactical approach find it difficult to withhold this information at the start of a lesson. Avoid providing too much information early in the lesson because it detracts from the problem-solving process. Conclude a lesson with game play that reinforces the skills practiced. The Planning Format for Tactical Games Lessons sidebar at the end of this chapter should help you identify and understand the phases of a lesson.

Your students' learning continues lesson by lesson, and you continue to modify the game so they can explore new aspects of tactical awareness. For example, you could introduce a 3v3 game, providing all players with an extra passing option so that they must effectively support the player with the ball. When students understand the need for good support, you can teach off-the-ball supporting movements before returning to the game. Thus you progressively develop game performance. You can extend the practice of maintaining possession by adding either a small goal or a target player at each end of a rectangular playing area. Ask your students, "How can you get the ball past the defense?" At this point students must think in terms of passing the ball between defenders, or of splitting the defense, an essential tactic for penetrating in attack.

IMPLEMENTING A TACTICAL GAMES APPROACH USING THIS BOOK

The chapters in this book provide suggestions for teaching tactically in a variety of games and sports. The chapters vary in length, and the levels of tactical complexity vary from game to game. For example, invasion games tend to be more tactically complex than net and wall games, so we have identified five levels of tactical complexity for soccer but only three for badminton.

Each chapter contains a framework of problems, movements, and skills to assist you in breaking down the game tactically. We also suggest levels of tactical complexity to give you an idea of how to developmentally sequence your teaching. We suggest several lessons for each level, but these are only outlines with little detail on equipment and management procedures. For the sake of space we have restricted each outline to the tactical problem being addressed, the lesson focus, the lesson objective, an initial game form, teacher questions with likely student responses, practice tasks with teaching cues, and a closing game form. This abbreviated format provides a greater breadth of material to get you started. This format is laid out in the Planning Format for Tactical Games Lessons sidebar, and following this should help you plan your own lessons. Major components of the plan are in bold text, followed by points to consider in developing a plan.

Finally, we suggest that before focusing on unit content, you take the first one or two lessons in each activity to teach students how to set up and run small-sided games. This will help them understand the playing boundaries, game rules, and routines, and make the learning environment run smoothly. If you choose to integrate tactical games teaching with the Sport Education model (more on this later), you should organize your environment so that students understand their roles and the routines for beginning and ending class. Have students practice their roles and go over class rules and routines during the first lesson or two.

SUMMARY

To conclude this chapter, we reemphasize the four things you need to do to address the essential points of a tactical approach to games teaching.

1. **Consider the tactical problems to address during your unit, and decide on the complexity of the solutions to these problems.** These

---

Planning Format for Tactical Games Lessons

Game _____ Lesson # _____ Grade level _____

Major components of the plan are bolded, and points for you to consider are italicized.

- **Tactical problem:** *What is the tactical problem addressed during the lesson?*
- **Lesson focus:** *What is the focus in terms of how the tactical problem will be solved?*
- **Objectives:** *What are the major cognitive and psychomotor learning objectives?*

1. **Game:** *What is the modified game being played?*

   Goal: *What performance goal will you give to the students?*

   Conditions: *What conditions will you put on the game to ensure that students address the tactical problem?*

   Questions: *After initial game play, what questions might you ask (and what answers do you anticipate) to help students focus on the tactical problem and its solution?*

2. **Practice task:** *What skill practice will help students solve the tactical problem when they return to game play?*

   Goal: *What performance goal will you give to the students for the skill practice?*

   Cues: *What teaching cues will you use to assist skill acquisition?*

   Extension: *How might you extend the skill practice to make it harder or easier to match the content with the varying abilities of students?*

3. **Game:** *What modified game may help students apply their newly learned skills to solve the tactical problem during play?*

   Goal: *What performance goal will you give to the students for the game?*

   Conditions: *What conditions will you put on the game to ensure that students use the skills they learned to address the tactical problem?*

4. **Closure:** *What would be an appropriate closure or ending discussion for the lesson?*

---

decisions depend on the experience and ability of your students. We provide tactical frameworks and levels of tactical complexity throughout this book, and you can easily develop these frameworks and levels for other games within the same category by using our examples.

2. **Within each lesson, have students practice skills after they have experienced a game form that presents a tactical problem requiring that skill.** In this way they appreciate the need for the skill and broaden their view of skill development to include both off-the-ball movements and on-the-ball skills. The timing of practice is a critical component of a tactical approach. As the teacher, you should modify initial game forms so your students can confront tactical problems.

3. **Link the initial modified game and the skill practice through your questions. The quality of these questions is critical.** Questions must

first draw students' attention to the tactical problem and then to potential solutions to the problem. You cannot assume that you will always get the answer you are expecting (these are students after all), but experience in this approach will enable you to think on your feet, probe further, and guide students to responses. Don't assume that students are versed in terminology, such as *overhead clear* or *drop shot*. Rather, expect students to talk about *long* and *short* shots, at which point you can introduce correct terminology before skill practice.

4. **After your students have practiced skills, give them the opportunity to apply their improved skills and tactical understanding in game play.** By providing your students with this opportunity, you increase the probability that they will understand the value of skills in the relevant game context.

Chapter 2

Principles of Games Teaching and Learning

This chapter addresses some principles of games teaching that are particularly important in a tactical games approach. In particular, the principle of transfer in tactical games teaching is sufficiently important to warrant its own discussion. *Transfer of learning,* a commonly applied principle in education, is well documented in the literature on motor learning as the basis for sequencing the skills and concepts to be learned (Magill 1993). Transfer may be positive when the learning of one skill or concept aids the learning of another. For example, learning to throw a ball overhand positively affects learning the tennis service because of the biomechanical similarities of these skills. Conversely, transfer might be negative when the learning of one skill or concept interferes with the learning of another, as is the case in which a novice performer moves from learning the badminton underhand forehand drive to learning the tennis forehand drive. Racket weight and technical differences (the wrist is used much more in badminton) might cause negative transfer. Transfer might also be zero if learning one skill or concept has no effect on learning another.

There is research literature supporting the principle of transfer in motor skill acquisition (Dan Ota and Vickers 1998; Singer, DeFrancesco, and Randall 1989; Wrisberg and Liu 1991), most of which investigates the relative effects of blocked or variable practice trials on transfer. However, there is a lack of research investigating the transfer of understanding in physical activity, which is surprising considering the abundance of literature confirming the transfer of learning in other educational areas. Studies in literacy suggest that children are able to transfer learning strategies across reading tasks and among subjects such as reading, writing, and world geography (Benson 1997;

McAloon 1994). Similarly, researchers in linguistics report that learning to read and write in one foreign language can benefit the learning of another (Berman 1994; Tucker 1996). Transfer has also been supported in technology. Beard (1993) argued for the positive transfer of computer skills to new computer tasks, and Harvey and Anderson (1996) identified positive transfer across computer languages. Finally, Toh and Woolnough (1994) determined that the science skills of planning, performing, communicating, and interpreting transfer to other scientific areas of study.

TRANSFER OF TACTICAL KNOWLEDGE IN GAMES

Given the findings just described, it seems reasonable to speculate that understanding transfers positively among tactically similar games. Although historically, games have been grouped in different ways for different reasons, we use the classification system suggested by Almond (1986), which is presented in table 2.1. The system divides games into invasion, net and wall, striking and fielding, and target games:

- **Invasion games**—In invasion games teams score by moving a ball (or other projectile) into another team's territory and either shooting into a fixed target (a goal or basket) or moving the projectile across an open-ended target (i.e., across a line). To prevent scoring, one team must stop the other from bringing the ball into its territory and attempting to score. Solving these offensive and defensive problems requires similar tactics in various invasion games even though many of the required skills are different. For example, although players must understand the need to shoot to score in both floor hockey and team handball, the

striking and throwing skills used to shoot in these two games are very different. Movement off the ball is common across all invasion games. Offensive players must move without the ball and position themselves so that they can receive passes from teammates and threaten the goal. The defensive components of invasion games are also similar in that players must mark, or guard, opponents and must pressure the ball carrier before attempting to win the ball. Effective decision making is critical; players must decide whether to pass, shoot, or move with the ball and decide when, where, and how to move when they do not individually possess the ball.

- **Net and wall games**—In net and wall games, teams or individual players score by hitting a ball into a court space with sufficient accuracy and power that opponents cannot hit it back before it bounces once (as in badminton or volleyball) or twice (as in tennis, racquetball, and squash). In all of these games shot placement is at a premium in that players must hit to open spaces to win points. Court awareness is important so that a player can move an opponent around the court to create the spaces needed to attack. On the other hand, players must also defend spaces, usually on their side of the net, to best position themselves to return the ball. Players need to evaluate their own strengths and weaknesses, and those of their opponents, before selecting and executing skills. Decisions by any player must also account for the court positioning of all players involved in the game.

- **Striking and fielding games**—In striking and fielding games such as softball, baseball, and cricket, players on the batting team must strike a ball with sufficient accuracy and power that it eludes players on the fielding team and gives the hitter time to run

Table 2.1   Games Classification

Invasion	Net and wall	Striking and fielding	Target
• Basketball (FT)	Net	• Baseball	• Golf
• Netball (FT)	• Badminton (I)	• Softball	• Croquet
• Team handball (FT)	• Tennis (I)	• Rounders	• Bowling
• Water polo (FT)	• Table tennis (I)	• Cricket	• Lawn bowling
• Soccer (FT)	• Pickleball (I)	• Kickball	• Pool
• Hockey (FT)	• Volleyball (H)		• Billiards
• Lacrosse (FT)	Wall		• Snooker
• Speedball (FT/OET)	• Racquetball (I)		
• Rugby (OET)	• Squash (I)		
• Football (OET)	• Handball (H)		
• Ultimate Frisbee (OET)			

FT = focused target; OET = open-ended target; I = implement; H = hand.

Adapted from L. Almond, 1986, Reflecting on themes: A games classification. In *Rethinking games teaching*, edited by R. Thorpe, D. Bunker, and L. Almond (Loughborough University), 71-72. By permission of D.L. Bunker.

between two destinations (bases or wickets). As in a net or wall game, players attempt to place the ball in gaps between fielders to maximize the run scoring of the hit. Decisions regarding where (accuracy) and how (power or placement) to hit a ball are based on the positioning of fielders and the type of ball or pitch delivered. To prevent scoring, players on the fielding team must position themselves so they can gather and throw a ball to the base or wicket to which the hitter is running before the hitter reaches it. Fielding decisions, particularly those concerning a fielder's positioning, are based on the relative strengths and weaknesses of the pitcher or bowler and of the batter, and also (perhaps) on the game score.

- **Target games**—In target games, players score by throwing or striking a ball to a target. Some target games are unopposed (e.g., golf, 10-pin bowling), whereas others are opposed (e.g., lawn bowling, croquet, shuffleboard) in that one participant is allowed to block or hit the opponent's ball. In opposed target games, players prevent scoring by hitting the opponent's object to a disadvantageous position relative to the target. Decision making in target games is much more individualized than in other game categories because of their primary focus on players' own personal strengths and weaknesses or perhaps on equipment, such as when a player selects a club before a shot in golf.

The classification system presented in table 2.1 was originally developed so that teachers could select from several game types to expose children to a variety of activities (Almond 1986). The weakness of selecting across types is that it is unlikely to lead to deep tactical learning and improved game performance within any category. Lack of depth is an issue because performance enhancement in any game will probably not result from the typical unit of six to eight lessons chosen to give students a variety of experiences.

Table 2.1 emphasizes game tactics rather than skills. Students who are well versed in tactics are more likely to be able to carry over their performance from one game to another within a category than will students who practice skills in isolation. To clarify, the skills used in soccer, basketball, and field hockey are different, and instruction focused on skills in these sports will result in little carryover among them. However, because the games are tactically similar, focusing on tactical problems can lead to positive transfer among games. Several teachers have found this transfer to be the greatest benefit of using a tactical approach to games teaching. For example, a

> ◇ **TIP BOX**
>
> Select from within rather than across game categories. Doing so provides students with a deeper understanding of effective game performance by identifying similarities among games within each category.

sixth-grade teacher began a series of units on invasion games by focusing eight lessons on the tactical problems of maintaining possession of the ball and attacking the goal in soccer. She then applied the same tactical problems to ultimate Frisbee and floor hockey during consecutive units of similar lengths. Her students were able to transfer their understanding of one game to another, particularly how to move when not in possession of the ball, Frisbee, or puck. Other teachers and student teachers have reported similar outcomes.

Considering the conceptual arguments we have just presented, it is perhaps surprising that only a few studies have investigated the extent to which knowledge and tactical understanding transfer from the performance of one game to another. One of our studies indicated a positive transfer of performance in high school students moving from badminton to pickleball (Mitchell and Oslin 1999b). Performance was videotaped for each game, and students answered structured questions regarding the similarities between badminton and pickleball and how learning one might help in performing another. The students demonstrated the transfer of both game performance and cognitive knowledge. Martin (2004) conducted a similar study using the invasion games of ultimate Frisbee and team handball, novel activities for the sixth-grade boys involved in the units. This study also noted positive transfer when students moved from ultimate Frisbee to team handball, particularly in passing decisions and offensive support.

IMPLICATIONS FOR CURRICULUM DEVELOPMENT

The concept of transfer underpins a tactical approach to games teaching. Given its support in the education literature, and more recently in the physical education literature, transfer has some implications for selecting content during curriculum development. Simply, if students transfer cognitive learning from one game to another, it might be wise to consecutively teach games with similar tactical goals to capitalize on their similarities. In addition to obtaining a breadth of experience across two or more games, students might achieve a depth of tactical learning within the same game category. Tables 2.2 and 2.3 demonstrate consecutive units in both invasion games and net games.

Table 2.2 presents sample content for eight lessons of soccer followed by eight lessons of field hockey for middle school students. Clearly, these students will develop the understanding that soccer and field hockey are essentially the same game played with different implements and that what they learn in solving the problems of one game applies to the other. We have not included a chapter on field hockey in this book, and again we emphasize that transfer is also a feature of tactical games teaching for you as the teacher. If you do not know much about field hockey, you could apply what you know about soccer (or basketball or ice hockey or team handball) to field hockey. In doing so you will realize that you know more than you think you do about many games.

Table 2.3 presents sample content for badminton and pickleball units. Again, we have not included a pickleball chapter in this book (it is very similar to tennis). As in the example of invasion games, students will soon appreciate the similarities of the two net games. The sequence of lessons in table 2.3 emphasizes three tactical problems of net games and their corresponding solutions, which are shown in greater detail in table 2.4.

TEACHING DURING GAME PLAY

An additional principle of effective games teaching involves teaching during game play. Too often, beginning teachers feel unsure of themselves while game play is in progress and ask themselves, what should I be doing? or, how can I teach during game play? Frequent and focused game play is essential for developing effective decision-making capabilities. Because students spend substantial amounts of time engaged in game play when learning a tactical approach, it is

Table 2.2 Consecutive Units on Invasion Games

	Soccer		Field hockey	
Lesson	Tactical problem	Solution—skill or movement	Tactical problem	Solution—skill or movement
1	Maintaining possession of the ball	Dribbling under control (using multiple surfaces of the foot to change direction)—practice and game settings	Maintaining possession of the ball	Dribbling under control (using correct side of the stick and stick manipulation)—practice and game settings
2	Maintaining possession of the ball	Passing and receiving with the inside and outside of the foot—practice and game settings	Maintaining possession of the ball	Passing and receiving (using the push pass and cushioning the ball)—practice and game settings
3	Maintaining possession of the ball	Supporting teammates who have the ball and moving to open space—practice and game settings	Maintaining possession of the ball	Supporting teammates who have the ball and moving to open space—practice and game settings
4	Attacking the goal	Shooting a static or moving ball—practice and game settings	Attacking the goal	Shooting a static or moving ball—practice and game settings
5	Attacking the goal	Dribbling around defenders to shoot (combining lessons 1 and 4)—practice and game settings	Attacking the goal	Dribbling around defenders to shoot (combining lessons 1 and 4)—practice and game settings
6	Defending space	Marking opponents and pressuring the ball in small-sided game play	Defending space	Marking opponents and pressuring the ball in small-sided game play
7 and 8	All	6v6 round-robin tournament play	All	6v6 round-robin tournament play

Table 2.3 Consecutive Units on Net Games

Lesson	Badminton		Pickleball	
	Tactical problem	Solution—skill or movement	Tactical problem	Solution—skill or movement
1	Setting up to attack	Overhead forehand clear for depth in the opponent's court and creating space in the frontcourt—practice and game settings	Setting up to attack	Forehand ground stroke for depth in the opponent's court and creating space in the frontcourt—practice and game settings
2	Setting up to attack	Overhead backhand clear for achieving depth in the opponent's court—practice and game settings	Setting up to attack	Backhand ground stroke for achieving depth in the opponent's court—practice and game settings
3	Setting up to attack	Initiating play with an underhand clear (service) to push the opponent back—practice and game settings	Setting up to attack	Initiating play with a flat underhand service to the receiver on the baseline—practice and game settings
4	Setting up to attack	Using a drop shot to bring the opponent forward to use the space in the frontcourt—practice and game settings	Setting up to attack	Using an approach shot to position at the net and threaten the space in the frontcourt—practice and game settings
5	Winning the point	Using a smash into the frontcourt to exploit a weak clear or poor drop shot—practice and game settings	Winning the point	Using a volley from the net to exploit the advantageous position at the net—practice and game settings
6	Defending space	Recovering to center court between skill attempts—practice and game settings	Defending space	Recovering to the center of the baseline between skill attempts—practice and game settings
7 and 8	All	Round-robin tournament play—preferably singles	All	Round-robin tournament play—preferably singles

Table 2.4 Tactical Problems and Solutions in Net Games

Tactical problem	Key question for players to ask themselves	Solution
Setting up to attack	How do I set myself up so I can attack my opponent?	Push my opponent to the back of his or her court to open up space in the front.
Winning the point	How do I take advantage of the space I created to win a point?	Attack the space I created in the frontcourt with a smash, drop shot, or volley. (Although these shots differ in the techniques used in various net games, the principle of attacking space in the frontcourt is the same.)
Defending space	How do I prevent my opponent from scoring?	Position myself in the best place from which to return most of my opponent's shots. (Again, the best position varies with different net games. The base position for badminton is the actual center of the court so a player can reach both drop shots and clears. In pickleball, because the ball is allowed to bounce once on the receiver's side, the base position is at the center of the baseline. Nevertheless, the principle of returning to a base position from which space is most easily defended is common to both games.)

appropriate to mention strategies for teaching within the game. First, it is important to observe your students in game play once they have begun. As you observe, ask yourself the following questions:

- What is happening in the game(s)?
- Is this what I want?
- What changes do I need to make to help students play more effectively? Do I need to change the rules or game conditions?

During game play, two important strategies for teaching within the game are freezing the game and reconstructing and rehearsing (which usually follow freezing the game).

- Freezing the game—Use freezing the game (stopping game play) to point out (in a constructive manner) appropriate, or perhaps inappropriate, performance. Bear in mind that students need a prearranged signal for freezing and that you need to stop game play immediately when you see a situation occur. It is also important that players freeze immediately in place so that the context of the situation is not lost.

- Reconstructing and rehearsing—Having frozen a game, you can now use the process of reconstruction to identify what happened and demonstrate appropriate game performance or critique inappropriate performance. After reconstructing for the sake of critique, you can use rehearsal to facilitate the learning of appropriate performance, taking a "this is what should happen" approach. Older students might even be encouraged to reflect on what is happening and develop their own performance alternatives, trying various solutions while remaining in game play. Reconstructing and rehearsing are potentially useful for teaching decision making, a critical component of game performance that should be taught during game lessons. To many teachers, this is synonymous with coaching. Indeed, teachers at our workshops have often said things such as, "I do this [reconstruction and rehearsal] all the time when I coach, but it never crossed my mind to do it during PE classes as well." We encourage you to teach decision making in your instruction.

SUMMARY

Clearly, the concept of transfer is central to teaching and learning games tactics, and the ability to teach during game play (i.e., provide immediate feedback) is important for student learning and performance. Although the research literature supporting the transfer of tactical understanding is limited, many can recall anecdotal examples of students who have successfully applied the knowledge of one game to another. In our experience, field hockey players easily adapt to the spatial aspects of soccer, despite being soccer novices, because of their good understanding of positions and movements. Likewise, we have witnessed a cross-cultural transfer when cricket players understand the principles of baseball and softball, including offensive principles such as ball placement and defensive principles such as backing up bases and adjusting fielding position for right- and left-handed hitters.

Several teachers have raised the concern that they are not games experts but instead possess expertise in a specific area such as swimming or gymnastics, and so they lack the confidence to teach games tactically. If this is true of you, we suggest that you learn one game from each category and apply your knowledge to other games within the same category as a way of getting started in tactical games teaching. Subsequent chapters cover each game category with first an elementary (in part II) and then a more sport-specific secondary focus (in part III), including at least two specific games per category, and have been written to simplify the task of transfer. For example, much of the chapter on soccer can be applied to teaching offensive and defensive principles in team handball or field hockey, and much of the chapter on tennis can be applied to pickleball. We hope these chapters are useful resources for your games teaching.

◈ TIP BOX

The principle of transfer applies to you, the teacher. Remember that because many games are similar, if you know one game from each category, you will know the principles of other games within the same category.

Chapter 3

Preparing Students for a Tactical Games Approach

This chapter is written primarily with elementary students in mind because of their need to be prepared for the independent activities and learning inherent in the tactical games approach. With young learners, you should not assume that they understand your expectations. Be prepared to direct activities, such as warming up and stretching in the early lessons, and to demonstrate and set up game play. A tactical approach requires that students engage in game play independently in small groups; this is a very different way of learning for most elementary students, whereas secondary students are more able to direct their own activity with some independence.

An additional concern for most elementary teachers is the time factor. Many elementary physical education teachers have back-to-back classes approximately 30 to 40 minutes long. When one class is finished, the next class is already lined up at the door ready to enter the gymnasium—a scenario familiar to many of you who teach in elementary schools. A first-grade class might be followed by a fourth-grade and then a third-grade class, making it virtually impossible to set up equipment and leave it for three classes in a row. The time factor is particularly problematic for games teaching, in which equipment setup is crucial. Especially specific to a tactical games approach is the problem of fitting the game–skill practice–game format into 30 to 40 minutes. The use of multiple small-sided games requires considerable coordination and training of students; and setting them up could be time consuming if you are not well organized.

This chapter provides suggestions to ease the transition to a tactical approach and to enable both teachers and students to manage a new environment for teaching and learning.

TRAINING STUDENTS TO PLAY SMALL-SIDED GAMES

This section outlines procedures for training students, as young as second grade (seven and eight years old), to play small-sided (usually modified or conditioned) games independently. In particular, young learners must learn simple rule structures and to respect the game play of other students on adjacent courts or fields, particularly when a ball enters another court. Second-grade students have shown us their ability to adhere to the following two simple rules:

- When your ball rolls into another game, wait at the edge of that court or field for the ball to be returned to you (move around the outside of the gymnasium if necessary).
- When a ball rolls into your game from another game, stop it and roll it back to that game (or to the nearest sideline if the other game is too far away).

Simple though they seem, these rules must be taught and reinforced in the early stages of games teaching, when multiple games are being played. We and other teachers at the elementary level have found young learners more than able to restrain themselves from rushing onto another court to retrieve a ball and also to resist the temptation to kick or throw a ball that has come into their game from another game. Once again, you must teach and reinforce these rules. Although secondary students might need reminders, these rules should not be new to them.

An additional challenge lies in having elementary students learn and understand the court or field boundaries. We advise assigning students to permanent courts or fields to aid in this learning. For example, in figure 3.1 the gymnasium is divided into four courts for invasion games teaching, presumably with taped lines on the floor, each of which is numbered. Play is conducted across the width of the gymnasium so that each court is longer than it is wide, and teams (which remain the same throughout a games unit) are permanently assigned to a home court for entry into the gymnasium and warm-up activities. This organization facilitates a smooth and active start to lessons because students know where to go immediately upon entry into the gymnasium.

Preset warm-up activities enable teams to enter the gym and begin activity immediately and independently. Attendance taking is usually unnecessary at the elementary level, but if required, this can be done while students are warming up. Learners at the second-grade level can work independently in this

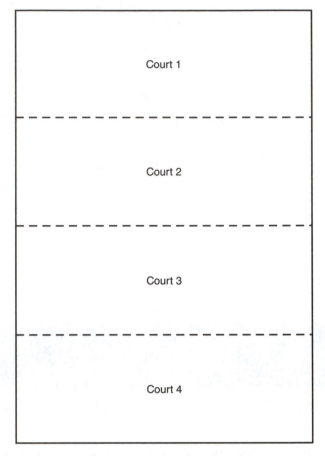

Figure 3.1 Permanent court or field assignments for invasion games.

way if organized and taught to do so. We stress that you can and should teach routines, rules, warm-up procedures, and other aspects of management in much the same way you might teach other lesson content. Provide plenty of opportunities for students to practice routines, and give appropriate feedback and praise for successful implementation.

Figure 3.2 illustrates possible setups for net games. In figure 3.2a, the gymnasium is divided into halves; an equal number of court spaces (6) in each half provides 12 small courts. Nets are spread across each half of the gymnasium, providing multiple playing areas. Note that in the early stages of net games learning (perhaps at second grade), you may decide to work without nets and instead use cones, ropes, or simply a line over which the ball must cross. This makes court setup easier for younger children. Figure 3.2b shows the nets set up over the length of the gymnasium, creating four court spaces.

Field arrangements for striking and fielding games can also be done to maximize young learners' opportunities for involvement in game play. Of course, for

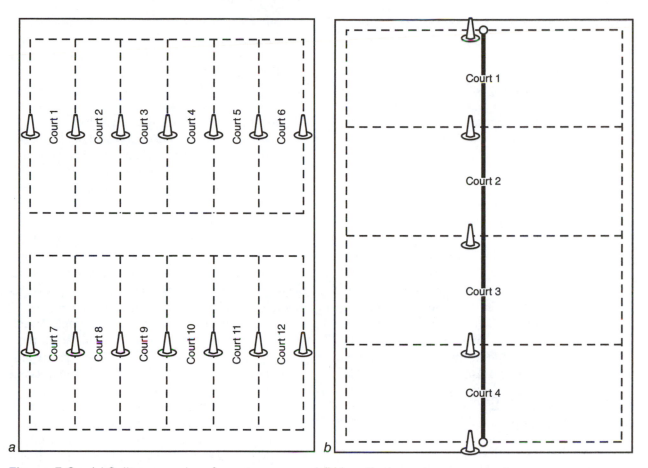

Figure 3.2   *(a)* Split gymnasium for net games and *(b)* lengthwise net arrangement.

this to occur, you must dispense with the traditional single-game approach, in which players receive very little ball contact, either in the form of batting or fielding. Figure 3.3 illustrates a triangular setup; three games back to back and a safety zone in the middle for batting teams are ideal. In this setup, batting teams are always hitting away from each other. Each field might be split in half so that even smaller spaces can be used for 2v2 or 3v3 games, as illustrated in chapter 9 on striking and fielding games.

TEACHING APPROPRIATE SPORT BEHAVIOR

Most second- and third-grade classes include children who have gained youth sport experience through programs run by the local parks and recreation department or perhaps by the YMCA or YWCA. However, these programs often have lower coach-to-player ratios than the 1:20 or 1:30 facing physical education teachers every day. Additionally, these programs

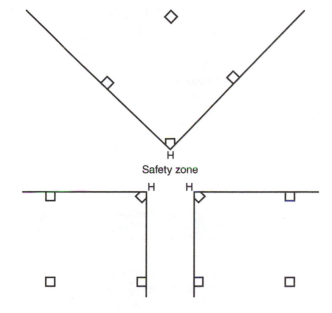

Figure 3.3   Multiple striking and fielding game-playing areas.

often involve large-sided games controlled by adults, alleviating the need for the players to be responsible for the conduct of the game.

The small-sided nature of a tactical approach, combined with the higher number of students per teacher, makes it necessary for students to learn to organize their own game play cooperatively so that they can play a purposeful game. In the following paragraphs, we suggest organizational strategies to accomplish this by describing appropriate and constructive sport behavior.

The organization of teams and the assignment of simple roles and responsibilities can facilitate students' learning game play and appropriate sport behavior. We advocate the use of the Sport Education curriculum model (Siedentop, Hastie, and van der Mars 2011), which outlines mechanisms for team, equipment, and game organization that help students develop appropriate sport behaviors. This model helps students develop into competent, literate, and enthusiastic players. Suggestions for doing this are described more fully in chapter 5, Tactical Games Curriculum Model.

TEACHING RULES AND ROUTINES

In this section we suggest some simple rules and routines that help make tactical games lessons run smoothly within the short time frame (30 to 40 minutes) available to the elementary, and increasingly the secondary, physical education teacher.

Entry Into the Gymnasium (or Playing Field) and Equipment Management

Routines have an enormous impact on the effective use of time in physical education. Many classes begin with students sitting in squads, on spots, or in a circle so the teacher can take attendance, explain what will happen in class, and distribute equipment. An example will illustrate the value of time-efficient routines for gymnasium entry.

> ### ◈ TIP BOX
> We advocate routines that allow for an active start to a lesson. Students enter the gymnasium and begin activity immediately by organizing their own equipment.

Consider a second-grade class of 24 students who are learning the tactics, skills, and movements of a modified net game against an opponent (singles play) in a designated playing area. Rather than use a net in the early stages of play, they engage in a simple throw-and-catch game across a line (or perhaps across a jump rope laid flat on the floor), which enables them to work on tactical aspects of play without having to worry about clearing the height of a net. The game also uses a mandatory "one bounce within the boundary" rule (i.e., the ball must bounce once on the opposite side of the "net").

Assuming that equipment has not been left out by the previous class (because this class might have been kindergartners or fifth-graders, who are learning something different), your first task is setting up 12 playing areas and getting play started as quickly as possible. Obviously, it is not time effective for you to set up all the playing areas; you need a simple system for your students to follow so they can set up their own playing areas. Using the available gymnasium floor lines, it is easy for the students to set up playing areas such as those in figure 3.2a.

Students enter the gymnasium and, in their established pairs, set up the court by taking cones from a predetermined location and placing them in the appropriate places. Small pieces of colored floor tape guide students in placing the cones in the right positions. Court setup can be accomplished independently by one player, while the opponent can locate the ball to be used. Play can begin immediately after the court is set up. Note that although we do not assume that secondary students do not need help organizing their equipment and playing spaces, they are likely to need less structured guidance and practice than young learners are.

Restart Rules

Games have natural breaks in play (frequent during the early stages of learning), so students must learn how to initiate their own game play and how to restart play when a natural break occurs, such as the ball going out of bounds or into the net. First, experienced players know that when one team causes a ball to go out of bounds in an invasion game, the game is restarted at the sideline by the other team. This concept will need to be taught and frequent reminders provided until the rule is understood regardless of the age of the students. As a principle, it is best to adapt restart rules to increase the likelihood that a team passing the ball into play can do so successfully so that the game can restart without the ball going immediately out of bounds again. You might stipulate that any defender must be at least one arm's length back from the player taking the inbound pass, or you might use a rule that the first pass into play is "free" (i.e., cannot be intercepted) but that it must go backward (i.e., toward the passer's own goal).

In a game such as soccer, in which a ball is thrown into play and must be controlled with the feet, we recommend the use of a free kick-in or roll-in, either of which would make it easy for the receiving player to control the ball. Options for restarting after a goal is scored can also vary between a restart at the center (as in soccer) and a restart from the goal line (as in basketball). The advantage of using a restart from the goal line in all invasion games is that it speeds up play; players learn to restart more quickly and make effective transitions from defense to offense before the opposing team recovers. The advantage of a restart at the center of the court or field is that it enables a team that has conceded a goal to restart from farther up the court or field. The choice is yours, and it may depend on the characteristics and preferences of your students.

Similarly, some sensible principles help with efficient restarts in net games. First, at the early stages of learning net games, all starts and restarts (i.e., service) should take the form of an underhand toss, or in volleyball, a rainbow toss. This provides a ball that is easier for the opponent to receive and therefore increases the likelihood of a longer rally or a point being played. Second, service should alternate every point so that no single player can dominate a game (or be dominated) as a result of a strong (or weak) serve. Third, always use a rally scoring system in which points can be scored on either team's serve. Most, although not all, net games now use rally scoring, but again, this rule provides more scoring opportunities for novice learners.

Defense Rules

The intensity of defense, particularly in invasion games, is often a hindrance to offensive performance. (We hear you saying, "As it is supposed to be!") Although high-intensity defense is necessary for effective game play, it lessens the likelihood of developing decision-making capacity and motor skill performance. We advocate the teaching and use of a graded system of defense, beginning with cold defense and moving through warm and hot defense. Cold defense is obviously the easiest type of defense to play against. In skill practice and game situations, this amounts to defenders simply being obstacles for players to have to pass or move around. Defenders can neither intercept passes nor knock balls from their opponents' hands when playing cold defense, making it somewhat inappropriate for game play situations.

Warm defense is ideal for novice players because it allows them to intercept passes but not knock the ball out of an opponent's hands or tackle an opponent. In warm defense, a defender must stay one arm's length away from the player in possession of the ball, providing some space and time for decision making and skill execution. Warm defense also provides an appropriate extension of skill practice tasks that begin with cold defense to facilitate skill performance.

Hot defense should be introduced once decision-making and skill learning have taken place. Players are permitted to intercept passes and to tackle in hot defense; tackling has implications for the teaching of appropriate sport behavior. Note that you will probably have to move to hot defense in game situations in which dribbling is allowed because the inability to tackle will make it too easy for players to advance the ball and score.

SUMMARY

The implementation of a tactical games approach across the elementary and secondary grade levels does require that students work independently in terms of organizing and running their own small game situations. Clearly, the sooner students are able to organize themselves the better, and the learning of simple rules, routines, and expectations at an early stage helps with this. We hope the suggestions given in this chapter will enable the learning of these organizational features to go smoothly.

Chapter 4

Getting Started With Tactical Games Teaching

Chapter 3 addressed important considerations for preparing students for a tactical games approach to learning. However, if this approach to teaching games is new for you, you may need to adjust your thinking. This chapter addresses several things to consider as you think about teaching using this approach—particularly, issues related to planning and implementing the content.

The tactical games approach is grounded in a constructivist learning perspective that recognizes the centrality of the learner to the construction of meaning across the psychomotor, cognitive, and affective domains. This approach places students in dynamic game play that requires them to make decisions and reflect on those decisions through assessment and teacher facilitation. All parts of the process are important, and you must take care in planning them.

CONCEPTUAL FRAMEWORK FOR PLANNING TACTICAL TEACHING

In this section we share a conceptual framework to guide your tactical thinking and planning (Griffin and Sheehy 2004) (figure 4.1). The primary features of this planning framework are the (a) games classification system, (b) game or game form focus, (c) tactical problems and levels of tactical complexity, (d) game or game form modifications, (e) questions for teaching, and (f) problem-solving skills as outcomes. Not only do you need to consider the goals and learning activities for the unit, but you also need to think about the length of the unit. If the duration of your unit is short (8 to 10 lessons), you will want to limit the number of tactical problems you address. Using the tactical problems as the organizing feature for the

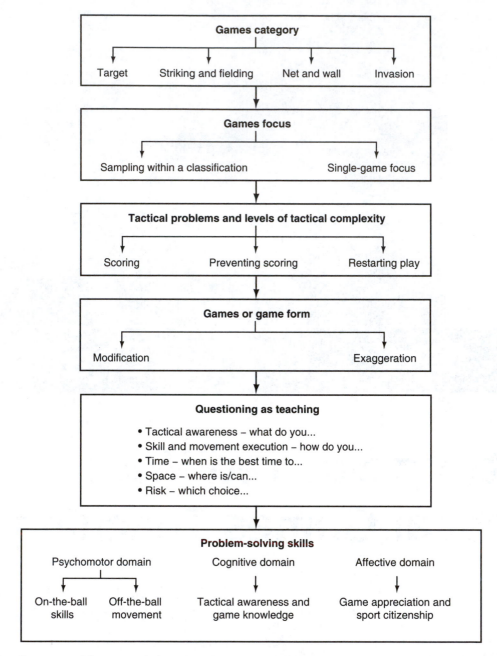

Figure 4.1   Conceptual framework for planning your teaching.

unit provides a clear match between unit length and goals. Limiting the number of tactical problems gives you the opportunity to add depth to your unit—that is, to do a few things well. We advocate establishing a block plan that outlines a progression of learning tasks for each day of your unit. A block plan provides a view of the big picture and can help you focus. Table 4.1 provides a sample block plan for volleyball.

Games Classification System

The first feature to consider in your tactical games planning is the games classification system, which is a categorization scheme based on similarities among the primary rules that define games (Bunker and Thorpe 1982). The primary rules of a game identify how the game is to be played (tactics) and how winning can be achieved. Classifying games provides students with a more expansive view of games and helps them identify similarities of games that are usually considered quite different in terms of specialized skills. In using this approach, you may explicitly teach students to transfer the knowledge they have about one game to another simply because the games are in the same classification. For example, you need to point out that volleyball is a net game that shares tactical similarities with tennis and badminton.

Table 4.1 Sample Volleyball Block Plan

Day 1	Day 2	Day 3	Day 4	Day 5

• Introduction to unit
• 3v3 game:
  ○ Base position
  ○ Free ball (toss)
• Closure
	• 3v3 game
	• Setting up to attack:
	  ○ Forearm pass (FAP)
	• Practice = FAP
	• 3v3 game
	• Closure
		• 3v3 game
		• Setting up to attack
		  ○ Setter open up
		• Practice = FAP and open up
		• 3v3 game
		• Closure
			• 3v3 game
			• Setting up to attack:
			  ○ Setter pass to hitter
			• Practice = open up and pass to hitter
			• 3v3 game
			• Closure
				• 3v3 game
				• Setting up to attack and winning the point:
				  ○ Transition by hitter
				• Practice = pass, open up, and transition
				• 3v3 game
				• Closure

Day 6	Day 7	Day 8	Day 9	Day 10
• 3v3 game • Winning the point by attacking the ball • Practice = hitting and spiking • 3v3 game • Closure	• 3v3 game • Attacking the ball: ○ Transition to hit or spike • Extend practice • 3v3 game • Closure	• 3v3 game • Review = setting up to attack and winning the point by attack • 3v3 game • Closure	• 3v3 game • Review = setting up to attack and winning the point by attack • 3v3 game • Closure	• 3v3 tournament • Closure

Game Focus

Game focus involves considering the intent of the unit (e.g., exploring tactical problems across games) and the various games and game forms you need to design to meet the goals of the lesson or unit. When creating game experiences, you may organize the unit in one of two ways: game sampling or single game.

• **Game sampling.** The purpose of game sampling is to provide students with a variety of experiences that show the similarities and differences among games (Holt, Strean, and Bengoechea 2002). The games classification system can facilitate the sampling process by providing a selection of games with similar tactical problems, in contrast to the traditional approach of teaching one specific sport as a unit topic. For example, you might want your students to experience solving the tactical problems of setting up to attack and winning the point across various net and wall games such as pickleball, badminton, and volleyball. To help them transfer learning from one game to another, students can encounter, and you can point out, the common tactical elements or problems in each of the three games.

• **Single game.** The purpose of a single-game focus within a unit is to provide students with an in-depth experience of the tactical problems and decision-making options associated with one particular game (e.g., volleyball). Selecting a single game for a unit with a high level of content knowledge is strongly advocated if you are a first-time user of the tactical games model. Either choice—game sampling or single game—provides a context in which to facilitate students' development and the effective use of problem-solving skills.

Tactical Problems and Levels of Tactical Complexity

The next feature to think about is the tactical problems and the complexity of the problems you want your students to solve. As you know, central to the tactical games model are the tactical problems presented by various games. Tactical problems are those that must be overcome to score, prevent scoring, and restart play. Having identified the relevant tactical problems that a game presents, students need to solve these problems by making appropriate decisions and applying appropriate movements and skills. Levels of tactical complexity help you match tactical complexity with your students' problem-solving development. As students develop an understanding of tactical problems and appropriate solutions, you can increase the complexity of the game; that is, working with levels of tactical complexity affords a way of teaching games in a developmentally appropriate manner.

Game and Game Form

Games refers to small-sided competitive challenges in teams with equal numbers of players (e.g., 3v3), whereas *game forms* refers to highlighted tactical situations, often encountered during a full version of the game, in which the numbers of players on the teams are uneven (e.g., 3v2). Game forms emphasize tactical problems, thereby giving students multiple opportunities to problem solve and practice the appropriate tactical response (French and McPherson 2003). Proponents of the tactical games model argue that all students can play a game if that game is modified to enable meaningful play to occur (Ellis 1986; Mitchell, Oslin, and Griffin 2003). This may mean beginning with few skills, few rules, and as few players as possible. Modified games or game forms, however, should be representative of the mature form of the sport, and conditioned (i.e., exaggerated by rule changes) to emphasize tactical problems encountered within the game (i.e., changing the secondary rules) (Mitchell, Oslin, and Griffin 2003). The following are five aspects of the game or game form that can help you exaggerate a particular tactical problem.

- *Rules*. Rules define what players can and cannot do in a game and can be changed (i.e., game conditions) to create specific learning emphases. For example, in 3v3 volleyball there might be a rule to alternate the serve using a free-ball toss. Alternating the serve using a free-ball toss makes starting the game simple and highly successful and gives both teams an equal chance to receive the serve.

- *Number of players*. Small-sided games or game forms (3v3 or 2v1) slow down the tempo and flow of a game, thus limiting the tactical complexity, which in turn simplifies the decision-making process. They also maximize the potential for every student to be a decision maker within a game or game form.

- *Playing area*. Altering the size of the playing area or changing the size of the goal may help students focus on learning a particular aspect of the game. For example, a 3v3 volleyball game may involve a narrow court (e.g., one-half of a regular court) and a lower net.

Narrowing the court and lowering the net allow the students to focus on a small playing area, making the game easier for novice players. Larger playing areas in invasion games provide players with more time for decision making and skill execution, whereas smaller areas have the opposite effect making the game harder.

- *Equipment*. Modifying the playing equipment to make the students feel safer allows for more successful execution of skills and movements. For example, students are more likely to attempt the forearm pass or dig when using trainer volleyballs.

- *Scoring or modifying the goal*. Changing scoring rules allows you to shape the game to reinforce practice. For example, in a volleyball lesson, teams can earn points for containing the first pass on their side of the court.

Questioning as Teaching

As mentioned in chapter 1, questioning is a critical teaching skill used in the tactical games model. Questions help you guide your students in identifying solutions to the tactical problem presented in the game. As a facilitator, you need to know when to use questions and when to provide answers. Literature on tactical games teaching has been consistent in emphasizing the importance of quality questions (Bunker and Thorpe 1982; Den Duyn 1997). The quality of questions is critical to problem solving in a tactical games model and should be an integral part of the planning process. These questions fall into five categories:

- Tactical awareness—What do you . . .?
- Skill and movement execution—How do you . . .?
- Time—When is the best time to . . .?
- Space—Where is . . .?
- Risk—Which is the best choice between . . .?

Each type of question is not necessarily asked during a single questioning session. You determine the number and types of questions based on the readiness of your students.

 TIP BOX

Games should be mostly small-sided and modified to present students with problems they must solve.

 TIP BOX

Good questioning is very important because questions help students understand the need for skill practice based on their performance in the game.

Problem-Solving Skills

The tactical games approach is a student-centered approach in that the teacher merely facilitates the learning process. As the facilitator, you set problems or goals by organizing the game or game form, and then give your students the opportunity to solve these problems. One of the basic premises of the tactical games approach is that to become good games players, students need to become good problem solvers. Students need to be able to define the problem, gather information about the problem, identify the decision-making options, make the decision, and put the decision into action. To do this, they need game experiences to help them develop their problem-solving skills. Through questions, you help your students explore possible solutions to the problem. These solutions then become the focus of a situated practice. You also facilitate practice by either simplifying the game or introducing more challenging game conditions to meet students' abilities. In this way you work with the student's prior knowledge to develop new knowledge.

PUTTING THE PLANNING FRAMEWORK INTO ACTION

Having explained the thinking behind the conceptual framework, in this section we provide an example of the decisions the teacher makes that put the tactical games planning framework into action. Using the conceptual framework (figure 4.1), let's say a physical education teacher at a middle school decides to further student understanding of net and wall games and chooses a single-game focus on volleyball because the students completed a net and wall game sampling unit last year. The sampling unit focused on setting up to attack and winning the point in pickleball, table tennis, and volleyball. The teacher knows that the students are novice players and selects scoring as the main tactical problem and determines the level of tactical complexity to be level I.

Now that the teacher has made decisions about the game category, game focus, tactical problems, levels of tactical complexity, and modifications, he will use questioning as opportunities occur during the first lesson within this volleyball unit. The tactical problem for the first lesson is setting up to attack, with a lesson focus on base position and containing the ball on one side of the net. The 50-minute lesson begins with students involved in 3v3 games, each of which is played on half a court (a total of 12 students per court), with the goal of attempting to contain the first pass on their team's side of the court. The conditions of the game include a narrow court with a lower net and

up to three hits per side. The game is initiated from a playable, two-handed, overhead toss (free ball), which then alternates between teams to begin each point. As the students play, the teacher observes.

After a short game of approximately seven minutes, the games break down (meaning that students cannot direct consistent passes to the middle, the ball doesn't go over the net, and so on). At that point, the teacher begins to ask students questions with the purpose of encouraging self-directed, reflective analysis of their game play. The following is a representation of a typical exchange:

- Teacher: What did you do to contain the ball on your side of the net? (tactical awareness)
  Students: Hit the ball high.

- Teacher: Where would be the best place to pass the ball? (space)
  Students: The middle of the court.

- Teacher: How did you hit the ball to keep control? (skill selection and execution)
  Students: Used hands (overhead pass) or bumped it using forearms (forearm pass).

As illustrated, through the questioning process, the students verbally identify issues related to solving the tactical problem of containing the first pass. Now that the students have identified these solutions, the teacher needs to situate them in practice situations that reward and reinforce good decision making, not just good skill execution (French and McPherson 2003). Further, when the skill is placed within the game context, the importance of being able to execute it consistently is highlighted, thereby increasing students' focus during practice.

At this point students return to their playing courts and practice in triad formations with one tosser, one passer, and one setter. From the location on the court that simulates actual game play, the tosser sends a rainbow toss to the passer, who uses a forearm pass to direct the ball to the setter. The setter then catches the ball and bounce passes it back to the tosser. After three trials, the students switch roles, allowing each student to practice each of the roles during the majority of the class time. During practice the teacher circulates and asks students what they are thinking. Just asking questions can focus their attention on tactics (French and McPherson 2003). The lesson then ends with a 3v3 game using the same conditions as the initial game; however, now teams earn points (i.e., change in secondary rule) when they attempt a forearm pass as a way to contain the ball on their side of the court.

THE TEACHER AND THE CHANGE PROCESS

As they say in Texas, "If all you ever do is all you've ever done, then all you'll ever get is all you ever got" (Friedman 2008, p. 6). The nature of change is crucial to physical education as a viable subject in P-12 schooling. In this section we present critical aspects of the multidimensional and complex nature of the change process (Fullan 2001; Sparkes 1990). According to Sparkes (1990), there are three necessary dimensions (materials, teaching approaches, and beliefs) of the change process that need to occur at deepening levels.

In their review of games research, Oslin and Mitchell (2006) found research on the perceptions of teachers (i.e., preservice and in-service) regarding the implementation of games-centered teaching approaches. Findings from this research on teacher change processes can inform you as you make the shift to teach using a tactical approach.

Preservice teachers enjoyed being taught via a games-centered approach (Light 2003) and showed better understanding of tactics through course work focused on tactical concepts (Howarth and Walkuski 2003). It appears that tactical concepts presented through various forms of preservice course work help teachers' tactical understanding develop. The caution raised by researchers is that preservice teachers with more experience grasp the tactical concepts faster than do those with less experience. In addition, some findings indicate that preservice teachers used more higher-order cognitive questions when teaching using a games-centered approach (Gubacs 1999; Light 2003; McNeill et al. 2004; Sullivan and Swabey 2003). Positive experiences for the preservice teachers were greatly increased by cooperating teachers' ability to identify similarities between a constructivist approach and a games-centered approach.

In-service teachers experienced similar adjustment times to those of preservice teachers in regard to shifting from a technical to a games-centered approach, developing new pedagogical content knowledge, and using varied higher-order questions (Brooker et al. 2001; Butler 1993; Doolittle 1983; Gubacs 2000; Gubacs et al. 1998). After gaining experience with the games-centered approach, in-service teachers were positive and reported having more time to observe and assess student performance. Teachers gained confidence in their ability to plan and implement a games-centered approach and expressed an appreciation for the student-centered nature of a games-centered approach.

Research on the teacher change process can guide the development of teacher knowledge and practices (Oslin and Mitchell 2006) particularly as they implement new approaches to teaching. We encourage you to consider these findings and to continually strive to reflect on and improve your performance, thus approaching your teaching as a learner. This section addresses the following four skills and attitudes identified by Joyce and Showers (1995) that might enhance your learning potential as a teacher: putting your learning into action, persistence, meeting the cognitive demands of instruction, and flexibility.

Putting Learning Into Action

You have probably attended many classes, conferences, and workshops and read books that have motivated you to consider changing the way you teach. But how do you turn your motivation into action? In other words, what do you need to consider as you begin your change journey? We invite you to consider the following aspects that are critical to the implementation of a new teaching approach: ownership of the change, teacher beliefs, pedagogical content knowledge, and persistence.

Ownership of Change

The teacher is the most important player in any effort to change a teaching approach (Hall and Hord 2001). Thus, the ownership of the innovation (i.e., change) is critical to the success of adopting it. Research suggests that several factors are critical to ownership for teachers: (a) the norms of the school culture (i.e., context matters) and the psychological temperament of the teachers (Rovegno and Bandhauer 1997a, 1997b); (b) informal opportunities to learn with and from other teachers (Armour and Yelling 2007); (c) shared vision and decision making and external support, and (d) the value physical education has in schools (Dyson and O'Sullivan 1998). Teachers need to determine what the change means to them personally, keeping in mind that making a significant change involves a certain amount of ambiguity, ambivalence, and uncertainty about the meaning of the change. Thus, successful implementation of a new teaching approach is truly a process of clarification (Fullan 2001).

Teacher Beliefs

Several assumptions about the nature of teacher change underlie current approaches to teacher professional development:

- Teachers' beliefs play a central role in the process of teacher development.

- Changes in teachers' beliefs precede changes in teachers' practices.
- The notion of teacher change is multidimensional and is prompted by personal factors and professional work contexts.

To move toward change, we need to examine our core beliefs. Beliefs are highly resistant to change and serve as a filter through which our experiences must pass (Lortie 1975; Pajares 1992). Beliefs help us understand our world and persevere even when contradictory evidence is presented (Nisbett and Ross 1980; Peterman 1991). Core beliefs form the center of a belief system. They are the most powerful beliefs and exert a strong influence over other beliefs. Core beliefs are also the most resistant to change because they become part of us at an early stage (Nisbett and Ross 1980; Rokeach 1968). Generally, beliefs are not explicit, discussed, or understood. Teachers are rarely asked about, or for that matter given sufficient time to reflect on, their beliefs about teaching and learning. Any significant innovation, if it is what Sparkes (1990) calls "real change," requires individuals to work out their own personal meanings (Fullan 1991).

Figure 4.2 offers a games teaching continuum to help you think about your core beliefs about games teaching.

On the left side of the continuum is the technical approach, on the right side is a tactical games approach, and in the middle is a progression of what we refer to as a gamelike approach. A gamelike approach shifts practice from isolated technical drills (e.g., shuttle or circle drills in volleyball, which focus on one skill) to drills arranged within the tempo and flow of the game (e.g., a triad drill in volleyball).

The games teaching continuum acts as a gauge to give you a reading of where you are and offers possible progressions for moving your games teaching toward a tactical approach. One teacher from our workshops and research shared her change in her core beliefs in this way (Berkowitz 1996, p. 44):

Until a few years ago, I taught technical skills in isolation; detached from the game or activity, such as, forearm passing to oneself or set to the wall . . . . The realization that I made very little impact on the level of skill improvement in my students has caused me to reconsider my philosophical perspective. I no longer expect my students to demonstrate a specified level of skill proficiency. Rather, the expectation is utilization of various skills to accomplish the tactics within the game.

Pedagogical Content Knowledge

Pedagogical content knowledge (PCK) is a specific category of knowledge (Grossman 1990; Shulman 1986) with the following key elements:

- Knowledge of strategies and representations for teaching particular topics
- Knowledge of students' understanding, conceptions, and misconceptions of these topics
- Knowledge of and beliefs about the purpose of teaching particular topics
- Knowledge of curriculum materials available for teaching

At the heart, PCK is made up of three related categories: subject matter knowledge, general pedagogical knowledge, and contextual knowledge.

Implementing a tactical games approach is a way of thinking and being as an educator. Think of adopting this approach as a new way of thinking and developing your PCK for games education. As teachers, we understand games education differently from how other experts, such as highly skilled performers, understand it. Highly successful teachers and coaches have well-developed PCK, which includes a knowledge of many ways to represent movement for learners. PCK is highly domain specific, so for example, teachers with rich soccer knowledge may not have rich knowledge about tennis or softball. The richest PCK about games education affords teachers the best opportunities to build bridges between students and physical activities, and to help students become skillful, thinking movers (Griffin, Dodds, and Rovegno 1996).

We view a tactical games approach as a way to help teachers integrate everything they know and to consider holistic curriculum models of PCK (i.e., curriculum models that integrate knowledge of content, teaching strategies, and how students learn the content). A tactical games approach, as a curriculum model for games teaching, takes into account students' needs

Technical	Gamelike	Tactical

Figure 4.2 Games teaching continuum.

and motivations to learn, thus informing teachers' PCK. The underlying constructivist learning theory, the rationale for the approach, and the organizing structures (games classification, frameworks, levels of tactical and game complexity, and assessment) provide a comprehensive way of thinking and being as a games educator.

Persistence

Persistence is what Joyce and Showers (1995) called "driving through" the initial trials in which performance is awkward. For example, as a player, you know how hard it is to change your golf swing or your tennis backhand. Think about how hard it is as a teacher to give up using calisthenics as warm-ups or to use a game *before* skill practice. The key to success often is pure determination (not necessarily talent); this will go a long way in helping you overcome the difficulty of changing behavior.

During a project that focused on learning to teach using a tactical approach, Danielle, a middle school physical education teacher, provided an example of persistence when we asked her how she felt about using a new approach with sixth-graders. Danielle answered, "When you have taught one way and you are in the pressure of the moment, you have to work hard not to go back to your old way."

> ### ◈ TIP BOX
>
> Change can be difficult. Start with small changes, build on them, and be persistent!

Meeting the Cognitive Demands of Instruction

Teachers have complained that their preservice programs have overemphasized theory and neglected the practical aspects of teaching (Joyce and Showers 1995). Nonetheless, teachers who acknowledge the importance of understanding theory can better meet the cognitive demands of instruction. When you know what to do and how to do it, you can be flexible and use the new knowledge appropriately in many situations.

Flexibility

Flexibility is the openness to consider that alternatives have something to offer. Being flexible is important in all aspects of teaching, and it can also serve you

well when you participate in the teacher-as-learner process. For example, a teacher who has always used a technical approach to games teaching starts his volleyball unit by teaching the forearm pass and setting students up to practice this skill. Generally, his role is that of *information giver* (direct instruction). Now this teacher shifts to implementing a tactical approach in the volleyball unit. He places students in small-sided games and, after game play, gathers them for discussion, using his questions to address the value of setting up to attack using the forearm pass. The teacher's role now shifts from information giver to *information processor* (indirect instruction). This role shift requires the teacher to be flexible.

IMPLEMENTING PRACTICES

Our teacher-development efforts have helped us identify some helpful implementation practices. These practices help create a safe learning-by-doing climate (Stallings 1989):

- Have a plan.
- Remember that change for you also means change for your students.
- Think gamelike.
- Make sure your lessons reflect a game-questions-practice-game progression.
- Develop professional learning communities (PLCs).

Let's discuss each of these practices in detail.

• **Have a plan.** You need to have a plan that is based on what you have learned in this chapter about change but also what you know about yourself and the change process. Keep in mind that change is a process of clarification and is likely to come through reflective practice (i.e., keeping a journal, discussing with a colleague).

　○ Select a sport-related game that you feel most comfortable with (i.e., your favorite or your best). This ensures that you start with strong content knowledge so you can link prior knowledge with new information (Stallings 1989). Our firsthand experience and our observations of and collaborations with preservice and in-service teachers as they grapple with a tactical games approach has shown that strong content knowledge makes transfer easier. For example, one teacher chose volleyball because she had played competitively at the college level and coached at the high school level. Because this was her strongest sport, she was able to break it down into smaller tactical parts such as setting up for a pass-set-hit, receiving a serve, and defending against a free ball.

○ Consider how you might plan a whole unit. First, consider your goals or objectives. Ask yourself what tactical problems you want your students to solve. Here you have two choices: consult our levels of tactical complexity, or use the tactical problems to organize your unit and develop your own levels. For example, if you are getting ready to teach a volleyball unit, you might focus only on the tactical problems of setting up to attack and winning the point. After you have decided on the tactical problems, you can consult this book about the levels of tactical complexity to establish the on-the-ball skills and off-the-ball movements appropriate for your students' level.

• **Remember that change for you also means change for your students.** Part of the difficulty in introducing a new teaching process into the classroom is students' discomfort with change (Joyce and Showers 1995). A new teaching approach for you is a new learning approach for your students, so it is a change for all of you. We advocate starting by piloting a unit with *one* class of your choice, preferably one in which students work well together (Griffin 1996). Because the primary structure of a tactical approach is the small-sided game or game form, you need to feel comfortable teaching many small groups or pairs (Berkowitz 1996). If you consider this a pilot test, then you may feel more open to the peaks and pits of the change process. You may decide to pilot a volleyball unit with one class before the actual unit is scheduled in the curriculum so that you can make changes and try them right away. In this way, you build a safe environment in which to explore an alternative approach to games teaching and learning.

• **Think gamelike.** Thinking gamelike means considering how you can arrange the skills and tactics for practice within the flow and tempo of the game (Griffin 1996). For example, gamelike practice for volleyball requires a triad formation. Figure 4.3 illustrates the triad with a focus on forearm passing. The triad formation involves a minimum of three players fulfilling three roles—initiator, performer, and target player—within each drill (Griffin 1994). If you have more than three players in the drill, you can add roles such as collector, feeder, or additional performer. Triad drills, such as toss and pass to a target, serve and serve receive to a target, toss-set-hit, pass-set-hit, or any other skill or tactical combinations of the game, simulate the tempo and flow of volleyball. Gamelike drills enhance the quality of practice.

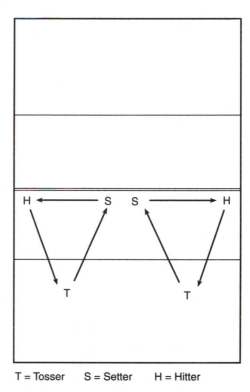

T = Tosser   S = Setter   H = Hitter

Figure 4.3 Focus on forearm passing in a triad.

Thinking gamelike increases the likelihood of carryover into the game. Drills such as practicing a volleyball skill against the wall, partners passing back and forth without the net, using a circle or semicircle to practice skills, and using a shuttle formation to practice skills provide many opportunities to practice, but clearly have nothing to do with the flow and tempo of a volleyball game. Gamelike practice allows students to develop skills within the context of the game. It also promotes a cooperative learning environment.

• **Make sure your lessons reflect a game-questions-practice-game progression.** Let's take a closer look at the lesson plan format used in this book.

• *Tactical problem (what you say to your students).* The tactical problem is the big-picture feature that guides each lesson plan. The tactical problem is what you say to the student when you start your lesson. For example, "Today we will be working on solving the problem of setting up to attack in volleyball."

• *Lesson focus (what you ask your students).* The lesson focus relates to the on-the-ball skills and off-the-ball movements you want your students to become aware of to solve a tactical problem. The lesson focus guides your questions. For example, if you want your students to understand the value of calling for the ball in volleyball, your questions should reflect that lesson focus, such as, "What should you do if two teammates are close to the ball?" or, "When is the best time to call for the ball?" The questions should align with the focus of the lesson.

- *Objective (what your students practice).* The objective should help you design your practice. For example, if the objective is for the students to call for the ball ("Mine"), then you should arrange a practice in which two players who are near each other work out who calls and when to call for the ball.

- *Initial game.* First, game conditions refer to the essential components, such as the number of students, size of the court or playing area, equipment type (e.g., regulation or modified ball) and modifications (e.g., net height), and specific conditions (e.g., two hits on a side, three passes before a shot). Second, the goal of the game will directly reflect the focus of the lesson. We continue with the volleyball example in which students are engaged in a small-sided volleyball game. Game conditions are lower net, narrow and short court, modified volleyball, game initiated from a free ball, alternating toss, and rotation after each point. The goal of the game is for teams to score a point each time the pass goes to the setter.

- *Questions.* We have learned that constructing questions presents some difficulty at first. Three key aspects to questioning are (a) limiting the number of questions to two or three, (b) working with (incorporating) students' answers, and (c) aligning questions with the lesson focus. Again, we offer these question stems to help guide you:
  - What do you . . .? (Tactical awareness)
  - How do you . . .? (Skill selection and execution)
  - When is the best time to . . .? (Timing)
  - Where is or can . . .? (Space)
  - Which choice . . .? (Risk)

- *Practice task.* Essential elements for quality practice involve (a) running drills on the field or court because this is where games are played, (b) organizing gamelike practices to match the game-playing goal, (c) using specific feedback related to key words, (d) providing goals for practice, and (e) keeping activity compatible with the skill levels of players. Going back to the volleyball lesson, students would practice the forearm pass in triads (see chapter 8, level I, lesson 1 for details).

- *Closing game.* The purpose of the closing game is to reinforce the focus or goal of your lesson and to give students a chance to practice their skills. The conditions of the game reflect all of the essential game components. This game may or may not be different from the initial game you have read about in the specific sport chapters. You can consider it a way of reinforcing the goal of the lesson, perhaps by having students keep track of the number of shots taken in basketball games or the number of passes completed in soccer. To finish the volleyball example, students return to the original game and the original conditions to reinforce the lesson goal. Students could compare their scores in the initial game to those in the closing game or count the number of successful forearm passes to a target.

- **Develop professional learning communities (PLCs).** Learning is a social process that may be viewed as activities in which learners participate in communities of practice, also referred to as professional learning communities (PLCs), and move toward full participation in the sociocultural practices of the group over time (Lave and Wenger 1991). PLCs can be places where teachers gather regularly to share the trials and tribulations of teaching and learning, take part in professional debate, and reflect on their practices with supportive colleagues. Following are several examples of PLCs related to games-centered teaching (i.e., the tactical games approach).

  - Media and materials: Many publications (written and video) published on this topic are resources to help you begin to think and believe differently about games education.

  - Conference presentations: Although conferences can be limited in effect, they do offer some connection to the concept and the people passionate about this work. The games-centered approach is a global movement that offers chances to meet and debate with a group of passionate people. We have never met a games-centered person who did not want to talk about his or her work.

> ◇ **TIP BOX**
>
> Finding company, in the form of other teachers, can help the process of curriculum change.

- Workshops or institutes: Various workshops and institutes provide camplike experiences in which you can immerse yourself in the concepts and be with like-minded people.

The possible benefits of teachers helping each other are endless. Knowing whom to approach, knowing what to ask for help with, and being sensitive to one another's needs will go a long way in building a strong professional culture. As teachers, we need to have others to share our successes with and to support us in taking risks.

SUMMARY

A tactical games approach with an emphasis on authentic performance provides an active, in-depth learning setting for students. An underlying goal of the tactical games approach is to appeal to students' interest in games playing so that they value working toward improved game performance.

We believe that a tactical games approach enables students to understand games more deeply than a technical approach does, to play more effectively, and to appreciate the similarities among games. Here, a teacher reflects on her feelings about implementing a tactical approach:

There have been a number of positive outcomes using this approach. If my goal was to have students play the game more effectively, then letting them play the game was critical. Because my students have had increasingly more opportunities to play games and solve tactical problems, they seem to have a better understanding of games in general. Technical skill work still occurs but never in isolation, always as it would in the game and mostly as a means to accomplish the tactical problems. Students come in excited, positive, and ready to go because they know they are going to get to play a game of some form. I no longer hear, "Are we going to play a game today?" (Berkowitz 1996, 45)

The tactical approach is a holistic approach that takes into consideration students' cognitive, psychomotor, affective development. It provides students of all developmental levels with a greater understanding of games and improved game performance by teaching them tactical awareness (Mitchell, Griffin, and Oslin 1994). The tactical approach also focuses on developmentally appropriate skill acquisition and ensures that students learn skills when they can appreciate their value to the game. Students then practice these skills under conditions that enable them to relate the skills to game contexts.

The process of teaching for tactical awareness is based on *playing the game*, an enjoyable activity for most students. The primary goal of physical education programs, to promote lifetime participation in physical activity, will only be achieved if students enjoy physical activity. The identification and assessment of outcomes based on tactical awareness can contribute to progressive gains in game performance, critical thinking, and enjoyment at successive stages of development. In this chapter we leave you with the challenge of matching content such as soccer, volleyball, and softball with a context that helps students make meaning—through playing games!

Tactical Games Curriculum Model

The previous chapters provided some food for thought regarding planning and implementing a tactical games approach, but focused primarily on teaching individual lessons and units. In this chapter we encourage you to go further and consider making the tactical games approach less of an innovation and more a normal part of your physical education curriculum. Kirk (2005) argued that tactical approaches to games teaching can become "mainstream practice" within physical education and youth sport programs. For this to become reality, Kirk suggested that, in addition to revising the research agenda, proponents of tactical approaches focus on conceptualizing a model for tactical games teaching and base instructional resources on this formalized approach.

In *Instructional Models for Physical Education,* Metzler (2011) called for "model-based instruction" as a means of focusing on long-term, holistic learning outcomes. He described a teaching model as a set of teaching patterns that "ties together theory, planning, classroom management, teaching-learning processes, and assessment" (p. xxiv). In this book we have attempted to tie together these facets of curriculum and instruction. We support Metzler's call for model-based instruction using a tactical games approach by proposing a conceptual framework for a tactical games model and linking the elementary and secondary levels to suggest how a tactical games model can span the physical education curriculum. In this chapter, we revisit the concepts underpinning the original model, simplify this model for the teacher, and reemphasize the ties among planning, management, and teaching–learning processes that have been described in the preceding chapters and introduce the issue of assessment that will be more fully addressed in the next chapter.

ASSUMPTIONS UNDERPINNING A TACTICAL GAMES CURRICULUM

A curriculum model is not values-free, and several assumptions underpin the tactical games model. To make our values clear, we should identify these assumptions.

First, proponents of the model believe that games are important to the physical education curriculum because they are enjoyable lifetime physical activities and they are based on sport, which is a prominent social institution in our society. Educators who implement games instruction in physical education at all levels value games playing as an activity in its own right. Proponents value games for their educational benefits, including emphases on decision making, problem solving, communication, teamwork, and skillfulness.

Second, all students can understand and play games at their particular ability levels. Unfortunately, it is not uncommon to hear that some students cannot play games because they lack skill (we have even been told this by high school teachers). This is exactly the reason for the small-sided game play and the distinct modifications to games made throughout chapters 7 through 22.

Third, and related to the previous assumption, games can be modified to represent their mature forms, and they can be conditioned (i.e., exaggerated by rule changes) to emphasize tactical problems encountered within the game. Each lesson in chapters 7 through 22 contains examples of modifications designed to place students in problem-solving situations.

◇ TIP BOX

Proponents of the tactical games model argue that younger students of perhaps lower abilities can play games if those games are modified to enable meaningful play.

Games have common tactical elements, or problems, and understanding these elements can help students transfer learning from one game to another.

Tactical problems form the basis of the games classification system presented in table 2.1. Some preservice teachers and experienced teachers express the concern that they don't know games well enough or, more frequently, do not know a particular game sufficiently enough to modify and teach with any expertise. Clearly, it is advantageous for teachers to be games players or at least to know games if they are to successfully use a tactical games model in their teaching.

Our response to the "knowledge" concern is that most teachers probably know a lot more about most games than they realize, particularly if they apply what they know about one game to another. For example, a college basketball player once told us that she was not sufficiently comfortable with the game of soccer to develop its scope and sequence and then teach it successfully. We suggested that she might begin by taking what she knew about basketball, which was extensive and specific, and applying it to soccer. Using this approach, she was able to develop lesson content based on deciding when to shoot, pass, or dribble and around defensive aspects of the game such as marking, or guarding. Although knowing a game will obviously help you teach it, you do not need to know all games well!

As we suggest in chapter 2, if you are not familiar with games content, try to learn one game from each category and then apply that knowledge to other games within the same category. Knowing one game gives you a good understanding of the main rules of game play, an appreciation for basic tactical considerations, knowledge of starting and restarting play, and an appreciation for the spirit in which games can and should be played. For teachers with little or no games experience, printed resources (including this book) are a good place to begin seeking lesson ideas.

CONCEPTUAL FRAMEWORK

A curriculum model is sometimes best understood by referring to a diagram, or conceptual framework, outlining its major components. A conceptual framework for the tactical games model is presented in figure 5.1. Central to the model are the tactical problems the various games present—problems that must be overcome to score, prevent scoring, and restart play. Having identified the relevant tactical problems of a game, students solve them by making appropriate decisions and applying appropriate movements and skills. Again, many games within each category have similar tactical problems, and understanding these similarities can assist in transferring performance from one game to another.

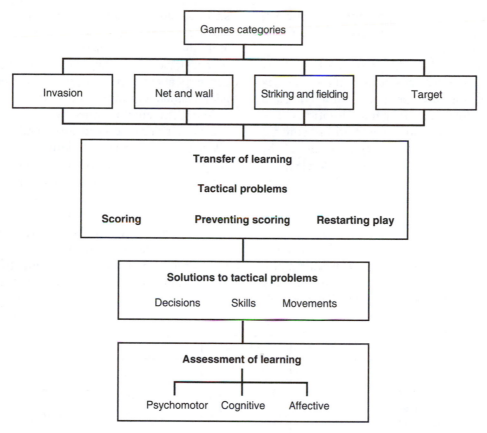

Figure 5.1 A conceptual framework for the tactical games curriculum model.

We believe that it is possible and desirable to develop a progressive and sequential tactical games curriculum across the compulsory education spectrum, beginning at second grade (about age 7). In part II of this book we suggest a thematic approach as a means of building sport foundations in children, whereas in part III we use a more sport-specific approach to allow for greater specificity and greater development of performance competence. Choosing an approach is clearly an issue of content development; the conceptual framework in figure 5.1 can help you identify relevant tactical content. Tactical frameworks are then used to develop levels of game complexity to ensure that content is planned in developmentally appropriate progressions based on the development of game understanding and performance skill.

MODEL-BASED INSTRUCTION

In this section we address the tactical games curriculum in light of Metzler's (2011) characteristics of model-based instruction. Our point in doing this is to emphasize the development of tactical games teaching from a teaching model (Bunker and Thorpe 1982) to a curriculum model.

Planning

Chapters in parts II and III of this book include numerous lesson outlines using the planning format presented in chapter 1. This format represents a simplification of the original six-stage Teaching Games for Understanding (TGfU) model (Bunker and Thorpe

> ◆ **TIP BOX**
>
> All parts of the tactical games model are important and must be planned so that
>
> - games are modified appropriately to encourage student thinking relative to the tactical problem on which instruction is focused,
> - questions are designed to develop tactical awareness (an understanding of what to do to solve a problem) and are well thought out, and
> - practice tasks teach essential skills to solve problems in as gamelike a manner as possible.

1982). This original model is presented in figure 5.2, with the simplified format again shown for comparison purposes in figure 5.3.

The original TGfU model presented by Bunker and Thorpe (figure 5.2) described a more complex six-stage model for developing decision making and improving performance in game situations. The simplified three-stage model presented in figure 5.3 focuses on the essential lesson components of the model—namely, modified game play, the development of tactical awareness and decision making through questioning, and skill development.

Management

In physical education, time constraints often mandate the creation of sound and efficient management procedures. Too often in both elementary and secondary gymnasiums, students enter the gym and immediately sit in squad lines for attendance and wait for the teacher to begin the lesson warm-up (often stretches and calisthenics). Teachers who adopt this and other time-inefficient procedures are usually the first to raise concerns about their ability to implement a tactical games lesson within the allocated time.

With students assigned to permanent "home" courts or fields, the need for attendance squads is alleviated. If attendance taking is required, it can simply be accomplished by observation once students are actively engaged in game play. The management structures that are an integral facet of Sport Education provide an effective framework through which a tactical games model can be implemented.

The organization of teams, assignment of simple roles and responsibilities, and identification and designation of field spaces and home fields or courts can facilitate effective management and place your

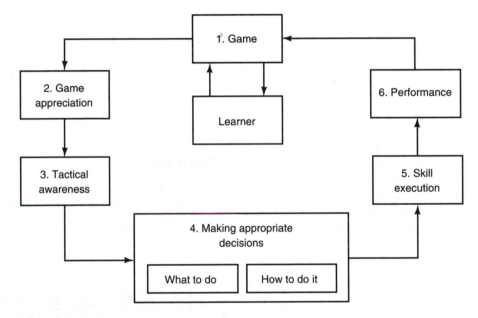

Figure 5.2 TGfU model.

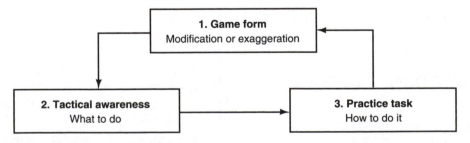

Figure 5.3 Simplified tactical games model.

Adapted from R.D. Thorpe and D.J. Bunker, 1986, A model for the teaching of games in secondary schools. In *Rethinking games teaching*, edited by R. Thorpe, D. Bunker, and L. Almond (Loughborough University), 8. By permission of D.J. Bunker.

tactical games teaching within an appropriate sport context. In this section we advocate the use of Sport Education (Siedentop, Hastie, and van der Mars 2011) to organize teams, equipment, and games to help students develop game play and sport behaviors. The Sport Education curriculum helps students develop into competent, literate, and enthusiastic participants. It is not our intention to describe all the features of this curriculum model in depth. Rather, we briefly describe the way we have used it to facilitate the use of a tactical approach to games instruction at both the elementary and secondary levels.

The team contract (reproducible 5.1) is a sample contract that might be used at the secondary level. In fact, we have used this type of contract with groups ranging from fourth-graders to undergraduate

students and across a range of games. Each student accepts responsibility for one of the roles on the contract and signs her name next to that role to confirm a willingness to carry out the necessary responsibilities. Once responsibilities are defined, students enter the gymnasium and begin play immediately under the direction of the team coach. Each team is assigned a home court to which team members go upon entering the gym. The equipment manager distributes vests of the appropriate color and sets up goals (if needed for the game being played). Coaches report to you, the teacher, to find out the introductory activity (game), or they might go to a "coaches' corner" to read the starting activity from the chalkboard. Alternatively, the coach might have some latitude to work with her team on things previously learned. The administrator takes attendance, and warm-up and stretching can begin under the direction of the athletic trainer. Teams remain the same throughout the sport "season," which includes both a regular season and a postseason. Introductory game play is often done within teams, as are skill practices, which are organized at the home court by the coach, eliminating the need for time-consuming transitions to alternative playing areas and avoiding confusion on the part of the students as to where they should conduct practices.

With all students aware of their responsibilities to the team, lessons can begin and run to conclusion smoothly and in a time-efficient manner. Small changes are communicated by the teacher to the coaches, thereby eliminating the need to communicate information by gathering in the whole class. Students, primarily each team's statistician, keep track of win–loss records and fair play or performance points (awarded by the teacher) to decide on a regular season champion prior to commencing "playoffs." In addition to providing effective management, this system also teaches appropriate sport behaviors. In using the Sport Education model, we have seen and heard quality discussions within and among teams concerning individual members' responsibilities and the importance of ensuring that these responsibilities are fulfilled. Sport behavior has also been discussed, and the importance of fair play and effective leadership by coaches becomes apparent. Disputes are resolved by a replay, and the value of shaking hands and congratulating opponents on a well-played game is also stressed.

Teaching and Learning

Using a tactical games model means using mixed teaching strategies, including direct and indirect

Reproducible 5.1

Team Contract

Class _____

Semester _____

Sport _____

Team name _____

The team members and especially the coaches should demonstrate the following:

1. Good sporting behavior.
2. Fair play—Know and play by class and game rules.
3. Hard work—Practice and work your hardest to be a good team player.
4. Cooperation—Whenever possible, team decisions should be made by all team members together.
5. Respect—For classmates, teachers, and equipment.
6. Positive attitude—Work hard to encourage team members to be positive.
7. Responsibility—Help with lesson organization by carrying out your role.

We will do our best to carry out our roles and to cooperate and work as a team under the leadership of our coach.

Team members' signatures:

_____ (Coach—Organize practices)

_____ (Assistant coach—Help coach as requested)

_____ (Athletic trainer—Organize warm-up and stretching)

_____ (Equipment manager—Give out and collect equipment)

_____ (Reporter—Sports reporting)

_____ (Statistician—Collect and organize team statistics)

From S.A. Mitchell, J.L. Oslin, and L.L. Griffin, 2013, *Teaching sport concepts and skills: A tactical games approach for ages 7 to 18*, third edition (Champaign, IL: Human Kinetics).

Reproducible 5.1   Team contract handout.

teaching styles and problem-solving strategies. Teachers trained in movement education should feel a high degree of comfort with this approach. In fact, some teachers have first come to understand tactical games teaching as a movement education approach to games instruction. Problems are set and students are given opportunities to seek solutions to these problems. Solutions to the problems are identified through the questioning process, and these solutions then become the focus of a practice task.

Direct instruction might be the preferred teaching style at this point, although this may depend on the specificity of the required solution. Take care to modify practice tasks to simplify or challenge students, as their abilities require. Lesson outlines in part II and part III chapters provide examples of task extensions, but be creative with this aspect of your teaching.

As stressed in chapter 1, the quality of the questions asked will be critical, and these should be an integral part of the planning process. Although we have provided many questions in the chapters, we encourage you to develop your own questions that are meaningful to your students.

Assessment

The issue of learner assessment in education is of such importance that assessment ideas are an integral component of K-12 National Content Standards for Physical Education (NASPE 2004; figure 6.1 in chapter 6 aligns tactical games instruction with the NASPE standards). Our concerns for learner assessment are threefold:

- **Assessment should be an ongoing part of instruction.** Because learner assessment takes time, it should not be left until the end of an instructional unit.

- **Assessment should be authentic and therefore related to instructional objectives.** When game performance improvement is the goal of instruction, assessment should be conducted within the context of the game.

- **Assessment of learning should be completed in all domains.** The original Teaching Games for Understanding model (Bunker and Thorpe 1982) focused on outcomes in all domains. Understanding of games was a key goal, as was the motivation to practice and become effective games players. Yet we encourage you to remember that what makes physical education unique is its opportunity to achieve learning

outcomes in the psychomotor domain. To this end, game performance assessment tools such as the Game Performance Assessment Instrument (GPAI) and the Team Sport Assessment Procedure (TSAP) (Grehaigne, Godbout, and Bouthier 1997) described in chapter 6 have been developed to measure psychomotor outcomes during game play.

Lastly, we must not forget the affective domain, because games are an ideal setting in which to promote appropriate sporting behavior. Sport settings require specific social behaviors that not all students are aware of, such as being quiet while someone is putting or teeing off in golf. These skills promote play outside the context of physical education. This is especially important for those who want to continue to be games players outside the confines of our gymnasiums. Affective assessments are addressed in chapter 6 along with assessments in all domains.

◇ TIP BOX

Making learner assessment an ongoing and habitual process, perhaps assessing one team during each lesson, ensures that the learning of all students is determined based on more than one occurrence, to account for uncharacteristically good or poor performances.

SUMMARY

We hope we have encouraged you not only to rethink the way you teach games, but also to view tactical games teaching as a curriculum model rather than simply a teaching method. Increasingly, the tactical games literature seeks to take the approach beyond planning for a single lesson by attempting to formulate ideas for constructing a curriculum scope and sequence based on the tactical similarities among games. Many physical educators now group games for instruction to maximize the principle of transfer. For example, following one invasion game with another in consecutive units of instruction enables students to see the common principles of play across invasion games, a key component of tactical games teaching. For reasons such as these, we believe that a tactical games model is a viable and increasingly mainstream way of organizing games curricula and games instruction within the context of physical education.

Chapter 6

Assessing Outcomes

This chapter addresses the role of assessment in teaching and learning games. How can we accurately and fairly assess what students have learned? When understanding is the purpose of instruction, assessment is more than evaluation; it is a substantive contribution to learning (Blythe and Associates 1998). Assessment that fosters understanding (i.e., that goes beyond evaluation) has to be more than a test at the end of the unit. It must inform students and teachers of what students currently understand and of how to proceed with subsequent teaching and learning. Integrated performance and feedback is exactly what students need as they develop their understanding of particular concepts. Ongoing assessment is the process of providing students with clear responses to their demonstrations of understanding in a way that improves subsequent performances.

Integrating assessment with instruction can help learning by providing feedback that teachers and their students can use to assess themselves and one another and to modify their activities. According to Black and colleagues (2004), there are two main problems with assessment: (a) the methods that teachers use do not promote good learning; and (b) feedback often has a negative impact, particularly on low-achieving students, who then believe that they lack ability and so are not able to learn. As Oslin (2005) pointed out, the role of assessment in tactical games teaching is that it ensures that students develop the skillfulness, competence, and confidence needed to play games. In this chapter we examine what to assess and what your students should know and be able to do (i.e., learning outcomes), aligning assessment with the National Association for Sport and Physical Education (NASPE) standards (National Association for Sport and Physical Education 2004). We share our beliefs about assessment and then outline practical considerations for assessing students.

ASSESSMENT BELIEFS

We have four major beliefs about assessment: (a) it should be ongoing and regular, (b) it should be authentic, (c) planning what to teach is the same as planning what to assess, and (d) assessment should serve as a system of checks and balances for teaching and learning.

We believe that assessment should be an ongoing and regular part of teaching sport-related games—ongoing in that it is an expected part of a unit, and regular in that it is routine to every lesson. Assessment can be for summative purposes (assigning grades) and for formative purposes (checking on student progress, providing feedback for diagnosing strengths and weaknesses). Summative assessment, usually evaluation, involves systematically determining the extent to which objectives have been met (Veal 1993). Summative assessment can be based on several formative assessments taken over the course of a unit. Formative assessment provides feedback for you and your individual students about the strengths and weaknesses of performances as well as checks on student progress. Every tactical games lesson includes a segment of questions and answers that is a measure of formative assessment. Using a variety of summative and formative assessments throughout a unit not only gives you a picture of your students' learning, but also provides your students with in-depth knowledge about what they should learn in the unit (Zessoules and Gardner 1991).

Another valuable aspect of ongoing assessment is that it gives you many opportunities to find out what your students already know about games. The role of prior knowledge in games teaching is important for two reasons. First, students generally know about games because they have played them in their neighborhoods or in community leagues or have watched them as spectators. Because of all of these possible experiences, students' knowledge may differ from the desired knowledge (Clement 1993; Griffin and Placek 2001; Wandersee, Mintzes, and Novak 1994). Second, students may have alternative conceptions about various aspects of game play. For example, they may have ideas about their roles in particular games positions or about how to get open in an invasion game to support teammates. Alternative conceptions are reasonably different ideas about an aspect of game play that are based on a learner's experience and are brought into formal instruction (Dodds, Griffin, and Placek 2001;

Wandersee, Mintzes, and Novak 1994). As a teacher, you should acknowledge that your students usually know something about games playing; you need to have a sense of this prior knowledge to build developmentally appropriate instruction.

Assessment should be authentic. When implementing a tactical games approach, because the goal is for students to focus on successful game play, your assessment should also focus on game play (Veal 1993).

Typically, physical educators rely on skills testing to assess game performance, and there are many examples of common skills tests in any measurement textbook. Using skills tests to assess game performance is problematic for four reasons: they do not predict playing performance, they do not take into account the social dimensions of games, they measure skills out of context, and they do not reflect a broader view of game performance (Mitchell, Oslin, and Griffin 2003; Oslin, Mitchell, Griffin 1998).

Planning what to teach is the same as planning what to assess. This notion of integrating instructional goals with instructional processes and assessment is known as instructional alignment (Cohen 1987). Instructional alignment helps the teacher establish a relationship of assessment to the goals and learning activities of a lesson or unit, thus informing students of expected learning outcomes. Each tactical lesson in part II begins with the tactical problem to be solved, a lesson focus, and specific lesson objectives. Considering these aspects of instructional alignment in your planning will help you limit your scope of content (to doing a few things well), allowing time for assessment and enhancing your ability to sequence the games' content appropriately. The relationship of the assessment criteria to what has been taught is critical for performance in game situations (Mitchell and Oslin 1999a). Ongoing assessment should have established criteria, and these criteria should be

- clear—articulated explicitly at the beginning of each performance,
- relevant—closely related to the goals for the unit, and
- public—all students in the class know and understand the criteria (Blythe and Associates 1998).

For example, in a tactical games lesson, you ask your students to confront a situation or problem, engage in an action situation (i.e., practice or game) to solve the problem, and reflect on their actions (i.e., critical thinking). This instructional process helps you and your students stay focused during each learning activity as you ask yourself, what aspects of the lesson

◇ TIP BOX

To assess improvement in student performance, assessment should (a) measure all aspects of performance and (b) measure game playing in context.

do I want my students to reflect on? Answering this question will help you decide what type of assessment measures (e.g., assessing game play, asking questions) to use.

Assessment can serve as a system of checks and balances for teaching and learning in that it holds you accountable for teaching and your students responsible for learning (James, Griffin, and France 2000). It helps you improve your instruction and helps your students understand the expected learning outcomes. As noted by Oslin, Collier, and Mitchell (2001), assessment is necessary not only to evaluate the extent to which students have learned lesson content, but also to ensure that they stay focused. Ongoing assessment should provide feedback that

- occurs frequently from the beginning to the end of the unit;

- is both formal and planned and more casual and informal;

- provides students with information not only about how well they have carried out performances but also about how they might improve them;

- informs the planning of subsequent classes and activities; and

- comes from a variety of perspectives, including from students' reflections, from peers, and from the teacher (Blythe 1997).

The goal of student assessment is not simply to measure student performance, but to improve it. The primary focus of a tactical games approach is to encourage students to become better games players (i.e., competent). Assessment helps you and your students establish ongoing feedback about solving a particular tactical problem and helps students demonstrate whether they have achieved particular goals or standards relative to game performance. These considerations are important to successfully using assessment in the everyday life of your classes.

Although we have shared why we believe assessment is vital to the teaching and learning process, we also recognize that there are practical considerations for making assessment work in your situation. Many teachers believe that there is too much paperwork and there is not enough time to make assessment part of gymnasium life. These factors should not keep you from providing your students with a complete learning experience, which includes assessment and accountability. The next section addresses the decisions you need to make about assessment and the various assessment strategies you can use.

ASSESSMENT STRATEGIES

As a teacher, you have many decisions to make, including keeping track of student learning. Your first assessment decision has to do with matching the assessment to the focus of the lesson (i.e., lesson objective). Next, you need to decide whether assessment will be formative or summative, and then to consider the assessment strategy you will use. The assessment strategy will take into account who will do the assessment and the type of assessment tool to use.

Who will do the assessment is one of the keys to addressing the issues of paperwork and time. Teachers can and should assess, but they should not do all the assessment, all the time. They can assess for both formative and summative purposes. Students can also assess and should do so in various formative situations. Students can assess themselves (i.e., self-assessment or reporting), assess each other (i.e., peer assessment), and assess as a group (i.e., group problem solving). Students can attain a specific learning goal only if they understand that goal and can assess what they need to do to reach it (Black et al. 2004), making self-assessment an important part of the learning process. Peer assessment adds value because students may accept feedback from one another that they might not take seriously from their teacher. When involving students in assessment, consider the following guidelines:

- Teach students how to assess, what assessment means, and how to use the information gathered from the assessment process. These three important considerations will set you up for success when involving students with assessment. Take the time to teach all three. For example, after the first two lessons of a badminton unit with a combined fifth- and sixth-grade class, a teacher introduced partner assessment to her students. The students were to keep track of overhead clears. The teacher set up a demonstration game for the students to practice. She organized the students to observe in pairs so that they could check for understanding, and then she had students share

TIP BOX

Involving students in assessment is cost-effective. In our work, students have shared how much they enjoy being involved in assessment and benefit from the opportunity.

their results as a class. The activity was repeated a second time to make sure students understood their roles and expectations. The time spent was short, but the teacher was clear about her expectations through practice. She used this example to teach the students what the information meant as well as to set up students to give feedback to each other in a meaningful way.

- Establish an assessment routine. For assessment to be a regular part of your class, you must create a solid routine. You will need a system for organizing students, equipment, and space. First, students need to know whom they are assessing. There are endless ways to organize; the following are just two examples:
  - In partner assessment, student A assesses student B, and then the two switch roles; they continue alternating roles throughout the unit.
  - In team assessment, teams take turns observing game play and assessing the members of another team.

A second consideration involves organizing the equipment for assessment. On what and with what will the students write? How will the assessment forms be collected? There are several options, such as pencils attached to clipboards, student or team portfolios, or envelopes taped to a wall (some for blank assessment sheets and some for completed sheets). Finally, you need to consider space in the assessment process. How will observers use the space? Where will they sit to assess each other? Where will the equipment be prior to the assessment and at the end of class? We trust that you know yourself as a teacher, your students, and your facilities well enough to develop a smooth routine.

- Hold students accountable. Simply put, you need to follow up on all aspects of assessment. If you do not value assessment and take care when integrating it into the teaching and learning process, neither will your students. Take time to briefly discuss the results and their meaning because this indicates the importance you place on the assessment process.

- Consider doability in assessment. Doability involves considering how much assessment to do and who will do it. You should limit how much to observe and measure in a particular lesson or across a whole unit regardless of whether the teacher or student is involved in the assessment. This will ensure that you set assessment tasks that can be accomplished within the constraints of available time, equipment, facilities, and people.

Next, we consider the type of assessment to use. Assessment might range from an observation instrument to student self-reporting. Table 6.1 shows various types of assessment and who is a better fit for administering each one—teacher or student.

Table 6.1 Types of Assessment for Teachers and Students

Assessment type	Teacher	Students	Explanation
Written test	Yes	No	Teachers would typically use this as either a formative or summative assessment.
Question–answer session	Yes	No	Typically used as a formative assessment by a teacher to determine the extent of student understanding.
Game Performance Assessment Instrument (GPAI)	Yes	Yes	Could be used by either teachers (formatively or summatively) or students as a formative or peer assessment.
Monitoring and observation	Yes	No	Teachers observe while students play. This enables teachers to decide which students or groups can best demonstrate tasks and also to determine whether the content is pitched at a developmentally appropriate level.
Rubric	Yes	Yes	Could be used by either teachers (formatively or summatively) or students as a formative or peer assessment.
Checklist	Yes	Yes	Could be used by either teachers (formatively or summatively) or students as a formative or peer assessment.
Self-report or journal	No	Yes	An appropriate form of assessment, particularly in the affective domain. Students record their thoughts, motivations, and level of understanding.

When considering the logistics of assessment, you need to consider yourself as the teacher, your students, and your equipment and facilities, but work with them and around them as needed. It is important to balance the type of assessment with who does the assessing because this balance provides you and your students with a broader picture of their progress toward becoming better games players.

ASSESSING LEARNING OUTCOMES

The three domains of learning—psychomotor, cognitive, and affective—help us identify the range of learning outcomes that reflects a broad view of game performance. Figure 6.1 presents our proposed learning outcomes and indicates the relationships among them. We have argued that improvement in game performance, the primary goal of a tactical games approach, will lead to increased enjoyment, interest, and perceived competence. These motivational outcomes increase the likelihood that students will play games later in life, hence increasing the likelihood that they will maintain a physically active lifestyle after school and into adulthood and achieve and maintain health-related fitness, as specified by NASPE content standards 3 and 4 (NASPE 2004). Figure 6.1 matches tactical games outcomes with the NASPE standards.

Improved game performance stems from increased tactical awareness, which is the ability to identify problems and their solutions in game situations and thus become a better decision maker. The link between tactical awareness and game performance occurs through the integration and interaction of the psychomotor, cognitive, and affective domains.

The psychomotor domain encompasses game performance; the cognitive domain reflects the understanding of game-related knowledge; and the affective domain considers the behavioral and social dimensions of sport and games, such as good sporting behavior, teamwork, and cooperation. In the end, the domains influence each other, which reflects the multidimensionality and complexity of game play. The following sections discuss assessment as it relates to each domain.

Psychomotor Domain

In teaching and learning tactical games, the psychomotor domain encompasses off-the-ball movement, such as support, and on-the-ball skills, which include skill selection and skill execution (figure 6.1). This domain parallels NASPE content standard 1 (NASPE 2004), which states, "A physically educated person demonstrates competency in motor skills and movement patterns needed to perform a variety of physical activities" (p. 11). A tactical games approach primarily focuses on improved game performance (i.e., competent players). Assessment of game-playing ability should include the decisions players make about what to do with the ball and the movements players make when they do not have the ball, because both on- and off-the-ball skills are vital to becoming competent or proficient games players (NASPE 2004). For example, in a small-sided (3v3) basketball game, we can assess what players are doing with the ball. But it is just as important to assess how players move in positive ways to get the ball.

Recent efforts to measure performance more completely in game play have included assessing aspects

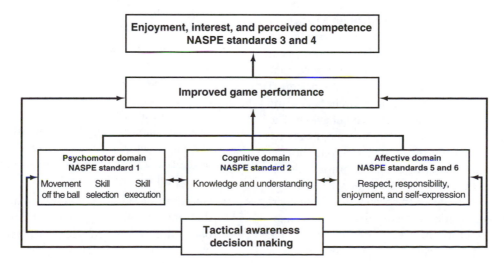

Figure 6.1　Anticipated learning outcomes.

of decision making, skill execution, and individual performance (French et al. 1996; Grehaigne, Godbout, and Bouthier 1997; Grehaigne, Richard, and Griffin 2005; Mitchell, Oslin, and Griffin 1995; Nevitt, Rovegno, and Babiarz 2001; Oslin 2005; Oslin, Mitchell, and Griffin 1998; Turner and Martinek 1992). These types of measurements are valuable for three reasons.

- They assess students in game play.

- They can provide information about a player's thinking process. For example, in an invasion game a player may receive credit for attempting to pass to an open player even if the pass is not well executed.

- They can be a valuable source of information for planning the next lesson.

As we have maintained, game play should be measured authentically; that is, within the context of actual game-playing situations (Oslin 2005). The authentic assessment of game performance requires observing participants when they are not in possession of the ball. Therefore, carefully planned observation is essential. In this section we introduce two formal methods for assessing both individual and team performance: the Game Performance Assessment Instrument (GPAI) and the Team Sport Assessment Procedure (TSAP) (Grehaigne, Godbout, and Bouthier 1997; Grehaigne, Richard, and Griffin 2005). We also share an invasion games rubric that we have used with students for peer assessment.

Game Performance Assessment Instrument (GPAI)

The GPAI was developed as a comprehensive assessment tool for teachers to use and adapt for a variety of games. This flexibility means that teachers can use the GPAI for various games across the classification system (e.g., invasion, net and wall) or within a particular classification (e.g., basketball, soccer). We designed the GPAI to provide teachers and researchers a means of observing and coding performance behaviors. The GPAI includes behaviors that demonstrate the ability to solve tactical problems by making decisions, moving appropriately, and executing skills. We initially developed performance components for the GPAI through consultation with five teacher-coaches who had expertise in each classification category discussed in chapter 2 (table 2.1). Our aim was to identify observable components of game performance that applied across game categories. After identifying seven components,

we formulated descriptions of each component and reformulated them until all experts reached consensus.

Seven components of game performance are defined in the GPAI, although not all components apply equally to all games. For example, in tennis the base component is critical to court coverage, but players do not have to guard, or mark, opponents. The seven components listed next constitute a broad definition of game performance that entails much more than skill execution (Mitchell and Oslin 1999a). The main value of this broad definition lies in the ability to give credit to students for all aspects of game performance, including the decisions they make and how hard they work both offensively and defensively, rather than just giving credit for the proficient execution of motor skills. This provides plenty of incentive for students who lack technical proficiency to be involved in game play. These lower-skilled students, perhaps even including students with disabilities, know that their efforts will be rewarded in the assessment process regardless of actual execution outcomes.

Following are brief descriptions and examples of each component of game performance. Table 6.2 provides examples of these components in each game category.

- Base is a position to which players should return between skill attempts. For example, in net games, players should return to a specific place on the court that provides optimal opportunity for court coverage.

- Decision making is choosing which movement or skill to execute in response to a tactical problem.

- Skill execution concerns actual motor performance. After players decide what they are going to perform, skill selection and execution must be efficient to achieve the desired outcome.

- Support is important primarily in invasion games, in which keeping possession is vital to scoring. To keep possession as a team, players with the ball must be able to pass to teammates who are ready and available to receive passes. Hence, being available to support teammates (an off-the-ball movement) is critical to keeping possession of the ball and scoring and thus to solid overall game performance.

- Guarding, or marking, are off-the-ball movements that are critical components of defensive game play. All invasion games require players to guard, or mark, their opponents to deny them the ball and prevent them from scoring.

Table 6.2 Examples of Performance Components in Games

Component	Invasion games	Net and wall games	Striking and fielding games	Target games
Base	Basketball player sets up in position in a zone defense.	• Badminton player returns to about the T at center court between shots. • Tennis player returns to the center of the baseline between shots. • Volleyball player returns to a designated playing area when the ball is returned over the net during a rally.	Softball player starts in base position (fielding position) before each pitch.	Golf player starts in a setup or stance position.
Decision making	Decide whether to shoot, pass, or dribble.	Decide shot selection and placement.	• Batters—decide pitch and placement of shot. • Fielders—decide where to throw the ball. • Pitchers—decide how to deliver the ball.	Golfers—decide which club to use.
Skill execution	• Player shoots on target. • Player passes accurately to an open player. • Player controls the ball from a pass.	• Player executes a clear to deep court. • Player executes a drop shot close to the net in front of the service line. • Player passes the ball to set up a move (more than one hit on a side).	• Player fields cleanly. • Player throws accurately to target. • Player hits effectively (maximizes scoring, minimizes outs).	• Player executes a chip to within 6 ft (1.8 m). • Player shoots an arrow and hits the target. • Player delivers the ball. • Player throws a horseshoe.
Supporting	Player moves into an open position to receive a pass in soccer.	Volleyball setter positions to receive the forearm pass from the backcourt.	Shortstop moves to be a "relay" fielder for an outfielder.	Shuffleboard partner executes a "clear out" for a teammate.
Guarding, or marking	Defender positions between the end zone and the receiver in flag football, closing the space as the receiver gets closer to the ball or to the end zone.	Blockers move to "guard" hitters in a volleyball game.	First- or second-base player stays at the base during the pitch to prevent an offensive player from stealing.	Bocce player positions the first ball in a protective position to block the path to the jack.
Covering	Basketball defender moves across to cover the "back door." Soccer "sweeper" or football "safety" covers the first defender.	Covering teammates position themselves behind volleyball blockers to retrieve balls that come off the block.	Softball, baseball, or cricket fielders back up the bases or stumps to prevent overthrows.	N/A
Adjusting	Ball at the opposite end of the field—defender adjusts position by moving at least to the halfway line in a position to support the attack if needed and to deny space should opponents counterattack.	• Badminton doubles players adjust offensive front–back formation to a defensive side–side formation when necessary. • Volleyball players in the front row adjust (open up) when the ball goes to the back row (face the ball).	Softball or cricket fielders adjust their positions according to the strengths and weaknesses of batters and to whether batters are left- or right-handed.	Bocce players adjust the angle of release based on where obstructing balls are lying, to either increase or decrease the flight.

- Covering, another defensive component, usually involves providing backup to teammates who make challenges for the ball. In invasion games defenders make a challenge for the ball and teammates cover the space behind them. In basketball this is called "help" defense, and in soccer it is simply known as cover. In striking and fielding games such as softball, the fielder making a play on a ball should have a teammate covering in case of a fielding error. In volleyball, a net game, players provide cover for teammates who are attempting to spike.

- Adjusting refers to the ability to adjust positioning as needed in the game. In other words, players should not stand rooted during a game.

The appeal of the GPAI is that you can adapt and use the instrument according to the type and aspect of the game being played, your students, and your gymnasium or playing area. The two basic scoring methods using the GPAI are the 1 to 5 system (reproducible 6.1) and the tally system (reproducibles 6.2, 6.3, and 6.4).

Mitchell and Oslin (1999a) pointed out that the 1 to 5 scoring system is efficient for two reasons. First, observers (primarily the teacher) do not have to record each time a player is involved in the game. In invasion games and some net and wall games, this is impossible to do effectively because of the tempo, flow, and unpredictability of such games when players have a wide range of skill levels. Simply, it is more efficient with some game types to observe carefully for a period of time and then record a score than it is to try to observe and then record every involvement of a player when a lot of action might be missed during the recording or writing process. Second, the 1 to 5 scoring system provides for a wide range of scoring but not so wide as to affect scoring consistency. You can create criteria for the five indicators—that is, from very effective performance to very weak performance—or use a modified scale from always to never. These indicators should be based on your objectives, your students' abilities, and the time available for physical education.

The tally system can be used with striking and fielding games and some net and wall games because they are played at a slower pace and have natural breaks (between pitches, bowls, or points), which gives the observer an opportunity to score or tally every event. The tally system also provides a more precise performance measure. As you can see in the net and wall and striking and fielding game GPAI forms (reproducibles 6.3 and 6.4), components are scored as either "appropriate" or "inappropriate," or "efficient" or "inefficient." You can then develop percentage scores for assessed GPAI components (Mitchell and Oslin 1999a). For example, an appropriate decision-making percentage would be calculated by dividing the number of appropriate decisions made by the total number of decisions made. Likewise, you could calculate a skill execution percentage by dividing the number of efficient execution attempts by the total number of execution attempts.

You can also give your students the bigger picture of their game play by calculating game involvement and overall game performance scores. Game involvement can be measured by adding all incidences of involvement in the game, including inappropriate decisions made and inefficient skill execution attempts. Do not include inappropriate guarding (or marking), supporting, adjusting, and covering because an inappropriate response in these components indicates that the player was not involved in the game. Game performance is a more precise measure and is calculated by adding the scores from all components assessed and dividing by the number of components assessed:

(% decisions made + % skill execution) / 2

Reproducible 6.1

**Game Performance
Assessment Instrument for Invasion Games**

Class _____ Evaluator _____ Team _____ Game _____

Observation dates   (a) _____   (b) _____   (c) _____   (d) _____

Scoring Key

5 = very effective performance (always)
4 = effective performance (usually)
3 = moderately effective performance (sometimes)
2 = weak performance (rarely)
1 = very weak performance (never)

Components and Criteria

- **Skill execution**—Students pass the ball accurately, reaching the intended receiver.
- **Decision making**—Students make appropriate choices when passing (i.e., passing to unguarded teammates to set up a scoring opportunity).
- **Support**—Students attempt to move into position to receive a pass from a teammate (i.e., forward toward the goal).

Name	Skill execution	Decision making	Support

From S.A. Mitchell, J.L. Oslin, and L.L. Griffin, 2013, *Teaching sport concepts and skills: A tactical games approach for ages 7 to 18*, third edition (Champaign, IL: Human Kinetics).

Reproducible 6.1   The 1 to 5 system.

Reproducibles 6.2-6.4   The tally system.

Following are examples of possible performance measures:

- Game involvement = number of appropriate decisions + number of inappropriate decisions + number of efficient skill executions + number of inefficient skill executions + number of appropriate supporting movements

- Decision-making index (DMI) = number of appropriate decisions made / (number of appropriate decisions made + number of inappropriate decisions made)

- Skill execution index (SEI) = number of efficient skill executions / (number of efficient skill executions + number of inefficient skill executions)

- Support index (SI) = number of appropriate supporting movements / (number of appropriate supporting movements + number of inappropriate supporting movements)

- Game performance = (DMI + SEI + SI) / 3

Let's now examine some GPAI data from a soccer unit in which the components measured were decision making, skill execution, and support (table 6.3).

The data in table 6.4 have been collected from observations of a team playing soccer. We have assessed players' decision making, skill execution, and support. Each X tally on the recording sheet represents one observation.

After adding up his scores for each component of Matthew's game performance, we applied the formulas suggested previously to come up with the following measures of his game play:

Game involvement = 7 + 7 + 6 = 20

Decision making = 6 / 7 = 0.86

Skill execution = 6 / 7 = 0.86

Support = 6 / 10 = 0.60

Game performance = (0.86 + 0.85 + 0.60) / 3 = 0.77

Table 6.3 GPAI Criteria for a Soccer Unit

GPAI component	Criteria
Decision making	Player attempts to pass to an open teammate. Player attempts to shoot when appropriate.
Skill execution	Reception—control of pass and setup of the ball. Passing—ball reaches target. Shooting—ball stays below head and is on target.
Support	Player appears to support the ball carrier by being in or moving to an appropriate position to receive a pass.

Table 6.4 Observation of Soccer Performance

Name	Decision made		Skill execution		Support	
	A	IA	E	IE	A	IA
Matthew	xxxxxx	x	xxxxxx	x	xxxxxx	xxxx
Nicholas					xxx	xxx
Katie	xxxxx	x	xxxxx	x	xxxx	x
Jamal	xx	x	xxx	x	xxxxx	xx
Jenn	xxx	xx	xx	xxx	xx	x
Sasha	x	xx	x	xx	xxxxxxx	x

A = appropriate

E = efficient

IA = inappropriate

IE = inefficient

Game performance is the arithmetical average of the decision making, skill execution, and support indexes. This calculation ensures that players whose scores indicate strong game performance do have contact with the ball, make good decisions, and execute skills well within the game. If percentages are easier to report (and for students to understand) for the DMI, SEI, and SI, simply multiply the figure you get by 100 in each case.

Matthew has been highly involved in the game, and his decision-making and skill execution scores indicate a high degree of success, although on some occasions he failed to give support to teammates. Nicholas, on the other hand, was not particularly involved in the game either with or without the ball. Using the formulas, his respective measures of game performance are 3, 0, 0, 0.5, and 0.17. Katie's performance was strong overall. Sasha's scores are interesting—although not particularly successful in either decision making or skill execution, Sasha was involved in the game. Her scores for support provide evidence of this, suggesting that she worked hard to be in a position to receive the ball, and she should be credited for her efforts. As you can see, the GPAI provides useful information about the strengths and weaknesses of students' game play.

GPAI scores can be used for both formative and summative purposes. You could set targets for students relative to GPAI scores; for example, you could tell students, "See if you can score 75% on decision making today." If you choose to use GPAI scores for grade assignment, we recommend reporting both game performance and game involvement scores to give students credit both for the quality of their performance and for attempts to be fully involved in game play. You can easily build criteria for assessment into a game-specific record sheet. For example, in table 6.4 we coded Matthew's supporting runs to space as appropriate, but we coded his lack of support for teammates as inappropriate. We can code appropriateness each time Matthew makes a decision about what to do with the ball. For example, when he passes to a teammate who is closely marked (guarded), we tally the decision as inappropriate. If such a pass is technically well struck, we code it as efficiently executed.

Each sport chapter has been designed to assist you in creating GPAIs that align with each lesson and across the unit. Let's take a closer look at the chapters and possible GPAI modifications for those chapters. For example, each sport-specific chapter has levels of game complexity. In chapter 11 on soccer, there are five levels of tactical (game) complexity, which provide a scope and sequence to your instructional unit. Table 6.5 shows only tactical complexity level II; as you can see, it limits instructional focus to two offensive tactical problems (maintaining possession of the ball and attacking the goal) and two defensive components (defending space and defending the goal). The level also limits the size of the games to be played (level II uses three- and six-sided games) as well as the skills and movements to teach.

You can limit the focus of your GPAI instrument to the objectives of the overall unit. Reproducible 6.1 is a possible GPAI for an invasion game unit. This GPAI focuses on the offensive components of level II skill execution, decision making, and support. Spaces are provided for six players because level II calls for three- or six-sided games. Now you have an idea of how the levels of tactical complexity can help you link assessment with instruction.

Next, we'll examine how the lessons are designed by looking at a specific lesson (soccer level II, lesson 9). All lessons begin with the same format by stating the tactical problem to be solved, the general lesson focus, and the specific objective for the lesson. The following is from lesson 9:

- Tactical problem—Maintaining possession of the ball
- Lesson focus—Supporting the ball carrier
- Objective—Support the player with the ball constantly.

In this lesson the focus is on providing constant support for any player in possession of the ball, which means that you should limit your GPAI use to support

Table 6.5 Tactical Complexity Level II in Soccer

	Tactical problem	Level II
Scoring	Maintaining possession of the ball Attacking the goal	Supporting Shooting, turning
Preventing scoring	Defending space Defending the goal	Marking, pressuring the ball Goalkeeper—Positioning, receiving, throwing

only. Games are complex, so we recommend that you limit the observation focus for yourself as well as your students (Mitchell and Oslin 1999a). In this lesson you might use the GPAI in reproducible 6.2 that focuses only on support and limit the number of students by observing just one team, or use this form as a peer assessment tool. The goal is always to align your instruction by linking objectives, instructional activities, and assessment.

At this point, you are probably asking yourself, can I really do this and be accurate? The answer is yes! Assessments by both teachers and students who used a version of the GPAI in live settings have been considered reliable. That is, in their assessment of performance, observers have been consistent with a fellow observer approximately 80% of the time (Griffin, Dodds, and James 1999; Oslin, Mitchell, and Griffin 1998). You can make your GPAI measures more objective and less subjective by having two observers independently collect GPAI data on the same performers and then compare scores to establish interobserver agreement. The key to establishing reliability is the quality of the criteria stated for observation: the criteria should be specific and observable (Mitchell and Oslin 1999a).

Team Sport Assessment

Grehaigne, Godbout, and Bouthier (1997) developed the Team Sport Assessment Procedure (TSAP) as another authentic assessment instrument to reflect student learning in relation to real-life applications. The TSAP was developed for use in formative and summative assessment scenarios in which tactical learning is the primary focus. It is a peer assessment procedure based on two basic questions: (a) How did the player gain possession of the ball (i.e., "conquering" the ball, receiving a pass from a teammate in the course of play)? and, (b) How did the player dispose of the ball (i.e., passing the ball off, playing an offensive pass or shot, or losing the ball)? According to these questions, a player's specific behaviors are observed and coded during the game play in six components to reflect offensive performance in invasion games. Table 6.6 identifies and defines the observed components, and reproducible 6.5 provides a recording sheet. The information provided by the individual variables, performance indexes, and performance score are all indicators of both technical and tactical performance, which are related to successful game play.

The TSAP combines "volume of play" and "efficiency" to compute team performance, or what Grehaigne and colleagues (1997) referred to as "rapport of strength." Table 6.7 provides formulas that you may want to use to help your students understand their data.

Let's take a closer look at a student's data after playing in a 3v3 game of basketball (table 6.8). Kevin's game-play data tell us the following:

- Volume of play (game involvement) = 5 + 7 = 12
- Efficiency index (effective play) = 5 + 4 + 3 + 10 = 22
- Performance score (overall performance) = (12 / 2) + (22 × 10) = 6 + 220 = 226

Table 6.6 TSAP Components of Game Play

Components	Definitions
GAINING POSSESSION OF THE BALL	
Conquering the ball (CB)	Interception, stealing the ball from the opponent, or recapturing the ball after an unsuccessful shot on goal or near-loss to the other team
Receiving the ball (RB)	Receiving the ball from a teammate and not immediately losing control of it
DISPOSING OF THE BALL	
Playing a neutral ball (NB)	Passing the ball to a teammate, or any pass that does not put the other team in jeopardy
Losing the ball (LB)	Losing the ball to the other team without having scored a goal
Playing an offensive ball (OB)	Passing the ball to a partner, thus pressuring the other team, which most often leads to a shot on goal
Executing a successful shot (SS)	Scoring or maintaining possession of the ball following the execution of a shot

Adapted from Grehaigne, Richard, and Griffin.

Reproducible 6.5 Recording sheet.

Sample Game Rubric for Peer Assessment

Another possibility when seeking to assess students in game play is to create game play rubrics. Reproducible 6.6 provides a sample invasion game rubric we developed for peer assessment in an ultimate Frisbee unit. This rubric focuses on solving the tactical problem of maintaining possession of the ball (i.e., Frisbee), particularly involving passing and supporting in game play. The rubric combines on-the-ball skills (pass and catch) and off-the-ball movements (support) to guide students in their decision making. Students have the opportunity to learn a hierarchy for decision making. In using this type of rubric, students are encouraged to examine all possible solutions, which guides their own work and helps them become independent learners through peer assessment.

Measuring a variety of performance components beyond skill execution provides an objective measure of participation, rewarding students who engage in game play on and off the ball. Students who have not had the opportunities to develop skills can be rewarded for moving into position to receive a pass (support play), making good decisions (when to pass,

Table 6.7 Formulas for Calculating TSAP Outcome Variables

Outcome variables	Calculation
Volume of play (VP)	CB + RB
Efficiency index (EI)	CB + OB + (SS / LB) + 10
Performance score (PS)	(Volume of play / 2) + (efficiency index × 10)

SS = executing a successful shot   LB = losing the ball
CB = conquering the ball   VP = volume of play
RB = receiving the ball   OB = playing an offensive ball

Table 6.8 Game Play Data From a 3v3 Basketball Game

Name	CB	RB	LB	NB	OB	SS
Kevin	5	7	2	5	4	6
Shelly	2	6	4	4	2	2
Karen	1	4	1	6	6	4

CB = conquering the ball   NB = playing a neutral ball
RB = receiving the ball   OB = playing an offensive ball
LB = losing the ball   SS = executing a successful shot

From S.A. Mitchell, J.L. Oslin, and L.L. Griffin, 2013, *Teaching sport concepts and skills: A tactical games approach for ages 7 to 18*, third edition (Champaign, IL: Human Kinetics).

Reproducible 6.6   A sample invasion game rubric.

when to shoot), or appropriately marking players to keep them from scoring or gaining possession of the ball for their team (Oslin 2005).

The GPAI and TSAP are primarily *product* measures, which make it easy for the observer to identify the effectiveness of the performance. For example, if a student scores low on supporting teammates and passing, both teacher and student will see that there is a need to work on those particular skills.

Process measures that focus on the execution of movements or skills are also important. Movement and skill forms can be assessed during practice situations using rubrics and checklists focused on critical elements of specific movements or skills. You probably use a number of these forms in your teaching on a regular basis. Both product and process measures can be used to develop a summative evaluation.

This section has familiarized you with two ways to assess game performance in the psychomotor domain that both you and your students can use successfully. Because the GPAI provides all players with credit for simple game involvement and for decisions and performance with and without the ball, all students—regardless of skill level—will value game improvement.

Cognitive Domain

The cognitive domain encompasses students' ability to know and articulate solutions to tactical problems (i.e., what to do) and explain how, when, and where to execute particular skills and movements (i.e., how to do it, when to do it, where to do it).

The cognitive domain parallels NASPE (2004) content standard 2, which states, "A physically educated person demonstrates understanding of movement concepts, principles, strategies, and tactics as they apply to the learning and performance of physical activities" (p. 11). This standard refers to students' ability to articulate aspects of game understanding.

As a teacher, you know that there are many ways to assess students' knowledge and understanding of sport-related games. You are familiar with many types of assessment tools such as written tests, reflective journals, checklists, portfolios, role playing, student logs, and demonstrations, to name a few. We encourage you to use other resources such as *Moving Into the Future: National Standards for Physical Education* (NASPE 2004), *Teaching Middle School Physical Education* (Mohnsen 1997), and *Teaching for Outcomes in Elementary Physical Education* (Hopple 1995) for additional assessment tools. Following are some ways to get started assessing cognitive aspects of game performance, which foreground a tactical approach.

• Question-and-answer sessions such as those found in our book provide two opportunities for formative assessment. The first opportunity is right after the initial game, when you can ask questions regarding what to do (i.e., tactical awareness) and how to do it (i.e., skill execution). A question-and-answer session that targets the specific objectives of the lesson serves three functions. First, it shifts the students to the center of the learning environment and you to the role of facilitator. Second, students share what they already know (prior knowledge) and begin to think critically about the tactical problem you have presented in the small-sided, conditioned game. Third, as students develop game understanding, they begin to recognize the tactical similarities between games, and this tactical understanding can transfer to other games (Mitchell and Oslin 1999b). The second opportunity in our lesson formats for a question-and-answer session is at the end of the lesson during closure. This is an opportunity to debrief your students by asking three questions: (a) what happened, (b) what does it mean, and (c) now what?

• A one-minute quiz is a written or verbal test used at the end of a lesson to check for understanding (Griffin and Oslin 1990). Quiz questions are simple and hold students accountable for lesson content. Think tactically when you design questions. For example, have your students solve a tactical problem, make connections among games from the same category, and describe various skills and movements practiced in class. The following are examples of questions with a tactical focus:

- *Q: What are the ways we tried to maintain possession of the ball?* The focus of this question is on the various skills or movements used to solve the tactical problem of maintaining possession of the ball in an invasion game (e.g., basketball, soccer, hockey).

  A: Pass, dribble, or support (depending on the lesson focus).

- *Q: How are volleyball, tennis, badminton, and handball similar?* The focus of this question is on the similarities among these games because they are in the same classification (net and wall games).

  A: They are all net or wall games in which the primary goal is to propel an object over a net or against a wall in such a way that the opponent cannot return it.

- *Q: What are the learning cues for support that we used today?*

  A: Quick, straight movement; call for a pass.

- In scenario activities, students are asked to solve tactical problems that you design. The figures on reproducibles 6.7 through 6.9 are examples of invasion game scenarios, whereas the figures on reproducibles 6.10 through 6.12 are net and wall game examples. Scenarios could be completed by students as a worksheet on which they draw and write, or they could be discussed orally as a class. Sometimes students know what to do in a game but cannot always execute it, so scenarios provide them with an opportunity to show their knowledge of game play.

- Self-report journals give you and your students a simple way to keep track of written assignments. Students can self-report or use their journals for the one-minute quizzes or to reflect on their game performance assessments (GPAI), such as how they might improve their performance. Self-report journals are a place where students can give you feedback about their own performances. In addition, they provide a permanent product that you can use either formally or informally and do not have to be evaluated immediately.

- The following is one way to use the self-report journal so that students reflect on their game understanding. Either at the end of class or at home, have students reflect on their game play. Ask students to reflect on the following questions:

- What does the information tell you about your game play?
- How can you improve your play?
- What would you do differently?
- How could you help your team's performance?

Affective Domain

The affective domain addresses, among other things, socialization into sport. Students need to be aware of not only their in-game knowledge (e.g., what to do, how to do it) but also their knowledge about games in general. For example, for competition to be good and appropriate, players need to cooperate with each other. The affective domain parallels NASPE (2004) content standard 5, which addresses personal and social responsibility, and standard 6 which focuses on valuing and enjoying physical activity. Thus, assessing the affective domain involves assessing rule and procedure adherence, cooperation, etiquette, good sporting behavior, fair play, and teamwork (including performing assigned or selected roles within teams such as equipment manager and statistician). These aspects of game performance are important. They do not just happen—they must be planned for and taught, and students must be held accountable for them.

The purpose of this section is twofold. First, we offer two ways to frame your game units to foster desirable sport behaviors and responsibility (i.e., sport citizenship). Second, we offer a few ways to assess your students for appropriate sport citizenship in a tactical games approach.

Promoting Sport Citizenship

Following are suggestions for fostering sport citizenship:

- **Integrate tactical games with Sport Education.** Sport Education (Siedentop, Hastie, and van der Mars 2011) has the personal and social dimensions of games built right in. Students form teams and take on roles such as coach, equipment manager, statistician, and so on. Teams can be assigned as special duty teams during tournaments to be officials and to keep score and game statistics. In Sport Education, students are placed in teams for the duration of a season, which allows them to get to know each other well (see Collier 2005, for example). This enables them to work on such things as teamwork and players' roles and responsibilities. Also, question-and-answer sessions that focus on positive sporting behavior, fair play, and etiquette are more meaningful when students are affiliated with teams.

Reproducible 6.7

Invasion Game Scenario 1

Solving the Tactical Problem: Attacking the Goal (or Basket)

Name _____ Date _____

Directions

Observe the student's game play and place a tally mark in the appropriate box.

Situation

This is a 2v2 situation in an invasion game such as soccer, team handball, or basketball. Team O is on offense and team X is on defense. You are player O1 with the ball. How can you and your teammate (O2) work together to beat the defenders on team X and attack the goal? Try to think of two different ways. Explain what you would do, and draw lines on the figure to show what you would do.

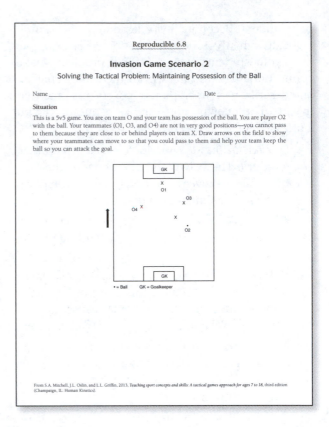

1. I could . . .

2. I could . . .

Reproducible 6.8

Invasion Game Scenario 2

Solving the Tactical Problem: Maintaining Possession of the Ball

Name _____ Date _____

Situation

This is a 5v5 game. You are on team O and your team has possession of the ball. You are player O2 with the ball. Your teammates (O1, O3, and O4) are not in very good positions—you cannot pass to them because they are close to or behind players on team X. Draw arrows on the field to show where your teammates can move to so that you could pass to them and help your team keep the ball so you can attack the goal.

Reproducible 6.9

Invasion Game Scenario 3

Solving the Tactical Problem: Defending Space

Name _____ Date _____

Situation

This is a 3v3 basketball game situation with team O on offense. You are on team X, and player O1 on team O has the ball. Team X is not defending very well! Draw arrows on the court to show where you and your teammates can position yourselves to make it harder for team O to attack your basket.

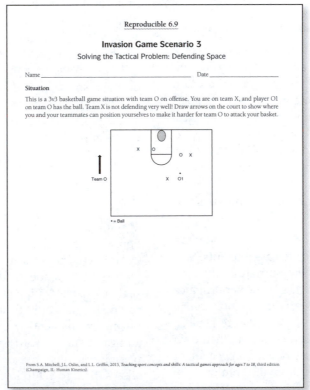

Reproducibles 6.7-6.9 Examples of invasion game scenarios.

Reproducible 6.10

Net and Wall Game Scenario 1

Solving the Tactical Problem: Creating Space in the Opponent's Court

Name _____ Date _____

Situation

This is a diagram of a court for a net game. The lines represent the boundaries of the court, and the thick line is the net. In this situation players A and B are playing a net game. You are player B. Player A hits the ball (or shuttle) to you.

1. Place an X where you want to make your next shot land.

2. Explain why you have placed the X in this position.

3. What type of shot would you need to use?

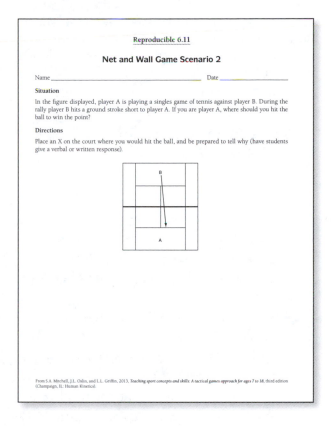

Reproducible 6.11

Net and Wall Game Scenario 2

Name _____ Date _____

Situation

In the figure displayed, player A is playing a singles game of tennis against player B. During the rally player B hits a ground stroke short to player A. If you are player A, where should you hit the ball to win the point?

Directions

Place an X on the court where you would hit the ball, and be prepared to tell why (have students give a verbal or written response).

Reproducible 6.12

Net and Wall Game Scenario 3

Situation

In the figure displayed, team ABC is playing team DEF in a 3v3 volleyball game. During a rally player E sends a free ball over the net to player C. What should player C do with the ball?

Directions

Draw a line to where player C should put the ball, and be ready to explain how player C will do this.

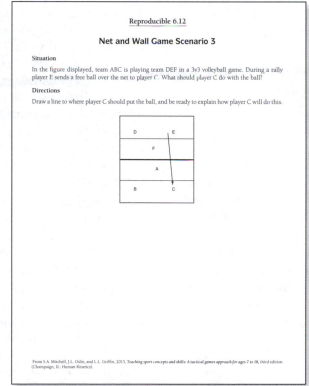

Reproducibles 6.10-6.12   Examples of net and wall game scenarios.

- **Introduce Teaching Personal and Social Responsibility (TPSR) levels.** There are five TPSR levels, which can be considered a progression (adapted from Hellison 1996):
  - Level 1: Respect
    - Self-control
  - Level 2: Participation and effort
    - Exploring effort
    - Trying new things
    - Developing a personal definition of success
  - Level 3: Self-direction
    - Demonstrating on-task independence
    - Developing a sound knowledge base
    - Developing, carrying out, and evaluating a personal plan
    - Balancing current and future needs
    - Striving against external forces
  - Level 4: Sensitivity and responsiveness to the well-being of others
    - Developing prerequisite interpersonal skills
    - Becoming sensitive and compassionate
    - Contributing to the community and beyond
    - Helping others without rewards
  - Level 5: Outside the gym
    - Trying out the levels in the gymnasium, on the playground, and at home
    - Making decisions about the usefulness of the levels outside the gym

We suggest two ways to implement the TPSR levels. First, students can report at the end of class by raising the number of fingers that corresponds to their perception of the level of their own behavior for the day or week. Second, students can complete journal entries regarding their levels, including a bit of reflection.

- **Integrate cooperative learning (CL).** There is significant evidence to support the idea that students working in small cooperative groups master material presented by the teacher better than students working on their own (Cohen 1994; Johnson and Johnson 1989; Slavin 1996). Dyson (2005) pointed to five main components of CL that can be integrated into the tactical games model:
  - Positive interdependence. Each group member learns to depend on the rest of the group while working together to complete the task.
  - Individual accountability. Teachers establish and maintain student responsibility for appropriate

behavior, task involvement, and outcomes (Siedentop and Tannehill 2000).
  - Face-to-face interaction. Group members have face-to-face discussions in close proximity to one another (e.g., think-pair-share).
  - Interpersonal and small-group skills. These include skills such as listening, sharing decision making, taking responsibility, learning to give and receive feedback, and learning to encourage each other (e.g., peer tutoring or coaching).
  - Group processing. Time is allocated for the group to share how well it achieved its goals and maintained effective working relationships. Group processing is similar to the processing or debriefing (e.g., what happened? and, now what?) that takes place in adventure education (see Dyson 2005, for example).

Assessing Sport Citizenship

Some of the tools and resources suggested for the cognitive domain can be redesigned to assess the affective domain. The following are ideas to get you started with assessment in this domain:

- Use a class circle discussion. The class circle discussion is similar to the question-and-answer sessions that are built into every lesson, and it could be used to discuss the social and behavioral dimensions of games. For example, one of your objectives for the lesson might be for students to demonstrate respect to their peers by making at least two supportive skill- or outcome-related statements to their classmates during a practice task or game. At the end of class you could then gather students into a circle to discuss some core values that make for appropriate sporting behavior; namely, caring, respect, integrity, and responsibility.

- Use self-report journals in which students reflect on or rate their sport citizenship (using TPSR levels) for a particular day, event such as a tournament, or overall unit. Students could describe both positive and negative sporting behaviors.

- Create a good citizenship rubric such as the one in table 6.9. This table has three indicators of good sport citizenship in game settings, and players can score from 3 to 1 on each indicator depending on the consistency of their behavior. Students record their levels in the left-hand column.

The affective domain also addresses the feelings and emotions students have developed about sport-related games. For example, you might ask your students how they feel when they win or lose or how they feel about themselves after learning a particular game.

Table 6.9 Good Sport Citizenship Rubric

Level 3—Uses indicators in an extremely consistent manner.
Level 2—Uses indicators with consistency most of the time.
Level 1—Uses indicators with occasional consistency.

Level	Indicators
	Makes no observational errors in interpreting or applying the rules of the game.
	Refrains from actions or behaviors that endanger or injure other students.
	Recognizes and acknowledges good play by a teammate or opponent.

The underlying goal of the tactical games approach is to appeal to students' interest in playing games so they value or appreciate the need to work toward improved game performance. Improving performance should lead to greater enjoyment, interest, and perceived competence to become lifelong games players.

Following are some examples for assessing these sort of outcomes:

- **Self-report journals.** Students may record the following:
  - How they felt about their particular games units
  - How they felt when they scored
  - How they felt playing against an opponent
  - How they felt when they tried a new game
  - Successes or challenges in learning a new skill or movement
  - Successes or challenges when playing a particular game
- **Role play.** Students create a play dealing with conflict resolution during a small-sided game that they usually play in class.
- **Affective domain rubric.** Reproducible 6.13 provides a sample rubric for assessing the affective domain.

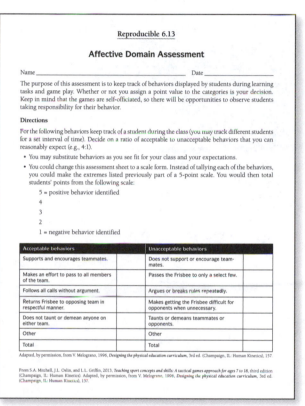

Reproducible 6.13   Sample rubric for assessing the affective domain.

SUMMARY

This chapter described ways to assess students' learning through a tactical games approach. We outlined the potential learning outcomes and aligned a tactical approach to three domains of learning (psychomotor, cognitive, and affective) as well as to the NASPE (2004) standards. Formal and informal measures allow for ongoing assessment and can help you provide a clear message to your students that the intent of teaching sport-related games is to improve performance. You should view yourself as an architect of games learning and create conditioned games and assessments that provide the skills, movements, and competencies students need to be successful games players (Oslin 2005). The take-home message is simply that assessment matters. The teaching and learning process is not complete without assessment. By building assessment into your daily teaching, you are making an investment in your students, in yourself as a teacher, and in physical education as a viable subject. Ongoing assessment ensures that students develop the competence and confidence to play games long after they leave your physical education program.

Part II

Lesson Plans for a Tactical Games Approach at the Elementary Level

Building Sport Foundations

Elementary physical education curricula typically introduce sport and games content at the second- or third-grade level. This introduction usually takes the form of teaching and learning manipulative skills through drill-type activities, as lead-up activities to game play, which comes later. In fact, we have heard some physical educators express the opinion that children as old as seven (second grade) are not capable of game play and should be restricted to skill practice only. Needless to say, we disagree with this viewpoint and argue that the teacher is responsible for modifying the game so that young students can play. These modifications involve changes to game goals, equipment, team size, scoring, and playing areas. Once a version of the game that is appropriate for the participants is created, further development of both tactical understanding and technical proficiency within the game is possible.

This section describes the thematic tactical games approach we advocate for teaching in the elementary grades. Other teaching approaches, such as the skill theme approach advocated by Graham, Holt/Hale, and Parker (2013), suggest that students learn best when content is collapsed into themes to emphasize common components. Similarly, for elementary grades, we advocate teaching not discrete games, such as soccer, volleyball, and softball, but rather, units of invasion games, net and wall games, and striking and fielding games centered on specified tactical problems. For example, in teaching invasion games such as soccer, hockey, and basketball, you might teach young students to keep possession of a ball by passing, receiving, and supporting. Depending on the length of your instructional unit, time spent on invasion games might also include learning shooting techniques. In this way, students learn to solve the tactical problems of invasion games play rather than looking only at the skills of a specific game in isolation.

This approach is intended to develop more knowledgeable and adaptable game players at the elementary level—players who can switch easily among various invasion games or net games and retain a degree of understanding of game play that transfers from one game to another. For example, because of the similarity among invasion games, students should be able to move from soccer to hockey and retain a degree of understanding of game tactics.

This thematic approach will be a different way of thinking for many teachers, many of whom voice concern about the lack of time for skill development in any one activity. Our response is simple: Because of the large amount of practice time required for skill development, competence is rarely (and proficiency is almost never) achieved in elementary games teaching and learning. Regardless of the approach used, there is insufficient curriculum time for skill learning to occur, but some depth of tactical learning is both possible and desirable. Once students perceive that they understand or know how to play a game, they are more likely to play in and outside the physical education context.

Chapter 7

Invasion Games at the Elementary Level

Invasion games, with their numerous simple and complex decision-making challenges, provide the early learner with more freedom of movement than other game types. They also offer opportunities to interact with peers in a socially oriented team environment. These features make invasion games wonderful vehicles for high levels of activity and for the achievement of psychomotor, cognitive, and affective learning outcomes. We begin this chapter by identifying relevant tactical problems and complexity levels for elementary children, and then provide suggestions for organizing elementary invasion games lessons, and for appropriate invasion game progressions. At the end of the chapter, sample lesson outlines are provided for invasion games at game complexity levels I, II, and III. Lessons are intended to provide a progression of tactical and skills learning and, as such, are sequential.

ELEMENTARY INVASION GAMES TACTICS

As addressed in part I of this book, games should be broken down into tactical problems. Solutions to these problems will be in the form of off-the-ball movements and the selection and execution of on-the-ball skills. These solutions represent the content of games instruction at the elementary level. Table 7.1 shows a tactical framework for elementary-level invasion games. This framework provides the scope of content for teaching invasion games at the elementary level by breaking them down according to the problems associated with scoring, preventing scoring, and starting or restarting play. The levels of game complexity described in the next section provide an appropriate sequence for this content. Taken together,

Table 7.1   Problems, Movements, and Skills in Elementary-Level Invasion Games

Tactical problems	Off-the-ball movements	On-the-ball skills
SCORING (OFFENSE)		
Keeping possession of the ball	• Supporting the ball carrier • Deciding when to pass	Passing and receiving the ball
Penetrating the defense and attacking the goal	• Using a target forward • Deciding when to shoot and dribble	• Moving with the ball • Shooting • Faking • Changing speed
Transitioning from defense to offense	Moving to space—deciding when and where to move	Quick outlet pass
PREVENTING SCORING (DEFENSE)		
Defending space	• Guarding a position • Footwork • Pressuring the ball carrier	
Defending the goal	Goalkeeping—positioning	Goalkeeping—stopping and distributing the ball
Winning the ball	Rebounding—boxing out	• Rebounding—taking the ball • Tackling and stealing the ball
RESTARTING PLAY		
Beginning the game	Supporting positions	Initiating play
Restarting from the sideline	Supporting positions	• Putting the ball in play • Quick restarts
Restarting from the end line	Supporting positions	• Putting the ball in play • Quick restarts
Restarting from violations	Supporting positions	• Putting the ball in play • Quick restarts

the framework and levels of game complexity provide a developmentally appropriate scope and sequence of invasion games content for elementary children. Ideally, games should be no larger than 3v3 at first, progressing to a maximum of 6v6 in games such as soccer and hockey.

LEVELS OF ELEMENTARY INVASION GAME COMPLEXITY

Tactical content should be sequenced to make games instruction developmentally appropriate. We recommend identifying the level of game complexity for each game category. These levels include the learning of concepts, movements, and skills across a variety of games. So, at level I you might teach your students to keep possession of a ball by passing, receiving, and supporting in soccer, hockey, and basketball. Depending on the length of time spent on invasion games, level I might also include learning shooting techniques in these games. Table 7.2 presents three possible levels of complexity for invasion games, on which you can base the development of unit and lesson plans.

Notice that we advocate beginning invasion games play with no more than three players per team. This

limit allows for some decision making (Should I pass to player A or player B?), but does not force a vast range of possibilities. We have even found two-a-side games to be effective because they decrease the passing options, forcing players to make straightforward decisions (Do I pass to my teammate, shoot, or dribble?). Such a limit represents decreased complexity in the early stages of invasion games learning. Table 7.2 shows how game complexity can increase as students progress through levels II and III. Transition is a more complex tactical problem and is addressed only at level III.

Using a tactical games approach, you can plan instructional units that enable students to learn to address similar tactical problems across a variety of invasion games. Looking at table 7.2, you can see that students' initial exposure to invasion games might address the concepts of possession, penetration, defending space, and simple starts and restarts while they play small, conditioned versions (2v2 or 3v3) of any invasion games. Although the game can be changed at any time (because the problems addressed are similar, regardless of the game), the skills taught would be different. For example, the skills needed to keep possession in soccer are different from those needed in basketball and hockey. However, the key to

Table 7.2 Levels of Tactical Complexity for Elementary-Level Invasion Games

Tactical goals and problems	Level I Three-a-side maximum	Level II Four-a-side maximum	Level III Six-a-side maximum
SCORING (OFFENSE)			
Keeping possession of the ball	• Passing and receiving the ball • Deciding when to pass	• Passing and receiving the ball • Supporting the ball carrier	
Penetrating the defense and attacking the goal	• Shooting • Moving with the ball • Deciding when to shoot and dribble	• Shooting • Faking	• Using a target forward • Shooting • Faking • Changing speed • Moving with the ball
Transitioning from defense to offense			• Moving to space—deciding when and where to move • Quick outlet pass
PREVENTING SCORING (DEFENSE)			
Defending space		• Guarding a position • Footwork • Pressuring the ball carrier	
Defending the goal		Goalkeeping—positioning	Goalkeeping—stopping and distributing the ball
Winning the ball			• Tackling and stealing the ball • Rebounding—boxing out • Rebounding—taking the ball
RESTARTING PLAY			
Beginning the game	Initiating play	Supporting positions	
Restarting from the sideline	Putting the ball in play	Supporting positions	Quick restarts
Restarting from the end line	Putting the ball in play	Supporting positions	Quick restarts
Restarting from violations	Putting the ball in play	Supporting positions	Quick restarts

this approach is that, by learning the general concepts, students more quickly understand what they need to do to play invasion games successfully.

MODIFICATIONS FOR ELEMENTARY INVASION GAMES

In the following sections, we suggest modifications (or conditions) for teaching invasion games. These are intended to ensure a developmentally appropriate progression of learning and an environment conducive to understanding invasion game play.

Equipment and Playing Areas

As a rule of thumb, early invasion game experiences should be of the throw-and-catch variety, such as a simple version of team handball. The reason is that this type of game incorporates manipulative skills that young elementary school students (again, we are thinking of second grade as a starting point) are able to perform in both practice and game situations played in confined space, as is typical in the average elementary school gymnasium. Medium-sized sponge balls (about 8 or 9 in., or 20 to 23 cm, in diameter) work well for throw-and-catch games because they are big enough to facilitate catching, small enough to not hinder throwing, and soft enough that no one will get hurt when hit with the ball. Several sizes of balls, as well as of Frisbees, made from foam are commercially available, and these should be in every elementary school physical educator's equipment storeroom.

In early throw-and-catch games, it is wise to eliminate movements with the ball, such as running or dribbling, so that passing, receiving, shooting, and movement by supporting teammates become the focus of the game. Allowing young players to move with the ball can lead to either excessive physical contact or to players simply running or dribbling down the court with their heads down. Once students start to become more competitive with each other, it is also wise to restrict defense to intercepting passes only. The section Defense Rules in chapter 3 provides some suggestions for using "cold," "warm," and "hot" defense.

Once students are accustomed to playing a simple throw-and-catch invasion game, you might progress to a different game that uses similar skills or perhaps to one that uses different skills but emphasizes similar tactical problems. By choosing a game that requires different skills, you emphasize the transfer of tactical understanding. The game can only require skills that young players are able to perform, such as a modified floor hockey game such as pillow polo, which uses sponge balls of varying sizes (depending on the students' ability to strike the ball) and commercially available pillow polo sticks, which have a Styrofoam head. At this point, the new game allows students to move with the ball by dribbling, opening up a range of new offensive possibilities as they penetrate the defense with the ball. It is, of course, important to revisit the rules regarding balls intruding onto neighboring courts because ball control is more difficult with sticks, and the ball will therefore go out of bounds more frequently. It is difficult to eliminate dribbling in games such as soccer and hockey, and increased movement increases the demands on the available space, suggesting that these games should be played outdoors where possible. Also, outdoor surfaces, particularly grass, slow the movement of the ball, making skill execution easier.

Notice that in the level I invasion game lessons, the first four lessons emphasize keeping possession in team handball—a throw-and-catch game requiring lower levels of skill. Once students are comfortable playing these games independently, the remaining lessons rotate team handball with pillow polo while focusing on the tactical problem of attacking the goal. Addressing the same tactical problem reinforces players' tactical understanding of game play; it reintroduces tactical problems in different invasion games to provide a depth of tactical learning and the transfer of tactical learning from one game to another.

As students become more independent games players, you can switch the equipment during a lesson so that more than one game is played addressing a particular tactical concept. Switching equipment during a lesson is more likely to be possible with level II or III learners than with those at level I. Where more space is available, in larger gymnasiums or outside areas, you can expand the range of invasion games played to include games such as soccer, in which the ball travels farther and faster and in which more time is needed to execute difficult ball-control skills.

Game Conditions

A critical aspect of a tactical approach to teaching games is the use of game conditions to increase the likelihood that players have to think about ways to overcome a problem and execute skills appropriately. Designing game conditions really involves little more

than applying simple rule modifications and adjusting the goal of the game, the scoring system, playing areas, and equipment, in any combination, so that players are faced with a problem that must be solved through the application of particular movements and skills. Think of yourself as an architect of task design. Consider these examples:

- If you want players to think about how to keep the ball as a team by supporting the player in possession, it makes sense to have them play a possession game with the goal of completing a certain number of consecutive passes in order to score a point. Restricted movement for the player with the ball also encourages supporting players to move to a space where they can receive a pass.

- Conditions related to defense, in addition to the use of cold, warm, or hot defense, can have a valuable effect on offensive play. For example, in basketball, you might want players (probably older elementary students) to think about and execute shots from outside the shooting key as a prelude to practicing jump shots in a skill practice setting. By establishing the condition that the defending team must stay inside the key, players on the offensive team will be less likely to try to shoot from close to the basket and more likely to shoot from outside, where they have space and time.

- When you add direction to the game by moving from a possession game to a game that involves shooting into a goal (see the following section), some players will attempt to shoot from a long distance. This cuts down on team play and eliminates some of the passing, receiving, and supporting work previously practiced. It is tempting to insert a condition that forces players to pass a certain number of times (say, three times) before any team member can shoot, but this might have two unintended negative effects:

  - First, it might actually penalize players who get the ball into a shooting position with one or two excellent passes to players who are supporting effectively. Not being allowed to shoot in this case can frustrate players.

  - Second, those quick-witted players seeking to take advantage of the condition might simply make three very quick, short passes before taking a long shot anyway.

Rather than a three-pass condition, it is probably better to stipulate an area of the court or field from which players must shoot in order to score, ensuring that the team works together to get the ball to this area. To prevent an excessive number of long shots, it might be best to stipulate that teams must get the ball across midcourt (at the halfway line) or perhaps into the offensive third of the court or field before a player takes a shot.

The previous examples illustrate the simplicity of setting game conditions. As the teacher, you should ask yourself the following two questions: what do I want my students to think about and do in this game? and, how do I design the game to make this happen? Although this may be a different way of thinking for you (at least initially), the more game conditions you devise, the easier it becomes to develop conditions that make students think about solving particular problems through the use of specific skills. The conditions of the game set the problem to be solved and help students see the value of using particular skills before these skills are then isolated for practice.

PROGRESSIONS FOR TEACHING ELEMENTARY INVASION GAMES

We and our colleagues in elementary schools have frequently raised the issue of the starting point and progressions for learning game play. Specifically, we have asked the following two questions:

- What type of invasion game provides the easiest introduction for the elementary school student?
- What types of invasion games best progress students' understanding of game playing to a more mature level?

The following suggestions represent our answers to these questions.

Possession Games

A 2v2 or 3v3 possession (keep-away) game is a sensible game form when you are beginning to teach the invasion game. Be aware that 3v3 is more complex than 2v2 because the extra player on each team provides an additional passing option. Early lessons in this chapter use a 3v3 format, but this format could be changed to 2v2 if simplification is necessary. The choice of game (i.e., two- or three-a-side) may also be determined by class numbers, gymnasium size, and available equipment. Regardless of team size, it should be possible to fit several small-sided possession games into a normal-sized elementary school gymnasium (assuming a class size of about 24 students). Figure 7.1 shows six games of 2v2 in a gymnasium, whereas figure 7.2 shows four games of 3v3. Floor tape can easily be used to mark playing areas for either format.

The benefit of the possession game is that young learners do not have to concern themselves with direction. They can simply move anywhere on the court and count the number of passes the team makes. You might notice any or all of the following things occurring early in the students' learning of possession games:

- Some players (say, at the second-grade level) might be reluctant to play against the other team to the point that they will stand and watch while opponents pass the ball back and forth. If this is the case, you will probably need to encourage them to try to "get" (intercept) the other team's passes.
- Players will stand still, hold out their hands, and yell, "Throw it here!" Assuming that the other team has responded to your previous (if necessary) prompts to intercept passes, the stationary player on the first team is very easy to guard simply because she is static. You will need to encourage these players to move into open space.

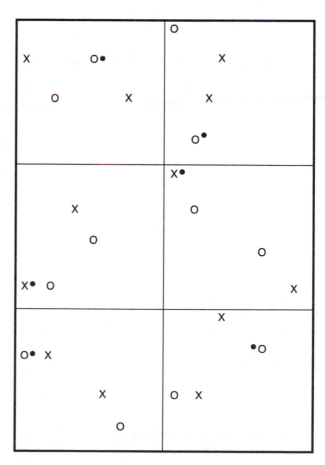

Figure 7.1 A gym floor layout for 2v2 invasion games.

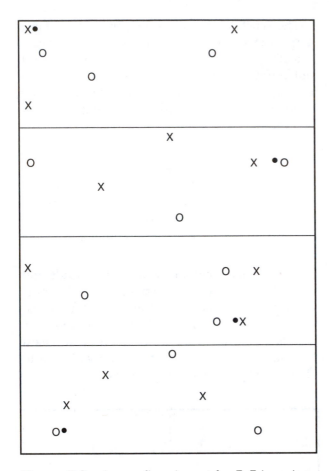

Figure 7.2 A gym floor layout for 3v3 invasion games.

- Not only will players stand still and expect to receive a pass, but they will also stand close to the player who has the ball, which sometimes happens because teachers have, perhaps rightly, suggested that short passes work better than long ones. This proximity makes the game very congested and decreases the likelihood of completed passes because the poor use of space decreases the amount of time available to throw. Try suggesting to players that they will actually be more helpful to a teammate who has the ball by moving away from him into open space. Be aware that some may take this as meaning "go to the next county" and move out of accurate passing range, so you will probably need to demonstrate appropriate distances.

- You will often notice that the player with the ball will take a long time to decide to pass to an open teammate. This can cause frustration because by the time the player in possession makes the pass, defenders have moved to guard the previously

open player. Remember that speed of thought in game play is developmental in the same way that motor skill is. It is only by being put in these decision-making situations that young games players develop the ability to make appropriate decisions with sufficient speed to allow for effective implementation. Occasionally freezing and reconstructing game situations to demonstrate appropriate decisions is a useful teaching strategy.

- You might notice that the player with the ball often goes unguarded. This actually represents some intelligent thinking on the part of novice players, which we have seen in students as young as second grade. It is an acknowledgment that the player with the ball cannot move (as per the rules you have established) and is, therefore, not a threat. What you will see in this case is an effective double-teaming of the other player (in a 2v2 game). This makes it very difficult for a team to keep possession of the ball, and the situation might require some intervention on your part. Try any or all of the following: require one-on-one guarding, encourage a lot of movement from the supporting player to make double-teaming harder, and allow the player with the ball to take three steps while in possession.

- Remember that you have to teach start and restart rules, particularly for out-of-bounds balls.

Games to a Goal

The best way to increase the complexity of invasion game play for young learners is to place a goal (using a pair of cones) at each end of the court or field and tell one team to try to throw the ball through one goal and the other team to try to throw the ball through the other goal. Some words of caution here:

- Some young learners need several reminders of the goal into which they are attempting to score.

- It is best to restrict movement with the ball to either one step or, to prevent arguments, to no movement at all.

- Insist that the ball must be traveling downward (unless it has bounced first) as it goes between the cones and that it must go cleanly through the cones (i.e., if the ball hits the cone, it does not count).

- Remember to specify warm defense and to teach restarts for out-of-bounds balls.

At first, it is best to restrict the width of the goal (to about 6 to 8 ft, or 1.8 to 2.4 m) so that a goalkeeper is not necessary. This goal size keeps all players active and involved in the decision-making aspects of the game. As game-playing proficiency improves, it becomes appropriate to widen the goal (12 to 16 ft, or 3.7 to 4.9 m) and include a goalkeeper. A goalkeeper creates a greater challenge for shooting accuracy and, as a by-product, is a useful strategy for taking a player out of field play to provide more space for field players to play the game. Again, some words of advice: first, make sure that the ball is sufficiently soft so that it will not hurt a goalkeeper on contact; second, for safety reasons, specify a line past which no player other than the goalkeeper can move (some teachers tape a goalie's box on the floor); and third, rotate the goalkeeper frequently.

Games to a Target Player

Moving on a little in complexity, all invasion games require that teams penetrate the opponent's defense to make progress toward the goal. A useful way of teaching penetration is to position a target player in the other team's half of the field or court and have students try to reach this player with an early pass. This is a good way of moving the ball forward quickly to transition from defense to offense. In soccer, this player is actually referred to as a target player, whereas basketball uses the term *post player*. Regardless of the term used (we use *target player*), the incorporation of the target player into a small-sided game is a useful way to teach penetration by encouraging players to look for gaps in the opposing team's defense through which to pass to the target player. In the 3v3 game, a team scores by getting the ball to its target player (OT or XT), as shown in figure 7.3.

The following are points to be aware of in target player games:

- Players need to be reminded that the target player is replacing the goal. The purpose of the game is no longer to shoot through the goal but to pass to their own target player, who is positioned behind an end line in the offensive end.
- Target players have an initial tendency to stand still (which will not help their teammates reach them with a pass) and need to be reminded that they can move at any time, anywhere along the end line to help open up gaps through which teammates can pass.
- It will be important to emphasize appropriate restarts after a team has reached the target player (target players must give the ball back to the other team after a score so that play changes direction).

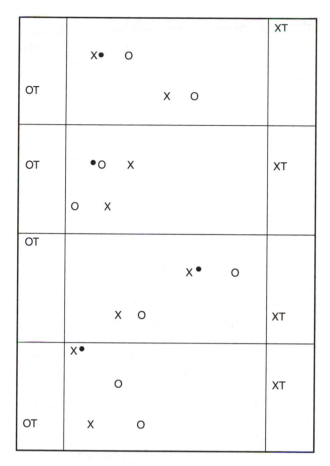

Figure 7.3 Court or field layouts for 3v3 invasion game with target players. XT and OT are target players positioned in their respective end zones.

Games to an End Zone

Some invasion games, such as American football, rugby, and ultimate Frisbee, involve scoring in an end zone. These games involve increased complexity because players must carry the ball (or Frisbee) into the end zone or receive it inside. Again, these games can easily be played using gymnasium lines and modified equipment. This type of game is also useful for emphasizing moving with the ball. If dribbling in soccer or basketball is the focus of instruction, it might be appropriate to have players score by dribbling the ball under control across the end line and into the end zone. Again, you should review restarts (giving the ball back to the other team after a score) to prevent a team from simply moving in and out of the end zone with the ball, claiming to have scored each time. In addition, stress safety in games such as ultimate Frisbee and football, in which players might be running forward but looking back to receive a pass.

SCOPE AND SEQUENCE

In developing the content suggestions for this and the next two chapters on net and wall games and striking and fielding games, we asked ourselves the following three questions:

1. What are the problems or concepts of invasion games that can be realistically addressed at the elementary level? (That is, how much can elementary students understand about game play?)

2. How are these problems solved by movements that occur without the ball (off the ball) and skills that are performed with the ball (on the ball)?

3. How can this content be sequenced in levels so that young learners can play a developmentally appropriate game at each level?

Note that in addressing the third question, we are suggesting a different approach to the development of the games curriculum. At the beginning of a typical games unit of instruction, teachers normally ask themselves, what skills should I teach? We advocate asking a different question: how do I want (or how can I expect) the game to look at the end of this unit? This question places a different emphasis on the development and sequencing of content because all content is chosen with the idea of enhancing the overall quality of game performance at each level rather than of enhancing skill alone.

The tactical framework for invasion games was presented in table 7.1, whereas table 7.2 sequenced this content into three levels of game complexity to allow for developmentally appropriate instruction. Note that in table 7.1 the scope of content is restricted to what is essential for a modified version of any invasion game. Teams must understand and be able to keep possession of the ball to be successful offensively and must then turn this possession into offense by attempting to penetrate the opposing team's defense and attack the goal. Frequent changes of possession are the norm at the elementary level, and an understanding of how to turn defense into offense (transition) is also beneficial. More advanced tactical aspects of offensive team play, such as creating and using space, are not as appropriate at the elementary level because they are needed less in the small-sided game.

For defense, players need to know how to defend space, defend the goal, and win the ball back when it has been lost. The decisions, movements (without the ball), and skills (with the ball) suggested as means of addressing the tactical problems are rudimentary and appropriate for the elementary level. Table 7.2 suggests that the game will look different at successive levels by virtue of the number of players on each team and the increased complexity of decisions, movements, and skills anticipated as solutions to tactical problems.

Introduce students to invasion games in a way that makes learning fun.

LEVEL I

Level I lessons (second and third grade or ages 7 to 9) focus on a game of three-a-side, beginning with a simple throw-and-catch version of team handball. Tactical problems addressed are limited to the essentials of invasion game play for novices: keeping possession, penetrating and attacking, and starting and restarting play. There are several points to note as you explore these lessons:

- Modified equipment, particularly more appropriate types of balls, enable young learners to play games more effectively.
- Changing from one game (team handball) to another (pillow polo) reinforces the similarities among invasion games.
- Only a limited number of teaching cues are suggested, providing the learner with just the essential input to assist in skill acquisition, thereby preventing information overload.

- Restarts, such as they are taught at this level, should be addressed primarily during game play as these situations arise. In particular, there will be numerous opportunities to address restarts from a ball that goes out of bounds.
- Some prior teaching and learning of the fundamental manipulative skills of throwing and catching is assumed.
- Notice that here, and in chapters 8 through 10, the first lesson (or sometimes two lessons) at each game complexity level is given over to organizing teams, assigning courts, and teaching students how to play the game. This involves teaching simple procedures, as outlined in chapter 3, to ensure that future lessons run smoothly. A lesson on these organizational matters will save time over the course of an instructional unit or season.

LESSON 1

Elementary Level I

Tactical Problems   Playing the game and keeping possession

Game   Team handball using a volleyball-sized sponge ball (8 to 9 in., or 20 to 23 cm, in diameter)

Lesson Focus   Court and team organization and passing

Objectives   Learn court spaces and complete successful passes to be able to play a keep-away game within a specified court.

START-UP

1. Begin the lesson with the designation and familiarization (as warm-up) of court spaces (1 through 4).
2. Mark the lines with floor tape and label the courts. Students jog to the appropriate court when that court number is called; frequent changes to the court number called make this an active warm-up. Exercises can be put in at particular stopping points in the warm-up.
3. Players form or are assigned to teams of three, and they choose or are assigned to home courts. Each team gets half a court as its home court (figure 7.4).

Court 1

Court 2

Court 3

Court 4

Figure 7.4   Home court setup.

PRACTICE TASK

Triangle passing (i.e., three players in a triangle formation)

Goal   Make 10, 15, or 20 consecutive passes without dropping the ball.

Condition   Players may not move with the ball.

Extensions

- Students pass and move to another space on the court.
- If their ability warrants it, students play 2v1 with a goal of eight passes in a row and then switch (the defender must go to the ball). They use cold (standing) going to warm (arm's length) defense.

GAME

If time permits, students play a 3v3 possession game (four passes in a row earns 1 point).

Goal   Keep the ball.

Conditions

- Players may not move with the ball.
- Players use a warm defense (start to teach this in game play).
- Players use a throw-in from the out-of-bounds line for a ball that is out of bounds.

CLOSURE

Question and a discussion about court spaces

> Q: What is an effective way to keep the ball away from another player in a game?
>
> A: Pass it to a teammate and then move to space.

LESSON 2

Tactical Problems   Playing the game and keeping possession

Game   Team handball (sponge ball)

Lesson Focus   Passing and moving in a 3v3 game

Objective   In a 3v3 game, pass the ball to keep it away from the other team.

GAME 1

Pass and move or 2v1 at home court

Goal   Make four passes in a row.

Conditions

- The defender must try to get the ball.
- Players use a warm (arm's length) defense; slapping the ball out of others' hands is not permitted.

GAME 2

3v3 possession game (four passes in a row earns 1 point)

Goal   Keep the ball.

Conditions

- Players may not move with the ball.
- Players use a warm defense.
- Use the usual boundaries and restart rules.

CLOSURE

- Questions and a discussion about any issues that arose during the lesson.
- Ask team members to describe how they work to keep the ball.

LESSON 3

Tactical Problem   Playing the game and keeping possession.

Game   Team handball (spongeball).

Lesson Focus   Passing and moving in a 3v3 game.

Objective   In a 3v3 game, students keep the ball away from the other team through effective passing and moving.

GAME 1

3v3 possession game (four passes in a row is 1 point).

Conditions

- Do not move with the ball.
- Use a warm defense.
- Use the usual boundaries and restart rules.

Goal   Keep the ball.

Questions

Q: *Where do your passes have to go so that your team can keep the ball?*

A: *To a teammate.*

Q: *Are two-hand passes better than one-hand passes for making sure the ball gets to a teammate? Why or why not?*

A: *Yes, because you can get the ball to your teammate more easily (more accurately).*

Q: *When are one-hand passes better?*

A: *When you have to throw a long way.*

PRACTICE TASK

Triangle passing using a two-hand chest pass.

Goal 10 passes in a row around the triangle (passes should go straight to the receiver).

Cues

- Chest pass:
  - Ball to the chest.
  - Step and push away.
  - Point fingers at the receiver.
- Receiving:
  - Watch the ball.
  - Move in front of the ball.
  - Keep hands out.
  - Put fingers up for high catch, down for low catch.
- Throw pass:
  - Take the ball back with elbow bent.
  - Step with the opposite foot.
  - Throw to your receiver.

Extensions

- One-hand pass
- Pass and move
- 2v1

Question

Q: How and where should you move?

A: Quickly to space.

GAME 2

Repeat game 1.

Goal Keep the ball as long as possible by making good passes to teammates.

CLOSURE

- Questions and discussion on boundaries and etiquette.
- Questions and discussion on good passing (which pass to use) and moving in game play.

LESSON 4

Tactical Problems Playing the game, keeping possession to make forward progress, and attacking the goal

Game Team handball (sponge ball)

Lesson Focus Passing and moving forward in a 3v3 game

Objectives

- In a 3v3 game, keep the ball and move it forward to score in the goal as a team.
- Work on timing the pass to beat a defender (passing at the right time).

GAME 1

2v1 at home court

Goal   Make eight passes in a row.

Conditions

- The defender must try to get the ball.
- Players use a warm (arm's length) defense.

Question

Q: When is a good time to pass?

A: As the defender comes toward you. (Set up a demonstration of this: As a defender, approach a player with the ball. Have all players who are watching say "Now" at the point when the player should give the pass to a supporting teammate.)

GAME 2

3v3 to a small goal (1 point per score)

Goal   Move the ball forward as a team and score in the goal with a downward shot.

Conditions

- Players may not move with the ball.
- Players must shoot from outside a designated point or line.
- Players must shoot down to score. A hit cone is no goal.
- Players use a warm defense.
- Usual boundaries and restart rules apply.

Cues

- Pass as the defender comes toward you.
- Pass the ball ahead of the receiver.

Extension   Widen the goal and put one player from each team in goal.

CLOSURE

Questions and a discussion about determining the right time to pass the ball in a game

Note   Now that students are playing a game, you can change to a different invasion game by simply changing the equipment. To this point players have become accustomed to playing small-sided games in defined spaces and are able to start, restart, and play independently; and they have learned that it is important to keep the ball. Now they are asked to move the ball forward to get into position to score. Students can address this problem in more than one invasion game, and it would now make sense to begin discussing similarities among games. Lessons now progress to address the problem of attacking and alternate between two invasion games, but bear in mind that these lessons can really be used with any invasion game.

LESSON 5

Tactical Problems   Keeping the ball and attacking

Game   Pillow polo (use pillow polo sticks and 6 in., or 15 cm, foam or gator balls)

Lesson Focus   Dribbling and stick control

Objective   In a 3v3 game, move the ball forward by dribbling under control with the stick.

Note This is a difficult skill, made more difficult by the pressure of a game situation. It may require two lessons of practice time and, hence, several practice task extensions.

GAME 1

3v3 to goal with goalkeeper

Goal Get the ball forward and score.

Conditions

- Sticks must always be below knee height.
- Players can move with the ball.
- Goalkeepers can save with feet or stick.
- Only the goalkeeper is allowed inside the goal box or line.

Questions

Q: How can you get the ball forward (other than passing, as you did before in handball)?

A: Run with the ball (dribble).

Q: When should you dribble?

A: When you have space in front of you.

PRACTICE TASK

Whole class dribbling

Goals

- Control the ball.
- Evade opponents.

Conditions

- Each student has a ball.
- Students free dribble in the gym.
- Students must avoid hitting anyone else's ball.

Cues

- Keep your hands apart on the stick.
- Push the ball forward (don't hit it).
- Keep the ball close.
- Push the ball left and right.
- Look up so that you don't hit others.

Extensions

- Players must stop the ball on your whistle by putting the stick on top of the ball (demonstrate control).
- Players must avoid you (acting as a tackler) as they go around.
- Decrease the playing area; this makes evasion harder.
- Players dribble and try to push others' balls away.

GAME 2

Repeat game 1.

CLOSURE

Question and a discussion about keeping the ball from an opponent

Q: If an opponent is trying to get the ball from you, how else can you move it forward?

A: By passing.

Tactical Problems   Keeping the ball and attacking

Game   Team handball (sponge ball)

Lesson Focus   Moving forward to support the passer

Objective   In a 3v3 game, keep the ball and attack the goal by moving forward to support the player with the ball.

GAME 1

3v3 to goal

Goal   Move when you don't have the ball.

Conditions

- Players may not move with the ball.
- Players use a warm defense (arm's length).

Questions

Q: What should you do after you have passed the ball?

A: Move.

Q: Where to (in which direction)?

A: Forward.

Q: Why forward?

A: To get closer to the goal to shoot.

Q: How should you move—quickly or slowly?

A: Quickly.

PRACTICE TASK

Team practice in which players pass and move up and down the home court (figure 7.5)

Goal   Make three passes between team players to get the ball to the other end of the home court.

Conditions

- Players may not move with the ball.
- Players pass and move to the end of the home court.
- Players pass and move back to the goal before shooting past the goalkeeper (of the three team members, one is goalkeeper and the other two are passers or shooters).

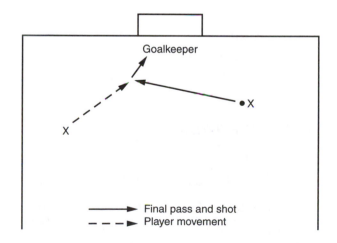

Figure 7.5   Floor diagram of a home court for the practice task.

Cues

- Pass and move forward into space.
- Receive and pass quickly.
- Pass ahead of the receiver (lead the receiver).

Extension   Players must make four passes using faster passing and faster movement.

GAME 2

Repeat game 1.

CLOSURE

Questions and a discussion about where to move after passing. Support the discussion with demonstrations and examples.

LESSON 7

Tactical Problems   Keeping the ball and attacking

Game   Pillow polo (use pillow polo sticks and 6 in., or 15 cm, foam balls)

Lesson Focus   Passing and receiving

Objective   In a 3v3 game, move the ball forward by dribbling, passing, and receiving.

GAME 1

3v3 to goal with goalkeeper

Goal   Get the ball forward and score.

Conditions

- Sticks must always be below knee height.
- Players can move with the ball (dribble).
- Goalkeepers can save with feet or stick.
- Only the goalkeeper is allowed inside the goal box or line.

Question

Q: *It is hard to dribble if someone is trying to get the ball away from you. How else can you get the ball forward as a team?*

A: *Pass it.*

PRACTICE TASK

Pairs passing

Goal   Make every pass go to your partner.

Conditions   Students are in pairs with one ball per pair. Partners stand about 5 yards apart and pass back and forth while moving around the gym (all pairs are working at the same time).

Cues

- Passing:
  - Step and push to your partner.
  - Push the ball ahead of your partner (lead your partner).
- Receiving:
  - Put your stick behind the ball.
  - Push the ball to get it ready for your next pass.

GAME 2

Repeat game 1.

Goal Perform good passing and dribbling to keep the ball and get it forward.

CLOSURE

Question and a discussion about where to pass the ball

> *Q: Where should you pass the ball if you are moving forward with a teammate?*
>
> *A: Ahead of that teammate.*

LESSON 8

Tactical Problem Attacking

Game Team handball

Lesson Focus Shooting

Objective In a 3v3 game, shoot the ball down into the goal when the opportunity arises.

GAME 1

3v3 to goal with goalkeeper

Goal Shoot when possible.

Conditions

- Players may not move with the ball.
- Players use a warm defense (arm's length).

Questions

> *Q: What should you do if you are open in front of the goal?*
>
> *A: Shoot.*
>
> *Q: Should you shoot up or down? Why?*
>
> *A: Down. It is harder for the goalkeeper to save the ball if it is low.*

PRACTICE TASK

Team shooting practice with a passer, a shooter, and a goalkeeper (rotate)

Goal Make all shots go down at the goal.

Conditions

- Two players make three or four passes to each other before one of them takes a shot.
- Players alternate shooting.

Cue Step and shoot down.

Extensions

- Players try to pass quickly to confuse the goalkeeper.
- Players fake shots and pass or shoot.

GAME 2

Repeat game 1.

CLOSURE

Questions and a discussion about attempting goals

> Q: What do you do when you have the ball in front of the goal?
>
> A: Shoot!
>
> Q: How can you confuse the goalkeeper?
>
> A: Fake.

LESSON 9

Tactical Problem   Attacking

Game   Pillow polo (use pillow polo sticks and 6 in., or 15 cm, foam balls)

Lesson Focus   Shooting (wrist shot)

Objective   In a 3v3 game, shoot at the goal when the opportunity arises.

GAME 1

3v3 to goal with goalkeeper

Goal   Get the ball forward and score.

Conditions

- Stick must always be below knee height.
- Players can move with the ball.
- Goalkeepers can save with feet or stick.
- Only the goalkeeper is allowed inside the goal box or line.

Questions

> Q: When you get close to the goal, what should you try to do?
>
> A: Score.
>
> Q: What do you have to do to score? What do we call it?
>
> A: Shoot.

PRACTICE TASK

Whole class dribbling and shooting

Goal   Score as many goals as you can.

Conditions

- Every student has a ball.
- Students perform free dribbling and shooting in the gym. They may dribble and shoot into any goal (these are set up already on each home court).
- After scoring in one goal, students dribble to another for their next shot.

Cues

- Keep your hands apart on the stick.
- Push the ball ahead.
- Push and flick your wrists.

Extensions

- Put in goalkeepers.
- Challenge students by saying, "How many goals can you score in 30 seconds?" Players cannot shoot into the same goal twice in a row.

GAME 2

Repeat game 1.

CLOSURE

Question and a discussion about attempting goals

> Q: What do you do when you get close to the goal?
>
> A: Shoot.

LESSON 10

Tactical Problem   Attacking

Game   Pillow polo (use pillow polo sticks and 6 in., or 15 cm, foam balls)

Lesson Focus   Shooting after a pass

Objective   In a 3v3 game, shoot after receiving a pass close to the goal.

GAME 1

3v3 to goal with goalkeeper

Goal   Get the ball forward by passing and score.

Conditions

- Sticks must always be below knee height.
- Players can move with the ball.
- Goalkeepers can save with feet or stick.
- Only the goalkeeper is allowed inside the goal box or line.

Question

> Q: If you receive a pass close to the goal, what should you do?
>
> A: Shoot the ball.

PRACTICE TASK

Whole class passing and shooting

Goal   Score as many goals as you can.

Conditions

- Each pair of students has a ball.
- Partners perform free passing and shooting in the gym, moving around the gym and shooting into any goal. After scoring in one goal, partners must pass and move to another for their next shot.

Cues

- Keep your hands apart on the stick.
- Pass the ball ahead of your partner.

- Receive and push ahead to get ready for the shot.

Extensions

- Put in goalkeepers.
- Challenge partners to see how many goals they can score in 30 seconds.

GAME 2

Repeat game 1.

CLOSURE

Question and a discussion about attempting goals

> *Q: What do you do when you receive a pass close to goal?*
>
> *A: Shoot.*

LEVEL II

Level II (third and fourth grades) invasion games are suitable for players who have experienced the content covered in level I, understanding that they may have acquired these skills in or outside of physical education. Lessons at level II focus on more sophisticated means of keeping possession and attacking the goal, and introduce aspects of defense and goalkeeping and some formal teaching of restarts.

Assuming a wider range of skill among students, it would be reasonable at this level to vary the game to reinforce to students the essential similarities of invasion games. If you wish to experience this flexibility by changing the game occasionally, we challenge you to teach the same game for no more than two consecutive lessons and also to change equipment, and therefore the game (e.g., from team handball to ultimate Frisbee), midway through a lesson. You might be impressed at your students' ability to transfer an understanding of one invasion game to performance in another.

If you wish to err on the side of caution and maintain the more traditional approach of teaching a single-game unit, the lessons in this section are written as flexibly as possible so that, with a change in equipment and teaching cues during skill practice, they can apply to any invasion game you are teaching for a complete unit. For example, if your preference is for basketball, lessons 11 through 18 can still apply, with some revi-

Level II students can use more varied equipment and apply the invasion games skills they learned in level I.

sion to allow for different types of passes (although these would be very similar to handball) and shots (which might not be so similar). We suggest organizing permanent teams on which players have defined roles and responsibilities, as outlined in chapter 3.

LESSON 11

Tactical Problem   Keeping the ball

Game   2v2 team handball (gator balls)

Lesson Focus   Court and team organization and the possession game (review of level I)

Objective   Recognize court spaces and complete successful passes within specified courts (1 to 3).

START-UP

Begin the lesson with the designation and familiarization (as warm-up) of court spaces (1 to 3). Players form or are assigned to teams of four, and they choose or are assigned to home courts 1, 2, or 3.

GAME

2v2 possession at home court (figure 7.1)

Goals   Earn 5 points per team, and complete the contract (see chapter 5). Responsibilities: coach, equipment manager, trainer, reporter.

Conditions

- Players may take only one step with the ball.
- Players use a warm defense (arm's length).
- Five passes in a row earns 1 point.

CLOSURE

Questions and a discussion about boundaries and responsibilities. Questions and a discussion (with coaches only) about the fairness of teams (e.g., are the teams equal in playing ability?).

LESSON 12

Tactical Problems   Playing the 4v4 game, keeping possession, and attacking the goal

Game   Team handball

Lesson Focus   Passing and receiving in a 4v4 game

Objective   In a 4v4 game, keep the ball and move it forward to score as a team in the goal or end zone.

GAME 1

2v2 at home court

Goal   Earn 5 points per team.

Conditions

- Player may take only one step with the ball.
- Players use a warm defense (arm's length).
- Five passes in a row earns 1 point.

Questions

Q: *What are the best types of passes to make to keep the ball?*

A: *Quick, chest, bounce.*

Q: *How should you catch the ball—by putting your hands out or by bringing the ball in?*

A: *Hands out.*

Q: *Why?*

A: *You can pass it again much faster that way.*

PRACTICE TASK

Passing and receiving in pairs with the goal of 10, 15, or 20 consecutive passes

Cues

- Passing:
  - Step to your target.
  - Push the ball away.
  - Use a firm pass.
- Receiving:
  - Show a "target hand."
  - Put your hands out to receive.
  - "Give" a little to absorb the force.
- Use a quick pass back.

Extension   Players pass and move to lead the receiver.

GAME 2

4v4 to the end zone (1 point per score)

Goal   Earn 5 points per team.

Conditions

- Players may take only one step with the ball.
- Players use a warm defense.
- Use the usual boundaries and restart rules.

Extension   Play is to the target player.

CLOSURE

Questions and a discussion about boundaries and etiquette

Note   This lesson can be done with any invasion game: ultimate Frisbee, floor hockey, ultimate football, soccer, speedball. Answers to questions might differ, as will teaching cues. The next two lessons show how the pass-and-receive theme might be addressed in ultimate Frisbee.

LESSON 13

Elementary Level II

Tactical Problems   Keeping possession and attacking

Game   Ultimate Frisbee (use sponge Frisbees)

Lesson Focus   Passing the Frisbee backhand

Objective   In a 4v4 game, pass accurately using short passes with a backhand technique.

GAME 1

4v4 to the end zone

Goal   Move the Frisbee forward and score in the end zone.

Conditions

- Players may not move with the Frisbee.
- Scoring happens in the end zone.
- Players use a warm (arm's length) defense.
- A dropped or knocked-down Frisbee results in a turnover.

Questions

Q: What type of pass do you need in this game—long or short?

A: Short.

Q: Why?

A: Because it is hard to throw the Frisbee a long way.

PRACTICE TASK

Triangle passing (demonstrate backhand pass)

Goal   Make 10 passes without dropping the Frisbee.

Cues

- Keep your thumb on top and fingers underneath.
- Step with the same foot as the hand you are throwing with.
- Reach across your body.
- Throw to your target.
- Let go level with your front foot.

Extension   Players pass and move.

GAME 2

Repeat game 1.

Goal   Use short backhand passes and forward supporting movements to space to score.

CLOSURE

Question and a discussion about the types of passes. Review cues.

Q: Are long or short passes best, and why?

A: Short ones; they're more accurate.

LESSON 14

Elementary Level II

Tactical Problems   Keeping possession and attacking

Game   Ultimate Frisbee (use sponge Frisbees)

Lesson Focus   Catching the Frisbee with two hands

Objective   In a 4v4 game, catch the Frisbee efficiently to move forward.

GAME 1

4v4 to the end zone

Goal Move the Frisbee forward and score in the end zone.

Conditions

- Players may not move with the Frisbee.
- Scoring happens in the end zone.
- Players use a warm (arm's length) defense.
- A dropped or knocked-down Frisbee results in a turnover.

Questions

Q: How should you catch the Frisbee—with one or two hands?

A: Two.

Q: Why?

A: Because it is easier and safer (but it is quicker with one hand).

PRACTICE TASK

Triangle passing (demonstrate the backhand pass)

Goal Make 10 passes without dropping the Frisbee.

Cues

- Move into line.
- Keep your thumbs down to catch a high Frisbee.
- Keep your thumbs up to catch a low Frisbee.
- Use a quick pass to your target.

Extensions

- Players pass to the receiver's side to make her move and catch.
- Players use one-handed catches for speed.

GAME 2

Repeat game 1.

Goal Use short backhand passes, safe catches, and good moves to space to score.

CLOSURE

Question and a discussion about the types of catches. Review cues.

Q: Are one- or two-handed catches better?

A: It depends on whether you need or want safety or speed!

LESSON 15

Elementary Level II

Tactical Problems   Keeping possession and attacking

Game   Team handball

Lesson Focus   Passing quickly in a 4v4 game

Objective In a 4v4 game, keep the ball and move it forward by passing to open players quickly after receiving the ball.

GAME 1

4v4 to goal

Goal   Find open players to pass to.

Conditions

- Players may take only one step with the ball.
- Players use a warm defense (arm's length).

Questions

Q: When you catch the ball, what should you do?

A: Pass it.

Q: When should you pass it? (Or how should you pass?)

A: Right away (quickly).

PRACTICE TASK

Players practice pressure passing and catching in a triangle. One passer and two feeders rotate after 30 seconds. Player A passes to player B, who passes back to player A, who then passes to player C, who passes back to player A, who passes to player B, and so on. Player D is the coach (figure 7.6).

Goal   Drop no passes in 30 seconds.

Cues

- Receiving:
  - Put two hands out and spread your fingers.
  - Keep your thumbs down for a high ball.
  - Keep your thumbs up for a low ball.
- Passing:
  - Step to your target and pass immediately.

Extensions   Most passes can be done in 30 seconds. Feeders move toward the goal after the feed and receive a return pass from player A (this extension requires two balls: one for player B and one for player C). Players then reverse direction.

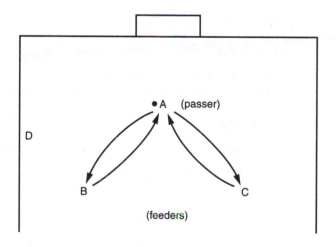

Figure 7.6

GAME 2

Repeat game 1.

Note   If it becomes necessary to spread out the 4v4 game, have students choose from these positions: one defender (must stay in own half), two middle players (can go anywhere), and one forward (must stay in opposing half).

CLOSURE

Questions and a discussion about passing

> Q: What is important about your passing in the game?
>
> A: Do it quickly.
>
> Q: Why?
>
> A: To move the ball over space faster.

Have students do the practice task from this lesson to warm up in the next class.

LESSON 16

Tactical Problems   Playing the 4v4 game and keeping possession

Game   Team handball

Lesson Focus   Moving and supporting in a 4v4 game and timing the pass

Objective   In a 4v4 game, keep the ball and move it forward to score as a team in the goal or end zone.

GAME 1

2v2 at home court

Goal   Earn 5 points per team.

Conditions

- Players may take only one step with the ball.
- Players use a warm defense (arm's length).

- Five passes in a row earns 1 point.

Questions

> Q: How can your teammates help you keep the ball and get it forward?
>
> A: Move to places to receive a pass.
>
> Q: Like where?
>
> A: Away from opponents and ahead of me.
>
> Q: When should you pass?
>
> A: As soon as my teammate is free and there is a passing lane.

PRACTICE TASK

Player A has the ball and says "Go." Players C and D can move to a supporting position. Player A must time the pass so that it is given when the passing lane is open. Player B (the defender) advances toward player A and tries to block the pass to player C or player D. Play restarts after player C or player D receives the ball. Players rotate roles every turn. In figure 7.7, player A has passed to player D.

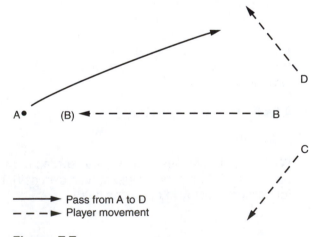

Pass from A to D
Player movement

Figure 7.7

Cues

- Supporting teammates (players C and D)—Move quickly from behind the defender (player B).
- Player A—Pass when the lane is open.

Extension Players play 3v1 up to six passes. After six consecutive passes, or a turnover, the defender is changed.

GAME 2

4v4 to the end zone (1 point per score)

Goal Earn 5 points per team.

Conditions

- Player may take only one step with the ball.
- Players use a warm defense.

Extension Play is to the target player (a permanent end zone player).

CLOSURE

Questions and a discussion about supporting movements, boundaries, and etiquette

Note This lesson can be done with any invasion game: ultimate Frisbee, floor hockey, ultimate football, soccer, and speedball. Answers to questions would be similar among these games, although teaching cues would differ because different skills are taught.

LESSON 17

Elementary Level II

Tactical Problem Attacking

Game Team handball

Lesson Focus Receiving and shooting quickly and accurately

Objective Transition to shoot, and shoot accurately, after receiving a pass.

GAME 1

4v4 to goal with goalkeeper

Goal Shoot when possible and be on target.

Conditions

- Players may take up to three steps with the ball.
- Players use a warm defense (arm's length).
- To score, players shoot downward from the outside shooting line or goal box.

Questions

Q: What should you do if you receive a pass close to the goal?

A: Shoot.

Q: Where do you aim—up or down? Why?

A: Down. It is harder for the goalkeeper to save.

PRACTICE TASK

Shooter A passes to feeder F, who passes the ball across to shooter A, who has advanced. Shooter A receives and shoots at goal. Player B shoots next (figure 7.8).

Cue   Pass, move, receive, step, and shoot downward.

Extensions

- Players feed from the other side.
- Players fake a shot before the actual shot.
- Players jump and shoot.

GAME 2

Repeat game 1.

CLOSURE

Questions and a discussion about shooting

> Q: When is the right time to shoot?
>
> A: As soon as you get the chance.
>
> Q: Where do you aim the shot, and why?
>
> A: Down, to make it harder for the goalkeeper.

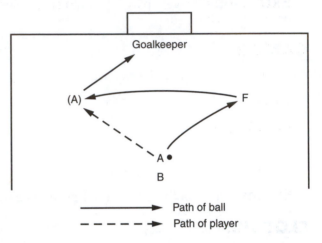

Figure 7.8

LESSON 18

Tactical Problem   Defending space in the game

Game   Ultimate Frisbee

Lesson Focus   Marking, or guarding, players

Objective   Guard an opposing player in open play to make it difficult for that player to find space to receive a pass.

GAME 1

4v4 to the end zone

Goal   Get close to an opponent when the other team has the Frisbee.

Conditions

- Players may take only one step with the ball.
- Players use a warm defense (arm's length) on players in possession.
- Use the usual boundaries and restart rules: a dropped or knocked-down Frisbee results in a turnover.

Questions

> Q: What is it called when you get close to an opponent?
>
> A: Guarding.

Teaching Sport Concepts and Skills

Q: Where should you stand to guard your opponent?

A: Between your opponent and your end zone (set up a demonstration of this) where you can see both the opponent and the Frisbee.

GAME 2

Repeat game 1.

GAME 3

Repeat game 1.

CLOSURE

Questions and a discussion about where to stand to guard an opposing player

Note   Again, the concept of guarding as a means of effective defense is common to all invasion games. Ultimate Frisbee is used only as an example in this lesson.

LESSON 19

Elementary Level II

Tactical Problem   Defending the goal

Game   Hockey, soccer, or team handball

Lesson Focus   Goalkeeper positioning

Objective   As goalkeeper, position to cut down the shooting angle.

GAME 1

4v4 to goal with goalkeeper

Goal   When in goal, make it as difficult as possible for the shooter to score.

Condition   Rotate the goalkeeper frequently so that all players get to play goalkeeper in this game.

Questions

Q: How can the goalkeeper make it hard for the shooter to score?

A: Stand in the right place.

Q: Where is the right place?

A: It depends on where the shooter is shooting from (demonstrate this with a shooter from the right side and a shooter from the left side).

PRACTICE TASK

Each player takes a turn in the goal. Three teammates (A, B, and C) pass the ball among themselves. They must make a minimum of three passes before shooting (figure 7.9).

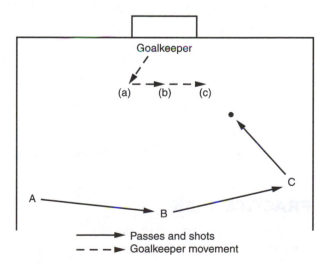

Figure 7.9

Goal   As goalkeeper, cut down the shooting angle by moving toward the player with the ball after each pass (get to positions a, b, and c for shots by players A, B, and C).

Cues

- Slide your feet across.
- Move toward the ball.

GAME 2

Repeat game 1.

CLOSURE

Question and a discussion about the goalkeeper's placement

> Q: What should the goalkeeper do to make it harder for a shooter?
>
> A: Move to the ball.

LESSON 20

Tactical Problem   Starting and restarting play

Game   Hockey, soccer, team handball, ultimate Frisbee, or any other invasion game

Lesson Focus   Positioning to get the ball into play

Objective   Provide two passing options for the inbound pass.

GAME 1

4v4 to goal with goalkeeper

Goal   Keep possession at each inbound pass.

Conditions

- Rotate goalkeepers.
- Have players restart quickly after the ball goes out of bounds.

Questions

> Q: Where do you take the inbound pass or throw-in (soccer) from?
>
> A: Where the ball went out of bounds.
>
> Q: How should you take it—quickly or slowly? Why?
>
> A: Quickly, to take advantage of possession.
>
> Q: With three players on the court, how many supporting players should the inbound passer have?
>
> A: Two.

PRACTICE TASK

Player A must get the ball to player B or C. Player D (the defender) begins by facing players B and C, and tries to guard them or block the pass. Players play 3v1 to four passes and then rotate the defender position (figure 7.10).

Teaching Sport Concepts and Skills

Goal Make a successful in-bounds pass each time.

Cues

- Players B and C:
  - Each go to a side.
  - Fake one way and move the other.
- As player A, pass as soon as a passing lane is open.

Extensions

- Players play 2v2 beginning with an in-bounds pass.
- Four consecutive passes results in a score and a turnover. The other team restarts with an inbound pass.

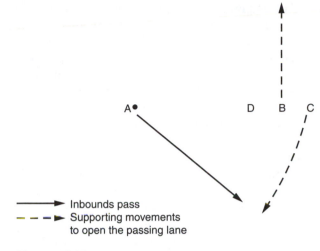

→ Inbounds pass
- - -► Supporting movements to open the passing lane

Figure 7.10

GAME 2

Repeat game 1.

CLOSURE

Question and a discussion about inbound passes

Q: What is important about the way you take an inbound pass?

A: Take it as soon as a passing lane opens.

LEVEL III

As elementary students develop their abilities to understand and play invasion games, you will be able to increase the complexity of the games they play. The most obvious way to increase complexity is to add to the number of players on each team. This increases the range of options available to players when they have the ball. It also makes it possible for more players to be involved in the game (especially when they don't have the ball) either as supporters to the ball carrier or as defending players. A move to playing 6v6 increases the range of offensive possibilities and defensive responsibilities.

Progress in game complexity at level III (fourth and fifth grades) is based on the assumption that students have become comfortable in game play of 4v4 or fewer. For this reason, you will probably not have to devote any lessons to teaching students to play the game. They will come to the unit already familiar with playing two or three games at the same time within the same gymnasium or in the same outdoor area. Level III picks up where level II ends. Defensively, students should have learned marking, or guarding, as a way of defending space; now it is time for them to further

address the problems of defending the goal through goalkeeping or rebounding (in basketball). Goalkeeping and rebounding are two of the most important aspects of invasion games, but they often are ignored in games education. On defense, it is also important to learn appropriate ways of winning the ball in games that allow tackling.

The offensive focus of the 6v6 game is on penetrating a defense to attack the goal and on transitioning from defensive situations to offense as quickly as possible without losing the ball. Of course, the field of play is larger to accommodate the increased number of players, making it more difficult for a team to transition from defense to offense. Players have greater freedom to move with the ball and more opportunities to give longer passes to transition effectively.

The lesson outlines presented in this section encompass a variety of possibilities. Some lessons (24 to 26) are written in a rather generic manner, emphasizing the point that lessons can be used with a variety of games. Others, particularly those relating to defense (21 to 23), are designated for specific games (soccer, basketball, floor hockey). Our goal here, difficult though it might be, is to develop a series of lessons that you can adapt to a single games unit.

At this point, you might be concerned that your students have not been sufficiently exposed to any single game, such as basketball, to be able to demonstrate any degree of game-playing proficiency. Do not be too concerned! Remember, they have learned to make appropriate decisions about shooting, passing, and dribbling; and they have learned how to move without the ball offensively to support and defensively to mark, or guard. The major feature of basketball not specifically addressed to this point has been shooting (set shots and layups) and dribbling, although this would have been possible with some adaptations of level I and level II lessons. Teams can remain at six-a-side for basketball, allowing for 3v3 within-team practices and scrimmage games. The use of the Sport Education model (Siedentop, Hastie, and van der Mars 2011) involving regular competition would provide responsibilities for players not actively playing during basketball game play if games were 5v5 or even 4v4. Alternatively, if warranted by student ability level, regular season play could remain 3v3 with two smaller teams made from the larger team.

Again, it is not necessary to teach specific lessons on restarts at level III. However, it is important to encourage players to take restarts, including throw-ins, corners, and restarts after violations, as quickly as possible to take the most advantage of possession at the restart.

Level III students should be ready for the complexity of playing invasion games on teams.

LESSON 21

Elementary Level III

Tactical Problem   Defending the goal

Game   Soccer (see the note at the end of the lesson on adaptations for floor hockey)

Lesson Focus   Goalkeeping and stopping shots

Objective   Get in line with the ball and hold the ball safely.

START-UP

Players form or are assigned to teams of six, and they choose or are assigned to home courts. Have students sign team contracts.

GAME 1

3v3 with goalkeepers (two field players and one goalkeeper per team)

Goals

- As goalkeeper, stop the shots.
- As field players, take lots of shots.

Conditions

- Rotate goalkeepers.
- Shorten the field to increase the number of shots.

Questions

Q: Where should the goalkeeper be to have the best chance of making a save?

A: In line with the ball (demonstrate this).

Q: How should the goalkeeper move into line?

A: Slide the feet.

Q: What is the best way for the goalkeeper to hold the ball safely once she has it?

A: Cradled in her arms and tucked into her chest.

PRACTICE TASK

Set up a partner practice in which one partner hand-feeds balls to the goalkeeping partner. Balls should be fed at low (feet), medium (waist), and high (chest) levels.

Goals

- Get your body in line with the shot.
- Save and hold the ball safely into your chest.

Condition   Use one ball per pair if possible.

Cues

- Slide your feet to get in line.
- Take the ball into your chest.

Extensions

- Have players vary the direction of the feeds to make their partners move into line as they improve.
- Increase the speed of the feeds to give further challenge.

GAME 2

Repeat game 1.

CLOSURE

Question and a discussion about the goalkeeper's movements

Q: How should the goalkeeper move to make saving easier?

A: Slide the feet to get in line with the ball.

Note   Given the amount of time taken for the initial organization of teams and home courts, this lesson is quite long and may require a second lesson to cover all the material. The lesson can be applied easily to floor hockey in a following lesson. The same game and practice task can apply, although questions and cues would need to address the goalkeeping stance in hockey and the importance of stopping and covering the ball with the hand. Softball gloves to catch or block and cover would be helpful.

Tactical Problems   Defending the basket and winning the ball

Game   Basketball

Lesson Focus   Defensive rebounding after shot attempts

Objectives   Face the basket after a shot attempt to box out the opponent and then jump to take the rebound and give an outlet pass.

GAME 1

3v3 half-court basketball

Goal   When defending the basket, win the rebounds so that the opposing team does not get the turnover.

Conditions   Apply conditions if necessary. Either of these conditions will increase the likelihood of shots that can be rebounded:

- Players may not dribble.
- Shots must be made from outside the key.

Questions

> Q: Once you have turned to see the shot, how can you make it harder for your opponent to win the rebound?
>
> A: Block him (box out).
>
> Q: Where should you be when you catch the ball—on the ground or in the air?
>
> A: In the air. Jump to take the rebound.

PRACTICE TASK

Three-player rebounding practice

Goal   Box out and win the rebounds.

Conditions

- Have one feeder (A and D) and two rebounders (B and C, E and F) per group (figure 7.11).
- Two separate groups of three are at one basket.
- Players A and D shoot against the backboard.
- Players B, C and E, F go for the rebound.
- Players rotate positions every three feeds.

Cues

- Defenders (players B and E)—Turn to see the ball and box out players C and F (demonstrate this).
- Jump to take the rebound.

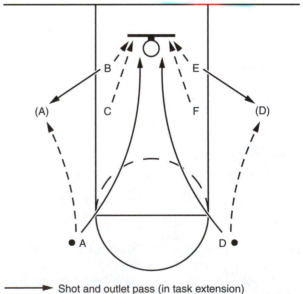

→ Shot and outlet pass (in task extension)
- - → Rebounding (B, C, E, F) and moving for outlet pass (A, D)

Figure 7.11

Extension   The rebounder takes the rebound and gives an outlet pass to the feeder, who has moved to the side.

GAME 2

Repeat game 1.

Condition   Award an additional point for every rebound taken.

CLOSURE

Questions and a discussion about rebounds

> Q: What are the two key points to winning a rebound?
>
> A: Box out and jump to take the ball in the air.
>
> Q: What do you do after you win a defensive rebound?
>
> A: Give an outlet pass.

LESSON 23

Tactical Problem   Winning the ball

Game   Soccer or floor hockey

Lesson Focus   Winning the ball with a block tackle

Objective   Use a strong block tackle to win the ball.

GAME 1

3v3 without a goal or goalkeeper

Goals

- On offense, dribble the ball across the end line under control.
- On defense, tackle the ball carrier to stop her.

Condition   Players try to dribble around opponents before passing.

Question

> Q: Where should you be to make a tackle—close up or back a bit?
>
> A: Close up to block.

PRACTICE TASK

Players perform 1v1 static block tackle practice; pairs are spread out in general space.

Goals   Sandwich the ball between your foot and your partner's foot (between sticks in hockey). Make a firm contact (you will be able to feel and hear this).

Conditions

- On a count of three, both partners make a solid block tackle.
- Players must use the same foot (in soccer) as their partners.

Cues

- Get close to the ball.
- Relax your knee a bit (in soccer).

- Keep firm contact with the ball.
- Push through.

Extensions

- Players alternate feet (in soccer).
- Players use a three-step approach to a tackle.

- Use 1v1 game play.

GAME 2

Repeat game 1.

CLOSURE

Question and a discussion about tackling

Q: What are the important things in tackling?

A: Stay on your feet (in soccer), get close to your opponent, make a firm contact, and push through.

LESSON 24

Elementary Level III

Tactical Problem   Transitioning from defense to offense

Game   Soccer, floor hockey, or basketball

Lesson Focus   Making a quick outlet pass and dribbling at speed

Objective   Move effectively from defense to offense by executing a quick outlet pass and dribbling at speed with the ball or puck.

GAME 1

6v6 including goalkeepers (where appropriate)

Goal   Move the ball forward as quickly as possible to move your team from defense to offense.

Condition   Players use a warm defense.

Questions

Q: How can you get the ball forward quickly to your own goal?
A: Pass.

Q: Where should the first pass go? Why?
A: Out to the side, because there will be more space outside than in the center.

Q: After the first pass, how can you get the ball forward?
A: Dribble.

PRACTICE TASK

Outlet pass and speed dribble

Goal   Perform the maximum number of passes or dribbles in one minute (team competition).

Conditions

- Players use a continuous outlet pass and dribble as a team.
- Two feeders (F1 and F2) feed players A, B, C, and D in turn.
- Player A takes the feed from feeder F1, speed dribbles to a designated point, and passes to feeder F2, who feeds player B.
- Player A then lines up behind player D; player B dribbles and passes to feeder F1, who feeds player C, and so on.
- Use two balls to provide more practice (players A and B could be dribbling at the same time) (figure 7.12).

Cues

- Make a quick pass.
- Push the ball ahead.
- Dribble at speed.

Extension   Players go the other way (pass to the left side).

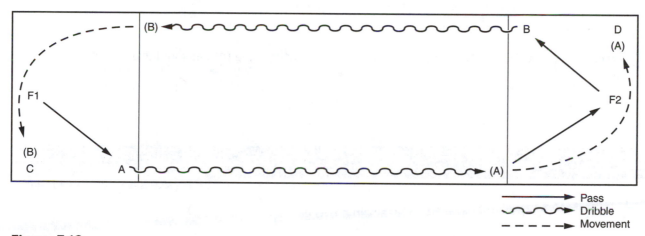

Figure 7.12

GAME 2

Repeat game 1.

CLOSURE

Question and a discussion about defensive and offensive positions

Q: How can you make a good transition from defense to offense?

A: Use a quick outlet pass to the side and dribble the ball forward.

LESSON 25

Tactical Problem   Penetrating to attack the goal in a 6v6 game

Game   Soccer, team handball, hockey, basketball, or ultimate Frisbee

Lesson Focus   Using a target or post player to penetrate and attack

Objective   Create depth in attack by using a target or post player.

GAME

6v6 (includes goalkeepers when appropriate)

Goal   Move the ball forward and score.

Extensions

- On offense, leave a target player in the opposing team's half of the field and try to reach this player as quickly as possible with the ball.
- On defense, guard the target player (use a warm or hot defense as abilities allow).

CLOSURE

Questions and a discussion about the role of target players

Q: How does having a target player help offensively?

A: She helps with transition by being forward.

Q: How can you use the target player most effectively?

A: Give an early pass to the target player.

Note   It is worthwhile to change the game at least once during this lesson. Include basketball, because a post player does differ a little from a target player: a three-second rule prevents the post player from staying too close to the opponent's basket. Sometimes you will want to freeze game play to reconstruct or rehearse ways of reaching the target early with the ball.

LESSON 26

Tactical Problem   Penetrating to attack in a 6v6 game

Game   Soccer, team handball, hockey, basketball, or ultimate Frisbee

Lesson Focus   Using a target or post player to penetrate and attack

Objective   Use a target or post player to create scoring chances.

GAME 1

6v6 (include goalkeepers when appropriate)

Goal   Move the ball forward and score by using the target player.

Conditions

- On offense, leave a target player in the opposing team's half of the field and try to reach this player as quickly as possible with the ball.
- On defense, guard the target player (use a warm or hot defense as abilities allow).

Questions

Q: How does having a target player help offensively?

A: It helps spread out your team from end to end (gives depth).

Q: How can you use the target player to set up shooting chances?

A: Give a pass to the target player and keep moving for a return pass.

PRACTICE TASK

When shooting from a target player feed, each player starts at position S, passes to the target player (Tg), runs to position S, and shoots the return pass (figure 7.13). Each player collects his own shot and returns to the back of the starting line.

Goal   Use the target player to create shooting opportunities.

Extension   Players shoot from the other side (their weaker hand or foot).

Cues

- Shooter:
  - Pass to the target.
  - Support for the return pass.
  - Shoot the return pass.
- Target player:
  - Receive and pass ahead of the shooter.

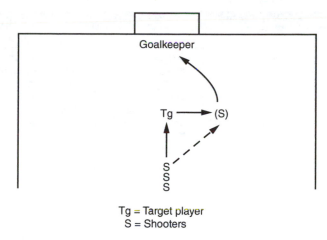

Tg = Target player
S = Shooters

Figure 7.13

GAME 2

Repeat game 1 with 6v6 (including goalkeepers when appropriate).

Goal   Use the target player to create shooting opportunities during game play.

Conditions

- Play with a target player in the attacking half.
- Goals or points from a target player feed count as double.

Cue   Use the target player to set up scoring chances.

CLOSURE

Questions and a discussion about the importance of getting the ball to the target player quickly with an early pass and using the target player to create scoring chances

TEACHING CUES FOR INVASION GAME SKILLS

As previously mentioned, we recommend a thematic approach to teaching games that addresses the tactical problems of game play using several games from the same category. This approach requires a knowledge of many skills and their associated teaching cues, particularly with invasion games. Remember our mandate that you change the game either between or during invasion game lessons. Therefore, in this chapter only we provide an overview of teaching cues for the skills of passing, receiving, shooting, dribbling, support play, and defensive play (table 7.3). We have deliberately limited cues to those six that are most critical to efficient technical performance. Be aware that some of these teaching cues can be used in other games; for example, many of the basketball and soccer cues could be used for speedball, as could many of the cues used in the team handball lessons.

SUMMARY

The invasion game category is the most complex, so we hope this chapter has given you some ideas of effective ways to introduce these games to elementary students. Organization is critical, and students need to develop the ability to have multiple games going at the same time within a gymnasium. Again, we have seen second-graders (seven- and eight-year-olds) do this without difficulty. Using appropriate game progressions helps students develop their game-related knowledge, and the progressions provided in this chapter should help.

Table 7.3 Teaching Cues for Invasive Games

Soccer	Hockey	Football (American)	Basketball	Ultimate Frisbee
BASIC PASSING				
• Place the nonkicking foot beside the ball, pointing to the target. • Point the toe of the kicking foot out (or in if passing with the outside of the foot). • Strike the center of the ball with the inside of the foot. • Follow through to the target.	• See the target. • Keep the blade on the ball or puck. • Push the ball and follow through to the target.	• Grip across the seams. • Keep the arm back and elbow bent. • Step with the opposite foot. • Throw and flick the wrist.	• Keep thumbs behind the ball, elbows in. • Step and extend. • Pass the ball flat (i.e., horizontally). • Finish with palms out.	• Grip with the thumb on top, forefinger along the outside of the rim. • Step with the same-side (as the throwing hand) foot. • Pass flat and follow through to the target.
RECEIVING				
• Move into line with the ball. • Receive with the inside or outside of the foot. • Push the ball away to set up the next pass or shot.	• Move into line with the ball or puck. • Keep the blade to the ground. • Push the ball or puck away to set up the next pass or shot.	• Move into line with the ball. • Palms to the ball. • Keep thumbs together (high ball) or little fingers together (low ball). • Cup hands around the ball. • Bend elbows to cushion the ball ("soft" hands).	• Move into line with the ball. • Palms to the ball, fingers spread. • Cup hands around the ball. • Bend elbows to cushion the ball ("soft" hands).	• Move into line with the Frisbee. • Point fingers to the Frisbee. • Keep thumbs down (high catch) or up (low catch). • Snap fingers and thumbs together onto the Frisbee.
SHOOTING				
• Take a long step to the ball. • Get close to the ball (nonkicking foot alongside the ball). • Strike the center of the ball with the laces. • Keep the toe down and follow through to the target.	• See the target. • Keep the blade on the ball or puck. • Take a long step. • Push the ball with a flick of the wrist. • Follow through to the target.		• Basic set shot: • See the ball in front of your eyes (for start position). • Keep the shooting hand under the ball and the supporting hand on the side of the ball. • Balance with feet shoulder-width apart. • Keep the elbow under the ball and pointing to the target. • Extend knees and arm. • Follow through (wrist points down after the shot).	
DRIBBLING				
• Push the ball with the inside or outside of the foot. • Keep the ball ahead, but close.	• Keep the stick on the ball or puck. • Keep the ball out to the side. • Protect the ball with the body.		• Keep the ball out to the side. • Protect the ball with the body. • Use the fingertips. • Keep the head up. • Dribble at waist height at speed. • Use a knee-high dribble to protect the ball.	
SUPPORT PLAY				
Off-the-ball support for all invasion games • Move out from behind defenders to open a passing lane. • Move quickly to support the ball carrier. • Signal or call for the ball.				
DEFENSIVE PLAY				
Positioning for all invasion games • Mark, or guard, the immediate opponent; stay between her and the goal. • Get closer to ("pressure") the opponent when he gets closer to his goal. • Pressure the opponent when he receives the ball. • Use a sideways stance, knees bent. • Position to one side to guide the opponent onto her weak side. • Tackle or intercept when the chance arises.				

Chapter 8

Net and Wall Games at the Elementary Level

To learn net and wall games, learners need the basic motor skills of catching, throwing, and covering the court. Novice learners playing the simplest form of a net or wall game need to understand the principles of (a) consistently returning the ball, (b) court positioning (spatial awareness), (c) ball placement, and (d) the flight and force (power) of the ball. These principles lay the groundwork for solving the tactical problems in net and wall games. Net and wall games provide learners with high levels of activity because they play in a single or small-sided team game (e.g., volleyball) format. These early game-playing experiences are, by necessity, limited by the fundamental skill levels of novice learners. In net and wall games at the elementary level, students progress from simple throw-and-catch games to striking (without and with

implements) games in both individual and team situations. Remember, the goal of a tactical games approach is to put the learner into progressively more complex games with clearly outlined tactical problems to be solved.

This chapter has four sections. First, we present the scope and sequence used to develop the lesson content (i.e., the framework and levels of game complexity). Second, we describe modifications to equipment and the playing area for teaching net and wall games. Third, we present game progressions, and finally, we provide lessons that you can implement across the three levels of game complexity. As in chapter 7, our goal is to provide sequenced content suggestions to assist you in developmentally appropriate instruction.

ELEMENTARY NET GAMES TACTICS AND LEVELS OF GAME COMPLEXITY

In developing the content for this chapter, we asked ourselves the following questions:

- What problems or concepts of net and wall games can be realistically addressed at the elementary level?

- How can these problems be solved in terms of movements that occur without the ball and skills that are performed with the ball?

- How can this content be sequenced in levels so that young learners can reasonably be expected to play developmentally appropriate games at each level?

Remember, in a tactical games approach, rather than learning discrete skills that are combined into games, learners are placed into progressively more complex games with clearly outlined objectives. The basic learning progression for net and wall games begins with the student throwing and catching over a net or against a wall. Next, the student focuses on underhand striking and team throwing and catching. Finally, the student focuses on striking with implements (e.g., pickleball, badminton, and tennis) and having more than one contact while striking with the hand(s) (i.e., volleyball).

Table 8.1 presents the tactical framework for net and wall games, and table 8.2 sequences the content into three levels of game complexity to allow for instruction that is developmentally appropriate for novice players.

MODIFICATIONS FOR ELEMENTARY NET AND WALL GAMES

To teach students to play net and wall games in their simplest form, you need to consider the range of possible equipment and playing area modifications. Also, as you plan your modifications, keep in mind the primary goal of net and wall games: to propel an object into space so that an opponent is unable to make a return (Griffin, Mitchell, and Oslin 1997).

Early net and wall games should include a variety of throw-and-catch games because these use the manipulative skills second-graders can perform in both practice and game situations. We strongly recommend that you modify the start and restart of the rally or game by eliminating the formal serve. The simplest and most successful way to get the game going is usually a throw. Such a modified serve allows students to begin play and then address tactical problems that are the very essence of net and wall games.

Table 8.1   Tactical Problems, Movements, and Skills for Elementary-Level Net and Wall Games

Tactical problems	Off-the-ball movements	On-the-ball skills
SCORING (OFFENSE)		
Maintaining a rally	• Moving to catch • Reading and anticipating	• Underhand throw • Underhand strike—forehand and backhand
Setting up an attack	• Seeing court spaces—long and short • Opening up to teammates	• Shots for depth—lob, drive, and clear • Approach shot • Drop shot • Service • Passing and setting
Winning a point	• Attacking spaces • Making power versus accuracy decisions	Downward hitting—volley, smash, and spike
PREVENTING SCORING (DEFENSE)		
Defending space	• Base positioning • Covering the court as a team • Sliding	
Defending against attacks	• Backing up teammates • Shifting to cover	Blocking downward hits
RESTARTING PLAY		
Initiating play	Receiving serve	Service

Table 8.2   Levels of Tactical Complexity for Elementary-Level Net and Wall Games

Tactical problems	Level I Throw-and-catch games with one bounce (throw tennis)	Level II • Striking-with-hand games with one bounce (hand tennis) • Throw-and-catch or no-bounce games with two contacts (deck tennis or volleyball)	Level III • Striking-with-implement games with no or one bounce (badminton, pickleball, or tennis) • Striking-with-hand games with two contacts (volleyball)
SCORING (OFFENSE)			
Maintaining a rally	• Underhand throw • Moving to catch • Reading and anticipating	Underhand strike—forehand (hand only)	Underhand strike—forehand and backhand (implement)
Setting up an attack	Seeing court spaces—long and short	• Shots for depth—lob, drive, and clear • Opening up to teammates	• Drop shot • Service • Passing and setting • Approach shot
Winning a point		Attacking spaces	• Downward hitting—volley, smash, and spike • Making power versus accuracy decisions
PREVENTING SCORING (DEFENSE)			
Defending space	Base positioning	• Covering the court as a team • Sliding	
Defending against attacks			• Blocking downward hits • Backing up teammates • Shifting to cover
RESTARTING PLAY			
Initiating play			• Service • Receiving serve

Here are possible modifications of equipment and playing area for net and wall games:

- *The balls should be soft and provide an easy bounce.* Consider offering a variety (i.e., smaller and larger) so that your students can make their own choices based on what works for them. This technique is known as teaching by invitation (Graham, Holt/Hale, and Parker, 2001).

- *When it is time to switch to using implements in net and wall games, be sure that rackets are light and have short handles.* Many teachers we have worked with have used racquetball rackets, badminton rackets, and tennis rackets with shorter handles.

- *Modifying the serve helps increase game play.* One of the complexities of net and wall games is that the skill of serving generally develops more quickly than other game skills and movements, thus making returning serve more difficult. We recommend simplifying the serve to increase skill and movement practice, thus enhancing game play development.

- *The playing areas should always be minicourts.* Your playing area can be short and wide, long and narrow, or somewhere in between, depending on your gymnasium or multipurpose room space. The size and shape of your court will depend on the tactical problem you want your students to work on and solve. You can set up the courts with tape, white shoe polish on a wooden gym floor (easy to remove), cones, or poly spots.

- *Instead of nets, use cones initially in early net game lessons.* Cones provide a simple barrier to play over. Once actual nets are used, we recommend badminton or volleyball nets. Both can be easily adjusted to tennis, badminton, or modified volleyball height.

Teach your students how to set up and break down the courts, especially when using cones or equipment that is easy to move. Students are capable and need to be held responsible for all aspects of their learning. Elementary physical education is often like a revolving door, with one class entering while the other class is departing, so you need students to help you maximize their learning time.

PROGRESSIONS FOR TEACHING ELEMENTARY NET AND WALL GAMES

Progressions begin with simple games that teach the basic concepts of net and wall games. Early game play should involve only a few skills, a few rules, and as few players as possible. As students gain competence in using skills and making decisions, the complexity of the game increases (i.e., increasingly complex skills, more players, and redefined rules).

You want to set up your students to use tactics even in the simplest games. The key to a tactical games approach is to focus on tactics as problems to be solved. With that in mind, it is important that students learn skills and movements in a game context (i.e., tactics drive the skills and movements to be practiced). In this way, they learn the reasons for using individual or combinations of skills and gain an understanding of the relationships among tactical problems across net and wall games. Teaching tactics in a game context leads to increased comfort for students because the game has been the primary learning activity throughout instruction. As in chapter 7, we are concerned with the starting point and progressions for learning the foundations of net and wall game play. The remainder of this chapter answers the following two questions:

- What type of net and wall game provides the easiest introduction for the elementary school student?
- What types of net and wall games best progress students' understanding of game playing to a more advanced level?

The following principles helped guide us in the development of appropriate progressions, represented by three levels of game complexity.

- *Move students from cooperative situations to competitive situations.* Cooperation (e.g., maintaining a rally) involves working with a partner toward a goal. Competition (e.g., 1v1 modified tennis) involves an opponent to work against. Students need to understand that good and appropriate competition requires cooperation; therefore, keeping a rally going is crucial to a competitive net or wall game.
- *Move from simple to complex.* This idea cuts across skills and movements as well as tactical problems and game conditions.

- *Move from individual (singles) to small-group games (2v2) to large-group games (4v4).* Fewer players will slow down the tempo and flow of the game, which makes it easier to play.

We advocate that at game complexity level I you begin with throw-and-catch games over a net or against a wall because these games are the easiest to introduce. Such simple games allow you to introduce about-game knowledge (what makes a game a game), such as court space, start–restart rules, and fundamental in-game knowledge (how to play throw-and-catch games). In this first step in the progression, we focus on cooperative situations, simple tasks, and singles games.

The second progression, level II, incorporates underarm striking and team throw-and-catch games. The progression principles we follow here relate to moving from cooperative to competitive situations and from simple to more complex tactical problems such as creating and defending space, which entail more movements and skills (e.g., underhand striking with the hand only). The focus of game play in this progression is on individuals and small groups.

Striking with implements in pickleball, badminton, and tennis; striking with the hand; and having more than one contact (i.e., in volleyball) are the foci of the final progression (level III). All progression principles are in full use at this level except playing in large groups. We do not advocate playing 6v6 volleyball at the elementary level because the goal is always to maximize involvement for all participants.

LEVEL I

After the initial lesson in which you establish equipment routines and teach the basic rules of the game, level I lessons (for second- and third-graders) focus on singles games, beginning with a simple one-bounce throw-and-catch game (e.g., "throw tennis" or one-wall handball). Tactical problems are limited to maintaining a rally, setting up an attack, and defending space. Throughout this level, much time is spent on the fundamental aspects of the game, such as court boundaries, etiquette, and start–restart rules. The two basic types of games introduced at level I are cooperative and competitive.

If you consider yourself a movement educator, feel free to intervene at any point during these level I lessons to teach movement concepts such as force and levels. These concepts are particularly applicable as students learn solutions to the tactical problem of setting up to attack because these solutions will include long and high shots to push an opponent toward the back of the court.

Students in level I learn the basic rules of net and wall sports.

LESSON 1

Tactical Problem   Maintaining a rally

Game   Throw tennis (singles game with players' choice of ball) using minicourts set up on a volleyball court

Lesson Focus   Court spaces, etiquette, and the cooperative game

Objectives   Recognize court spaces and play a cooperative game while keeping the ball in one's own court.

START-UP

Students select partners and balls and engage in a throw-and-catch warm-up using different sizes of balls and a one-bounce rule. Explain court spaces. Cones mark the "net" of each court (figure 8.1).

GAME

Throw and catch over the "net"

Goal Complete rallies of 10 throws while keeping the ball in the court.

Conditions

- All throws must be underhand and upward; players must throw from where they catch (i.e., no moving with the ball).
- Players throw over the net; the ball must bounce only once on the other side of the net.
- The ball cannot bounce on the thrower's side of the net.

CLOSURE

Discuss the width of the court (in line with the cones) and the depth of the court. Set up and take down practice.

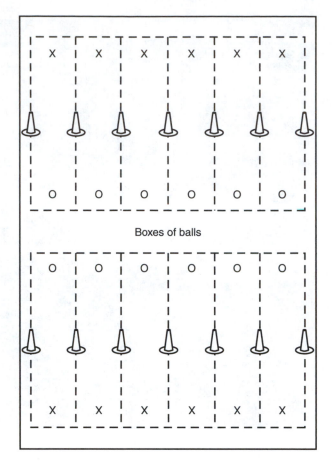

Boxes of balls

Figure 8.1

LESSON 2

Tactical Problem Maintaining a rally

Game Throw tennis (singles)

Lesson Focus Court spaces, etiquette, and the cooperative game

Objective Play a cooperative game while keeping the ball within the defined court.

GAME 1

Throw and catch over the "net"

Goal Complete rallies of 10 throws keeping the ball in the court.

Conditions

- All throws must be underhand and upward; players throw from where they catch.
- Players throw over the net; the ball must bounce only once on the other side of the net.
- The ball cannot bounce on the thrower's side of the net.

Questions

Q: What makes it easier to keep the ball in the court when you are throwing?

A: One or two hands (depending on the ball chosen).

Q: What should your throw look like? (Perhaps present some options here: one-handed or two-handed throw, feet still or stepping, and so on.)

A: Step as you throw (step with the opposite foot).

Q: What makes it easier to catch the ball? Where should you be?

A: After it bounces, let it come up and then down so it is falling when you catch it. (This makes it easier to catch and encourages the students to move their feet. Get students to think in a type of rhythm, or flow, of toss-bounce-catch.)

PRACTICE TASK

Partner throw-and-catch over the net

Goal   Complete rallies of 10 throws while keeping the ball in the court.

Cues

- Throwing:
  - Step with the opposite foot (to the throwing hand).
  - Swing through to your target.
- Catching:
  - Let the ball drop after the bounce.

GAME 2

Repeat game 1.

CLOSURE

Discuss the width of the court (in line with the cones) and the depth of the court.

Q: Where would you throw the ball if you wanted to make it harder for your partner to get it before it bounced twice?

A: Away from your partner into space.

LESSON 3   🛈 DVD   *Elementary Level I*

Tactical Problem   Playing a competitive game and setting up to attack.

Game   Throw tennis (singles).

Lesson Focus   Game rules and use of court spaces.

Objective   Students play a competitive game, with appropriate rules, and move their opponent to the back of the court.

GAME

Throw and catch over the "net."

Conditions

- All throws must be underhand and upward; throw from where you catch.
- Throw over the net; ball must bounce only once on the other side of the net.
- Ball cannot bounce on thrower's own side of the net.

Goal   Make your opponent move around the court.

Questions

Interjected Throughout Game

Q: What spaces are on the court for you to throw the ball into?

A: Front and back because the court is long and narrow.

Q: Is it harder to make a good throw from the front or from the back?

A: From the back.

Q: So where should you try to make your opponent move (front or back)?

A: Back. Try to get the ball to bounce close to the back line.

Q: What must you do to be in the best place to catch the ball?

A: Figure out where the ball will bounce and move to the right place.

After Continuing Game

Q: When you get your opponent to move back, where is the space now?

A: In the front.

Q: So to make it hard for your opponent, where should you throw now?

A: To the front.

Q: Should you throw quickly or should you wait to throw? Why?

A: Quickly, because your opponent will be farther away.

Q: When should you stop and restart a rally?

A: Restart a rally if . . .

  - *the ball bounces twice on opponent's side.*
  - *opponent throws the ball out of court.*
  - *opponent makes the ball bounce on her own side.*
  - *opponent throws overhand.*
  - *opponent catches the ball before it bounces.*

Note   Set up demonstrations of these restart rules.

CLOSURE

Review restart rules.

Tactical Problem   Defending space

Game   Throw tennis (singles)

Lesson Focus   Recovering to a base position

Objectives   Play a competitive game, with appropriate rules, and defend one's own space by moving back to the center of the baseline between throws.

GAME 1

Throw and catch over the "net"

Goal   Make your opponent move around the court.

Conditions

- All throws must be underhand and upward; players throw from where they catch.
- Players throw over the net; the ball must bounce only once on the other side of the net.
- The ball cannot bounce on the thrower's side of the net.

Cue   Move back to the line between throws (base position).

Questions

Interjected during game play:

Q: *If your opponent is moving you around your court, where should you move between your own throws?*

A: *The middle of your court at the baseline.*

Q: *Why?*

A: *So you can move up or back easily to get the next ball.*

GAME 2

Three-minute games against rotating opponents (i.e., rotate the opponent every three minutes)

Goal   Move your opponent, recover, and score the game.

Conditions

- Alternately, each player serves underhand.
- Players follow rules and score the game according to the restart rules.
- The following result in a point scored:
  - The ball bounces twice on the opponent's side.
- An opponent throws the ball out of court.
- An opponent makes the ball bounce on his own side.
- An opponent throws overhand.
- An opponent catches the ball before it bounces.

CLOSURE

Review court spaces, recovery, and scoring.

Note   With a competitive game now in full swing, it is worthwhile to move to a wall game to help students understand the tactical similarities between net and wall games. This move is made in lesson 5.

Tactical Problem   Setting up an attack

Game   One-wall handball (singles throw-and-catch)

Lesson Focus   Court spaces

Objectives   Play a cooperative and competitive game of one-wall handball and try to move opponents around the court.

GAME

Throw and catch against the wall

Goals

- Complete a 20-throw rally (cooperative game to introduce the shift to a wall game).
- Try to make your opponent move around the court (competitive game).

Conditions

- All throws must be underhand and upward; players throw from where they catch.
- The ball must bounce once *after* hitting the wall (cannot bounce before hitting the wall).
- The ball must bounce inside the boundaries (cones).

Questions

Interjected throughout game play:

Q: Where should you try to make the ball bounce to make it difficult for your opponent?

A: Near the back.

Q: Where on the wall do you need to aim to do this—high or low?

A: High up.

After continuing game play:

Q: When you get your opponent to move back, where is the space now?

A: In the front.

Q: So, to make it difficult for your opponent, where should you throw now?

A: To the front.

Q: Where on the wall should you aim—high or low?

A: Low.

Q: When do you score a point?

A: You score a point when any of the following happen:

- *The ball bounces twice in the court.*
- *The ball bounces outside the court lines.*
- *The ball bounces before it hits the wall.*
- *An opponent throws overhand.*
- *An opponent catches the ball before it bounces.*

Note   Set up demonstrations of these scoring rules.

CLOSURE

Review the use of court and restart rules.

Tactical Problem   Defending space

Game   One-wall handball (singles throw and catch)

Lesson Focus   Recovering to a base position

Objectives   Play a competitive game, with appropriate rules, and defend one's own space by moving back to the center of the court between throws.

GAME 1

One-wall handball

Goal   Try to make your opponent move around the court (competitive game).

Conditions

- All throws must be underhand and upward; players throw from where they catch.
- The ball must bounce once after hitting the wall.
- The ball must bounce inside the boundaries (cones).

Cues

- Move back to the center between throws (base position).
- Read and anticipate.

Questions

Interjected during game play:

Q: *If your opponent is moving you around your court, where should you move between your own throws?*

A: *To the middle of the court.*

Q: *Why?*

A: *So that you can move up or back easily.*

GAME 2

Three-minute games against rotating opponents

Conditions

- Players alternate underhand serves.
- Players follow rules and score the game according to the restart rules.

- The following result in a point scored:
  - The ball bounces twice in the court.
  - The ball bounces outside the court lines.
  - The ball bounces before it hits the wall.
  - An opponent throws overhand.
  - An opponent catches the ball before it bounces.

Note   Set up demonstrations of these scoring rules.

CLOSURE

Review recovery (to the center of the court).

Tactical Problem   Creating space

Game   Throw tennis (doubles or team)

Lesson Focus   Court spaces (these are wider, with two small courts combined, introducing playing in wider spaces)

Objectives   Play a competitive game, with appropriate rules, and set up attacks by moving the opposing team from back to front and side to side on the court to create space.

GAME 1

Throw tennis (2v2 or 3v3) over tennis-height net

Goal   Complete a 20-throw rally.

Conditions

- Alternate throw and catch (players take turns throwing and then moving to the back of their own line).

- The game is cooperative.
- The ball must bounce once inside court lines.

Cues

- Throw to space.

- Read and anticipate.

Extension   Players can catch the ball without a bounce.

Questions

> Q: *Now, how can you make it harder for your opponents to catch the ball before the second bounce?*
>
> A: *Throw the ball into space.*
>
> Q: *Where are the spaces?*
>
> A: *Front and back and at the sides.*

GAME 2

Newcome (2v2 or 3v3; plastic ball or deck ring)

Goal   Make the ball bounce in the opposing team's court.

Conditions

- The ball must not bounce.

- Use a badminton-height net.

Extension   Allow two contacts (i.e., players can throw the ball or ring to a teammate, who then throws it over).

Questions   Same as in game 1

CLOSURE

Review the use of spaces. Question and a discussion about moving opponents.

> Q: *How can you use the two contacts (throws) to help move your opponents and make space on the other side of the net?*
>
> A: *Change the direction with the second throw.*

LEVEL II

Level II (third and fourth grades) game progressions move from one-bounce games involving striking with a hand to two-contact games (i.e., two hits or throws per side before the ball crosses the net) using throwing and catching with no bounce. Again, the first lesson establishes the environment and the game. To focus on maintaining a rally, the students play games that involve underhand striking with the hand only. It is possible to repeat everything done at level I using striking with the hand as the means of moving the ball over the net or at the wall. This would present an effective progression to the use of modified rackets. However, the focus of level II lessons presented here moves to team games, though still using throw-and-catch skills. Offensively, the focus of these lessons is to maintain a rally and win points. The defensive (score prevention) concepts focus on covering the court as a team. At this level the students have the opportunity to work with actual nets at varying heights (tennis or badminton heights).

In level II, elementary students learn to focus and work on offensive and defensive teamwork by playing deck tennis, a catch-and-throw game.

LESSON 8

Elementary Level II

Tactical Problems   Playing a game and maintaining a rally

Game   Deck tennis

Lesson Focus   Keeping the projectile (deck ring or quoit) in the court

Objective   Maintain a rally of throw-and-catch deck tennis.

START-UP

Begins with the designation and familiarization of court spaces (1 through 4). Players form or are assigned to teams of three, and they choose or are assigned to home courts where they can go straight into the practice task as an instant activity.

PRACTICE TASK

Triangle passing

   Goal   Complete 10, 15, or 20 consecutive passes.

GAME

3v3 deck tennis (cooperative)

Goal Complete 10, 15, or 20 consecutive passes.

Condition Vary the serving (throws).

CLOSURE

Question and a discussion about throwing

Q: What are the best ways to throw the ring to keep it in the court?

A: Backhand or forehand.

Note Use the same game to start the next lesson.

LESSON 9
Elementary Level II

Tactical Problem Creating and defending space

Game Deck tennis

Lesson Focus Throwing quickly to space, judging the lines, and covering the court

Objective Play a 3v3 competitive game.

GAME 1

3v3 cooperative game

Goal Complete 10, 15, or 20 consecutive passes.

Condition Players vary the throws (backhand and forehand).

Question

Q: How would you win a point while playing against the other team?

A: You win a point when you land the ring inbound on the other side of the net, or when the other team throws the ring out of bounds or into the net.

GAME 2

3v3 competitive game

Goal Be aware of court spaces and the importance of quick catches and throws (i.e., game tempo).

Condition Players alternate serve, with each team serving in turn using an underarm throw from the midcourt or backcourt.

Questions

Interjected during game play:

Q: To score a point, where should you try to throw the ring?

A: Into a space.

Q: What should you do as soon as you catch the ring?

A: Quickly throw it back into a space.

Q: Why quickly?

A: To catch the other team out of position.

Q: What should you do if the ring comes over the net but is going out of bounds?

A: Leave it.

Q: How can you best cover your own court?

A: In a triangle (one in front, two in back usually works best).

Q: Where should the one front player stay?

A: At the net. (You need to emphasize this because the front player will initially drift back, getting in the way of teammates and taking catches that she shouldn't. This also leaves the frontcourt uncovered.)

CLOSURE

Questions and a discussion about appropriate sport behavior

Q: What should you do if you cannot decide on a point?

A: Replay the point.

Q: What should teams do after any game?

A: Find an opponent and shake hands.

LESSON 10

Elementary Level II

Tactical Problems   Maintaining a rally and creating space

Game   Deck tennis

Lesson Focus   Backhand and forehand throwing technique

Objective   Use backhand and forehand throws to maintain a rally and create space.

GAME 1

3v3 competitive game

Goal   Score points but keep the ring in the court (i.e., don't lose points by throwing out of court).

Condition   Alternate serves (backhand and forehand).

Question

Q: Which is the easier way to throw accurately—forehand or backhand?

A: Backhand. (Some might answer forehand. Practice order doesn't matter.)

PRACTICE TASK 1

Triangle passing using a backhand throw

Goal   Complete 10, 15, or 20 consecutive passes with appropriate technique.

Extension See how many backhand passes the team can throw in 30 seconds.

Cues

- Step with the same foot as the hand holding the ring.
- Throw low to high.
- Let go level with the front foot.
- Follow through to the target.

PRACTICE TASK 2

Triangle passing using forehand throws

Goal Complete 10, 15, or 20 consecutive passes with appropriate technique.

Extension See how many forehand passes the team can throw in 30 seconds.

Cues

- Step with the foot opposite the hand holding the ring.
- Throw low to high.
- Let go level with the front foot.
- Follow through to the target.

Note The cues used here for backhand and forehand resemble those that might be used in teaching tennis backhand and forehand.

Question

Q: *If you are trying to throw quickly, how should you catch the ring?*

A: *One-handed is quickest; two-handed is safest.*

Note Discuss the trade-off between speed and safety.

GAME 2

Repeat game 1.

CLOSURE

Review cues and ask a question and have a discussion about throwing.

Q: *What is the best way to win points in a game?*

A: *Throw quickly into space away from opponents.*

Note Use practice tasks 1 and 2 to start the next lesson.

LESSON 11

Elementary Level II

Tactical Problem Defending space on one's own side of the net

Game Deck tennis

Lesson Focus Court coverage and sliding movements

Objective Cover the court using a one-forward, two-back formation and sliding movements to make catches.

Teaching Sport Concepts and Skills

GAME 1

3v3 competitive game

Goal   Prevent the ring from hitting the floor on your own side of the net.

Condition   Alternate serve.

Questions

> Q: What is the best way to position yourselves as a team to keep the ring from hitting the floor on your side? **(Ask this during game play.)**

> A: One up and two back.

> Q: What type of movement should you use to get to the ring to make a catch? **(Ask this after the game.)**

> A: Slide.

PRACTICE TASK

Pressure passing

Goal   Drop no passes in 30 seconds.

Conditions

- Teams practice on their home courts.
- Players perform pressure passing and catching practice in a triangle.
- Use one passer (A) and two feeders (B and C), who rotate after 30 seconds.
- Player A passes to player B, who passes back to player A, who then passes to player C, who passes back to player A, who passes to player B, and so on.

Note   Feeders (B, C) should pass to the side of a passer (A) to force sliding movements by player A (figure 8.2).

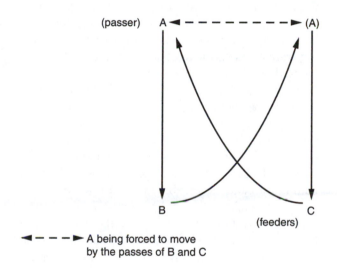

Figure 8.2

Extension   See how many passes teams can do in 30 seconds.

Cues

- Slide into line.
- Catch and pass quickly.

GAME 2

Repeat game 1.

Goal   Prevent the ring from hitting the floor.

Condition   Use one-up, two-backcourt coverage.

CLOSURE

Question and a discussion about defense

> Q: What is the best formation for defensive coverage?

> A: Two at the back and one at the front.

LEVEL III

Level III (fourth and fifth grades) games progress from one-bounce to no-bounce games, in which players strike with a racket (badminton, pickleball, and tennis), to two-contact games involving striking with the hands (volleyball). All offensive (scoring) concepts are addressed at this level. To maintain a rally, the students play games that involve underhand striking with a racket. Setting up an attack involves the introduction of deep, short, and approach shots (in tennis and pickleball); service; passing; and setting (in volleyball). The tactical problem of winning a point includes downward hitting, which comprises the volley, smash, and spike, as well as issues related to power versus accuracy. The defensive (score-preventing) concepts of defending space and defending against attacks are also discussed. Defending space includes the decisions and movements associated with backing up teammates and shifting to cover. Defending against attacks includes decisions and movements focused on blocking downward hits.

Note that lessons 12 through 15 are designed for tennis or pickleball; and lessons 16 through 18, although very similar, are designed for badminton. The changes that you see in the specific lessons involve the specific skills and movements taught (such as ground strokes in tennis versus overhead clears in badminton) and various base positions (recovery) in tennis and pickleball versus badminton. Because the skills learned at this level are more difficult than those learned in earlier levels, they require additional time in practice tasks. You may have to spread one lesson over two class periods to allow for this additional practice time.

In level III, students learn offensive concepts for net or wall games.

LESSON 12

Elementary Level III

Tactical Problem   Maintaining a rally

Game   Tennis or pickleball (minicourts set up on badminton or volleyball courts; use low nets)

Lesson Focus   Court spaces, etiquette, and the cooperative game

Objectives   Recognize court spaces and play a cooperative game while keeping the ball in one's own court and striking with a racket.

GAME 1

No-racket game (toss-bounce-catch game). Students select partners. Use a throw-and-catch warm-up, and have students play with a variety of balls; allow only one bounce. Explain court spaces.

Goal   Complete rallies of 10 throws while attempting to keep the ball in the court (discuss court width).

Conditions

- Have players start the rally with an underhand throw over the net.
- On the serve, the ball cannot bounce on the server's side of the net.
- The ball must bounce only once on the other side of the net.

Question

Q: What did you do to keep the rally going?

A: Throw to each other.

GAME 2

Tennis or pickleball (singles; short racket and soft-bounce tennis or sponge ball)

Goal   Complete rallies of 6 to 10 while attempting to keep the ball in the court using a racket.

Conditions

- Have players start the rally with an underhand throw over the net.
- The ball cannot bounce on the server's side of the net.
- The ball must bounce only once on the other side of the net.
- Players may use only ground strokes (forehand and backhand).

Cues

- Let the ball fall after the bounce.
- Keep your racket back and down.
- Step with the foot opposite the hitting arm (forehand).
- Step with the same foot as the hitting arm (backhand).
- Swing low to high.
- Contact the ball level with your front knee.

Questions

Q: What makes it easier to keep the ball in the court when you are using a racket?

A: Pointing the racket (up, down, or toward the net).

Q: Where should you make contact?

A: Level with the front knee.

Note   This will be a source of difficulty and possibly inconsistent striking accuracy.

CLOSURE

Review ground-stroke technique. Set up and take down practice.

Tactical Problem Maintaining a rally

Game Tennis or pickleball (minicourts set up on badminton courts or volleyball courts; use low nets)

Lesson Focus Court awareness

Objective Create space by using underhand striking with a racket (forehand and backhand ground strokes) in tennis or pickleball.

GAME 1

Tennis or pickleball (singles; short racket and soft-bounce tennis ball)

Goal Complete rallies of 6 to 10 while attempting to keep the ball in the court using a racket.

Conditions

- Have players start the rally with an underhand throw over the net.
- The ball cannot bounce on the server's side of the net.
- The ball must bounce only once on the other side of the net.
- Players must use ground strokes.

Cues

- Recite "bounce-hit" (having the hitter say this to herself helps focus attention).
- Keep your racket back and down.
- Step and swing low to high.

Question

Q: What is the best (most reliable) way to hit the ball with your racket?

A: Forehand or backhand ground stroke.

PRACTICE TASK 1

Using an underhand toss, partner A feeds three or four balls to partner B, who focuses on the forehand ground stroke. The feeder should begin with three or four balls to create a short, intense trial; then players collect balls and switch roles. Partner A calls, "Ball" to prompt partner B to be ready for the next ground stroke.

Cues

- Let the ball fall after the bounce (move your feet).
- Keep your racket back and down.
- Step with the foot opposite the hitting arm (same foot on backhand).
- Swing low to high.
- Contact level with your front knee.
- Follow through to the target.

PRACTICE TASK 2

Partners practice the backhand ground stroke. Partner A tosses (feeds) three to five balls to partner B, who focuses on backhand ground strokes. Players switch roles.

Cues Same as in practice task 1

GAME 2

Tennis or pickleball (singles; short racket and soft-bounce tennis ball)

Goal   Complete rallies of 10 to 15 using forehand or backhand ground strokes.

Conditions

- Players alternate serves; they start the rally with a bounce-hit serve or an underhand throw over the net if needed.
- The ball cannot bounce on the server's side of the net on the serve.
- The ball must bounce only once on the other side of the net.
- Players must use ground strokes.

CLOSURE

Review forehand and backhand technique.

LESSON 14

Elementary Level III

Tactical Problem   Setting up to attack in a competitive game

Game   Tennis or pickleball (singles)

Lesson Focus   Game rules and use of court spaces

Objectives   Play a competitive game, with appropriate rules, and try to move the opponent to the back of the court.

GAME 1

Tennis or pickleball (singles; short racket and soft-bounce tennis ball)

Goal   Make the opponent move around the court.

Conditions

- Players alternate serve; they start with a bounce-hit serve or an underhand throw over the net.
- The ball cannot bounce on the server's side of the net on the serve.
- The ball must bounce only once on the other side of the net.
- Players must use ground strokes.

Extension   Players can come to the net and volley (hit the ball before it bounces).

Questions

Interjected throughout game play:

> *Q: When should you stop and restart a rally?*
>
> *A: Restart a rally when any of the following happen:*
>
> - *The ball bounces twice on the opponent's side.*
> - *An opponent hits the ball out of the court.*
> - *An opponent makes the ball bounce on her own side.*
>
> *Q: What spaces are on the court for you to hit the ball to?*
>
> *A: Front and back.*

Q: Where should you try to make your opponent move—front or back?

A: Back. Try to get the ball to bounce close to the end line (baseline).

Q: Why?

A: It's harder to return the ball deep from a deep position.

After continuing game play:

Q: When you get your opponent to move back, where is the space now?

A: In the front.

Q: So, to make it hard for your opponent, where should you hit the ball?

A: To the front.

Q: What type of shot can you use?

A: Drop shot or volley.

CLOSURE

Review rules.

LESSON 15

Elementary Level III

Tactical Problem   Defending space

Game   Tennis or pickleball (singles)

Lesson Focus   Recovering to a baseline position

Objectives   Play a competitive game, with appropriate rules, and defend one's own space by moving back to the center of the baseline between hits.

GAME 1

Tennis or pickleball (singles; short racket and soft-bounce tennis ball)

Goal   Make the opponent move around the court.

Conditions

- Players alternate serve with a bounce-hit serve or an underhand throw over the net.
- The ball cannot bounce on the server's side of the net on the serve.
- The ball must bounce only once on the other side of the net on the serve.
- Players can volley.

Cue   Move back to the baseline between shots.

Questions

Interjected throughout game play:

Q: If your opponent is moving you around your court, where should you move to between hits?

A: The middle of the court at the baseline.

Q: Why?

A: It's the best place to be to cover the court by moving forward rather than by moving back.

GAME 2

Three-minute games against rotating opponents

Goals

- Move the opponent, recover, and keep score accurately.
- After coming forward to get a short ball, stay at the net and volley.

Conditions

- Players alternate serve with a bounce-hit serve or an underhand throw over the net.
- The ball cannot bounce on the server's side of the net on the serve.
- The ball must bounce only once on the other side of the net.

CLOSURE

Review court spaces, recovery, and scoring.

LESSON 16

Elementary Level III

Tactical Problem   Maintaining a rally

Game   Badminton (minicourts set up on badminton or volleyball courts with nets at approximately badminton height)

Lesson Focus   Court spaces, etiquette, and the cooperative game

Objectives   Recognize court spaces and play a cooperative game while keeping the shuttle (or soft ball) in one's own court and striking with an implement.

Note   You can use a soft ball instead of a shuttle if students find the ball easier to hit. However, the ball must be light enough to fly slowly.

GAME 1

Badminton (singles; short racket and shuttle or soft ball)

Goal   Complete rallies of 6 to 10 using either underhand or overhead strokes.

Conditions

- Players start the rally by either striking the shuttle with the racket or using an underhand throw over the net.
- The shuttle cannot land on either side of the net.

Cue   Ready position = racket up.

Questions

Q: Which is a stronger shot to use—the underhand or overhead stroke?

A: Overhead.

Q: What do you have to do to use an overhead stroke?

A: Move quickly with the racket up, get under shuttle, line up to shuttle, hit hard (like a throw), and snap the wrist.

GAME 2

Badminton (singles; short racket and shuttle or soft ball)

Goal   Complete rallies of 6 to 10 using an overhead stroke only.

Conditions

- Players start the rally either by striking the shuttle with the racket or by using an underhand throw over the net.
- The shuttle cannot land on either side of the net.

CLOSURE

Review the need for the overhead stroke (i.e., for power). Set up and take down practice.

LESSON 17

Elementary Level III

Tactical Problem   Maintaining a rally

Game   Badminton (minicourts set up on badminton or volleyball courts with nets at approximately badminton height)

Lesson Focus   Court awareness

Objective   Create space by using the overhead clear in badminton.

GAME 1

Badminton (singles; short racket and shuttle or soft ball)

Goal   Complete rallies of 10 while using a racket and attempting to keep the shuttle in the court.

Conditions

- Players start the rally either by striking the shuttle with the racket or by using an underhand throw over the net.
- The shuttle cannot land on either side of the net.

Cues

- Keep the racket up.
- Get under the shuttle.

Question

Q: How do you push your partner back?

A: Use an overhead (also known as a clear because you clear the opponent and get the shuttle to the back of the court with this stroke).

PRACTICE TASK

Partner A feeds (hits with the racket) three or four shuttles to partner B, who focuses on the overhead clear. The feeder should begin with three or four shuttles at a time to create a short, intense trial; then players collect shuttles and switch roles. Partner A calls "Shuttle 1-2-3-4" to prompt partner B to be ready for the next shot. Partner B scores 2 points for landing the shuttle within 3 feet (0.9 m) of the baseline and 1 point for landing it within 6 feet (1.8 m) of the baseline.

Cues

- Keep your racket up.
- Get under the shuttle using long strides.
- Line up the shuttle with your nonhitting arm.
- Bend your elbow.
- *Throw* the racket head at the shuttle.
- Snap your wrist.

GAME 2

Badminton (singles; short racket and shuttle)

Goal Complete rallies of 10 to 15 using the forehand or backhand clear.

Conditions

- Players alternate serve either by striking the shuttle with the racket or by using an overhand throw over the net.
- The shuttle cannot land on either side of the net.

CLOSURE

Review the reason for pushing the opponent to the back of the court, and the best way to do so.

Q. Why do you want to try and push your opponent back?

A. To make it harder for them to play and to keep them away from the net.

Q. What is the easiest way to do this?

A. By using a clear to get the shuttle over the opponent's head.

LESSON 18

Elementary Level III

Tactical Problem Setting up to attack in a competitive game

Game Badminton (singles)

Lesson Focus Game rules and use of court spaces

Objectives Play a competitive game, with appropriate rules, and try to move the opponent to the back of the court.

GAME

Badminton (singles; short racket and shuttle or soft ball)

Goal Make the opponent move around the court.

Conditions

- Players alternate serve either by striking the shuttle with the racket or by using an overhand throw over the net.
- The shuttle cannot land on either side of the net.

Questions

Interjected throughout game play:

Q: When should you stop and restart a rally?

A: Restart a rally when any of the following occurs:

- The shuttle lands on the court on either side.
- An opponent hits the shuttle out of the court.
- The shuttle hits the net during a rally (if it hits and goes over, it is good).

Q: What spaces are on the court for you to hit the ball to?

A: Front and back.

Q: Where should you try to make your opponent move—front or back?

A: Back. Try to get the shuttle close to the end line.

Q: Why?

A: It is harder to return.

After continuing game play:

Q: When you get your opponent to move back, where is the space now?

A: In the front.

Q: So, to make it hard for your opponent, where should you hit the ball?

A: To the front.

Q: How do you do that?

A: Soft shot (drop shot). Continued game play with a focus on trying to land the shuttle in the front of the court when the opponent is at the back.

CLOSURE

Review rules.

LESSON 19

Elementary Level III

Tactical Problem   Defending space

Game   Badminton (singles)

Lesson Focus   Recovering to a base position

Objectives   Play a competitive game, with appropriate rules, and defend one's own space by moving to the center of the court.

GAME 1

Badminton (singles; short racket and shuttle or soft ball)

Goal   Make the opponent move around the court.

Conditions

- Players alternate serve either by striking the shuttle with the racket or by using an underhand throw over the net.
- The shuttle cannot land on either side of the net.

Cue   Recover to center between shots.

Questions

Interjected during game play:

> *Q: If your opponent is moving you around your court, where should you move between hits?*
>
> *A: The middle of the court.*
>
> *Q: Why?*
>
> *A: To be able to move up or back easily for the next shot.*

GAME 2

Three-minute games against rotating opponents

Goal   Make the opponent move around the court.

Conditions

- Players alternate serve either by striking the shuttle with the racket or by using an overhand throw over the net.
- The shuttle cannot land on either side of the net.

CLOSURE

Review court spaces, recovery, and scoring.

Note   The recovery position in badminton (center of the court) is different from that in pickleball or tennis (center of the baseline) because the shuttle is not allowed to land in badminton. The bounce of the ball makes the baseline a better recovery position in tennis.

LESSON 20

Elementary Level III

Tactical Problem   Setting up an attack

Game   Volleyball

Lesson Focus   Game rules, court space, player rotation, base position

Objective   Learn the basic concept of volleyball, focusing on volleying the ball over the net.

Note   As we move to volleyball lesson outlines, it is worth considering the complexity of skill involved. The need for greater practice time may require spreading some of the following lessons over two classes.

GAME

Volleyball (3v3 using a soft, light ball or large trainer volleyball)

Goal   Make the ball bounce in the opposing team's court.

Conditions

- Use a badminton court or half a volleyball court.
- Place the net at badminton height.
- Players start in the base position (triad) (figure 8.3).
- Explain the base position (triad) and rotation before play begins. Players start in the base position, and play begins with a free-ball toss (rainbow toss) over the net. Alternate which side makes the initial free-ball toss, and have players rotate after each rally.
- The serve is a free-ball or rainbow toss (two-handed soccer throw-in).
- The back right player tosses from a designated "success" spot.
- Use a maximum of three contacts.
- No one player can have consecutive contacts.
- Add the following conditions later, as the game progresses:
  - Players practice calling "Mine" anytime the ball is hit to them.
  - Players not playing the ball should turn (pivot) to watch their teammates hit the ball (this is known as opening up).

Note   If you have large classes, we recommend that you play 3v3 but rotate players into the game versus adding more players to the game. Such games move quickly because you are rotating after each point and alternating serve.

Cues

- Be in a ready position (knees flexed).
- Be prepared to go after a ball hit in your direction.
- Stand at your assigned point (known as the base or home position).
- Return to your point after playing the ball.

Extension   Require a minimum of two contacts on a side.

Questions

Q: How do you win the rally against the other team?

A: A rally is won when the ball lands on the other side of the net or when the opposing team hits the ball out of bounds or into the net.

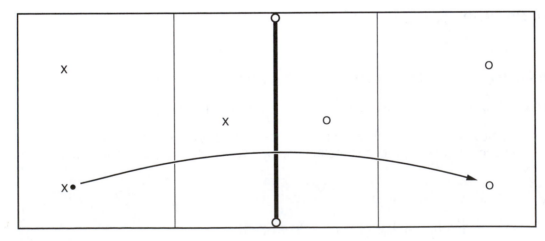

Figure 8.3

Teaching Sport Concepts and Skills

Q: How do you hit the ball to land it on the other side?

A: Move your feet toward the ball and strike the ball with hands and fingers upward or with a flat surface (off the forearms).

Q: What should you do when the ball is coming over the net but is going out of bounds?

A: Leave it.

Q: Is a ball that lands on the line good or out?

A: Good.

After continuing game play:

Q: Who should play the ball?

A: The player who calls "Mine."

Q: How do you know when to call "Mine"?

A: Call "Mine" if the ball is coming into your court area. Players who play the ball while moving in the direction of the target have the priority in playing it.

Q: What should players do when they do not play the ball?

A: Turn (pivot) to watch their teammates hit the ball (this is known as opening up).

CLOSURE

Review the base position and rules.

LESSON 21

Elementary Level III

Tactical Problem   Setting up an attack

Game   Volleyball

Lesson Focus   Setting up for an attack by using the overhead pass

Objective   Play a game using the overhead pass (set).

GAME 1

Volleyball (3v3 using a soft, light ball or large trainer volleyball)

Goal   Get two contacts on your own side of the court before putting the ball over the net.

Conditions

- Use a badminton court or volleyball court.
- Set the net at badminton height.
- Players start in the base position (triad) (figure 8.3).
- The serve is a free-ball or rainbow toss (two-handed soccer throw-in).
- The back right player tosses from a designated "success" spot.
- Players call "Mine."
- Require a maximum of three contacts.
- No one player can have consecutive contacts.

Question

Q: What do you have to do to get two contacts on your side?

A: The serve receiver calls "Mine," moves his feet toward the ball, and strikes the ball with hands upward or with a flat surface. The second player calls for and moves to play the serve receiver's hit.

PRACTICE TASK

Players practice overhead passes in their triads using a toss-pass-catch drill. T (tosser) tosses a free ball (rainbow toss) over the net for P (passer) to overhead pass to Tg (target player), who catches and bounce-passes the ball back to T (tosser). Players do three or four trials and then rotate positions (figure 8.4).

Cues

- Use fingerpads.
- Bend your legs.

- Extend your arms and legs (fly like a superhero).
- Give the ball a quick tap; this is not a catch-and-throw.

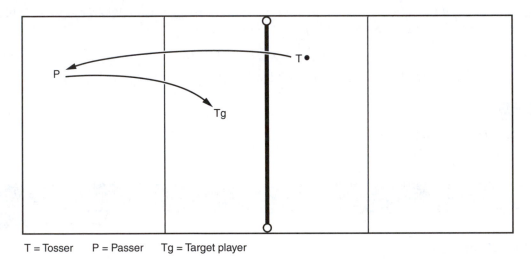

T = Tosser   P = Passer   Tg = Target player

Figure 8.4

GAME 2

Volleyball (3v3 using a soft, light ball or large trainer volleyball)

Goal   Team scores a point when they attempt two hits on a side.

Conditions

- Use a badminton court or volleyball court.
- Set the net at badminton height.
- Players start in the base position (triad) (figure 8.3).
- The first ball is a free-ball toss (two-handed soccer throw-in) or rainbow toss.
- The back right player tosses from a designated "success" spot.
- Players should practice calling "Mine" anytime the ball is hit to them.
- Require a maximum of three contacts.
- No one player can have consecutive contacts.

CLOSURE

Questions and a discussion about getting two hits on a side

LESSON 22

Tactical Problem   Winning the point

Game   Volleyball

Lesson Focus   Attempting to spike to win a point

Objective   Set up to spike in a game.

GAME 1

Volleyball (3v3 using a soft, light ball or large trainer volleyball)

Goal   Team earns a point for two hits on a side.

Conditions

- Use a badminton court or volleyball court.
- Set the net at badminton height.
- Players start in the base position (triad) (figure 8.3).
- The serve is a free-ball or rainbow toss (two-handed soccer throw-in).
- The back right player tosses from a designated "success" spot.
- Players call "Mine."
- Require a minimum of two contacts and a maximum of three contacts.
- No one player can have consecutive contacts.

Questions

Q: To score a point, where should you try to place the ball?

A: In open space.

Q: What other type of hits are there in volleyball besides the overhead pass?

A: Spike.

Q: Which is harder to return, an overhead pass or a spike?

A: Spike.

Q: Why?

A: It's a hard, downward ball.

PRACTICE TASK

In pairs, one player initiates a practice spike with a high self-toss; then moves to the ball, faces the net, and either swings or jumps and swings, spiking the ball over the net. The other player collects the ball and returns it to the spiker. Players switch positions after three to five tries.

Cues

- Move your feet to the ball.
- Face the net.
- Swing or jump and swing (depending on the developmental level of the student).

GAME 2

Volleyball (3v3 using a soft, light ball or large trainer volleyball)

Goals   Team members raise their hands when attempting a spike.

Conditions

- Team scores a point when the ball bounces on the opponents' side of the net.
- Use a badminton or volleyball court.
- Set the net at badminton height.
- Players start in the base position (triad) (figure 8.3).
- The first ball is a free-ball toss (two-handed soccer throw-in) or rainbow toss.

- The back right player tosses from a designated "success" spot.
- Players should practice calling "Mine" anytime the ball is hit to them.
- Require a minimum of two contacts and a maximum of three contacts.
- No one player can have consecutive contacts.

CLOSURE

Questions and a discussion about setting up to spike

Q: Where should you be facing when you spike?

A: Toward the net.

Q: If you jump to spike, in which direction should you jump?

A: Straight up (so that you don't hit the net on the way back down).

LESSON 23

Tactical Problems   Winning the point and defending against the attack

Game   Volleyball

Lesson Focus   Attempting to spike to win a point

Objective   Set up to spike in a game.

GAME 1

Volleyball (3v3 using a soft, light ball or large trainer volleyball)

Goals   Team members raise their hands when attempting a spike.

Conditions

- Team scores a point when the ball bounces on the opponents' side of the net.
- Use a badminton court or volleyball court.
- Set the net at badminton height.
- Players start in the base position (triad) (figure 8.3).
- The serve is a free-ball or rainbow toss (two-handed soccer throw-in).

- The back right player tosses from a designated "success" spot.
- Players should practice calling "Mine" anytime the ball is hit to them.
- Require a minimum of two contacts and a maximum of three contacts.
- No one player can have consecutive contacts.

Questions

Q: *What does your team have to do so that a teammate has a good chance to spike?*

A: *Get the ball high in the air.*

Q: *What can the opposing team do to play a spiked ball?*

A: *Play low or block it.*

Q: *Who would block the ball?*

A: *The front-row player.*

PRACTICE TASK

Form groups of three to set up to spike and block. Player S (setter) self-tosses to overhead pass (set) the ball to player H (hitter), who attempts to spike the ball over the net. Player B/C (blocker/collector) attempts to block and then collects the ball and returns it to player S. Allow players three to five trials; then have them rotate through positions from setter to hitter to blocker/collector (figure 8.5).

Cues

- Overhead pass (set):
  - Use fingerpads.
  - Bend your legs.
  - Extend your arms and legs (fly like a superhero).
  - Give the ball a quick tap; this is not a catch-and-throw.
- Spike:
  - Move your feet to the ball.
  - Face the net.
  - Swing or jump and swing (depending on the developmental level of the student).
- Block:
  - Keep your hands high.
  - Front the hitter.
  - Jump on the arm swing of the hitter.
  - Press the ball to the center of the court.

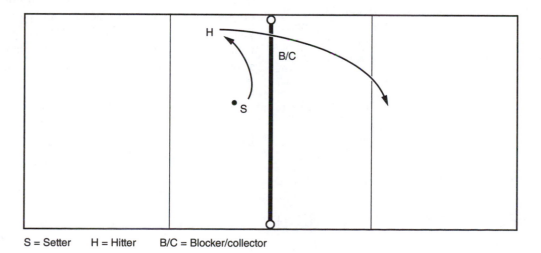

S = Setter   H = Hitter   B/C = Blocker/collector

Figure 8.5

GAME 2

Volleyball (3v3 using a soft, light ball or large trainer volleyball)

Goals

- Players jump when attempting a spike.
- Players raise their hands to block the ball.

Conditions

- Team scores a point when the ball bounces on the opponents' side of the net.
- Use a badminton or volleyball court.
- Set the net at badminton height.
- Players start in the base position (triad) (figure 8.3).
- The serve is a free-ball or rainbow toss (two-handed soccer throw-in).
- The back right player tosses from a designated "success" spot.
- Players should practice calling "Mine" anytime the ball is hit to them.
- Require a minimum of two contacts and a maximum of three contacts.
- No one player can have consecutive contacts.

CLOSURE

Questions and a discussion about spiking and blocking

> Q: *Where do you jump on a spike?*
>
> A: *Straight up.*
>
> Q: *When do you jump on a block?*
>
> A: *On the arm swing of the hitter.*

SUMMARY

Decision making is at the heart of all games, which is what makes them challenging and interesting. Our goal is to provide students with many opportunities to learn what to do in various net and wall games. These opportunities will lead to an understanding of these games and develop students' sense of com-petence, which will increase the likelihood that they will want to continue playing net and wall games. We recommend that you use one level of complexity and individualize your instruction as needed based on your students and your facilities and equipment. If your students complete the three levels of game complexity provided in this chapter, they will have gained a fundamental understanding of net and wall games.

Striking and Fielding Games at the Elementary Level

Chapter 9

Striking and fielding games such as baseball, softball, cricket, and rounders, because of their deeply entrenched connection to their respective cultures, have been considered essential content within the physical education curriculum. The format, equipment, and pace of these games, however, make them less than ideal in primary and elementary physical education contexts. Through significant modification, however, striking and fielding games can emphasize the development of numerous fundamental motor skills such as throwing, catching, striking, and running, and increase opportunities to perform these skills. At the same time, students can develop cognitive, psychomotor, and affective learning outcomes.

This chapter begins with a description of how we approach striking and fielding games using game situations (e.g., runner on first, no outs) to organize the content and progressions. We then describe modifications to equipment and playing area as well as the number of players per team that is ideal for teaching striking and fielding games. Framework and levels of game complexity then illustrate the scope and sequence used to develop lesson content. Finally, we present 35 lesson outlines covering four levels of game complexity. Bear in mind that in the early stages you may have to devote additional time to training students to play multiple games simultaneously.

ELEMENTARY STRIKING AND FIELDING GAMES TACTICS

Tactically, striking and fielding games involve situations, such as "one out and a runner on first base." In this example, a number of elements are involved. First, breaking the situation into offense and defense, there are two aspects of each. Offensively, there are the tactics, movements, and skills related to the batter and to the runner. If successful, the batter becomes the runner, and sometimes there is more than one runner. Defensively, there are tactics, movements, and skills related to the player fielding the ball as well as to the players providing support in the form of backing up a play or base coverage. Support can be verbal as well—for example, teammates can tell the player fielding the ball where to throw the ball.

Table 9.1 lists tactical problems according to a variety of offensive and defensive game situations associated with baseball, softball, T-ball, and kickball (see chapter 20 for a cricket-specific framework). Offensive players (i.e., the batter or batsman and runner) must consider the game situation related to scoring when making tactical decisions (column 2) and selecting and adjusting elements of skill execution (column 3). Similarly, defensive players must consider the game situations related to preventing scoring when making tactical decisions and selecting elements of skill execution. Note that this table is a little different from those in the preceding two chapters, where problems are broken down based on scoring and preventing scoring. Here the solutions to game problems, both offensively and defensively, are really based on the situation within the game, such as how many runners are on base and how many are out. In each situation both batters and fielders have to respond based on the game situation.

LEVELS OF ELEMENTARY STRIKING AND FIELDING GAME COMPLEXITY

The complexity of striking and fielding games depends on the game situation. For example, a situation in which there is a runner on first with no outs is less complex than a situation in which there are runners on second and third and one out. Table 9.2 identifies four levels of game complexity, suggesting a possible progression of game play development for striking and fielding games. The framework (table 9.1), along with the levels of game complexity, provides a developmentally appropriate progression of striking and fielding games content for elementary students, beginning at second grade. The lessons in this chapter correspond to these levels of game complexity. The first few lessons, in which students roll a ball to a partner, are actually target games for practicing accuracy. Initially, the objective is for students to learn how to consistently send a ball, whether rolling, tossing underhand, or throwing overhand, at the appropriate speed and in the appropriate direction. The skills and tactics (or concepts) needed to accurately send an object to a target are transferable to practically any game, making target games a good starting point in the elementary physical education curriculum.

Levels of complexity can also be changed by adjusting the type of skill used in any of the following games. At level I, for example, players can throw underhand, kick, or even strike a ball with a racket or off a batting tee. Repeating games using different skills helps students review tactical problems and reduces the time needed to teach a new game. In addition, the time needed to manage equipment can be reduced when students in different grade levels play the same or similar games, although with different skills. Individual games also allow for differentiated instruction as the complexity of one game can be increased or reduced to accommodate the skill level of the players. Thus, some can be throwing while others are kicking (same game, different skills). At levels II, III, and IV, changing the game situation to accommodate the different skill levels and abilities of the students increases learning as well as their engagement in game play.

MODIFICATIONS FOR ELEMENTARY STRIKING AND FIELDING GAMES

A key characteristic of a tactical games approach is the use of conditioned, or modified, games. Conditioned games are intended to highlight specific situations found in the formal, full-sided version of the game and can be designed as progressions (i.e., a progression of games) from 1v1 to 10v10. Even advanced players can create gamelike conditions during practice to improve particular aspects of, and address weaknesses in, their game play. In fact, every traditional baseball practice includes the coach calling out situations (e.g., runner on first, no outs) while hitting grounders to the infield.

The following guidelines will assist you in modifying striking and fielding games appropriately:

• *Consider the number of players.* When modifying or designing conditioned games, the first consideration

Table 9.1 Game Situations in Elementary Striking and Fielding Games

Tactical problems	Tactical decisions (off the ball)	Elements of skill execution (on the ball)
SCORING (OFFENSE)		
Game situation: cooperative games		
Accuracy		• Rolling for accuracy • Using an intermediate target • Rolling to open space
Combining skills		Rolling and running to first base
Game situation: 0-1 out, 0 runners		

Batting	Determining the best place to roll, kick, or hit the ball to get on base	• Combining skills—transition from:
		  ○ Roll to run
		  ○ Kick to run
		  ○ Hit to run
		  ○ Hit and run to first base.
		• Hitting to the outfield

Base running	Determining when to run through or round first base	Running through first base
Game situation: 0-1 out, runner on first		
Batting	Determining the best place to hit to in order to move the runner	Hitting to the right side of the field (behind the runner)
Base running	Determining whether to run on a grounder or stay on base on a line drive or fly ball	Combining skills: • Running from first to second • Start position for take-off • Pushing off base and driving the • opposite arm and knee • Stopping at second and keeping contact with the base
Game situation: 0-1 out, 0-2 runners (variable), infield grounder		
Batter		Rounding first and running to second base
Base running	Determining whether to run through or round first base	
Game situation: 0-1 out, 0-1 runner on base, outfield hit		
Batting	Determining where to hit	Hitting a ball to the outfield: • Line drive • Fly ball
Batting and base running	• Determining when to run • Anticipating where to hit the ball • Watching and listening to the coach	Tagging up on a fly ball: • Quick starts from base • Stopping and maintaining contact with the base (second and third base)
PREVENTING SCORING (DEFENSE)		
Game situation: cooperative games		
Adjusting for various situations	Reading and anticipating the ball when fielding	
Combining skills		Combining skills: catching and tagging first base
Game situation: 0-1 out, 0 runners, infield grounder		
Fielding	Determining (before the pitch) where to throw (first or second base)	Fielding a grounder; then tagging first base

Supporting players	• Determining:
	  ○ Where to back up
	  ○ Best angle for backup
	  ○ Whether bases need to be covered
	  ○ Best angle for base coverage
	• Communicating:
	  ○ Number of outs to teammates (signal)
	  ○ Where to throw the ball
		• Tagging plays at second, third, and home
		• Cutting off plays:
		  ○ Second base
		  ○ Shortstop
		• Relays
		• Moving to back up in the infield
		• Moving to back up in the outfield
		• Base coverage (footwork) on a force play

(continued)

Table 9.1 *(continued)*

Tactical problems	Tactical decisions (off the ball)	Elements of skill execution (on the ball)
PREVENTING SCORING (DEFENSE) *(CONTINUED)*		
Game situation: 0-1 out, runner on first, infield grounder		
Fielding	Determining: • Where to throw the ball • How to throw the ball (throw, flip, or tag the base)	• Fielding fly balls • Fielding line drives • Looking back at the runner (body and ball position) • Tag play (sweep tag): ○ Second base ○ Third base • Combining skills—catch and shovel pass, flip, toss • Base coverage on a tag play • Fielding in the outfield: ○ Adjusting angle prior to the catch ○ Adjusting body position to make a throw to third
Supporting players	• Determining: ○ Where to position for backup and base coverage ○ Which base to cover and how • Communicating: ○ Number of outs ○ Where to throw	• Covering second on a force play: ○ From an infield throw (second-base player and shortstop) ○ From an outfield throw • Cutting the lead runner at third: ○ Third-base player fields and covers third. ○ Infielders field and throw to third. ○ Adjust body. ○ Position to make the throw to third. • Moving into position for backup
Game situation: 0-1 out, 0-2 runners (variable), infield grounder		
Fielding		• Looking back at the runner • Tag play (sweep tag) • Combining skills: ○ Catch and shovel pass ○ Catch and toss ○ Catch and flip
Supporting players	• Base coverage • Shortstop coverage of second base on a force play • Second-base player coverage of second base on a force play	• Positioning for a backup play (adjust with the situation) • Moving into an appropriate position to cover base (adjust with the situation)
Game situation: 0-1 out, 0-2 runners (variable), outfield hit		
Fielding	Deciding where to throw	• Combining skills—fielding and throwing quickly • Fielding fly balls and line drives and throwing quickly to: ○ Second base ○ Cutoff ○ Relay • Covering base on a tag play • Tagging plays at second, third, and home
Supporting players	• Moving quickly with appropriate angles into position for backup of: ○ Adjacent players ○ Bases when runners are advancing • Backup • Communication	
RESTARTING PLAY		
Play starts or restarts on every pitch or roll.		

Table 9.2 Levels of Tactical Complexity for Elementary-Level Striking and Fielding Games

Tactical problems	Level I	Level II	Level III	Level IV
SCORING (OFFENSE)				
Game situation: cooperative games				
Accuracy	• Rolling for accuracy • Using an intermediate target • Rolling to open space			
Combining skills	Rolling and running to first base			
Game situation: 0-1 out, 0 runners				
Batting	Determining the best place to roll, kick, or hit the ball to get on base	Combining skills—transitioning from: • Hit to run • Hit and run to first base		Hitting to the outfield
Base running	Combining skills: • Roll to run • Kick to run	• Determining when to run through or round first base • Running through first base		
Game situation: 0-1 out, runner on first				
Batting			Determining the best place to hit to in order to move the runner Hitting to the right side of the infield (behind the runner)	

Base running		• Combining skills:
		  ○ Running from first to second base
		  ○ Start position for take-off
		  ○ Pushing off base and driving the opposite arm and knee
		  ○ Stopping at second and keeping contact with the base
		• Determining whether to run on a grounder or stay on base on a line drive or fly ball		

Game situation: 0-1 out, 0-2 runners (variable), infield grounder				
Batting			Rounding first and running to second base	
Base running			Determining whether to run through or round first base	
Game situation: 0-1 out, 0-1 runner on base, outfield hit				
Batting			Determining where to hit	Hitting a ball to the outfield: • Line drive • Fly ball
Base running			• Determining when to run • Anticipating where to hit the ball • Watching and listening to the coach	Tagging up on a fly ball: • Quick starts from base • Stopping and maintaining contact with the base (second and third base)

(continued)

143

Table 9.2 *(continued)*

Tactical problems	Level I	Level II	Level III	Level IV
PREVENTING SCORING (DEFENSE)				
Game situation: cooperative games				
Adjusting for various situations	Reading and anticipating the ball when fielding			
Combining skills	Catching and tagging first base			
Game situation: 0-1 out, 0 runners, infield grounder				
Fielding	Determining (before the pitch) where to throw (first or second base)	Fielding a grounder; then tagging first base		
Supporting players			• Determining: ○ Where to back up ○ Best angle for backup ○ Whether bases need to be covered ○ Best angle for base coverage • Communicating: ○ Number of outs to teammates (signal) ○ Where to throw the ball	• Tag plays at first, third, and home • Cutoff plays: ○ Second base ○ Shortstop • Relays • Moving to back up in the infield • Moving to back up in the outfield • Base coverage (footwork) on a force play
Game situation: 0-1 out, runner on first, infield grounder				
Fielding		Determining: • Where to throw the ball • How to throw the ball (throw, flip, or tag the base)	• Fielding fly balls • Fielding line drives • Looking back at the runner—body and ball position • Tag play (sweep tag): ○ Second base ○ Third base • Combining skills—catch and shovel pass, flip, toss • Base coverage on a tag play	Fielding in the outfield: • Adjusting angle prior to the catch • Adjusting body position to make the throw to third
Supporting players		• Communicating: ○ Number of outs ○ Where to throw • Covering second on a force play: ○ From an infield throw (second-base player and shortstop) ○ From an outfield throw • Cutting the lead runner at third base: ○ Third-base player fields and makes a force play at third. ○ Infielders field and throw to third. ○ Adjust body position to make the throw to third. • Moving into position for backup	Determining: • Where to position for backup and base coverage • Which base to cover and how	Moving into position for backup

Tactical problems	Level I	Level II	Level III	Level IV
Game situation: 0-1 out, 0-2 runners (variable), infield grounder				

Fielding			• Looking back at the runner
			• Tag play (sweep tag)
			• Combining skills:
			  ○ Catch and shovel pass
			  ○ Catch and toss
			  ○ Catch and flip	

Supporting players		• Base coverage • Shortstop coverage of second base on a force play • Second-base player coverage of second base on a force play	• Positioning for backup play (adjusting with the situation) • Moving into an appropriate position to cover the base (adjusting with the situation)	
Game situation: 1 out, 0-2 runners, outfield hit				

Fielding			• Combine skills—fielding and throwing quickly
			• Deciding where to throw
				• Fielding fly balls and line drives and throwing quickly to:
				  ○ Second base
				  ○ Cutoff
				  ○ Relay
				• Covering the base on a tag play
				• Tagging plays at second, third, and home

Supporting players			• Backup • Communication	Moving quickly with appropriate angles into position for backup of: • Adjacent players • Bases when runners are advancing
RESTARTING PLAY				
Play starts or restarts on every pitch or roll.				

should be given to the number of players. Games can be played 1v1, 3v3, or even 3v1, depending on the situation you are focusing on. Games for most seven- and eight-year-olds need no more than six players (an infield) because kids at this age rarely hit out of the infield, as most Little League spectators can attest. If they do hit to the outfield, you can either call it a home run or let the infield chase the ball and throw it in to stop the runner from advancing. Small-sided games (say, with only six players) give players more opportunities to actually catch and throw the ball as well as bat. It is also important to rotate players so everyone gets to play every position.

• *Modify the playing area.* The distances between bases can be shorter than regulation. Field sizes for players who have difficulty throwing and running can be smaller than fields for more skillful players. Fields can also be made smaller using only first, second, and home base, for example, to emphasize a particular aspect of play. For classes of 20 or more students, position fields in a cloverleaf design, with a large safety zone in the middle (figure 3.3), and stagger the fields to limit the potential of an errant throw striking a player on an adjacent field. The safety zone is for members of the batting team as well as for you. Be very strict about safety rules, and never tolerate a player who throws the bat.

• *Modify the equipment.* The lessons given in this chapter are prepared with roll and run, kickball, T-ball, softball, or baseball in mind. In the early stages, students often find kicking a larger ball easier than striking a smaller ball. Their understanding of game-play situations also develops more quickly when fielding a bigger ball. As students progress to batting, the use of batting tees, even for the most advanced players, is a must. Tees keep games going quickly and help batters send the ball to the appropriate area depending on the situation. If pitching is provided, limit the number of pitches as well as the number of foul balls, and consider a no-walk rule. Soft bats and balls are available at most discount and toy stores. Also consider a variety of lengths, weights, and sizes to accommodate each player. Gloves are optional. Depending on the composition of the ball, gloves can be a deterrent, and they encourage catching one-handed rather than with two hands. If your students are using gloves, teach them how to transfer the ball from the glove to the throwing hand, a skill essential to successful fielding.

• *Modify the rules, and whenever possible, implement rules to speed up play.* The rules should be limited to whatever is necessary to play a particular conditioned game. Additional rules can be added later, when a particular situation requires another rule or a modification to existing rules. Rules should be taught as specific tactics, movements, and skills are introduced. For example, when teaching hitting and running to first base, present the rule about not running inside the base path as well as the rationale for the rule. Putting another base outside of the first base line (that is, one inside the line for the base player and one outside for the runner) can protect the player covering first base as well as encourage the runner to run outside the base path.

• *Use situations to design or modify conditioned games.* As mentioned previously, all of the tactical problems related to striking and fielding games evolve from situations. One advantage of teaching from game situations relates to the need to individualize games. The whole class can be working on a particular situation, but more advanced players can work on more complex tactics, movements, and skills, while novice players work on more basic skills. For example, players on field A can work on fielding, while players on field B can work on base coverage in the same situation.

PROGRESSIONS FOR TEACHING ELEMENTARY STRIKING AND FIELDING GAMES

Most elementary specialists recommend focusing on the development of fundamental skills in kindergarten, first grade, and second grade, with some intro-

duction of sport skills and sports in third grade. This is not to say that sport skills and movements cannot be learned earlier, because many children do learn these as a result of participating in youth sports and having other more advanced movement experiences. For the most part, the introduction of a sport skill depends on the complexity of the tactic or skill and the context in which it is used. With this in mind, the level I lessons in this chapter use 1v1 games of roll and run. This encourages students to learn the fundamental skills and tactics involved in sending a ball to a target, fielding, tagging a base, running to a base, and so on. Again, these lessons can be repeated using kickball, T-ball, or other modification; although the game involves different skills, the tactics remain the same. Such repetition helps students develop tactical awareness while they are learning to become more skillful.

LEVEL I

Level I lessons (second and third grades) begin with partner games that focus on rolling for accuracy; then progress to 1v1 roll and run games. Tactical problems emphasize offensive skills of ball placement relative to the defender or fielder and running to the base ahead of the ball. Defensively, level I lessons focus on fielding and tagging the base ahead of the runner. Level I games also emphasize combining fundamental skills (e.g., roll and run, run-catch-run, catch-run-tag a base) and challenge students to improve from game 1 to game 2 by keeping track of points scored.

In level I, students work on developing accuracy with their aim.

Tactical Problems   Rolling for accuracy (target games) and ball placement (striking and fielding games)

Game   Rolling to a V (angle formed by a partner's feet)

Lesson Focus   Selecting an intermediate target

Objective   Select the intermediate target that will result in consistently sending the ball to the V formed by a partner's feet.

GAME 1

V-3

Goal   Roll the ball and hit the V three times in a row.

Conditions

- Students work in pairs; one rolls the ball and the other creates a target by putting her heels together and toes outward to form a V with her feet. Place a sticker on the floor right where the heels meet.
- Pairs begin 15 to 20 feet (4.6 to 6 m) away.
- Players take turns rolling and being the V target. The sticker can also be used by the roller, with the toe of the nonstepping foot on the sticker. This helps maintain a consistent start position.
- Class is set up with pairs parallel to each other, all rolling the same direction (figure 9.1). Place a poly spot or sticker on the floor to serve as a starting point.
- Make stickers available at multiple locations throughout the movement space so the students can get stickers when ready to do so.

Questions

Q: At first, was it easy or hard to hit the V three times?

A: Hard

Q: Why was it so hard to hit the V three times in a row?

A: It was so far away.

Q: Instead of aiming at the V way down there, what else could you aim at?

A: A line, a mark on the floor, or something closer.

X	X
X	X
X	X
X	X
X	X
X	X

Figure 9.1

PRACTICE TASK

First, rollers should be sure to use stickers at the V where the heels meet and at the toe of the nonstepping foot. They should place a sticker between them and the V target formed by their partner's feet. After rolling three times, they may adjust the sticker and roll three more times. If necessary, they may adjust the sticker again and roll three more times. Rollers then switch with their partners, who repeat the placement of the intermediate target.

Cues

- Roll the ball over the intermediate target.
- Use stickers for the starting point and the V target.

GAME 2

Repeat game 1.

CLOSURE

Review key points related to selecting an intermediate target when using the same starting point and target.

LESSON 2

Tactical Problems Rolling for accuracy (target games) and ball placement (striking and fielding games)

Game Moving target

Lesson Focus Adjusting an intermediate target when the location of the primary target changes

Objective Adjust the intermediate target to hit the V formed by a partner's feet consistently.

GAME 1

Goal Roll the ball twice in a row to each of the three targets.

Conditions

- Students work in pairs; one rolls the ball, and the other creates a target by putting his heels together and toes outward to form a V with his feet. Place three stickers approximately 12 inches (30 cm) apart to create three targets (figure 9.2). Demonstrate where the stickers go and then allow students to place their own.
- Pairs begin 15 to 20 feet (4.6 to 6 m) away.
- Players take turns rolling and being the V target. The stickers can also be used by the roller, with the toe of the nonstepping foot on the sticker. This will help maintain a consistent start position.
- Class is set up with pairs parallel to each other, all rolling in the same direction.
- Make stickers available at multiple locations throughout the movement space so the students can use them as needed.
- Ask students to keep score, adding 1 point to their score each time they hit the intended target and subtracting 1 point each time they miss the intended target. They score 5 points for hitting the target twice in a row.

■ = Sticker

Figure 9.2

Questions

Q: When the target changes, what do you need to change?

A: The intermediate target.

Q: How many of you used stickers to create intermediate targets for each of the primary targets?

A: (Some may have, and some may not have.)

*Q: Why is it important to think about your intermediate target **before** you roll the ball?*

A: Helps to hit the target more often (more consistently).

Teaching Sport Concepts and Skills

PRACTICE TASK

Students are in pairs and begin by focusing on the center target. They select start positions and roll three balls. They place intermediate targets between their start positions and the primary targets and take three rolls; then adjust the intermediate targets and roll three more balls. Students take turns with their partners until both have selected an intermediate target for each of the primary targets. They keep adjusting their intermediate targets until they are able to hit each target twice in a row. Partners let you know when they are done by standing at the start point with hands raised.

If possible, observe one or two trials before directing students to return to the game.

Goal   Hit each target twice in a row using a sticker to position an intermediate target.

Cues

- Use the same start position on each roll.
- Roll the ball over the intermediate target to hit the primary target.

- Sweep fingers along the floor, and follow through both targets (target line).

GAME 2

Repeat game 1.

CLOSURE

Review how to adjust the intermediate target when sending a ball to a different target. Emphasize the need to think about these things before rolling the ball.

Q: Can you think of any games in which you would need to use an intermediate target to roll (or throw) a ball accurately to a target?

A: Some examples of correct answers are bowling and golf.

LESSON 3

Elementary Level I

Tactical Problem   Defending space

Game   Watch and go

Lesson Focus   Reading (watching) the body movements of students rolling the ball to determine where they intend to send it

Objective   Read the movements of the roller and then move to the roller's intended target before the ball arrives.

GAME 1

Setup

- Students work in pairs. One rolls the ball and the other creates a target by putting her heels together and toes outward to form a V with her feet. Place three stickers approximately 12 inches (30 cm) apart to create three targets and place a poly spot 1 yard behind the three targets (figure 9.3).
- Make stickers available at multiple locations throughout the movement space so students can use them as needed.
- Ask students to keep score for four minutes of game time.

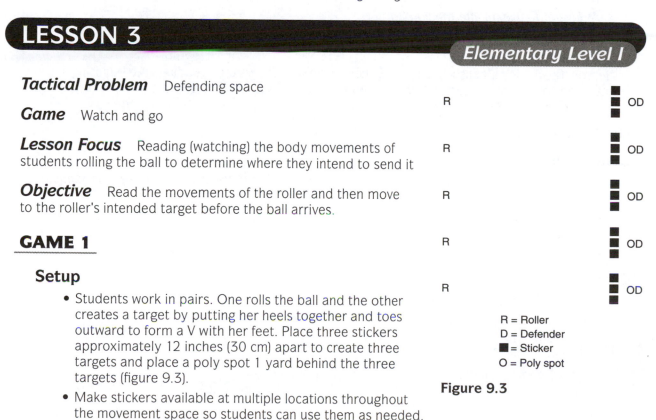

R = Roller
D = Defender
■ = Sticker
O = Poly spot

Figure 9.3

Goal   Score as many points as possible.

Conditions

1. Pairs begin 20 to 25 feet (6 to 7.6 m) away.
2. To begin, one partner is designated as the roller; the other, as the defender.
3. The defender starts on the poly spot behind the three targets and cannot move until the roller releases the ball. The roller picks one of the targets and then attempts to roll the ball to that target.
4. The defender attempts to move to the target spot and form a V with his feet. If the ball rolls over the target, the roller gets a point. If the defender successfully stops the ball from rolling over the target or the ball does not roll over the target, no points are scored.
5. The defender then becomes the roller; and the roller, the defender.

Questions

Q: *Show me with your fingers how many points you scored.*

A: *(Students hold up fingers.)*

Q: *When you were the defender, how did you know what target the roller was aiming at?*

A: *Watched the rollers eyes, arm, body position, or ball.*

Q: *When you were the roller, what did you do to keep the defender from knowing where you were aiming?*

A: *Looked away from the target or looked at different targets; rolled fast; faked or pretended to roll to a different target.*

Q: *Did anyone have difficulty hitting their target? Why?*

A: *Forgot to use an intermediate target.*

GAME 2

In this lesson, the game establishes the perfect context in which to practice reading and disguising. If some students need to work on accuracy, direct them to do so (as in lesson 2) and then return to the game when they are ready.

Goal   Score more points than you did in the first game.

Conditions

- Same as game 1, emphasizing closely watching the roller to determine where she is going to throw as well as emphasizing ways the roller can disguise where she intends to roll.
- Students who still need to work on establishing intermediate targets should do some practice rolls before returning to the game.
- Students can play four-minute games, attempting to better their scores in each game.

Cues

- Watch (read) the eyes and body for clues.
- Trick the defender with your eyes, with your movements, or by using quick throws.

CLOSURE

Review ways of reading the defender as well as ways of disguising the roll.

Q: *What other games involve reading (or watching) and disguising?*

A: *Some examples are basketball (and other invasion games) and tennis (and other net and wall games).*

LESSON 4

Tactical Problems   Ball placement and defending space

Game   Roll and run

Lesson Focus

- Tactical skill: rolling the ball away from the defender.
- Offensive skill: combining roll and run
- Defensive skill: Retrieve/catch ball and tag poly spot.

Objective   Roll the ball away from the defender to allow more time to run to the poly spot (and score) ahead of the tag.

GAME 1

Setup

- Students work in pairs.
- Pairs begin 20 to 25 feet (6 to 7.6 m) away, in a 2- to 3-yard-wide space. Each student has one poly spot from which to start; another poly spot is placed in the center between the two students (figure 9.4).
- If rollers roll the ball slowly, add a game condition that players cannot run until the ball has passed the centerline.

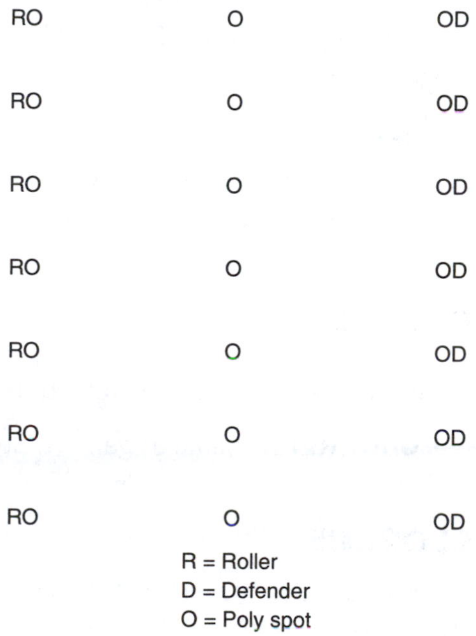

Goal   Score as many points as possible in the allotted time.

Conditions

1. To begin, one partner is designated as the roller; the other, as the defender.
2. The roller rolls the ball and must run to the center poly spot and back to the starting poly spot before the defender catches the ball and tags the center poly spot. If successful, the roller scores 1 point.
3. The roller now becomes the defender; and the defender, the roller.

RO	O	OD
RO	O	OD
RO	O	OD
RO	O	OD
RO	O	OD
RO	O	OD
RO	O	OD

R = Roller
D = Defender
O = Poly spot

Figure 9.4

Questions   Questions can be broken up to emphasize run and roll first, and then receiving and tagging the poly spot.

Q: Show me with your fingers how many points you scored.

A: (Students hold up fingers.)

Q: Rollers, how were you able to score points? What did you do, or what did you think about doing?

A: Rolled ball away from defender; faked throwing one direction; ran really fast.

Q: Why do you want to roll the ball away from the defender?

A: Gives you more time to run.

Q: What kinds of movements did you use to get from one poly spot to the other as fast as possible? (Have a student demonstrate as others observe. Pinpoint how feet move when transitioning from rolling to running and when using the pivot to change directions while running.)

A: Kept moving my feet when rolling the ball; used a pivot at the center poly spot.

Q: Defenders, how were you able to keep the roller from scoring points? What did you do, or what did you think about doing? (Have a student demonstrate as others observe. Pinpoint how the defender reads, or watches, the roller and then moves to the ball, catches it, and moves to tag the poly spot in one continuous movement.)

A: Watched the roller, ran to ball as fast as possible to catch it, and then ran to the base.

PRACTICE TASK

Students work in pairs in the same space as game 1. One student rolls and runs, working on continuous movement throughout the roll and run as well as using a pivot to change directions while running. The other student works on reading, or watching, and moving through the ball during the catch and toward the center poly spot, using one continuous movement. After five trials, pairs switch roles.

Goal   Score 5 points in a row.

Cues

- Keep your feet moving.
- Read, or watch, the roller.
- Disguise the roll.

GAME 2

Goal   Same as game 1, keep to the allotted time to allow students to assess.

Conditions   Same as game 1. Students can play more than one game if time allows, which challenges them to improve with each game.

CLOSURE

Review transition movements from roll and run, pivot, run-retrieve-run, and tag poly spot. Use a demonstration to show the continuous movement of feet throughout the roll and run and retrieve and tag. Also review reading, or watching, and disguising the roll from the previous lesson.

LESSON 5

Elementary Level I

Tactical Problem   Ball placement with no outs and no runners on base

Game   Roll and run to first

Lesson Focus   Ball placement

Objective   Roll the ball away from the defender, to the farthest location from the poly spot, to allow more time to run to the poly spot (and score) ahead of the tag.

GAME 1

Setup Same as game 1 in lesson 4, except that the poly spot is set to the left (first-base side) of the playing field (figure 9.5)

Goal Score as many points (runs) as possible.

Conditions

1. The roller must roll the ball and tag the poly spot before the defender catches the ball and tags the poly spot adjacent to the runner's poly spot. (A pin or wicket can also be used, with players required to knock it down before the runner tags his poly spot.)

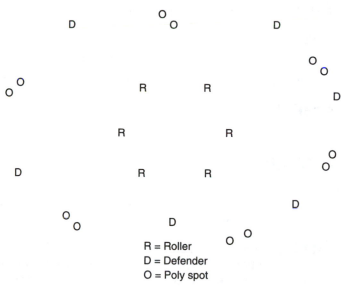

R = Roller
D = Defender
O = Poly spot

Figure 9.5

2. If the roller gets to the poly spot before the defender tags his poly spot, a run is scored. If the defender gets to his poly spot ahead of the runner, an out is declared.

3. After three runs or three outs, whichever comes first, students switch roles.

Questions

Q: Where was the best place to roll the ball to score a run?

A: Farthest away from the poly spot.

Q: Why?

A: Gives more time to get to the base.

Q: Think about what you learned in lesson 4. What did you learn in lesson 4 that could help you in this game?

A: How to roll and run in as fast as possible; how to retrieve and tag a poly spot as fast as possible.

Q: What about watching the roller and disguising the roll?

A: Watch the roller's eyes and movements, fake a throw in one direction, or look one way and throw another.

PRACTICE TASK

1. The roller rolls to a pin placed opposite the poly spot to which she is running; then transitions to a run and runs to and through the poly spot, just like a run to first base. The defender retrieves the ball and resets the pin. After three trials the two switch roles. After each partner has had two trials of three, extend the game.

2. In the next game, the roller does the same thing, but the defender's role changes. A ball is placed next to the runner's target poly spot. The defender begins at the runner's starting poly spot, and when the roller releases the ball, the defender runs and picks up the ball (at the target spot) and tags the poly spot next to the pin. If the defender tags the poly spot ahead of the roller tagging her poly spot, the roller/runner is out and does not score a point.

3. Partners alternate, with each getting an equal number of turns.

Goal   Be the first to score 5 points.

Cues

- Keep your feet moving while changing from one skill to another.
- Run through the poly spot (if modifying for baseball).

GAME 2

Repeat game 1.

CLOSURE

Review why placing the ball farthest from the poly spot (base) is the best way to score a point. Review the movement transitions needed when combining skills: roll and run, run-retrieve-run-tag a poly spot. Review reading the situation and disguising when and how they are going to roll or throw.

> **Note**   To modify this game so it is more similar to cricket, move the runner's poly spot closer and have the runner run to the poly spot and back to the starting point. Require the defender to retrieve the ball and then knock down a pin or wicket to get the runner out.

LEVEL II

The game situation of no outs, no runners on base, and a grounder to an infielder drives the tactical decisions, movements, and skills needed at level II (third and fourth grades). The first several lessons at this level focus on fielding, which extends the skills of catching and throwing to include a transition from receiving the ball to throwing the ball. This transition requires using the proper angle to approach the ball as well as positioning the body and the ball (once it is caught) to throw quickly and accurately. We recommend that you teach this transition directly.

The first few level II lessons focus on the on-the-ball skill of fielding, and then the off-the-ball skill of base coverage. Proper base coverage is important for safety as well as keeping runners off the bases and out of scoring position. An extra base positioned outside the base path (figure 9.6) can help keep the first-base player from colliding with or tripping the runner. It also trains runners to run outside the base path so they do not interfere with the play, which according to the rules would result in an out.

The later level II lessons focus on offensive elements of the game, first on base running and then on kicking or batting. Having the offensive team "roll and run" to first during the first few lessons helps maintain the focus on defense while allowing the offense to practice base running. Roll and run also eliminates the need to deal with bats, which can be a safety hazard, or large balls (if playing kickball), which can be difficult to throw.

The final few lessons focus on advancing to second base, which extends the role of the base runner both physically (rounding first) and cognitively (deciding to stay or run to second). The defense must also decide where to throw. Thus, the concept of cutting the lead runner to keep runners out of scoring position is

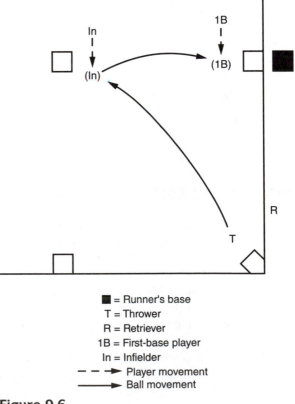

= Runner's base
T = Thrower
R = Retriever
1B = First-base player
In = Infielder
- - -▶ Player movement
——▶ Ball movement

Figure 9.6

Level II introduces students to actual game situations, although you can choose to focus on one or more elements of a particular situation.

important for students to learn at this level. Allowing the runner to advance increases the complexity of the tactical decisions. As the complexity of the game situations increases, so does the complexity of the tactical decisions and the skills required.

Game situations should be used to set up lesson progressions within and across units of instruction. Each situation involves defensive play, on- and off-the-ball, and offensive play, as a base runner and as a batter. As the teacher, you decide whether to focus on one or more elements of a particular situation; then allow that situation to naturally unfold and lead to the next likely situation. For example, when there are no outs, no runners on base, and a grounder is hit to the infield, the next situation is likely to involve no outs and a runner on first. The batter must then consider the best place to hit the ball to advance the runner, and the fielders must consider where to throw the ball. Extending the situation automatically extends the tactical decisions and skills needed to play the game.

LESSON 6

Tactical Problem   Throwing out the lead runner

Game   Kickball, throwball, T-ball, softball, or baseball

Situation   No outs, no runners on base, grounder to second-base player

Lesson Focus   Fielding transition from catch to throw

Objective   Receive the ball with two hands and immediately bring the ball into a throwing position; then step and throw to the player covering the base.

GAME 1

2v2 half-infield game

Goal   Get three outs before the offense scores three runs.

Conditions

- Offensive players throw, kick, or bat a ground ball to the second-base player; then run to first base, attempting to beat the throw.
- Defensive players field the ball and attempt to get it to first base ahead of the runner to get the runner out.
- Offense and defense switch after three runs or three outs, whichever comes first.

Questions

Q: How many of you were able to get three outs before the other pair scored three runs?

A: No one.

Q: Why not?

A: Throw was too late, throw was not caught or was off target, misplay at first.

Q: What can you do to get the throw to the base more quickly?

A: Make a good, quick throw to the player at first and a good catch at first.

PRACTICE TASK

The thrower rolls grounders to the infielder. As he catches with two hands, the infielder scoops and lifts the ball into a throwing position; then steps and throws to the target—the first-base player. The first-base player rolls ball back to the retriever, who feeds it to the thrower. Defensive players rotate after five trials at second base, and then rotate with offensive players who are throwing the ball (figure 9.1).

Goal   Demonstrate a smooth transition from catch to throw, and throw the ball accurately to first base.

Cues

- Use two hands.
- Scoop it up.

- Step to the target and throw.

Extension   After the throw, the thrower runs to first, and the fielder attempts to get the ball to first ahead of the runner.

GAME 2

Same as game 1 (2v2 half-infield game)

Goal   On defense, get three outs before the offense gets three runs.

Condition   The runner must run outside the base path to be considered safe at first base.

CLOSURE

Lead a discussion about the importance of getting to the ball quickly and getting into position to throw the runner out at first base. To assess, compare students' performances in game 1 to those in game 2.

Q: Why is it important for fielders to get to the ball quickly?

A: The quicker the fielder reaches the ball, the quicker the throw can be made to get the runner out.

LESSON 7

Elementary Level II

Tactical Problem   Supporting and covering the base on a force play

Game   Kickball, throwball, T-ball, softball, or baseball

Situation   No outs, no runners on base, grounder to second base

Lesson Focus   Covering first base on a force play

Objective   Cover first on a force play using a two-handed target and a foot on the inside edge of the base.

GAME 1

2v2 half-infield game

Goal   Get three outs before the offense scores three runs.

Conditions

- Offensive players throw, kick, or bat a ground ball to the second-base player; then run to first base, attempting to beat the throw.
- Defensive players field the ball and attempt to get the ball to first base ahead of the runner to get the runner out.
- Offensive and defensive players switch after three runs or three outs, whichever comes first.

Questions

Q: What is a force-out?

A: You just have to touch the base for the out when the runner must run to a base.

Q: What should the first-base player do when she is not fielding the ball?

A: Cover first base (catch the ball and tag the base).

Q: How can the first-base player help the fielders make an accurate throw?

A: Give a good target.

PRACTICE TASK

The thrower rolls grounders to the infielder, who fields and throws to first base. As soon as the first-base player sees the throw going to second, he moves to first and puts a foot on the inside edge of base and gives the fielder a big two-handed target (big hands, arms extended at chest level). After catching, the first-base player then rolls the ball to the retriever. After each defensive player has five trials at first base, players rotate; offensive players and throwers also rotate (figure 9.1).

Goal   Get to base quickly and receive and control the ball.

Cues

- Move quickly to cover first.
- Keep one foot on the inside edge of the base.
- Make a big, two-handed target.
- Watch the ball into the glove (absorb).

Extension   Have players use the foot opposite the throwing hand to tag first base, or add a runner.

GAME 2

2v2 half-infield game

Goal   Get three outs before the offense gets three runs.

Conditions   Same as game 1, but spread second and first farther apart as players improve.

Extension   Encourage runners to run it out: run through first, perhaps past a cone placed beyond first.

CLOSURE

Lead a discussion about first-base coverage and presenting a big target to throw to. Emphasize what to do when not fielding.

Q: How can the first-base player make it easier for the other fielders to be accurate with their throws?

A: Use the glove to provide a target.

Tactical Problem   Defending space and the base

Game   Kickball, throwball, T-ball, softball, or baseball

Situation   No outs, no runners on base, grounder to first base

Lesson Focus   Fielding grounders at first base and then tagging first for the force-out

Objective   Move quickly to the ball, field cleanly, and then run safely to first and tag the inside edge of the base.

GAME 1

2v2 half-infield game

Goal   Get three outs before the offense scores three runs.

Conditions

- Offensive players throw, kick, or bat a ground ball to the first-base player; then run to first base, attempting to beat the first-base player to the bag.
- Defensive players field the ball and attempt to get it to first base ahead of the runner to get the runner out.
- Offensive and defensive players switch after three runs or three outs, whichever comes first.

Questions

Q: If a player throws or hits a ball toward first base, what should the first-base player do?

A: Field the ball; then run and tag first base.

Q: What should the second-base player do?

A: Back up the first-base player who is fielding the ball.

PRACTICE TASK

The thrower rolls grounders between the first- and second-base players and runs to first base. The first-base player fields; then runs to first to tag the base ahead of the runner. The fielder (first-base player) should take a curved path (U or C) toward the baseline and then run parallel with the baseline to tag the base. The second-base player should back up, providing support for the first-base player. The first-base player then rolls the ball to the retriever. Defensive players rotate with offensive players after each defensive player has had five trials at first base (figure 9.7).

Goal   Get to the ball quickly, field cleanly, and run to first ahead of the runner.

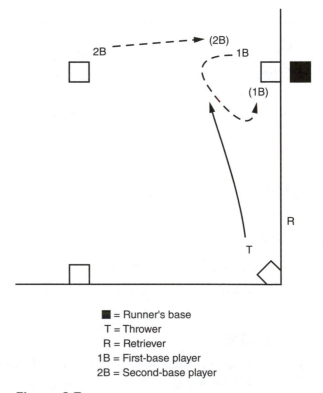

■ = Runner's base
T = Thrower
R = Retriever
1B = First-base player
2B = Second-base player

Figure 9.7

Cues

- Move quickly to the ball.
- Catch it first; then run to the base.
- Touch the inside edge of the base.
- Stay *inside* the base path.

Extension Players run a U or C pathway to get the runner out.

GAME 2

2v2 half-infield game

Goal Get three outs before the offense gets three runs.

Condition Throws should be modified to challenge both fielder and runner. For example, runners who are fast should throw the ball closer to the fielders; those who are slower should throw the ball farther from the fielders.

CLOSURE

Lead a discussion about fielding by the first-base player.

Q: How should the first-base player field a grounder that won't reach the base?

A: Charge the ball, pivot, and throw to the infield side of the base to avoid interference with the runner.

LESSON 9

Tactical Problem Scoring (hitting and running to first base)

Game Kickball, throwball, T-ball, softball, or baseball

Situation No outs, no runners on base, grounder to second base

Lesson Focus Transitioning from hit to run

Objective Hit and run as fast as possible through first base (drive right knee and left arm and keep head and eyes along the line).

GAME 1

2v2 half-infield game

Goal Get three runs before the defense gets three outs.

Conditions

- Offensive players hit or kick a ground ball to the second-base player; then run to first base, attempting to beat the throw.
- Defensive players field the ball and attempt to get it to first base ahead of the runner to get the runner out.
- Offensive and defensive players switch after three runs or three outs, whichever comes first.

Questions

Q: After hitting the ball, what should you do to get to first base as fast as possible?

A: Run fast.

Q: What's the first thing you need to do to run fast?

A: Get a good start.

PRACTICE TASK

All four players start at home plate, or three are at home and one is in the coaching box to coach the runner to run hard through the base and past the cone. In kickball, work on the transition from kicking to running. From a batting stance, the player imitates the swing (without bat or ball) and then "drives" (knee and opposite arm to first base). After three practice trials, the player repeats three more times with a bat and two players in the field. Have players repeat running trials three to five times.

Goal Hit and run to first.

Cues

- Drive knee and arm.
- Focus eyes along the line.

- Run hard through first base.

Extension Use a stopwatch to time from contact with the ball to contact with the base.

GAME 2

2v2 half-infield game

Goal Get three outs before the offense gets three runs.

Conditions Same as game 1; extra players can coach first base.

CLOSURE

Lead a discussion about hitting and running to first base.

> Q: Where should your eyes be focused while running to first base?
>
> A: Focus eyes along the line.

LESSON 10

Elementary Level II

Tactical Problem Scoring by hitting and running fast through first base

Game Kickball, throwball, T-ball, softball, or baseball

Situation No outs, no runners on base, grounder to second base

Lesson Focus Hitting and running through first base

Objective After hitting, run hard through first base.

GAME 1

2v2 half-infield game

Goal Get three runs before the defense gets three outs.

Conditions

- Offensive players throw, hit, or kick a ground ball to the second-base player; then run to first base, attempting to beat the throw.
- Defensive players field the ball and attempt to get it to first base ahead of the runner to get the runner out.
- Offensive and defensive players switch after three runs or three outs, whichever comes first.

Question

Q: Besides getting a good start, what else should you do to get to first base quickly?

A: Run hard, focus forward, listen to and watch the coach, and run through first base.

PRACTICE TASK

This is the same practice as the previous lesson, but it emphasizes running hard "through" first base. Put a cone about 5 feet (1.5 m) beyond first base, and encourage the runner to run as fast as possible past the cone. All four players start at home plate, or three are at home and one is in the coaching box to coach the runner to run hard through the base and past the cone. From a batting stance, each player imitates the swing (without bat or ball) and then "drives" (knee and opposite arm to first base). After three practice trials, each player repeats three more times with a bat. Put two players in the field and have each player repeat with a bat and ball. Repeat three to five times for each player.

Note   Adapt this if using throwing or running.

Goal   Hit and run fast through first base.

Cues

- Hit and run hard.
- Run "through" the base and past the cone.

Extension   Use a stopwatch to time from contact with the ball to reaching the cone beyond the base.

GAME 2

2v2 half-infield game

Goal   Get three runs before the defense gets three outs.

Conditions   Same as game 1; extra players can coach first base.

CLOSURE

Lead a discussion about the importance of speed and running through first base.

Q: How do you run through first base?

A: Run without breaking your stride or hesitating.

LESSON 11

Tactical Problem   Advancing a runner from first to second

Game   Kickball, throwball, T-ball, softball, or baseball

Situation   No outs, runner on first, grounder to second base

Lesson Focus   Offense running from first to second base

Objective   Start quickly from first base, run hard, and stop suddenly at second base.

GAME 1

3v3 half-infield game (adding a shortstop)

Goal   Advance the runner to second base.

Conditions

- Play starts with a runner on first base.
- Offensive players hit or kick a ground ball to advance the runner to second base; the offense scores a run when the runner is safe on second.
- Defensive players field the ball and attempt to get the lead runner out.
- Offensive and defensive players switch after three runs or three outs, whichever comes first.

Questions

Q: What are some things you can do to help you run faster from first to second base?

A: Get a good take-off, run hard, and don't stop too soon or overrun the base.

Q: According to the rules, when can you leave first base?

A: When the ball is hit or when it passes the batter.

PRACTICE TASK

For take-off practice, one player is a runner on first in a ready position. Two players are waiting. One player is at the plate with a bat imitating a swing. Players rotate after six to nine swings.

For practicing stops, about two steps before second base, runners should lean backward and get the heel down ahead of the toe. One step past is allowed, but the runner must keep one foot on the base. During practice, emphasize starting, then stopping, then both. Continue to focus on running hard.

Goal   Make a quick start, run hard, and stop suddenly.

Cues

- Start when the batter steps.
- Run hard.
- Lean back and put heels down to brake.

Extension   Use a stopwatch to time from contact with the ball to reaching the cone beyond the base.

GAME 2

3v3 half-infield game

Goal   Get three runs before the defense gets three outs.

Conditions   Same as game 1; adjust the size of the field to accommodate the level of play.

CLOSURE

Question and a discussion about advancing the runner from first to second

Q: Where's the best place for the batter to hit to move a runner at first to second?

A: Behind the runner.

LESSON 12

Tactical Problem   Cutting the lead runner

Game   Kickball, throwball, T-ball, softball, or baseball

Situation   No outs, runner on first, grounder to right infield

Lesson Focus   Shortstop coverage of second base on a force play

Objective   As the shortstop, cover second base properly on a force play from the right side of the infield.

GAME 1

3v3 half-infield game

Goal   Get three runs before the defense gets three outs.

Conditions

- Play starts with a runner on first base.
- Offense:
  - Players hit or kick a ground ball to the right side of the infield to advance the runner to second base.
  - Runs are scored when the runner is safe at second.
- Defense—Players field the ball and attempt to get the runner out at second base.
- Offensive and defensive players switch after three runs or three outs, whichever comes first.

Questions

Q: In this situation, which runner should you try to put out first?

A: The runner going to second.

Q: Who covers second when the ball is hit to the right side of the infield?

A: The shortstop.

Q: If you field the ball close to the base, do you need to throw the ball overhand?

A: No, you can just "flip" it.

PRACTICE TASK

Use a shortstop, a second-base player, and a thrower; runners are on first. The thrower throws grounders to the second-base player, and runners rotate running from first. Focus on the second-base player timing the flip to the base and the shortstop placing a foot on the edge of the base closest to the fielder making the play. Rotate players after six trials (figure 9.8).

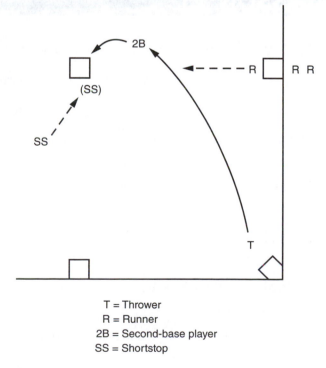

T = Thrower
R = Runner
2B = Second-base player
SS = Shortstop

Figure 9.8

Goal   As shortstop, cover second base on a force play without interfering with the runner.

Cues

- Second-base player:
  - Watch the ball go into the glove.
  - Flip it to the shortstop covering second base.
- Shortstop:
  - Get to the base quickly.
  - Place a foot on the edge closest to the play.
  - Give a good target.
  - Watch the ball go into the hands.

Extension   Add a base runner.

GAME 2

3v3 half-infield game

Goal   Get three runs before the defense gets three outs.

Conditions   Same as game 1

Extension   The offense must get the runner on first from home; then she can advance to second to score. Once on second, the runner does not advance. The offense can hit ground balls anywhere in the infield.

CLOSURE

Questions and a discussion about shortstop coverage of second base on a force play when the ball is hit to the right side of the infield

LESSON 13

Elementary Level II

Tactical Problem   Cutting the lead runner

Game   Kickball, throwball, T-ball, softball, or baseball

Situation   No outs, runner on first, grounder to left infield

Lesson Focus   Second-base player's coverage of second base on a force play when the ball is hit to the left side of the infield

Objective   Demonstrate proper coverage of second base on a force play from the left side of the infield.

GAME 1

3v3 half-infield game.

Goal   Get three runs before the defense gets three outs.

Conditions

- Play starts with a runner on first base.
- Offense:
  - Players hit or kick a ground ball to the left side of the infield to advance the runner to second base.

- Runs are scored when the runner is safe at second.
- Once on second, the runner does not advance.
- Defense—Players field the ball and attempt to get the runner out at second base.
- Offensive and defensive players switch after three runs or three outs, whichever comes first.

Questions

Q: In this situation, which runner should you try to put out first?

A: The runner going to second.

Q: Who covers second when the ball is hit to the left side of the infield?

A: The second-base player.

PRACTICE TASK

Use a shortstop, a second-base player, and a thrower. Focus on timing the flip or throw to the base and placing a foot on the edge of the base closest to the play. Rotate players after three to five trials.

Goal Cover second place properly on a force play from the left side of the infield.

Cues

- Get to the base quickly.
- Put a foot on the edge closest to the play.
- Give a good target.
- Watch the ball go into the hands.

Extension Add a base runner.

GAME 2

3v3 half-infield game

Goal Get three runs before the defense gets three outs.

Condition Throw, hit, or kick to the left side of the infield to advance the runner.

Extensions The offense must get the runner on first so he can then advance to second to score. Once on second, the runner does not advance. The offense can hit ground balls anywhere in the infield.

CLOSURE

Lead a discussion about covering second base on a force play when the ball is hit to the left or right side of the infield. Demonstrate each situation for players.

Q: Who covers second base when the ball is hit to the right side of the infield?

A: The shortstop.

Q: Who covers second base when the ball is hit to the left side of the infield?

A: The second-base player.

LESSON 14

Tactical Problem Cutting the lead runner

Game Kickball, throwball, T-ball, softball, or baseball

Situation No outs, runner on first, grounder to left infield

Lesson Focus Cutting the lead runner when the ball is hit to the third-base player

Objective Demonstrate the proper transition from a catch to a throw (from third to second base) to cut the lead runner.

GAME 1

4v4 infield game

Goal Get three outs before the offense scores three runs.

Conditions

- Play starts with a runner on first base.
- Offense:
  - Players hit or kick a ground ball toward third base to advance the runner to second base.
  - Runs are scored when the runner is safe at second.
- Defense—Players field the ball and attempt to get the runner out at second base.
- Offensive and defensive players switch after three runs or three outs, whichever comes first.

Questions

Q: In this situation, which runner should you try to put out first?

A: The runner going to second.

Q: Who covers second when the ball is hit to the third-base player?

A: The second-base player.

Q: What does the shortstop do?

A: Backs up play; then covers third base.

Q: Why is it more difficult to get a runner out at second from third base than it is from the shortstop position?

A: Third base is farther away.

Q: What can you do to improve the speed of the throw?

A: Charge the ball, watch the ball go into the hands, catch first, and then throw.

PRACTICE TASK

Three players are at third, one on the field and two waiting; three players are at second, one playing second base and two waiting. Two players are throwing and retrieving. Throw a ball to the third-base position. The third-base player charges the ball, scoops it up, steps toward second base, and throws to the base. Extra players rotate in after each trial, and all players rotate after nine throws. Or, after fielding the ball at third, that player plays second base and the second-base player goes to the third-base baseline.

Goal Make the force play at second from third base.

Cues

- Charge the ball.
- Scoop it up with two hands.
- Step to the target and throw.

Extension Add a base runner.

GAME 2

4v4 infield game

Goal   Get three runs before the defense gets three outs.

Conditions   Same as game 1

Extensions   The offense must get a runner on first so she can advance to second to score. Once on second, the runner does not advance. The offense can hit grounders anywhere in the infield.

CLOSURE

Lead a discussion about cutting the lead runner and fielding grounders from third base.

> Q: If you are fielding at third base and a runner is on first base, to which base do you throw in order to get that lead runner out?
>
> A: Second base.

LESSON 15

Tactical Problem   Cutting the lead runner

Game   Kickball, throwball, T-ball, softball, or baseball

Situation   No outs, runners on first and second, grounder to the infield

Lesson Focus   Cutting the lead runner when ball is hit to the third-base player

Objective   Demonstrate the proper transition from a catch to a throw (from third to second base) to cut the lead runner.

GAME 1

4v4 infield game

Goal   Get three runs before the defense gets three outs.

Conditions

- Play starts with runners on first and second base.
- Offense:
  - Throw, hit, or kick a ground ball anywhere in the infield to advance the runner to third.
  - Runs are scored when the runner is safe at third.
- Defense—Players field the ball and attempt to get the runner out at third base.
- Offensive and defensive players switch after three runs or three outs, whichever comes first.

Questions

> Q: In this situation, which runner should you try to put out first?
>
> A: The runner going to third.
>
> Q: Who covers third?
>
> A: The third-base player.

Q: What if the third-base player fields the ball?

A: Then the shortstop covers third.

Q: Why should you cut the lead runner whenever possible?

A: To keep the other team from scoring.

Q: In this situation, what should the third-base player do to help the player fielding the ball?

A: Get to the base quickly, give a good target, and catch and control the ball.

PRACTICE TASK

Thrower alternates grounders to the shortstop and second-base player, who field and throw to third base. The third-base player moves quickly to the base; uses a foot to touch the inside edge of the base closest to the play; and gives a big, two-handed target. Emphasize watching the ball go into the hands and positioning away from the incoming runner. After three to five trials at third, rotate infield, throwing, and retrieving duties.

Goal   Make the force play at third base to cut the lead runner.

Cues

- Move quickly to the base.
- Place a foot on the inside edge closest to the play (but out of the runner's path so the runner cannot block the throw).
- Make a *big,* two-handed target.
- Watch the ball go into the hands.

Extension   Add a base runner.

GAME 2

4v4 infield game

Goal   Get three runs before the defense gets three outs.

Conditions   Same as game 1

Extension   The offense must get runners on first and second so a runner can advance to third to score. Once on third, the runner can advance to home plate and score an additional run. The offense can hit grounders anywhere in the infield.

CLOSURE

Lead a discussion about cutting the lead runner and covering bases on force plays.

Q: If there are runners on first and second base, where is the force play?

A: Third base.

LEVEL III

Level III lessons (fourth and fifth grades), beginning where level II left off (with no outs, runner on first or second, and an infield grounder), review the tactics, movements, and skills needed for throwing out the lead runner. This series of lessons highlights offensive play during the early lessons, because most students should be ready to demonstrate some degree of bat control and hit and run and be able to decide whether to run through or to round first base.

Most level III lessons focus on tag plays (i.e., tagging a runner who is not forced to run). These lessons include coverage of second base by the shortstop as well as the second-base player. The situations expand to include tag plays at third and home plate and expand the number of players in the modified games as well as in practice situations.

The number of players for each situation can be easily adjusted with the addition of a player from the offensive team (offensive players can rotate or take turns playing for the defensive team). Remember that conditions can be adjusted to accommodate any situation, and students can also be quite helpful when asked for suggestions on modifying game conditions.

Finally, level III lessons also focus on outfield play. It is important here to emphasize getting the ball into the infield quickly. Off-the-ball communication is important here as well as backing up the player fielding the ball, which is another off-the-ball skill and should be taught as such. Good teams communicate, provide plenty of backup, and always know where to throw the ball *before* the batter hits the ball. These are tactics and skills that anyone can master.

Level III students learn tagging and outfield skills.

LESSON 16

Elementary Level III

Tactical Problems   Defending space and bases and throwing out the lead runner

Game   T-ball, softball, or baseball

Situation   No outs, runner on first, infield grounder

Lesson Focus   Fielding grounders and base coverage on force plays

Objective   When fielding a grounder hit to the infield, move to the ball, field it cleanly, and throw it accurately, making the correct play for the situation.

GAME 1

4v4 infield game

Goal   On defense, get the lead runner out.

Conditions

- Play starts with a runner on first.
- Offense:
  - Players hit a ground ball to the infield; then run to first base, attempting to beat the throw.
  - If a runner advances to second and the batter is out at first, the offensive team must fill the empty base to create a force situation.
- Defense—Players get the runner out, field the ball, and attempt to get the ball to the base ahead of the runner.
- Offensive and defensive players switch after three runs or three outs, whichever comes first.

Questions

Q: How many of you were able to get three outs before the other pair scored three runs?

A: (Most will not get three outs before the opponents score.)

Q: Why not?

A: The throw was too late, the throw was not caught or was off target, or there was a misplay at first.

Q: What can the fielder do to get the ball to the base more quickly?

A: Get to the ball as quickly as possible and make a clean catch and a good throw.

Q: What can the player covering the base do to support the fielder?

A: Get to the base quickly, give a good target, stop, and catch the ball.

PRACTICE TASK

Divide the infield in half; one thrower throws to the left side (shortstop; second-base player covers second), and one thrower throws to the right side (first and second base) (figure 9.9). An extra player can be a retriever or coach. Players on the left side make plays at second base, and players on the right side make plays at first base. The throwers roll grounders to an infielder; with two hands, she scoops and lifts the ball into a throwing position, and then steps and throws to the target (second-base player or first-base player). The first-base player rolls the ball back to the retriever, who feeds it to the thrower. Defensive players rotate after five trials at second base; then rotate with offensive players who are throwing the ball.

Note   It may be necessary to review cues for fielding (i.e., transition from catch to throw) as well as base coverage on a force play.

Goal   Demonstrate a smooth transition from a catch to a throw, and throw the ball accurately to first base.

Cues

- Thrower:
  - Use two hands.
  - Scoop it up.
  - Step to the target and throw.
- Base player:
  - Move quickly to cover the base.
  - Keep a foot on the inside edge of the base (the edge closest to the play).
  - Use a big, two-handed target.
  - Watch the ball into the glove (absorb).

Extension   Have players hit off a tee instead of using a throw.

GAME 2

Repeat game 1.

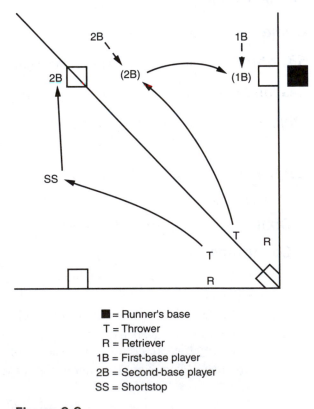

■ = Runner's base
T = Thrower
R = Retriever
1B = First-base player
2B = Second-base player
SS = Shortstop

Figure 9.9

CLOSURE

Discuss the importance of getting to the ball quickly and into position to throw the runner out, as well as supporting players covering the bases. Also, review proper base coverage.

Q: Why is it important to get to the ball quickly?

A: To get the runner out and keep any other runners from advancing.

LESSON 17

Tactical Problem   Scoring by hitting to get on base and advancing the runner

Game   T-ball, softball, or baseball

Situation   No outs, runner on first, infield grounder

Lesson Focus   Hitting to get on base and advance the runner

Objective   Hit the ball where it is most likely to advance the runner to get on base.

GAME 1

4v4 infield game

Goal   On offense, get on base *and,* when possible, advance the runner to the next base.

Conditions

- Play starts with a runner on first.
- Offense:
  - Players throw, kick, or bat a ground ball to the infield; then run to first base, attempting to beat the throw.
  - If a runner advances to second and the batter is thrown out at first, the offensive team must fill the empty base to create a force situation.
- Defense—Players field the ball and attempt to get it to the base ahead of the runner to get the runner out.
- Offensive and defensive players switch after three runs or three outs, whichever comes first.

Questions

Q: If there are no outs and no runner at first, where is the best place to hit the ball? Why?

A: To the left side of the infield, because the play is farther from first.

Q: What if there is a runner on first? Where is the best place to hit the ball? Why?

A: To the right side of the infield, behind the runner. This allows the runner to get to second base.

Q: Why is it important to get the runner to second base?

A: To give the runner a better chance of scoring on the next hit.

PRACTICE TASK

Arrange batting practice from a tee, with a fence 8 to 10 feet (2.4 to 3 m) in front of the tee. Mark three areas indicating left, center, and right fields on the fence. Each player hits three left, three center, and three right; then rotates with the second player. It is best to have students work in pairs, but they can also work in fours with a batter on deck and two players on safety patrol or coaching.

Goal   Hit the ball at least two out of three times to left, center, and right.

Cues

- Align your stance with the tee (to position the ball in the appropriate area of the contact zone).
- Spot the ball (i.e., focus on the place where you want to hit the ball).
- Step, hit, and follow through to the infield target.

Extension   Players hit off a tee to the infield.

GAME 2

Same as game 1 (4v4 infield game)

Goal   Score by getting on base and advancing the runners.

Conditions   Same as game 1

CLOSURE

Discuss the importance of getting runners into scoring position. Review batting technique.

> *Q: To where should you hit if there is a runner on first base?*
>
> *A: Hit the ball behind the runner, to the right side of the field and, if possible, down the first-base line.*

LESSON 18

Elementary Level III

Tactical Problem   Scoring by base running and advancing past first base

Game   T-ball, softball, or baseball

Situation   No outs, runners variable, infield grounder

Lesson Focus   Base running

Objective   Run through and make the turn to run to second base, according to the situation.

GAME 1

4v4 infield game

Goal   On offense, get runners to second base.

Conditions

- Offense:
  - Players throw, kick, or bat a ground ball to the infield; then run to first base, attempting to advance to second if possible.
  - Runs are scored when the offensive team gets a runner to second base safely. Once at second, base runners can continue running and score again if they reach home plate.
  - A coach must be on first at all times.
- Defense—Players field the ball and attempt to get it to the base ahead of the runner to get the runner out.
- Offensive and defensive players switch after three runs or three outs, whichever comes first.

Questions

Q: As a base runner, how do you know when to run through first base and when to make the turn?

A: Watch and listen to the coach; when the ball gets through the infield or on an overthrow.

Q: How should you run to first when you need to make the turn or go to second base?

A: Curve out before getting to the base.

PRACTICE TASK

Players line up behind home plate; one at a time they step up to the tee, imitate a swing, and run to first base. They listen for the coach and follow his instructions and hand signals ("Run it out," "Make the turn," "Go two"). The runners continue around the base path and get back in line. The first player around replaces the coach.

Goal Act immediately on the coach's signals and commands, and adjust your running path to make the turn toward second base.

Cues

- Look and listen for the coach.
- Start a C-turn three steps before first base.

Extension Players hit the ball off a tee.

GAME 2

Repeat game 1.

CLOSURE

Discuss running technique and the importance of watching the coach.

Q: How should you alter your running path if you are rounding first base?

A: Begin the turn two or three steps before reaching first base.

LESSON 19

Elementary Level III

Tactical Problem Defending space or the base in a tag situation

Game T-ball, softball, or baseball

Situation No outs, runners variable, infield grounder

Lesson Focus Tag plays

Objective Demonstrate the proper position to receive a throw and make a tag on an incoming runner.

GAME 1

4v4 infield game

Goal On defense, keep the runner from advancing to second base.

Conditions

- Offense:
  - Players throw, kick, or bat a ground ball to the infield; then run to first base, attempting to advance to second if possible.
  - Runs are scored when the offensive team gets a runner to second base safely. Once at second, base runners can continue running and score again if they reach home plate.
  - A coach must be on first at all times.
- Defense—Players field the ball and attempt to get it to the base ahead of the runner to get the lead runner out.
- Offensive and defensive players switch after three runs or three outs, whichever comes first.

Questions

Q: How can you keep the runner from advancing to second base?

A: Get the runner out at first by getting the ball to base ahead of the runner.

Q: If the batter hits and chooses to run to second base, what does the infielder have to do to get the runner out?

A: Tag the runner.

PRACTICE TASK

For offense, on the signal, the runner takes off, and then the thrower sends grounders to players on the left side of the infield (third and shortstop), who then throw to the second-base player moving to cover second base for the tag play. Runners start halfway down the first base line. The thrower times the throw to a make tag play close at second base. Players rotate after three to five trials by the second-base player. Focus on safe positioning to avoid interference from the runner. The sweep tag (catch and sweep the ball back and down to tag the runner) is recommended.

Goal Catch and tag the runner before he reaches the base.

Cues

- Quickly move into position (so the runner cannot come between you and the fielder).
- Catch first; then tag.
- Sweep low (at the edge of base closest to the runner).

Extension Players hit the ball off a tee.

GAME 2

Same as game 1 (4v4 infield game)

Goal On defense, tag the runner out at second base.

Conditions Same as game 1

CLOSURE

Discuss various tag situations and proper, safe technique.

Q: What is good technique to use in a tag situation at second base?

A: Sweep low and toward the side of the base from which the runner is approaching.

LESSONS 20 AND 21

Tactical Problem   Defending space or the base in a tag situation

Game   T-ball, softball, or baseball

Situation   No outs, runner on second, infield grounder

Lesson Focus   Tag plays

Objective   Make the appropriate decision, depending on the situation and position of the ball.

Note   Two lessons are devoted to this situation because of the complexity of possible solutions. Following are three possibilities for fielders to defend space or the base:

- Look the runner back and throw to first or hold the ball.
- Field and throw to third.
- Field and throw to first; then throw to third or home.

GAME 1

4v4 infield game

Goal   On defense, keep the runner from advancing to third base.

Conditions

- Offense:
    - Play starts with a runner at second base.
    - Players throw, kick, or bat a ground ball to the infield and attempt to advance the runner *and* get on first.
    - Runs are scored when the offensive team gets a runner to third base safely.
    - Once at third base, runners can continue running and score again if they reach home plate.
- Defense—Players field the ball and attempt to get the lead runner out.
- Offensive and defensive players switch after three runs or three outs, whichever comes first.

Questions

Q: *How can you keep the runner from advancing to third base?*

A: *Catch the ball and look back at the runner before throwing to first; throw the ball to third base as soon as you catch it.*

Q: *What does the third-base player need to do to get the runner out?*

A: *Tag the runner.*

PRACTICE TASK

The offense starts with a runner on second. The thrower sends grounders to players on the left side of the infield (third base and shortstop); then runs to first base. The fielder catches the ball and looks the runner back; then makes the throw or holds the ball depending on the situation. When the runner attempts to advance to third, the ball is thrown to third and the third-base player attempts to position and tag the runner out. Focus on safe positioning to avoid interference from the runner. The sweep tag is recommended.

Goal   On defense, keep the runner from reaching third base safely.

Cues

- Fielding by shortstop or third-base player:
  - Get to the ball quickly.
  - Look at the runner as you bring the ball back.
  - If in doubt, hold the ball (to keep the runner from advancing to third).
- Third-base coverage:
  - Quickly move into position (so that runner cannot come between you and the fielder).
  - Catch first; then tag.
  - Sweep low (at edge of base closest to the runner).

Extension   Players hit the ball off a tee.

GAME 2

Repeat game 1.

CLOSURE

Lead a discussion about tag situations; looking back at the runner; and proper, safe technique.

> Q: *How can you keep a runner from advancing while attempting to throw the batter out at first base?*

> A: *Field the ball and hold it in a throwing position as you look at the baserunner; if there is time, fake a throw.*

LESSON 22

Elementary Level III

Tactical Problems   Defending space or the base in a tag situation; advancing runners into scoring position

Game   T-ball, softball, or baseball

Situation   No outs, runner on second, infield grounder

Lesson Focus   Tag plays; fakes and feints to draw the throw

Objective   Make appropriate defensive and offensive decisions, depending on the situation and position of the ball.

GAME 1

4v4 infield game

Goals

- On defense, keep the runner from advancing to third base.
- On offense, get to third base to score.

Conditions

- Offense:
  - Play starts with a runner at second base.
  - Players throw, kick, or bat a ground ball to the infield and attempt to advance the runner and get on first.
  - Runs are scored when the offensive team gets a runner to third base safely.
  - Once at third base, runners can continue running and score again if they reach home plate.

- Defense—Players field the ball and attempt to get the lead runner out.
- Offensive and defensive players switch after three runs or three outs, whichever comes first.

Questions

Q: How can you keep the runner from advancing to third base?

A: Catch the ball and look back at the runner before throwing to first; throw the ball to third base as soon as you catch it.

Q: What does the third-base player need to do to get the runner out?

A: Tag the runner.

Q: As a runner on second base, what can you do to distract the fielder so that you can run to third or your teammate can get on first safely?

A: Fake like you're running to third, or wait for the throw then run to third.

PRACTICE TASK

The offense starts with a runner on second; the thrower sends grounders to players anywhere in the infield, and then runs to first base. The fielder catches the ball and looks back at the runner; then makes the throw or holds the ball depending on the situation. When the runner attempts to advance to third, the ball is thrown to third and the third-base player attempts to position and tag the runner out. Focus on safe positioning to avoid interference from the runner. The runner fakes the run and attempts to draw or delay the throw to first.

Goal   On defense, keep the runner from reaching third base safely. Base runners draw or delay the throw.

Cues

- Fielder:
  - Get to the ball quickly.
  - Look at the runner as you bring the ball back.
  - If in doubt, hold the ball (to keep the runner from advancing to third).
- Base coverage:
  - Quickly move into position at the base.
  - Catch first; then tag.
  - Sweep low (at the edge of the base closest to the runner).

- Runner:
  - Use a one-step fake.
  - Stay balanced.
  - Watch the ball.

Extension   Players hit the ball off a tee.

GAME 2

Same as game 1 (4v4 infield game)

Goal   On defense, keep the runner from advancing to third base. Runners draw or delay the throw.

Conditions   Same as game 1

CLOSURE

Lead a discussion about using a fake throw with a runner on second, tag situations, looking back at the runner, and drawing or delaying the throw.

Q: If you are a runner on second base, what can you do to help your batter get on first base?

A: Take a quick step toward third base and fake like you are going to run.

Tactical Problem   Defending space

Game   T-ball, softball, or baseball

Situation   No outs, runner on first, ball hit to right side of outfield

Lesson Focus   Outfield play

Objective   Move to the ball or position as quickly as possible to catch the ball and *immediately* throw the ball to second base.

GAME 1

4v4 half-field game (right center, right field, shortstop, second base)

Goal   On defense, get the runner out at second.

Conditions

- Offense:
    - Play starts with a runner at first base.
    - Players throw, kick, or bat a ground ball to the right side of the field and attempt to advance the runner *and* get on first.
    - Runs are scored when the offensive team gets a runner to second base safely.
    - Once at second base, runners can continue running and score again if they reach home plate. (A third-base player and catcher can be added from the batting team.)
- Defense—Players field the ball and attempt to get the lead runner out.
- Offensive and defensive players switch after three runs or three outs, whichever comes first.

Questions

Q: As an outfielder, what is your objective?

A: Catch the ball and get it to the infield as soon as possible.

Q: What are some things you can do to get to the ball quickly?

A: Watch it off the bat; know the situation.

Q: What are some things you can do to throw the ball quickly?

A: Catch it over the throwing shoulder; position the body to transition the ball quickly to the throwing hand.

PRACTICE TASK

One partner throws high fly balls to a partner. The partner should move under and catch the ball in position to throw quickly; then throw quickly and accurately (within one step) back to the partner. Players rotate after five trials.

Cues

- Move quickly to the ball.
- Time the catch.

- Catch over the throwing shoulder.
- Throw immediately to the base or cutoff player.

Extension   Add a base runner.

GAME 2

Same as game 1 (4v4 infield game)

Goal   On defense, keep the runner from advancing to second base.

Conditions   Same as game 1

CLOSURE

Lead a discussion about fielding fly balls and the advantage of getting the ball to the infield quickly.

> Q: What should an outfielder do once he or she has fielded the ball?

> A: Get the ball into the infield as quickly as possible.

LESSON 24

Tactical Problem   Defending space

Game   T-ball, softball, or baseball

Situation   No outs, runner on first, ball hit to left side of outfield

Lesson Focus   Outfield play

Objective   Move to the ball or position as quickly as possible to catch the ball and *immediately* throw the ball to second base.

GAME 1

4v4 half-field game (left center, left field, shortstop, second base)

Goal   On defense, get the runner out at second.

Conditions

- Offense:
  - Play starts with a runner at first base.
  - Players throw, kick, or bat a ground ball to the left side of the field and attempt to advance the runner *and* get on first.
  - Runs are scored when the offensive team gets a runner to second base safely.
  - Once at second base, runners can continue running and score again if they reach home plate. (A third-base player and catcher can be added from the batting team.)
- Defense—Players field the ball and attempt to get the lead runner out.
- Offensive and defensive players switch after three runs or three outs, whichever comes first.

Questions

> Q: As an outfielder, what is your objective?

> A: Catch the ball and get it to the infield as soon as possible.

> Q: What are some things you can do to get to the ball quickly?

> A: Watch it off the bat; know the situation.

> Q: What are some things you can do to throw the ball quickly?

> A: Catch it over the throwing shoulder; position the body to transfer the ball quickly to the throwing hand.

PRACTICE TASK

1. In outfield practice, three people are in left center field (one ready to field and two waiting). Other players should be playing second and third, and a runner should be at first.
2. The designated thrower stands at about the shortstop position and throws fly balls, line drives, and grounders between the left and left center fielders.
3. On the throw, the runner takes off from first and attempts to advance to second and third if possible.
4. One player calls the ball and fields it, and the other backs up and communicates where to throw the ball. These two fielders switch positions and wait until the other two players take their turns before having another trial.
5. After 15 balls are thrown, players switch roles until all players have had five opportunities to field or back up in the outfield.

Cues

- Call the ball and move quickly to it.
- Time the catch.
- Catch over the throwing shoulder and throw immediately to the base or the cutoff player.

GAME 2

Same as game 1 (4v4 infield game)

Goal   On defense, keep the runner from advancing to second base.

Conditions   Same as game 1

CLOSURE

Discuss fielding fly balls, the advantage of getting the ball to the infield quickly, and the off-the-ball responsibilities of backing up and communicating where to throw the ball.

> Q: *How should an outfielder decide where to throw the ball?*
>
> A: *Anticipate where the play will be before the batter hits the ball; listen to your teammates who should be telling you where to throw.*

LEVEL IV

Level IV (fifth and sixth grades) play focuses primarily on outfield play. Activities also entail support, or off-the-ball, play, such as backing up, base coverage, cutoffs, and relays. Although it takes time to develop the strength and accuracy to consistently perform these skills, it takes very little time to develop the movements needed for support play. Yet support play is essential to successful team play and often is not addressed with novices. Players who move on every play feel more involved in the game, which keeps their attention focused on the game.

Organizing teams of 5v5 allows for an easy shift to 10v10 play. When additional defensive players are needed, members of the offensive team can step in. But remember to rotate these players so that everyone gets an opportunity to play key defensive positions and the same player doesn't always get sent to the other team. Students who have played organized T-ball, baseball, or softball are more likely to request the "real" game (to which you might reply, "What's not real about this game?"). Occasionally you might want to provide an opportunity for full-sided game play, perhaps as a reward for highly engaged practices or significant improvement from game 1 to game 2. However, the decrease in opportunities to respond severely limits the degree to which a 10v10 game is useful in an instructional and practice setting where the emphasis is on learning how to play the game. If all small-sided games, drills, and practices reflect specific aspects of the "real" game, shifting from small-sided games to the full game should not pose a problem for novice or experienced players.

The form of the game, such as kickball, T-ball, or baseball, depends on the students, teacher, and context. Some forms, such as kickball and Wiffle ball, are better for indoor play than for outdoor play and can be used when outdoor play is prohibitive. When forced to play indoors, also consider setting up specific situations. However, you do not have to wait for inclement weather to chase you indoors to set up small areas or stations in which students can practice situations. Regardless of the game form or context, the tactics, movements, and skills needed for successful play are very similar, and there is no need to take a day off when inclement weather keeps you indoors.

Students in level IV have fun playing games and honing their outfield skills.

LESSON 25

Tactical Problem   Defending space

Game   T-ball, softball, or baseball

Situation   No outs, runner on first, ball hit to the left side of the field

Lesson Focus   Outfield play (extend and review content from previous lessons)

Objectives   Move to the ball or position as quickly as possible to catch the ball and *immediately* throw the ball to second base. When not fielding the ball, provide support by backing up the play or covering a base and communicating where to throw the ball.

GAME 1

5v5 half-field game (left center, left field, pitcher, second, shortstop)

Goal   On defense, get the runner out at second.

Conditions

- Offense:
  - Play starts with a runner at first base.
  - Players hit a ground ball to the left side of the field and attempt to advance the runner *and* get on first.
  - Runs are scored when the offensive team gets a runner to second base safely.
  - Once at second base, runners can continue running and score again if they reach home plate. (A third-base player can be added from the batting team.)

- Defense—Players field the ball and attempt to get the lead runner out.
- Offensive and defensive players switch after three runs or three outs, whichever comes first.

Questions

Q: As an outfielder, what is your objective?

A: Catch the ball and get it to the infield as soon as possible.

Q: What are some things you can do to get to the ball quickly?

A: Watch it off the bat; know the situation.

Q: What are some things you can do to throw the ball quickly?

A: Catch it over the throwing shoulder; position the body to transfer the ball quickly to the throwing hand.

PRACTICE TASK

1. In outfield practice, three people are in left center field; one is ready to field, and two are waiting. Other players should be playing second and third, and a runner should be at first.
2. The designated thrower stands at about the shortstop position and throws fly balls, line drives, and grounders between the fielders.
3. On the throw, the runner takes off from first and attempts to advance to second and third if possible.
4. One player calls the ball and fields it, and the other backs up and communicates where to throw the ball. These two fielders switch positions and wait until the other two players take their turns before having another trial.
5. After 15 balls are thrown, players switch roles until all players have had three to five opportunities to field or back up in the outfield.

Cues

- Call the ball and move quickly to it.
- Time the catch.
- Catch over the throwing shoulder and throw immediately to the base or cutoff player.

GAME 2

Same as game 1 (4v4 infield game)

Goal   On defense, keep the runner from advancing to second base.

Conditions   Same as game 1

CLOSURE

Discuss fielding fly balls, the advantage of getting the ball to the infield quickly, and the off-the-ball responsibilities of backing up and communicating where to throw the ball.

Q: What should the other fielders do to get runners out or keep them from advancing?

A: Let teammates know where to throw the ball and if there is a runner advancing.

LESSON 26

Tactical Problem   Advancing the base runner

Game   T-ball, softball, or baseball

Situation   No outs, runner on first, ball hit to the left side of the field

Lesson Focus   Hitting to the outfield

Objective   Hit the ball through or over the infield (a line drive or fly ball).

GAME 1

5v5 half-field game (second, third, shortstop, left field, left center)

Goal   On offense, advance the base runner from first to second base.

Conditions

- Offense:
  - Play starts with a runner at first base.
  - Players hit the ball to the left side of the field and attempt to advance the runner *and* get on first.
  - Runs are scored when the offensive team gets a runner to second base safely.
  - Once at second base, runners can continue running and score again if they reach home plate. (A first-base player can be added from the batting team.)
- Defense—Players field the ball and attempt to get the lead runner out at second base.
- Offensive and defensive players switch after three runs or three outs, whichever comes first.

Questions

Q: In a no outs, runner on first situation, what is the batter's responsibility?

A: Move the runner to second base.

Q: What do you have to do to do this?

A: Hit the ball past the infield into the outfield.

PRACTICE TASK

Students work in threes (a hitter, a coach, and a safety patrol). The hitter hits a ball suspended from a rope or pole so that it swings around the pole as many times as possible. This requires a fast bat and solid contact. A second station can include a batting tee, from which the batters hit Wiffle balls as far as possible. In either drill, the coach observes the point of contact to ensure that the ball is being struck in the power zone (waist level), and the safety patrol is watching to be sure no one else is in the area and is ready to yell, "Freeze!" if anyone comes near the batter.

Cues

- Watch the center of the ball.
- Swing fast.
- Contact the ball in the power zone.

GAME 2

Same as game 1 (5v5 half-field game)

Goal On defense, keep the runner from advancing to second base.

Conditions Same as game 1

CLOSURE

Lead a discussion about hitting line drives and fly balls through or past the infield by making contact with the ball in the power zone?

> Q: Where is the power zone?

> A: Out in front of the body to take advantage of the bat's momentum.

LESSON 27

Tactical Problems Advancing the base runner; defending space (outfield)

Game T-ball, softball, or baseball

Situation No outs, runner on first, ball hit to the left side of the field

Lesson Focus Hitting to the outfield; fielding a ball in the outfield

Objectives

- Hit the ball through or over the infield (line drive or fly ball).
- Move to the ball or position as quickly as possible to catch the ball and *immediately* throw it to second base.
- When not fielding the ball, provide support by backing up the play or covering a base and communicating where to throw the ball.

GAME 1

5v5 half-field game (second, third, shortstop, left center, left field)

Goals

- On offense, advance the base runner from first to second base.
- On defense, keep the runner from advancing to second base.

Conditions

- Offense:
  - Play starts with a runner at first base.
  - Players throw, kick, or bat the ball to the left side of the field and attempt to advance the runner *and* get on first.
  - Runs are scored when the offensive team gets a runner to second base safely.
  - Once at second base, runners can continue running and score again if they reach home plate. (A first-base player can be added from the batting team.)
- Defense—Players field the ball and attempt to get the lead runner out at second base.
- Offensive and defensive players switch after three runs or three outs, whichever comes first.

Questions

Q: What does the batter do in this situation, and how?

A: Moves the runner to second base with a hit through or over the infield.

Q: What does the fielder do in this situation, and how?

A: Fields the ball to catch and throw immediately.

PRACTICE TASK

Two stations (one batting station and one fielding station)

Station 1 Students work in threes (a hitter, a coach, and a safety patrol).

- Hitters hit a ball suspended from a rope or pole.
- Hitting the ball so that it swings around the pole as many times as possible requires a fast bat and solid contact.
- To accommodate more students, set up a second activity such as a batting tee from which batters can hit Wiffle balls as far as possible.

In either drill, the coach observes the point of contact to ensure the ball is being struck in the power zone. The safety patrol is watching to be sure no one else is in the area and is ready to yell, "Freeze!" if anyone comes near the batter.

Station 2

1. In outfield practice, three people are in left center field (one is ready to field, and two are waiting). Other players should be playing second and third, and a runner is at first.
2. The designated thrower stands at about the shortstop position and throws fly balls, line drives, and grounders between the fielders.
3. On the throw, the runner takes off from first and attempts to advance to second and third if possible.
4. One player calls the ball and fields it, and the other backs up and communicates where to throw it. These two fielders switch positions and wait until the other two players take their turns before having another trial.
5. After 15 balls are thrown, players switch roles until all players have had three to five opportunities to field or back up in the outfield.

Cues

- Station 1:
  - Watch the center of the ball.
  - Swing fast.
  - Contact the ball in the power zone.
- Station 2:
  - Call the ball and move quickly to it.
  - Time the catch.
  - Catch over the throwing shoulder.
  - Throw immediately to the base or cutoff player.

GAME 2

Same as game 1 (5v5 half-field game)

Goals

- On defense, keep the runner from advancing to second base.
- On offense, get the runner to second base and into scoring position.

Conditions   Same as game 1

CLOSURE

Discuss defending and fielding in the outfield, and hitting for power.

> *Q: When there is a runner on first base and the ball is hit past or through the outfield, where should the outfielder throw the ball?*
>
> *A: To the cutoff (i.e., the shortstop on the left side of the field and second-base player on the right side of the field).*

LESSON 28

Elementary Level IV

Tactical Problem   Tagging up on a fly ball to advance to the next base

Game   T-ball, softball, or baseball

Situation   No outs, runner on first, ball hit to the left side of the field

Lesson Focus   Tagging up on a fly ball

Objective   Tag up on a fly ball; then advance to the next base.

GAME 1

5v5 half-field game (second, third, shortstop, left field, left center)

Goal   On offense, attempt to advance on a fly ball.

Conditions

- Offense:
  - Play starts with a runner at first base.
  - Players hit the ball to the left side of the field and attempt to advance the runner *and* get on first.
  - Runs are scored when the offensive team gets a runner to second base safely.
  - Two runs are scored if the runner tags and advances to second base on a fly ball.
  - Once at second base, runners can continue running and score again if they reach home plate. (A first-base player can be added from the batting team.)
- Defense—Players field the ball and attempt to get the lead runner out at second base.
- Offensive and defensive players switch after three runs or three outs, whichever comes first.

Questions

> *Q: What does the runner on first do when the batter hits a fly ball?*
>
> *A: Waits in the start position until the ball is touched by a fielder; then runs to the next base.*
>
> *Q: What if the base runner doesn't think she will beat the throw to the base?*
>
> *A: She can stay on base; she does not have to run.*

PRACTICE TASK

A player stands at the shortstop position and throws fly balls to the left fielder and then to the left center fielder. A runner tags up and attempts to run to second ahead of the throw. A player can also be at second base to make the play on the runner. Extra runners should stand in the coach's box and step in as soon as the previous runner takes off.

Cues

- Be in a ready position.
- Go on contact.

GAME 2

Goal   On offense, get the runner to second base on a tag-up. Same as game 1 (5v5 half-field game)

Conditions   Same as game 1

CLOSURE

Lead a discussion about tagging up and advancing to the next base on a fly ball.

> *Q: What should base runners do if there are no outs or one out and the ball is hit in the air to the outfield?*
>
> *A: Tag up and advance if possible. If not, fake a run to draw the throw.*

LESSON 29

Tactical Problem   Defending second on a hit up the middle

Game   T-ball, softball, or baseball

Situation   No outs, runner on first, ball hit to center field

Lesson Focus   Covering second base on a force play when the ball is hit up the middle of the field; reviewing outfield hitting and fielding skills

Objective   Demonstrate proper coverage of second base from the second base and shortstop positions when a ball is hit to the center of the field.

GAME 1

5v5 half-field game (first, second, shortstop, left center, right center)

Goal   On defense, get the runner out at second.

Conditions

- Offense:
  - Play starts with a runner at first base.
  - Players hit the ball to center field and attempt to advance the runner *and* get on first.
  - Runs are scored when the offensive team gets a runner to second base safely.
  - Runners can continue running and score again if they reach home plate (third and catcher positions can be added from the batting team).

- Defense—Players field the ball and attempt to get the lead runner out at second base.
- Offensive and defensive players switch after three runs or three outs, whichever comes first.

Questions

Q: When a ball is hit to right center field, who covers second?

A: Shortstop.

Q: When a ball is hit to left center field, who covers second?

A: Second-base player.

Q: Where and how should second base be played in these situations?

A: Position outside second base, on the edge closest to the play. Give a good target and call for the ball. Put the foot opposite the glove hand on the outside edge of the base to make the force play.

PRACTICE TASK

1. Five players practice defense, and five players serve as throwers, runners, and retrievers and run the drill or practice. The defensive positions include a left center fielder, right center fielder, shortstop, and second-base player. Extra players can step in at any position and alternate with the player.

2. The thrower throws fly balls, line drives, or ground balls from the pitcher's mound alternately to left and right center field.

3. The runner at first takes off with the throw. The fielder who calls the ball catches it and throws to second to get the runner out.

4. An adjacent fielder backs up the play and communicates where to throw the ball. The shortstop and second-base players make the play at second base; when off the ball, they back up the throws to second base.

5. Players rotate after 8 to 10 throws to the outfield. Emphasize backup on every play and communication.

Goal To force the runner out at second base 6 out of 10 times

Cues Force play at second base:
- Position quickly outside the base path (between the fielder and the base).
- Show a target (signal with the glove) and call for the ball.
- Position the right foot on the edge of base (left foot if left-handed).
- Watch the ball into the glove.

GAME 2

Return to a 5v5 three-quarter-field game.

CLOSURE

Discuss force plays at second when there are no outs, a runner is on first, and the ball is hit to center field.

Q: Where should a center fielder throw the ball when there is a runner on first base?

A: Second base.

LESSON 30

Tactical Problem   Advancing the runner to second (scoring position)

Game   T-ball, softball, or baseball

Situation   No outs, runner on first, ball hit to right field

Lesson Focus   Offense hitting behind the runner to the right side of the field

Objective   Advance the runner to second base by hitting behind the runner.

GAME 1

5v5 three-quarter-field game (first, second, shortstop, right center, right field)

Goal   On offense, advance the runner to second base.

Conditions

- Offense:
  - Play starts with a runner at first base.
  - Players hit the ball to center field and attempt to advance the runner *and* get on first.
  - Runs are scored when the offensive team gets a runner to second base safely.
  - Runners can continue running and score again if they reach home plate. (Third-base and catcher positions can be added from the batting team.)
- Defense—Players field the ball and attempt to get the lead runner out at second base.
- Offensive and defensive players switch after three runs or three outs, whichever comes first.

Questions

Q: In a no out, runner on first situation, where is the best place to hit the ball to advance the runner to second base?

A: To the right side of the field behind the runner.

Q: As a batter, what do you need to do to hit to right field?

A: Adjust stance; look for outside pitch to hit; contact the ball on the right side of the plate (left-handed players should contact the ball on the left side of the plate).

PRACTICE TASK

Use multiple stations; for example, have three to five batting tees and three to five balls suspended from ropes and two to three pitching stations. Extra players can serve as coaches or safety patrol.

- Station 1: Use batting tees, and position batters so they contact the ball in front and to the right of home plate.
- Station 2: Suspend the ball on a horizontal pole or rope. Players practice adjusting their stance and contact point to hit the ball to the right side of the field.
- Station 3: Once the batter is ready, move her to a station where she can hit a pitched ball.

Cues

- Determine the contact point and adjust your stance.
- Contact the ball in the power zone to the right of, or in front of, the plate (left-handed batters should contact the ball to the left of, or in front of, the plate).
- Step and swing.
- Have a fast bat.

GAME 2

Return to a 5v5 half-field game.

CLOSURE

Lead a discussion about hitting behind the runner and critical elements for hitting to right field.

> Q: Where should the batter hit the ball to help advance a runner from first base to second base?

> A: Hit the ball behind the runner, to the left side of the field, and, if possible, down the first-base line.

LESSON 31

Tactical Problem   Defending bases on a tag play

Game   T-ball, softball, or baseball

Situation   No outs, no runner on first, ball hit to left field

Lesson Focus   Defense: tagging plays at second, third, and home

Objective   Cover the base (second, third, or home) to efficiently and safely tag out the advancing runner.

GAME 1

5v5 half-field game (second, third, shortstop, left, left center)

Goal   On defense, get the runner out at second.

Conditions

- Offense:
  - Play starts with no runner at first base.
  - Players hit the ball to left or left center field and attempt to advance to as many bases as possible.
  - Runs are scored when the offensive team gets a runner to second base safely, and additional runs are scored for advancing to third and again to home plate.
- Catcher, right-center, and first-base positions can be added from the batting team.
- Defense—Players field the ball and attempt to get the runner out.
- Offensive and defensive players switch after three runs or three outs, whichever comes first.

Questions

> Q: In a no out, no runners on, hit to left-field situation, where should the ball be thrown?

> A: To second base.

> Q: Because the runner is not forced to run in this situation, what does the second-base player need to do to get the out?

> A: Tag the runner.

PRACTICE TASK

1. Players are in left and left center field, two players are at second base to alternate (after each play), and one player is at third.

2. The designated thrower stands at about the shortstop position and throws fly balls, line drives, and grounders between the fielders.

3. On the throw, the runner takes off from first and attempts to advance to second and third if possible.

4. One player calls the ball and fields it, and the other backs up and communicates where to throw the ball. The second-base player positions himself between the ball and the bag, retrieves the throw, and attempts to tag the runner. After each attempt, the second-base player serves as a coach as the next player takes a turn.

5. Players rotate after each second-base player has had three to five practice opportunities.

Cues

- Position quickly between the base and the ball.
- Present a target and communicate where to throw the ball.
- Catch and sweep low (to the edge of the base closest to the incoming runner).

GAME 2

Return to a 5v5 half-field game.

CLOSURE

Lead a discussion about tag plays.

> Q: How do you get a runner out if it isn't a force play?
>
> A: Tag the runner.

LESSON 32

Tactical Problem   Defending bases with a cutoff

Game   T-ball, softball, or baseball

Situation   No outs, no runner on first, ball hit to left field

Lesson Focus   Defense uses a cutoff play to keep runners from advancing.

Objective   Throw to cut off when a runner is, or will be, safe at second.

GAME 1

5v5 half-field game (second, third, shortstop, left, left center)

Goal   On defense, get the runner out at second.

Conditions

- Offense:
  - Play starts with no runner at first base.
  - Hit the ball to left or left center field, and attempt to advance to as many bases as possible.
  - Runs are scored when the offensive team gets a runner to second base safely, and additional runs are scored for advancing to third and again to home plate.
- Catcher, right-center, and first-base positions can be added from the batting team.
- Defense—Field the ball and attempt to get the runner out.
- Offensive and defensive players switch after three runs or three outs, whichever comes first.

Questions

Q: In a no outs, no runners on, hit to left-field situation, where should the ball be thrown?

A: To second base.

Q: If it is obvious that the runner is or will be safe at second, where should the ball be thrown to keep the runner from advancing?

A: To second base, third base, or shortstop.

Q: What are the advantages of throwing to shortstop?

A: It keeps the runner from advancing, and the shortstop can redirect the throw if necessary.

PRACTICE TASK

1. Players in left field, in left-center field, at second base, and at third should rotate in after each play.
2. The designated thrower stands to the left-field side of the pitcher's mound and throws fly balls, line drives, and grounders between the fielders.
3. On the throw, the runner takes off from first and attempts to advance to second and third if possible.
4. One player calls the ball and fields it, and the other backs up and communicates where to throw the ball. The second-base player positions herself between the ball and the bag, retrieves the throw, and attempts to tag the runner. The shortstop moves toward left field and prepares to receive the cutoff if the pitcher or thrower calls for the cutoff. After each attempt, the second-base player serves as a coach as the other players take their turns.
5. Rotate after each player has had two or three practice opportunities at shortstop.

Cues

- Position quickly between the play and second base.
- Target and call for the ball.
- Catch and turn (left or glove side) toward the target.
- Run the ball in quickly (if not throwing).

GAME 2

Return to a 5v5 half-field game.

CLOSURE

Discuss cutoffs.

Q: If an outfielder can't reach the base with a throw, where should he or she throw?

A: Throw to the cutoff player.

Tactical Problem   Defending bases with a cutoff and relay

Game   T-ball, softball, or baseball

Situation   No outs, no runner on first, ball hit to right field

Lesson Focus   Using the cutoff play to keep runners from advancing, and the relay to put out the advancing runner

Objective   Throw to the cutoff when the runner is or will be safe at second. That player will relay the ball to third when the runner attempts to advance.

GAME 1

5v5 half-field game (second, third, shortstop, right field, right center)

Goal   On defense, get the runner out at second.

Conditions

- Offense:
  - Play starts with a runner at first base.
  - Players hit the ball to right field or right center and attempt to advance to as many bases as possible.
  - Runs are scored when the offensive team gets a runner to second base safely, and additional runs are scored for advancing to third and again to home plate.
- Catcher, right-center, and first-base positions can be added from the batting team.
- Defense—Players field the ball and attempt to get the runner out.
- Offensive and defensive players switch after three runs or three outs, whichever comes first.

Questions

Q: *In a no outs, no runners on, hit to left-field situation, where should the ball be thrown?*

A: *To second base.*

Q: *Who covers second base?*

A: *Shortstop.*

Q: *If it is obvious that the runner is or will be safe at second, where should the ball be thrown to keep the runner from advancing?*

A: *To second base, third base, or shortstop.*

Q: *What are the advantages of throwing to the second-base player if there is no play at second?*

A: *It keeps the runner from advancing, and the second-base player can redirect the throw if necessary.*

Q: *What if the runner continues to run to third?*

A: *The second-base player can relay the throw to third.*

PRACTICE TASK

1. Players are in right field and right center, and at second and third base.
2. The designated thrower stands to the right-field side of the pitcher's mound and throws fly balls, line drives, and grounders between the fielders.
3. On the throw, the runner takes off from first and attempts to advance to second and third if possible.
4. One player calls the ball and fields it, and the other backs up and communicates where to throw the ball. The shortstop positions himself between the ball and the base, retrieves the throw, and attempts to tag the runner. The second-base player moves toward right field and prepares to receive the cutoff or relay if the pitcher or thrower calls for the cutoff or a relay to third base. After each attempt, the second-base player serves as a coach as the other players take their turns.
5. Players rotate after each has had two or three practice opportunities at shortstop.

Cues

- Position quickly between the play and second base.
- Target and call for the ball.
- Catch, turn (left or glove side), and step toward the target.
- Use a throwing motion (don't release if no play).
- Run the ball in quickly if not throwing.

GAME 2

Return to a 5v5 half-field game.

CLOSURE

Lead a discussion about cutoffs and relays.

> Q: What is the cutoff player's job once he or she has the ball?
>
> A: Make a play at a base. If no play is possible, stop the runners from advancing by running the ball into the infield and, if necessary, toward the runner with the ball held in a throwing position.

LESSON 34

Tactical Problem   Defending space

Game   T-ball, softball, or baseball

Situation   No outs, no runner on first (but possible runners on other bases), hit according to where runners are positioned

Lesson Focus   On defense, use off-the-ball play as a team.

Objective   In a full-field game, provide appropriate backup for players fielding the ball and cover for base players in all fielding situations.

GAME 1

10v10 full-field game

Goal On defense, get three outs before the offense gets five runs.

Conditions

- Offense:
  - Play starts with no runners on base.
  - Players throw or bat the ball depending on the situation and attempt to advance to as many bases as possible.
  - Runs are scored when the offensive team gets a runner to any base safely, but score one run for first, two runs for second, three runs for third, and four runs for home.
- Defense—Players field the ball, attempt to get the runners out, and keep runners from advancing.
- Offensive and defensive players switch after five runs or three outs, whichever comes first.

Questions

Q: Who moves when the ball is hit?

A: Everyone should move.

Q: Where should they move?

A: It depends on the situation, but off-the-ball players should back up, cover bases, set up for cutoff or relay plays, and communicate.

PRACTICE TASK

Set up a situation practice of 10 players on the field; one, two, or three players set up and run situations. The defensive team scores runs for performing proper backups and coverage in each situation, but all 10 players must perform properly to score. One run is scored each time all 10 defensive players provide proper support for the player fielding the ball. Players rotate positions after five situations, with the one to three players who are setting up situations rotating in as well.

Cues

- Know the situation and where to throw.
- Watch the ball and move on contact.
- On first, make the play or back up the play.
- If not fielding, move to or toward the nearest base to back up or cover (except for the second-base player and shortstop).
- Communicate.

GAME 2

Return to a 10v10 game.

CLOSURE

Discuss off-the-ball play.

Q: How do the players fielding the ball and the rest of the team work together to field as a team?

A: Move to back up the play and cover the bases. Never stop moving until the umpire calls time out.

SUMMARY

This chapter has provided sample lessons for teaching striking and fielding games using a tactical approach. You can extend or refine many of these lessons to create new ones focusing on a variety of off-the-ball movements and on-the-ball skills. The key to creating new lessons is to remember that for each situation (e.g., one out, runner on first), every offensive and defensive player has a role. As you examine a situation, ask yourself, what off-the-ball movements or on-the-ball skills does the player need to adequately perform her role? Having identified these movements and skills, you can create game and practice conditions to help your students understand what to do and how to do it.

Perhaps the most important consideration in striking and fielding games is their minimal intensity. To mitigate this issue, you might consider integrating rules that speed up play. For example, you could use a countdown between innings at the end of which the pitcher is allowed to pitch. If there is no batter when the ball crosses the plate, it counts as an out. You might also consider asking students to make up their own striking and fielding games or practice drills, with emphasis on sustaining moderate to vigorous activity. Teaching students how to play, whether our game or theirs, is perhaps more important than teaching them what to play.

Chapter 10

Target Games at the Elementary Level

This chapter provides a rationale for including target games in the elementary physical education curriculum and also provides a scope and sequence of target game activities to help students understand the tactical problems common to most target games. Just as in invasion, net and wall, and striking and fielding games, tactical similarities across target games can help the transfer of learning not only from one target game to another but across games categories as well.

There are two subcategories of target games (Almond 1986). In one, the player performs independently of the opponent (*unopposed,* such as in golf, bowling, archery, and darts). A second subcategory, *opposed,* includes games such as billiards, horseshoe throwing, bocce, croquet, and shuffleboard, which allow the performer to counterattack. This means a player can choose to challenge an opponent's shot by blocking, knocking away a disk, or sending a croquet ball out of a playing area. Ring toss, beanbag toss, and rolling or bowling at a pin or target are examples of some of the less complex target game activities that are frequently found in elementary physical education.

Target games are frequently included in elementary curricula to develop and refine manipulative skills with little if any consideration given to the concepts or tactical problems common to most target games. However, these types of games provide a perfect context for developing the decision-making skills needed for game play. Compared with other games, such as invasion and net and wall games, in which decision making is more spontaneous, decision making in target games is done before performing the skill. Consequently, target games provide an excellent context for young learners to develop manipulative skills as well as basic decision-making skills, which can serve as a basis for more complex skills and tactics.

ELEMENTARY TARGET GAMES TACTICS AND LEVELS OF GAME COMPLEXITY

Similar to invasion, net and wall, and striking and fielding games, target games involve tactical problems or concepts and skills. Target games provide more time to make decisions before executing the skill. As shown in table 10.1, several preshot decisions are needed to solve the tactical problems. The primary tactical problem in target games is accuracy, which involves determining the proper direction and distance of the shot. The more proficient the learner becomes at making preshot decisions, the more likely she is to put herself into position to execute the skill successfully.

Students should learn skills and tactics together within a game context. If they do this consistently, they will come to understand the relationship between tactics and skills as well as the similarities among games. Table 10.2 illustrates a possible progression for tactics and skills, from level I to level III. Children, even as young as four years of age, can understand tactics related to a consistent starting point, a target line, and an intermediate target. Initially, you should use instructional aids to give them the idea and then gradually withdraw them. For example, use footprints to mark the starting point and an arrow or line taped on the floor as a target line.

MODIFICATIONS FOR ELEMENTARY TARGET GAMES

All that is needed for a target game is a target and an object to roll, toss, or slide. Targets can range from a single bowling pin to a box, hoop, or target drawn on the floor. Several inexpensive games can be found at toy or discount stores that include objects and targets (e.g., Tic Tac Throw, 10-pin bowling sets, dart games, and plastic golf sets). Many of these games have been designed specifically for young children, and others have been designed as leisure activities that families can play outdoors.

When setting up multiple target games in a gymnasium, remember that objects can roll or slide into other playing areas; therefore, it is useful to have some long objects, such as two-by-fours or noodle pool floats, to serve as barricades and to define and divide the playing areas. Figure 10.1 shows how a gym might be

Table 10.1   Tactical Framework for Elementary-Level Target Games

Tactical concepts for accuracy	Preshot decisions	Skill execution (on-the-ball)
Direction	Determine: • Starting point • Target line • Intermediate target • Release point	Grip—adjust (closed and open contexts): • Starting point • Target line • Intermediate target • Release point
Distance	Determine: • Length of backswing • Force • Arm swing	Approach: • Establish consistency in the step and arm swing. • Adjust the backswing, step, and approach relative to the shot requirements.

Table 10.2   Levels of Tactical Complexity for Elementary-Level Target Games

Tactical problems and concepts for accuracy	Level I One player unopposed	Level II 1v1 unopposed	Level III 1v1 opposed
Direction	Determine: • Starting point • Target line • Intermediate target • Release point • Grip	Adjust (in closed-context game such as bowling): • Starting point • Target line • Intermediate target • Release point	Adjust (in varied open-context games such as bocce): • Starting point • Target line • Intermediate target • Release point
Distance	Determine: • Length of backswing • Force • Arm swing	Approach: • Establish consistency in the step and arm swing.	Adjust the backswing, step, and approach relative to the shot requirements.

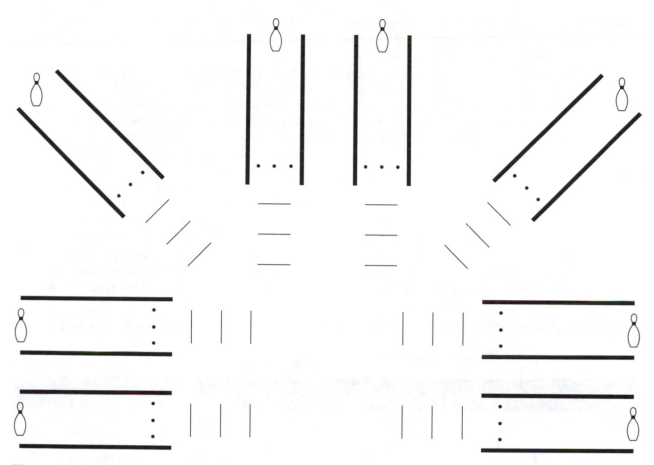

Figure 10.1 Organization of space and equipment for teaching target games in elementary physical education.

set up during a target games lesson. Notice that the stations are set up so that the objects are sent outward, toward the wall, allowing the teacher to easily monitor from the center of the activity area. Two to four students can be assigned to a station, and at least one student is responsible for returning the object safely to a partner or partners.

The courts should be arranged so you can lengthen them as students' skill and accuracy improve. Again, this is a good reason to have students send objects from the center toward the wall. Target sizes should also vary to accommodate the skill level of each student; for example, you can use different sizes of boxes or a target with various-sized concentric rings (such as an archery target) on the floor or wall. The type, size, and weight of the objects can also vary, or the students can have a variety of objects (e.g., different-sized balls, beanbags, or rings) to select from.

Several targeting aids should also be available, such as footprints drawn on the floor (or mat) to mark the start position, arrows taped to the floor to identify the target line, or stickers that can be used to mark an

intermediate target. Use colored floor tape to designate various distances from the target (figure 10.1). This allows students to move back after a certain number of successful rolls or tosses.

PROGRESSIONS FOR TEACHING ELEMENTARY TARGET GAMES

Target games are appropriate for very young learners (ages 4 and up) because they involve basic sending skills, such as rolling a ball, sliding a puck, or throwing or tossing underhanded. These are essentially the same skills needed to play even the most advanced forms of target games, although the objects may be heavier and the distances may be longer. It is easiest to begin with rolling a ball at a target or pin. Initially, the target should be close and large, and the ball should be small enough to grip with one hand. Wiffle balls, tennis balls, and soft foam balls are excellent because they are easy to manipulate.

A developmental task analysis (Siedentop, Herkowitz, and Rink 1984) can be used to determine how to increase and decrease the complexity of a target game activity (table 10.3). Significant elements of the task are listed across the top, and criteria are listed from simple to complex. Other criteria, such as ball weight and color, could also be added here. An initial task might require the student to roll a 5-inch (12.7 cm) Wiffle ball at a small target from 10 feet (3 m), with the tactical focus on the starting point. To increase or decrease task complexity, change *one* element at a time. Thus, you can modify task complexity to accommodate individual learners as they improve in skill and accuracy.

As with invasion, net and wall, and striking and fielding games, principles guide the development of appropriate progressions in target games.

First, *move from cooperative to competitive situations.* Competition should begin with the individual learner,

who is challenged to improve his own score. As the students improve, include competition against other students.

Second, *move from simple to complex.* This principle applies to both tactics and skills (tables 10.2 and 10.3).

Third, *move from unopposed to opposed target games.* The game form should be the primary basis for increasing complexity. Begin with very basic target games, such as rolling a ball at a pin or sliding a beanbag at a target on the floor. Then, introduce variations of more advanced target games, such as five-pin bowling or lawn darts (with weighted ends in place of pointed darts). Games that are opposed (e.g., horseshoe throwing, ring toss, shuffleboard, and bocce) should then be introduced. As shown in table 10.4, some target games are naturally more complex than others mostly because of the type of game and

Table 10.3 Developmental Task Analysis for Increasing and Decreasing the Complexity of a Target Game

Task complexity	TASK ELEMENTS				
	Ball size	Ball composite	Distance from target	Target size	Tactic
Simple	3 in. (7.6 cm) 5 in. (12.7 cm) 7 in. (18 cm)	Foam ball Wiffle ball Team handball	5 ft (1.5 m) 10 ft (3 m) 15 ft (4.6 m)	Large Medium-large Medium	Starting point Target line Intermediate target
Complex	9 in. (23 cm)	Playground ball	20 ft (6 m)	Small	Release point

Table 10.4 Target Games From Simple to Complex and Related Preshot Decisions

Target game	Skill	PRESHOT DECISION					
		Setup	Target line	Intermediate target	Release point	Point of contact	Length of backswing and step or speed of approach
Bocce, bowling, skittles, 10-pin	Rolling a ball	Y	Y	Y	Y	N	Y
Horseshoe throwing, ring toss, lawn darts	Tossing underhand	Y	Y	N	Y	N	Y
Shuffleboard	Pushing a cue	Y	Y	Y	Y	N	Y
Curling	Sliding a stone	Y	Y	Y	Y	N	Y
Golf	Putting	Y	Y	Y	N	Y	Y
Croquet	Hitting with a mallet	Y	Y	Y	N	Y	Y
Billiards, pool, snooker	Shooting with a cue	Y	Y	Y	N	Y	Y
Golf	Swinging a club	Y	Y	Y	N	Y	Y

age appropriateness of the equipment, yet all target games share many tactical similarities. Manufacturers have produced smaller versions of these games (e.g., golf bags and plastic, large-faced clubs and miniature pool tables) to encourage children to play target games that are similar to those played by their parents.

BOWLING AS AN EXEMPLAR FOR TEACHING TARGET GAMES

Bowling is the quintessential target game and exemplifies the relationship between preshot decisions and skill execution. In bowling, spots on the approach lane help the bowler position the feet when shooting strikes and spares, and arrows serve as intermediate targets. In addition, a row of spots just beyond the foul line serves as a marker for the release point. Rolling the ball over an arrow, rather than shooting at the pins, increases accuracy. This combination of spots and arrows allows the bowler to consistently shoot for strikes and the various spares. Of course, this assumes that the delivery is consistent not only in the grip or hand position but also in the point of release. Thus, the greater the alignments among the starting point, point of release, and intermediate target, the greater the accuracy.

We can take this concept of spots (as starting points) and arrows (as intermediate targets) and apply it to all target games. When putting, for instance, the golfer locates a spot (i.e., a mark on the green or a few blades of grass) just in front of the ball along the path he wants the ball to travel, and he uses this as an intermediate target. The golfer's stance or start position is determined once the ball path has been determined, because the stance must be parallel to the ball path. Once the start position and intermediate target are determined, the performer needs only to execute the putt or, as in the case of other target games, execute the shot, throw, push the cue, or roll the object to hit the target.

Target games that involve throwing, such as horseshoes and darts, do not have an intermediate target per se, but they do require a specific release point. Identifying a specific, consistent spot or area in the background during the release of the object may improve the consistency of the release and may well serve as an intermediate target. Most often the release point depends on the kinesthetic sense of the performer.

Although some target games involve a release point, others, such as golf, billiards, and croquet, involve a contact point. The contact point is the point on the ball that must be struck to send the object in the desired direction with the appropriate spin. During a pitch shot, for example, the golfer must strike below the midpoint of the ball and with a downward motion to send the ball up and land it on the green with enough backspin that it stays on the green and does not roll off.

Target games that include counterattacks by an opponent also require the selection of a starting point, intermediate target, and release point. To counterattack, the performer must make a number of tactical adjustments and precisely execute the shot. For example, in shuffleboard a player may want to knock the opponent out of scoring position, which requires that she adjust her stance and the intermediate target and judge the distance and speed (power) needed to not only reach the opponent's disk but also send her disk and her opponent's disk to the desired locations.

We must reiterate that even the most novice players can play target games quite successfully. The tactical problems are basic, easy-to-understand concepts that can easily be extended to challenge more advanced players. The lesson activities in this chapter illustrate how you might introduce tactical concepts to primary- and elementary-aged children. By using different objects, such as deck rings, beanbags, and horseshoes, the same lesson can be taught several times and in several contexts to provide the repetition young children need to develop motor skills and realize the tactical similarities among games.

Keep one thing in mind: many of the concepts that apply to target games also apply to other game categories. For example, striking a ball with a paddle or bat, executing a forearm pass in volleyball, and throwing a baseball, which represent more "open" skills (Gentile 1972), all incorporate the tactical concepts related to accuracy, direction, and distance. To promote competency in motor skills and movement patterns (NASPE 2004), we must teach skill development *and* tactical understanding intentionally as well as integrate them in kindergarten through 12th-grade physical education curricula.

TARGET GAMES LESSONS

Target games differ from games in other categories in that skill execution is similar across games. For example, rolling or bowling a ball is very similar to tossing a bocce ball, throwing a horseshoe, and striking a ball with a club. The only difference is the concept of the intermediate target, which does not apply to most tossing and throwing games, such as horseshoe throwing and darts. With most target games that involve tossing or throwing, the concept of the release point can be applied. Similarly, in target games that involve striking, the concept of the contact point applies along with that of the intermediate target.

Another difference between target games and other categories of games is that they involve basically *one* tactical problem—accuracy. For this reason, target games tend to be far less complex than other games, particularly at the elementary level. Because of their simplicity, we present five level I lessons focusing on accuracy (distance and direction) as the main tactical problem; many of these lessons can be combined depending on the age or grade level at which they are introduced. The same sequence of lessons can be used to teach the underhand toss, ring toss, and numerous other activities related to target games, which could perhaps be considered level II lessons. In fact, the same sequence of lessons can be used to teach horseshoe throwing, although the nature of the equipment would not make this game appropriate until level III.

LEVEL I

Target games present great challenges for children and are generally games that most can play due to the limited range of motor skills required for performance. Consequently, teachers could easily include target games as part of the early games experiences for primary or elementary children. Accuracy is obviously the first thing to be addressed, and young children will find themselves able to improve this quite quickly.

Level I starts students off on their quest to improve accuracy with their aim.

Tactical Problem Rolling for accuracy and direction

Game Rolling a ball at a pin

Lesson Focus Setting up and determining a start position

Objective Demonstrate a consistent start position (same spot, balanced stance, same grip and hand position on the ball, eyes focused on the target) before executing the roll.

GAME 1

Knockdown (roll a ball to knock down a pin)

Goal Knock down the pin three times in a row.

Conditions

- Position a pin and a partner at one end and a roller at the other end, approximately 10 to 15 feet (3 to 4.6 m) apart.
- Partners switch after five trials.

Questions

Q: How many of you were able to knock down the pin three times in a row?

A: (No one or only a few of them.)

Q: If you want to knock down the pin every time, what should you do before you roll the ball? **(Have children stand and pretend they are getting ready to roll.)** *What are you doing?*

A: Aiming, holding the ball, standing still.

Q: How are you standing, holding the ball?

A: Standing still, holding the ball with both hands in front of my body.

Q: Where are you standing? Where are you aiming?

A: Standing in line with the pin, aiming at the pin.

Q: When do you decide where and how to stand?

A: Before rolling the ball.

PRACTICE TASK

A partner stands 10 to 15 feet (3 to 4.6 m) away and forms a V with his feet (heels together and toes pointing out). The other partner should think about where and how to stand before rolling the ball. Players should start in the same place every time, stand the same way, hold the ball the same way, and aim the same way on every roll.

Goal Roll the ball so that it goes exactly to the V formed by the partner's feet, five times in a row. (The partner forming the V must stand perfectly still until the ball hits his feet.)

Cue *Same* start, *same* stance, *same* hold.

GAME 2

Knockdown (roll a ball to knock down a pin)

Goal   Same as game 1

Conditions   Same as game 1

CLOSURE

Review what to do to roll the ball the same way every time. Have students think about where and how to stand before rolling.

LESSON 2

Tactical Problem   Rolling for accuracy and direction

Game   Rolling a ball at a pin

Lesson Focus   Stepping and swinging the arm

Objective   Demonstrate smooth and consistent form and rhythm on the step and arm swing (swing back, step forward, swing forward, follow through toward the target, and release the ball low).

GAME 1

Knockdown (roll a ball to knock down a pin)

Goal   Knock down the pin three times in a row.

Conditions   Position a pin and a partner at one end and a roller at the other, approximately 10 to 15 feet (3 to 4.6 m) apart. Partners switch after 10 trials.

Questions

> Q: *How did you roll the ball to knock down the pin?*
>
> A: *Stepped and rolled the ball at the pin.*
>
> Q: *Did you start with your feet together or apart?*
>
> A: *Together.*
>
> Q: *What foot did you step with?*
>
> A: *The foot opposite the throwing hand.*
>
> Q: *Stand and show me your start position. Now show me your backswing. When do you do your backswing—before or after your step?*
>
> A: *Before.*
>
> Q: *What do you do when your arm swings forward?*
>
> A: *Step and release the ball.*

PRACTICE TASK

As students roll the ball, they sing, "Swing back" and then step long and low (bend to get low) and swing forward and release. They should release the ball low and smooth so that it rolls *all* the way to the partner without bouncing. Then the partner returns the ball in the same manner.

Goal   Roll the ball low and smooth with no bounces.

Cues

- Roll low and smooth.
- Swing back and step.

GAME 2

Repeat game 1.

CLOSURE

Review the backswing and step and forward swing, as well as a low, smooth, no-bounce release.

LESSON 3

Tactical Problem   Rolling for accuracy and direction

Game   Rolling a ball at a pin

Lesson Focus   Stepping and following through toward the target

Objective   Identify the target line and then send the ball in the direction of the pin by stepping and following through along the target line.

GAME 1

Knockdown (roll a ball to knock down a pin)

Goal   Knock down the pin three times in a row.

Conditions   Position a pin and partner at one end and a roller at the other, approximately 10 to 15 feet (3 to 4.6 m) apart. Partners switch after 10 trials. Tape or draw a line from the foul line to the pin to serve as a target line.

Questions

> Q: How did you roll the ball to knock down the pin?
>
> A: Got in a start position, aimed, stepped, and rolled the ball at the pin.
>
> Q: In which direction did you step?
>
> A: Straight, toward the pin.
>
> Q: What other body parts went straight toward the pin?
>
> A: The hand on the forward swing and follow-through.
>
> Q: When is the best time to think about the direction of your step and follow-through?
>
> A: Before rolling the ball.

PRACTICE TASK 1

Students perform five rolls, freezing at the end of each roll to have a partner check to see whether the step and release hand are pointing directly toward the pin. If the pin is knocked down, the student takes one step back. Students who miss the pin take one step forward. After five rolls, students switch with their partners. They need to think about and pick a good start position before rolling the ball and see how far back they can go and still knock down the pin.

Goal   Get three steps back from the starting point in five rolls.

Cues

- Step *to* the target.
- Follow through *to* the target.
- Think before you roll.

Question

Q: *Besides stepping and following through to the target, was there anything else you used to get the ball to roll straight to the target?*

A: *The target line.*

PRACTICE TASK 2

Repeat the practice with players using the target line as they step and follow through to the target. They freeze at the end of the roll and have their partners check to see if the step and release hand are pointing directly toward the pin. Those who knock down the pin take one step back. Those who miss the pin take one step forward. After five rolls, players switch with their partners and try to get farther back than they did before.

Goal   Get three steps back in five rolls.

Cues

- Step *to* the target.
- Follow through *to* the target.
- Think before you roll.

GAME 2

Knockdown (roll a ball to knock down a pin)

Goal   Knock down the pin three times on three rolls from three increasingly longer distances.

Conditions   Players who knock down the pin three times in a row should step back one step and roll again. Once they miss, they switch places with their partners.

CLOSURE

Review the key elements of the roll (step and follow through *to* the target) and target line that influence the direction in which the ball travels. Emphasize looking where to throw (use the target line) before throwing.

LESSON 4

Elementary Level I

Tactical Problem   Rolling for accuracy and direction

Game   Rolling a ball at a pin

Lesson Focus   Selecting an intermediate target

Objective   Select the intermediate target that will result in consistently knocking down the pin.

GAME 1

Knockdown (roll a ball to knock down a pin)

Goal   Roll the ball and knock down the pin three times in a row.

Conditions

- Students work in pairs; one rolls the ball and the other retrieves the ball, rolls it back, and sets up the pin.
- The pin is approximately 15 to 20 feet (4.6 to 6 m) away.
- Students switch after three turns.
- The class is set up with pairs parallel to each other, all rolling in the same direction (figure 10.2).
- Place three stickers on the floor to designate a start position behind the foul line; place three stickers slightly ahead of the foul line, 6 to 18 inches (15 to 46 cm), to serve as intermediate targets.
- Use one plastic bowling pin per pair and an assortment of balls so that the children can choose the one that works best for them (Graham, Holt/Hale, and Parker 2013).

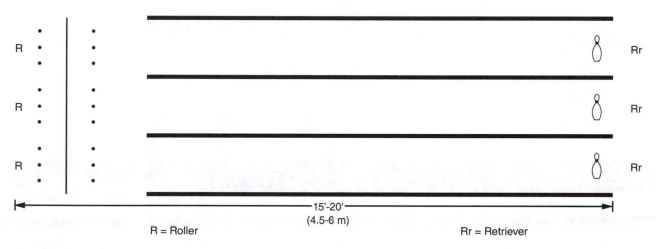

Figure 10.2

Questions

Q: How many of you were able to knock down the pin three times in a row?

A: (No one or very few.)

Q: Why is it so hard to hit the pin three times in a row?

A: It is too far away.

Q: Instead of aiming for the pin, way down there, where else could you aim?

A: At the stickers in front of the line.

Q: Which sticker would work best?

A: Don't know.

PRACTICE TASK

Students select one of the stickers behind the line so they have the same starting place every time. They roll two balls over the first sticker, two over the second sticker, and two over the third sticker to determine which works best to help them knock down the pin. Make sure they roll the ball right over the intermediate target sticker.

Goal   Roll over the intermediate target three times in a row.

Cues

- Start the *same*.
- Roll the ball *over* the sticker.

Questions

Q: Which sticker worked the best for you?

A: (Left, right, or middle.)

Q: Why does aiming at the sticker work better than aiming at the pin?

A: Because it is closer.

Q: Does anyone know what you call a target that is closer?

A: An intermediate target.

Q: Why do you want to always start the same and use an intermediate target?

A: So that you can knock down the pin on every roll.

GAME 2

Repeat game 1.

CLOSURE

Review the key points related to starting in the same spot and using an intermediate target.

LESSON 5

Tactical Problem   Rolling for accuracy and distance

Game   Rolling a ball at a pin

Lesson Focus   The relationship of the length of the backswing and the step to the force needed to roll the ball a greater distance

Objective   Demonstrate an understanding of the concept that the longer the backswing is, the greater the force and the farther the ball will roll; and adjust the backswing relative to the distance needed to consistently knock down the pin.

GAME 1

Knockdown (roll a ball to knock down a pin)

Goal   Roll the ball and knock the pin down twice from each distance.

Conditions

- Students work in pairs; one rolls the ball and the other retrieves the ball and rolls it back and sets up the pin.
- Students switch after two turns at each of the three distances.
- The pin is set at the closest spot for the first two trials, the middle spot for the next two trials, and the farthest spot for the last two trials (figure 10.3).
- Remind students to start the same each time and to use an intermediate target to send the ball in the right direction.

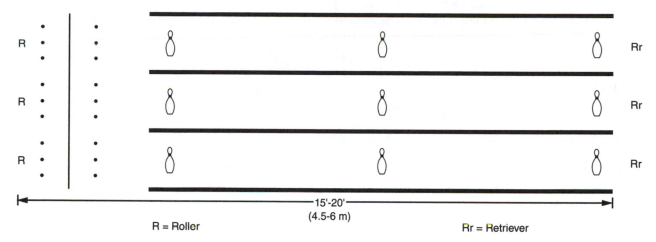

R = Roller   15'-20'
(4.5-6 m)   Rr = Retriever

Figure 10.3

Questions

Q: How did you swing your arm when you rolled the ball at the spot nearest you, compared to when you rolled the ball at the spot farthest from you? Stand up and show me how you moved your arm when the spot was near. Now, show me how you moved your arm when the spot was far away.

A: More arm swing when the pin is far away, and less when it is near.

Q: Why does the ball go farther, or a longer distance, when your arm goes back farther?

A: It gives more power and speed.

Q: When would you want more force?

A: When the pin is far away.

Q: How do you swing your arm when you want more force?

A: Way back.

Q: When would you want less force?

A: When the pin is near.

Q: How do you swing your arm back when you want less force?

A: Just a little bit.

PRACTICE TASK

Have students practice using a shorter backswing when the pin is near and a longer backswing when the pin is far away. If they reach the goal, they ask their partners to set the pin back one step. They should determine the farthest distance they can roll the ball and still hit the pin.

Goal   Knock down the pin two times in a row from each distance.

Cues

- Big swing *far.*
- Little swing *near.*

Questions

Q: Besides swinging your arm back farther, what can you do to roll the ball a farther distance?

A: Use a longer step; use a longer forward swing and follow-through.

Q: Besides helping you create more force and roll the ball a farther distance, how does the step and follow-through help you knock down the pin?

A: It helps to roll the ball in the right direction toward the pin.

GAME 2

Knockdown (roll a ball to knock down a pin)

Goal   Knock down the pin from as far away as possible.

Conditions

- Return to game 1, except have players set up the pin one step farther every time they knock it down.
- Partners switch after two misses in a row.
- Students use a longer step when the pin is far away and a shorter step (or no step) when the pin is near.

CLOSURE

Review the key points related to the concept that the longer the step and arm swing are, the greater the force and the farther the roll will be.

LEVEL II

Level II lessons emphasize the need to adjust the starting point, target line, and intermediate target. Although three pins may seem to be a bigger target, more accuracy is required to knock down all three pins because of the need to hit the "pocket." You may choose to use terms similar to those used in bowling, such as *headpin* and *pocket*. We do recommend referring to the pins by number: number 1 for the headpin, number 2 for the 2-pin, and number 3 for the 3-pin. Level II lessons can be expanded to include more pins, with 5-pin being the most logical extension. This will involve more adjustments in preshot decisions and will be a good lead-in to 10-pin bowling. Scoring can also be added when students are ready, and it is often good content to integrate into the classroom setting.

Level II students work on striking more difficult targets.

LESSON 6

Tactical Problem   Rolling for accuracy and direction

Game   3-pin

Lesson Focus   Adjusting the start position, target line, and intermediate target

Objective   Adjust the start position, target line, and intermediate target to consistently hit the pocket.

GAME 1

3-pin

Goal   Knock down all three pins three times in a row.

Conditions

- Three pins (1, 2, and 3) and a partner are at one end, and a roller is at the other end approximately 15 to 20 feet (4.6 to 6 m) away.
- Partners switch after every three trials.

Questions

Q: *(Pointing to the 3-pin setup) Will someone show me the best place to hit the pins so that they all fall down?*

A: *Between the 1 and 2 (2 and 3 for left-handed rollers).*

Q: *When you had just one pin, you rolled the ball right down the middle. Where do you want to roll the ball to hit between the 1- and 2-pins?*

A: *From the right side of the lane.*

Q: *If you want to roll the ball down the right side, where should you stand?*

A: *On the right side of the lane.*

PRACTICE TASK 1

Have students use footprints to help them find a good starting point. They put the footprints in what they think will be a good spot and try them out by taking two rolls. If after two rolls they do not hit between the 1- and 2-pin, they should adjust the footprints and take another two rolls. Once they have their footprints at a good starting point, their partners set up their footprints.

Goal   Adjust the footprints to obtain a good start position.

Condition   Adjust the footprints and take two rolls.

Questions

Q: *How many of you were able to find a good starting point?*

A: *(All.)*

Q: *Besides a starting point, what should you think about before you roll?*

A: *The target line and the intermediate target.*

Q: *Where is the target line?*

A: *Between the ball (where the ball is released) and the 1- and 2-pins.*

Q: What is the intermediate target?

A: The dot (marked on the lane) that goes along that line.

Q: Why do you want to use an intermediate target?

A: It is closer to aim at than the pins way down the lane.

PRACTICE TASK 2

Students go back to their lanes and look for a target line and the dot (intermediate target) they will use to aim. They try out their intermediate target twice to see if it works. If not, they pick another intermediate target and try it twice. After they find their intermediate target, they mark it (with a sticker) so they will know where it is when they roll the ball. Next their partner takes a turn while they go to the other end to set pins and roll the ball back.

Goal   Use the intermediate target to improve accuracy.

Cues

- Pick an intermediate target.
- Take two rolls.

GAME 2

Repeat game 1.

CLOSURE

Review how to make adjustments to the starting point, target line, and intermediate target when shooting at three pins instead of one pin. Emphasize thinking about where and how to stand before rolling the ball.

LESSON 7

Elementary Level II

Tactical Problem   Rolling for accuracy and direction

Game   3-pin

Lesson Focus   Adjusting the start position, target line, and intermediate target

Objective   Adjust the start position, target line, and intermediate target on the second roll to consistently hit the remaining pin(s).

GAME 1

3-pin

Goal   If you do not knock down all three pins with the first ball, knock down the remaining pins with the second ball.

Conditions

- Three pins (1, 2, and 3) and a partner are at one end, and a roller is at the other end approximately 15 to 20 feet (4.6 to 6 m) away.
- Players attempt to knock down all three pins with the first ball and the remaining pins with the second ball.
- Partners switch after every six trials.

Questions

> Q: *Is knocking down three pins the same as knocking down one pin?* **(Point to a 3-pin setup and a setup with one pin remaining.)**
>
> A: *No.*
>
> Q: *If you do not knock down all the pins with the first ball, what should you do to be sure you knock down the remaining pins?*
>
> A: *Change the start point and the intermediate target.*
>
> Q: *What if you have the 1-pin (headpin) and another pin remaining? Do you need to change your starting point and the intermediate target?*
>
> A: *No.*

PRACTICE TASK 1

Players use the footprints to find a starting point and dots to find an intermediate target when aiming for the 3-pin. They place the footprints in what they believe will be a good spot and try them out by taking two rolls. If after two rolls they do not hit the 3-pin, they adjust the footprints again and take another two rolls. Once they have their footprints at a good starting point, their partners set up their footprints.

Goal   Knock down all pins in two rolls

Cue   Line up your footprints with your intermediate target.

Questions

> Q: *How many of you were able to find a good starting point and intermediate target to knock down the 3-pin?*
>
> A: *(All.)*
>
> Q: *If you left the 2-pin, would your start position and intermediate target be the same?*
>
> A: *No.*
>
> Q: *Where would they be?*
>
> A: *Not sure.*

PRACTICE TASK 2

Players use the footprints to find a starting point and dots to find an intermediate target when aiming for the 2-pin. They place the footprints in what they believe will be a good spot and try them out by taking two rolls. If after two rolls they do not hit the 2-pin, they adjust the footprints again and take another two rolls. Once they have their footprints at a good starting point, their partners set up their footprints.

Cue   Line up your footprints with your intermediate target.

GAME 2

Repeat game 1.

CLOSURE

Review how to make adjustments to the starting point, target line, and intermediate target when shooting at three pins instead of one pin. Emphasize thinking about where and how to stand before rolling the ball.

Tactical Problem   Rolling for accuracy and direction

Game   3-pin

Lesson Focus   Adjusting the start position, target line, and intermediate target

Objective   Adjust the start position, target line, and intermediate target on the second roll to consistently hit the remaining pin(s).

GAME 1

3-pin

Goal   If you do not knock down all three pins with the first ball, knock down the remaining pins with the second ball.

Conditions

- Three pins (1, 2, and 3) and a partner are at one end, and a roller is at the other end approximately 15 to 20 feet (4.6 to 6 m) away.
- Players attempt to knock down all three pins with the first ball and the remaining pins with the second ball. They keep score to see how many pins they have knocked down after four rolls.
- If they do not knock down all three pins after the second roll, they set up three pins for a third roll.
- Partners switch after every four rolls.

Questions

Q: *How many of you were able to knock down 12 pins on four rolls?*

A: *(No one.)*

Q: *How many of you are hitting between the 1- and 2-pin when three pins are standing?*

A: *(Some.)*

Q: *What should you do before you roll to knock down the pins?*

A: *Find a starting point, target line, and intermediate target.*

Q: *What happens to your starting point, target line, and intermediate target when you're aiming at the 2-pin or the 3-pin?*

A: *They are different.*

PRACTICE TASK

Players use the footprints to find a starting point and dots to find an intermediate target when aiming for the three setups (all three pins, 2-pin, and 3-pin). First, they must figure out where their footprints and intermediate target need to be when all three pins are standing. They take two turns to be sure they are right. Then, they let their partners have a turn to figure out where their footprints and intermediate targets need to be. They repeat the process for the 2-pin and 3-pin. (Different-colored dry-erase markers can be used to mark start positions and intermediate targets.)

Goal   Best use of footprints and intermediate target to improve accuracy

Cue   Line up your footprints with your intermediate target.

GAME 2

3-pin

Goal   Same as game 1. Compare the scores of game 1 and game 2.

Conditions   Same as game 1

CLOSURE

Review how to make adjustments to the starting point, target line, and intermediate target when shooting at three pins instead of one pin. Emphasize thinking about where and how to stand before rolling the ball.

LEVEL III

Level III lessons involve a different game, bocce. However, bocce skills and tactics transfer easily from bowling. The emphasis here should be on adjusting the starting point, target line, and intermediate target as the target changes, and on adjusting the speed of the arm swing and the length of the backswing as the target gets closer or farther away. Although this sounds simple enough, accuracy requires control and consistency, which takes considerable practice and time to develop. Initially, some students may have to be prompted to take their time and intentionally think through their preshot decisions.

Level III students learn a fun new game—bocce!

LESSON 9

Elementary Level III

Tactical Problem   Rolling for accuracy and direction

Game   Bocce

Lesson Focus   Adjusting the start position, target line, and intermediate target

Objective   Determine the start position, target line, and intermediate target to get the ball close to the jack on each roll.

GAME 1

Bocce

Goal Score 2 points on every roll.

Conditions

- Play on grass or carpet.
- Foam balls can be used on a fast surface.
- Place the jack in a permanent position; players, who each have two balls, try to get their balls closest to the jack.
- Players alternate until each player has rolled two balls.
- The ball closest to the jack scores 2 points.
- A player with two balls closer than the balls of the other player scores 4 points—2 points for each ball that is closest to the jack.

Questions

Q: How many of you were able to score 2 points on every roll?

A: (No one.)

Q: If you were rolling a ball to knock down some pins, what would you do before you rolled?

A: Pick a starting point, target line, and intermediate target.

Q: Because this too is a target game, do you think that tactic will work here?

A: Yes.

PRACTICE TASK

Players use the footprints to find a starting point and dots to find an intermediate target when aiming for the jack. First, they must figure out where their footprints and intermediate targets are and then let their partners figure out where to place their footprints and intermediate targets. Each player takes two or three turns to be sure the placements are right. (You can use stickers to mark start positions and intermediate targets.)

Goal Use footprints and intermediate target to improve accuracy.

Cue Line up your footprints with your intermediate target.

GAME 2

Bocce

Goal Same as game 1. Compare the scores of game 1 and game 2.

Conditions Same as game 1

CLOSURE

Review how to make adjustments to the starting point, target line, and intermediate target when shooting at the jack. Emphasize the similarities among target games.

Tactical Problem   Rolling for accuracy and direction

Game   Bocce

Lesson Focus   Adjusting the start position, target line, and intermediate target

Objective   Determine the start position, target line, and intermediate target to get the ball close to the jack on each roll.

GAME 1

Bocce

Goal   Score 2 points on every roll.

Conditions

- Play on grass or carpet.
- Foam balls can be used on a fast surface.
- The player who will go second rolls the jack out about 15 to 20 feet (4.6 to 6 m).
- Players try to get each of their two balls closest to the jack.
- Players alternate until each has rolled two balls.
- The ball closest to the jack scores 2 points. A player with two balls closer than the balls of the other player scores 4 points—2 points for each ball that is closest to the jack.

Questions

Q: How many of you were able to score 2 points on every roll?

A: (No one.)

Q: What happens to your starting point, target line, and intermediate target when the jack is in a different place?

A: They change.

Q: What should you do before you roll?

A: Figure out the new starting point, target line, and intermediate target.

PRACTICE TASK

Players play three rounds using footprints and dots to mark their intermediate targets. Every time the jack is in a new position, players must figure out where their footprints and intermediate targets are and then let their partners figure out where to place their footprints and intermediate targets. Then they play the round and repeat the process on each new roll of the jack.

Goal   Use footprints and intermediate target to improve accuracy.

Cue   Line up your footprints with your intermediate target.

GAME 2

Bocce (without footprints, but intermediate target can still be used)

Goal   Compare the scores of game 1 and game 2.

Conditions   Same as game 1.

CLOSURE

Review how to make adjustments to the starting point, target line, and intermediate target when shooting at the jack. Emphasize the similarities among target games.

LESSON 11

Tactical Problem   Rolling for accuracy and distance

Game   Bocce

Lesson Focus   Adjusting the speed of the arm swing and the length of the backswing

Objective   Adjust the speed and length of the backswing and arm swing depending on the distance from the jack.

GAME 1

Bocce

Goal   Score 2 points on every roll.

Conditions

- Play on grass or carpet.
- Foam balls can be used on a fast surface.
- Place the jack in a permanent position; players try to get each of their two balls closest to the jack.
- Players alternate until both have rolled both balls.
- The ball closest to the jack scores 2 points.
- A player with two balls closer than the balls of the other player scores 4 points—2 points for each ball that is closest to the jack.

Questions

Q: *How many of you were able to score 2 points on every roll?*

A: *(No one.)*

Q: *Why aren't you getting your ball close to the jack?*

A: *Rolling too long or too short or not consistently.*

Q: *In the last lesson we worked on adjusting the starting point and intermediate target. What do you need to adjust when the roll is too long or too short?*

A: *The arm swing.*

Q: *Watch my arm as I roll the ball at the jack 20 feet (6 m) away, then 10 feet (3 m) away. How is it different?*

A: *Faster at 20 feet (6 m) and a longer backswing.*

PRACTICE TASK

Place jacks at 10, 15, and 20 feet (3, 4.6, and 6 m). Players throw six balls (two balls at each jack). Combine two teams and have them take turns rolling and retrieving. Players adjust the speed of the arm swing and the length of the backswing according to the distance from the jack.

Goal   Hit each jack with at least one ball.

Cue   The farther the jack is, the faster and longer the backswing must be.

GAME 2

Bocce

Goal   Same as game 1. Compare the scores of game 1 and game 2.

Conditions   Same as game 1

CLOSURE

Review how to make adjustments to the varying distances of the jack by changing the speed of the arm swing and the length of the backswing. Emphasize the use of feedback from the previous throw to adjust the next throw.

SUMMARY

In closing, we emphasize the fact that the tactical problems related to target games transfer across game categories to invasion, net and wall, and striking and fielding games. For example, the concept of a contact point is applicable to batting, volleyball, tennis, soccer, and many other games. The concept of a release point relates to throwing a baseball and shooting a basketball, just to name a couple. This provides further justification for including target games in the elementary physical education curriculum.

Part III

Lesson Plans for a Tactical Games Approach at the Secondary Level

Developing Sport Performance

The 12 chapters in part III focus on building sport performance within specific games at the secondary level, beginning with five chapters on select invasion games. Invasion games have many similarities, particularly in terms of game decisions and both offensive and defensive off-the-ball movements. Obviously, the skills employed vary tremendously from game to game, but in terms of decisions and movement, students can easily transfer learning from one invasion game to another.

Of the five chapters on invasion games, the soccer chapter is probably the best for teaching other games such as hockey because of the tactical similarities of the games. A game such as ultimate Frisbee also uses many of the offensive and defensive concepts that soccer does. The other invasion games in this part—in particular, rugby and flag football—have specific rules that affect the way the game is played and contribute to its uniqueness. Situations such as setting screens in basketball; playing behind the goal in lacrosse; only passing backward (or sideways) in rugby; and starting, stopping, and resetting in flag football are not replicated in other invasion games.

The chapters on net games include volleyball, badminton, and tennis. Although there is a certain degree of skill transfer across these games it is perhaps not to the same extent as in invasion games. Likewise, the striking and fielding games of softball and cricket have some similarities in their basic concepts while also possessing their own uniqueness as do the target games of golf and bowling. We hope these sport-specific chapters will help develop the sport performance of your students.

Chapter 11

Soccer

This chapter illustrates a tactical approach to teaching soccer, an invasion game. Before starting, remember that two critical points form the basis for the lesson format. First, students practice for skill development *after* they have played a game form that presents a tactical problem requiring that skill. As the teacher, you can modify game forms so that students confront various problems. You can also ask questions that encourage students to think of solutions. Second, having practiced a skill gives students the opportunity to apply that skill and tactical awareness in a game. By providing this opportunity, you increase the probability that students will understand the value of skills in the relevant game context.

In this chapter, we make the following assumptions about facilities, equipment, and students' experience:

- Soccer is taught outdoors, although you can teach some lessons indoors.

- There is one soccer ball for every two students. If you must have more than two students for one ball, you can modify most activities to accommodate the situation.

- Cones are available for marking the suggested playing areas. It would be advantageous to permanently mark a series of 10-by-10-yard grids (10 by 10 yards is ideal, but you could vary the grids according to your available space). The 10-yard markings on an American football field can be useful for marking play areas.

- The size and weight of the soccer balls match students' development (i.e., younger students use smaller and lighter balls). It may also be necessary to use smaller or larger playing areas, depending on student development. Bear in mind that players with lower abilities need more space, not less, because greater space gives them more time to control and use the ball (assuming they stay spread out).

- Students have some experience playing soccer. We assume this because soccer was probably addressed to some extent at the elementary level, perhaps in combination with other invasion games as discussed in part II. Therefore, games start with 1v1 but move quickly to 3v3 and 6v6.

It is up to you to ask questions and give answers that will give students the fullest and most useful experience.

We do not overtly address the 11v11 game but accept that at the high school level, both teachers and students will want to spend some time in full-field play (if class size permits). We have limited

games to 6v6 because games of this size require less extensive positional knowledge on the part of either the teachers or the players. For a better understanding of the positional demands of the full-field game, consult one of the many available texts on soccer coaching.

All the lessons in this chapter begin with a game form. When determining the size of the teams for these game forms, consider the appropriate group size for skill practice. Keep students in their teams during skill practice to facilitate transitions among lesson stages.

For ease of reference, we include the tactical framework and levels of tactical complexity for soccer once more in tables 11.1 and 11.2. We briefly describe activities before beginning the specific lesson at each level.

LEVEL I

At level I, we suggest that students focus on maintaining possession of the ball and attacking the goal, because these are the fundamental tactical problems for invasion games. At this level we answer the questions of what to do and how to do it by focusing on

Table 11.1 Tactical Problems, Movements, and Skills in Soccer

Tactical problems	Off-the-ball movements	On-the-ball skills
SCORING (OFFENSE)		
Maintaining possession of the ball	• Dribbling for control • Supporting the ball carrier	• Passing—short and long • Control—feet, thigh, chest
Attacking the goal	Using a target player	Shooting, shielding, turning
Creating space in attack	• Crossover play • Overlapping run	• First-time passing • Crossover play • Overlapping run
Using space in attack	Timing runs to goal, shielding	• Width—dribbling, crossing, heading • Depth—shielding
PREVENTING SCORING (DEFENSE)		
Defending space	Marking, pressuring, preventing the turn, delaying, covering, making recovery runs	Clearing the ball
Defending the goal	Goalkeeping—positioning	Goalkeeping—receiving the ball, making saves, distributing (throwing and punting)
Winning the ball		Tackling—block, poke, slide
RESTARTING PLAY		
Throw-in—attacking and defending	Defensive marking at throw-ins	Executing a quick throw
Corner kick—attacking and defending	Defensive marking at corners	• Short corner kick • Near-post corner kick • Far-post corner kick
Free kick—attacking and defending	• Defending—marking at free kicks • Defending—setting a wall	Attacking—shooting from free kicks

Table 11.2 Levels of Tactical Complexity for Soccer

Tactical problems	Level I	Level II	Level III	Level IV	Level V
SCORING					
Maintaining possession of the ball	• Dribbling for control • Passing (short) • Control (with the feet)	Supporting the ball carrier		• Passing—long • Control—thigh, chest	
Attacking the goal	Shooting	• Shooting • Turning • Shielding	Using a target player		
Creating space in attack			First-time passing	Overlapping run	Crossover play
Using space in attack				Width—dribbling, crossing, heading	• Depth—shielding • Timing of runs to goal, shielding
PREVENTING SCORING					
Defending space		Marking, pressuring	Preventing the turn	Clearing the ball	Delaying, covering, making recovery runs
Defending the goal		• Goalkeeper positioning and receiving the ball • Distributing—throwing			• Goalkeeping—making saves • Distributing—punting
Winning the ball			Tackling—block, poke	Tackling—slide	
RESTARTING PLAY					
Throw-in—attacking and defending	Executing a quick throw	Defensive marking at throw-ins			
Corner kick—attacking and defending	Short corner kick	Defensive marking at corners	Near-post corner kick		Far-post corner kick
Free kick—attacking and defending			Attacking—shooting from free kicks		Defending—marking and setting a wall

players' actions when they possess the ball. Dribbling, passing, controlling the ball, and shooting are the primary solutions to maintaining possession and attacking the goal. We suggest beginning with dribbling because it is the natural inclination of the novice soccer player upon receiving the ball, and it allows players to move the ball away from opponents who are trying to regain possession. Adding simple restarts when the ball goes out of bounds at the sideline or goal line enables you to evolve a small-sided game at this level.

We do not recommend that you pay attention to defense at level I, although you could easily do so by using level II lessons. Our rationale for focusing only on the tactical problems of scoring is threefold. First, besides making students aware that each team should try to prevent the other from scoring, spending time on defense is not necessary for a modified game of soccer. Players need only focus on the essential tactical problems for a game to take place, which are maintaining possession and attacking the goal. Unless teams seek solutions to these problems, a modified game does not represent the mature form. Second, we believe that early success motivates students and that it is counterproductive to focus on preventing offensive success at level I. Third, because of time constraints, it is not possible to focus on all aspects of the game during an initial instructional unit.

When students are first learning soccer, they should focus on the fundamentals of dribbling.

LESSON 1

Tactical Problem   Maintaining possession of the ball

Lesson Focus   Dribbling to control the ball

Objective   Move the ball into space to avoid opponents and move the ball forward using controlled actions.

GAME 1

Setup   1v1 played in an area 20 by 10 yards marked with cones at each end. The dimensions can vary for this beginning game. It is possible to play without lines—just spread out the cones marking each game to allow for movement between them (from end to end), and don't be too concerned if one game overflows into another (overflow will only be temporary, and the players will still be working on their dribbling).

Goal   Stop the ball on the opponent's line (between the cones) to score.

Conditions

- After a goal is scored, the ball is returned to the player who conceded the goal.
- The player who scored must retire to halfway down the playing area.

Questions

Q: What is the goal of this game?

A: Get to the opponent's line and stop the ball.

Q: So, how do you get the ball to the line?

A: Dribble.

Q: What problem does the opponent give you?

A: She's in the way. You have to keep the ball away from her while you dribble.

Q: How many parts of the foot can you use as you dribble?

A: Six—the inside, outside, instep (i.e., the laces), sole, heel, and toe. (Teachers often fail to consider all of these surfaces as useful for ball manipulation, instead focusing on the inside of the foot. Although the inside of the foot is important, the outside is equally important for dribbling, and the other surfaces are crucial for changing direction.)

PRACTICE TASK

Setup   Students perform free dribbling within a specified area (of sufficient size matched to the number of students). Give one ball to each student or have students share a ball if necessary. Call "Turn" or "Speed up" or "Slow down" (or anything else that forces a change in direction or speed).

Goals

- Closely control the ball while dribbling.
- Quickly change speed and direction.

Cues

- Keep the ball close.
- Use all parts of both feet.
- Turn and move away at high speed.

Extensions

- You become the defender (along with some other students)—the dribbler has to dribble the ball past the defenders.
- Use a 1v1 possession game in 10 by 10 yards. Player A tries to keep the ball away from player B for five seconds.

GAME 2

Repeat game 1.

LESSON 2

Secondary Level I

Tactical Problem   Maintaining possession of the ball

Lesson Focus   Passing and receiving balls on the ground with the inside of the foot

Objectives

- Make accurate and firm, short passes.
- Use one touch to control and set up the next move.

GAME 1

Setup   3v3 possession game in 30 by 20 yards (figure 11.1)

Goal   Make five consecutive passes.

Questions

Q: *What must you do in this game?*

A: *Keep the ball.*

Q: *How can your team keep the ball?*

A: *Pass.*

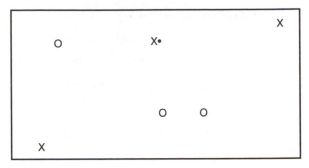

• = Ball

Figure 11.1

PRACTICE TASK

Setup   Partner (or triad) practice with players approximately 10 yards apart; players practice passing and controlling.

Goals

- Use one touch to control and set up the next pass.
- Firmly and accurately pass using the insides of both feet.

Cues

- Passing:
  - Face the direction in which you are passing.
  - Keep the nonkicking foot next to the ball.
  - Use the inside of the foot and square the foot to the ball.
  - Strike the ball through its center.

- Receiving:
  - Get in line with the ball as it comes.
  - Use one touch with the inside of the foot to set yourself up for the next pass.

Extension   Players pass and move to another space. The receiver has to look up and find the player who moved to give the next pass. Encourage the receiver to look twice—once as the ball is on the way and once after he has it under control—before passing.

GAME 2

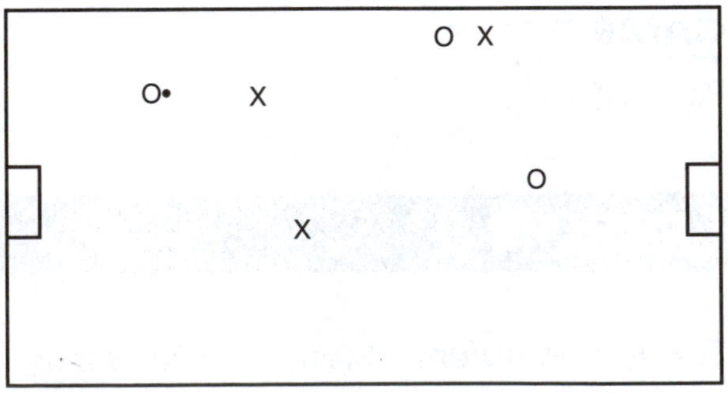

Setup   3v3 in 30 by 20 yards, narrow goal, no goalkeeper (figure 11.2)

Goals

- Use quick control and setup.
- Use firm and accurate passing.
- Keep your head up for vision.
- Score in the small goal.

• = Ball

Figure 11.2

Conditions

- Require a maximum of three touches before passing (depending on students' abilities).
- The ball must stay below head height (the head-height rule).

LESSON 3

Tactical Problem   Maintaining possession of the ball

Lesson Focus   Passing and receiving balls on the ground with the outside of the foot

Objectives

- Make accurate and firm, short passes.
- Use one touch to control and set up for the next move.

GAME 1

Setup   3v3 possession game in 30 by 20 yards (figure 11.3)

Goal   Make five consecutive passes.

Questions

Q: What must you do in this game?

A: Keep the ball.

Q: How can your team keep the ball?

A: Pass.

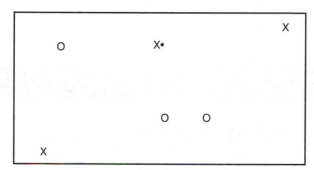

• = Ball

Figure 11.3

PRACTICE TASK

Setup   Partners practice passing and controlling or setting up when 5 to 10 yards apart.

Goals

- Use one touch to control and set up.
- Use firm and accurate passing with the outsides of both feet.

Cues

- Passing:
  - Face the direction in which you are passing.
  - Keep the nonkicking foot next to the ball.
  - Use the outside of the foot and point the toe inward.
  - Strike the ball through its center.
- Receiving:
  - Get in line with the ball as it comes.
  - Use one touch with the outside of the foot to set yourself up for the next pass.

GAME 2

Setup   3v3 in 30 by 20 yards, narrow goal, no goalkeeper (figure 11.4)

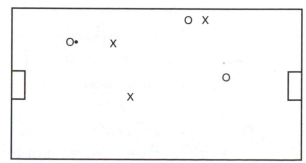

• = Ball

Figure 11.4

Goals

- Use quick control and setup.
- Use firm and accurate passing with the inside or outside of the foot as appropriate.
- Keep your head up for vision.
- Score in the small goal.

Conditions

- Require a maximum of three touches before passing (depending on students' abilities).
- Use the head-height rule.

LESSON 4

Tactical Problem   Attacking the goal

Lesson Focus   Shooting

Objectives   Learn the three principles of good shooting:

- Shoot on sight.
- Hit the target.
- Keep the shot low.

GAME 1

Setup   6v6 on small field of 30 by 30 yards with large goals (8 yards) (figure 11.5)

Goals

- Shoot when possible.
- Hit the target (the whole goal).

Questions

Q: *What should you do when you're this close to the goal?*

A: *Shoot.*

Q: *Why should you shoot?*

A: *Because if you don't shoot, you won't score!*

Q: *Where should you aim when you shoot?*

A: *At the whole goal so you can force the goalkeeper to make a save.*

Q: *Should you aim high or low?*

A: *Low.*

Q: *Why should you shoot low?*

A: *It's harder for the goalkeeper to go down to make a save.*

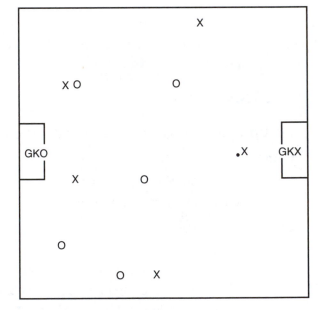

• = Ball   GK = Goalkeeper

Figure 11.5

PRACTICE TASK

Setup Partners practice (figure 11.6) with a static or moving ball (with goalkeepers if groups of three are needed).

Goals

- Shoot the ball between two posts or cones.
- Keep all shots below waist height.

Cues

- Take a long step to the ball.
- Keep the nonkicking foot next to the ball.
- Use the instep (or laces).
- Keep the head and toe down.

X   X   X   X   X

Cone   Cone   Cone   Cone   Cone   Cone

•X   •X   •X   •X   •X

Figure 11.6

GAME 2

Repeat game 1.

Goals

- Use a specific number of shots, depending on your ability.
- Make a specific number of on-target shots.

LESSON 5

Tactical Problem   Attacking the goal

Lesson Focus   Using a target player to create shooting opportunities

Objective   Use a target player to lay (pass) the ball off for a shot by a supporting player (see practice task).

GAME 1

Setup   6v6 in 50 by 40 yards, full-size goals (figure 11.7)

Goal   Get an early pass to a target player; then move to support the target player.

Conditions

- One target player per team (OT, XT).
- One defender marks the target player.

Questions

Q: What should other players do when their own target player has the ball?

A: Provide support.

Q: Where is a good place to support?

A: In a position to receive a pass and shoot.

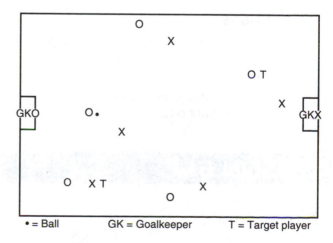

• = Ball   GK = Goalkeeper   T = Target player

Figure 11.7

PRACTICE TASK

Setup Students practice shooting from a target player layoff (pass) (figure 11.8); use one goalkeeper, one collector, one target player, and three or four shooters.

Goals

- Make an accurate pass to a target.
- As the target player, make a firm layoff (to the side).
- As the shooter, makes a clean strike of a moving ball.
- Make a specific number of shots on-target.

Cues

- Shooter:
    - Pass firmly to the target.
    - Run to the side of the target to receive the return pass.
- Shoot the moving ball immediately.
- Target player—Pass firmly to the side.

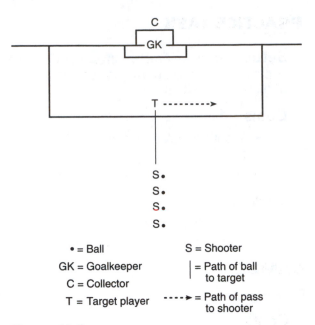

• = Ball	S = Shooter
GK = Goalkeeper	❘ = Path of ball to target
C = Collector	
T = Target player	----▶ = Path of pass to shooter

Figure 11.8

GAME 2

Setup 6v6 in 50 by 40 yards, full goal (figure 11.9)

Goals

- As the target player, shield or lay off.
- Support the target player.
- Make a specific number of shots on goal per team.

Conditions

- Players rotate being the target player.
- The target player cannot turn with the ball.
- Goals scored from a layoff by the target player count double.

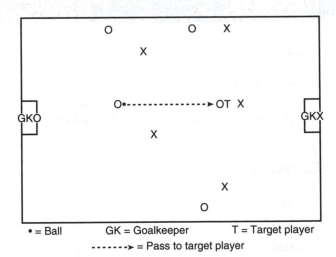

| • = Ball | GK = Goalkeeper | T = Target player |
| ------▶ = Pass to target player | | |

Figure 11.9

LESSON 6

Tactical Problem Restarting play

Lesson Focus Throwing in

Objective Quickly make a correct throw-in to move the attack forward.

Teaching Sport Concepts and Skills

GAME 1

Setup   6v6 in 60 by 30 yards, full goal (figure 11.10), narrow field so the ball goes out of play often and players must take many throw-ins

Goal   Take quick throw-ins.

Question

Q: *How can you quickly get the ball into play on a throw-in?*

A: *Player O1 throws to the nearest player (O2), who passes it back to O1.*

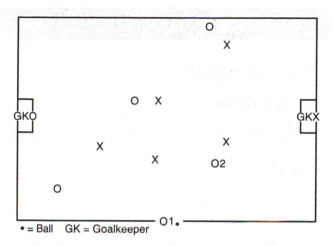

• = Ball   GK = Goalkeeper

Figure 11.10

PRACTICE TASK 1

Setup   Partners practice throwing, controlling, and returning.

Cues

- Thrower:
  - Use two hands.
  - Take the ball behind the head.
  - Keep two feet on the ground at all times.
  - Throw to the receiver's feet and move onto the field.

- Receiver—Control and return the ball to the thrower.

PRACTICE TASK 2

Setup   2v1 (defender O) in 30 by 10 yards (figure 11.11)

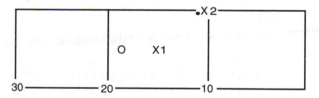

Figure 11.11

Goals

- As the receiver (X1) of the throw-in, turn with the ball or pass the ball back to a teammate (X2).
- Players X1 and X2 try get the ball to the 30-yard line under control by combining together against the defender (2v1).

Conditions

- The attack starts with a throw-in at the 10-yard line.
- The support player (X2) must get free to receive the return pass.

Cues

- Thrower (X2):
  - Use two hands.
  - Take the ball behind the head.
  - Keep two feet on the ground at all times.
  - Throw to the receiver's feet and move onto the field.

- Receiver (X1)—Control and return the ball to the thrower.

GAME 2

Repeat game 1.

Tactical Problem   Restarting play

Lesson Focus   Attacking at corner kicks, the short corner

Objective   Use corners to create scoring opportunities.

GAME 1

Setup   6v6 in 40 by 50 yards, full goal, referee calls many corners (figure 11.12)

Goal   Be aware of the corner kick as a chance to score.

Question

Q: *How can you use a corner to score?*

A: *Get the ball into the center.*

PRACTICE TASK

Setup   Team practice, unopposed (no goalkeeper), short corners (figure 11.13)

Goal   Use short corners to attack the goal.

Cues

- The two attackers (X5, X6) go to the corner.
- Attacker X5 quickly passes to attacker X6.
- Attacker X6 dribbles closer to the goal before passing or shooting.

GAME 2

Repeat game 1.

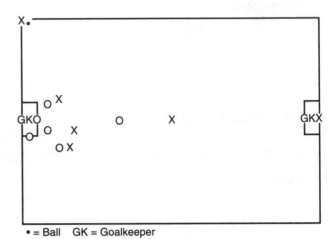

• = Ball   GK = Goalkeeper

Figure 11.12

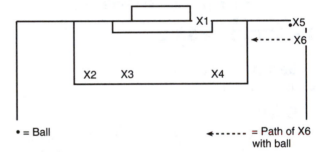

• = Ball

◄------ = Path of X6 with ball

Figure 11.13

LEVEL II

At level II, students again focus on the tactical problems of maintaining possession of the ball and attacking the goal, but they progress to defending the goal and defending space. The focus of maintaining possession now shifts from solutions for players who have the ball to contributions of teammates without the ball. This early focus on off-the-ball movement is critical because soccer players spend much more time without the ball, and they should spend this time in productive movement. As in all invasion games, players need to learn when and where they should move to help their team keep possession of the ball.

After paying additional attention to attacking the goal, students focus on defending space and the goal. It is appropriate to shift the focus to defense because students will understand that they must solve defensive problems for their team to succeed. Modified games at level II enable students to see the value in marking, or guarding, opponents and in having the goalkeeper properly positioned to receive the ball when it comes. Brief attention to the goalkeeper's distribution of the ball allows the game to develop in complexity by the end of level II. Distribution at this level consists of rolling or throwing the ball, which is more appropriate than kicking in small-sided games.

It is important for players to learn to pay attention to those without the ball for potential plays.

LESSON 8

Tactical Problem   Maintaining possession of the ball

Lesson Focus   Supporting the ball carrier

Objective   Be positioned to receive a pass.

GAME 1

Setup   3v3 in 30 by 20 yards, narrow goal (figure 11.14)

Goals

- Accurately pass with the insides and outsides of the feet.
- Move into position to receive a pass.
- When you have the ball, look for support.

Conditions

- Require three touches (each player has two touches to receive the ball and one to pass or shoot).
- Use the head-height rule.

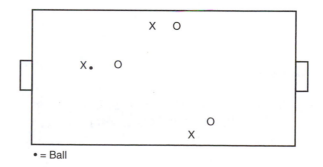

• = Ball

Figure 11.14

Questions

Q: How can players without the ball help a player who has the ball?

A: Be in a position to receive a pass.

Q: Where should supporting players go?

A: Away from defenders into open space.

Q: Any open space?

A: Anywhere you can receive a pass—into a passing lane (this could be behind a teammate with the ball if necessary).

PRACTICE TASK

Setup 2v1 in 20 by 10 yards, pass and support (figure 11.15), two attackers (X and S). On the signal, the defender (O) attacks the ball, the supporter (S) moves to one side, and the attacker (X) draws the defender and passes. Players play for six passes or until player O wins the ball.

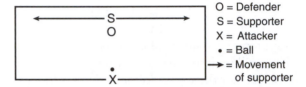

Figure 11.15

Goals

- The supporting player moves to a good position.
- The attacker (X) waits for the defender (O) to close in before passing.

Condition Players perform three repetitions and rotate.

Cues

- The defender attacks the ball on the signal.
- The supporter moves quickly to the side.
- The attacker passes as the defender advances.

GAME 2

Repeat game 1.

LESSON 9 🔵

Tactical Problem Maintaining possession of the ball

Lesson Focus Supporting the ball carrier

Objective Support the player with the ball constantly.

GAME 1

Setup 4v4 (minimum) or 6v6 (maximum) in 40 by 30 yards, full or narrow goal (figure 11.16)

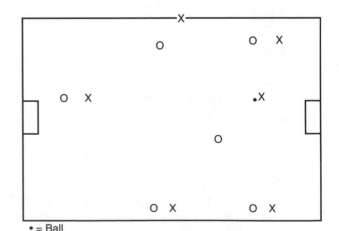

Figure 11.16

Teaching Sport Concepts and Skills

Goals

- Be in a position to receive a pass.
- Be aware that the ball carrier needs support to be able to pass.

Conditions

- Require three touches (depending on abilities).
- Use the head-height rule.

Questions

Q: How can players without the ball help a player who has the ball?

A: Be in position to receive a pass.

Q: Where should supporting players go?

A: Away from defenders and into a passing lane.

PRACTICE TASK 1

Setup 3v1 (passive defender) in 10 by 10 yards, unopposed possession (figure 11.17)

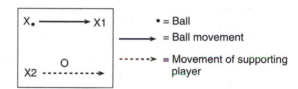

Figure 11.17

Goals

- Be aware of the best location for support.
- Provide two options for the ball carrier.

Cues

- As the ball is passed, player X2 moves to support the player who will give the next pass (X1).
- Move quickly and call for the ball.

PRACTICE TASK 2

Setup 3v1 (active defender) in 10 by 10 yards, possession (figure 11.18); rotate the defender at 10 passes or when the ball goes out of the grid.

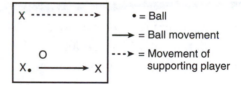

Figure 11.18

Goals

- Make 10 consecutive passes with the ball in the grid.
- Provide two options for the ball carrier.
- Use the maximum possible angle of support.

Condition The defender must attack the ball.

Cues

- Move to support the passer (don't get stuck with a defender between you and the ball).
- Move quickly and call.
- Wait for the defender to come to you before passing.
- Use firm passes.

GAME 2

Repeat game 1.

Goals

- Give the ball carrier two open receivers.
- Support quickly and call for the ball.

LESSON 10

Tactical Problem   Attacking the goal

Lesson Focus   Turning with the ball

Objective   Make quick turns while in possession of the ball.

GAME 1

Setup   1v1 in 20 by 10 yards, two feeders (F) (figure 11.19). If player O wins the ball from player X, she becomes the attacker.

Goal   Receive a pass from a feeder and turn to pass to the other feeder.

Questions

> Q: What does the attacker need to do in this situation?
>
> A: Turn quickly.
>
> Q: How can the attacker turn past the defender?
>
> A: Flick with the outside of the foot and move forward onto the ball.

Figure 11.19

PRACTICE TASK

Setup   Partners 10 yards apart practice receiving passes and turning.

Cues

- Receive and turn in one move.
- Push the ball with the outside of the foot.
- Use a clock analogy (receive the ball from 12 o'clock and push it to 4 or 8 o'clock).

GAME 2

Setup   3v3 in 20 by 20 yards, two feeders (figure 11.20)

Goals

- Receive the pass from a feeder.
- Work as a team to pass to the other feeder.

Conditions

- Each pass to a feeder earns 1 point.
- Players cannot return a pass to the feeder who gave the pass.

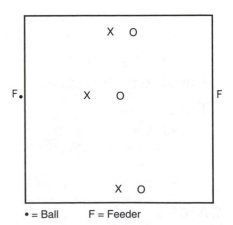

Figure 11.20

LESSON 11

Tactical Problem   Attacking the goal

Lesson Focus   Shooting

Objectives

- Receive the ball and execute a quick shot on target.
- Follow the shot for a rebound.

GAME 1

Setup   Shooting derby, 2v2 in 30 by 20 yards (figure 11.21), with two feeders, one goalkeeper, and one collector (eight players total) and a full goal. Players switch every eight trials.

Goal   Use one touch to control; then shoot on target.

Question

Q: *If you receive the ball this close to the goal, what should you do?*

A: *Turn and shoot.*

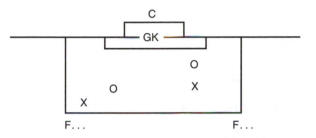

GK = Goalkeeper
C = Collector
F = Feeder
. . . = Several soccer balls

Figure 11.21

PRACTICE TASK

Setup   Pressure shooting in a penalty area (figure 11.22), with three shooters (alternating every three shots), two feeders, one goalkeeper, and two collectors. Players switch every eight trials.

Goal   Make a specific number of shots on target.

Cue   Set up for a shot with one touch to the right or left (left if the pass is from the left feeder, right if the pass is from the right feeder).

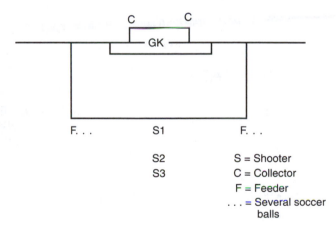

S = Shooter
C = Collector
F = Feeder
. . . = Several soccer balls

Figure 11.22

GAME 2

Setup   4v4 in 30 by 20 yards, full goal

Goals

- Make an even number of shots from 10 and 20 yards.
- Make a specific number of shots on target.

LESSON 12

Tactical Problem   Defending space

Lesson Focus   Marking (guarding) and pressuring the ball

Objective   Understand the need to mark players and to pressure the ball to defend space.

GAME 1

Setup   4v4 in 40 by 30 yards, full goal

Goals

- Be in position between an opponent and your own goal.
- Be in position so you can see the opponent and the ball.

Condition   Mark (or guard) an opposing player.

Questions

Q: How can you make it hard for opponents to receive the ball?

A: Mark (or guard) them.

Q: Where should you stand to mark them?

A: Between the opponent and the goal.

Q: As the ball nears your opponent, what should you do?

A: Get closer to the opponent.

Q: As your opponent nears your goal, what should you do?

A: Again, get closer to the opponent.

PRACTICE TASK

Setup   1v1 plus two feeders in 20 by 10 yards (figure 11.23)

Goals

- Prevent the opponent from turning.
- Keep an appropriate distance.
- Use an appropriate stance.

Conditions

- Position feeders at 0 and 20 yards.
- Have players alternate feeds.

Cues

- Close down the opponent quickly.
- Stop one arm's length away.
- Get low.

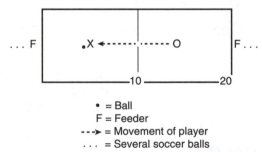

- • = Ball
- F = Feeder
- - - ➤ = Movement of player
- . . . = Several soccer balls

Figure 11.23

- Use a staggered stance.
- Wait for the opponent to try to turn.
- Don't dive into the tackle.

GAME 2

Repeat game 1.

Goals

- Close the space between you and the opponent as the ball is played.
- Prevent the opponent from turning.

LESSON 13

Tactical Problem   Defending the goal

Lesson Focus   Goalkeeping and positioning

Objective   As goalkeeper, be positioned to narrow the angle.

GAME 1

Setup   2v2 in 20 by 20 yards, full goal with one goalkeeper per team (figure 11.24)

Goal   Give the attacker as little a target to shoot at as possible.

Condition   The goalkeeper cannot come past the 10-yard line.

Question

> Q: How can the goalkeeper give the attacker less area to shoot at?
>
> A: Move out or sideways to narrow the angle.

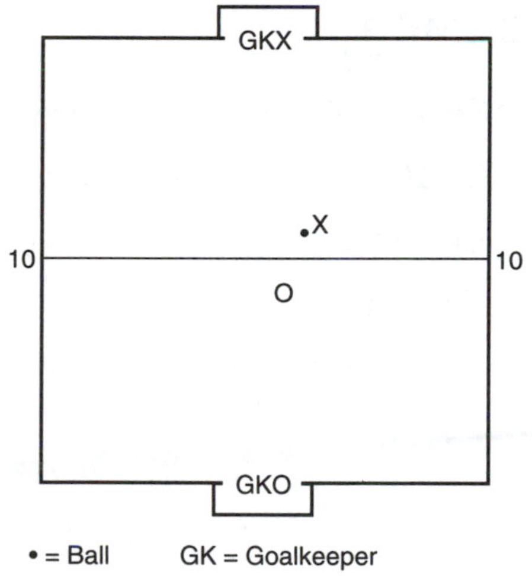

PRACTICE TASK

Setup   Goalkeeper versus goalkeeper (1v1) in 20 by 20 yards, full goal (figure 11.25)

Goals

- Move to narrow the angle.
- Move side to side and off the line.

Conditions

- Players start dribbling from 0 yards each time.
- Players shoot from a different point outside 10 yards each time.

Cues

- Come off the goal line toward the ball.
- Stay low.

• = Ball   GK = Goalkeeper

Figure 11.24

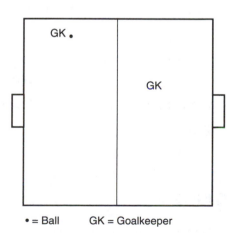

• = Ball   GK = Goalkeeper

Figure 11.25

GAME 2

Setup 4v4 in 40 by 30 yards, full goal, rotate goalkeepers

Goals

- Move to narrow the angle.
- Move side to side and off the line.

LESSON 14

Tactical Problem Defending the goal

Lesson Focus Goalkeeping, gathering the ball

Objectives

- Get the body behind the ball.
- Bring the ball into the chest.

GAME 1

Setup Goalkeeper versus goalkeeper (1v1) in 20 by 10 yards

Goal Get in line with the oncoming shot.

Condition Players use cooperative shots at half pace.

Questions

Q: Where should the goalkeeper be positioned to stop the ball?

A: In line with the ball.

Q: What is the best way to securely hold the ball?

A: Cradled into the chest.

PRACTICE TASK

Setup Partner practice (hand feeds at low, medium, and high heights)

Goals

- Get your body behind the ball (in line with the shot).
- Take the ball into your chest.

Condition Players make their partners move as they improve.

Cues

- Get in line with the oncoming shot.
- Take the ball into your chest.
- Cradle the ball.
- Protect the ball.

GAME 2

Setup 2v2 in 20 by 20 yards, full goal plus goalkeepers

Goals

- Narrow the angle.
- Put your body behind the ball.
- Take the ball into your chest.

LEVEL III

Level III builds directly on level II, further investigating the tactical problems of attacking the goal and defending space. We increase tactical complexity by adding the issues of creating space in attack and winning the ball. We investigate additional methods of restarting play—specifically, using restarts to score. Because we are increasing tactical complexity at level III, skill requirements also increase. We assume that students have learned the material covered in levels I and II and therefore have some degree of technical competence accompanying their developing understanding. Although technical and tactical competencies develop at different rates for different students, level III is likely suitable for upper middle school or beginning high school students (about ages 13 through 15).

Introducing an offensive target player at level III shows students how to create shooting opportunities as a team. An emphasis on one-touch passing enables them to more effectively create space to increase their opportunities for shooting. With the introduction of the target player, students must investigate solutions to prevent this target player from turning with the ball and attacking the space between them and the goal. At level III, the game looks more developed both offensively and defensively.

Level III introduces free kicks, of which there are two types:

- The direct free kick is awarded for most offenses, including pushing, tripping, and using hands on the ball. The player taking the free kick may shoot directly at goal.

- The indirect free kick is awarded for offenses such as unsporting conduct or obstruction (of an opponent when the ball is not playable). The ball must be touched by two players before a goal can be scored.

Learning how to create space and form an attack is important to achieving a goal.

LESSON 15

Secondary Level III

Tactical Problem   Maintaining possession of the ball

Lesson Focus   Supporting the ball carrier

Objective   Provide support so the passer can split the defense (i.e., pass the ball between two defenders).

GAME 1

Setup 2v2 to target player in 30 by 20 yards, with two target players (OT and XT) along the end line (a total of 3v3) (figure 11.26)

Goal Get the ball to the target player (who can move along the end line).

Conditions

- Require three touches.
- Use the head-height rule.

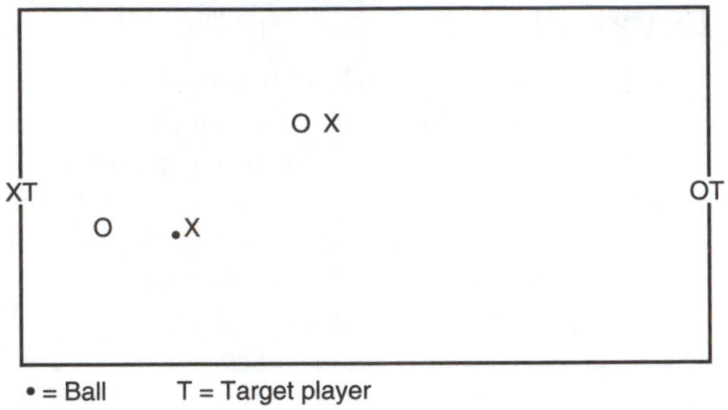

Question

Q: How can the target player help teammates find him?

A: Constantly move sideways along the end line to support teammates.

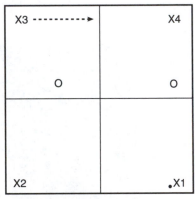

• = Ball   T = Target player

Figure 11.26

PRACTICE TASK

Setup 4v2 (defenders) possession game in 20 by 20 yards (figure 11.27)

Goals

- Make 10 consecutive passes (splitting defenders with a pass counts as two passes).
- Give an angle of support so the passer can split the defense.

Condition Defenders must attack the ball.

Cues

- The passer splits the defenders.
- Supporters position themselves so the passer can split the defenders.

• = Ball

- - - - - ▶ = Movement of supporting player (X3) so passer (X1) can split defenders

Figure 11.27

GAME 2

Setup 6v6 in 50 by 40 yards, full goal

Goal Split defenders with a pass to put a teammate in a scoring position.

Condition Use the head-height rule.

LESSON 16

Tactical Problem Attacking the goal

Lesson Focus Penetrating using a target player

Objective Use a target player for early penetration.

Teaching Sport Concepts and Skills

GAME 1

Setup   4v4 in 30 by 20 yards, full goal (figure 11.28)

Goals

- Get the ball to the target player quickly with an accurate pass.
- As the target player, hold the ball and threaten the goal.

Condition   Each team must leave a target player in the opponent's half and a central defender in its own half.

Question

Q: *What can the target player do when she receives the ball?*

A: *Hold (keep possession of the ball), turn, or lay off.*

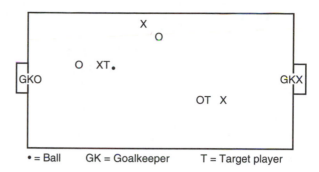

• = Ball   GK = Goalkeeper   T = Target player

Figure 11.28

PRACTICE TASK

Setup   2v1 to goal (plus one goalkeeper) in 20 by 10 yards (figure 11.29). Play starts with a feed to the target player by a support player, and players switch roles every four trials.

Goal   As the target player, hold, shield and turn, or lay off (make a short sideways pass) to a teammate.

Cues

- Target player:
  - Hold.
  - Turn and shoot.
  - Look for support.
  - Follow the shot for a rebound.
- Support player—Support the target player.

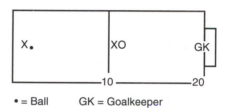

• = Ball   GK = Goalkeeper

Figure 11.29

GAME 2

Repeat game 1.

Goal   As the target player, hold and turn or hold and lay off to supporting players.

LESSON 17

Secondary Level III

Tactical Problem   Creating space in attack

Lesson Focus   One-touch (or first-time) passing

Objective   Use a first-time pass to create space (a first-time pass is one given immediately without using any touches to control the ball).

GAME 1

Setup   2v2 plus two players per team at the outside corners in 20 by 20 yards for a total of 4v4 (figure 11.30)

Goals

- Take possession.
- Make 10 passes.

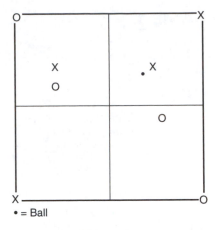

Conditions

- Four players in the grid can use only the first-time pass. Outside players can move 10 yards along each line.
- Inside players cannot tackle outside players.

Question

Q: *What does the first-time pass enable you to do?*

A: *Move the ball quickly.*

Figure 11.30

PRACTICE TASK

Setup   3v1 pressure pass using two balls (figure 11.31) with first-time passes (alternate balls)

Goal   Accurately redirect the ball using a first-time pass to the player without the ball.

Figure 11.31

Cues

- Decide early where the ball has to go.
- Redirect the ball with the inside or outside of the foot.

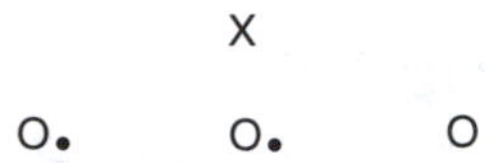

GAME 2

Setup   4v4 in 40 by 30 yards, small goals, no goalkeeper

Goals

- Move the ball quickly.
- Offer quick support.

Condition   Two players per team must play one touch (designate one of these players as a target player) and then rotate.

LESSON 18

Secondary Level III

Tactical Problem   Creating space in attack

Lesson Focus   One-touch passing

Objective   Use a first-time pass to beat a defender (one-two play).

Teaching Sport Concepts and Skills

GAME 1

Setup   2v1 to a target player (T) in 30 by 10 yards (figure 11.32). Play starts with a feed to a defender (O) at 20 yards; the defender gives a first-time pass back and moves forward.

Goal   As a team, players X1 and X2 must get the ball to the target player.

Condition   The defender must go to the ball.

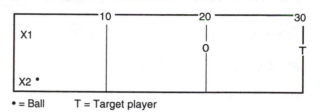

Figure 11.32

Question

Q: How can two players help each other beat one defender?

A: Use a give-and-go, or one-two play.

PRACTICE TASK

Setup   2v2 with passive defenders on 10 and 30 yards in 40 by 10 yards (figure 11.33)

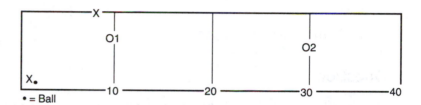

Figure 11.33

Conditions

- The defenders must go to the ball.
- Each defender can advance only a maximum of 10 yards.
- Attackers must beat each defender with a give-and-go play.
- Player O1 stops once beaten. Player O2 moves only when the ball crosses the 20-yard mark.

Cues

- Supporter:
  - Position yourself ahead of the ball.
  - Return the pass (first time) behind the defender.
- Ball carrier:
  - Draw the defender toward you.
  - Give (pass) and go (for return).

GAME 2

Repeat game 1.

Goal   Use appropriate timing in the give-and-go play.

GAME 3

Setup   4v4 in 40 by 30 yards, small goals, no goalkeeper

Goal   Use a give-and-go play at appropriate times to beat opponents.

Conditions

- Two players per team play one touch and then rotate.
- An extra goal is awarded for a give-and-go play that beats an opponent.

Tactical Problem   Winning the ball

Lesson Focus   Containing and tackling

Objectives

- Stay on one's feet.
- Make a solid tackle.

GAME 1

Setup   3v3 in 30 by 20 yards, no goal (figure 11.34)

Goal   Control the ball and get it to the 30-yard line.

Condition   Take on an opponent (try to dribble around her) before passing.

Question

> Q: How can you slow an attacker and win the ball?
>
> A: Channel (i.e., guide the opponent in a particular direction) and tackle.

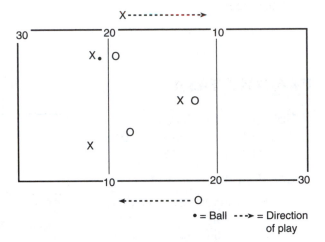

Figure 11.34

PRACTICE TASK 1

Setup   1v1 in 20 by 10 yards. The defender (O) passes the ball to an attacker (X) and advances to close him down. The attacker (X) tries to dribble around the defender (O) to the 20-yard line (figure 11.35).

Goal   Channel and tackle.

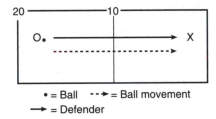

Figure 11.35

Conditions

- The defender feeds from 20 yards.
- The defender can move to close down the attacker when the ball crosses 10 yards.

Cues

- Close quickly to about 6 feet (2 m).
- Adopt a staggered stance in front and to one side of the opponent.
- Channel the attacker to his weak side (i.e., to his left if he is right-footed).
- Stay on your feet and wait for the attacker to move (to go around you).
- Get your foot in for a solid tackle (or poke the ball out of play).

PRACTICE TASK 2

Setup 1v1 block tackle practice (standing). On a count of three, both players use the inside of the same foot to make a solid tackle on the ball.

Goal Make a firm tackle.

GAME 2

Repeat game 1.

LESSON 20

Tactical Problem Restarting play

Lesson Focus Using a near-post corner kick

Objective Use a near-post corner to create scoring opportunities.

GAME 1

Setup 6v6 in 40 by 50 yards, full goal, referee calls many corners

Goal Be aware of a corner as a chance to score.

Condition Place an offensive player on the near (front) post for each corner.

Question

> Q: How can the near-post corner be effective?

> A: The near-post player can redirect the ball for incoming attackers.

PRACTICE TASK

Setup Team practice, unopposed, at the near-post corner (figure 11.36)

Goal Use a near-post corner to score.

Cues

- Corner taker (X1)—Aim for the head of the near-post player (X2).
- Near-post player (X2)—Redirect the ball back and out with the head or foot (a flick).
- Attackers (X3, X4, and X5)—Run to meet the flick.

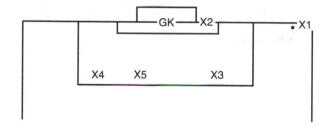

• = Ball   GK = Goalkeeper

Figure 11.36

GAME 2

Repeat game 1.

LESSON 21

Secondary Level III

Tactical Problem Restarting play

Lesson Focus Attacking with free kicks

Objective Use free kicks to score.

GAME 1

Setup 6v6 in 60 by 40 yards, full goal, referee calls many free kicks while players are in a variety of positions on the field

Goal Be aware of free kicks as scoring opportunities.

Question

Q: How can you use a free kick to threaten the goal?

A: Shoot, pass, or cross depending on the position of the free kick.

PRACTICE TASK

Setup Team practice, opposed, direct or indirect free kicks from a variety of angles, three teams working at each goal. All free kicks are from outside the penalty area (figure 11.37).

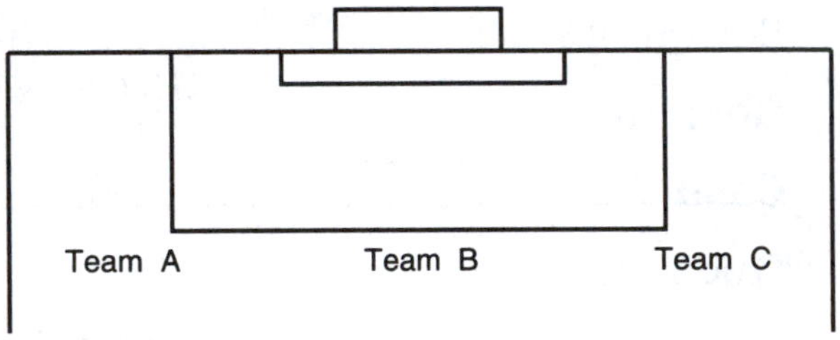
Team A
Team B
Team C

Figure 11.37

Goal Attack from a free kick using different strategies (including the shot, chip, and cross) depending on the angle and type of kick.

Cues

- When shooting, hit the target.
- Pass the ball into the shooter's path.
- Cross to the center of the goal area.

GAME 2

Repeat game 1.

LEVEL IV

At the beginning of level IV, students revisit maintaining possession of the ball because they are able to investigate this tactical problem in a larger playing area. Solutions to the problem include controlling the ball with the thigh and chest and long passing. A focus on using the overlapping run to create space provides additional width in attack, which students must now use effectively. Solutions to the problem of using this space include dribbling, crossing the ball, and heading toward the goal. These skills are used in bigger playing spaces, making level IV more suitable for high school students with some soccer experience and ability.

The offensive focus on crossing and heading necessitates further attention to the defensive problems this focus creates. These problems are defending space in the penalty area and winning the ball from offensive opponents in wide positions. Solutions include clearing the ball and making sliding tackles.

Maintaining possession of the ball is an important skill to hone.

LESSON 22

Secondary Level IV

Tactical Problem   Maintaining possession of the ball

Lesson Focus   Long passing

Objective   Use a long pass to keep possession and switch play.

GAME 1

Setup   6v6 in 60 by 40 yards, full goal

Goal   Use the long pass to switch defense to attack quickly.

Condition   Require one target player per team (have players rotate into this position).

Questions

Q: How can you use the space on the field?

A: Stay spread out.

Q: How can a long pass help you?

A: It reaches teammates who are away from the ball and helps you quickly move from defense to attack.

PRACTICE TASK

Setup   Long pass, partner practice, static and rolling balls

Goal   Make a long and accurate pass above head height.

Cues

- Take a long step to the ball.
- Keep the nonkicking foot next to the ball.
- Place the kicking foot under the ball.
- Contact the ball with the top of the foot (laces of the shoe).
- Lean back as you follow through.

GAME 2

Repeat game 1.

LESSON 23

Tactical Problem   Maintaining possession of the ball

Lesson Focus   Receiving the long pass

Objective   Control and set up the ball with feet, thigh, and chest.

GAME 1

Setup   4v4 throw and control game in 50 by 40 yards, no goals

Goal   Control the ball and stop it on the goal line.

Condition   Players practice throwing and controlling. Player A throws to player B, who controls the ball with any part of her body and then picks it up and throws it to another player on her team. In this way players progress down the field.

Question

Q: What must you do to succeed in receiving a long pass?

A: Receive and control the ball from the air.

PRACTICE TASK

Setup   Partner practice, hand-feeding to feet, thigh, chest

Goals

- Bring the ball down to your feet quickly.
- Kill the bounce and set up for the next move to right, left, or front.

Cues

- Foot:
  - Kill the bounce with the inside or outside of the foot.
  - Drag the foot across the ball to kill the bounce.

- Thigh:
  - Bring the thigh up to the ball.
  - Withdraw the thigh on impact.
  - Kill the bounce when the ball falls.
- Chest:
  - Bring the chest out to the ball.
  - Withdraw the chest on impact.
  - Kill the bounce when the ball falls.

GAME 2

Setup 4v4 in 60 by 40 yards, no goals

Goal Control the ball and stop it on the goal line.

Conditions

- Each team has a target player (players rotate into this position).
- Require a 10-yard dribble maximum.

LESSON 24

Tactical Problem Maintaining possession of the ball

Lesson Focus Combining short and long passing

Objective Use a combination of short and long passes to maintain possession.

GAME 1

Setup 6v6 possession game in 60 by 40 yards, no goal (figure 11.38)

Goal Control the ball and stop it on the goal line.

Conditions

- Require three touches.
- Teams consist of two forwards, two players midfield, two defenders.

Questions

Q: Is it best to use long or short passes or a combination of both?

A: Combination.

Q: What do short passes do to the defenders?

A: Bring them in toward the ball.

Q: Leaving space for what?

A: Longer passes to space behind the defenders.

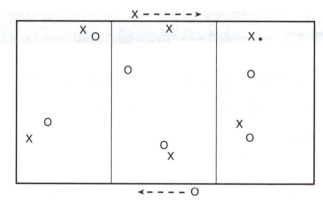

• = Ball   - - - ➤ = Movement of player

Figure 11.38

PRACTICE TASK

Setup 4v4 possession game plus two outside corner players per team in 30 by 20 yards for a total of 6v6 (figure 11.39)

Goals

- Combine short and long passes to keep the ball.
- Use short passes to draw opponents.
- Follow with long pass to open up the game.

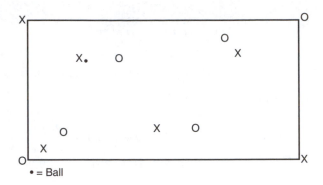

• = Ball

Figure 11.39

Conditions

- Corner players can move 10 yards along each sideline.
- Inside players cannot tackle players at outside corners.

Cue Short, short, short (passes to draw in opponents), long (pass to the space that has been created).

GAME 2

Setup 6v6 in 60 by 40 yards, full goals, no restrictions

Goal Combine short and long passes to maintain possession and move the ball into a scoring position.

LESSON 25

Secondary Level IV

Tactical Problem Creating space in attack

Lesson Focus Overlapping run

Objective Use overlapping runs to create space at the flanks (overlapping is made by a supporting player around the side of a teammate with the ball, usually at the side of the field).

GAME 1

Setup 6v6 in 30 by 50 yards, short and wide, full goal

Goal Be aware of the need to use width to best advantage in attack.

Questions

Q: *Where is the most space on the field?*

A: *In wide areas.*

Q: *How can you use this space?*

A: *Get players into wide areas to receive a pass.*

Q: *What can wide players do when they get the ball?*

A: *Cross the ball into the center.*

PRACTICE TASK

Setup Overlap and cross drill (figure 11.40). Passer (X) passes to target player (T); player X overlaps, receives a return pass from player T, and crosses the ball. Nonpasser (Y) and target player (T) run to the center of the goal to meet the cross.

Extension Player Y overlaps, receives a pass from player T, and crosses. Player X passes to player T, and players X and T run to the center of the goal.

Goals

- Make quick overlapping runs.
- Use good timing when passing to the runner.

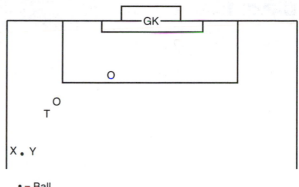

• = Ball
GK = Goalkeeper
T = Target player
Y = Nonpasser

Figure 11.40

Conditions

- Use static defenders (O) at first; then change to active defenders (O).
- Player X passes to player T and runs wide around player T (using an overlapping run down the sideline).
- Player T receives and passes the ball back into player X's path.
- Player Y sprints to the center of the goal area.

Cues

- Pass and go round
- Receive and give it back
- Go hard to the goal

GAME 2

Repeat game 1.

Goal Use the overlapping run in game situations.

Condition When passing to the wing, players must follow the pass to overlap the receiver.

LESSON 26

Tactical Problem Using space in attack

Lesson Focus Using width in attack

Objectives

- Be aware of areas of the field best suited to dribbling.
- Acquire dribbling skills.

GAME 1

Setup 6v6 in 50 by 50 yards, short and wide, full goal

Goal Be aware of the areas of the field that contain the most space in attack (i.e., the flanks or wings).

Question

Q: Other than making a cross, what do wide players have space to do?

A: Run at and around defenders; dribble.

PRACTICE TASK 1

Setup Players are in threes doing a continuous dribbling relay.

Goals

- Control with the insides and outsides of both feet.
- Work on pace and change of pace.

Cues

- Push or stroke the ball.
- Keep the ball close.

PRACTICE TASK 2

Setup Repeat task 1 with a cone for a defender.

Goals

- Beat the defender (i.e., the cone) with the ball.
- Perform a push and run, fake shot and push, and step over and push.

Cues

- Push and run.
- Fake the shot and push (the ball around the cone with the outside of the foot).
- Accelerate.

GAME 2

Repeat game 1.

Goal Attack the space behind the opponent whenever possible.

Condition Mark or guard 1v1.

LESSON 27

Secondary Level IV

Tactical Problem Using space in attack

Lesson Focus Using width in attack

Objective Beat a defender with the dribble.

GAME 1

Setup   2v2 to the opposite goal line in 30 by 20 yards

Goal   Be aware of the need to move forward when teammates are marked and of the need to get past an opposing defender while keeping the ball under control.

Condition   Mark or guard 1v1.

Questions

> Q: *If there is space behind your opponent, what can you do?*
>
> A: *Go around her.*
>
> Q: *How?*
>
> A: *Dribble, push the ball past, and accelerate.*

PRACTICE TASK 1

Setup   1v3 in 30 by 10 yards, static defenders on 10, 20, and 30 yards (figure 11.41)

Goals

- Beat each defender in turn and cross the 30-yard line with the ball under control.
- If tackled, retrieve the ball and continue to the next defender.
- Use the push and run, feint shot and push, and step over and push.

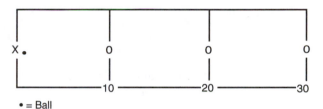

Figure 11.41

Condition

- Defenders cannot move.
- Defenders must give the ball back to the attacker if they win a tackle.

Cues

- Push and run.
- Feint and push.
- Accelerate.

PRACTICE TASK 2

Setup   Extend practice task 1.

Condition   Defenders can move only along their lines.

GAME 2

Setup   4v4 in 40 by 30 yards, small goals (no goalkeeper)

Goal   Beat opponents in a 1v1 game situation.

Conditions

- Use 1v1.
- Players attempt to beat an opponent before passing.

Tactical Problem   Using space in attack

Lesson Focus   Using width in attack

Objective   Deliver an accurate cross after the dribble.

GAME 1

Setup   4v3 (including goalkeeper) in 20 by 40 yards, short and wide. One feeder (F) feeds to any player X (figure 11.42).

Goals

- Attack to score from a cross.
- Be aware of the need for a good cross.
- In defense, bring the ball under control to the 20-yard line.

Question

Q: If you have a chance to deliver a cross, where should you aim?

A: Toward the center of the goal but away from the goalkeeper.

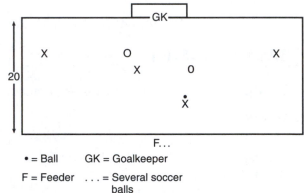

• = Ball   GK = Goalkeeper

F = Feeder   . . . = Several soccer balls

Figure 11.42

PRACTICE TASK

Setup   Continuous crossing drill in 60 by 50 yards, two full goals (figure 11.43). Crossers (X) dribble and cross away from the goalkeeper. The goalkeeper collects and feeds player X waiting at the side of the goal, and player X proceeds down the side of the field to cross the ball. After making a cross, player X moves to the side of the goal and waits for the next feed from the goalkeeper. Numbers in this practice can vary; figure 11.43 shows an eight-player drill rotating counterclockwise. Crosses come from right.

Goals

- Send a flighted ball from the wings.
- Cross the ball away from the goalkeeper.

Cues

- Move down the field quickly.
- Cross the ball away from the goalkeeper.

GAME 2

Setup   6v6 in 60 by 50 yards (plus one coach and one feeder per team). Alternate feeds for each team. The feeder must feed to either the right or left winger.

Goal   Maximize the use of the width of the field.

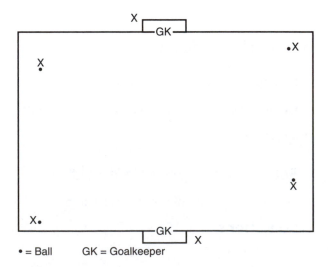

• = Ball   GK = Goalkeeper

Figure 11.43

Conditions

- Each team has two permanent wingers.
- Feeders give alternate feeds to each team and must feed to wingers.

LESSON 29

Tactical Problem   Using space in attack

Lesson Focus   Using width in attack

Objective   Score with the head.

GAME 1

Setup   Heading game, 3v3 in 30 by 20 yards, small goal

Goals

- Score with the head.
- Become aware of the need to use the head to change the direction of the ball.

Conditions

- The thrown ball must be headed to another teammate and caught (throw, head, throw, head).
- The game includes only throwing, heading, and catching (progress is made up the field in this way).
- Players must head the ball into the goal to score.

Questions

Q: When might you be able to score with your head?

A: From a cross.

Q: Where should you head the ball to?

A: At the goal and down.

Q: Why head it down?

A: To make it harder for the goalkeeper to make a save.

PRACTICE TASK 1

Setup   Static practice (figure 11.44) with one header (X) and two feeders (O). Each feeder has a ball. Player X receives alternating feeds from each player O and heads the ball back to the feeder.

Goals

- Use the correct contact point (hairline).
- Use the body for momentum.
- Head the ball down to a receiver.

O.   X   .O

Figure 11.44

Cues

- Get behind the ball.
- Contact the ball on the hairline.
- Use the trunk of your body for momentum.
- Head the ball down.

PRACTICE TASK 2

Setup   Three players set up in a right-angle (figure 11.45) with one header (X) and two feeders (O) and only one ball per group

Goal   Change direction with a header.

Cues

- Get behind the ball.
- Head across the ball's line of flight to change its direction.
- Contact the ball on the hairline.
- Use the trunk of your body for momentum.
- Head the ball down.

X   •O

O

Figure 11.45

GAME 2

Setup   6v6 in 60 by 40 yards, full goals

Goals

- Score with the head.
- Understand the value of using the full width of the field.

Conditions

- Have two permanent wingers per team.
- Players can only score with their heads.
- Players can pick up and hand-feed inside 10 yards if necessary because of low-quality crosses.

LESSON 30

Tactical Problem   Defending space

Lesson Focus   Clearing the ball

Objective   Clear the ball from danger using height, width, and length.

GAME 1

Setup   4v4 (three defenders plus goalkeeper), attack versus defense in 30 by 50 yards (figure 11.46)

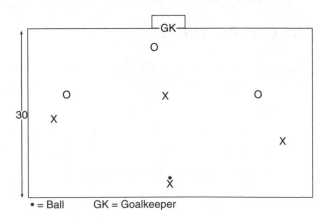

Figure 11.46

Goals

- Attack and score.
- As a defender, keep the ball away from the goal.

Conditions

- Play offense against defense. Offense restarts after a goal or if the ball goes out of bounds at the end line.
- Attack restarts at 30 yards.
- Players throw in as normal for a ball out at the sideline.
- Change offense and defense after three attacks.

Questions

Q: If a cross comes in, what should you do?

A: Clear it.

Q: Where should you clear to?

A: High, wide, and long, in that order.

Q: Why is the order important?

A: High gives you time to get under the ball again. Wide moves the ball away from the goal to the side. Long adds distance between you and the goal.

PRACTICE TASK

Setup   Clearances practice (figure 11.47) with high-thrown (for accuracy) feeds to the feet or head of each defender (O), with one feeder (F from wing). The defender clears the ball and goes to the back of the line to wait for the next feed. Also include one collector behind the goal and one behind the feeder.

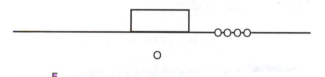

Figure 11.47

Goals

- As a defender, clear with height, width, and length.
- Clear the ball out of play at the nearest point if necessary (back over the feeder's head is ideal).

Cues

- Accelerate to meet the ball.
- Clear as high, wide, and long as possible.
- Clear away from, not across, the goal.

GAME 2

Repeat game 1.

LESSON 31

Tactical Problem   Winning the ball

Lesson Focus   Slide tackle

Objective   Tackle at a stretch using poke and slide tackles.

GAME 1

Setup   All-in tackling in 20 by 20 yards

Goal   Tackle at a stretch with the poke or block.

Conditions   Players knock out other balls but keep their own. Once a ball is out, players go to an adjoining 20- by 20-yard grid and start again.

Questions

> *Q: If you cannot stay on your feet to tackle, what must you do?*
>
> *A: Go down on the ground to tackle, but make sure you win the ball.*
>
> *Q: How should you go down?*
>
> *A: Slide.*

PRACTICE TASK

Setup   1v1 slide tackle practice in 20 by 10 yards (figure 11.48)

Goals

- Use the correct position and technique for the slide tackle.
- Make slide tackles inside 20 yards.

Conditions

- Both defender (O) and attacker (X) start at 0 yards.
- Player O can only tackle after player X starts to run with the ball at medium speed.

Cues

- Get close to the ball carrier.
- Fold under the leg nearest to your opponent as you slide.
- Knock the ball with your other leg (left leg in figure 11.48).

GAME 2

Setup   5v5 in 60 by 40 yards, full goal with goalkeeper

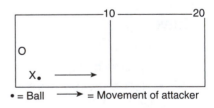

Figure 11.48

Goals

- Mark, channel the opponent, and tackle using the most appropriate technique.
- Use the slide tackle as a last resort.

Condition   Use the head-height rule.

LEVEL V

By the time students reach level V, the game is tactically complex and approaching its mature form. There is more large-field play, and solutions to tactical problems require more advanced movements and teamwork. For example, additional solutions for creating space include the crossover play for either a shot or a cross. Additional use of space includes adding depth to the attack by appropriately timing supporting runs toward the goal.

Defending space also becomes more complex at this level, as students learn how to cover each other and how to recover to provide depth in defense. Because attacking players are shooting more effectively at this level, goalkeeping should develop to include diving to make saves and distributing the ball over greater distances. Level V culminates with a further investigation of offensive and defensive aspects of restarting play.

Level V represents content for advanced soccer players and might be most appropriate for an elective class of experienced players. The atmosphere in this type of class might resemble that of a coaching environment.

Once ready, students can use all they have learned by practicing in large fields of play.

LESSON 32

Secondary Level V

Tactical Problem   Using space in attack

Lesson Focus   Using depth in attack

Objective   Understand the value and use of support from behind.

GAME 1

Setup   4v4 in 40 by 30 yards, full goal

Goal   See the value of supporting from a defensive position.

Conditions
- Have a target player on each team.
- Players cannot turn with the ball.

Question

Q: What options are available to the target player when he receives the ball?

A: Pass to the side or passing back.

PRACTICE TASK 1

Setup   3v1 in 30 by 20 yards (figure 11.49)

Goals

- Get the ball to 30 yards.
- As the target player, control and shield the ball, pass to either teammate (X), and run forward or diagonally for the return pass.

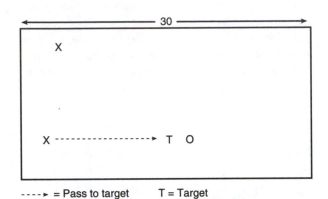

Figure 11.49

Conditions

- Play starts with a feed to the feet of the target player (T) at 15 yards.
- Allow only three touches (two touches to control the ball, one to pass) to speed up the game.
- The defender (O) must go to the ball.

Cues   Target player—Look for support at the side and behind.

PRACTICE TASK 2

Setup   4v2 in 40 by 30 yards (extension of practice task 1)

Goals

- Get the ball to 40 yards.
- As the target player, control and shield the ball, pass to a teammate, and run forward or diagonally for the return pass.

Conditions

- Play starts with a feed to the feet of the target player (T) at 20 yards.
- Allow three touches.
- Defenders must go to the ball.

GAME 2

Repeat game 1.

LESSON 33

Secondary Level V

Tactical Problem   Using space in attack

Lesson Focus   Using depth in attack

Objective   Make well-timed attacking runs to the penalty area.

GAME 1

Setup Groups of eight, 2v2 plus two crossers (CO and CX) and two goalkeepers in 30 by 50 yards, short and wide (figure 11.50)

Goal Understand that a static attacker is easier to mark than a moving one.

Conditions

- The goalkeeper must feed a crosser (who is unopposed).
- The crosser serves the ball toward the opposing goal.

Questions

Q: Where should you (X1 and X2) be located as the ball is crossed—level with, behind, or in front of the ball?

A: Behind the ball.

Q: Why?

A: So you can move forward onto the cross.

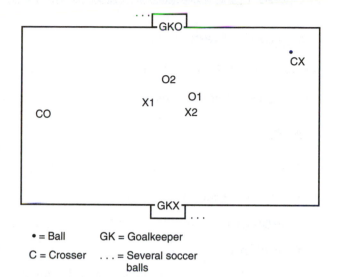

• = Ball   GK = Goalkeeper

C = Crosser   . . . = Several soccer balls

Figure 11.50

PRACTICE TASK

Setup In pairs (figure 11.51), the striker feeds the winger, the winger crosses, and the striker finishes. Players switch roles.

Goals

- Time the run so the striker moves onto the cross.
- Score with the head or foot.

Cues

- Striker:
  - Hold the run and stay behind the ball.
  - Wait for the cross and move onto it.
- Winger: Cross away from the goalkeeper.

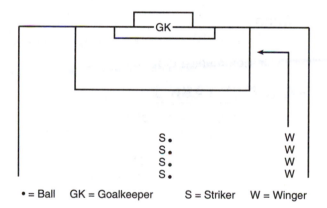

• = Ball   GK = Goalkeeper   S = Striker   W = Winger

Figure 11.51

GAME 2

Setup 4v4 in 40 by 50 yards, full goal

Goal Time runs to meet the crosses.

Condition Players use a maximum of three touches in central 20 yards (middle of field).

Tactical Problem   Creating space in attack

Lesson Focus   Crossover play

Objective   Use the crossover play to create space.

GAME 1

Setup   3v3 possession game in 20 by 20 yards

Goal   Be aware of the need to create space in a confined area.

Condition   Passes must be 10 yards or shorter.

Question

> Q: How can you create space in a confined area?
>
> A: Use short passes, crossover.

PRACTICE TASK 1

Setup   Free dribbling in 30 by 20 yards with crossovers, one ball per two players

Goal   Exchange possession by using a crossover with any player.

Cues

- Passer—Leave the ball for the receiver.
- Communicate by calling "Leave it" or "Mine," or call your name.

PRACTICE TASK 2

Situation drill, crossovers leading to a shot and cross (figure 11.52)

Goal   Be aware of situations in which the crossover play is most useful.

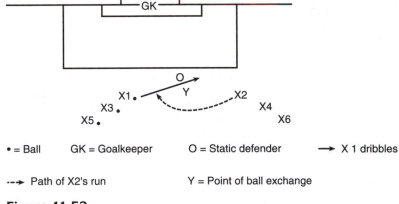

Conditions

- Receiving and shooting:
  - The passer (X1) leaves the ball for the receiver (X2).
  - Players communicate by saying "Leave it" or "Mine."
  - Player X2 receives and shoots.
- Receiving and crossing:
  - The drill begins with the ball in a wide position.
  - Passer (X2) leaves the ball for the receiver (X1).
  - Players communicate by saying "Leave it" or "Mine" or calling their own names.

• = Ball   GK = Goalkeeper   O = Static defender   → X 1 dribbles

--→ Path of X2's run   Y = Point of ball exchange

Figure 11.52

- Player X1 receives and crosses.
- Player X2 continues toward the goal to meet the cross.

Cues

- Takeover and shoot
- Communicate
- Receive and go wide
- Cross and finish

GAME 2

Setup   6v6 in 50 by 40 yards, full goal

Goal   Use crossover play to create space and a chance to score.

Condition   Players must perform one crossover play in the attacking half before approaching the goal in each attack.

LESSON 35

Tactical Problem   Defending space

Lesson Focus   Delaying the attack

Objectives

- Understand that the first role of the individual defender is to delay the attack, keeping the ball in front of him, to give teammates time to recover.
- Delay and channel.

GAME 1

Setup   3v3 (including goalkeeper) in 30 by 20 yards (figure 11.53) with one full goal, attack versus defense

Goal   Create uneven numbers.

Condition   Use the head-height rule (the ball must stay below head height).

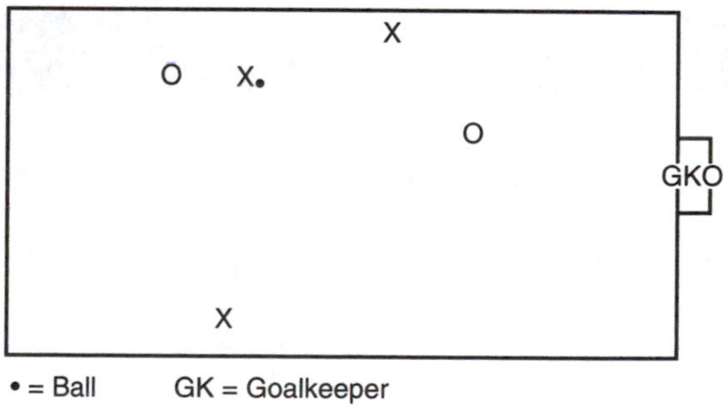

Questions

Q: What should you do if you have fewer defenders than your opponents have attackers?

A: Delay the attack to give teammates time to recover.

Q: How can you delay your opponents?

A: Use channeling to make the opponent go where you decide.

• = Ball   GK = Goalkeeper

Figure 11.53

PRACTICE TASK

Setup 2v1 in 30 by 10 yards, no goal (figure 11.54)

Goals

- Close space quickly.
- Don't dive in for a tackle; stay on your feet.
- Channel the path of the ball between your opponents to delay the attack (also known as jock-eying).
- Challenge for the ball at the appropriate moment.

Condition Attackers must control the ball and get it to the end line.

Cues for Defenders

- Close the space.
- Position to force the sideways pass.
- Move across and back; slide and drop back.

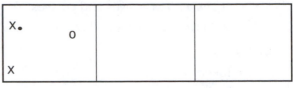

• = Ball

Figure 11.54

GAME 2

Setup 3v3 in 30 by 20 yards, two small goals (no goalkeeper)

Goals

- Close space quickly.
- Don't dive; stay on your feet.
- Channel the path of the ball.
- Challenge for the ball at the appropriate moment.

Condition Use the head-height rule.

LESSON 36

Secondary Level V

Tactical Problem Defending space

Lesson Focus Making recovery runs

Objective Make appropriate recovery runs to get between the ball and the goal and to cover the first defender.

GAME 1

Setup 2v2 in 30 by 10 yards

Goals

- Get the ball to the end line.
- Understand the need to cover teammates.

Condition Use the head-height rule.

Questions

Q: What should forward players do if one teammate is trying to delay an attack?

A: Recover to help defensively.

Q: Where should the recovering defenders recover to?

A: Behind the first defender.

PRACTICE TASK

Setup 2v1 plus one retreating defender in 30 by 10 yards (figure 11.55)

Goals

- Defenders should work as a pair to stop the attackers from reaching the end line (tandem defense).
- One defender goes to the ball; the other covers and stays with the opponent.

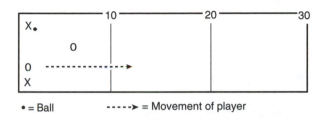

Figure 11.55

Conditions

- The retreating defender cannot move until the attackers start.
- The retreating defender must get goal side of (i.e., behind) the first defender before challenging for the ball.

Cues

- First defender—Delay the attack.
- Recovering defender—Recover quickly, moving behind teammate.
- Take your own opponent.
- Cover your teammate.
- Communicate.

GAME 2

Setup 4v4 in 40 by 30 yards, full goal with goalkeeper

Goals

- Defend in numbers.
- Get goal side.
- Cover for the first defender.
- Communicate.

Condition Use the head-height rule.

LESSON 37

Tactical Problem Defending the goal

Lesson Focus Goalkeeping, diving to save

Objectives

- Know when and how to dive to tip a ball around or over the goal.
- Work on saving in 1v1 situations.

GAME 1

Setup 2v2 in 20 by 10 yards, full goal plus goalkeeper (figure 11.56)

Goals

- Shoot on sight.
- Hit the target to force a save.

Question

Q: What are a goalkeeper's priorities in saving a shot?

A: Hold the ball if possible; tip the ball out of play if necessary. Do not give up rebounds.

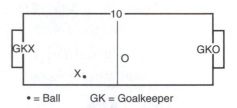

Figure 11.56

PRACTICE TASK

Setup Goalkeeper versus goalkeeper (1v1) in 20 by 10 yards, two full goals

Goals

- Tip the ball around the goal if you cannot hold it.
- If diving, take off from the foot nearest the ball.
- In 1v1, smother the ball at the attacker's feet.

Condition A player who takes the ball across the 10-yard line must go around the goalkeeper; otherwise, she shoots from outside the 10-yard line.

Cues

- Hold or tip the ball out of play.
- Take off on the foot nearest to the ball when diving.

GAME 2

Repeat game 1.

LESSON 38

Tactical Problem Defending the goal

Lesson Focus Goalkeeping, distributing the ball

Objective Distribute quickly, accurately, and efficiently.

GAME 1

Setup 4v2 (three defenders plus one goalkeeper versus two attackers) in a penalty area (approximately 20 by 40 yards; figure 11.57)

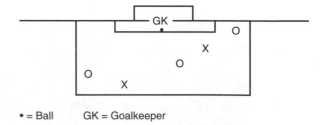

• = Ball   GK = Goalkeeper

Figure 11.57

Goals

- As a defender, move away from the goalkeeper to provide an outlet for the goalkeeper.
- As the goalkeeper, use effective distribution to get the ball away from the goal.
- As an attacker, win the ball and shoot.

Conditions

- The attacker feeds the ball to the goalkeeper from 20 yards.
- The goalkeeper may not kick the ball out.

Questions

Q: Whom should the goalkeeper give the ball to?

A: The first available player.

Q: How should the goalkeeper give the ball?

A: Roll it if possible.

Q: Why is rolling best?

A: It gets the ball to the ground quickly. It is easier to receive and control a rolling ball than a bouncing ball.

PRACTICE TASK

Setup   Partner practice, rolling, overarm throws

Goal   Distribute quickly and accurately so the receiver can easily control the ball.

Cues

- Roll the ball firmly and flat.
- Keep your arm straight during overarm throws for increased distance.
- Use a bent-arm throw for speed.

GAME 2

Repeat game 1.

LESSON 39

Secondary Level V

Tactical Problem   Restarting play

Lesson Focus   Attacking with corner kicks to the far post

Objective   Use far-post corners to create scoring opportunities.

GAME 1

Setup   6v6 in 40 by 50 yards, full goal, referee randomly calls many corners

Goal   Be aware of the corner as a chance to score.

Question

Q: What is the advantage of a far-post corner?

A: The ball moves away from defense.

PRACTICE TASK

Setup   Team practice, unopposed, at far-post corners (figure 11.58)

Goal   Use far-post corners to score.

Cues

- Corner taker—Cross away from the goal-keeper to the far-post area.
- All players at the edge of the penalty area—Attack the far-post area when the kick is taken.

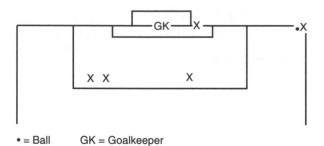

• = Ball   GK = Goalkeeper

Figure 11.58

GAME 2

Repeat game 1.

LESSON 40

Secondary Level V

Tactical Problem   Restarting play

Lesson Focus   Defending corner kicks

Objective   Prevent scoring at corners.

GAME 1

Setup   6v6 in 40 by 50 yards, full goal, referee randomly calls many corners

Goal   Be aware of the need to defend against corners.

Question

Q: How can you effectively defend corners?

A: Mark opponents and clear the ball.

PRACTICE TASK

Setup   Team practice, opposed (figure 11.59)

Goal   Appropriately mark and position defenders for near-post, far-post, and short corners.

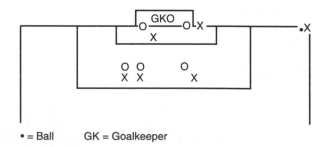

• = Ball   GK = Goalkeeper

Figure 11.59

Teaching Sport Concepts and Skills

Cues

- Mark an opponent.
- Be the first to meet the ball when it is crossed.
- Clear the ball high, wide, and long.

GAME 2

Repeat game 1.

LESSON 41

Tactical Problem   Restarting play

Lesson Focus   Defending free kicks

Objectives

- Efficiently defend free kicks.
- Set a wall.

GAME 1

Setup   6v6 in 60 by 50 yards, full goal, referee calls many free kicks

Goal   Set up defense efficiently.

Question

Q: How can you successfully defend a free kick?

A: Mark opponents or set a wall.

PRACTICE TASK

Setup   Team practice, opposed, with direct or indirect free kicks from a variety of angles. The attacking team decides from where to take each free kick and whether to use a direct or indirect kick.

Goals

- Mark correctly.
- Set two-, three-, four-, and five-player walls (five players if the free kick is central, two if it is wide, three or four if it is in between).

Cues

- Set the wall quickly.
- Use the tallest players to form the outside of the wall.
- Mark opponents if you are not in the wall.
- Line up the outside of the wall with the near post so that the wall covers half the goal (figure 11.60).

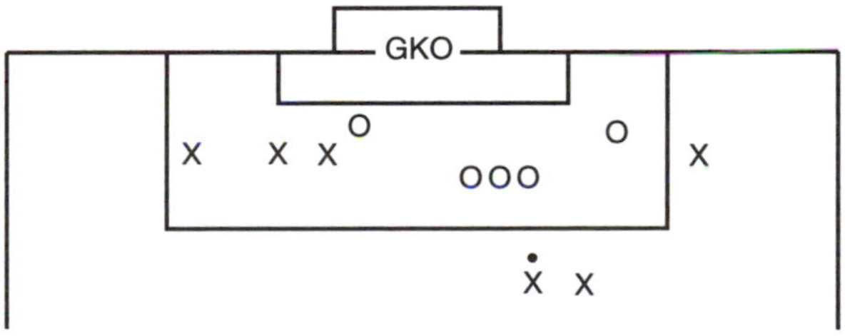

• = Ball   GK = Goalkeeper

Figure 11.60

GAME 2

Repeat game 1.

SUMMARY

This chapter has covered the five levels of tactical complexity for teaching soccer. You may choose to base an instructional unit on one particular level. For example, with novice players you would focus on level I. We recommend focusing a unit on one level of tactical complexity to help your students develop both their offensive and defensive performance as they progress in their understanding of the game.

Nevertheless, you may choose to develop your students' understanding of one specific tactical problem during a unit. In this case you could select the material related to the tactical problem from across the five levels of tactical complexity. Whichever approach you choose, base your instruction on developing tactical awareness and an understanding of the game of soccer and not simply on performing isolated kicking, trapping, and heading skills.

You can use many, if not most, of the lessons in this chapter with other invasion games such as floor or field hockey, team handball, and ultimate Frisbee. Although we have not included specific chapters for these games in this book, they are similar to soccer in tactical complexity. Their tactical problems are the same as those in soccer even though the solutions may require different on-the-ball skills. You will see this in chapter 12, which is on basketball.

By following levels of tactical complexity, you help your students progressively increase their understanding and performance. The levels presented in this chapter are comprehensive, and although games might break down because of inadequate skill execution, student performance will improve with increased understanding of what to do in game situations.

Chapter 12

Basketball

As an invasion game, basketball shares many of the tactics found in soccer. In this chapter we apply several strategies from chapter 11 to games and practices specific to basketball. Once you have taught the similar tactics in soccer and basketball, it should be easy to apply these tactics to other invasion games such as ultimate Frisbee, floor hockey, and team handball.

Our recommended lesson format for basketball follows the game, practice, game sequence outlined in chapter 2. If you are thinking, I don't have enough baskets for teaching these lessons, you are not alone. Some practitioners we have worked with have (a) bolted extra hoops on the wall; (b) rotated teams onto a court; (c) rotated players into a game; (d) assigned four teams (of two or three students) to one basket or two teams to each side of a basket; (e) used stations that alternate game play and practice; (f) played on half-courts; (g) assigned extra students responsibilities such as coaching, scoring, officiating, and serving as team trainer; and (h) used targets painted on the wall such as those used in WallTar (Stevens and Collier 2001).

As in the soccer chapter, we assume that you will use balls of appropriate size and weight to facilitate game play and skill development and to foster success. The sizes of the teams used in the conditioned games depend on the tactics and skills you want to emphasize. For example, a 1v1 game forces students to dribble to get away from or around their defenders, whereas a 3v3 game has more opportunities for passing, setting screens, and using a give-and-go. You can assign players or teams a court or basket at the beginning of a unit, and they can remain there for most game and practice activities. Assigning baskets or courts eliminates reorganizing and helps your lessons run smoothly.

We present the tactical framework and levels of tactical complexity for basketball in tables 12.1 and 12.2. We briefly describe each level before outlining its associated lessons.

LEVEL I

We suggest that students at level I focus on offense. Defensive qualities are important, but if introduced too soon, defense may prohibit the development of offensive skills, especially if peers play defense aggressively. Introduce defense after students have developed some proficiency with on-the-ball skills. Rather than eliminate defense, control defensive play by instituting three levels of involvement:

1. Cooperative defense, in which the defensive player stays two arm's lengths away from the opponent and is relatively passive. At times the defensive player even coaches the opponent.

2. Active defense, in which the defensive player stays about one arm's length away from the opponent and has active hands and feet but makes no attempt to intercept the ball.

3. Competitive defense, in which the defensive player assumes the appropriate position depending on whether the opponent has the ball, and attempts to intercept the ball.

One of our local practitioners refers to these defensive levels as *cold, warm,* and *hot*. She assigns defensive levels according to each student's ability. Doing so has helped her challenge more skilled players while providing successful and equally challenging experiences for novice players.

One way to teach students how to play offensively is to assign specific defensive levels that provide a challenging experience.

Table 12.1   Tactical Problems, Movements, and Skills in Basketball

Tactical problems	Off-the-ball movements	On-the-ball skills
SCORING		

Maintaining possession of the ball	• Create passing lanes to support the ball carrier:
	  ○ Fake and replace
	  ○ Juke step
	  ○ Cut away, then back to the ball
	• Determine when and where to use various passes
		• Chest pass
		• Bounce pass
		• Overhead pass

Attacking the basket	• Identify an open lane in which to dribble; then drive and shoot
	• Fast break:
	  ○ Position to receive the outlet pass
	  ○ Fill lanes (down court)
		• Shooting (3-8 ft, or 1-2.4 m)—short shot close to the basket (3-9 ft, or 1-2.7 m)
		• Give-and-go:
		  ○ Ball fake
		  ○ Cuts
		  ○ Lead pass
		• Shoot off the pass
		• Jump shot (12-15 ft, or 3.7-4.6 m)
		• Fast break:
		  ○ Rebound
		  ○ Pivot
		  ○ Outlet pass

Creating space to attack	• Pick away from the ball
	• Pick on the ball
	• Clear out to create space for a layup
	• Offense against 2-1-2 zone defense:
	  ○ Picks
	  ○ Screens
		• L-Cut
		• V-cut
		• Offense against 2-1-2 zone defense:
		  ○ Ball movement
		  ○ Skip pass

Using space in attack	Offense from player-to-player defense:
	• Pick-and-roll
	• Setting a screen
	  ○ On the ball
	  ○ Off the ball
		Dribble to reposition

PREVENTING SCORING		
Defending space	• Player-to-player defense • Moving around picks and screens	2-1-2 zone defense: • Movement as a team • Player responsibilities • Communication
Winning the ball	• Defense off the ball • Defense on the ball	Transition from defense to offense: • Follow the shot • Box out • Rebound • Outlet pass
RESTARTING PLAY		
Jump ball—offensive and defensive		Offensive and defensive positioning for jump

Inbound pass	Inbound sideline play—pick away from the ball	• Inbound end-line plays:
		  ○ Set picks
		  ○ Cutting off the pick
		  ○ Screens
		  ○ Inbound passes
		• Inbound sideline play—inbound pass

Foul shot		• Positioning for free throws • Rebounding from foul shot position

Table 12.2 Levels of Tactical Complexity for Basketball

Tactical problems	Level I	Level II	Level III	Level IV
SCORING				
Maintaining possession of the ball	• Create passing lanes to support the ball carrier: ○ Fake and replace ○ Juke step ○ Cut away, then back to the ball • Determine when and where to use various passes ○ Chest pass ○ Bounce pass ○ Overhead pass			
Attacking the basket	• Shooting (3-8 ft, or 1-2.4 m)—short shot close to the basket (3-9 ft, or 1-2.7 m) • Identify an open lane in which to dribble; then drive and shoot	• Give-and-go: ○ Ball fake ○ Cuts ○ Lead pass • Shoot off the pass	Jump shot (within 12-15 ft, or 3.7-4.6 m)	Fast break: • Rebound • Pivot • Outlet pass • Position to receive an outlet pass (off the ball) • Fill lanes (down court)
Creating space to attack		• L-cut • V-cut • Pick on the ball • Pick away from the ball		• Clear out to create space for a layup • Offense against 2-1-2 zone defense: ○ Picks ○ Screens ○ Ball movement ○ Skip pass
Using space in attack	Dribble to reposition		• Offense from player-to-player defense: ○ Pick-and-roll • Setting a screen: ○ On the ball ○ Off the ball	
PREVENTING SCORING				
Defending space			• Player-to-player defense • Moving around picks and screens	2-1-2 zone defense: • Movement as a team • Player responsibilities • Communication
Winning the ball		• Defense on the ball • Defense off the ball	Transition from defense to offense: • Follow the shot • Box out • Rebound • Outlet pass	
RESTARTING GAME				
Jump ball				Offensive and defensive positioning for the jump
Inbound pass			Inbound sideline plays: • Pick away from the ball • Inbound pass	Inbound end-line plays: • Set picks • Cutting off the pick • Screens • Inbound passes
Foul shot				• Positioning for free throws • Rebounding from foul shot position

Tactical Problem   Attacking the basket

Lesson Focus   Shooting within the zone, which is 3 to 8 feet (1-2.4 m) from the basket

Objective   Receive the pass, square the body to the basket, and shoot accurately.

GAME 1

Setup   3v3, half-court, five-minute scoring game

Goal   Score as often as possible.

Conditions

- Players must complete three consecutive passes before shooting.
- Players score 1 point for each shot attempted, 2 points for each basket made.
- All restarts begin at half-court.
- Dribbling is not permitted.

Questions

Q: What was the goal of your game?

A: Score as many points as possible.

Q: From where on the court did you score most of your points?

A: Close to the basket.

Q: Why is it better to shoot near the basket rather than far from the basket?

A: More likely to score—higher-percentage shot.

Q: What else can you do to increase your chances of scoring?

A: Use good shooting form. Use the backboard as a target.

PRACTICE TASK

Setup   All players shoot three shots from each of the five spots marked around the basket (3-8 ft, or 1-2.4 m, away). The partner rebounds the ball and passes accurately to a teammate. The shooter provides target hands, squares up, and shoots.

Goal   Score on two of three shots at each spot.

Cues   Shooting—square up, remember BEEF:

- **B**ase firm.
- **E**lbow under the ball.
- **E**xtend the arm.
- **F**ollow through toward the target (square above the rim on the backboard).

GAME 2

Setup   3v3, half-court, five-minute scoring game

Goal   Score as many field goals as possible.

Basketball

Tactical Problem   Maintaining possession of the ball

Lesson Focus   Creating passing lanes by using on-the-ball skill execution and off-the-ball movement

Objectives

- Present a target hand to show the passer where to pass.
- Receive the ball in the triple-threat position.
- Perform a ball fake before passing.
- Make a lead pass just ahead of the target hand.

GAME 1

Setup   3v3, half-court, possession game

Goal   Complete three passes before shooting.

Conditions

- Players score 1 point for each successful pass and 2 points for a basket.
- Dribbling is not permitted.
- All restarts occur at half-court.

Questions

Q: What was the goal of your game?

A: Complete three passes before shooting.

Q: When you were passing, what did you do to keep the defense from stealing the ball?

A: Used arms and body to protect the ball; used ball fakes and jukes to throw off the opponent.

Q: Did you use any signals to let your teammates know you wanted to receive the pass?

A: Held hand up or out to let the passer know where to pass the ball.

PRACTICE TASK

Setup   Use 3v3 and have players practice passing and moving from point to wing, baseline, and high and low posts (no passes between post positions). Mark positions with tape, poly spots, and so forth (figure 12.1). The player passes and then moves to another position. The player receiving the ball must (a) present a target for the passer, (b) receive the ball in a triple-threat position and jump stop, (c) give a ball fake or juke (fakes and jukes are also known as feints—body movements to fool opponents) before passing, and (d) perform a quick, accurate lead pass to a partner. Players use cooperative to active defense and switch from offense to defense after 10 passes or two minutes. Continue as time allows.

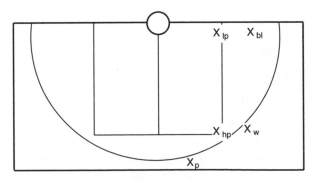

bl = Baseline   lp = Low post   p = Point
w = Wing   hp = High post

Figure 12.1

Goals

- Present a target hand to the passer.
- Receive the ball in a triple-threat position.
- Perform a ball fake or juke before passing.
- Make a lead pass ahead of the target hand.

Cues

- Receiver—Present a target hand.
- Passer—Assume the triple-threat position (ball at the hip, knees bent, elbows out).
- Passer—Fake a pass, make a pass.

GAME 2

Setup   3v3, half-court, possession game

Goal   Complete three passes before shooting.

Conditions

- Players score 1 point for each successful pass and 2 points for a basket.
- Dribbling is not permitted.
- All restarts occur at half-court.
- Players maintain possession by providing a target for the passer, receiving the ball in a triple-threat position, and using a ball fake.

LESSON 3

Secondary Level I

Tactical Problem   Maintaining possession of the ball

Lesson Focus   Creating passing lanes while off the ball

Objective   Use quick cut or fake-and-replace movements to get open to receive a pass.

GAME 1

Setup   3v3, half-court, possession game

Goal   Complete three consecutive passes on three consecutive possessions.

Conditions

- Players must complete at least three passes before shooting.
- Players score 1 point for three consecutive passes, 2 points for a basket.

Questions

Q: What was the goal of the game?

A: Complete three consecutive passes and shoot.

Q: What did you have to do to get three consecutive passes?

A: Move to an open space and get away from the defense.

Q: How were you able to get away from the defender?

A: By using cuts and fakes.

PRACTICE TASK 1

Setup   Players start at one of the five offensive positions (figure 12.1) in a 3v3 gamelike practice task with cooperative to active defense. The ball starts at the top of the key, with the point guard slapping the ball, signaling teammates to cut away from their defenders and move back (to get open for a pass, or to move toward the basket). The player receiving the pass does the same thing, slapping the ball and passing to an open teammate. Players switch from offense to defense after 10 passes or two minutes, and continue as time allows.

Goal   Use quick jab steps and fake movements to create a passing lane and receive a pass.

Conditions

- Players provide a target for receiving the ball.
- Players receive the ball in triple threat.
- Players use a ball fake before passing.

PRACTICE TASK 2

Setup   Repeat practice task 1, but allow players to shoot when in the zone (3-8 ft, or 1-2.4 m, from the basket).

Goal   Use quick jab steps and fake-and-replace movements to create a passing lane and receive a pass.

Cues

- Make quick cuts.
- Present target hands.
- Fake a pass, make a pass.

GAME 2

Setup   3v3, half-court, possession

Goal   Complete three consecutive passes on three consecutive possessions.

Conditions

- Players must complete at least three passes before shooting.
- Players score 1 point for three consecutive passes, 2 points for a basket, and 5 points for three consecutive passes on three consecutive possessions.

LESSON 4

Tactical Problem   Maintaining possession of the ball

Lesson Focus   Decision making before passing

Objectives

- Determine the appropriate situations for using overhead, bounce (using one or two hands), and chest passes during game play.
- Perform passes accurately and appropriately during game play.

GAME 1

Setup   3v3, half-court, possession game

Goal   Complete three consecutive passes on three consecutive possessions.

Conditions

- Players must complete at least three passes before shooting.
- Players score 1 point for three consecutive passes, 2 points for a basket, and 10 points for three consecutive passes on three consecutive possessions. (Ask students to be aware of the types of passes they use during game play.)

Questions

Q: What was the goal of the game?

A: Complete three consecutive passes on three consecutive possessions.

Q: What types of passes did you use during your game?

A: Overhead, bounce, and chest passes.

Q: Why did you use all these types of passes?

A: To throw the ball long, to get around a defender, or to throw a hard or quick pass.

PRACTICE TASK

Setup   Players start at one of the five offensive positions (figure 12.1) in a 3v3 gamelike practice task with cooperative to active defense (same as previous lesson). The ball starts at the top of the key, with the point guard slapping the ball to signal teammates to cut away from their defenders and then to cut back (to get open for a pass, or move toward the basket). The pass must be a skip pass— that is, a long pass that goes over or past one teammate and on to another. The player receiving the pass does the same thing until 10 consecutive overhead passes have been completed. Players repeat this task for the bounce pass, using active defense to create the need for the bounce pass, but this time passing to adjacent players. Finally, players repeat this task for the chest pass, using cooperative to active defense, and pass to teammates as they cut away from their defenders.

Goal   Make 10 consecutive passes during each passing rotation.

GAME 2

Setup   3v3, half-court, possession game

Goal   Complete three consecutive passes on three consecutive possessions.

Conditions

- Players must complete at least three passes before shooting.
- Players score 1 point for three consecutive passes, 2 points for a basket, and 10 points for three consecutive passes on three consecutive possessions.

Extension   Defense scores 2 points for each steal and 1 point for tipping or touching the ball.

LESSON 5

Tactical Problem   Attacking the basket

Lesson Focus   Identifying an open lane to the basket and dribbling to drive and shoot

Objective   Use a power dribble to drive and score.

GAME 1

Setup   3v3, half-court game

Goal   Score as often as possible.

Condition   Dribbling is not permitted except to drive to the basket.

Questions

Q: When you receive the ball, what are your three options?

A: Shoot, pass, dribble.

Q: When should you dribble?

A: To drive to the basket.

Q: When you have the ball and an open lane to the basket, what should you do?

A: Drive quickly toward the basket and shoot.

PRACTICE TASK 1

Setup   Students are in pairs, with one ball per pair. The player with the ball must use a ball fake, make a juke or jab step, and drive to the basket and then jump stop and shoot while the partner is a cooperative defender.

Goals

- Make a strong dribble and drive toward the basket.
- Demonstrate good form while performing the jump stop and shot.
- Use the square on the backboard to aim and shoot.

Cues

- Keep the ball down, eyes up.
- Use a two-foot jump stop.
- Shoot for the square.

Question

Q: How does the dribble change when someone is guarding you?

A: You keep the ball closer to your body and keep your body between the defender and the ball.

PRACTICE TASK 2

Setup   Use 1v1, one ball per pair. Players start at the foul line, check the ball, and get in a triple-threat position.

Goal   Score in 15 seconds or less.

GAME 2

Setup 3v3, half-court game

Goal Shoot as often as possible using a dribble and drive.

Conditions

- Dribbling is not permitted except to drive to the basket.
- Players can only score from a drive to the basket.

LESSON 6

Tactical Problem Using space in the attack

Lesson Focus Using the dribble for repositioning to make a pass

Objectives

- Use proper dribbling technique.
- Position the body between the defensive player and the ball.
- Identify the need for repositioning to create passing lanes.

GAME 1

Setup 3v3, half-court game

Goal Score without dribbling.

Conditions

- Players must make three consecutive passes before shooting.
- Players may dribble when needed.
- Players use active defense on the ball and competitive defense off the ball (no contact).

Questions

Q: Why was it difficult to score without dribbling?

A: Teammates were covered.

Q: What can players with the ball do when teammates are covered?

A: Dribble to reposition until the off-the-ball players are able to cut and create passing lanes.

Q: What can players off the ball do to open passing lanes?

A: Use feints, jukes, and cuts.

PRACTICE TASK

Setup Use a 2v2 dribble reposition drill with a passive to active defense. The player with the ball starts from the point position and dribbles to find an open pass to her teammate. The off-the-ball player uses various cuts to get open and receive a pass from the on-the-ball player. The extra players are coaches. One watches the defenders and makes sure they position appropriately and safely and do not make contact with the ball or ball carrier; the other watches the offense to see if they use jabs, jukes, cuts, and so on to effectively reposition themselves to create open passing lanes. Players can shoot when open. They switch roles after three shot attempts.

Goal

- As the on-the-ball player, dribble to reposition.
- As the off-the-ball player, create a passing lane.

Cues

- Make quick cuts.
- Dribble with the body between the defender and the ball.
- Watch the belly button of the offensive player attempting a fake.
- Read and anticipate.

GAME 2

Setup   3v3, half-court, possession game

Goal   Dribble only when there are no open passing lanes (off-the-ball players need to create passing lanes).

Conditions

- Dribbling is not permitted except to drive to the basket or to reposition to make a pass.
- Players use active defense on the ball and competitive defense off the ball (no contact).

LEVEL II

We recommend reviewing level I content (the triple threat, the ball fake, etc.) so students can refine and integrate these skills as they practice and play the game. You may need to repeat or extend one or two lessons from level I to improve your students' skills or tactical understanding.

Level II focuses on preventing scoring, specifically by winning the ball and defending space. If games break down because the defense is too active, you may want to restrain the defensive players by assigning degrees of intensity (passive, active, or competitive). Have students focus on their form and their positioning relative to the ball, the basket, and other defensive players.

Two lessons in this level are on attacking the basket. Unlike the individual skills covered in level I, the offensive skills here involve other team members and require teamwork. You may find that this is a good time to talk about the meaning of being a member of a team and the importance of working together.

In level II, students learn how to prevent the other team from scoring through winning the ball or defending space.

LESSON 7

Tactical Problem   Creating space to attack

Lesson Focus   Creating passing lanes in the zone

Objective   Use cuts (L-cut or V-cut) to elude a defender and get open for a shot.

GAME 1

Setup   3v3, half-court game

Goal   Get open to receive a pass in the zone.

Conditions

- Players shoot only from the zone (3-8 ft, or 1-2.4 m, around the basket).
- Players score 1 point for attempting a shot and 2 points for making a basket.

Questions

Q: What was the goal of the game?

A: To get open to receive a pass in the zone.

Q: How do you do that?

A: Move fast, use a fake or juke, run one way and then change directions really fast.

Q: What do you need to consider before making a cut?

A: The position of the ball and of the defenders.

PRACTICE TASK

Setup   Use 2v1 with one active defender and two offensive players. The ball begins at the point position, and the passer waits until the defender is guarding her before passing. Then, when she sees her teammate fake or juke, she ball fakes and times the pass to the open receiver. The receiver cuts toward the defender and then away with target hands up to communicate where the passer should pass the ball. The defender stays between the passer and the receiver, using active defense about an arm's length away. After the receiver catches a pass three times, all players rotate positions. Groups of three can rotate on and off the court and serve as coaches when on the sidelines.

Goals

- As an off-the-ball player, use quick cuts to elude the defender and get open in the zone.
- As an off-the-ball player, show target hands.
- As an on-the-ball player, use a ball fake and anticipate when and where to pass.

GAME 2

Setup   3v3, half-court game

Goal   As an off-the-ball player, get open in the zone.

Conditions

- Players shoot only from the zone.
- Players score 1 point for attempting a shot and 2 points for scoring a basket.

University Elementary Content and Methods. Lesson contributed by Christin Palumbo, student, Fall 2004.

LESSON 8

Tactical Problem   Attacking the basket

Lesson Focus   Using the give-and-go to score

Objectives

- Fake, pass, and cut to the basket.
- Time and throw a lead pass back to the cutter.
- Shoot off the pass.

GAME 1

Setup   3v3, half-court game

Goal   As an off-the-ball player, get open in the zone.

Conditions

- Players must complete at least two passes before shooting.
- All shots must be made within 3 to 5 feet (1-1.5 m) of the basket.

Questions

Q: Off-the-ball players, how were you able to get open in the zone?

A: Pass and cut or fake or juke away from the basket and then move quickly toward the basket.

Q: What did you do to keep the defender from getting between you and the ball?

A: Used a strong juke or jab step, crossover step, or quick move toward the basket.

Q: What did you need to consider before driving to the basket?

A: The position of the ball and of the other defenders.

PRACTICE TASK

Setup   Use 2v2 with active defenders and one ball. Two players serve as coaches. Each offensive player practices the give-and-go three times and then rotates into the coaching role. Players then move to the other side of the basket and repeat. They practice the give-and-go three times first with cooperative and then with active defense.

Goal   Score off a give-and-go.

Cues

- Pass and cut.
- Use a target hand.
- Keep the defender behind you.

Question

Q: What did you do to complete the give-and-go when there was competitive defense?

A: Used more fakes, dribbled to create passing lanes, and got open to support the player with the ball.

Cues

- Make quick cuts.
- Present target hands.
- Anticipate when and where to pass.

GAME 2

Repeat game 1.

Goal   Score off a give-and-go.

Condition   Players earn 1 extra point if they use a give-and-go to score.

LESSON 9
Secondary Level II

Tactical Problem   Creating space to attack

Lesson Focus   Setting a pick to create space

Objectives

- Set a pick on the opponent defending the on-the-ball player.
- On-the-ball player fakes or jukes and drives off the pick and shoots.

GAME 1

Setup   3v3, half-court game

Goal   Get the on-the-ball player open so he can shoot.

Conditions

- A different team member restarts play on each possession.
- Players earn 1 point for hitting the rim and 2 for getting the ball through the hoop.
- Players call their own fouls.

Questions

Q: How were you able to get the on-the-ball player open to shoot?

A: Performed a pick.

Q: What is a good body position for the player setting a pick?

A: Wide base, bent knees, arms across the body for self-protection.

Q: What is the best way for the player with the ball to use the screen?

A: Fake and then brush off the screen to create an open space to drive to the basket or shoot.

PRACTICE TASK

Setup   Use 2v1, active defense, one ball. The off-the-ball offensive player executes a pick, and the on-the-ball offensive player uses the pick to move to open space and score. The defense is active, supporting yet challenging the opponents. After the shot, another 2v1 group moves onto the court and runs the same drill. When on the sidelines, players each pick a player on the court to coach and give feedback to when the play ends. One coach watches to see whether the pick is set correctly, one watches to see whether the offensive player uses the screen correctly, and the third watches the defense to ensure it is at an appropriate level.

Goal   Successfully execute a screen three times in a row.

Cues

- Stand firm; straddle your feet.
- Keep your hands across the trunk (girls high, boys low), ready to take a charge.
- Shooter—Fake, cross step, and drive or shoot.

GAME 2

Repeat game 1.

LESSON 10

Secondary Level II

Tactical Problem   Creating space to attack

Lesson Focus   Getting open in the zone

Objective   As an off-the-ball player, use picks to get open in the zone.

GAME 1

Setup   3v3, half-court game

Goal   As an off-the-ball player, get open in the zone.

Conditions

- Dribbling is not permitted.
- Players use active to competitive defense on off-the-ball players.
- Players may shoot only in the zone.
- Players score 1 point for hitting the rim and 2 points for making a basket.

Questions

Q: Off-the-ball players, how were you able to get open in the zone?

A: By setting a pick on a teammate's defensive player to free the teammate up.

Q: How did you determine where to set the pick?

A: Considered the positions of the ball and of the defensive players.

Q: What should you do while your teammate is approaching to set a pick on your defender?

A: Fake or juke the defender away from the pick or basket.

PRACTICE TASK

Setup   Use 3v2, with two cooperative defensive players covering off-the-ball players and one coach observing the timing and form of the pick. The ball starts at the guard position, and the point passes to the wing and moves to pick the defender of the third offensive player, who is positioned near the baseline. Once the pick is set, the third offensive player cuts into the zone, receives a pass from the wing, and shoots. Players rotate after three trials and continue until all have had three chances to set a pick away from the ball. They can repeat the drill with active or competitive defense.

Goals

- Determine the best location for the pick.
- Set a strong pick.
- Set a defender up for the pick and then brush off the pick and cut into the zone.
- Shoot off the pass.

GAME 2

Setup   3v3, half-court game

Goal   As an off-the-ball player, use picks to get open in the zone.

Conditions

- Dribbling is not permitted.
- Players use active to competitive defense on off-the-ball players.
- Players may shoot only in the zone.
- Players earn 1 point for receiving a pass in the zone, 1 point for hitting the rim, and 2 points for making a basket (figure 12.2).

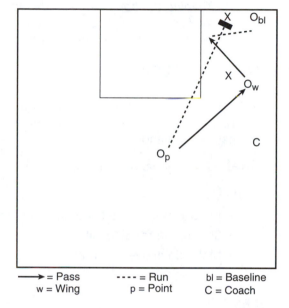

⟶ = Pass	---- = Run	bl = Baseline
w = Wing	p = Point	C = Coach

Figure 12.2

LESSON 11

Tactical Problem   Winning the ball

Lesson Focus   Defensive positioning when off the ball

Objectives

- Demonstrate proper defensive positioning, placing the body between the defender and the basket and keeping the ball-side hand between the defender and the ball.
- Watch the ball.
- Maintain active feet and hands.

GAME 1

Setup   3v3, half-court game

Goal   Keep the opponent from scoring.

Conditions

- Players use a competitive defense to guard opposing players.
- Dribbling is not permitted.
- Players must complete at least three passes before shooting.
- The defensive team scores 1 point if the offensive team does not complete three passes.

Questions

Q: What did you do to keep the opposing team from scoring?

A: Closely guarded and rebounded so they wouldn't get a second shot.

Q: What defensive positions or actions interfered with the offense the most and kept your opponent from scoring?

A: Keeping the body between the opponent and the goal, positioning the ball-side hand between the ball and the opponent, maintaining a ready position (medium body posture, weight forward, ready to move), keeping hands and feet active.

PRACTICE TASK

Setup   In pairs, players practice off-the-ball defensive positioning (partners can also coach each other). Players can dribble, but as soon as they pick up the dribble, the defensive player moves closer and has active hands and feet.

Goal   Either steal the ball without fouling or cause a turnover.

Cues

- Keep your body between the opponent and the goal.
- Stay in the ready position.
- Maintain active hands and feet.
- Watch the ball.

GAME 2

Repeat game 1.

LESSON 12

Secondary Level II

Tactical Problem   Winning the ball

Lesson Focus   On-the-ball defense

Objectives

- Use body angles to force movement away from the basket. (*Note:* This is similar to channeling in soccer.)
- Use the ball-side hand to deny a passing lane to off-the-ball players.

GAME 1

Setup   3v3, half-court game

Goal   Prevent the on-the-ball player from passing.

Conditions

- Dribbling is not permitted.
- Players must complete at least three consecutive passes before shooting.
- The defensive team receives 1 point for turnovers and 2 points for steals (without fouling).

Question

Q: How did you prevent the on-the-ball player from passing?

A: Overplayed to limit potential passing lanes, closely guarded the player with the ball, and used hands to block potential passing lanes.

PRACTICE TASK

Setup   Use 2v2 and active to competitive defense. The player with the ball starts at the point position and attempts to pass to a teammate. The defensive player assumes a defensive posture and attempts to prevent the pass for five seconds (the defender can count "one Mississippi, two Mississippi," and so on). The two players waiting off the court coach and then rotate into the drill after the offensive team has had three possessions. The offensive team becomes the defense, and the defensive team rotates off the court to coach.

Allowing students to group themselves into varying levels of skill-based groups creates a positive experience.

Goal   Either steal the ball without fouling or cause a turnover.

Cues

- Position your body to block passing lanes.
- Use your hands to block passing lanes.
- See the ball.
- Anticipate.

GAME 2

Repeat game 1.

LEVEL III

The lessons at level III continue to increase in tactical complexity. The game forms involve 4v4 situations emphasizing player-to-player defense and offense. Tactics such as creating space and using space in attack require greater skill and tactical understanding. We introduce jump balls for starting and restarting play. Lessons at level III may require more space than those at levels I and II.

As with level II, you may want to review the content from previous levels. If you discover that some students are not ready for level III, consider grouping students by abilities so that advanced players have an opportunity to improve and less-advanced players can continue to refine basic skills and tactical knowledge. When using the tactical approach, grouping by ability is easy because you can assign teams to individual courts or half-courts and each team can work on independent tasks or tactical problems.

Our experiences with grouping have been mostly positive. Discretion is the key to successful grouping by ability. A teacher at a local high school assigns levels to different courts: a high school court, a college court, and a pro court. She directs the students to assign themselves to courts. In many cases, self-selection by students is better than assignment by teachers. Of course, certain classes and students will need your guidance to attain effective groupings.

The tactical approach promotes the game-practice-game format for most middle school students and novice performers. However, high school students and experienced players love to play the game and have the capacity to learn through the game. With older and more experienced players, consider returning them to game play after the question segment of the lesson. During the question segment, ask students to identify solutions and then attempt to implement these solutions as they play. If teams or players are still having difficulty, then set them up to practice. Observe closely to identify a team that is performing well, and then ask those players to repeat the performance. We sometimes refer to this as an instant replay or an ESPN highlight. Having players repeat the play or performance may take a bit of guidance, but once they can reconstruct it, have them demonstrate to other teams.

Allowing students to group themselves into varying levels of skill-based groups creates a positive experience.

LESSON 13

Tactical Problem   Restarting play

Lesson Focus   Inbound (sideline) pass

Objective   Pick away from the ball to create space for an inbound pass when restarting play.

GAME 1

Setup   3v3, half-court game

Goal   Score within three passes.

Conditions

- Restart play from the sidelines on all violations and fouls.
- An inbound pass counts as one pass.
- If no shot is attempted within three passes, the offensive team has made a turnover and the ball must be taken out at the sideline.
- The player inbounding the ball must remain stationary until the ball is passed.
- Players use an active defense.
- Dribbling is not permitted.

Questions

Q: What did your team do to score within three passes?

A: Got open and created space near the ball.

Q: What did your team do to get open and create space, particularly during inbound plays?

A: Faked and cut to the ball and picked teammates' defenders so teammates could get away and come to the ball.

Q: If the ball is on the sideline at about midcourt, how should your team set picks to create space for the inbound pass?

A: Spread out, pick away to create space toward the ball, and cut toward the ball.

PRACTICE TASK

Setup   Teams create an inbound play that provides two options (using two players) for allowing a shot within three passes.

GAME 2

Repeat game 1.

Note   Allow teams to show their inbound plays during lesson closure.

LESSON 14

Secondary Level III

Tactical Problem   Attacking the basket

Lesson Focus   Jump shot

Objective   Use a jump shot to shoot over the defense when shooting within 12 feet (3.7 m) of the basket.

GAME 1

Setup   3v3, half-court game

Goal   Score on three consecutive possessions.

Conditions
- All shots must be taken from within 12 feet (3.7 m) of the basket.
- Off-the-ball defense is cooperative to active, and on-the-ball defense is active to competitive.
- The defensive team receives 2 points for blocking a shot (no contact).
- The offensive team receives 1 point for hitting the rim and 2 points for making a field goal.

Question

Q: What were some things you did to score when closely guarded?

A: Used fakes and jukes and used a jump shot.

PRACTICE TASK

Setup Arrange five or six spots around the perimeter of the basket, keeping within 6 to 12 feet (1.8-3.7 m). Players pair up and play 1v1, beginning with cooperative defense. The defender passes the ball to the offensive player; plays defense, turns, and follows the shot to the basket; retrieves the ball; and again passes the ball to the offensive player. Players rotate after three to five shots and repeat the drill with active and then competitive defense.

Goal Score on three consecutive possessions.

Cues

- Receive the pass in triple threat.
- Square shoulders to the basket.
- Jump straight up.
- Shoot at the peak of the jump.

GAME 2

Repeat game 1.

LESSON 15

Secondary Level III

Tactical Problem Winning the ball

Lesson Focus Defensive positioning following a shot to regain possession of the ball

Objectives

- Box out the opposing player at the release of the shot.
- Rebound the ball and make an outlet pass.

GAME 1

Setup 3v3, half-court game

Goals

- Prevent the offensive team from scoring.
- If the offense shoots, do not allow a second shot.

Conditions

- Dribbling is not permitted.
- Players must complete at least three consecutive passes before shooting.
- The defensive team receives 1 point for winning or rebounding the ball after only one shot.

Questions

Q: *What was the goal of the game?*

A: *To prevent scoring and prevent a second shot.*

Q: *What did you do to prevent a second shot?*

A: *Rebounded the first shot.*

Q: *How did you position yourself to get the rebound?*

A: *Moved between the defensive player and the basket.*

PRACTICE TASK

Setup   Use 2v2, plus one shooter and one outlet. Player O3 shoots the ball (figure 12.3). On the release, players X1 and X2 turn and box out the offensive players. Player X3 moves right or left, depending on which side of the basket the rebound occurs. The player rebounding the ball turns and passes to the outlet, player X3. Players repeat three times and then rotate.

Goal   Successfully rebound the ball and make an outlet pass three times in a row.

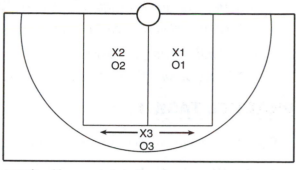

= Movement of player

Figure 12.3

GAME 2

Repeat game 1.

Condition   The defensive team gets 1 point for a successful rebound and 1 point for a successful outlet pass.

LESSON 16

Secondary Level III

Tactical Problem   Defending space

Lesson Focus   Player-to-player defense

Objectives

- Call picks and screens.
- Move around picks and screens.
- Stay with the player.

GAME 1

Setup   4v4, half-court

Goals

- On defense, use player-to-player competitive defense to keep the opponent from scoring.
- On offense, use picks to score and to create passing lanes in the attack.

Conditions

- Players call their own fouls.
- Dribbling is permitted only when driving to the basket.

Questions

Q: What are the advantages of player-to-player defense?

A: All players are closely guarded, which increases the chances to win the ball, and all defensive members know their responsibilities.

Q: What are the disadvantages?

A: Defense can get spread out too far away from the basket, and it's difficult to match players of equal abilities.

Q: How can you help your teammates while in player-to-player defense?

A: Let them know when a pick is being set, and pick up the offensive player threatening to score.

Q: What should you do when you're picked or screened?

A: Move around the pick so you can stay with your player.

PRACTICE TASK 1

Setup   Players review and practice on- and off-the-ball defensive positions in 3v3.

PRACTICE TASK 2

Setup   Use 3v3, two coaches, one ball, and a competitive defense. Offensive players execute on-the-ball screens. Defensive players being screened must fight around the screen and stay with their opponents. Coaches evaluate defenders' abilities to get around the screen.

Goal   Keep the opponent from getting an open shot.

PRACTICE TASK 3

Setup   Use 3v3, two coaches, one ball, and a competitive defense. Offensive players execute off-the-ball screens. Defensive players that are screened must fight around the screen and stay with their opponents. Coaches evaluate defenders' abilities to get around the screen.

Goal   Keep the opponent from getting an open shot.

Cues

- Call "Screen left" or "Screen right."
- Fight around the screen.
- Stay between your player and the basket.

GAME 2

Setup   Combine practice tasks 2 and 3. Rotate coaches into the game after two minutes.

Goal   Keep the offensive team from scoring for 30 seconds.

LESSON 17

Secondary Level III

Tactical Problem   Using space in the attack

Lesson Focus   Using offense against a player-to-player defense

Objective   Use picks or screens to free on- and off-the-ball players to create support and scoring opportunities.

GAME 1

Setup   4v4, half-court

Teaching Sport Concepts and Skills

Goals

- On defense, play competitive player-to-player defense.
- On offense, score as many points possible.

Conditions

- A different team member restarts play on each possession.
- Players call their own fouls and use a 30-second offensive clock (i.e., they must shoot within 30 seconds).
- The defensive team gets 3 points if the offensive team does not get a shot off within 30 seconds.

Question

Q: What did you do to score against the player-to-player defense?

A: Set picks or screens to free teammates, used cuts to get away from defenders, and moved the ball quickly and accurately.

PRACTICE TASK 1

Setup   Players practice an offensive play that you design: offense against a player-to-player defense, 4v4, active defense, one ball, full or half-court.

Goal   Score three times in a row using offensive play.

PRACTICE TASK 2

Setup   Teams create and practice their own offensive plays against a player-to-player defense. Each team of four creates an offensive play and practices it against the opponent (the other four players). Teams use an active defense.

Goal   Score three times in a row using offensive play.

Cues

- Anticipate the ball and player movements.
- Identify opportunities to get a player open.

GAME 2

Repeat game 1.

Condition   Teams score an extra point when they execute a play successfully.

LESSON 18

Tactical Problems   Winning the ball and using space in the attack

Lesson Focus   Transitioning from defense to offense

Objectives

- Rebound and make an outlet pass.
- Set up the offense as quickly as possible.

GAME 1

Setup 4v4, half-court

Goals

- On defense, use the outlet pass after rebounding the ball.
- On offense, score as many points as possible.

Conditions

- Players need to remember to box out and use the outlet pass on a defensive rebound.
- Players call their own fouls and a 30-second offensive clock.
- The defensive team gets 1 point for a successful rebound and outlet pass.

Questions

Q: Why should you make an outlet pass after rebounding the ball?

A: To get the ball out of the key and away from opponents and to get the ball down the floor faster.

Q: Which player should get the outlet pass?

A: A player who is not involved in the rebound and is on the same side of the key where the ball rebounds.

Q: Where and how should the outlet player go to receive the outlet pass?

A: To the sideline nearest the player rebounding the ball; he should move quickly to create a passing lane.

PRACTICE TASK 1

Setup Use 4v4, with one shooter and one outlet; player O4 shoots the ball (figure 12.4). On the release, players X1, X2, and X3 turn and box out the offensive players. Player X4 moves right or left, depending on where the rebound occurs. The player rebounding the ball turns and passes to the outlet, player X4. Players repeat three times and then rotate.

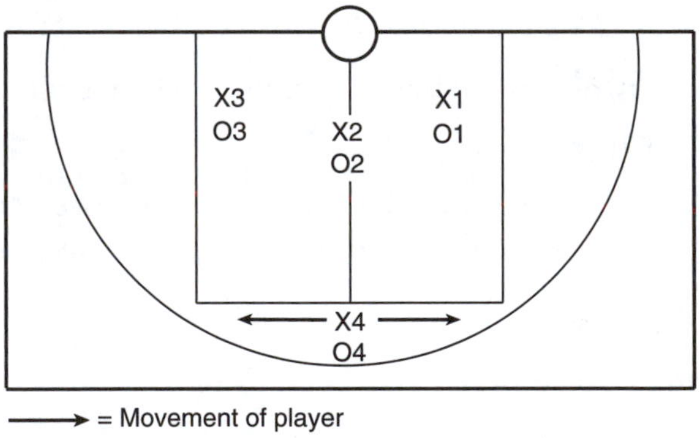

Goal Successfully complete three consecutive outlet passes.

Cues

- Rebound.
- Protect the ball.
- Pivot away from the basket.

———▶ = Movement of player

Figure 12.4

PRACTICE TASK 2

Setup Extend practice task 1. After the outlet pass, the guard moves toward center court to create a passing lane. The next available player fills the outside lane, opposite the rebound. Trailing players move down the court as quickly as possible and assume offensive positions.

Goal After rebounding the ball, use no more than five passes to score.

Cues

- Use the get-and-go.
- Move down the court quickly.
- Stay wide and spread out to maintain passing lanes.

GAME 2

Repeat game 1.

LEVEL IV

Lessons in level IV require 5v5 game play. The first few lessons emphasize starting and restarting play in the full court. Students may remain in half-court games unless the tactical problem dictates a full court, such as when learning the fast break. When using a full court, try rotating teams on and off the court. Allowing only one shot at the basket can also make games move more quickly and can optimize playing time for all students. Consider using the curriculum model in *Complete Guide to Sport Education* (Siedentop, Hastie, and van der Mars 2011), which advocates using students to coach, officiate, record statistics, keep score, act as trainers, and fulfill other responsibilities of team management. Following this model maintains high levels of student involvement while exposing students to other aspects of sport participation.

A primary tactic addressed in level IV is defending the basket, specifically, using 2-1-2 zone defense and defensive alignment during a free throw. On the offensive side, we introduce scoring tactics that use space in the attack, including offensive plays to use against a 2-1-2 zone defense, offensive alignments to use during a free throw, and a fast break. Of course, a number of other zone defenses or offensive alignments can be addressed at level IV.

Students in level IV learn offensive tactics that will help them move the ball and score past defense.

LESSON 19

Tactical Problem   Winning the ball

Lesson Focus   Positioning to gain possession of a jump ball

Objectives

- Match with a player on the circle.
- Position for offensive jump balls.
- Position for defensive jump balls.

GAME 1

Setup 4v4, half-court

Goal Gain possession of the ball off the jump ball.

Conditions

- After every basket, players use a jump ball to restart play.
- Players rotate so that each participates in the jump ball.
- The team gaining possession of the jump ball continues offensive play until it scores or until the other team wins the ball.

Questions

Q: What did you and your teammates do to win the jump ball?

A: Matched up with opponents on the circle for the jump ball.

Q: If you thought your team would win the jump ball, how did you line up on the circle?

A: Close to the basket so we could turn and score.

Q: If you thought your team would lose the jump ball, how did you line up on the circle?

A: Between the offense and the basket so we could defend the goal.

PRACTICE TASK 1

Setup Players practice the jump ball; they match up according to height. Use four players per group and one ball and one circle. Two players jump, another player tosses, and the other coaches. Players perform three jumps before rotating. Rotate through all players twice, allowing six jumps each. Jumping players try to tip the ball to the coach.

Goal Win three of six jump balls.

Cues

- Match up.
- Bend your knees.
- Jump when the tosser releases the ball.

PRACTICE TASK 2

Setup Players practice offensive and defensive jump balls, 3v3, with one tosser, one coach, one ball, one circle, and one basket. They play jump ball until one team scores or the other team wins the ball. Players rotate after each jump ball.

Goal Win the jump ball and score.

Cues

- Match up.
- Anticipate offensive or defensive jump balls.
- React.
- Transition quickly.

GAME 2

Repeat game 1.

LESSON 20

Tactical Problem   Winning the ball

Lesson Focus   Rebounding from the foul lane

Objective   Position offensively and defensively for free throws.

GAME 1

Setup   5v5, full court

Goal   Win rebounds on foul shots.

Condition   Free throws are awarded for all fouls and violations.

Questions

Q: How should the offensive team line up on a free throw?

A: Between the defensive players on the sidelines of the key, with one player at half-court to defend against a potential fast break.

Q: How should the defensive team line up on a free throw?

A: Begin with a player on the block next to the basket; then position one player on the other side of the offensive player, with one player close to the shooter, ready to block out.

PRACTICE TASK

Setup   Offensive and defensive teams alternate free throws. Players practice defensive positioning after the ball release and making outlet passes, as in a fast break. If the offensive team gets the rebound, play continues until the offense scores or until the defense wins the ball.

Goals
- On defense, get all rebounds off the free throws.
- On offense, regain possession of missed free throws.

Cues
- Step in at ball release.
- Step in quickly and firmly hold your position.
- Keep your body against the opponent.

GAME 2

Repeat game 1.

LESSON 21

Tactical Problems   Using space in the attack and attacking the basket

Lesson Focus   Outlet pass and fast break

Objectives

- Execute a pivot and outlet pass from the rebound.
- Move the ball down the floor using a wide formation.
- Score from a break.

GAME 1

Setup   5v5, full court

Goal   On defense, use an outlet pass after rebounding the ball, and score before the opponent sets up.

Conditions

- Players call their own fouls and use a 30-second offensive clock.
- The defensive team gets 1 point for a successful rebound and outlet pass and 3 points for scoring off the break (within eight seconds of the rebound).

Questions

Q: After the rebound, what did you do to get the ball down the floor quickly?

A: Used fast, accurate passes and quickly created open passing lanes down the court.

Q: What was the best way to create these passing lanes?

A: By moving down the court, spreading out, and using the whole court.

PRACTICE TASK

Setup   Use 5v5, with one shooter (O5) and one outlet (X5) (figure 12.5). On the ball release, players X1, X2, X3, and X4 turn and box out offensive players. Player X5 moves right or left, depending on which side of the basket the rebound occurs. The player rebounding the ball turns and passes to the outlet, player X5. Then the point guard or off-guard moves up the court and toward center court to create a passing lane. The next available player fills the outside lane, opposite the rebound. Trailing players move down the court as quickly as possible and assume offensive positions. Players repeat the task three times and then rotate.

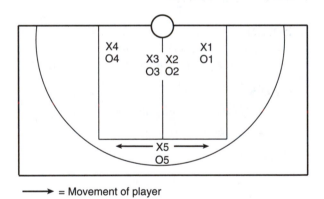

Figure 12.5

Goal   Score off three consecutive fast breaks.

Cues

- Anticipate.
- Move quickly to support.
- Support down the court, toward the basket.
- Stay wide.

GAME 2

Repeat game 1.

Tactical Problems Attacking the basket and creating space to attack

Lesson Focus Layup and clear-out

Objective Use a clear-out to create space for a teammate to drive to the basket and score using a layup.

GAME 1

Setup 5v5, half-court

Goal Score off the dribble.

Conditions

- Play restarts at half-court.
- After one scoring attempt, defense goes on offense and offense rotates out while a new team of five rotates in at half-court and plays defense.
- Teams use player-to-player defense.
- The offensive team must score off the dribble.
- Players earn 1 point for hitting the rim and 2 points for making a field goal.

Questions

Q: What did the off-the-ball players do to allow the on-the-ball player to score off the dribble?

A: Cleared the lane so the on-the-ball player could drive to the basket.

Q: What type of shot was used to score?

A: A layup.

PRACTICE TASK 1

Setup Players pair up and play 1v1, using cooperative defense. The offensive player starts at the 3-point line with the ball, fakes or jukes, and drives to the basket. Players use right hands when shooting from the right side of the basket and left hands when shooting from the left side of the basket. They rotate after each drive and begin the drive from different areas of the 3-point line. Increase the intensity of the defense to active and then to competitive as play improves.

Goal Score on three consecutive possessions.

Cues

- Fake, use the crossover step, dribble, and drive.
- Take off from the left; then shoot right (right side of the basket).
- Take off from the right; then shoot left (left side of the basket).

PRACTICE TASK 2

Setup Add players to the game (3v3, 4v4, or 5v5). Begin with a cooperative defense. Allow teams to devise different methods of clearing and distracting defenders. Teams can also design plays. Encourage teams to work on reading the defense and encourage the on-the-ball player to anticipate cuts and picks.

Goal Score on three consecutive possessions.

Cues

- Fake toward the basket and then cut away.
- Create space in which the driving player can lay off (in case the defender stops the drive).

GAME 2

Repeat game 1.

LESSON 23

Tactical Problem   Restarting play

Lesson Focus   Inbound pass from the offensive end line

Objective   Run a set play to achieve an inbound pass.

GAME 1

Setup 5v5, full court

Goal Score within 10 seconds of inbounding the ball from the end line.

Conditions

- Dribbling is not permitted except to drive to the basket.
- Teams use a 2-1-2 defense to defend the space around the basket.
- Play restarts from the end line.

Question

Q: What did your team do to score within 10 seconds of the inbound pass?

A: Passed quickly, moved quickly, and set up screens and picks to create open passing lanes.

PRACTICE TASK 1

Setup   At the end line, players practice a play against a 2-1-2 defense that you design. They play 5v5 with an active defense on a half-court.

Goal Score three times in a row against a 2-1-2 defense.

PRACTICE TASK 2

Setup   Teams create and practice their own end-line plays against a 2-1-2 defense. Each team of five creates an offensive play and then practices it against the opponent. They use an active defense.

Goal Score three times in a row against a 2-1-2 defense.

Cues

- Know your role.
- Execute your role.
- Remember that timing is everything.

GAME 2

Repeat game 1.

Condition   Teams score an extra point when they successfully execute a play.

LESSON 24

Secondary Level IV

Tactical Problem   Defending space

Lesson Focus   2-1-2 zone defense

Objectives

- Execute a 2-1-2 zone defense (teams).
- Execute proper defensive positioning when on and off the ball (individual players).

GAME 1

Setup   5v5, full court

Goal   Use a 2-1-2 defense to keep the opponent from scoring.

Conditions

- Dribbling is not permitted in the frontcourt.
- Players must complete at least three passes to different players before attempting a shot.

Questions

Q: Where did the offensive team take most of its shots?

A: Outside the key area.

Q: Was the zone defense easier or harder to play than the player-to-player defense?

A: Easier, because we didn't have to move as much and it was easier to keep the offense away from the basket and to get rebounds because we were closer to the basket.

Q: What were the disadvantages of the zone defense as compared with the one-on-one defense?

A: We couldn't always get to the ball, it was hard to defend long-range shooters and hard to play when two players were in our zone, and we couldn't see all offensive players at once.

PRACTICE TASK 1

Setup   Players practice a 2-1-2 zone shift with one team playing defense and the other team standing around the perimeter. The offensive team passes the ball quickly around the perimeter, allowing the defensive players to practice positioning and covering opponents inside their areas of the zone. Players practice talking to each other, communicating the positions of offensive players.

Goal   Give the offensive team no open shots within 15 feet (4.6 m) of the basket.

PRACTICE TASK 2

Setup   Players repeat task 1, but focus on positioning for on-the-ball and off-the-ball defense, picking up or escorting players as they pass through their areas of the zone, and knowing when not to pick up an offensive player (e.g., not guarding players too far from the basket to be shooting threats).

Goal   Know the positions of off-the-ball players at all times.

Cues

- Talk.
- Anticipate.
- Play aggressive on-the-ball defense.
- Cover players in your zone.

GAME 2

Repeat game 1.

LESSON 25

Tactical Problem   Creating and using space in the attack

Lesson Focus   Offense against a 2-1-2 defense

Objectives

- Run offensive plays against a 2-1-2 defense.
- Identify the strengths and weaknesses of a 2-1-2 defense.

GAME 1

Setup   5v5, full court

Goals

- On defense, use a 2-1-2 defense to defend the space around the basket.
- On offense, score off the 2-1-2 defense.

Conditions

- Dribbling is not permitted in the frontcourt.
- Players must complete at least three passes to different players before attempting a shot.

Question

Q: What did you do to score off the 2-1-2 zone defense?

A: Moved the ball quickly, drew one or more defenders to create passing lanes, and used screens to create shooting opportunities.

PRACTICE TASK 1

Setup   Players practice an offensive play against a 2-1-2 defense that you design. They play 5v5 with an active defense on a full court or half-court.

Goal   Score three times in a row against a 2-1-2 defense.

Cues

- Move the ball quickly.
- Use lots of off-the-ball movement.
- Pick or screen.

PRACTICE TASK 2

Setup Teams create and practice their own offensive plays against a 2-1-2 defense. Each team of five creates an offensive play and then practices it against an opponent. Teams use an active defense.

Goal Score three times in a row against a 2-1-2 defense.

Cues

- Pass quickly.
- Cut quickly.
- Support.
- Screen.

GAME 2

Repeat game 1.

Condition Teams score an extra point when they execute a play as planned and score a basket off the play.

SUMMARY

This chapter has provided four levels of lessons. The lessons do not encompass the full range of teaching possibilities, and you can develop many other lessons and sequences. We hope we have given you a starting point for developing your own sequence of lessons at four or even more levels, depending on the time you have available and the abilities of your students or players.

Let students play at a level at which they are comfortable. Impose only those conditions that they are ready to handle. If you or your students become frustrated, stand back and assess the situation. Talk to your students. They need to understand how to modify games so everyone can play and be successful. Remember, it is not participation but *success* that increases the likelihood of your students' future involvement in basketball. So sound the buzzer and let the games begin!

Chapter 13

Lacrosse

Kath Howarth
State University of New York
Cortland, New York

This chapter continues to explore a tactical approach to teaching invasion games at the secondary level, focusing on lacrosse. Lacrosse creates some interesting challenges for the teacher. First, the adult game has a distinct form for men and another for women. Second, because lacrosse requires a stick, fostering early success in the game can be a little more challenging for the teacher. Lacrosse is an exciting and unusual game in which students run fast while using the basic skills of catching and throwing. The use of space behind the goal is unique and creates special problems for the defense. With careful planning and modified equipment, you can introduce a generic form of lacrosse to coed classes with the understanding that as students begin to enjoy the game, they may want to learn the specific skills and tactics of women's and men's lacrosse in club or varsity teams.

The facilities and equipment needed for an introduction to lacrosse include the following:

- Either a large indoor space with a high roof or a space outdoors.
- Modified equipment including beginner sticks or short-handled youth sticks.
- One soft ball per student, either normal size or slightly larger than a lacrosse ball (beginner sticks come with larger lacrosse balls).
- Several small goals, preferably enough for small-sided games of three to seven players per side, with safe space to play in behind each goal.
- At least one full-size set of goalposts (more if possible) to show how the goal affects the placement of attack and defense players around the goal and

goalie. Shooting nets, which cover the center of the goal but have open edges, are good for creating a challenge to scoring goals. Marking a centerline and a fan in front of the goal circle is desirable.

- Markers for extra goal circles, such as spots, rubber lines, and so on.
- A variety of balls, such as small foam balls and handballs, that can be used for throwing and catching games. These remove the technical frustrations of using sticks when exploring some tactical situations.

All lessons in this chapter start with a game, although you may need to insert some simple warm-up activities using the stick and ball to allow for extra individual practice. Older students will likely be familiar with some aspects of lacrosse, and frustration levels may vary among students as you introduce the game problems. Allow students to play some games without sticks so they can feel the flow of the game without the technical problems sometimes posed by the sticks. Many lessons in this chapter have diagrams to help you visualize the field of play and players' posi-

Sticks can be shortened to a length appropriate for your students' level.

tions. Not all players' stick positions are shown—only those of key players (such as the player with the ball and the next player to receive).

Safety is a priority, especially when implements are used in invasion games. For a coed class to play lacrosse safely, the authentic ball should not be used. Authentic sticks, particularly men's sticks, are also unsafe unless the safety precautions required for the adult sport are followed. Remember to follow school district rulings about eye protection and mouth guards. Only a noncontact form of lacrosse should be introduced in physical education. This form does not reduce, but rather enhances, the fun of the game at a beginning level.

Table 13.1 presents the tactical problems, movements, and skills in lacrosse. A detailed outline of the levels of complexity for each tactical problem appears in table 13.2. Some concepts take more time to develop than others, particularly because of the associated stick skills that must be acquired. You may need to repeat or extend lessons to give students time to develop confidence in the requisite techniques.

LEVEL I

The most important goals at level I are maintaining possession and protecting the ball. Lacrosse is fun because there are usually lots of opportunities to score. Thus, attacking the goal is also a priority. Because passing and catching with the lacrosse stick present particular problems, lessons for level I focus on developing safe passing and catching skills, especially those related to accuracy and to creating open passing lanes. Games in level I can be started simply with a pass rather than with the more difficult draw or face-off starts used in the women's and men's competitions. In fact, the shape of some of the modified beginner sticks can hinder these starting techniques. When play goes out of bounds, the nearest player can bring the ball onto the field, or the ball can change possession.

Emphasis on defense is low in level I because the game needs to flow and the technical problems of passing and catching are sufficient handicaps at first. However, there is good reason to emphasize what the defender can do when the ball is in the air or on the ground, because the skill of catching can be practiced in defense as intercepting. Also, picking up the ball is an important part of the beginner game, whether it is done on offense to maintain possession or on defense to win the ball and regain possession. Success when in possession of the ball is the key to motivation in the early stages of lacrosse.

Table 13.1 Tactical Problems, Movements, and Skills in Lacrosse

Tactical problems	Off-the-ball movements	On-the-ball skills
SCORING (OFFENSE)		
Maintaining possession of the ball	• Supporting the ball carrier • Signaling	• Protecting the ball—cradling • Safe passing and catching • Passing—long, short, back, feed, swing • Variety of cradling and passing under pressure • Picking up the ground ball • Changing hands when running • Changing hands to pass
Attacking the goal	Passing patterns	• Variety of shots • Fakes • Passing patterns • Feeding the cutter • Turning • Rolling • Dodging
Creating space in attack	• Dodging • Clearing patterns • Triangle shape in attack • Cutting and replacing • Overlaps • Picks • V-cut • Settled attack • Fast break • Transition to attack	Passing—long, short, back, feed, swing
Using space in attack	• Give-and-go • Timing the cuts • Using width and depth • Pick-and-roll • Swinging play in attack • Creating overlaps	• Driving to the goal • Drawing defenders away
PREVENTING SCORING (DEFENSE)		
Defending space	• Marking, pressuring, denying, covering the passing lane • Intercepting, sliding • Backing up • Team defense	Clearing the ball away from the goal
Defending the goal	• Player-to-player defense • Ball, player, goal position • Zone defense • Team defense • Communication	• Intercepting, clearing the ball • Picking up a loose ball
Winning the ball	Double-teaming	Blocking the pass Ground ball control
RESTARTING PLAY		
Draw or face-off	• Positioning • Supporting the ball carrier	Taking the draw or face-off
Free position	• Positioning • Supporting the ball carrier	
Off-side or out of bounds	• Positioning • Supporting the ball carrier	

Table 13.2 Levels of Tactical Complexity for Lacrosse

Tactical goals and problems	Level I	Level II	Level III	Level IV
SCORING (OFFENSE)				
Maintaining possession of the ball	• Safe passing and catching • Picking up the ground ball • Protecting the ball—cradling • Signaling	• Supporting the ball carrier • Changing hands when running • Passing—long, short, back, feed, swing	Changing hands to pass	Variety of cradling and passing under pressure
Attacking the goal	Variety of shots	• Variety of shots • Turning • Rolling • Dodging	Feeding the cutter	• Variety of shots • Fakes • Passing patterns
Creating space in attack	• Triangle shape in attack • Passing—long, short, back, feed, swing • Dodging	V-cut	• Fast break • Cutting and replacing • Overlaps • Clearing patterns	• Settled attack • Picks • Transition to attack
Using space in attack		• Give-and-go • Timing the cuts	Using width and depth	• Swinging play in attack • Creating overlaps • Driving to the goal • Drawing defenders away • Pick-and-roll
PREVENTING SCORING (DEFENSE)				
Defending space		• Marking, pressuring, denying • Intercepting	• Covering the passing lane • Sliding • Intercepting • Clearing the ball away from the goal	• Backing up • Team defense
Defending the goal	• Intercepting, clearing the ball • Picking up a loose ball	Ball, player, goal position	• Team defense • Player-to-player defense	• Player-to-player defense • Zone defense • Communication • Team defense
Winning the ball	Ground ball control	Blocking the pass		Double-teaming
RESTARTING PLAY				
Draw or face-off	Positioning			• Taking the draw or face-off • Supporting the ball carrier
Free position	Positioning			Supporting the ball carrier
Off-side or out of bounds	Positioning			Supporting the ball carrier

A focus on learning to catch and pass properly will later help students enjoy the fast pace of the game.

LESSON 1

Tactical Problem   Maintaining possession of the ball

Lesson Focus   Passing, signaling, receiving, and controlling the ball

Objectives

- Protect the ball.
- Signal for and control the ball.
- Pass quickly and accurately.

GAME 1

Setup   1+1+1 (figure 13.1)

Goals

- Keep the ball in the air or in the stick.
- Score by successfully passing the ball among the three players.

Conditions

- Players must stay in a restricted area.
- Five passes without a miss equals 1 point.

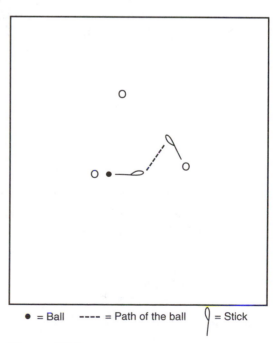

● = Ball   ---- = Path of the ball   ⧙ = Stick

Figure 13.1

Questions

Q: What was the goal of your game?

A: To keep the ball safe.

Q: How did you score?

A: By successfully passing the ball.

Q: What did you have to do when the ball was missed and was on the ground?

A: Scoop it up.

PRACTICE TASK 1

Setup   In groups of three, practice passing to the left and right.

Goals

- Catch the ball safely.
- Pass accurately to the side of the player signaling for the ball.
- Lead the catcher by sending the ball away from the catcher's body.

Cues

- Catching:
  - Present a target by reaching out to the ball and opening the face of the stick to the ball.
  - Point your feet and the stick in the same direction.
  - Cushion the ball as it enters the stick.
  - Take both hands to your nondominant side to catch, or try to change hand position.
- Throwing:
  - Throw side-on to the target, taking the head of the stick back and pointing the bottom of the stick toward the target (the partner's stick).
  - Make a high overarm throw with the top hand and pull the bottom hand in as the top hand moves toward the target.

PRACTICE TASK 2

Students practice picking up a ground ball on their own.

Goal   Pick up the ball smoothly and continue running.

Cues

- Point the head of the stick at the ball.
- Lower the stick to the bottom-hand side and push firmly with the bottom hand through the pickup.
- Place one foot level with the ball.
- Raise the stick quickly to maintain control and to prepare to pass or shoot.

GAME 2

Setup   2v1 using a hoop as a goal (figure 13.2)

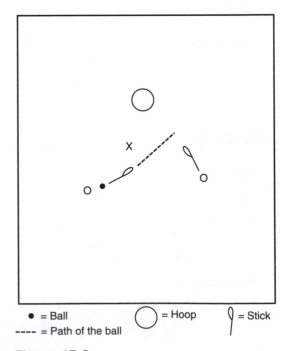

● = Ball   ◯ = Hoop   ⌇ = Stick

---- = Path of the ball

Figure 13.2

Goals

- Score as many goals as possible in the set amount of time.
- Pass accurately to a partner and away from the defender.

Conditions

- Teams score 1 point for every goal and an extra point for three passes made without interception by the defender and without dropping the ball.
- The defender must stay a stick's length away from the hoop.
- Only one person can go for the ground ball (the nearest person).

Questions

Q: Why was this game harder than the first?

A: Because there was a defender and we had to score as many goals as possible in a set time.

Q: How did you keep the ball?

A: By keeping passes short and accurate.

Q: What difference did the defenders make?

A: They made us move in order to pass and catch safely.

LESSON 2

Secondary Level I

Tactical Problem   Maintaining possession of the ball

Lesson Focus   Passing from the nondominant side, signaling, and receiving and controlling the ball

Objectives

- Protect the ball.
- Signal for and control the ball.
- Pass quickly and accurately from both sides of the body.

GAME 1

Setup   2v1 (figure 13.3)

Goals

- Keep the ball in the air or in the stick.
- Score by successfully passing the ball between partners four times.

Conditions

- Players must stay in the restricted area.
- Players use a cool defense (defenders stay one arm's length away).

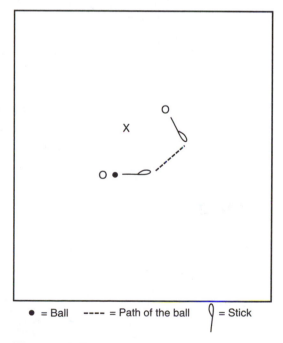

● = Ball   ---- = Path of the ball   ﾖ = Stick

Figure 13.3

Questions

Q: What was the goal of your game?

A: To keep the ball safe and away from the defender.

Q: How did you score?

A: By passing the ball between us four times.

PRACTICE TASK

Setup   In a triad, players throw the ball from the right or left side depending on where the defender stands (i.e., throw from the free side).

Goals

- Pass accurately from the free side (the side away from the defender) to the player signaling for the ball.
- Catch the ball safely.
- Signal for the pass.
- Get to the ball first when it's on the ground.

Cues

- Throwing:
  - When throwing from the dominant side, step with the opposite foot toward the target, move the head of the stick back and point the bottom of the stick toward the target (partner's stick), perform a high overarm throw with the top hand, and pull the bottom hand in as the top hand moves toward the target.
  - From the nondominant side, try a shovel pass. Swing the stick across your body, drop the head of the stick down, and shovel the ball toward the receiver (like shoveling snow).
- Catching:
  - Signal by reaching out to the ball and opening the face of the stick to the ball.
  - Point your feet and stick in the direction the thrower is moving so you are not blocked by the defender.
  - Cushion the ball as it enters the stick.
  - Take both hands to the nondominant side to catch, or try to change hand position.
  - React quickly after a missed pass. When there is a ground ball, the first person to the ball gets possession.

GAME 2

Setup   3v3 keep-away (no goals), played with sticks or with no implement depending on the skills of the students (figure 13.4)

Goals

- Score as many points as possible in the set amount of time.
- Pass accurately to teammates and away from defenders.

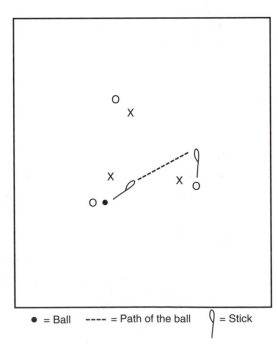

● = Ball   ---- = Path of the ball   ⎝ = Stick

Figure 13.4

Conditions

- Teams score 1 point for every three successful passes made without an interception by the defender or without dropping the ball.
- The defender must stay a stick's length away from the opponent.

Questions

Q: Why was this game harder than the first?

A: Because there was a defender and we had to score as many points as possible in a set time.

Q: How did you keep the ball?

A: By keeping passes short and accurate and away from the defender.

Q: What difference did the defenders make?

A: They made us move in order to pass and catch safely. We had to pass from and to the free side.

LESSON 3

Tactical Problem   Creating space in attack

Lesson Focus   Creating passing lanes

Objectives

- Move to open space.
- Make safe passes.

GAME 1

Setup   Use 1v1 with a feeder (three players total) behind a marker and with a goal (hoop or line). See figure 13.5.

Goal   Get open, receive the pass, and go to the goal.

Condition   The feeder cannot move over the line until a pass has been made.

Questions

Q: How did you get open?

A: Moved and signaled into open space away from the defender.

Q: How did the feeder know when to pass the ball?

A: There was an open space (passing lane) between the feeder and the receiver's stick. The receiver watched and made eye contact with the feeder.

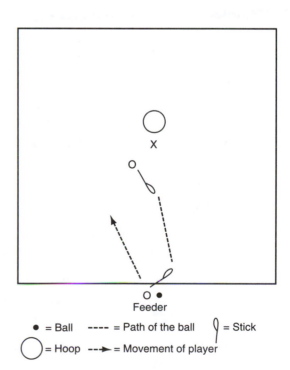

Figure 13.5

PRACTICE TASK

Setup   In a triad, players throw the ball to the receiver's stick as the receiver signals and moves away from a stationary defender. Increase the defender's role from stationary to moving as the attack becomes more successful (figure 13.6).

Goals

- Pass accurately to the free side of the player signaling for the ball.
- Lead the attack away from the defense by passing ahead of her outstretched stick.
- Signal for the pass and catch the ball safely.

Cues

- Dodging:
  - Use a sudden fake or sharp sprint to get into open space.
  - Lead with the stick held out as a target.
- Catching:
  - Signal by reaching out and opening the face of the stick to the ball.
  - Keep the stick as still as possible to give a good target.

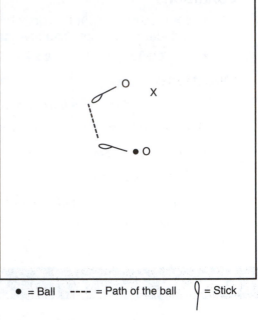

● = Ball   ---- = Path of the ball   ⎧ = Stick

Figure 13.6

GAME 2

Setup   3v3 keep-away (no goals)

Goals

- Score as many points as possible in the set amount of time.
- Pass accurately to teammates and away from defenders.

Conditions

- Teams score 3 points for three successful passes made without an interception by the defender and without dropping the ball.
- Teams score 2 points if one pass was dropped within the three completed possessions.
- Teams score 1 point if two passes were dropped within the three completed possessions.
- The defender must stay a stick's length away from the opponent.

Questions

Q: Why was this game harder than the first?

A: Because there was a defender and we had to score as many points as possible in a set time.

Q: How did you score the most points?

A: By passing and catching accurately without dropping the ball or losing possession.

Q: What did the defenders make you do?

A: They filled the space between us and made us dodge and move quicker in order to pass and catch safely.

Q: What is a passing lane?

A: An open space between the player with the ball and the receiver.

Tactical Problem   Attacking the goal

Lesson Focus   Shooting

Objectives

- Shoot with control.
- Cut, control, and shoot on target.

GAME 1

Setup   Use 1v1 with a feeder (three players total) behind a marker and with a goal (e.g., a street hockey or real lacrosse goal with the center area marked with pinnies to represent a goalie). See figure 13.7.

Goal   Get open, receive the pass, and shoot.

Conditions

- The feeder cannot move over the line until a pass has been made.
- Players use a static defense.

Questions

Q: When did you shoot and why?

A: When in front of the goal because this position gave the most space to aim at.

Q: Where did you aim the ball?

A: Into the corners and angled downward.

PRACTICE TASK

Setup   Use individual practice. Each player has a ball (figure 13.8). Make sure there are lots of targets.

Goals

- Run toward the goal or target and bounce the ball into the corners of the goal.
- Shoot from the optimal position in front of the goal.

Cues

- Maintain speed through the shot.
- Follow through to make the ball go downward.
- Practice in pairs and receive the ball from a partner; then run to the goal to score.

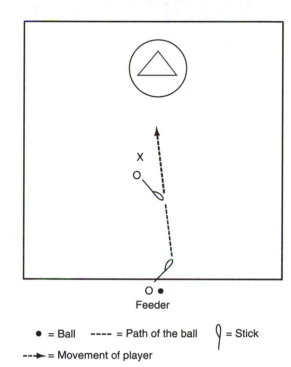

● = Ball   ---- = Path of the ball   ⊋ = Stick

--▶ = Movement of player

Figure 13.7

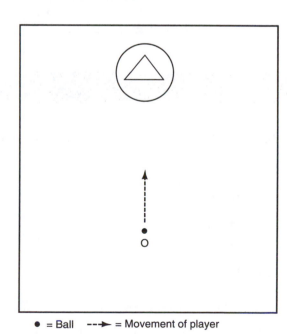

● = Ball   --▶ = Movement of player

Figure 13.8

GAME 2

Setup   3v3 with one goal and with a cone at the other end of the space to mark the start of the game (figure 13.9)

Goals

- Score as many times as possible.
- Keep the shooting space open and ready for the shooter to move into and receive the ball.

Conditions

- The three attackers become defenders after scoring.
- The game starts from the cone after each goal.
- Players must pass at least once before taking a shot.
- No defender is allowed to stand in front of the goal.

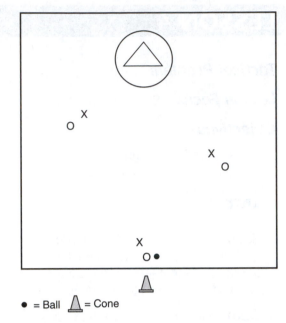

● = Ball   △ = Cone

Figure 13.9

Questions

Q: What was the primary aim for the attacking team?

A: To get a player in front of the goal and ready to take a shot.

Q: How did you do this?

A: By keeping that space open so someone could dodge or cut away from the defender into that space and receive the ball.

Q: What was hard about this game?

A: Timing the move to receive and shoot the ball from the best spot in front of goal and keeping the space open for the person to run into and score.

LESSON 5

Secondary Level I

Tactical Problem   Creating space in attack

Lesson Focus   Giving passing options for the ball carrier

Objectives

- Use the attack triangle.
- Create passing lanes.

GAME 1

Setup   3v3 keep-away with no goal (figure 13.10)

Goal   Offer options for the ball carrier by forming a triangle shape in attack.

Condition   Players change possession of the ball after five successful passes. (Five passes is 1 point—keep score.)

Questions

Q: Why is a triangle important for your game?

A: It gives the ball carrier two directions in which to pass the ball.

Q: What else do you have to think about when you are helping your teammate make a safe pass?

A: Opening up space for the pass by creating a passing lane between me and the ball.

Q: In which direction should the ball carrier pass, if possible?

A: Away from the defender and into the open space.

PRACTICE TASK

Setup   Players are in threes. The defender marks the receiver (from front or behind). The receiver moves suddenly away from the defender to signal and receive the ball (figure 13.11). The pie shape on the diagram represents the free side of the player who is moving to receive the ball.

Goals

- Create space by dodging away from a defender.
- Create space by moving with the ball away from the defender.

Cues

- Receiver:
  - Make the move very sudden.
  - Lead with the open stick.
  - Fake if necessary.
  - Move in the direction in which the thrower is open (the thrower's free side).
- Defender—Mark the thrower (front or side).
- Thrower—Pass to the receiver only if there is no defender between you and the receiver (i.e., there is a passing lane).

GAME 2

Setup   3v3 with one goal and one hoop (figure 13.9)

Goals

- Score as many goals as possible.
- Keep the triangle shape while on offense, and help the ball carrier by creating passing lanes and open spaces.
- On defense, regain possession and take the ball to the hoop.

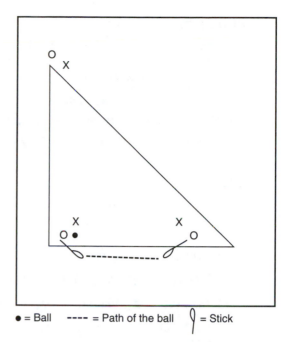

● = Ball   ---- = Path of the ball   = Stick

Figure 13.10

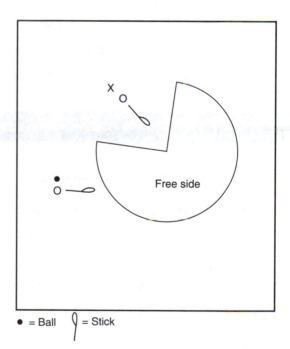

● = Ball   = Stick

Figure 13.11

Conditions

- The three attackers become defenders after five minutes of play, at which time scoring starts over.
- The game starts from the hoop after each goal is scored.
- Players must pass at least once before taking a shot.
- No defender is allowed to stand in front of the goal.
- The defending team can score by taking the ball away from the offense and putting it in the hoop.

Questions

Q: What was the primary aim for the attacking team?

A: To score.

Q: How did you score?

A: By keeping space open and giving options to the passer by using a triangle shape in offense.

Q: How else did you create space?

A: By opening up passing lanes among teammates and taking the ball away from the defender to pass.

Q: What is a passing lane?

A: The open space between the ball and the receiver (free of defense players).

Q: What do you do to create that space?

A: Use dodging and fakes and move the stick away from the defender to pass or to signal for the pass.

LESSON 6

Tactical Problem   Attacking the goal

Lesson Focus   Using the space behind the goal

Objectives

- Feed the ball to a cutter.
- Use the player behind the goal as a safety.

GAME 1

Setup   3v3 with one goal (figure 13.12)

Goal   Offer options behind the goal for the ball carrier by forming a triangle shape in attack.

Conditions

- One attacker must always be behind the goal.
- Players change possession after a goal has been scored.
- The ball must be passed at least once to the person behind the goal.

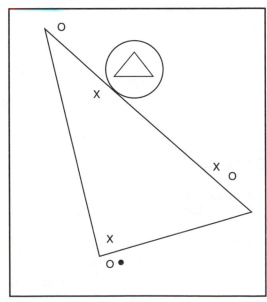

• = Ball

Figure 13.12

Questions

Q: Why is a triangle important for your game?

A: It gives the ball carrier two directions in which to pass the ball.

Q: What is the point of having a player behind the goal?

A: To feed the ball to players who are in positions to score.

Q: Anything else?

A: He can be a safety receiver because his defender will probably not mark him as closely behind the goal.

PRACTICE TASK

Setup   Players are in threes. The defender marks the receiver at the start. The receiver moves suddenly away from the defender and toward the goal to signal and receive the ball from the feeder, who stands behind and to the side of the goal (figure 13.13).

Goal   Feed the cutter at the right moment so she can score.

Cues

- Cutter:
    - Make the move very sudden.
    - Lead with the open stick.
    - Fake if necessary.
- Feeder:
    - Make the pass flat and direct.
    - Time the pass so the receiver is in the best shooting position.

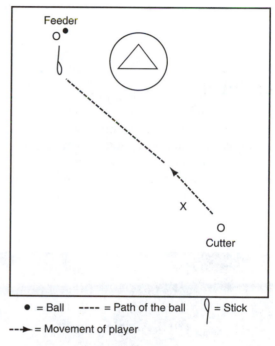

● = Ball   - - - - = Path of the ball   ⎰ = Stick

- - -► = Movement of player

Figure 13.13

GAME 2

Setup   3v3 with one goal and one hoop at the opposite end of the playing area

Goals

- On offense, score in the goal as many times as possible.
- On offense, keep the triangle shape and help the ball carrier by creating passing lanes and open spaces.
- On defense, score by regaining possession and taking the ball to the hoop.

Conditions

- The game starts from behind the goal.
- There must be an attack player behind the goal at all times.
- The three attackers become defenders after five minutes of play, at which time scoring starts over.
- Players must pass at least once before taking a shot.

Questions

Q: What was the primary aim for the attacking team?

A: To score.

Q: How did you do this?

A: By keeping space open and giving options to the passer by using a triangle shape in offense.

Q: What was the role of the player behind the goal?

A: To be a feeder and a safety receiver.

Q: What important skills does that player need?

A: Accurate passing and good timing.

LEVEL II

At level II the major focus is still on maintaining possession and scoring. However, lessons start looking at simple tactical concepts for defending the player and the goal. As students become more successful in scoring, they need to study the roles of offensive players who are off the ball, particularly because play can continue behind the goal. Thus, using and creating space in lacrosse have an added dimension around the goal. As the defense improves, attack players have to help each other more by considering when and where to move. Students need to develop attacking skills such as changing hands on the stick as well as a variety of passing options. Attackers also need to work on scoring goals when less time and space are available.

Students need to learn attacking skills such as various hand placements and passes.

LESSON 7

Tactical Problem   Maintaining possession

Lesson Focus   Supporting the ball carrier

Objectives

- Help a teammate under pressure.
- Pass under pressure.

GAME 1

Setup   3v3 in a square area

Goals

- Offer options for the ball carrier by creating passing lanes.
- Score by making four successful passes.

Conditions

- The ball changes possession after four passes.
- The ball must be passed at least once to each person.

Questions

Q: How can you support your teammates?

A: Signal clearly with the stick away from the defense, and change position to keep the defender busy.

Q: What can the ball carrier do to maintain possession when under pressure from a defender?

A: Pull the stick away from the defender and keep the feet moving while looking for help.

PRACTICE TASK

Setup   Players are in threes. The defender marks the ball carrier, who is trying to move toward the goal (a hoop). One offensive player tries to dodge past the defense, and the second one moves to help the ball carrier (figure 13.14).

Goal   Support the offense.

Cues

- Receiver:
  - Move very clearly and early.
  - Lead with the open stick to the side away from the defender to create a passing lane.
  - Change position when the ball carrier changes stick position to keep the passing lane open.
- Passer:
  - Keep your head up and look for help.
  - Pass only if the offense has opened a clear passing lane.
  - Keep the stick and ball away from the defense.
  - Keep your feet moving.

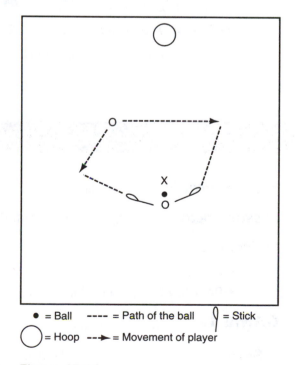

● = Ball   ---- = Path of the ball   ⏐ = Stick

◯ = Hoop   --▶ = Movement of player

Figure 13.14

GAME 2

Setup 4v3 with one goal and a hoop for the defense to take the ball to when they regain possession (figure 13.15)

Goals

- On offense, score in the goal as many times as possible.
- On offense, keep the triangle shape and help the ball carrier by moving and creating passing lanes and open spaces.
- On defense, score by regaining possession and taking the ball to the hoop.

Conditions

- The game starts from behind the goal.
- There must be an unmarked attack player behind the goal at all times, and each player fills this role in turn.
- The three attackers become defenders after five minutes of play, at which time scoring starts over.
- Players must pass at least once before taking a shot.

Questions

Q: *How did you score?*

A: *By keeping the shooting space open and giving options to the passer by using a triangle shape in offense.*

Q: *What was the role of the player behind the goal?*

A: *To support a player under pressure by being a safety receiver.*

Q: *What important skills does that player need?*

A: *Accurate passing and good timing.*

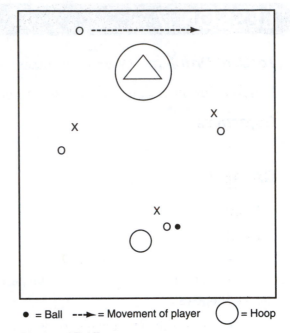

● = Ball ---➤ = Movement of player ◯ = Hoop

Figure 13.15

LESSON 8

Secondary Level II

Tactical Problem   Defending space

Lesson Focus   Marking an opponent off the ball and pressuring the opponent with the ball

Objectives

- Pressure the pass.
- Be ready to intercept the ball.

GAME 1

Setup   3v3 with one goal for the offense and a line to which the defense can take the ball to safety (figure 13.16)

Goals

- Prevent scoring.
- Keep the opponent from receiving the ball.

Conditions

- No body contact allowed.
- No stick checking allowed.
- Players score 1 point for intercepting a ball, getting a ground ball, or taking a ball to safety.

Questions

Q: What do you do when your opponent has the ball?

A: Stay between her and the goal and follow her stick with my stick.

Q: What do you do in defense when your opponent does not have the ball?

A: Stop her from receiving a pass either by marking her and forcing the pass to go elsewhere or by intercepting the pass.

PRACTICE TASK 1

Setup Players are in pairs with one ball. The attacker runs down a line or a channel of space with the ball. The defender tries to position himself so that the attacker is forced to stay on one side of the line or channel (this may be the attacker's weak side or the area away from the middle of the field or the goal). See figure 13.17.

Goals

- On defense, control the attacker's movement through body positioning.
- On defense, reduce the options for the attacker.

Cues

- Mirror the attacker's movement and stick position.
- Go hip to hip.

PRACTICE TASK 2

Setup Players are in threes with one ball. Two attackers pass the ball back and forth. The defender starts at right angles to and 2 yards away from the attack (figure 13.18). As the passes are made, the defender times a fast run to try to intercept the ball. If she intercepts, she passes the ball back and tries again with the other attacker. Players change roles after five tries.

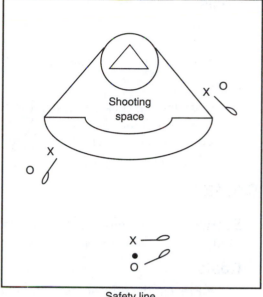

● = Ball   ꪀ = Stick

Figure 13.16

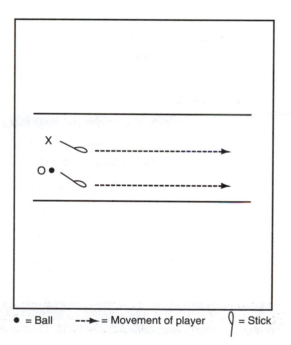

● = Ball   ---▶ = Movement of player   ꪀ = Stick

Figure 13.17

Goals

- Time the run to the preparation movement of the passer.
- Keep running once the ball is in the stick.

Cues

- Stretch the stick out, watch the passer carefully, and accelerate.
- Keep the stick still and don't try to knock the ball down.

GAME 2

Setup 3v3 with one goal for the offense and a line to which the defense can take the ball to safety

Goals

- Prevent the offense from entering the shooting area to score.
- Keep the opponent from receiving the ball.

Conditions

- No body contact allowed.
- No stick checking allowed.
- Players score 1 point for intercepting, getting a ground ball, or taking the ball to the safety line.

Questions

Q: How do you decide where to force your offense to move with the ball?

A: Force the offense away from the shooting area, and make offensive players move their sticks to their weak (nondominant) sides.

Q: Where on the field is it safest to go for an interception?

A: Away from the scoring area and away from the center of the field.

Q: If your opponent has the ball, where should you be and why?

A: Between him and the goal to slow him down and force him away from a shooting position.

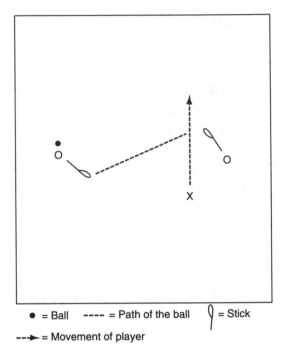

● = Ball   ---- = Path of the ball   ⸮ = Stick

--➤ = Movement of player

Figure 13.18

LESSON 9

Secondary Level II

Tactical Problem   Winning the ball

Lesson Focus   Regaining possession of a loose ball and gaining possession in transitions

Objectives

- Win the draw or face-off.
- Win the ground ball.

GAME 1

Setup 3v3 keep-away with no goals

Goals

- Reduce the number of passes the opposition can make.
- Regain possession of the ball.

Condition No body or stick contact allowed.

Questions

Q: What do you do to regain possession of the ball?

A: Intercept or be the first on the ball when it goes on the ground.

Q: How can you make it harder for your opponents to pass?

A: Mark them closely both on and off the ball.

Q: What should you do when you lose the ball?

A: Quickly try to get it back and become a defender.

PRACTICE TASK 1

Setup Players are in threes with one ball (figure 13.19). Player O1 rolls the ball between players O2 and O3, who both try to get to the ball, pick it up, and gain possession (the first player there gets the ball). The winner passes the ball to player O1.

Goals

- Get to the ball first.
- Pick up the ball and keep moving.

Cues

- Move quickly.
- Lower the head of the stick and push it strongly under the ball to scoop the ball up.
- If the ball is moving away too fast, quickly stop it and then scoop it up.

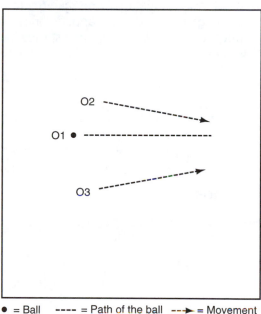

● = Ball   ---- = Path of the ball   --→ = Movement of player

Figure 13.19

PRACTICE TASK 2

Setup Players are in threes with one ball (figure 13.20). Set up the draw (rather than the face-off because the draw gets the ball into the air). One player acts as the official and places the ball between the backs of the other players' sticks. The other two players draw and try to get the ball toward their wings.

The two player O's in the center represent the two players who take the draw (in the women's game) or the two midfielders who take the face-off (in the men's game). Until this happens, they are both on offense. Once the game begins, they become offense or defense depending on whose team wins the draw or face-off.

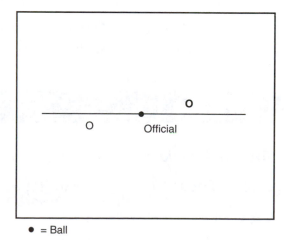

● = Ball

Figure 13.20

Goal   Win the ball either by moving it toward the goal or by catching it.

Cues

- Bend your knees and stay balanced to hold the ball between the backs of the sticks.
- Listen for the whistle (official can say "Whistle").
- Pull the stick quickly up and away.
- Try different pressures and speeds to control the ball.

GAME 2

Setup   3v3 with a line for a goal plus three extra players (one is the official and the other two are extra defenders guarding their own goal line; figure 13.21)

The two player O's in the center represent the two players who take the draw (in the women's game) or the two midfielders who take the face-off (in the men's game). Until this happens, they are both on offense. Once the game begins, they become offense or defense depending on whose team wins the draw or face-off.

Goals

- Win the draw and score by carrying (not throwing) the ball over the goal line.
- Regain possession by being the first on any ground ball or by intercepting a pass.

Conditions

- No body contact allowed.
- No stick checking allowed.

Questions

Q: When is your first chance to win the ball?

A: At the draw.

Q: Are there other opportunities to win the ball?

A: Yes, if the ball goes on the ground and if there is a bad pass that can be intercepted.

Q: What happens if the ball goes out of bounds?

A: The game stops and one of the teams is given the ball.

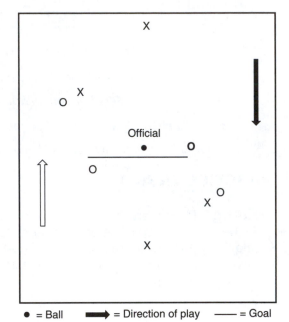

● = Ball   ➡ = Direction of play   ─── = Goal

Figure 13.21

LESSON 10

Secondary Level II

Tactical Problem   Creating space in attack

Lesson Focus   Making space to get free to receive the pass

Objective   Use a V-cut.

GAME 1

Setup   1v1 with a feeder (three players total) and with a hoop or goal or line (figure 13.22)

Goal   Get free to receive the ball and go to the goal.

Condition   The original feeder cannot continue in the game unless it is to receive the ball from the defense if the defense gains possession.

Questions

> Q: How can you create space for yourself to get free from your defender?
>
> A: Move in one direction and then quickly move in another.
>
> Q: Where do you want the ball to be passed?
>
> A: Into the space where I am moving away from my defender.

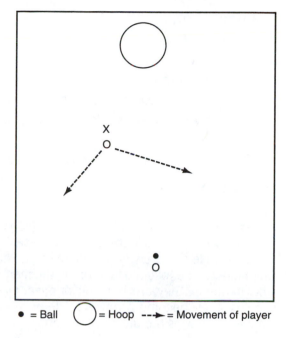

● = Ball   ◯ = Hoop   --▶ = Movement of player

Figure 13.22

PRACTICE TASK

Setup   Players are in threes practicing the V-cut; the final move is toward the ball (figures 13.23 and 13.24).

Goal   Create space in which to receive the ball.

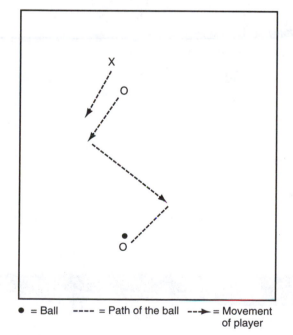

● = Ball   ---- = Path of the ball   --▶ = Movement of player

Figure 13.23

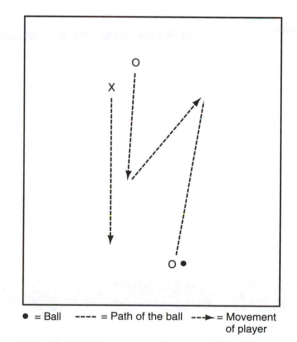

● = Ball   ---- = Path of the ball   --▶ = Movement of player

Figure 13.24

Cues

- Receiver:
  - Make the move very sudden and partially signal with the stick to make the defender follow.
  - Cut forward with a stronger signal into the space you create.
  - Once you are successful, try other directions for the V-cut.
  - Always receive the ball while moving away from the defender.
- Passer:
  - Pass only if the offense has opened a clear passing lane and given a convincing signal.

GAME 2

Setup 5v5 game with two goals (figure 13.25)
The two player O's in the center represent the two players who take the draw (in the women's game) or the two midfielders who take the face-off (in the men's game). Until this happens, they are both on offense. Once the game begins, they become offense or defense depending on whose team wins the draw or face-off.

Goal Help your team by creating space and cutting to the ball.

Conditions

- The game starts from the goal line.
- Teams must make at least three passes before they can score.

Questions

Q: What was the primary aim for the attacking team?

A: To score.

Q: How did you do this?

A: By cutting and recutting to open up spaces.

Q: Which cut is the hardest to mark?

A: The one that goes upfield toward the ball.

Q: Why is that hard?

A: Because at first the V-cut takes the defender toward her goal, which leaves the space between the passer and the ball uncovered.

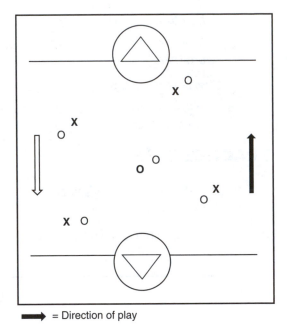

→ = Direction of play

Figure 13.25

LESSON 11

Tactical Problem Creating space in attack

Lesson Focus Creating and using space with the pass

Objective Use a give-and-go.

GAME 1

Setup   2v2 with a hoop or goal or line (figure 13.26)

Goal   Pass to a teammate, move to receive the ball, and go to the goal.

Conditions

- The ball must be passed twice before a goal can be scored.
- The player who starts the play with the ball is the only player who can score.

Questions

Q: How can you open up space to free yourself?

A: By passing the ball to another player.

Q: What does the defense do?

A: Move and look toward the ball.

PRACTICE TASK

Setup   Players are in fours practicing the give-and-go with a cool (almost stationary) defense (figure 13.27).

Goal   Create a space in which to receive the ball by deflecting the defender's attention from the space.

Cues

- Passer:
  - Send the ball out to the receiver on the wing.
  - When the defender looks after the ball, cut behind him and move again to receive the ball.
- Receiver—Control the ball quickly and keep your head up to see the runner moving for the give-and-go.

GAME 2

Setup   Use 4v4 with two goals (or hoops) at both ends of the field. (Having two options for scoring at each end keeps the game wide.) See figure 13.28.

Goal   Create space using the give-and-go midfield.

Conditions

- The game starts from the goal line.
- Teams must make at least three passes before they can score.

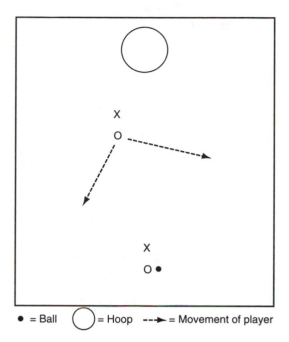

● = Ball   ◯ = Hoop   ---▶ = Movement of player

Figure 13.26

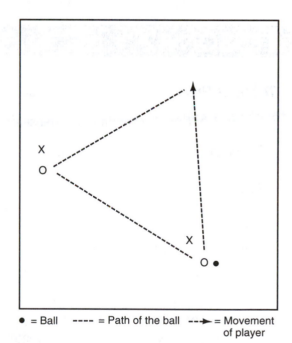

● = Ball   ---- = Path of the ball   ---▶ = Movement of player

Figure 13.27

Questions

Q: What was the primary aim for the attacking team?

A: To create space and score.

Q: How did you do this?

A: By opening up space with give-and-go moves.

Q: How did this help you?

A: The ball moves across the field and makes the defensive players move their focus. It gives us a chance to move and lose our defenders midfield.

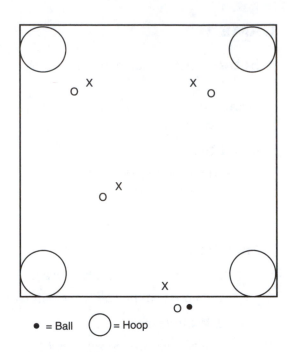

● = Ball   ◯ = Hoop

Figure 13.28

LESSON 12

Secondary Level II

Tactical Problem   Defending the goal

Lesson Focus   Preventing the offense from entering the goal area with or without the ball

Objective   Defend opponents on goal side and ball side when both on and off the ball.

GAME 1

Setup   3v3 with a goal

Goal   Prevent the offense from moving into the shooting area.

Conditions
- Defense starts with 10 points.
- Defense loses a point for every goal scored against them.
- Defense wins a point for every interception or other possession gained.

Questions

Q: How can you keep your opponents from scoring?

A: By preventing them from getting into a scoring position.

Q: What does the defense need to do?

A: Place themselves between offensive players and the goal area and closely mark the offensive player with the ball.

PRACTICE TASK

Setup   Players are in threes. With a hoop or cone as a goal, they practice correct goal-side and ball-side defensive positioning (figure 13.29).

Goals

- Force attackers away from the dangerous shooting area by being goal side.
- Move ball side to make passing as difficult as possible for attackers.

Cues

- Place your feet within the angle made by drawing lines from the goal to the player and from the player to the ball. Standing in this angle is standing in the goal-side, ball-side position.
- Try to see the ball as well as the opponent. As the player moves from one side to another, change your position so that you are always covering the player's line to the goal.
- Use the stick to reach into the passing lane if possible.

GAME 2

Setup   3v3 with one goal (figure 13.30)

Goal   Keep the offense from scoring a goal.

Conditions

- The ball starts at different points (e.g., from the center, from behind goal, and so on).
- Players play short, intense games (e.g., five minutes) to see if the defense can be successful.

Questions

Q: What was the primary aim for the defending team?

A: To keep the offense out of the scoring area.

Q: How did you do this?

A: By marking the opponent goal side and ball side whenever possible.

Q: How did doing this help you?

A: The offensive players always had a defender between them and their goal, and so they had to make passes away from the target area.

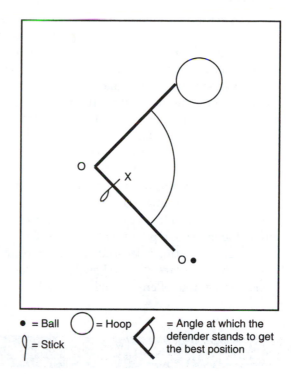

● = Ball   ◯ = Hoop   ⊲ = Angle at which the defender stands to get the best position

◖ = Stick

Figure 13.29

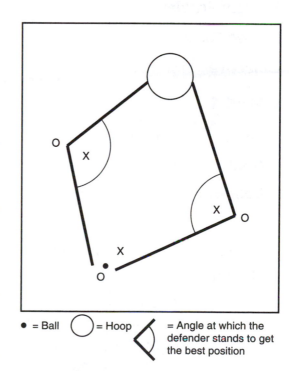

● = Ball   ◯ = Hoop   ⊲ = Angle at which the defender stands to get the best position

Figure 13.30

LEVEL III

Level III develops general offensive and defensive tactics into more team-oriented concepts. As the numbers of players on teams increase, so does the need to anticipate future plays two or three moves ahead. Working on offense may mean having more, equal, or fewer numbers than the defending team has, depending on the situation. Using a fast break or creating width and depth of support for the person with the ball demands an awareness of several options by off-the-ball offensive players. Similarly, defensive players begin working together to cover a free offensive player or begin working as a unit in a zone. In level III the tactical use of a free position or a turnover after a foul is added to the repertoire of solutions for restarting the game. At this level students can explore the roles of various players as well as the importance of transitioning from offense to defense.

Team-oriented plays require players to think ahead.

LESSON 13

Secondary Level III

Tactical Problem   Maintaining possession

Lesson Focus   Protecting the ball

Objective   Change hands to protect the ball.

GAME 1

Setup   3v3 within a square area marked by cones

Goal   Protect the ball and keep possession.

Conditions

- A successful pass to each player (minimum of three passes, but could include more) scores a point.
- Defense cannot touch a stick or person.

Questions

Q: How can you keep the ball safe?

A: Keep the stick and ball away from the defense.

Q: How do you do that?

A: Pull the stick to the side that is away from the defender, and run away from the defender.

PRACTICE TASK

Setup   Players are in pairs. The player in possession practices taking the ball away from the defender's stick by moving his own stick away and changing his top hand to the side the stick is moved to (i.e., the top hand on the left of the body is the left hand).

Goal   Change hands smoothly and keep control of the stick.

Cue   Slide the bottom hand up to switch hands so the stick remains under control.

GAME 2

Setup   3v3 in a square area marked by cones

Goal   Protect the ball by switching hands.

Conditions

- Teams score by keeping the ball for at least three successful passes.
- Players score 1 extra point by switching hands to protect the ball.

Questions

Q: How did you keep possession?

A: By changing hands and taking the ball away from the defender.

Q: What do you now need to learn?

A: How to make an overarm pass from the nondominant side.

LESSON 14

Tactical Problem   Maintaining possession

Lesson Focus   Variety in passing

Objectives

- Change hands to pass.
- Pass to a trail player.

GAME 1

Setup   3v3 within a rectangular area, with goals marked by cones at each end

Goal   Protect the ball and keep possession.

Conditions

- Players must change hands to protect the ball.
- Players score points for changing hands and for carrying the ball through the goals marked by cones.

Questions

Q: How can you keep the ball safe?

A: Keep the stick and ball away from the defense.

Q: What about passing the ball? How do you pass safely?

A: Pass the ball from the side away from the defender.

Q: Which passes can be used?

A: The overarm from each side and the shovel pass from the nondominant side.

PRACTICE TASK 1

Setup   Players are in threes practicing passing the ball from the nondominant side after changing hands. A static defender stands on the dominant side (figure 13.31).

Goals

- Change hands smoothly and keep control of the stick.
- Pass away from the defender.

Cues

- Slide the bottom hand up to switch hands so the stick is under control.
- Step onto the opposite foot to throw.
- Begin with short passes.

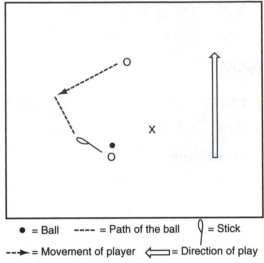

● = Ball ---- = Path of the ball ♀ = Stick
--▶ = Movement of player ⟨══ = Direction of play

Figure 13.31

PRACTICE TASK 2

Setup   Players are in threes and practice passing the ball to a person behind them (a trail player) while a defender is in front (figure 13.32).

Goal   Use the player behind as a safety or for changing the point of attack.

Cue   Use a shovel pass to speed up the pass (which will be short) and to protect the stick from the defender.

GAME 2

Setup   Use 3v3 in a large square area marked by cones. If possible, place a goal in the middle of the area (figure 13.33).

Goal   Protect the ball by switching hands to pass and by using the trail player.

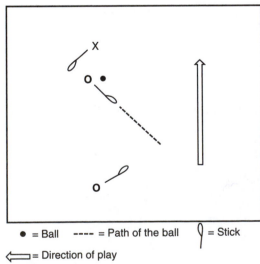

● = Ball ---- = Path of the ball ♀ = Stick
⟨══ = Direction of play

Figure 13.32

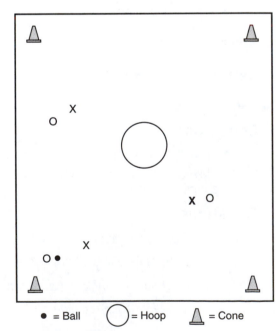

● = Ball ◯ = Hoop ▲ = Cone

Figure 13.33

Condition   Players must keep the ball for at least three successful passes before scoring in the goal.

Questions

> Q: How did you keep possession?
>
> A: By changing hands, passing from the side away from the defender, and using the trail player.
>
> Q: How will you know there is a trail player?
>
> A: The trail player will call.

LESSON 15

Tactical Problem   Defending space

Lesson Focus   Covering the most dangerous spaces

Objectives

- Cover the passing lanes.
- Move over to cover the most dangerous players.

GAME 1

Setup   3v2 within a rectangular area with a goal at one end

Goal   Defend the most dangerous spaces.

Condition   The offensive team must make three passes before shooting at the goal.

Questions

> Q: Where are the most dangerous spaces?
>
> A: In front of the goal and between the ball and the opponent.
>
> Q: How do you defend these spaces?
>
> A: Mark goal side and ball side.
>
> Q: What happened when offensive players got past their defenders?
>
> A: They ran to the goal and scored.
>
> Q: How can defenders cope with this?
>
> A: Leave their own opposing players and go to the offensive player with the ball.

PRACTICE TASK

Setup   Players are in threes. The free attacker with the ball runs toward a goal (cone or hoop). The defender decides when to leave the second attacker to prevent the free attacker from scoring (figure 13.34).

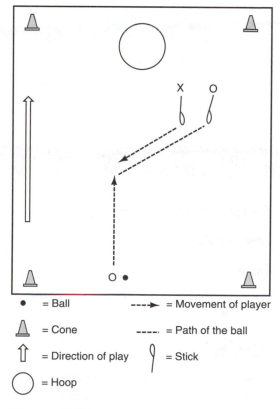

● = Ball	----► = Movement of player
△ = Cone	----- = Path of the ball
⇧ = Direction of play	Ɋ = Stick
◯ = Hoop	

Figure 13.34

Goal   Slide when there is time to take on the new attacker, but do not allow an easy pass to the other opponent, who would then have an open goal.

Cues

- Keep the stick high to cover the passing lane.
- Move diagonally, but be ready to switch directions and stay with the new attacker.
- Use quick and balanced footwork.

GAME 2

Setup   3v2 in a large square area marked by cones, one goal (figure 13.35)

Goals

- Keep the player you are guarding from attacking the goal.
- Be ready to take on any player who is free and moving toward the goal with the ball.

Condition   The game starts with the free player holding the ball at the far end from the goal.

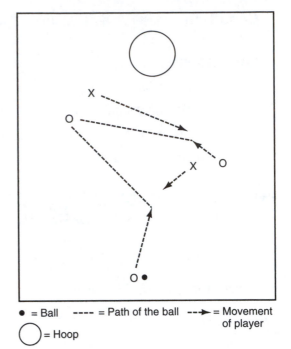

● = Ball   ---- = Path of the ball   --➤ = Movement of player

◯ = Hoop

Figure 13.35

Questions

Q: How did you defend space?

A: By making sure my opponent did not get into a shooting area.

Q: What other job did you have as a defender?

A: To watch for any other player who was free and moving into a danger area.

Q: Why did you decide to slide onto that player?

A: She was more dangerous than my player—that is, she had the ball, was free, and was going toward the goal.

LESSON 16

Secondary Level III

Tactical Problem   Attacking the goal and creating space

Lesson Focus   Working as a team to score

Objectives

- Feed a cutter to give the optimum shot.
- Cut and replace.

GAME 1

Setup   Use 5v5 with a goal at each end. If possible, mark a fan in front of the goal circle as is done in women's games (figure 13.36).

The two player O's in the center represent the two players who take the draw (in the women's game) or the two midfielders who take the face-off (in the men's game). Until this happens, they are both on offense. Once the game begins, they become offense or defense depending on whose team wins the draw or face-off.

Note   This game may be played without sticks by using a ball such as a handball. Doing so removes the frustration of not being able to control the passing well enough to achieve teamwork.

Goal   Work as a team to create chances to score.

Condition   No player can stand in the fan or run into the goal circle.

Questions

Q: *Why is standing in the fan not allowed?*

A: *Because it is dangerous and reduces the shooting space for the attack.*

Q: *How can you work as a team to create scoring chances?*

A: *Give the player with the ball good space to run into for scoring. Keep moving to give passing options in case the player needs to pass.*

Q: *What can you do to help your teammate with the ball?*

A: *Be a trail or a cutter, or be mobile to keep my defender from being able to go to the player with the ball.*

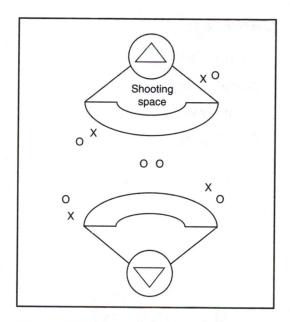

Figure 13.36

PRACTICE TASK

Setup   Players are in fives (with one ball). One player stands behind the goal and acts as a feeder. Two attackers, each with a defender, practice cutting into the scoring area (the fan) to receive the ball and score (figure 13.37).

Goals

- Work as a team so the feeder can pass to a cutter in the best position to score.
- Cutters work out who is in the best place to cut to the ball.
- The other cutter replaces and balances the game.

Cues

- Cutter—Stand diagonally opposite the feeder (this makes it hard for the defender to see both the ball and the cutter).
- Feeder—Wait for the best cut and then make a flat and direct pass.

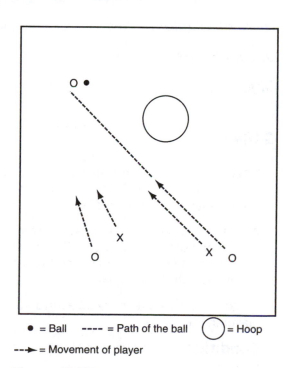

● = Ball   ---- = Path of the ball   ◯ = Hoop

--►= Movement of player

Figure 13.37

GAME 2

Setup 5v5 with one goal

Note This game can also be played without sticks until the players gain more confidence.

Goal Work as a team to score a goal.

Conditions

- The game starts at the far end from the goal.
- Players try to score quickly.
- If the first run fails, the team takes the ball behind the goal for safety and tries to send cutters through.

Questions

Q: How did you work as a team to attack the goal and score?

A: We kept the shooting area open and made good decisions about when and where to move.

Q: What jobs did you have as an attacker?

A: I could be the cutter, the trail, the free player with the ball, the feeder behind the goal, or the helper on either side of the player with the ball.

Q: How did you create space to help the teammate with the ball?

A: I cut into a scoring position. I kept my defender away from my teammate and the shooting area by making myself dangerous. I used the space behind my teammate and let her know I was trailing.

LESSON 17

Tactical Problem Creating space in attack

Lesson Focus Fast break

Objective Overlap with a free player and create space that is hard to defend.

GAME 1

Setup Use 4v3 with a goal at one end. If possible, mark a fan in front of the goal circle as is done in women's games (figure 13.38).

Note This game may be played without sticks by using a ball such as a handball. Doing so removes the frustration of not being able to control the passing well enough to achieve the goal.

Goal Work as a team to take advantage of an extra player in the attack.

Condition No player can stand in the fan or run into the goal circle.

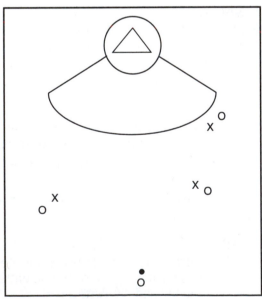

● = Ball

Figure 13.38

Questions

Q: If you are the free player with the ball, what should you do?

A: Look toward the goal and score if possible.

Q: What if you are too far away from the goal to score? Should you pass?

A: No, because then you lose the extra attack by passing to a marked player.

Q: What should you do instead?

A: Run toward the goal until a defender has to move over to defend me and then look for the next free player.

PRACTICE TASK

Setup Players are in fives, with three attackers and two defenders. Use one goal. Player O1 is free with the ball, players O2 and X2 are next in line toward the goal, and players O3 and X3 are nearest to the goal (figure 13.39).

Goals

- Work as a team so the player with the ball drives to the goal and forces player X2 to move toward him (to slide).
- As player O1, pass to player O2 once that player is free.
- As player O2, force player X3 to slide and then pass to player O3, who scores the goal.

Cues

- Follow the three Ds: drive, draw, and dunk.
- Drive toward the goal looking to score.
- Use your movement to draw a defender over to you to stop your progress.
- Dunk (pass) the ball to the new free player.
- Time the pass so it occurs before the defender can block but after the defender has decided to slide.

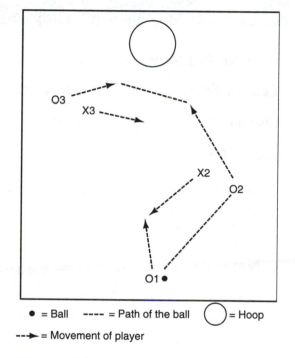

● = Ball   ---- = Path of the ball   ◯ = Hoop

--→ = Movement of player

Figure 13.39

GAME 2

Setup 5v5 with one goal

Note This game can be played without sticks until the players feel confident enough to try sticks.

Goal Work as a team to score a goal.

Conditions

- The game starts at the far end from the goal.
- Players try to score quickly by recognizing the fast break.
- If the first run fails, the team takes the ball behind the goal for safety, settles the attack around the goal, and tries to send cutters through.

Questions

Q: How did you work as a team to attack the goal and score?

A: By driving toward the goal to get away from my opponent and to create a fast break.

Q: What do you do as the free attacker with the ball?

A: The three Ds: drive, draw, and dunk.

Q: How did you help the teammate who had the ball?

A: I kept my defender away from her by pulling out to the side and making myself dangerous. When my opponent left me to slide over to her, I signaled for the ball.

LESSON 18

Secondary Level III

Tactical Problem   Using space in attack

Lesson Focus   Width and depth of attack in transition from defense to offense

Objective   Connect and overlap in the midfield.

GAME 1

Setup   Use 5v5 with a goal at each end. If possible, mark a fan in front of the goal circle as is done in women's games. Begin the game in a diamond shape, or a 1-3-1 formation (figure 13.40).

Note   This game may be played without sticks by using a ball such as a handball. Doing so removes the frustration of not being able to control the passing well enough to achieve the goal.

Goal   Work as a team to use all available space in attack.

Condition   No player can stand in the fan or run into the goal circle.

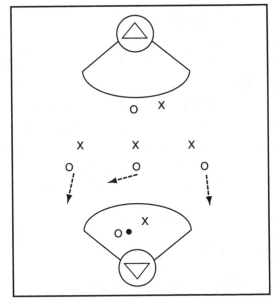

● = Ball   ---► = Movement of player

Figure 13.40

Questions

Q: If one of your teammates suddenly gets the ball from the opposition, what should you do?

A: Quickly help him.

Q: Where are good places to help?

A: Along the sides of the field or from behind the goal.

Q: Why are these good spaces?

A: Because they are safe and open, and opponents are more likely to use spaces nearer to the goal.

PRACTICE TASK

Setup   Players are in fives. One player starts with the ball on the ground near the goal the team is defending. Three players set up in midfield: two on the wing and one in the center. One player waits near the goal the team is attacking (figure 13.41).

Goals

- Work as a team so the player who picks up the ball has passing options across the whole width of the field.
- After passing the ball, continue behind the ball carrier as a trail to create depth in attack.

Cues

- Watch the direction of the pickup, which indicates where the player will look first.
- Start to move early, and if you do not receive the ball, move to support the ball carrier at the side.
- Follow the game so there is width and depth of support.
- Use the entire field.

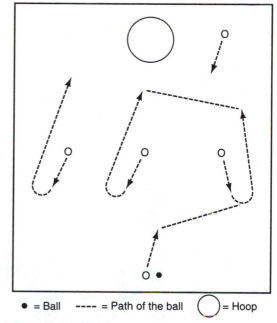

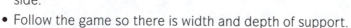   = Ball   ---- = Path of the ball   = Hoop

Figure 13.41

GAME 2

Setup   5v5 with two goals

Note   This game can be played without sticks until the players feel confident enough to try sticks.

Goal   Work as a team to use all the space on the field.

Conditions

- Players toss for first possession, which starts at the defending goal.
- The game restarts at the goal where the previous goal was scored.

Questions

Q: How did you work as a team to use space, attack the goal, and score?

A: By making sure we had players on each wing to create width and also in front of and behind the ball to create depth.

Q: What did you do as the attacker with the ball?

A: Looked up quickly to see where my team was on the field.

Q: How did you help the teammate who had the ball?

A: Used a space different from the rest of my team to provide lots of options.

LEVEL IV

Games at level IV are typically larger, and the overall pattern and detail of the game are more developed. Greater skill is required to meet the greater options available in level IV. For example, players begin using a long but risky pass from wing to wing. Shooting is harder because the defense is stronger at defending the goal. Using full-size goals is important at this stage. The offensive players learn some simple plays that occur in a settled attack around the goal so that if their first run fails, they can still confuse and out-maneuver the defense. The defense needs to clear the ball, using the goalie as the first line of attack (a player can be designated to take this role if there is no goalie in your game). Students can practice simple plays for opening up attack positions in front of the goal and can consider their various roles as offense near the goal, offense in the midfield, and defense near the goal in terms of risks, responsibilities, and required skills.

Having more players on the field increases the level of difficulty and options for play.

LESSON 19

Secondary Level IV

Tactical Problem   Creating space in attack

Lesson Focus   Passing patterns

Objective   Clear the ball from the goal and move it to the attacking end.

GAME 1

Setup   Use 5v5 with a goal at each end of the field. If possible, mark a fan in front of the goal circle as is done in women's games. Play the game in a diamond shape, or a 1-3-1 formation (figure 13.42).

Note   This game may be played without sticks by using a ball such as a handball. Doing so removes the frustration of not being able to control the passing well enough to achieve the goal.

Goal   Work as a team to clear the ball from the goal and move it into attack.

Condition   A player starts the game by passing the ball from inside the goal circle.

Questions

Q: Where is the safest place to clear the ball to?

A: Out to the wing away from the shooting area.

Q: Where should players move to help?

A: Out to the sides of the field away from their opponents.

Q: What should the attackers do as they see the ball being cleared to the sides of the field?

A: Get ready to meet the ball and then take it to the goal.

PRACTICE TASK

Setup   Players are in fours with a goalkeeper in the goal with the ball. The three players act as defense, with two playing on the wings and one playing in the center. More defensive players wait their turn to play behind the goal (figure 13.43).

Goal   Work as a team so the goalie has a safe clear and the player who receives the ball has backup and a player to pass to.

Cues

- Defenders—Cut away from the goal and lead to the outside of the field with sticks.
- When not receiving the pass, roll around and support the ball carrier from the side and from behind.

GAME 2

Setup   6v6 game with two goals

Note   This game can be played without sticks until the players feel confident enough to try it with sticks.

Goal   Work as a team to clear the ball up the field to the attack.

Conditions

- The game starts when a player in one of the goal circles clears the ball.
- The player in the goal circle then moves out and becomes a field player for the rest of the game.
- No player should remain in the goal.

Questions

Q: How did you work as a team to create space to clear the ball?

A: Moved to the outside of the field to create width.

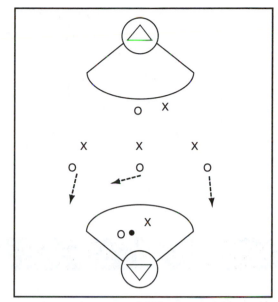

● = Ball   ---▶ = Movement of player

Figure 13.42

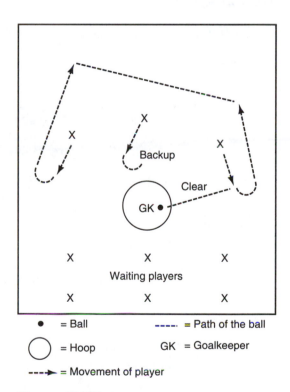

● = Ball   ----· = Path of the ball

◯ = Hoop   GK = Goalkeeper

---▶ = Movement of player

Figure 13.43

Q: What did you do if you were not used by the goalie?

A: Looked to see where my team was and either dropped back as the safety player or cut again to receive the next pass.

Q: What did the attack players do to help the team?

A: Cut toward the person bringing the ball up the field to offer lots of options.

Q: What happened then?

A: They took the ball toward the goal to score.

Q: What patterns did your team make?

A: A basic diamond that widened at the wings and narrowed at the goals.

LESSON 20

Tactical Problems   Defending space and winning the ball

Lesson Focus   Team defense

Objectives   Back up a defender and double-team.

GAME 1

Setup   Use 6v6 with a goal at each end of the field. If possible, mark a fan in front of the goal circle as is done in women's games. Play the game in a diamond shape, or a 1-3-1 formation (figure 13.44).

Goal   Work as a team to defend space and win the ball.

Conditions

- A player starts the game by passing the ball from inside the goal circle.
- No player can remain in the fan without an opponent.

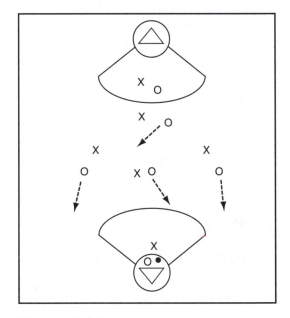

Figure 13.44

Questions

Q: What should your team do when a player with the ball gets past one of your players?

A: Help out by sliding.

Q: How can you provide help before a player has gotten past a defender?

A: Double-team the ball carrier.

Q: Where should you try to be, relative to the ball, to be able to double-team?

A: Between the goal and the ball carrier and behind my defender.

PRACTICE TASK

Setup Players are in threes. One attacker has the ball, and one defender is marking goal side. The second defender calls to the first defender, who guides the attacker into the double-team (figure 13.45).

Goal Work as a team so the attacker is guided into the second defender and has no forward passing lane.

Cues

- First defender—Use your body as a barrier (no contact) to force the attacker in the direction of the second defender.
- Second defender—Verbally communicate that you are there as the double-team helper.

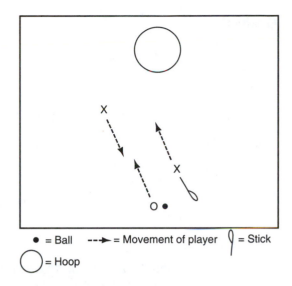

● = Ball   ---▶ = Movement of player   ⎇ = Stick

◯ = Hoop

Figure 13.45

GAME 2

Setup 6v6 game with two goals

Goal Work as a team to back up each other when playing defense, using the slide and the double-team.

Conditions

- The game starts with a clear by a player in a goal circle.
- The player in the goal circle then moves out and becomes an extra field player for the rest of the game.
- No player should remain in the goal.

Questions

Q: How did you work as a team to give support and backup?

A: We had defenders behind us to slide or to double-team.

Q: When is a double-team most likely to happen?

A: When the attacker nears a shooting opportunity and when the attack is in a smaller area (e.g., around the goal).

Q: What key elements make team defense work well?

A: Positioning and communicating with the defender marking the ball carrier.

LESSON 21

Secondary Level IV

Tactical Problem Creating space in attack

Lesson Focus Balance in team attack

Objective Create a settled attack.

GAME 1

Setup   Use 5v5 with a goal. If possible, mark a fan in front of the goal circle as is done in women's games (figure 13.46).

Goal   Work as a team around the goal to score.

Conditions

- A player starts the game by passing the ball from behind the goal.
- No player can remain in the fan without an opponent.

Questions

Q: *What should your team do when a player has the ball behind the goal?*

A: *Cut into the shooting area to receive and shoot.*

Q: *What do the other players do as the cutter goes through?*

A: *Keep the shooting area open by staying out of it, move to fill the space left by the cutter and balance the attack, or help the feeder by offering another passing option on the outside of the shooting area.*

Q: *If an open cutter does not emerge, what can you do?*

A: *Pass the ball around the outside of the circle and wait for another cutter, or go in with the ball.*

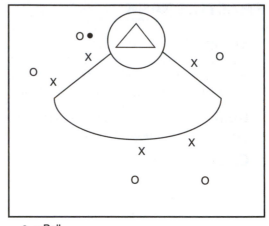

● = Ball

Figure 13.46

PRACTICE TASK

Setup   Players are in fives. One attacker stands behind the goal with the ball, and all other attackers circle the goal (figure 13.47).

Goal   Work as a team to keep the ball moving among the attack players.

Cues

- Keep the ball moving as quickly as possible.
- Keep the circle big to make it harder for defenders to cover the space.
- Keep changing the direction of the pass.

Extension   Players are in fives. If the settled attack is working, add cutters.

Goal   Work as a team to pass the ball around the circle and to feed into a cutter who is in a position to shoot.

Cue   If you are opposite the ball, you are in a strong position to cut because it is hard for the defender to see both you and the ball.

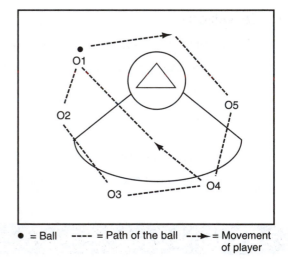

● = Ball   ---- = Path of the ball   --▶ = Movement of player

Figure 13.47

GAME 2

Setup   5v5 game with two goals

Goal   Work as a team to play a settled attack.

Conditions

- The game starts with a clear by a player in a goal circle.
- The ball must go behind the attacking team's goal once before the team can settle around the goal and try to score.

Questions

Q: How did you work as a team to score a goal?

A: We balanced ourselves around and behind the goal.

Q: Why is doing this helpful for the offense?

A: It creates space in the shooting area and gives a lot of options for passing and cutting.

Q: What key elements help the offense succeed?

A: Keeping the offense balanced when cutters go through, and keeping the ball moving so it's hard for the defenders to watch both the ball and their opponents.

LESSON 22

Tactical Problem   Defending the goal

Lesson Focus   Defending dangerous shooting spaces

Objective   Play a team defense.

GAME 1

Setup   Use 5v5 with a goal. If possible, mark a fan in front of the goal circle as is done in women's games.

Goal   Work as a team around the goal to defend the goal.

Conditions

- A player starts the game by passing the ball from behind the goal.
- No player can remain in the fan without an opponent.

Questions

Q: What should you do as the defense when a player has the ball behind the goal?

A: Position to see the ball and the opponent, and hold our sticks high to cover space.

Q: What does the defender of the feeder do?

A: Wait level with the goal in case the feeder tries to circle to score.

Q: How can you hinder passing into the shooting area?

A: Hold my stick up and toward the shooting area and follow my player through the shooting area, staying between her and the ball.

PRACTICE TASK

Setup   Use 3v3 with a goal. One attack player starts with the ball behind the goal (figure 13.48).

Goal   Work as a team to keep the ball from being passed or taken into the shooting area.

Cues

- Position yourself so that you can see the ball and your player.
- Keep your stick high to cover any passes made into the danger area.
- Communicate where the ball is, who is marking the ball carrier, when there is a cutter, and so on.

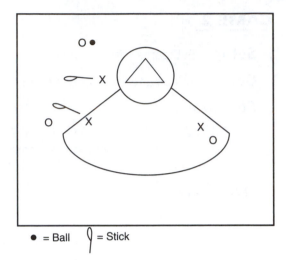

● = Ball   ⑨ = Stick

Figure 13.48

GAME 2

Setup   5v5 game with one goal (figure 13.49)

Goal   Work as a team to defend the goal.

Conditions

- The game starts at the centerline.
- The offense must take the ball behind the goal once before scoring.

Questions

Q: *How did you work as a team to defend the goal?*

A: *We positioned ourselves so that we could see the ball and our opponents.*

Q: *How did you help each other?*

A: *We talked to each other.*

Q: *What did you tell your teammates?*

A: *Where the ball was, who was marking the ball carrier, and whether there was a cutter or a free player.*

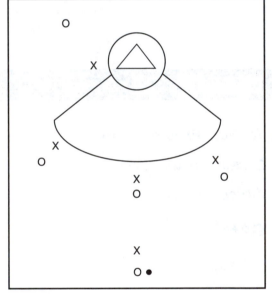

● = Ball

Figure 13.49

LESSON 23

Tactical Problem   Restarting the game

Lesson Focus   Using the restart to the team's advantage

Objectives

- Take the draw.
- Take a free position.

GAME 1

Setup   Use 7v7 with two goals (figure 13.50). If possible, mark a fan in front of the goal circle as is done in women's games.

Goal   Take advantage of a possession from a restart.

Conditions

- The game starts with a center draw.
- If the game goes out of bounds or there is a foul, a free position is given to restart play.

Questions

Q: What should your team do when the centers are taking the draw?

A: Try to get into good positions to catch the ball.

Q: Who are the major players at this moment?

A: The midfielders on the wings. The centers also have to control the draw.

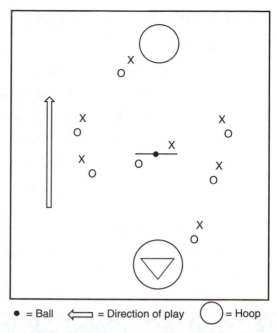

● = Ball   ⇐ = Direction of play   ◯ = Hoop

Figure 13.50

PRACTICE TASK

Setup   Players are in sevens. Two players take the draw while two midfielders (and their defenders) wait on the wings to receive the draw. One person acts as the official and sets up the draw (figure 13.51).

The two player O's in the center represent the two players who take the draw (in the women's game) or the two midfielders who take the face-off (in the men's game). Until this happens, they are both on offense. Once the game begins, they become offense or defense depending on whose team wins the draw or face-off.

Goal   Work as a team to get possession of the draw.

Cues

- Try to hold your stick still until the whistle.
- Practice a draw with your left hand at the top and a draw with your right hand at the top.
- During the draw, try to catch the ball yourself as well as to get it to your attacker.

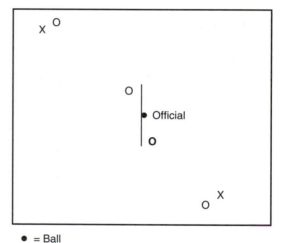

● = Ball

Figure 13.51

GAME 2

Setup   7v7 game with two goals

Goals

- Work as a team to win the draw and get early possession.
- Help when the game is restarted (e.g., for an infringement, a play out of bounds, and so on).

Condition   Teams score an extra point for getting possession at the draw.

Questions

Q: How did your team get the draw?

A: We balanced ourselves around the circle according to where we thought the ball would go.

Q: Who are important players in winning the draw?

A: The wings and the center players.

Q: What can they do to be ready?

A: Hold their sticks high and have their feet ready with their weight forward to take quick action toward the ball.

Q: What should you do at any restart?

A: Look around, see who can help the player with the ball, and see if the team is spaced to give width and depth to support.

LESSON 24

Tactical Problem   Creating space in attack

Lesson Focus   Using plays to create space in front of the goal

Objective   Use picks.

GAME 1

Setup   Use 5v5 with one goal. If possible, mark a fan in front of the goal circle as is done in women's games (figure 13.52).

Goal   Create space in front of the goal for a shot.

Condition   No player can remain in the fan without an opponent.

Questions

Q: What should your team do to create space?

A: Make an open space in front of the goal.

Q: How do you do that?

A: Draw our defenders away and create a settled attack around the goal.

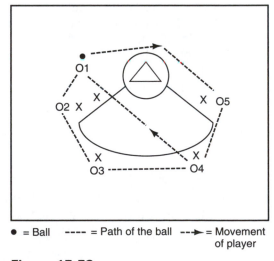

● = Ball   ---- = Path of the ball   --➤ = Movement of player

Figure 13.52

Teaching Sport Concepts and Skills

PRACTICE TASK

Setup   Players are in fours and pick opposite (like an off-ball screen, or pick, in basketball). The feeder behind the goal receives the ball from player O1, who is on the same side of the goal area. Player O1 moves across the front of the goal as if cutting for the ball. When the cut is not used, player O1 picks the defender (player X) of player O3, who then cuts to receive the feed (player O2) from behind the goal (figure 13.53).

Goal   Work as a team to create space for shooting using a pick.

Cues

- Move safely into the pick.
- Keep the stick close to your body.
- Make the first cut convincing.
- Player O2—Signal clearly to receive and shoot.

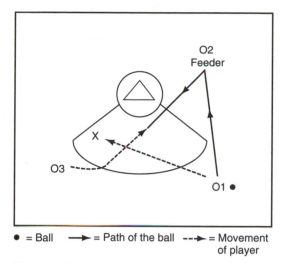

● = Ball   ⟶ = Path of the ball   ⇢ = Movement of player

Figure 13.53

GAME 2

Setup   7v7 game with two goals

Goal   Work as a team to score using a pick.

Condition   Teams score an extra point for using the pick in front of the goal.

Questions

Q: How did your team create space in front of the goal?

A: We used picks.

Q: What is important about using picks?

A: Making them safe (i.e., performing them in view of the defender, using a controlled run, and correctly timing the move away from the pick when receiving the ball).

SUMMARY

The levels of tactical complexity covered in this chapter should help you present lacrosse to secondary students in coed physical education classes so they experience both the fun and challenges of a unique sport that uses an implement to catch the ball.

Remember that at any time lacrosse sticks can be put aside so students can try out tactical problems free from technical constraints. When necessary, take extra time to establish confidence in stick handling through small games and gamelike practices rather than pushing toward a larger game. If the tactical insights gained through more familiar games such as soccer and basketball are included in the introduction to lacrosse, students' confidence to try something new will grow as they see that invasion games have many similar concepts. Lacrosse can then be taught as a game with familiar tactical concepts but presenting unique challenges such as the use of a stick to catch and maintain possession of the ball and the use of space behind the goal.

Although at the competitive level lacrosse is different for men and women, the basic tactical concepts remain the same. The specific equipment for and rules of either game would be inappropriate for the majority of your students. However, their interest in and motivation to continue playing recreationally or competitively can be developed through careful presentation of levels of tactical complexity and, of course, through your assessment of the level of their abilities and experience.

Chapter 14

Rugby

Rugby will be unfamiliar to many of you, yet once you are introduced to the game, you will find it fast paced and action packed. This chapter introduces the game so you can teach it to your students. In fact, this chapter was requested by one of our recent student teachers, who had taught a rugby unit in a middle school. Upon hearing our plans for this book, she said, "Please tell me you're including a chapter on rugby!"

Rugby has some similarities to American football, particularly the shape of the ball and the method of scoring. In fact, American football developed from rugby. Rugby was first played in 1823 at Rugby School (hence the name of the game) in when, during a soccer (football) game, it is said that a boy named William Webb Ellis picked up the ball and ran with it. The game became known as rugby football and grew in popularity as rules developed to distinguish it from soccer. The full name of the game is rugby union, and its rules are governed internationally by the International Rugby Board. In the mid- to late 19th century a slightly different version of the game emerged, which in 1893 became known as *rugby league*. Rugby league became a professional game while rugby union was played only by amateurs until the 1990s, when it too became a professional game. Rugby union and rugby league are distinguished by the number of players on a team (15 in rugby union and 13 in rugby league) and by the restart rules. This chapter focuses only on rugby union.

The rules of rugby might confuse teachers and students who are new to the game, so we introduce rules in stages and only when they are needed to shape the developing game. However, to give you a general picture of the game and to distinguish rugby from American football (for the American reader), we first overview some key rules:

- A regulation game of rugby uses 15 players per team, but for this chapter we provide instructional content for a maximum of 7 players per side, and we use a noncontact tag (RFU 2012) version of the game that is similar to the flag football played in the United States (in fact, flag belts can easily be used in this rugby version).

- The ball must be passed backward or sideways. This rule sometimes causes problems in early learning because progressing seems difficult when the ball cannot be passed forward. This rule can make for interesting problem-solving experiences for students.

- A fumbled pass that goes forward and hits the ground is a knock-on, which results in a restart being awarded to the opposing team.

- A try is scored when the ball is placed on the ground behind the try line (think of a touchdown in American football that has to be placed, not thrown or dropped, onto the ground in the end zone).

- Players can support and assist teammates only from behind (i.e., blocking is not permitted as it is in American football).

- In tag rugby, players must stay on their feet. If a player in possession of the ball goes down to the ground (even when scoring a try) or if a player dives to retrieve a ball, a free pass is awarded to the nonoffending team.

- After having his tag pulled, the player with the ball has been tagged and must pass within three seconds and three strides. The tagger must call "Tag" (so the player with the ball knows he has been tagged) and return the tag to its owner before either player can resume involvement in the game.

- When a tag is made, the players from both teams must return to their respective sides of the ball before resuming involvement in the game.

- The player with the ball cannot shield the flag and should always carry the ball in two hands.

- Players may not kick the ball in tag rugby.

The scope and sequence of the lessons on rugby are broken down tactically in tables 14.1 and 14.2. From a tactical perspective, rugby is very much a possession game. It is all about keeping and advancing the ball to score. This focus is clearly reflected in the framework shown in table 14.1 and in the tactical levels in table 14.2, in which much of the content involves ball possession. Early lessons shape the game as primary rules are introduced in level I. At this level, students learn the importance of moving forward with the ball, passing, and supporting the ball carrier so that when a tag is made, the player in possession has a teammate to pass to. With some simple restarts, the game of tag rugby starts to take shape at level I. At level II players learn how to defend space, although the savvy games player at the secondary level will no doubt understand the need for 1v1 coverage at an earlier stage (i.e., they may cover instinctively at level I). With improved defense, students should begin to learn ways to create space and penetrate defense, such as by using the dummy (fake) pass. The game continues to take shape at level II with more sophisticated restarts

Table 14.1   Tactical Problems, Movements, and Skills in Rugby

Tactical problems	Off-the-ball movements	On-the-ball skills
SCORING (OFFENSE)		
Maintaining possession of the ball	Support—running with the ball carrier	• Running with the ball • Passing
Advancing the ball		• Drawing a defender • Running forward in possession • Scoring a try
Creating and using space to penetrate and score	• Dummy passes • Looping moves • Scissors moves	• Looping moves • Scissors moves
PREVENTING SCORING (DEFENSE)		
Defending space	• 1v1 coverage • Making the tag	
RESTARTING PLAY		
In-field restarts Out-of-bounds restarts		• Free pass • Tap back • One-player scrum • Three-player scrum • Line-out

Table 14.2   Levels of Tactical Complexity for Rugby

Tactical problems	Level I—4v4	Level II—4v4 to 7v7	Level III—7v7
SCORING (OFFENSE)			
Maintaining possession of the ball	• Running with the ball • Passing • Supporting—running with the ball carrier		
Advancing the ball	• Running forward in possession • Drawing a defender • Scoring a try		
Creating and using space to penetrate and score		Dummy passes	• Looping moves • Scissors moves
PREVENTING SCORING (DEFENSE)			
Defending space	Making the tag	1v1 coverage	
RESTARTING PLAY			
	• Free pass • Tap back	• One-player scrum • Three-player scrum	Line-out

and with the introduction of a one-player scrum and then a three-player scrum (don't worry, scrums are explained and illustrated later in the chapter). The scrum requires body-to-body contact, so some safety precautions are necessary.

Assuming that students develop the ability to defend space and tag the ball carrier, instruction at level III should focus on more sophisticated ways of creating space to penetrate and score. Two-player moves such as the loop and the scissors are challenging, requiring on-the-ball skills and off-the-ball movements by both players. Level III also adds the line-out as a way of restarting when the ball goes out of bounds.

LEVEL I

Level I lessons provide a simple introduction to the game of rugby. In lesson 1, students play a simple possession game with several extensions so that a modified game of rugby can take place in subsequent lessons. The remaining level I lessons focus on moving the ball forward as a team and scoring.

LESSON 1

Secondary Level I

Tactical Problems   Playing the game and maintaining possession of the ball

Lesson Focus   Team organization and shaping the game

Objective   Understand game rules and basic passing.

GAME 1

Setup   4v4 possession game in 30 by 20 yards (figure 14.1)

Goal   Keep the ball away from the other team.

Conditions

• Players can run and pass in any direction, but they must stop and pass to a teammate when their tag is pulled off by an opponent.

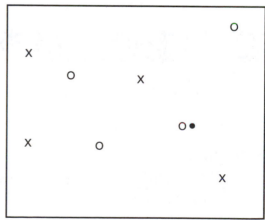

● = Ball

Figure 14.1

- The tagger must return the tag to its owner before either player can resume involvement in the game.
- A dropped ball goes to the other team.
- If the ball goes out of bounds (including if the ball carrier puts a foot on the line), the other team gets a free pass to restart from where the ball went out.
- At any restart, opposing players must be 5 yards back.

Questions

Q: What must you do in this game?

A: Keep the ball.

Q: How can your team keep the ball?

A: Run and pass.

Extensions   Introduce the game extensions one at a time to allow the game to gradually take shape. Introducing these extensions will take time and may even require another lesson (depending on your available time) as players adjust to each new rule.

- Players play 4v4 across a line (now we add direction to the game but still allow the ball to be passed in any direction—figure 14.2). They cross the line while carrying the ball to score.
- Players may not pass the ball forward and may support and assist the ball carrier only from behind (i.e., no blocking as seen in American football).
- Players score a try by placing the ball down behind the line.

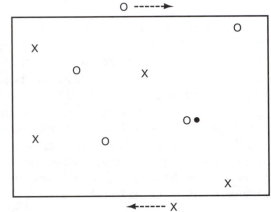

● = Ball   ---▶ = Movement of player

Figure 14.2

Questions

Q: If you cannot pass the ball forward, how do you get it to the other end of the field?

A: By running forward with the ball.

Q: Where do your teammates need to be to help you?

A: Behind or to the side.

LESSON 2

Tactical Problems   Maintaining possession and advancing the ball

Lesson Focus   Running forward, passing backward, and scoring a try

Objectives

- Score a try by placing the ball down.
- Run forward and accelerate when in possession of the ball.
- Look behind and pass to teammates.

GAME 1

Setup 4v4 in 30 by 20 yards (figure 14.3)

Goal Move the ball forward to score a try.

Conditions

- A try is scored by placing the ball down behind the line.
- The ball cannot be passed forward.
- The ball carrier must stop and pass to a team-mate when her tag is pulled off by an opponent.
- The tagger must return the tag to its owner before either player can resume involvement in the game.
- A dropped ball goes to the other team for a free pass (restart from where the ball was dropped).
- At any restart, opposing players (Xs in figure 14.3) must be 5 yards back from the horizontal line along which the ball is positioned. (Note that this is not the same as being 5 yards from the ball. In a game played with 15 players per side on a full-size field, this distance would be 10 yards, and you can increase to this distance if your players need more space.)
- Out-of-bounds balls restart with a free pass.
- Players can support and assist teammates with the ball only from behind (i.e., no blocking).

Note These conditions are the basic conditions for all games from this point on. To avoid repetition, we refer to them as game conditions.

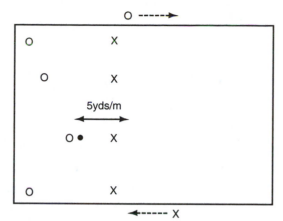

● = Ball   ---▶ = Movement of player

Figure 14.3

Questions

Q: *How do you score a try?*

A: *By placing the ball down with pressure (not dropping the ball) behind the line.*

Q: *If you cannot pass the ball forward, how do you get it to the other end of the field?*

A: *By running forward with the ball.*

Q: *Where do your teammates need to be to help you?*

A: *Behind or to the side.*

PRACTICE TASK

Setup In teams, players practice running single file and scoring a try (figure 14.4). Players O1, O2, O3, and O4 run forward at the same pace, with the ball beginning with player O4. Player O4 places the ball down and moves to the side while slowing down so the rest of the team can pass. Player O3 picks up the ball and runs on before placing the ball down, moving to the side, and slowing down.

Goal Use downward pressure to correctly score a try.

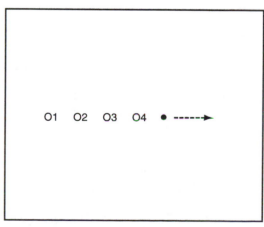

● = Ball   ---▶ = Movement of player

Figure 14.4

Cues

- Place the ball down.
- Pick up and accelerate.

Extension   Instead of placing the ball down, the ball carrier turns and passes to the next player in line.

Cues

- Hold the ball with two hands across the seams (figure 14.5).
- Turn to look at the receiver.
- Pass underhand (for a quicker release than overhand) and aim for the receiver's chest.
- Accelerate when you receive the ball.

GAME 2

Repeat game 1.

Goals

- Use correct technique to score a try.
- Support from behind the ball carrier.
- Run forward and pass accurately.

Figure 14.5   Hold the ball with two hands across the seams.

LESSON 3

Tactical Problems   Maintaining possession and advancing the ball

Lesson Focus   Running forward, passing sideways or backward, and providing support

Objectives

- Ball carrier—Run forward and accelerate.
- Support the ball carrier by positioning to the side and slightly behind.

GAME 1

Setup   4v4 in 30 by 20 yards (figure 14.3)

Goal   Move the ball forward to score a try.

Conditions   Game conditions

Questions

Q: Where are the most effective locations for supporting teammates to help the passer?

A: Behind and to the side.

Q: Why is being to the side important?

A: So a team does not pass the ball too far backward.

Q: So, as the ball carrier runs forward, what do the teammates have to do?

A: Run with the ball carrier.

PRACTICE TASK

Setup Teams practice running in a staggered line and passing (figure 14.6). Players O1, O2, O3, and O4 run forward at the same pace, and player O1 begins with the ball. With player O2 off her shoulder, player O1 passes to player O2, who accelerates to get ahead of player O3 before passing. Player O3 accelerates and passes to player O4. Switch the middle players and restart.

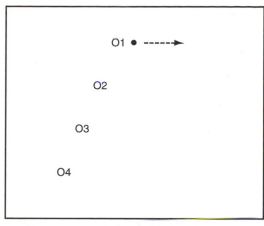

● = Ball   ---▶ = Movement of player

Figure 14.6

Cues

- Accelerate when you receive.
- Slow after you pass.
- Swing your arms across your body (figure 14.7).
- Aim in front of the receiver's chest.

Extension Players pass down the line and back. Player O4 sends the ball back to player O3 after receiving, and the practice ends with player O1 scoring a try.

Figure 14.7 Swing the arms across the body when passing the ball.

GAME 2

Repeat game 1.

Goal Move the ball forward to score a try and support teammates in possession of the ball.

LESSON 4  Secondary Level I

Tactical Problem Advancing the ball

Lesson Focus Drawing a defender

Objective Draw the defender to the ball carrier before passing.

GAME 1

Setup 4v4 in 30 by 20 yards (figure 14.3)

Goal Find ways to beat defenders with a pass.

Conditions Game conditions

Questions

Q: How can you beat a defender by passing?

A: By running at the defender.

Q: When should you pass?

A: When you get close to the defender (but not so close that the pass will be intercepted).

Q: What do you need from your teammates?

A: Support (i.e., someone to pass to).

PRACTICE TASK

Setup Groups of four play 2v1v1 in 20 by 10 yards (figure 14.8).

Goal Players O1 and O2 combine to beat players O3 and O4 by passing.

Conditions

- Player O3 can move forward only when player O1 starts to move.
- When beaten by the pass, player O3 cannot recover (i.e., player O3 is out of the game).
- Player O4 can only move once player O3 has been beaten.

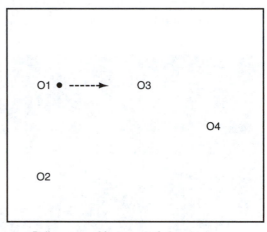

● = Ball   --→ = Movement of player

Figure 14.8

Cues

- Player O1 runs at player O3 while player O2 supports.
- Player O1 times the pass as player O3 advances (when player O3 is about 1 yard away).
- Player O2 runs at player O4 while player O1 supports, and then player O2 passes back to player O1.

Note Defenders (players O3 and O4) might start intercepting the pass because they know it is coming. At this point players O1 and O2 could fake a pass (i.e., make the passing motion without actually passing). A fake is called a dummy pass and is formally taught at level II, but do not be surprised if some of the more savvy games players begin using the dummy pass now, and do not discourage its use.

GAME 2

Repeat game 1.

Goals

- Beat defenders with passes where possible.
- Run at defenders and commit them to the tag.

LESSON 5

Tactical Problem   Restarting play

Lesson Focus   Restarting play with a tap back to simulate the scrum restart (introduced later)

Objectives

- Restart play using a tap back involving two players.
- Advance the ball quickly from the restart.

GAME 1

Setup   4v4 in 30 by 20 yards (figure 14.3)

Goals

- Score.
- Retain possession and move forward after restarts.

Conditions   Game conditions

Question

> Q: How can you restart and make good use of the space ahead of you?
>
> A: Get the ball into the space as quickly as possible.

PRACTICE TASK

Setup   Pairs practice the tap back (figure 14.9), getting the ball to a player who then passes it out to teammates (figure 14.10).

Goals

- Use quick passes and movements.
- As player O4, receive the ball before the gain line (i.e., before running past player O1).

Note   This practice enables you to start building understanding of basic positions in the game. The player receiving the tap back (player O2 in figure 14.10) is called the scrum half, and the player receiving the pass (player O3) is known as the fly half. Player O4 is the center. Knowing these positions is important when you start developing the seven-a-side version of the game at the next level.

Cues

- Player O1—Place your foot on the ball and roll it back.
- Scrum half (player O2)—Get the line moving with a pass ahead of the fly half (player O3).

Figure 14.9   Tap back.

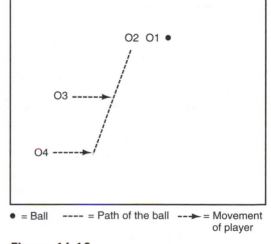

● = Ball   ---- = Path of the ball   --▶ = Movement of player

Figure 14.10

GAME 2

Repeat game 1.

Goal   Effectively restart and move the ball to space.

Note   The tap back is now the restart when any rule infractions occur, when the ball goes out of bounds (taken from inside the sideline), and when a team scores (taken from the center of the field).

LEVEL II

Well done! You have introduced your students to a basic game of rugby with rules that are easily understood and implemented. Although you have taught only five lessons, bear in mind that this is a new game for most students and learning it may take time. You may need to spread one lesson over two classes (depending on the length of the class) to help students gain sufficient understanding. Nevertheless, the content of level I should enable your students to play and officiate their own games, leaving you free to instruct and provide feedback as needed.

Lessons in level II focus first on defending space, which in turn requires more creativity by attacking players if they are to penetrate and score. We then address restarts, specifically by introducing the scrummage, or scrum for short. In the full (15-sided) version of rugby there are eight players in a scrum. However, in the seven-sided game there are only three: two props on the outside and a hooker in the middle. These players (three from each team) bind together (figures 14.11 and 14.12) and lean against each other until the ball is put into the middle of the scrum by the scrum half (figure 14.13). Each player in the scrum places her head to the left of the opposite player's head so that she leans against the opposite player with her right shoulder contacting her opponent's (as shown with just two players in figure 14.14). Once the scrum is set, the ball is put in and the two sets of players push against each other. The hooker uses his foot to hook the ball and push it through the back of the scrum for the scrum half to pick up and begin the attack.

A scrum is used to restart the game following a rule infraction, with the put-in awarded to the team that did not break the rule. Scrums can also be used to restart when the ball goes out of bounds; the put-in is awarded to the team that did not cause the ball to go out. The advantage of putting the ball into the scrum is one of positioning. The ball is always put in from the left of the put-in team's scrum, and the hooker can hook the ball more easily with the right foot when the ball comes from the left side. There is also an advantage in timing in that, with more advanced

Figure 14.11   Binding together to make a scrum.

Figure 14.12   What binding together to make a scrum looks like from behind.

Figure 14.13 Players in the scrum leaning against the other until the ball is put into the middle of the scrum by the scrum half.

Figure 14.14 Two players showing how to lean against the opposite player's shoulders.

thinking, the hooker can signal with his left hand when he wants the ball to be put in and so will know when to raise his foot.

Important rules regarding the scrum are that (a) the ball must be rolled down the midline between the two sets of players and (b) the hooker cannot raise her foot until the ball enters the middle of the scrum. Violating either of these rules results in a free kick to the other team. A free kick is taken by one player who puts the ball down at the place of the infraction, taps it with her foot, picks it up, and begins play. Lastly, if the ball is not hooked between the legs of the scrummaging players (the ball sometimes rebounds off players' legs and back out of the tunnel), the scrum is retaken and the put-in stays with the same team.

Some important safety concerns arise from the scrum, particularly of a scrum collapsing when players push against each other. A collapse might lead to injury, but you can decrease the likelihood of a collapsed scrum by teaching players to keep their shoulders higher than their hips and by allowing players to lean against each other and support the hooker only when the ball is put in. The scrum then becomes a contest between the two hookers.

LESSON 6

Tactical Problem   Defending space

Lesson Focus   1v1 coverage

Objective   Cover each offensive player with a marking defender.

GAME 1

Setup   4v4 in 30 by 20 yards (figure 14.3)

Goal   Match up players at every restart.

Conditions   Game conditions

Question

> Q: What is the best way to defend your space when the other team has the ball?
>
> A: 1v1. Match up across the field with the other team so they cannot get through easily.

GAME 2

Setup   4v4 in 30 by 20 yards (figure 14.3)

Note   The game continues with the same conditions as game 1. Encourage players to match up with opponents, particularly at restarts, to ensure 1v1 coverage that will make penetration by the offensive team more difficult. This lesson does not include a skill practice because defending space is best practiced within the game, but you might need to freeze play at times to illustrate where you are or are not seeing effective one-on-one coverage. The extended game play can also serve to review previously learned content and to emphasize that improved defense requires more creativity from the offensive team (the focus of lesson 7).

LESSON 7

Tactical Problem   Creating space to penetrate

Lesson Focus   Dummy passes

Objective   Beat a defender with either a pass or a dummy pass.

GAME 1

Setup   4v4 in 30 by 20 yards (figure 14.3)

Goal   Find ways to beat defenders.

Conditions   Game conditions

Questions

> Q: Now that the defense is better, how can you beat defenders?
>
> A: With a pass.

Q: What can you do if defenders try to intercept your passes?

A: Fake the pass and keep the ball.

PRACTICE TASK

Setup   Groups of four play 2v1v1 in 20 by 10 yards (figure 14.8).

Goal   Players O1 and O2 combine to beat players O3 and O4 with passes or with dummy passes if players O3 and O4 try to intercept.

Conditions

- Player O3 can move forward only when player O1 starts to move.
- When beaten, player O3 cannot recover (i.e., player O3 is out of the game).
- Player O4 can move only once player O3 has been beaten.
- Attackers and defenders rotate every two repetitions.

Cues

- Player O1 runs at player O3 while player O2 supports.
- Player O1 times the pass as player O3 advances (about 1 yard away).
- If player O3 moves to intercept, player O1 does the show (fake a pass) and go (keep the ball).
- Players O1 and O2 go on and beat player O4.

GAME 2

Repeat game 1.

Goals

- Beat defenders with passes or dummy passes.
- Run at defenders and commit them to the tag.

LESSON 8

Tactical Problem   Restarting play

Lesson Focus   One-player scrum

Objective   Use correct binding technique against an opponent.

GAME 1

Setup   4v4 in 30 by 20 yards (figure 14.3)

Goal   Restart with one heel back and one-on-one coverage.

Conditions   Game conditions

Question

Q: Does anyone know of another way players restart the game in rugby?

A: With a scrum. (Note that this response is a bit optimistic because it is unlikely that any of the students will have watched rugby. Still, some students may have seen rugby and may answer, "Players pile up and fight for the ball," which is what a scrum looks like to the uninitiated. You will probably have to provide the term scrum.)

PRACTICE TASKS

Setup

- Use a 1v1 scrum. Players practice binding and leaning against an opponent (figure 14.14).
- Use a 1v1 scrum with the ball put in and heeled back (figure 14.15). Players work cooperatively, alternating put-ins.

Extension
Players perform competitive repetitions in which the other team's hooker also tries to hook the ball.

Goals

- Demonstrate a strong scrummaging position.
- Put the ball down the middle, heeled back, and retrieve behind the scrum.

Figure 14.15 1v1 scrum with the ball put in and heeled back.

Cues

- Binding—place your right shoulder against the right shoulder of your opponent.
- Place your head below your opponent's arm.
- Keep your shoulders above your hips.
- Keep your knees bent, back straight.
- Scrum half—Put the ball in straight and move to the back of the scrum.

Note The scrummaging position of the player on the left in figure 14.14 is better than that of the player on the right (who is the taller of the two). The player on the left is in a stronger position, with hips lower than the shoulders and a straighter back.

GAME 2

Setup Repeat game 1 using a one-player scrum for all restarts.

Goal Appropriately use a one-player scrum to restart and initiate the attack.

Condition Scrummaging players may only lean; they may not push.

Note The 1v1 scrum is the first step in introducing formal restarts, and it has implications for the tagging feature of tag rugby. You need to stipulate that players can be tagged only in open play (i.e., tags cannot be pulled in scrums, or later, in line-outs).

LESSON 9

Secondary Level II

Tactical Problem Restarting play

Lesson Focus Three-player scrum

Objective Use correct binding technique with teammates and against opponents.

Teaching Sport Concepts and Skills

GAME 1

Setup 4v4 in 30 by 20 yards (figure 14.3)

Goal Restart with a 1v1 scrum and one-on-one coverage.

Conditions Game conditions with a 1v1 scrum to restart

Questions

> Q: If we increase the number of players on each team to seven, we need to increase the size of the scrum to how many?
>
> A: Three. (Students may or may not know this answer, so you might have to provide it.)
>
> Q: How can the three players in each team's scrum work to win the ball?
>
> A: Together.
>
> Q: How?
>
> A: Designate one player to hook the ball and two players to support the hooker.

Note At this point you can introduce the positions of the two props (who prop up the hooker on either side) and the importance of these players binding together to function as a unit.

PRACTICE TASKS

Setup

- In a 3v3 scrum, players practice binding together as a unit (figures 14.11 and 14.12) and leaning against opponents (figure 14.13).
- In a 3v3 scrum with the ball put in and hooked back, players work cooperatively, alternating put-ins between teams. Only the possession team's hooker hooks the ball.

Extension Players perform competitive repetitions in which the other team's hooker also tries to heel the ball.

Goals

- Demonstrate a strong scrummaging position.
- Use correct binding and head placement within the scrum.
- Put the ball down the middle, heeled back, and retrieve behind the scrum.

Cues

- Bind around the waist (figure 14.12), with the hooker's arms over those of the props.
- Place your right shoulder to the right shoulder of the opponent (heads to the left).
- Keep your head below the opponent's arm.
- Keep your shoulders above your hips.
- Keep your knees bent and back straight.
- Scrum half—Put the ball in straight and move to the back of the scrum.

Note Both of the two players closest to the camera in figure 14.13 have reasonable scrummaging positions, with their knees bent, backs straight, and shoulders above their hips. The player on the left has a slightly stronger position, because his legs are farther back.

GAME 2

Setup　7v7 in 50 by 30 yards, using a three-player scrum for all restarts (figure 14.16)

Note　The progression to a 7v7 game requires reorganization. The simplest way to accomplish this transition is to combine teams of four into teams of eight. Doing so leaves one player per team off the field. These two players can act as referees (two referees per game) or coaches (one coach per team). Using teams of eight also keeps skill practice at four players per group, which is a number students will have become accustomed to by now.

Goal　Appropriately use a three-player scrum to restart and initiate the attack.

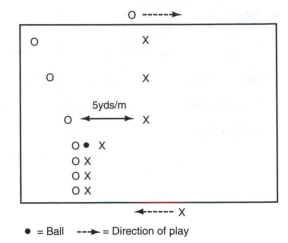

● = Ball　 - - -▶ = Direction of play

Figure 14.16

Conditions

- Use game conditions with a three-player scrum for all restarts.
- Scrummaging players may only lean; they may not push.

Note　This lesson requires additional time and should be spread over two sessions so that students can learn the intricacies of binding together against the opposing scrum. In addition, players should have the opportunity to experience all positions in the scrum (which is also known as the "forwards") and in the "backs" (the players outside the scrum). The individual positions within the backs are known as the scrum half (the player who puts in and receives from the scrum), the fly half (the player who receives the outlet pass from the scrum half), the center (the player next in the line), and the winger (the player on the end, with the most space to run).

LEVEL III

At this point your students have come a long way. They are able to play a 7v7 game with appropriate restarts, and they understand basic positions. However, they will find it increasingly difficult to penetrate the opposition in the 7v7 game because more players are on the field and therefore less space is available for offense (even though the field is now slightly bigger than in the 4v4 game previously played). Greater creativity in attacking is called for, and attack becomes the focus of the early lessons in level III; players (particularly the backs) learn to work together to create and use space to penetrate and score. Learning the scissors and loop moves will be easy for students who have played American football because of their similarities with the reverse moves sometimes performed by wide receivers. Again, these moves are complex, and you

might need an extra lesson to progress from unopposed performance to game play.

Further attending to the appropriate restart for the out-of-bounds ball completes the seven-a-side version of tag rugby. A line-out is illustrated in figures 14.17 and 14.18. The team that did not move the ball out of bounds gets the throw-in, which is usually taken by the hooker. The opposing hooker stands just inside the sideline and does not rejoin the game until after the throw, leaving two players (the two props) to contest the line-out. The goal is to catch the ball and pass it to the scrum half, who then distributes it to the backs. Remember that at restarts the opposing backs must be 5 yards (10 yards on a full-size field) away from the horizontal line on which the ball lies. The same rule applies to line-outs, and you can increase the distance to give more space to the attacking team if necessary.

Figure 14.17 A line-out.

Figure 14.18 A different view of the line-out.

LESSON 10

Tactical Problem   Creating space to penetrate

Lesson Focus   Drawing the defender and using dummy passes in a 7v7 game

Objective   Run at defenders and beat them with a pass or dummy during open 7v7 play.

GAME 1

Setup 7v7 in 50 by 30 yards, using a three-player scrum for all restarts (figure 14.16)

Goal Penetrate the opponent's backs.

Conditions Use game conditions with a 3v3 scrum to restart.

Questions

Q: If spaces are tight and it is difficult to get through the defense, what tactics have you previously learned that will help?

A: Drawing the defenders and passing or using a dummy pass.

Q: Which of the opposition's players should you run at? (**Another way of asking this is,** Where is the most space to attack?)

A: The outside player (the winger). (The most space to attack is at the wing or wide area of the field.)

PRACTICE TASK

Setup 4v4 in 30 by 30 yards or in half of the game field (figure 14.19), restarting with free passes or tap backs

Goal Attack the outside player, where there is the most space to exploit.

Cues

- Run diagonally at the outside player.
- Draw (the defender) and pass or dummy pass.

GAME 2

Repeat game 1.

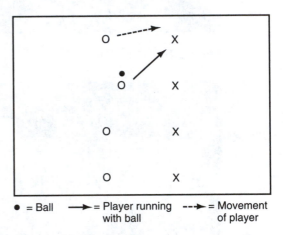

● = Ball ⟶ = Player running with ball ⇢ = Movement of player

Figure 14.19

LESSON 11

Tactical Problem Creating space to penetrate

Lesson Focus Switching the direction of play with a scissors move

Objective Employ a scissors move in practice and game play (see Practice Task).

GAME 1

Setup 7v7 in 50 by 30 yards, using a three-player scrum for all restarts (figure 14.16)

Goal Penetrate the opponent's backs.

Conditions Use game conditions with a 3v3 scrum to restart.

Question

Q: If spaces are tight and you run out of space on the outside of the field, what can you do?

A: Switch play. (This can be done with a scissors move.)

PRACTICE TASK

Setup Set up an unopposed four-player practice (figure 14.20). Player O1 runs at the outside player; player O2 cuts inside and behind player O1; player O1 passes to player O2 so that player O1 is shielding the ball from the defender; player O2 continues the movement by passing to player O3, who passes to player O4, who scores in the corner. The middle players rotate every two repetitions.

Goal Perform one scissors move while moving the ball from one end of the practice area to the other (the move needs about 30 yards of space).

Note Practicing the scissors move is best done at walking speed until students understand the pattern.

Cues

- Ball carrier (O1):
  - Run diagonally at the outside player.
  - Give the pass so that you shield the ball with your body.
- Player O2:
  - Call "Inside" and cut in.
  - Receive the ball and move diagonally to link up with player O3.
- Players O3 and O4—Support player O2 and be prepared to execute another scissors move if necessary.

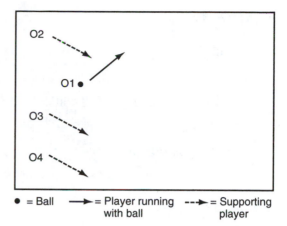

● = Ball   → = Player running with ball   ⇢ = Supporting player

Figure 14.20

EXTENSION

Setup 4v4 in 30 by 30 yards or in half of the game field (figure 14.19), restarting with free passes or tap backs

Goal Attack the outside player and use scissors to change the direction of play.

Cues

- Run diagonally at the outside player.
- Draw the defender and execute scissors where possible.

Note As defenders begin to anticipate the scissors, the offense may use the dummy scissors (i.e., instead of passing, the ball carrier fakes the pass and continues running).

GAME 2

Repeat game 1.

LESSON 12

Tactical Problem Creating space to penetrate

Lesson Focus Creating a player-up situation by using a loop move

Objective Employ a loop move in practice and game play (see Practice Task).

GAME 1

Setup 7v7 in 50 by 30 yards, using a three-player scrum for all restarts (figure 14.16)

Goal Penetrate the opponent's backs.

Conditions Use game conditions with a 3v3 scrum to restart.

Question

Q: If you are the ball carrier, how can you create space after you have passed the ball?

A: Loop around the player you just passed to.

PRACTICE TASK

Setup Set up an unopposed four-player practice (figure 14.21). Player O1 runs forward and passes to player O3. Player O1 loops around player O3 to receive a pass before linking with player O4. The middle players rotate every two repetitions.

Goal Perform one loop move while moving the ball from one end of the practice area to the other (the move needs about 30 yards of space).

Note The loop can be performed in the outside areas of the field (i.e., by looping around the outside player, perhaps player O2 in this case, and exploiting any available space on the wing). Like the scissors move, the loop move is best practiced at walking speed until students understand the pattern.

Cues

- Ball carrier (O1):
  - Run at the opposite player.
  - Pass to O3 and loop around.
  - Receive and pass to O4.
- Player O3:
  - Receive the pass and wait.
  - Return the pass to player O1.

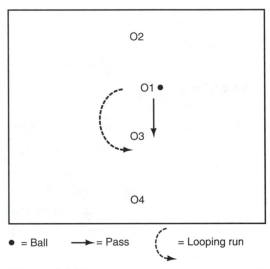

• = Ball   ⟶ = Pass   ⌒ = Looping run

Figure 14.21

- Player O4:
  - Support player O1 and be prepared to receive.
  - Start the next repetition with player O4.

EXTENSION

Setup 4v4 in 30 by 30 yards or in half of the game field (figure 14.19), restarting with free passes or tap backs

Goal Use a loop move to penetrate.

Cue Loop and rejoin the attack.

Note Although figure 14.21 shows player O1 looping around one teammate (in this case, player O3), player O1 can always loop around both players to the outside and receive a pass from player O4 at the end of the line. Encourage such creativity.

GAME 2

Repeat game 1.

LESSON 13

Tactical Problem   Restarting play

Lesson Focus   Restarting play from out of bounds using a two-player line-out

Objective   Employ a line-out to restart play in practice and game play (figures 14.17 and 14.18).

GAME 1

Setup   7v7 in 50 by 30 yards, using a three-player scrum for all restarts (figure 14.16)

Goal   Review the scrum restart.

Conditions   Use game conditions with a 3v3 scrum to restart.

Question

> Q: How do invasion games usually restart after the ball goes out of bounds?
>
> A: The ball is thrown in (the same happens in rugby).

PRACTICE TASK

Setup   Pairs practice throwing and catching for the line-out. Partners stand 5 to 7 yards apart and use a straight throw so that the receiver must jump to catch the ball above his head.

Goals

- Make a straight throw at jumping height.
- Throw underhand (two hands) or overhand (one hand).

Cues

- Throw straight.
- Throw at jumping height.
- Catch and turn 90 degrees while still in the air (for a pass to the scrum half, see the extension).

Extensions

- Players perform unopposed practice in groups of four. The hooker throws and the props jump to catch and pass to the scrum half. Players rotate positions.
- Players perform an opposed practice (4v4) with contested line-outs.

GAME 2

Setup   7v7 in 50 by 30 yards, using scrum and line-out restarts as appropriate

Goal   Use both scrums and line-outs to restart the game and initiate attacks.

SUMMARY

The 13 lessons in this chapter give you and your students a basic understanding of rugby. Remember that we have limited the content to a seven-a-side, non-contact version of the game, so there is a lot involved in the full game that was not included. Nevertheless, tag rugby provides a safe, skillful, fast, and exciting game for students to play, and it makes for a rewarding teaching experience as well. Good luck!

Chapter 15

Flag Football

Although flag football involves the same broad principles as other invasion games, it does set up a little differently. This is largely due to the start-stop-reset structure of the game, which is built into the rules. This structure perhaps makes it a tactically simpler game given the many natural breaks in play that allow for preplanned plays to be set up. One might also argue that flag football is technically simpler than other invasion games because it is essentially a throw-and-catch game, even though it can be difficult for novices to acquire the technique of throwing a spiral pass. That said, although flag football involves only a limited range of offensive skills, the game requires a significant understanding of decision making and space creation, and in fact it is an ideal game for teaching and learning off-the-ball movements because of the 1v1 matchups that begin every play. Defensively, flag football is similar to other invasion games in that players need to understand the concepts of defensive space, distance, pressure, and timing, to be successful.

As with all physical education content, ensuring developmentally appropriate activity is critical and is accomplished through skillful game design, equipment modification, and the use of appropriate playing spaces. Flag football does require space, and so is best taught in outdoor areas. If it must be taught indoors, a 3v3 or 4v4 game could be played in a space about the size of half a basketball court or on a volleyball court (or in any space of approximately 30 by 20 yards). As a general guide for games of more than 3v3, it is best to allow for at least 8 yards of length and 5 yards of width for each of 3 players on a team. The use of smaller spaces would make it difficult for players to execute plays involving passing and running routes. The type of ball used can also be a factor in helping novices execute the necessary passing and catching skills. A range of smaller and softer balls are available, as are easily detachable flags. Once game play begins, players with the ball are not permitted to protect these flags with their hands.

Table 15.1 breaks flag football down from a tactical perspective in the same way other tactical frameworks have done, and table 15.2 outlines the two levels of tactical complexity beginning with 3v3 and leading to a simple 6v6 version of the game. At level I the 3v3 setup suggests that offensively each team would have a quarterback (QB), a running back (RB, also eligible to receive), and a wide receiver (WR), adding a second wide receiver if playing 4v4. In level II games the 6v6 setup requires a quarterback, running back (eligible to receive), center, and three wide receivers when on offense. At each level, defensive players should match up with each individual offensive player. In both level I and level II games, defending players cannot cross the line of scrimmage for three seconds (a count of "3 Mississippi") after the ball is snapped. Other rule variations necessary for smaller versions of the game are identified within the levels and lessons in the following sections.

LEVEL I

Although this part of the book focuses mainly at the secondary level, level I lessons in this chapter are introductory lessons that could be implemented as early as third or fourth grade (eight or nine years old). The lessons are also certainly easy to understand at the secondary level, though the game has less transfer than other invasion game forms. Unique elements that make flag football stand alone among invasion games include the stop/start nature of the game, which comes from the use of set plays on every "down."

At the younger ages the game should not exceed 4v4 (QB, RB, WR, WR); 3v3 is actually the preferred format (QB, RB, WR). It is tempting to assume that many secondary students, particularly in North America, will be familiar with aspects of the game of (American) football such as a line of scrimmage (which marks the furthest point forward at which a pass can be made), scoring by touchdowns (in contrast to rugby, the ball simply has to cross the line under control of the offensive team for a score), and having four downs in which to move the ball 10 yards. However, we try to avoid these assumptions, and instead introduce and modify rules as needed to shape the game. For example, the four-downs rule might be modified on a small field, especially after students have been taught how to throw a spiral pass; a modified rule might be that a team has only one or two sets of four downs (known as a series) in which to score. This speeds up the game and creates more changes in possession.

Table 15.1 Tactical Problems, Movements, and Skills in Flag Football

Tactical problems	Off-the-ball movements	On-the-ball skills
SCORING (OFFENSE)		
Maintaining possession of the ball		• Handoffs and running with the ball • Center snap
Advancing the ball, or attacking	Passing routes—slant, down and in or out, hook, fly	• Passing—spiral and shovel • Catching
PREVENTING SCORING (DEFENSE)		
Defending space	• 1v1 coverage • Pressuring and closing on receivers	Deciding to switch or stay
Winning the ball	Breaking on the ball	Intercepting

Table 15.2 Levels of Tactical Complexity for Flag Football

Tactical goals and problems	Level I—3v3 or 4v4	Level II—6v6
SCORING (OFFENSE)		
Maintaining possession of the ball	Handoffs and running with the ball	Center snap
Advancing the ball, or attacking	• Passing routes—down and in or out • Passing—spiral • Catching	• Passing routes—slant, hook, fly • Passing—shovel
PREVENTING SCORING (OFFENSE)		
Defending space	• 1v1 coverage • Pressuring and closing on receivers	Deciding to switch or stay
Winning the ball		• Breaking on the ball • Intercepting

Limit team sizes to three players in level I to make sure all students become familiar with the rules and tactics of flag football.

The level I lessons are based on a 3v3 game, moving later to 4v4, in a playing area of 30 by 20 yards, which includes a 5-yard end zone in which scoring takes place. This is really the minimum space needed because the end zone actually takes up a third of the playing area; if you have more space available to add to the length of the field, you should do so. An additional line should be marked 5 yards into the field from each end line, identifying the place where play restarts following a touchdown (or even after interceptions if you modify the rule). Figure 15.1 shows a field of 30 by 20 yards plus end zones. Additional parallel fields, with shared sidelines, could be added as necessary depending on the number of students and games to be played.

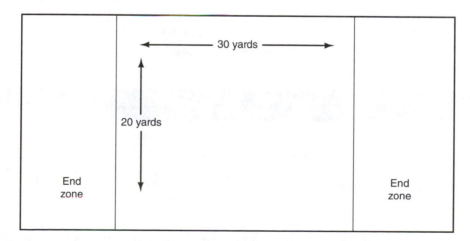

Figure 15.1　Field dimensions for games with as many as four players per team.

LESSON 1

Tactical Problem   Maintaining possession of the ball

Lesson Focus   Introducing game rules

Objectives   Play a fair game and explore possession possibilities.

GAME

Setup   3v3 in 30 by 20 yards

Goal   Retain possession for four downs and move the ball forward from the 5-yard line.

Conditions

- Each team has the following configurations:
  - On offense—QB, RB, WR; players rotate positions every down.
  - On defense—three defensive players who line up horizontally (on the line of scrimmage) opposite the offense.
- Each team has four downs in which to score, and then possession changes hands.
- The QB has the ball at the line of scrimmage and says "Go" to begin each down.
- A down ends at the point a flag is pulled; the new down starts from where the flag is pulled.
- All new (change of) possessions (i.e., a new four downs) begin at the 5-yard line.
- Possession changes hands after
  - a touchdown,
  - four downs if a touchdown is not scored, or
  - the defending team intercepts or recovers a fumbled ball.
- Defenders cannot cross the line of scrimmage until after three seconds (a count of "3 Mississippi").

Note   The preceding rules will be standard for all level I and level II lessons unless otherwise stated. In reality, you will probably have to have students spend the entire first lesson in the game to ensure that they understand and can independently implement the rules in a fair and appropriate manner. A sensible teaching strategy is to vary the opponents by rotating teams. If the class is ready to move on, then you can use content from lesson 2.

LESSON 2

Tactical Problem   Maintaining possession of the ball

Lesson Focus   Maintaining possession and gaining ground by using the running game

Objectives

- Understand that running is safer (i.e., less risk of a turnover) than throwing the ball.
- Use appropriate handoff technique.

GAME 1

Setup 3v3 in 30 by 20 yards

Goal Keep the ball and move it forward.

Conditions See lesson 1.

Questions

> Q: To keep the ball, is it safer to run or to pass it?
>
> A: Run.
>
> Q: Why?
>
> A: Because a longer pass can be intercepted.
>
> Q: So, how do you get the ball from the QB to the RB?
>
> A: Hand it off.
>
> Q: How should the RB carry the ball?
>
> A: Protected by the carrying arm.

PRACTICE TASK

Setup Players perform handoff practice in teams—each team in its own space.

Conditions

- Have one QB, one RB, and one cold defender at the line of scrimmage.
- Players rotate positions every "play."

Extension The defender can become a warm defender and try to take the flag when the RB crosses the line of scrimmage.

Cues

- QB:
  - Turn and shield the ball with your body.
  - Place the ball in the hands of the RB.
- RB—Take the ball and cover it.

GAME 2

Repeat game 1.

Goal Gain possession and move the ball forward by running.

LESSON 3

Secondary Level I

Tactical Problem Advancing the ball

Lesson Focus Advancing the ball by the WR running simple passing routes.

Objectives

- As WR, run a simple down-and-out passing route.
- Execute the pass–catch.

GAME 1

Setup 3v3 in 30 by 20 yards

Goal Score by either running or throwing the ball.

Conditions See lesson 1.

Questions

Q: What is the fastest way to advance the ball down the field, and why?

A: Pass, because the ball moves faster that way.

Q: Who does the QB pass to?

A: The WR.

Q: Where does the WR move to before the pass?

A: Down the field.

Q: And then where, to get away from defenders?

A: Change direction and speed—either in or out, by changing direction and speed.

Q: Where is there usually the most space—inside or outside?

A: Outside, away from defenders.

PRACTICE TASK

Setup Team practice: one QB and two WRs who alternative receiving

Goals

- As WR, run two out of three successful down-and-out routes.
- As QB, throw two out of three catchable passes to each WR.
- As WR, catch two out of three catchable passes.

Condition The QB says "Go," and the WR runs 7 to 8 yards down the field and cuts to the outside quickly.

Extension Add a warm defender.

Cues

- WR:
  - Move downfield quickly.
  - Turn to the outside and look for the ball.
  - Watch the ball into the hands.

- QB:
  - Grip the ball across the seams.
  - Step and throw.
  - Release off the fingertips.
  - Aim ahead of the receiver and for the chest area.

GAME 2

Repeat game 1.

Goal Score off a passing play.

Condition Players must throw at least two passes in every four downs.

LESSON 4

Tactical Problem Advancing the ball (essentially the same as lesson 3 with the focus on a down-and-in passing route)

Lesson Focus Advancing the ball by the WR running simple passing routes

Objectives

- As WR, run a simple down-and-in passing route.
- Execute the pass–catch.

GAME 1

Setup 3v3 in 30 by 20 yards

Goal Score either by running or throwing the ball.

Conditions See lesson 1.

Question

Q: If there is no space to the outside for the receiver to use, where does she turn?
A: Inside.

PRACTICE TASK

Setup Team practice: one QB and two WRs who alternate receiving

Goals

- As WR, run two out of three successful down-and-in routes.
- As QB, throw two out of three catchable passes to each WR.
- As WR, catch two out of three catchable passes.

Condition The QB says "Go," and the WR runs 7 or 8 yards down the field and cuts to the inside quickly.

Extension Add a warm defender.

Cues

- WR:
  - Move downfield quickly.
  - Turn to the inside and look for the ball.
  - Watch the ball into the hands.
  - Catch and move away at speed.
- QB:
  - Grip the ball across the seams.
  - Step and throw.
  - Release off the fingertips.
  - Aim ahead of the receiver and for the chest area.

Flag Football

GAME 2

Repeat game 1.

Goal   Score off a passing play.

Condition   Players must throw at least two passes in every four downs.

LESSON 5

Tactical Problem   Defending space

Lesson Focus   Defenders guarding receivers in 1v1 situations

Objective   As defenders, take up appropriate positions at the line of scrimmage and track WR passing routes.

GAME 1

Setup   3v3 in 30 by 20 yards

Goals

- WR—Get free from defenders.
- Defenders—Stay close to the WRs.

Condition   The QB must pass on every down.

Questions

Q: Where should defenders position themselves at the start of each down?

A: Opposite the WR at the line of scrimmage.

Q: What should the defender do as the WR runs downfield?

A: Go with the WR to cover the run.

PRACTICE TASK

Setup   Team practice: QB, WR, DB (defensive back)

Goal   For the DBs to prevent successful pass completions by the WRs

Conditions

- All players set up at the line of scrimmage.
- The DB covers the WR route to prevent a reception if possible.

Cues

- DB:
  - Line up opposite the WR.
  - Follow the run, staying between the WR and the end zone.
  - Watch for the change in direction and go with the WR.

GAME 2

Repeat game 1.

Goal   As DB, allow no passing touchdowns.

Condition   The QB must throw at least two passes in every four downs.

LESSON 6

Tactical Problem   Defending space

Lesson Focus   DB adjusts position by pressuring and closing gaps at appropriate times.

Objective   As DB, close in on the WR when the WR is nearer to the end zone.

GAME 1

Setup   3v3 in 30 by 20 yards

Goals

- WR—Score on a pass play.
- DB—Prevent the touchdown.

Condition   The QB throws only passes.

Question

Q: When should the DB close in on the WR?

A: When the WR is nearer the end zone or when the QB gets ready to throw.

PRACTICE TASK

Setup   Team practice: QB, WR, DB

Goals

- As WR, score from a pass reception.
- As DB, be close enough to apply pressure and prevent the touchdown.

Condition   Players run pass plays from various positions on the field.

Cue   DB—Be closer when the WR is approaching the end zone.

GAME 2

Repeat game 1.

Goal   As DB do not allow the receiver to score from pass plays.

Condition   The QB must throw at least two passes in every four downs.

LESSONS 7 AND 8

Tactical Problems   Maintaining possession and advancing the ball

Lesson Focus   Developing the play book and tournament play

In these lessons, each team works independently to develop two running plays (plays 1 and 2) and two pass plays (plays 3 and 4), practices them, and then implements them during a tournament situation. A play sheet, such as that in figure 15.2, can easily be developed and given to teams to hold them accountable for their work.

Figure 15.2

LEVEL II

As indicated in table 15.2, lessons in level II see the game move from 3v3 to a 6v6 format. This is easily accomplished by adding two more WRs and also including a center (C) to snap the ball for the QB. Offensively, this gives each team a QB, RB, C, and three WRs. Defensively, players again just line up opposite one of the offensive players, but an additional defensive rule will probably be necessary in this larger game. The more tactically aware defensive players will likely forgo adopting positions at the line of scrimmage but will drop off to cover the back field, taking up the position of a safety (think sweeper in soccer). This might particularly be the case for players defending against the QB, C, and RB because these offensive players are less likely to receive deep thrown passes. The following additional rules will help structure the

6v6 game, particularly by keeping a less cluttered back field so the WRs can run passing routes:

- The defending team must have three players at the line of scrimmage when the ball is snapped.
- The three remaining defenders (defensive backs; DB) guard 1v1 against the WRs.
- After the snap the center becomes an eligible receiver (good for short yardage situations using a shovel pass).
- The QB can run with the ball after three seconds (a count of "3 Mississippi").

Tactically, the 6v6 game expands the range of options available to the offensive team and the level of challenge faced by the defensive team. With multiple possible receivers, offensive players can learn to work together to create space as well as run more complex passing routes. Defense of space also becomes more complex because the DBs may face WRs who interchange positions and run at angles, forcing the DBs to make decisions about whether they should stay with their opponents or switch and just defend spaces. With more passing options, the DBs will also have more opportunities to make interceptions, and instruction at this level will address the issue of breaking on the ball.

It goes without saying (but we will say it anyway) that the playing space for a 6v6 game needs to be bigger than that for a 3v3 game. A field size of about 50 by 30 yards would be a minimum to ensure sufficient space for players to move and especially to execute passing plays. Again, a 5-yard line is required for restarts. Given the length of the field, it would also be appropriate to change the possession limit for each offensive series, perhaps allowing two sets of four downs in which to score. This would allow players to run a range of plays, of both short and long yardage, but still allow for quite frequent changes of possession.

Level II students can start playing 6v6 games.

LESSON 9

Secondary Level II

Tactical Problem   Maintaining possession

Lesson Focus   Playing the game and keeping the ball at the start of each play

Objective   Execute a snap (from C to QB) without dropping the ball.

GAME 1

Setup   3v3 (within teams) in 30 by 20 yards

Goal   Start each play with a successful snap.

Conditions

- Each team has the following configurations:
  - On offense—QB, C, WR; players rotate positions every down.
  - On defense—three defensive players who line up opposite the offense.
- The C begins each play with a pass or snap to the QB at the line of scrimmage.
- The C can receive after the pass or snap.
- Each team has four downs in which to score, and then possession changes hands.
- A down ends at the point a flag is pulled; a new down begins from where the flag is pulled.
- All new (change of) possessions (i.e., a new four downs) begin at the 5-yard line.
- Possession changes hands after
  - a touchdown is scored,
  - four downs if a touchdown is not scored, or
  - the defending team intercepts or recovers a fumbled ball.
- Defenders cannot cross the line of scrimmage until after counting "3 Mississippi."

Questions

Q: What is the safest way of passing the ball from the C to the QB?

A: Hand it, don't throw it.

Q: If the C is going to then receive, which way does he need to face to get moving?

A: Forward.

Q: How can you face forward but pass it backward safely?

A: Through the legs.

PRACTICE TASK

Setup   Team practice

Goal   Successfully snap the ball so that it is not dropped in the exchange.

Condition   Pairs in self-space execute the 3-point stance and center snap to the QB.

Cues

- C:
  - Adopt the 3-point stance (feet shoulder-width apart, one hand on the ground leaning on the ball).
  - On the signal, snap the ball back between your legs with a quarter turn so it is parallel to the ground.
- QB:
  - Have hands ready behind the C.
  - Keep the heels of your hands together and your hands parallel to the ground.
  - Feel the ball into your hands.

GAME 2

Setup   6v6 on 50 by 30 yards

Goal   Start each play with a successful snap.

Conditions

- Each team has the following configurations:
  - On offense—QB, C, RB, three WRs; players rotate positions every down.
  - On defense—three defensive players who line up opposite the offense.
- Each team has two sets of four downs in which to score, and then possession changes hands.
- A center snap begins each play.
- A down ends at the point a flag is pulled; a new down begins from where the flag is pulled.
- All new (change of) possessions (i.e., a new four downs) begin at the 5-yard line.
- Possession changes hands after
  - a touchdown is scored,
  - four downs if a touchdown is not scored, or
  - the defending team intercepts or recovers a fumbled ball.
- Defenders cannot cross the line of scrimmage for three seconds (a count of "3 Mississippi").
- The defending team must have three players at the line of scrimmage when the ball is snapped. The three remaining defenders (defensive backs; DB) guard 1v1 against the WRs.
- After the snap the center becomes an eligible receiver.
- The QB can run with the ball after three seconds ("3 Mississippi").

Note   These rules are retained for the 6v6 game throughout the level II lessons.

LESSON 10

Secondary Level II

Tactical Problem   Advancing the ball

Lesson Focus   Straight-line passing routes (slant and fly)

Objective   As WR, run slant and fly routes to receive passes.

GAME 1

Setup   6v6 in 50 by 30 yards

Goal   Score from touchdown passes.

Conditions   See lesson 9.

Question

> Q: If you are a WR with speed, what directions can you run in to find space?
>
> A: Straight (fly) or diagonally (slant).

PRACTICE TASK

Setup   See figure 15.3.

- Players are in groups of three or four (within teams).
- Positions are QB and two WRs (with an optional C to snap the ball).

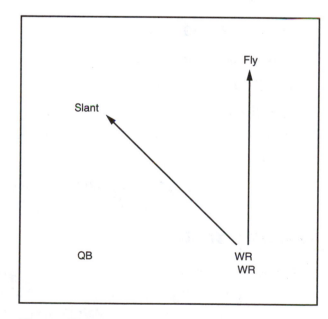

Figure 15.3

Goal   WRs make successful receptions after running patterns.

Condition   The WRs alternately run slant and fly routes.

Extension   Have WRs defend each other alternately.

Cues

- WR:
    - Fly (run straight at speed).
    - Look over your shoulder for the ball.
    - Have hands ready to catch, and watch the ball in.
    - Slant (run diagonally at speed).
    - Angle your body to see the QB's throw.
    - Have hands ready to catch, and watch the ball in.

- QB:
    - Drop three steps after saying "Go" (or after taking the snap).
    - Step and throw in front of the WR.

GAME 2

Repeat game 1.

Goal   Score from slant and fly routes.

Condition   Players perform three pass plays in every four downs.

LESSON 11

Tactical Problem   Advancing the ball

Lesson Focus   Curved passing routes, hook pattern

Objective   As WR, run successful hook patterns to receive passes.

GAME 1

Setup   6v6 in 50 by 30 yards

Goal   Score from passing plays.

Condition   Players may use only passing plays.

Questions

Q: As well as straight routes, what other kinds of routes are there?

A: Curved.

Q: So, if a receiver runs out straight and then curves back to the ball, what does that look like?

A: A hook.

PRACTICE TASK

Setup   See figure 15.4.

- Players are in groups of three or four (within teams).
- Positions are QB and two WRs (with an optional C to snap the ball).

Goal   WRs make successful receptions after running hook patterns.

Conditions   The WR runs a hook pattern, turning to receive the pass.

Extension   Have WRs defend each other alternately.

Cues

- WR:
    - Run straight at speed.
    - Hook back to the ball.
    - Have hands ready to catch, and watch the ball in.
- QB:
    - Drop three steps after saying "Go" (or after taking the snap).
    - Step and throw direct to the WR's hands.

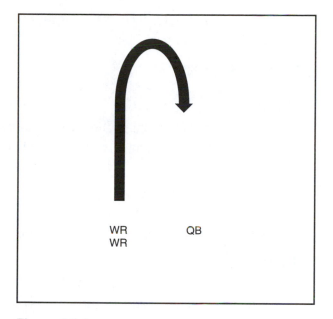

Figure 15.4

GAME 2

Repeat game 1.

Goal   Score touchdowns using any passing routes.

Condition   Three out of every four downs must be passing plays.

LESSON 12

Tactical Problem   Advancing the ball

Lesson Focus   Short yardage gains using a shovel pass

Objective   As QB, execute a shovel pass to both the C and the RB for short yardage gains.

GAME 1

Setup   6v6 in 50 by 30 yards

Goal   Use a variety of short and long passing plays.

Conditions

- All plays must be passing plays.
- In two of every four downs, QBs must throw long (slant, fly hook).
- In two of every four downs, QBs must throw short.

Questions

Q: Who are the best players to receive if you want to gain only a few yards?

A: The C and RB.

Q: What type of pass is best, especially when there isn't much time for a windup?

A: A push, or shovel pass.

PRACTICE TASK

Setup

- Players are in groups of three within teams—QB, RB, and C.
- Each team is working in its own space but playing towards an end zone.

Conditions

- The C snaps the ball and moves forward 2 or 3 yards and turns.
- On the snap, the RB runs diagonally forward to the side of the QB.
- The QB plays a shovel pass to either the C or RB.

Cues

- C—Snap, go, and turn with hands ready.
- RB—Go sideways and forward, hands ready.
- QB—Throw a push pass one handed (palm facing outwards) to the C, or throw underhand with two hands (rugby style) to the RB.

GAME 2

Repeat game 1.

Goal   Score from both long and short yardage plays.

Conditions

- All plays must be passing plays.
- In two of every four downs, QBs must throw long (slant, fly hook).
- In two of every four downs, QBs must throw short (shovel pass).

LESSON 13

Secondary Level II

Tactical Problem   Defending space

Lesson Focus   Working together on defense to cover the runs of WRs

Objective   DBs communicate and decide whether to stay with their own opponents or switch when WRs make crossing runs.

GAME 1

Setup   6v6 in 50 by 30 yards

Goal   Score and prevent scoring.

Conditions

- Every down must be a passing play.
- At least two WRs must run diagonal and crossing routes (like an X).

Questions

Q: *What should the DBs do when the WRs cross over each other? What choices do DBs have?*

A: *Either go with their players or switch players.*

Q: *How do they decide what to do?*

A: *They communicate.*

PRACTICE TASK

Setup Team practice with six players: C, QB, two WRs, two DBs (figure 15.5)

Goal DBs decide and communicate whether to switch or stay to defend against WRs running crossover patterns.

Conditions

- On the snap, the WRs make diagonal crossing runs.
- DBs decide whether to switch or stay and defend accordingly.

Cues

- WRs—Cross over.
- DBs:
  - Communicate.
  - Switch or stay and try to prevent the reception.

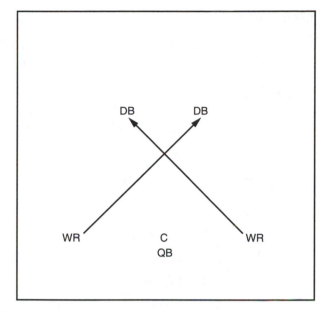

Figure 15.5

GAME 2

Repeat game 1.

Goals

- As DB, prevent scoring.
- As DB, switch or stay when necessary.

Conditions

- Every down must be a passing play.
- The offense can now mix up and start to design plays with multiple receivers.

LESSON 14

Secondary Level II

Tactical Problem Winning the ball

Lesson Focus As DB, recognizing when to attempt interception and knowing how to "break on the ball."

Objectives

- As DB, see the QB as she prepares to throw.
- As DB, read the flight of the ball and intercept if possible.

GAME 1

Setup   6v6 in 50 by 30 yards

Goal   As DB, intercept whenever possible.

Condition   All plays must be passing plays beyond the line of scrimmage.

Questions

Q: As a DB, what do you have to watch if you are going to try to intercept a pass?

A: The QB and the ball (but always know where your WR is).

Q: What do you look at in the QB?

A: The preparation to throw—move as the QB steps.

Q: What do you need to notice about the pass?

A: Its speed and flight (i.e., can I get to the ball before it gets to the receiver?).

PRACTICE TASK

Setup   Team practice with six players: C, QB, two WRs, two DBs (figure 15.5)

Goal   As DB, intercept the pass.

Condition   On the snap, the WRs run any routes they choose.

Cues
- DBs:
  - Know where your WR is.
  - Watch the QB's preparation to throw.
  - Judge the flight of the ball and time your interception.

Note   In all likelihood this will lead to DBs getting beaten by WRs frequently at first as they attempt to intercept passes they shouldn't. This is part of the learning process as they start to realize which passes they can intercept and which they can't. Patience is a prerequisite here.

GAME 2

Repeat game 1.

Goal   As DB, intercept whenever possible.

Condition   Every interception earns 2 points.

LESSONS 15 AND 16

Tactical Problem   All

Lesson Focus   Developing the playbook and tournament play

In the two closing lessons, as in level I, each team works independently to develop plays and then implements these plays during a tournament situation. Given that the offensive focus of level II has been on passing plays, both long and short, it might be appropriate to require four short-yardage plays (including both running and passing plays) and four long-yardage plays. Again, a play sheet, such as the one in figure 15.2, can easily be developed and given to teams to hold them accountable for their work.

SUMMARY

This chapter provides just two levels of tactical complexity for flag football, thus focusing on the essential elements of the game and enabling students to develop the building blocks for football in general, from a question-driven perspective. Clearly, the intent here is to provide foundational content for a noncontact version of football, similar to the approach taken in chapter 14 for rugby. This version makes the game enjoyable for all and provides multiple roles for students to fill.

Students come to (American) football with a vast range of experience gained from either playing or watching the game. As a result, some students will be able to progress very quickly, and others will take longer to develop both understanding and skill performance. We recommend that you make good use of the more experienced and higher-skilled players as assistant teachers or team coaches if you are working with a Sport Education framework.

Chapter 16

Volleyball

A tactical games approach is a problem-solving approach that places students at the center of deciding *what* to do (tactical awareness), *how* to do it (skill execution), *when* to do it (timing), *where* to do it (space), and *when* to try it (risk). For students to think tactically, they must ask, what should I do in this situation? When you focus on getting students to think tactically, you move away from simply saying, do this. As the teacher, you design a situation (a set of playing conditions) that highlights the game problem you want students to solve. Placing students in these situations emphasizes the decision making and social dynamics of sport-related games.

As you may know, there are six basic skills in volleyball (the pass, set, attack, serve, dig, and block); however, there is some uniqueness to the game that merits consideration (Kessel 2008).

- Players must rebound and strike the ball. Most sports allow players to hold or pause with the ball. However, in volleyball, no matter what happens on the second hit, the third has to go over the net; players have no chance to regroup and try again.

Also, unlike the majority of rebound and striking sports, volleyball does not provide players with an implement with which to rebound or strike the ball (i.e., an object).

- The game at the novice level is often won by the lesser-skilled team. You need to be patient with beginners to help them strive for three touches.
- Volleyball has the world's biggest court because, once the ball is in play with the serve, the court boundaries extend beyond the actual court lines.
- Volleyball can be played on any surface, yet the ball can never touch the floor, something that is legal in other sports.
- The fact that the player must rebound or strike the ball directly makes volleyball a complex challenge for any novice player. Reading and anticipating become the other essential skills. Ninety-nine percent of the game is spent moving to be in a better position and to touch the ball better.

The major changes in volleyball in recent years (beginning in 1999) have been in serving and scoring.

Teachers must incorporate instruction with hands-on learning.

First, changes in serving rules enacted in 2000 included (a) allowing serves in which the ball touches the net, as long as the ball goes over the net into the opponents' court and (b) expanding the service area to allow players to serve anywhere behind the end line within the extensions of the sidelines. Second, before 1999, points could be scored only when a team had the serve, known as side-out scoring, and all games were played to 15 points. The current scoring system (formerly known as the rally point system) states that a point is awarded to the team that does not make the error. The team that won the point serves for the next point. Scoring changes made the length of games and matches more predictable, thus making volleyball more spectator friendly.

To help students begin solving the problem of setting up to attack in volleyball, you could place them in a 3v3 game on a modified court (narrower and shorter with a lower net). Initiate the game with a free toss (used as the serve), and have teams alternate serves on every point. The goal of this game is for players to contain the first pass on their side of the court. The situation and conditions help teams of students identify what movements and skills are needed to contain the ball in order to set up for an attack.

VOLLEYBALL TACTICS

There are two basic types of game knowledge. First is *about-game knowledge,* which includes the rules and procedures that make games work, such as ways of starting and restarting play and the locations of boundaries. Second is *in-game knowledge,* which includes the skills and movements related to the specific game. Table 16.1 accounts for both types of knowledge; it presents our framework of the tactical problems of volleyball and their required off-the-ball movements and on-the-ball skills.

Let's take a closer look at the fundamental offensive tactic of any volleyball game, the pass-set-attack. Setting up to attack involves the on-the-ball skills of forearm and overhead passing and attacking. The relevant off-the-ball movements, which are often overlooked, involve opening up (establishing an unobstructed space), transitioning (establishing a new position), supporting (backing up teammates), pursuing (following and saving the ball to continue play), and constantly reading and anticipating through movement. A player who does not receive the serve needs to support teammates, be ready to pursue a difficult pass, and transition for the next play. If taught, these off-the-ball movements optimize students' tactical awareness and thus improve overall game play. You also need to consider what about-game knowledge is developmentally necessary, such as knowing how to rotate and knowing boundaries and the rules of starting and restarting play. You should also teach appropriate terms such as *base, free ball,* and *serve receive.* These terms can be viewed as tactical concepts to assist your students' understanding.

As in chapters 11 through 15, lessons progress in the number of players (i.e., 2v2, 3v3, 4v4) and present questions and answers, practices, and games. Games should be modified (i.e., lower net, smaller court) to represent the advanced form and exaggerated (e.g., contain the first contact on one side of the net or use

Table 16.1 Tactical Problems, Movements, and Skills in Volleyball

Tactical problems	Off-the-ball movements	On-the-ball skills
SCORING (OFFENSE)		
Setting up to attack	• Open up • Base • Support • Pursue and save • Transition • Read and anticipate	• Forearm pass • Set

Winning the point	• Transition:
	  ○ To attack
	  ○ To base
	• Read and anticipate
		• Down ball
		• Spike:
		  ○ Standing
		  ○ Open space
		  ○ Crosscourt
		  ○ Line
		  ○ Roll
		  ○ Tip
		• Serve:
		  ○ Underhand
		  ○ Overhand

Attacking as a team	• Serve receive (3v3 and 6v6) • Cover • Transition • Communication	• Attack coverage • Play sets
PREVENTING SCORING (DEFENSE)		
Defending space on your own court	• Base • Open up • Read and anticipate • Free ball • Support • Pursuit	
Defending against an attack	• Base • Read and anticipate • Adjust • Transition	• Dig • Solo block

Defending as a team	• Base:
	  ○ Floor defense
	  ○ Up defense
	  ○ Back defense
	• Communication
		Double block

a two-contact rule) to present students with tactical problems (Thorpe, Bunker, and Almond 1986).

Basic Triad Formation

Using a basic triad formation in volleyball provides many options for situated learning. Figure 16.1 shows the triad for practicing setting. The triad involves a minimum of three players fulfilling three roles described as initiator, performer, and follow-through player (Griffin 1994). The initiator starts practice with a skill or simulated skill such as a toss or serve. The initiator provides the game tempo for the practice to create the intensity for the performer. The performer is the primary player and the focus of the practice. The follow-through player could act either as the target who stops and retrieves the ball or as a performer who executes the next logical skill or movement. In figure 16.1 the initiator is labeled with a T (tosser), the performer with an S (setter), and the follow-through player with an H (hitter).

The power of the triad formation is that it is game-like. You can conduct it on a volleyball court using the net and simulating the flow of a volleyball game. It has sequences such as toss and pass to target; toss and set to target; serve and pass (serve and receive) to target; or pass, set, and hit (or spike). For example, practicing forearm passing in this format makes students aware of where to set up to attack. You can adapt the triad formation to meet the contextual needs of your students, facilities, and equipment.

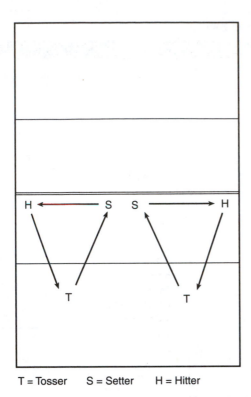

T = Tosser   S = Setter   H = Hitter

Figure 16.1 Triad for volleyball practice setting.

The following are suggestions for working in the triad formation:

- *Use more than three students.* The triad does not necessarily use *only* three students. Adding another performer, collector, or feeder can help the flow of practice when you have limited space (e.g., few courts), limited equipment (e.g., few balls and nets), and large numbers of students. Including more players is especially useful when students are novice players because, as you know, the ball does not always go where they want it to go. Using extra players can decrease the time required for ball retrieval and maintain the flow of the activity.

- *Organize the triad by teams,* depending on the type of drill and the size of the class. If you have teams of six to eight players, it is easy to divide these teams for triad work. You should also be able to have two or three small groups working on one regular volleyball net and court.

- *Have a two-ball minimum rule.* The two-ball rule allows the practice to run smoothly. The target player should have one ball ready to go and bounce that ball to the feeder or tosser to help the practice run smoothly. Using a bounce pass is a built-in safety feature because it allows sufficient time for the tosser to react and catch the ball.

- *Modify the formation.* If students are unable to toss the ball over the net, modify the drill by having the tosser duck under the net and toss the ball from the net to the back row. This modification still uses a gamelike triad but may be more developmentally appropriate for your students.

When structuring net games, be mindful of the court dimensions, available equipment, and number of students. Modifications simplify and slow the game, giving students the opportunity to think tactically (i.e., problem solve). Remember that small-sided volleyball games played in reduced court areas with a lower net and a larger, softer ball use the same regulations, solutions, and skills as the full game.

TEACHING VOLLEYBALL

Volleyball is a difficult game for novice players for two reasons. First, it is a rebounding and striking game. Second, if students cannot hit the ball in the right direction, at the right angle, and with the correct amount of force, a game cannot take place. Students can experience great frustration as a result of their inability to keep the ball in play individually and as a team. Here are several suggestions for increasing the likelihood of successful modified game play:

- *Modify the ball.* Because players must rebound or strike the ball directly, modifying the ball (i.e., using a larger, softer ball) can make all the difference in their willingness to play.

- *Initiate games from a free-ball toss.* Teaching the serve to novice students is not necessary for maximizing game play in small-sided games. When working with novice players or beginning a unit, the free ball (i.e., an easy rainbow toss over the net) facilitates game play. Remember that receiving the serve is one of the most difficult skills of the game. Beginning games with a free toss encourages success and enables students to focus on solving the tactical problems of volleyball.

- *Encourage a no-ace, or cooperative-serve, rule.* After you introduce the serve, you should establish a no-ace rule (i.e., a point cannot be scored directly from a serve), which makes receiving the serve easier for a while.

- *Teach students how to toss.* Take the time to teach your students how to toss, and provide them with practice. Insist that they toss with two hands (overhead if necessary) and with no spin. A one-handed spinning toss is difficult to receive and decreases the likelihood of the ball being returned. View tossing as an essential skill in volleyball, because students need to be able to initiate games and practices.

- *Add volleyball courts by using badminton courts.* Use badminton courts (nets and lines) to maximize the use of facilities and equipment and to allow for more game play and practice.

- *Practice variations.* Here are several ways you can vary tasks:

  - Vary the number of passers.
  - Vary the initial starting point for serving or receiving.
  - Vary the flight of the ball.
  - Vary the speed of the ball.
  - Vary the sides of the court (one or two sides).

- Vary the serve.
- Vary the areas of the court to serve to or receive in.
- Vary the players involved (add hitters, blockers, and diggers).

LEVELS OF TACTICAL COMPLEXITY

You should never teach tactics that exceed the abilities of your students, and you should always promote safety and success. Table 16.2 presents the levels of tactical complexity you can use to develop your students' tactical awareness. You can view these levels as the possible scope and sequence for teaching volleyball in your physical education program.

Table 16.2 Levels of Tactical Complexity for Volleyball

Tactical problems	Level I	Level II	Level III	Level IV	Level V
SCORING (OFFENSE)					
Setting up to attack	• Forearm pass • Set • Open up • Base • Read and anticipate	• Transition • Pursue and save • Support			

Winning the point	• Down ball
	• Standing spike
	• Transition:
	  ○ To attack
	  ○ To base
	• Read and anticipate
		• Transition:
		  ○ To attack
		  ○ To base
		• Down ball
		• Spike
			Serve:
			• Underhand
			• Overhand
				Spike:
				• Open space
				• Crosscourt
				• Line
				• Roll
				• Tip	

Attacking as a team		Transition	Serve receive (3v3)	• Serve receive (6v6) • Cover • Communication	• Attack coverage • Play sets
PREVENTING SCORING (DEFENSE)					
Defending space on your own court		• Base • Open up • Read and anticipate • Free ball • Support • Pursuit			
Defending against an attack		• Base • Read and anticipate • Adjust • Transition	Dig	Solo block	

Defending as a team					• Base:
					  ○ Floor defense
					  ○ Up defense
					  ○ Back defense
					• Communication
					• Double block

The following principles can guide you in developing appropriate lesson progressions. We encourage developmentally appropriate practice, which means adjusting the situated learning both across grade levels and within each class.

- Move students from cooperative to competitive situations. In cooperative play (i.e., maintaining a rally), students work in pairs or teams toward a goal. In competitive play (e.g., a 3v3 volleyball game), students work in teams against opponents. Students should explore the idea that cooperation is an essential component of good competition. This idea speaks to the social and behavioral dynamics of sport-related games (e.g., teamwork, good sporting behavior, fair play, game etiquette).

- Move from simple to complex skills and movements. By doing so you provide students with the opportunity for early success, which results in perceived competence. Continually ask yourself what your students need to know to challenge their knowledge and improve their game performance. This simple to complex principle applies to skills and movements within each game as well as across tactical problems.

- Move from smaller (2v2 or 3v3) to larger (4v4 or 6v6) games. Including fewer players increases overall game involvement and slows the pace of the game, which makes it easier for students to experience the problems and play the game.

LEVEL I

The lessons in level I set students up to play the simplest form of volleyball and teach them the principles of ball placement and court positioning. These principles lay the groundwork for solving the tactical problems of setting up for attack and winning the point. The on-the-ball skills include the basic forearm (free-ball) and overhead (set) pass and the attack (down ball and hit or spike). Off-the-ball movements include returning to base position, opening up, reading and anticipating through movement, and transitioning. Note that the early lessons progress slowly to match the complexity of volleyball skills, moving from the concept of containing the ball on one's own side of the court to setting up using the forearm pass to attack (down ball and spike). We have found that students are motivated by learning to attack. This motivation makes teaching skills such as the set easier. This notion builds on the assumption of the tactical approach that students learn best if they know what to do before they understand how to do it.

In level I, students work on the fundamental skills for volleyball placement, such as forearm passing.

LESSON 1 💿 DVD

Tactical Problem   Setting up to attack

Lesson Focus

- Base positions and containing the ball on one's own court
- Reading and anticipating through movement (watching the flight of the ball and getting the feet to the ball)

Objective   Make the initial pass high and in the middle of the court (playable ball).

GAME 1

Setup   3v3

Goal   Set up to attack the ball.

Conditions

- Make the court narrow and short, set up as seen in figure 16.2.
- Each team alternately initiates points with an easy playable toss (free ball).
- Have a serving team.

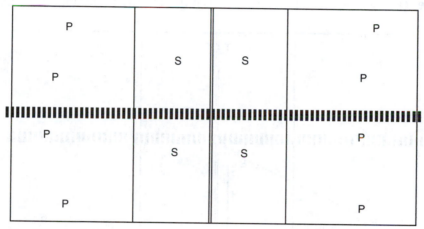

S = Setter   P = Passer

Figure 16.2

Notes

- An easy toss is a two-handed soccer throw-in (rainbow toss).
- The base position is a player's home, or recovery, position during a game.

Questions

Q: What did you do to contain the ball on your side of the court?

A: Controlled the ball and hit it high.

Q: What did you have to do to play the ball?

A: Read the flight of the ball, anticipate where it was going, and move to it.

Q: How did you accomplish this?

A: With an overhead or forearm pass. (Note that the novice might not know the terms but will possibly say, "Like this," while showing you the actions.)

Q. Which way is best for receiving the serve?

A. Using the forearms.

Q: Where is a safe place to pass?

A: Into the middle of the court.

PRACTICE TASK

Setup   Players are in a triad and use a forearm pass.

Goals

- Pass a playable ball, one that is high and in the middle of the court, so that another player can hit it.
- Focus on a medium body posture (knees bent, arms loose, and hands ready) and a flat platform.

Conditions

- Players perform three trials before rotating.
- The tosser prompts by hitting the side of the ball and then gives a playable toss to the passer, who passes the ball to the target (setter).
- The setter catches the ball and then bounces it back to the tosser (figure 16.3).

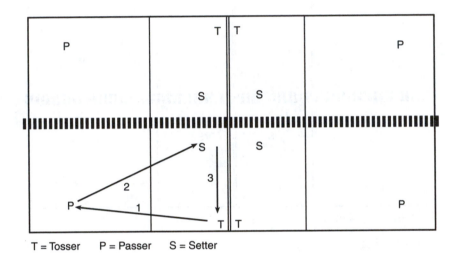

T = Tosser   P = Passer   S = Setter

Figure 16.3

Cues

- Use a medium body posture.
- Move your feet to the ball (read and anticipate).
- Point your belly button to the target.
- Keep your thumbs together, and make a flat platform (i.e., forearms level).

GAME 2

Setup   3v3

Goals

- Attempt a forearm pass as the first contact on your side of the net.
- Players earn 1 point for attempting a forearm pass (i.e., for trying the forearm pass, even if the result is not playable).

LESSON 2

Tactical Problem   Setting up to attack

Lesson Focus   Learning the base position and containing the ball on one's own court using the forearm pass

Objective   Select the forearm pass and execute a playable ball in the middle of your court.

GAME 1

Setup 3v3

Goal Set up to attack the ball.

Conditions

- Make the court narrow and short.
- Each team alternately initiates points with an easy playable toss (free ball).
- Rotate the serving team (figure 16.2).

Notes

- An easy toss is a two-handed soccer throw-in (rainbow toss).
- The base position is a player's home, or recovery, position during a game.

Questions

Q: What did you do to set up a playable ball on your side of the court?

A: Hit the ball high to the middle of the court using the forearm pass.

Q: What did you do to read and anticipate the movement of the ball?

A: Tracked the ball with my eyes and moved into position.

Q: How do you perform the forearm pass?

A: Use a medium body posture and a flat platform and point the belly button at the target.

Q: Why should you use the forearm pass?

A: The flat platform has a larger, flatter surface that makes it easier to block the ball (i.e., to receive).

PRACTICE TASK

Setup Players are in triads practicing the forearm pass.

Goals

- Perform three trials or two playable balls before rotating.
- Hit a playable ball, one that is high and in the middle of the court, so another player can hit it.
- Focus on a medium body posture and pointing the belly button to the target.

Conditions

- The tosser prompts by hitting the side of the ball and then gives a playable toss to the passer, who passes the ball to the target (setter).
- The setter catches the ball and bounces it back to the tosser (figure 16.3).

Extension Move the passer to other positions in the back row.

Cues

- Use a medium body posture.
- Move your feet to the ball.
- Make a flat platform.
- Point the belly button to the target.

GAME 2

Setup 3v3

Goals

- Use a forearm pass as the first contact on your side of the net.
- Teams earn 1 point if the first pass is a playable forearm pass.

LESSON 3

Tactical Problem Setting up to attack

Lesson Focus Learning the base position and containing the ball on one's own court using the forearm pass

Objective Call the first ball and execute a playable forearm free pass to the middle of one's own court.

GAME 1

Setup 3v3

Goal Set up to attack the ball.

Conditions

- Make the court narrow and short.
- Each team alternately initiates points with an easy playable toss (free ball).
- Rotate the serving team (figure 16.2).

Notes

- An easy toss is a two-handed soccer throw-in (rainbow toss).
- The base position is a player's home, or recovery, position during a game.

Questions

Q: How do you know it is your ball to play?

A: By reading (tracking) the path of the ball during the serve (toss).

Q: What do you do to be sure you get to the ball? So you perform the forearm pass?

A: Anticipate and move my feet to align with the path of the ball and call the ball "Mine."

PRACTICE TASK

Setup Players are in triads practicing the forearm pass.

Goals

- Complete three trials before rotating.
- Pass a playable ball, one that is high and in the middle of the court, so another player can hit it.
- Move the feet to the ball and call the ball ("Mine").

Conditions

- The tosser prompts by hitting the side of the ball and then gives a playable toss that forces the passer to move his feet (e.g., two steps side to side or up or back).
- The passer calls the ball.
- The target (setter) catches the ball and bounces it back to the tosser (figure 16.3).

Cues

- Use a medium body posture.
- Move your feet to the ball.
- Make a flat platform.
- Point the belly button to the target.
- Call "Mine."

GAME 2

Setup 3v3

Goals

- Call the ball and select and execute the forearm pass as the first contact on your side of the net.
- Teams earn 1 point if the passer calls the first ball and executes a playable forearm pass.

LESSON 4

Tactical Problem   Winning the point

Lesson Focus   Attacking the ball

Objective   Select and execute a down ball (i.e., a standing spike) or spike (with a jump).

Note   Again, in this lesson we shift from setting up to attack to the attack itself, a skill that we might be introducing earlier than you are accustomed to when teaching volleyball. Our reason for this is motivational: students get a lot out of learning to attack, and once they are able to attack, they see greater value in quality setting as you work backward from the spike (or down ball).

GAME 1

Setup 3v3

Goals

- Set up to attack.
- Teams earn 1 point when they have two hits on their side.

Conditions

- Make the court narrow and short.
- Each team alternately initiates points with an easy playable toss (free ball).
- Rotate the serving team (figure 16.2).
- Players may use up to three hits.

Note   An easy toss is two-handed soccer throw-in (rainbow toss).

Questions

Q: What are you setting up to do when you get two hits on your side?

A: To attack.

Q: How do you attack in volleyball?

A: With a hit, spike, or down ball.

Q: How does an attack help you win the point?

A: It's hard to return.

PRACTICE TASK

Setup   Players are in triads practicing the toss to attack.

Goals

- As hitter, perform three to five trials.
- As tosser, toss a high ball (1 yard high, near the spiking line) for the hitter to attack.

Conditions

- Organize two teams of three players on each of two courts.
- The tosser (setter) tosses a high ball near the spiking line for the hitter to attack (figure 16.4). The toss should simulate a set.
- The hitter selects to hit a down ball or a spike.
- The feeder keeps the balls from becoming a danger in the field of play and gives the balls, one at a time, to the tosser.
- A collector scoops up the balls after the hit and rolls them to the feeder.

Note   For safety during hitting practice, have two teams work together on the same side of the court, and be sure that all teams hit the same way.

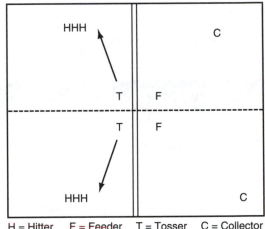

H = Hitter   F = Feeder   T = Tosser   C = Collector

Figure 16.4

Cues

- Down ball (i.e., a hit without the jump):
  - Move your feet to the ball.
  - Throw your hands high.
  - Swing fast.

- Hitting (with a jump):
  - Move your feet to the ball.
  - Jump.
  - Throw your hands high.
  - Swing fast.

GAME 2

Setup   3v3

Goals

- Set up to attack to win the point.
- Teams earn 1 point when they attempt to attack the ball.

LESSON 5

Tactical Problem   Setting up to attack

Lesson Focus   Setting up to overhead pass (set) the ball

Objective   Select and execute an overhead pass from a playable forearm pass.

GAME 1

Setup   3v3
Goals
- Use a forearm pass as the first contact on your side of the net.
- Teams earn 1 point by attempting to attack the ball.

Conditions
- Make the court narrow and short.
- Each team alternately initiates points with an easy playable toss (free ball).
- Rotate the serving team (figure 16.2).
- Players may use up to three hits.

Note   An easy toss is a two-handed soccer throw-in (rainbow toss).

Questions

Q: What is the purpose of the second hit?

A: To set up a player to attack.

Q: Where and how should you set up the player to attack?

A: Close but not tight to the net (about 1 yard away) and by using a high rainbow ball.

Q: How should you set up the player?

A: With the overhead pass or set.

PRACTICE TASK

Players in triads practice the toss, overhead pass (set), catch.

Goal   Perform three of five trials successfully and then rotate.

Conditions
- The passer prompts by hitting (slapping) the side of the ball and then tosses a playable forearm pass to the setter.
- The setter sets the ball to the target (target hitter) (figure 16.5).

Cues
- Use a medium posture.
- Keep your hands high (at your forehead).

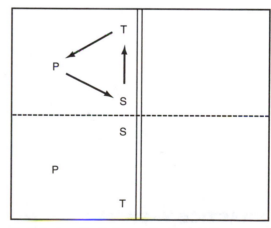

P = Passer   S = Setter   T = Target hitter

Figure 16.5

- Use volleyball-shaped hands.
- Be square to the target.
- Extend your arms and legs (finish like Superman).

GAME 2

Setup   3v3

Goals

- Set up for an attack by using the overhead pass (set).
- Teams earn 1 point if they have two hits on their side.

LESSON 6

Tactical Problem   Setting up to attack

Lesson Focus   Setter moving (opening up) into position to set up

Objective   Open up to set.

GAME 1

Setup   3v3

Goals

- Set up for an attack using the overhead pass (set).
- Teams earn 1 point if the they have two hits on their side.

Conditions

- Make the court narrow and short.
- Each team alternately initiates points with an easy playable toss (free ball).
- Rotate the serving team (figure 16.2).
- Players may use up to three hits.

Note   An easy toss is a two-handed soccer throw-in (rainbow toss).

Questions

Q: What direction does the setter face when the ball is on the other side of the net?

A: She faces the net.

Q: What does the setter need to do once the ball is on her side of the net?

A: Turn to see the ball.

Q: How does the setter do this?

A: Pivots, turns, and calls "Here."

PRACTICE TASK 1

Setup   Players are in triads practicing opening up and setting.

Teaching Sport Concepts and Skills

Goals

- Open up.
- Make three or four sets to the target hitter.
- Perform a good set, which is a rainbow ball (1 yard high and 1 yard off the net).

Conditions

- The tosser prompts by hitting (slapping) the side of the ball and then gives a playable toss (simulates a good forearm pass) to the setter, who sets the ball to the hitter.
- The setter is in a ready position at the net.
- When the ball is hit, the setter opens up and sets the ball to the hitter, who catches it and bounces it back to the tosser (figure 16.6).

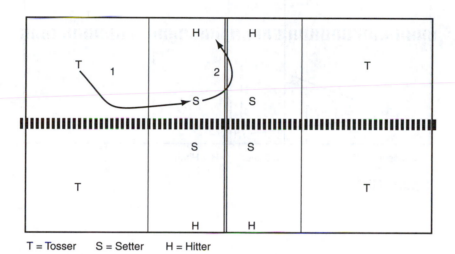

T = Tosser   S = Setter   H = Hitter

Figure 16.6

Cues

- Opening up
  - Be in a ready position at the net.
  - Use a medium to high posture.
  - Keep hands high for a block.
  - Pivot (turn) to the passers.
  - Call "Here."
  - See the passer play the ball.
  - Adjust to set the ball (happy feet).

- Setting
  - Use a medium posture.
  - Keep hands high (at forehead).
  - Use volleyball-shaped hands.
  - Be square to target.
  - Finish like Superman (extend arms and legs).

PRACTICE TASK 2

Setup   Extend the previous drill (only if students are ready for the challenge).

Goals

- Open up.
- Make three or four good sets to the hitter.
- Perform a good set, which is a rainbow ball (3 to 6 feet high).

Conditions

- The target (hitter) prompts by hitting (slapping) the side of the ball and then gives a playable toss (free ball) to the passer, who passes to the setter.
- The setter is in a ready position at the net.
- When the ball is hit, the setter opens up and sets the ball to the hitter, who catches it and starts again (figure 16.7).

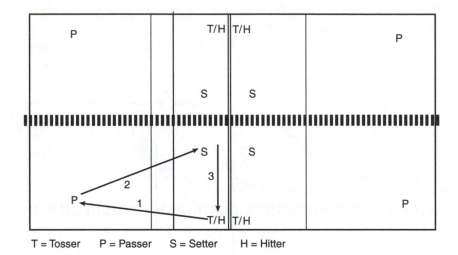

T = Tosser   P = Passer   S = Setter   H = Hitter

Figure 16.7

GAME 2

Setup   3v3

Goals

- Select and execute skills to set up the pass-set-attack on your side of the net.
- Teams earn 1 point for an attempt at pass-set-attack.

LESSON 7

Tactical Problem   Winning the point

Lesson Focus   Transitioning to attack

Objective   As passer, make a successful transition to the hitter.

GAME 1

Setup   3v3

Goals

- Set up to attack.
- Teams earn 1 point when they attempt to set up to pass-set-attack.

Conditions

- Make the court narrow and short.
- Each team alternately initiates points with an easy playable toss (free ball).
- Rotate the serving team (figure 16.2).
- Players may use up to three hits.

Note An easy toss is a two-handed soccer throw-in (rainbow toss).

Questions

Q: Where should you be while waiting for the ball?

A: In base position, ready to move.

Q: How do you get ready to attack (spike or hit) the ball?

A: Move to where the set is going and transition.

PRACTICE TASK

Setup Players are in triads; passers practice transitioning to attack.

Goals

- Perform three to five trials.
- Pass and then transition to attack (hit).

Conditions

- Organize on courts A and B (two teams of three players on each court). See figure 16.8.
- The tosser tosses a free ball to the passer–hitter, and the passer uses the forearm pass to get the ball to the setter.
- The setter catches the ball and tosses a rainbow set (1 yard high and 1 yard off the net).
- As the setter catches, the passer–hitter transitions to hitter for the attack.
- After attacking the ball, the hitter returns to the passing line.

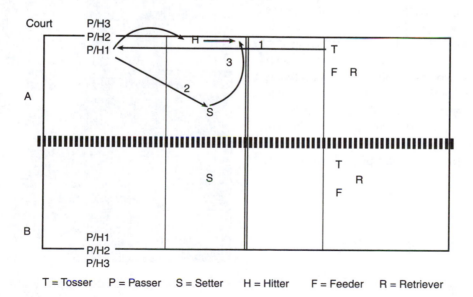

T = Tosser   P = Passer   S = Setter   H = Hitter   F = Feeder   R = Retriever

Figure 16.8

Note   For safety during hitting practice, have two teams work together on the same side of the court; all teams should hit in the same direction.

Cues

- Hitting:
  - Move your feet to the ball.
  - Jump.
  - Throw your hands high.
  - Swing fast.
- Transitioning—Establish a new position.

GAME 2

Setup   3v3

Goals

- Set up to attack.
- Teams earn 1 point for getting two hits on a side and 2 points for executing a pass-set-attack.

LEVEL II

Having introduced volleyball in its most basic tactical form in level I, you can further students' understanding in level II. Begin level II by using a few of the lessons from level I as a review. Have students continue to solve the tactical problem of setting up to attack and winning the point by focusing more on the on-the-ball skill of attack (e.g., hit, down ball, tip) and on the off-the-ball movement of transitioning (establishing a new position). Also, get your students to solve the problem of how to pursue and save a ball off the playing court to keep the rally going for their teams.

Introduce the problem of defending space on their own court, which involves the off-the-ball movements of base and adjust. Tactical problems at level II include defending space against a free ball to set up to attack. Doing this involves understanding many off-the-ball movements such as base positioning, pursuing, and transitioning. Continue to initiate play with a free toss.

Honed spiking skills require students to learn how to defend their side of the net.

LESSON 8

Tactical Problem   Setting up to attack

Lesson Focus   Reviewing setting up to attack

Objectives   Select and execute the forearm pass and the opening up by the setter.

GAME 1

Setup   3v3

Goals

- Set up to attack.
- Teams earn 1 point by attempting to use two hits (contacts) on their side.

Conditions

- Make the court narrow and short.
- Initiate the game from a playable toss (free ball).
- Alternate a free ball after each rally.
- Rotate the serving team (figure 16.2).
- Players may use up to three hits.

Note   An easy toss is a two-handed soccer throw-in (rainbow toss).

Questions

Q: What are you setting up to do?

A: Attack and win a point.

Q: Where should the first pass go?

A: High in the air and into the middle of the court.

Q: Who should play the second ball?

A: The setter (a person close to the net).

PRACTICE TASK

Setup   Players are in triads practicing setting up to attack.

Goals

- Perform two or three trials or two playable balls before rotating.
- Set up a playable ball, one that is high and in the middle of the court, so another player can hit the ball.
- Focus on a medium posture, feet to ball, a flat platform, belly button to target, and calling the ball.

Conditions

- The tosser stands behind the 10-yard line and tosses a free ball to the passer.
- The tosser moves the passer up and back and laterally.
- The passer uses a forearm pass to get the ball to the setter.
- The setter catches the ball (figure 16.9).
- The tosser can also move the ball from side to side and up and back to increase difficulty for the passer.

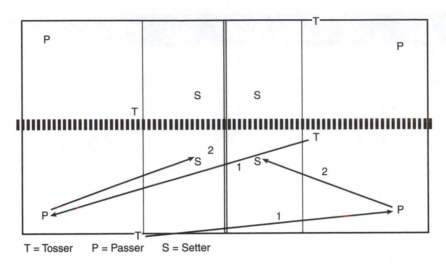

T = Tosser   P = Passer   S = Setter

Figure 16.9

Cues

- Medium posture
- Feet to the ball
- Use a flat platform
- Belly button to target
- Call for the ball

GAME 2

Setup   3v3

Goal   Earn 1 point by making two hits (contacts) on a side.

LESSON 9

Secondary Level II

Tactical Problem   Setting up to attack

Lesson Focus   Pursuing and saving

Objective   Successfully pursue and save a ball off the court and make it playable.

GAME 1

Setup   3v3

Goal   Earn 1 point by making two hits (contacts) on a side.

Conditions

- Make the court narrow and short.
- Each team alternately initiates points with an easy playable toss (free ball).
- Rotate the serving team.
- Players may use up to three hits.

Note   An easy toss is a two-handed soccer throw-in (rainbow toss).

Questions

Q: When can you save a ball that is not in the court but is still in the air?

A: When the first or second passes stay in playable territory but go outside the boundaries of the court.

Q: What do you do when your teammate passes the ball into playable territory but off of the actual playing court?

A: Read, anticipate, and chase it (pursue).

Q: How do you do this?

A: Run forward quickly.

Q: What skill do you use to make the save?

A: Get into a medium posture and execute the reverse forearm pass.

PRACTICE TASK

Setup Players are in triads practicing pursuing and saving.

Goals

- Pursue and save the ball for three of five trials.
- Use two hits to send the ball over the net to reinforce moving as a system.

Conditions

- The tosser tosses a high, playable ball out of bounds for passers to pursue and save.
- After the toss, the tosser returns to the setter base to play the setter role (figure 16.10).

Cues

- Individual:
  - Use a medium posture.
  - Run toward the ball.
  - Run with hands apart.
  - Use the reverse forearm pass.
  - Get back to the court.
  - Keep your platform parallel to the ground.
  - Pass a high, playable ball.

- Team:
  - Move as a system.
  - Use a contact player as the point.
  - All players shift.

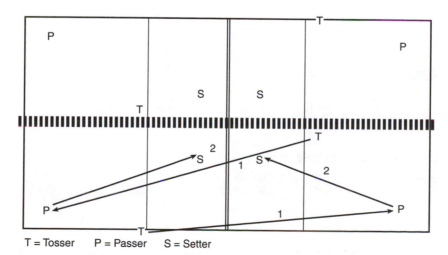

T = Tosser   P = Passer   S = Setter

Figure 16.10

GAME 2

Setup   3v3

Goals

- Pursue and save a ball to the middle of the court.
- Play a continuous rally.

LESSON 10

Tactical Problem   Winning the point

Lesson Focus   Transitioning to attack

Objective   As passer, successfully transition to hitter.

GAME 1

Setup   3v3

Goals

- Set up to attack.
- Teams earn 1 point by attempting to pass-set-attack.

Conditions

- Make the court narrow and short.
- Each team alternately initiates points with an easy playable toss (free ball).
- Rotate the serving team (figure 16.2).
- Players may use up to three hits.

Note   An easy toss is a two-handed soccer throw-in (rainbow toss).

Questions

Q: Where should you be while waiting for the ball?

A: In base position, ready to read and anticipate.

Q: How do you get ready to attack (spike or hit) the ball?

A: Move to where the set is going and transition.

PRACTICE TASK

Setup   Players are in triads; the passer practices transitioning to attack.

Goals

- As passer–hitter, execute three to five trials.
- As passer–hitter, pass and then transition to attack (hit).

Conditions

- Organize players on courts A and B (two teams of three players).
- The tosser tosses a free ball to the passer–hitter.
- The passer uses the forearm pass to get the ball to the setter.
- The setter catches the ball and tosses a rainbow set (1 yard high and 1 yard off the net).
- As the setter catches, the passer–hitter transitions to hitter for the attack.
- After attacking the ball, the hitter returns to the passing line (figure 16.8).

Note To ensure safety during hitting practice, have two teams work together on the same side of the court, and have all teams hit in the same direction.

Cues

- Hitting:
  - Move your feet to the ball.
  - Jump.
  - Throw your hands high.
  - Swing fast.
- Transitioning—Establish a new position.

GAME 2

Setup 3v3

Goals

- Set up to attack.
- Teams earn 1 point for making two hits on a side and 2 points for executing a pass-set-hit.

LESSON 11

Tactical Problem Winning the point

Lesson Focus Approaching for attack (spike approach)

Objective As hitter, successfully transition off the net and approach.

GAME 1

Setup 3v3

Goals

- Select and execute an attack (pass-set-hit).
- Teams earn 1 point for attempting to attack (down ball, hit, or spike).

Conditions

- Make the court narrow and short.
- Each team alternately initiates points with an easy playable toss (free ball).
- Rotate the serving team.
- Players may use up to three hits.

Notes

- An easy toss is a two-handed soccer throw-in (rainbow toss).
- You can change the size of the court to meet students' needs.
- Arrange players in positions of passer, setter, and hitter as shown in figure 16.11.

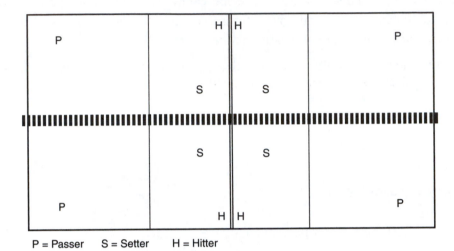

P = Passer   S = Setter   H = Hitter

Figure 16.11

Questions

Q: *Where is the front hitter's base position?*

A: *Facing the net to see how play develops on the opponent's side and to block a bad pass.*

Q: *What should the hitter do when the ball crosses the net?*

A: *Transition and move off the net.*

Q: *How does the hitter approach to attack?*

A: *Runs three strides and ends on two feet ready to jump.*

Practice Task   Players practice approaching to attack.

Goal   As a hitter, perform three successful trials out of five and then rotate.

Conditions

- Two teams practice together (teams A and B).
- The setter slaps the ball (to prompt the hitter to move back from the net) and tosses a high, outside set after the hitter has transitioned off the net.
- The hitter approaches to attack (hit or spike) the ball (figure 16.12).

Extensions

- Teams continue hitting practice by switching sides to experience hitting from both the left and right front positions.
- Teams hit from behind the 10-yard line, with the setter tossing a high set at the 10-foot (3 m) line to allow hitters to swing fast and through without hitting the net.

Cues

- Move your feet to the ball.
- Jump.
- Throw your hands high.
- Swing fast.
- Strike the ball with the heel of your open hand.
- Snap your wrist.

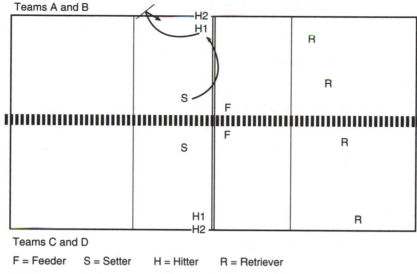

Teams A and B

H2
H1

R

R

S

F

F

S

R

H1
H2

R

Teams C and D

F = Feeder   S = Setter   H = Hitter   R = Retriever

Figure 16.12

GAME 2

Setup   3v3

Goals

- Select and execute an attack (pass-set-hit).
- Teams earn 1 point when they set up and attack (down ball, hit, or spike).

LESSON 12

Tactical Problem   Winning the point

Lesson Focus   Setting to attack

Objectives

- Execute a hittable set and successfully transition off the approach to attack (hit or spike).
- Set a hittable ball that is high and 0.5 to 1 yard off the net (rainbow set).

GAME 1

Setup   3v3

Goals

- Use the forearm pass as the first contact.
- As hitter, transition off the net.
- Teams earn 1 point by attempting to attack (hit or spike).

Conditions

- Make the court narrow and short.
- Each team alternately initiates points with an easy playable toss (free ball).
- Rotate the serving team.
- Players may use up to three hits.

Note   An easy toss is a two-handed soccer throw-in (rainbow toss).

Questions

Q: *Where should the setter set the ball?*

A: *0.5 to 1 yard off the net.*

Q: *How should the hitter get ready to hit?*

A: *Transition off the net.*

Q: *When should the hitter approach?*

A: *When the ball is at its apex (highest point).*

PRACTICE TASK

Setup   Players practice setting and hitting.

Goal   Execute the pass and hit successfully for three trials before rotating.

Conditions

- Use two teams and three balls.
- The tosser slaps the ball (prompts) so that the setter and hitter make off-the-ball movements (open up, transition).
- The tosser tosses the ball to the setter, using a good forearm pass.
- The setter sets (forearm or overhead pass), and the hitter hits a down ball or spikes (figure 16.13).

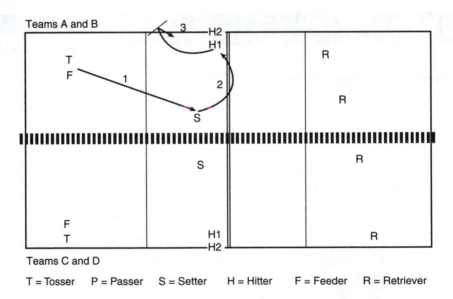

Figure 16.13

GAME 2

Setup   3v3

Goal   Teams earn 1 point for two hits and 2 points for a successful attack.

Tactical Problem   Defending space on one's own court

Lesson Focus   Defending against a free ball, using base positions, opening up, and supporting

Objective   Successfully defend space on one's own court.

GAME 1

Setup   3v3

Goals

- Start in base positions.
- Use the forearm pass as first contact.
- As setter, open up.
- Two hits (contacts) earn 1 point.

Conditions

- Make the court narrow and short.
- Each team alternately initiates points with an easy playable toss (free ball).
- Rotate the serving team.
- Players may use up to three hits on a side.
- The setter is in a ready position.

Note   An easy toss is a two-handed soccer throw-in (rainbow toss).

Questions

Q: What do you do when a free ball comes over the net?

A: Read, anticipate and move to play the ball in your area.

Q: What does the setter do?

A: Opens up.

Q: What does the hitter do?

A: Transitions off the net.

Q: What does the passer do?

A: Splits the court, balances the court, and plays in the middle of the court.

Q: What should players be doing if the ball does not come directly to them?

A: Move to support teammates by backing them up if they need help playing the ball.

PRACTICE TASK

Setup   Players practice defending against a free ball.

Goal   As a team, perform three trials successfully, move correctly as a team, and then rotate positions.

Conditions

- Use two teams and three balls.
- The passer for team A is the tosser for team B.
- The tosser slaps the ball as a prompt for everyone to be ready.
- The setter, hitter, and passer call "Free" and make appropriate off-the-ball movements.
- The setter opens up and calls "Here."
- The hitter transitions off the net.
- The passer balances the court by playing in the middle back.
- The tosser tosses the ball (a free ball).
- The passer, setter, and hitter attempt a pass-set-hit (figure 16.14).

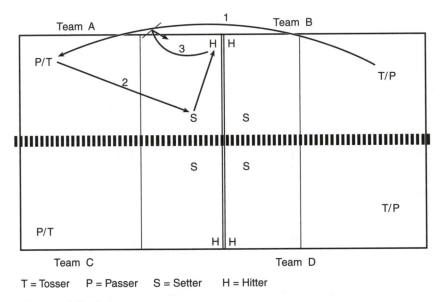

T = Tosser   P = Passer   S = Setter   H = Hitter

Figure 16.14

GAME 2

Setup 3v3

Goals

- Defend space in your court against a free ball.
- Teams earn 1 point for calling "Free."

LEVEL III

The time has come to introduce the serve (underhand or no-ace overhead). Changes in the serving rules to consider at this level include (a) allowing serves in which the ball touches the net, as long as it goes over the net into the opponents' court and (b) expanding the service area to allow players to serve anywhere behind the end line within the extensions of the sidelines. We suggest that you start with what was considered the traditional serving area and introduce the tactic of moving the server's placement slowly. Keep in mind, though, that some students may have more success serving from different places along the end line.

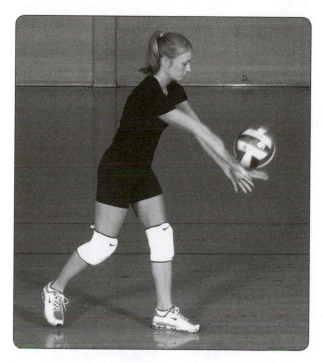

A solid serve is necessary to keep the game active.

At level III, students should begin to understand the difference between receiving a free ball and receiving a serve. Introduce them to a basic serve-receive formation. You may also introduce the dig, which is a type of forearm pass for receiving balls that are attacked (hit or spiked). At level III you should challenge your students with more complicated gamelike practices (skill and movement combinations) to increase their action profiles. Feel free to have them play 3v3 or move to 4v4 as larger teams become necessary for meeting their developmental needs. Remind them that if they are not doing something (playing the ball, moving to base, transitioning, or adjusting), they are doing something wrong. Volleyball is a read, anticipate, and move game!

LESSON 14

Secondary Level III

Tactical Problem   Attacking as a team

Lesson Focus   Using two players to receive a serve

Objectives   Practice the serve receive, the forearm pass, and supporting as a team.

GAME 1

Setup   3v3

Goal   To use a minimum of two hits on a side every time a team receives the ball.

Conditions

- Use a narrow court.
- Teams earn 1 point by making two hits (contacts) on a side.
- Each team alternately initiates points with an easy playable toss (free ball).
- Teams alternate free balls and rotate before giving each free ball.
- Players may use up to three hits on a side.
- The setter is in a ready position.

Note   Arrange players in positions of passer, setter, and hitter as shown in figure 16.15.

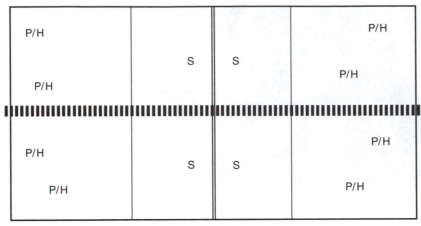

P = Passer   S = Setter   H = Hitter

Figure 16.15

Questions

> Q: *What do players do to serve receive as a team?*
>
> A: *Organize, play a position, and set up in a formation.*
>
> Q: *How do you serve receive as a team?*
>
> A: *Call the ball, open up, and support.*

PRACTICE TASK

Setup   Two players practice the serve receive.

Goal   Perform three successful trials out of five and then rotate.

Conditions

- Use two teams and three balls.
- The tosser slaps the ball (prompts) and tosses a free ball or makes an easy underhand or overhead serve for passers 1 and 2 to receive.
- The setter is a target setter and catches the ball (figure 16.16).

Teams A and B

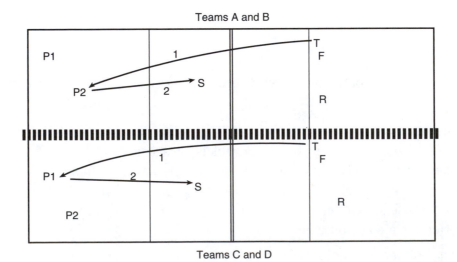

Teams C and D

Figure 16.16

Cues

- On-the-ball skills—Block the ball with your forearms.
- Off-the-ball movements:
  - Call the ball using "Mine," "Good," or "Out."
  - Open up.
  - Support.

Note If you can, use a full court.

GAME 2

Setup 3v3

Goals

- Use the forearm pass as the first contact.
- As a nonpasser, open up or support.
- Teams earn 1 point when a support player calls "Good" or "Out" or a passer calls "Mine."

LESSON 15

Tactical Problem   Winning the point

Lesson Focus   Starting the point on the attack

Objective   Serve overhead and into the court.

GAME 1

Setup   3v3

Goal   Successfully serve into the court to begin each point.

Conditions

- Use a narrow court.
- Start the game with either an underhand or overhead no-ace serve.
- Alternate serves and rotate on regaining the serve (side-out).
- Players may use up to three hits on a side.
- The setter is in a ready position.

Note   Arrange players in positions of passer, setter, and hitter as shown in figure 16.17.

Questions

Q: What serve gives you the most options?

A: The overhead serve.

Q: How do you make an overhead serve?

A: Perform a throwing action, tee up the ball, lift the ball, make firm contact, and finish to the top of the net.

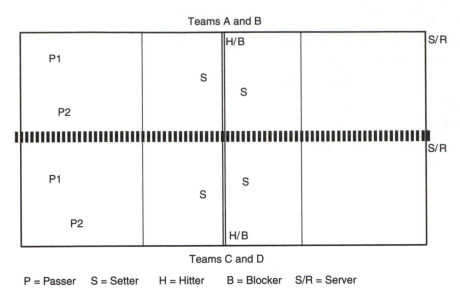

Teams A and B

P = Passer　　S = Setter　　H = Hitter　　B = Blocker　　S/R = Server

Figure 16.17

PRACTICE TASK 1

Setup　Players practice the overhead serve.

Goal　Gradually move back to the end line.

Conditions

- Students work in pairs, starting at the spike line and gradually moving back to the end line.
- Students should be encouraged to serve from different places along the end line.

Cues

- Tee up the ball.
- Lift the ball.
- Make firm contact.
- Finish toward the top of the net.

PRACTICE TASK 2

Setup　Players practice the overhead serve.

Goals

- As server, hit an overhead serve over the net into the middle of the backcourt.
- As passer, hit a playable ball, one that is high and in the middle of the court, so another player can hit it.

Conditions

- The tosser prompts by hitting the side of the ball and then executes a modified overhead serve from the spiking line.
- The passer receives the serve and passes it to the target (setter).
- The setter catches the ball and bounces it back to the tosser (figure 16.16).
- The server gradually moves back to the end line.

Cues

- Overhead serve:
  - Tee up the ball.
  - Lift the ball.
  - Make firm contact.
  - Finish to the top of the net.
- Receiving the serve:
  - Use a medium body posture.
  - Block the ball.
  - Point your belly button to the target.

GAME 2

Setup   3v3

Goal   Accurately and successfully serve into the court.

Conditions

- Start the game with an overhead serve.
- Introduce different end line serving places into the game to challenge students.
- Give players a choice of two serving places to start with so there is some consistency for tracking the serve.

LESSON 16

Secondary Level III

Tactical Problem   Winning the point

Lesson Focus   Starting the point on the attack

Objective   Execute the overhead serve and transition into the court.

GAME 1

Setup   3v3

Goal   Force passers to move for the serve receive.

Conditions

- Use a narrow court.
- Initiate the game from a playable no-ace serve.
- Alternate serves and rotate on regaining the serve (side-out).
- Players may use up to three hits on a side.
- The setter is in a ready position.

Note   Arrange players in positions of passer, setter, and hitter as shown in figure 16.17.

Questions

Q: *To where do you serve to get the passers to move?*

A: *To open spaces.*

Q: *How do you do that?*

A: *Position feet and follow through.*

PRACTICE TASK

Setup Players practice serving and transitioning to the court.

Goal Execute three of five trials successfully, and rotate.

Conditions

- Use two teams and three balls.
- The server serves and transitions into the court to receive a free ball from the tosser (i.e., the server now becomes a passer).
- The passer passes to the setter.
- The setter catches the ball, and the next server begins her turn (figure 16.18).

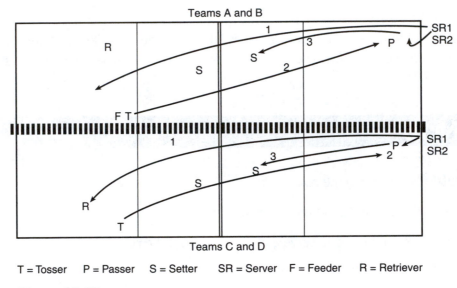

T = Tosser   P = Passer   S = Setter   SR = Server   F = Feeder   R = Retriever

Figure 16.18

Cues

- Tee up the ball.
- Lift the ball.
- Make firm contact.
- Finish to the top of the net.

Note If you can, use a full court.

GAME 2

Setup 3v3

Conditions

- Start the game with an overhead serve.
- Introduce different end line serving places into the game to challenge students.
- Give a choice of two to start with so there is some consistency for tracking the serve.

LESSON 17

Tactical Problems   Setting up to attack and winning the point

Lesson Focus   Combining skills and movements

Objective   Perform pass-set-hit combinations.

GAME 1

Setup   3v3

Goals

- Successfully serve and receive with two players.
- Earn 1 point with each pass, set, and attempted hit.

Conditions

- Use a narrow court.
- Initiate the game from a no-ace serve.
- Alternate serves and rotate on regaining the serve (side-out).
- Players may use up to three hits on a side.

Questions

Q: What does a team need to do to win a point when receiving a serve?

A: Make a forearm pass, set, transition, open up, communicate, and support.

Q: What would make a team win more points?

A: Being consistent, communicating, and working as a team.

PRACTICE TASK 1

Setup   Players practice the pass-set-hit.

Goal   Pass and hit successfully for three of five trials before rotating.

Conditions

- Use two teams and three balls.
- The tosser slaps the ball (prompts) so the setter and hitter make off-the-ball movements (open up, transition).
- The tosser tosses the ball to the passer, who uses a forearm pass to get the ball to the setter.
- The setter sets (using a forearm or overhead pass), and the hitter hits or spikes (figure 16.19).

Note   The tosser can also use a modified overhead serve.

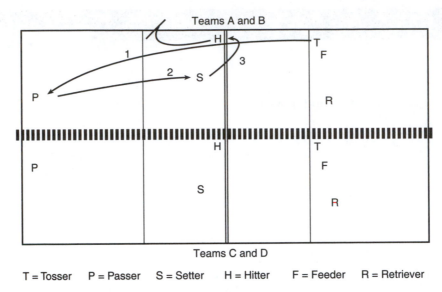

Teams A and B

Teams C and D

T = Tosser   P = Passer   S = Setter   H = Hitter   F = Feeder   R = Retriever

Figure 16.19

PRACTICE TASK 2

Setup   Players practice serving and a receive-set-hit combination.

Goal   Pass and hit successfully for three of five trials before rotating.

Conditions

- Use two teams and three balls.
- The server slaps ball (prompts) so the setter and hitter make off-the-ball movements (open up, transition).
- The server tosses the ball to the passer, who uses a forearm pass to get the ball to the setter.
- The setter sets (using a forearm or overhead pass), and the hitter hits or spikes (figure 16.20).

Note   The server can also use any easy underhand or overhead serve.

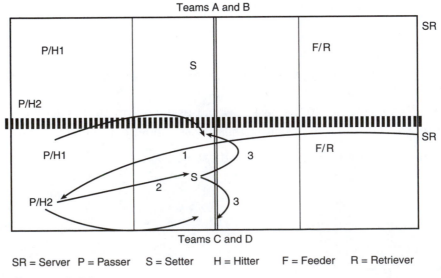

Teams A and B

Teams C and D

SR = Server   P = Passer   S = Setter   H = Hitter   F = Feeder   R = Retriever

Figure 16.20

GAME 2

Setup 3v3

Conditions

- Start the game with an overhead serve.
- Introduce different end line serving places into the game to challenge students.
- Give a choice of two serving places to start with so there is some consistency for tracking the serve.

LESSON 18

Secondary Level III

Tactical Problem Defending against an attack

Lesson Focus Digging

Objective Contain the dig on one's own court.

GAME 1

Setup 3v3

Goals

- Win a point with a hit, down ball, or tip if possible.
- Be aware of the need to contain the dig on your side of the court.

Conditions

- Use a narrow court.
- Initiate the game from a no-ace serve.
- Teams rotate on regaining the serve (side-out).
- Players may use up to three hits on a side.

Note Arrange players in positions of passer, setter, and hitter as shown in figure 16.21.

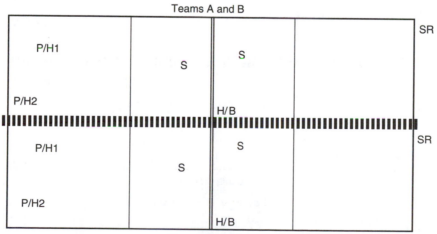

Figure 16.21

Questions

Q: What is your role as a player in the back row?

A: To dig the ball, keep the ball in play, and save the ball.

Q: How can you dig a spike ball and contain it on your side of the court?

A: Be low and dig to myself.

Q: Why should you contain the ball on your side of the court?

A: To counterattack and to set and hit.

PRACTICE TASK

Setup   Players practice digging in a triad.

Goal   Perform three of five trials successfully, and rotate.

Conditions

- Use one team and three balls.
- The tosser slaps the ball (prompts) so the digger adjusts to a low posture.
- The tosser tosses or hits a down ball (mock spike) to the digger across the court.
- The digger digs the ball to himself (figure 16.22).

Note   This task may not seem gamelike, but focusing on digging to themselves helps players learn to contain the ball on their side of the court. If players can dig high to themselves, then the next progression is to dig to the center of the court.

Cues

- Adopt a low posture.
- Use the J-stroke.
- Dig to the center of the court.

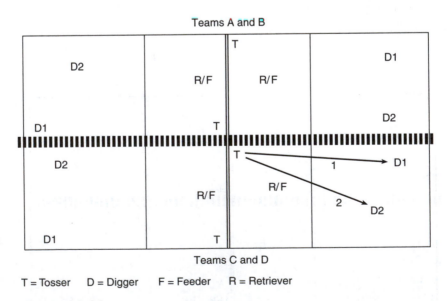

Figure 16.22

GAME 2

Setup 3v3

Goal Successfully dig the ball to keep the point alive after a spike.

Conditions

- Use regulation scoring (formerly known as rally scoring).
- Use a regular serve.

Note Regulation scoring (formerly known as rally scoring) states that a point is awarded to the team that does not make the error. The team that won the point serves for the next point.

LESSON 19

Tactical Problem Defending against an attack

Lesson Focus Containing a dig on one's own court

Objective Dig a spiked ball.

GAME 1

Setup 3v3

Goals

- Win a point with a hit or spike when possible.
- Be aware of the need to contain the dig on your side of the court.

Conditions

- Use a narrow court.
- Initiate the game from a no-ace serve.
- Teams rotate on regaining the serve (side-out).
- Players may use up to three hits on a side.

Note Arrange players in positions of passer, setter, and hitter as shown in figure 16.23.

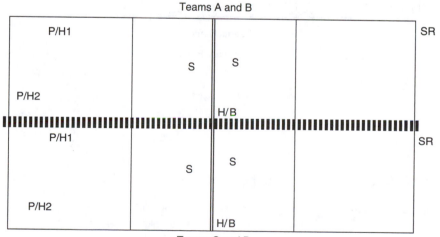

Teams A and B

P = Passer   S = Setter   SR = Server   B = Blocker   H = Hitter

Figure 16.23

Questions

Q: How do you get ready to dig?

A: Read and anticipate by watching the attacker (hitter), and dig low before the hitter spikes.

Q: How do you contain a dig on your side of the court?

A: Be low and dig to the center of the court.

PRACTICE TASK

Setup   Players practice digging a spike.

Goal   Dig for three of five trials successfully, and rotate.

Conditions

- Use two teams and three balls.
- The setter slaps the ball (prompts) so the hitter transitions off the net to hit.
- The setter tosses a high, outside set.
- The hitter hits or spikes the ball.
- The digger adjusts to a low posture.
- The digger digs to herself (figure 16.24).

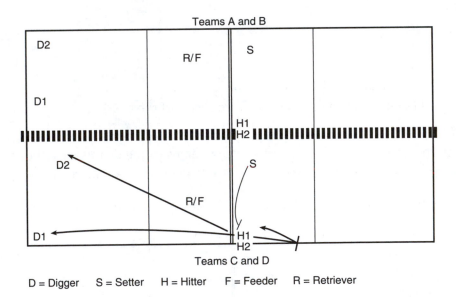

D = Digger   S = Setter   H = Hitter   F = Feeder   R = Retriever

Figure 16.24

GAME 2

Setup   3v3

Goal   Successfully dig the ball to keep the point alive after a spike.

Condition   Use the current scoring system (i.e., rally scoring).

LEVEL IV

Tactical complexity in level IV addresses the problem of attacking as a team by increasing the number of players on a team to four or six and by expanding the court. Games of 4v4 or 6v6 should feel comfortable if they meet the developmental needs of your students. Revisit the basic problems of setting up for attack and winning the point. You may also introduce an offensive serve-receive pattern (i.e., the W). Practicing a serve-receive pattern provides students with the opportunity to problem solve opening up, transitioning, providing support, and using base positions in the advanced game form. This level allows you to introduce a specialized setter position that increases the attack possibilities to include left, right, and middle attack. We encourage you to again initiate games from a free ball to maximize game play before gradually returning to a serve. If you did not introduce the expanded service area with your students in level III, we encourage you to consider implementing this rule (tactic) in level IV.

Once students are ready, begin introducing more players.

LESSON 20

Secondary Level IV

Tactical Problem   Attacking as a team

Lesson Focus   Performing the serve receive as a team

Objective   Serve receive and transition to attacks.

GAME 1

Setup 6v6

Goal Set up to attack.

Conditions
- Use a full court.
- Use regulation rules and scoring.
- Initiate the game from a free ball from the server position.

Questions

Q: What is the best way to organize your team to receive the serve?

A: Use the W serve-receive formation and playing positions.

Q: What is the advantage of the W formation for the serve receive?

A: All players can see the serve (i.e., they are not standing one in front of the other), and each player has his own area to cover.

Q: How does using a serve-receive formation help your team?

A: It helps with communication, and all players know their roles.

PRACTICE TASK

Setup Players are in a serve-receive formation with a free ball used to start each point.

Goal As base player, return to a home or recovery position when the ball passes over the net.

Conditions
- Use two teams and three balls.
- The server first serves an easy ball to team A, and team A sets up to attack and transitions to base (figure 16.25).
- The server then tosses a free ball, and team A sets up to attack (figure 16.26).
- Each team has three trials at three serve-receive positions (rotations).

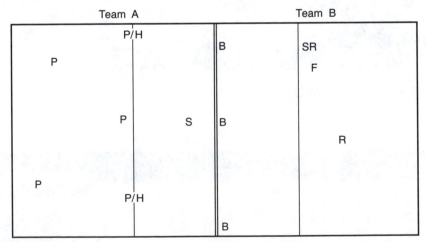

F = Feeder   P = Passer   S = Setter   H = Hitter   B = Blocker   R = Retriever

SR = Server

Figure 16.25

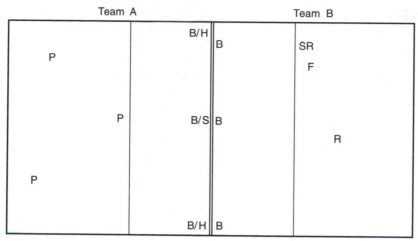

F = Feeder   P = Passer   S = Setter   H = Hitter   B = Blocker   R = Retriever
SR = Server

Figure 16.26

GAME 2

Setup   6v6

Condition   Use a regulation game.

LESSON 21

Tactical Problem   Winning the point

Lesson Focus   Practicing attack variations and ball placement (e.g., open space, crosscourt, and down the line).

Objective   Use attack variations.

GAME 1

Setup   6v6

Goal   Win the point by attack.

Conditions

- Use a regulation court (if possible).
- Use regulation rules and scoring.
- Initiate the game from a free ball from the server position.

Note   Teams can implement the no-ace serving rule as a variation.

Questions

Q: What do you want to do when you attack (spike) the ball to win a point?

A: Kill the ball, spiking it so that players cannot return it.

Q: What are different ways to attack?

A: Tip, down ball, spike (crosscourt, down the line, roll shot).

PRACTICE TASK

Setup Players practice varying the attack.

Goal As hitter, execute three of five trials successfully; then rotate.

Conditions

- Use two teams and three or four balls.
- The tosser tosses a good pass to setter 1; then tosses a pass to setter 2.
- Setter 1 sets a high, outside ball for the hitter to spike down the line or crosscourt, or to tip (figure 16.27).

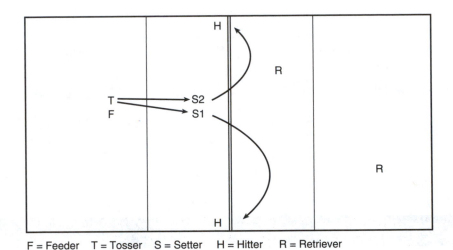

F = Feeder   T = Tosser   S = Setter   H = Hitter   R = Retriever

Figure 16.27

GAME 2

Setup 6v6

Goal Successful pass, set, hit combinations in the game.

Condition Use the no-ace serve or the regulation serve.

LESSON 22

Secondary Level IV

Tactical Problem Defending against an attack

Lesson Focus Practicing the solo block

Objective Attempt to front the hitter and block.

GAME 1

Setup 4v4

Goal Defend against a spike.

Conditions

- Use a narrow court, slightly lower net, and regulation rules.
- Initiate the game from a free ball from the server position.
- Use rally scoring.

Questions

Q: What is the first-line defense against an attack?

A: Blocking.

Q: How do you block?

A: Put your arms up before the hit or spike.

PRACTICE TASK

Setup   Players practice the solo block against a spike.

Goal   As blocker, execute three of five trials successfully, and then rotate.

Conditions

- Use two teams and three or four balls.
- The setter tosses high, outside sets for the hitter to hit or spike.
- The blocker blocks (figure 16.28).

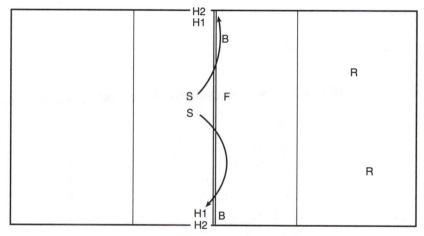

F = Feeder   S = Setter   H = Hitter   B = Blocker   R = Retriever

Figure 16.28

Cues

- Hold hands high.
- Front the hitter.

- Jump when the hitter swings her arm.
- Press to center court.

GAME 2

Setup   Players play two games of 4v4.

Goal   Successful outside blocking in the game

Conditions

- Use the no-ace serve.

- Use rally scoring or the regulation game.

Tactical Problem   Attacking as a team

Lesson Focus   Serve receiving as a team

Objective   Serve receive and transition to attack.

GAME 1

Setup   6v6

Goal   Serve receive and set up to attack.

Conditions

- Use a full court.
- Use regulation rules and scoring.
- Use the no-ace serve.

Question

Q: What does your team need to do to set up for an attack?

A: Serve receive, set, hit, support teammates, and communicate.

PRACTICE TASK

Setup   Players practice the free-ball wash.

Goal   Earn 2 consecutive points.

Conditions

- Use two teams and three or four balls.
- Initiate the game from a free ball.
- A wash is an attempt to earn 2 consecutive points. For example, team A starts by receiving a free ball. Team A wins the rally and earns the right to receive the next free ball. Team B now has the opportunity to wash out, or nullify, team A's second point. If team A wins the second point, it wins the game; but if team B washes team A's second point, the game begins again. If team A does not win the first point, then the game starts over with team B receiving the first free ball.

Note   Implement a game manager to toss free balls from the sideline near the net standard. As the teacher, you can manage and coach one game while the other court manages itself. Remember to switch and coach the other court after five to seven minutes.

GAME 2

Setup   6v6

Goal   Serve receive and set up to attack.

Conditions

- Use a full court.
- Use regulation rules and scoring.
- Use the no-ace serve.

LEVEL V

The problem of team defense becomes the primary focus at level V, which introduces defensive systems. You should feel free to have your students play 4v4 or 6v6 if doing so meets their developmental needs. If they are ready, you can introduce the double block and complete the tactical levels by teaching attack coverage (players supporting hitters when they are blocked). You can provide an additional challenge for your students by introducing various plays for setting up to attack.

The double block can help stop a spiked ball before it reaches the floor.

LESSON 24

Tactical Problem   Setting up to attack

Lesson Focus   Play sets

Objective   As setter, come from the back row to work on sets.

GAME 1

Setup   6v6

Goal   Set up to attack.

Conditions

- Use a full court.
- Use regulation rules and scoring.
- Initiate the game from a free ball or no-ace serve.
- Players toss a free ball from the server position; the setter plays in the server position.
- Players rotate around the setter.

Questions

Q: What can teams do to vary their tactics in setting up attacks?

A: Change sets; use different attack variations.

Q: How do you change sets?

A: Have the setter come from the back row, or vary the set height.

PRACTICE TASK

Setup   Players play sets.

Goal   Execute three of five successful setter trials, and then rotate.

Conditions

- Use two teams and three or four balls.
- The tosser slaps the ball (prompts) for hitters to transition off the net and for setter 1 to transition to the net.
- The tosser tosses a good pass to the setter target spot.
- The setter calls and sets a four, then two, and then red ball.
  - A four ball is a high, outside set (for the left front hitter).
  - A two ball is 0.5 yard high and 0.5 yard out from the setter (for the middle hitter).
  - A red ball is a high ball to the back (for the right front hitter).
- The hitter hits.
- Play repeats for setter 2 (figure 16.29).
- Players play out each set.

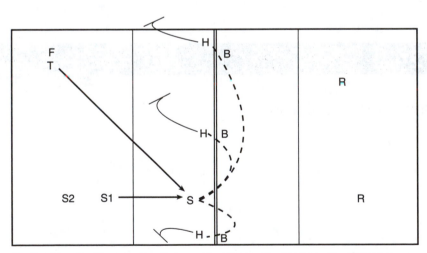

F = Feeder   T = Tosser   S = Setter   H = Hitter   B = Blocker   R = Retriever

Figure 16.29

GAME 2

Setup   6v6

Goal   Vary the positioning of the sets during the game.

Condition   Use a regulation game.

LESSON 25

Tactical Problem   Attacking as a team

Lesson Focus   Attack coverage

Objective   Play sets and attack coverage

GAME 1

Setup   6v6

Goal   Teams earn 1 point with a four ball, two ball, or red ball (see previous lesson) and a spike.

Conditions

- Use a full court.
- Use regulation rules and scoring.
- Initiate the game from a free ball or no-ace serve.
- Players toss a free ball from the server position; the setter plays in the server position.
- Players rotate around the setter.

Question

> Q: What should teams do to protect hitters who get blocked?
>
> A: Cover them.

PRACTICE TASK

Setup   Players practice free-ball transitions and attack coverage

Goal   Perform three of five trials successfully, and then rotate.

Conditions

- Use two teams and three or four balls.
- The tosser slaps the ball for the team to call "Free" and for the hitter to transition off the net and the setter to transition to the net.
- The passer passes a free ball to the target spot for the setter.
- The setter calls and sets a four, two, and red ball.
- The hitter hits, and the team covers the hitter.

Cue   Form a funnel around the hitter.

Extension 1   Use base positions (figure 16.30).

Note   Numbers represent positions in rotation.

Extension 2   Players transition to attack (figure 16.31).

Extension 3   Players practice attack coverage if the hitter four-hit or spiked (figure 16.32).

GAME 2

Repeat game 1.

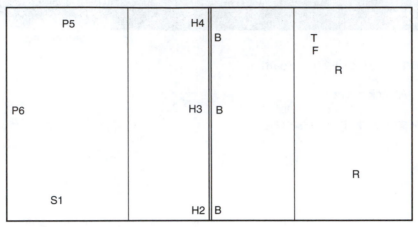

F = Feeder   P = Passer   S = Setter   H = Hitter   B = Blocker   R = Retriever
T = Tosser

Figure 16.30   Base positions.

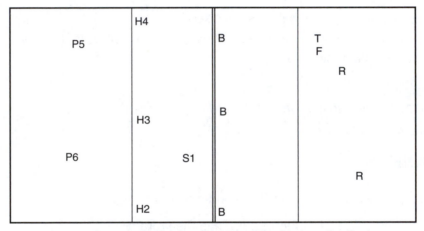

F = Feeder   P = Passer   S = Setter   H = Hitter   B = Blocker   R = Retriever
T = Tosser

Figure 16.31   Players transition to attack.

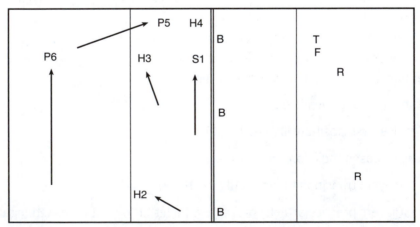

F = Feeder   P = Passer   S = Setter   H = Hitter   B = Blocker   R = Retriever
T = Tosser

Figure 16.32   Players practice attack coverage if the hitter four-hit or spiked the volleyball.

LESSON 26

Tactical Problem   Defending as a team against an attack

Lesson Focus   Floor defense

Objective   Use a floor defense against an attack.

GAME 1

Setup   6v6

Goals

- Defend against the attack.
- Earn 1 point with a dig-set-hit or a block.

Conditions

- Use a full court.
- Initiate the game from a free ball or no-ace serve.
- Players toss a free ball from the server position.

Question

Q: What should teams do to defend against an attack?

A: Organize a defense and play positions.

PRACTICE TASK

Setup   Players practice attack defense.

Goal   Perform three of five trials successfully, and then rotate.

Conditions

- Use two teams and three or four balls.
- The tosser slaps the ball (prompts) for the hitter to transition off the net and the setter to open up to set.
- The tosser tosses a good pass to the setter.
- The setter calls and sets a four, two, and red ball.
- The hitter hits.
- The defense plays the ball out (pass, dig-set-hit) (figure 16.33).

Cues

- Start in base, read the play, adjust, and make the play.
- Use floor positions.
- Diggers 1 and 5 cover crosscourt and line while digger 6 patrols the tip and roll shot.
- Blockers 2 and 4 block when on the ball and cover the angle shot when off the ball.
- Setter or blocker 3 solo or double blocks and transitions to set.

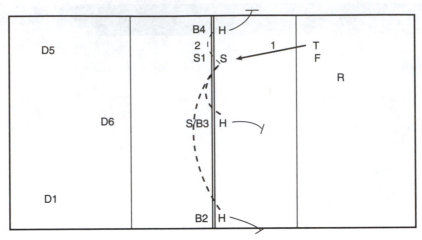

F = Feeder   D = Digger   S = Setter   H = Hitter   B = Blocker   R = Retriever
T = Tosser

Figure 16.33

GAME 2

Setup   6v6

Goals

- Defend against the attack.
- Earn 1 point with a dig-set-hit or a block.

Conditions

- Use a full court.
- Initiate the game from a free ball or no-ace serve.
- Players toss free balls from the server position.

LESSON 27

Secondary Level V

Tactical Problem   Attacking and defending as a team

Lesson Focus   Team tactics and communication

Objective   Successfully implement team concepts.

GAME 1

Setup   6v6

Goal   Learn team tactics.

Conditions

- Use a full court.
- Use regulation rules and scoring.
- Use the no-ace serve.

Question

Q: *What are the goals of the game?*

A: *Receiving the serve, setting up to attack, winning the point, and so on.*

PRACTICE TASK

Setup   Players practice the free-ball wash (refer to level IV, lesson 23, for a description).

Goal   Earn 2 points in a row.

Condition

- Use two teams and three or four balls.
- Initiate the game from a free ball.

Note   Implement a game manager to toss free balls from the sideline near the net standard. You can manage and coach one game while the other court manages itself and switch after five to seven minutes.

GAME 2

Setup   6v6

Goal   Serve receive and set up to attack.

Conditions

- Use a full court.
- Use regulation rules and scoring.

Game Extensions   An additional game to introduce to your students is *continuous volleyball,* or *king (or queen) of the court.* The game uses 1-point games with either quick scoring (every point scores) or regulation volleyball scoring. You can use one or more courts and label one side of the court winners and the other side challengers. Winning teams move or stay on their own courts. Losing teams try again by joining the challengers' line. The game can focus on various components of the real game, such as the following:

- You can begin it from a serve, modified or no-ace serve, free ball, down ball, or spiked ball.
- You can teach other critical elements of game play such as pursuing (for a ball out of control), transitioning off the net, receiving the serve, or floor positioning for defense.
- You can help students hone their skills by playing a form of triples known as *cheap shot* that moves the end line to the 10-foot (3 m) line.
- You can regulate the offense in another modification of triples by creating rules such as (a) only the back row can attack, (b) the attack must go beyond the 10-foot (3 m) line, (c) the attack must be from the middle or back row, or any combination of these. These modifications enable the teams to focus on specific offensive strategies.

SUMMARY

The levels of tactical complexity and their accompanying lessons in this chapter are the building blocks for your volleyball unit. The lessons are specifically designed to solve problems at various levels of tactical complexity, not in units organized from the first to last lesson. For example, we encourage you to include tournament play in your units. The following are suggestions for keeping score during tournament play:

- Use goals from an earlier game.
- Increase the number of players on each team from three to four to six. The number of players changes the pace and momentum of the game.
- Use regulation games, but initiate games from a free ball or no-ace serve.
- Either score games (i.e., play to 5, 11, or 15 points) or time games (i.e., play for 5, 7, or 10 minutes).

We encourage you to make these materials meet the contextual needs of you, your students, your facilities, and your equipment. We view 3v3 as the basic game that develops students' abilities to solve other aspects of volleyball. Although this chapter is comprehensive, it is not exhaustive, and an endless number of variations and extensions for these lessons are possible. We encourage you to design your units, mixing levels and creating your own lessons. For example, you might organize a unit primarily around level IV but include parts or variations of earlier lessons for review.

Implement the levels as a way of sequencing your games curriculum. Do not get trapped into teaching the same lessons to each grade level or you will perpetuate the existing problem in games teaching (introducing the same skills over and over). Remember, teach the game with the game!

Chapter 17

Badminton

Badminton is a game for students of all abilities. It can be played at any level, and it is well suited to teaching students with varying abilities. Unfortunately, some students believe that badminton is a technically difficult game they cannot play.

It is common to see the initial lesson in a badminton unit begin with a lecture on the parts of the racket, which is not stimulating and not information that students need or want to know. An introduction to the underhand serve often follows because it is a necessary skill for beginning a point. Many students have difficulty performing the underhand serve, either mis-hitting the shot or missing the shuttle completely. Teachers sometimes continue instruction in the underhand serve until the students reach satisfactory competence, at which point they plan to move to the next skill. The problem is that many students might not get to the next skill because they never learn to serve. As a result, they simply experience frustration and come to believe that they lack the necessary skills to play the game.

The tactical approach we suggest in this chapter avoids scenarios such as this one. Students are immediately placed in modified, or conditioned, game situations. They begin a point in whichever way they find successful—even by placing the shuttle on the racket and throwing it over the net or by tossing it with the hand. The singles game is the primary focus of instruction, because it is tactically simpler than the doubles game and it ensures maximum participation. As in other chapters, the tactical complexity of the game increases as the students progress. New skills are taught after students understand the necessity of having these skills for solving tactical problems in the game. Tournament play can take place at any level, but the type of game used in a tournament should not exceed the tactical complexity that students have experienced. For example, tournament play at level I should focus on the half-court singles game. We begin with alternate serving at level I. You can introduce the correct scoring and serving (i.e., score on your own service) later, preferably when students can return the shuttle well enough for rallies to take place.

Students ideally work in pairs during badminton instruction. This enables them to play singles games and practice the related tactics and skills. Using pairs also makes it easy for you to later combine groups for doubles practice and competition. Singles games should take place on a half-court to provide a long, thin playing area that emphasizes the front and back of the court as primary spaces for attack. One court for every four participants is ideal, although these facilities may not be available to you. If space is short, you have several options:

- You can set up nets down the length of a court and, by adding some lines, create minicourts that run across the regulation court. Although not ideal for high school students, these minicourts do give middle school students sufficient space in which to play.

- You can use spaces between courts by using string to connect net posts.

- You can rotate players on and off the court, although this will decrease activity time for all students and thus is not preferable.

We assume that each student has a badminton racket and that each pair of players has a shuttle. Students will not likely have prior badminton experience because the game is not typically taught at the elementary level due to the prohibitive length of the racket for younger learners. However, students might be familiar with some of its tactical principles through net and wall game instruction of the kind advocated in *Sport Foundations for Secondary Physical Education: A Tactical Games Approach (2003)*. In particular, they might be familiar with the concept of creating space through hitting long and short. We present the framework of the tactical problems, movements, and skills in badminton in table 17.1 and the levels of tactical complexity in table 17.2.

LEVEL I

At level I students focus on setting up to attack by creating space on the opposite side of the net and on defending space on their side of the net. These are the two tactical problems fundamental to badminton. Creating space is accomplished by being aware of open areas on the court. In the half-court singles game, these spaces are at the back and the front of the long, narrow court. Students become aware of these spaces through appropriate questioning, after which they can be introduced to the overhead clear and drop shot. While learning how to create space, students also see the need to defend space on their side of the net. As players create space by moving their opponents up and down the court, their opponents will be doing the same. Hence, they must defend their space. This is when you introduce the concept of recovery.

Focusing on these two tactical problems enables the basic form of badminton to take shape. At this

Table 17.1 Tactical Problems, Movements, and Skills in Badminton

Tactical problems	Off-the-ball movements	On-the-ball skills
SCORING (OFFENSE)		
Setting up to attack by creating space on the opponent's side of the net		• Overhead clear—forehand, backhand • Overhead drop shot—forehand, backhand • High service • Underarm clear—forehand, backhand
Winning the point		• Smash • Attacking the short serve • Attacking the drop shot
Attacking as a pair	• Front, back offense • Communication	
PREVENTING SCORING (DEFENSE)		
Defending space on your own side of the net	Recovery to center court—footwork	Low service
Defending against an attack		• Returning the smash • Returning the drop shot
Defending as a pair	• Side-to-side defense • Communication	

Table 17.2 Levels of Tactical Complexity for Badminton

Tactical goals and problems	Level I	Level II	Level III
SCORING (OFFENSE)			
Setting up to attack by creating space on the opponent's side of the net	• Overhead clear—forehand, backhand • Overhead drop shot—forehand, backhand	• High service • Underarm clear—forehand, backhand	
Winning the point		• Smash • Attacking the short serve	Attacking the drop shot
Attacking as a pair			• Front, back offense • Communication
PREVENTING SCORING (DEFENSE)			
Defending space on your own side of the net	Recovery to center court—footwork	Low service	
Defending against an attack		Returning the smash	Returning the drop shot
Defending as a pair			• Side-to-side defense • Communication

level students can serve underarm, overarm, or any way (even with a throw) that gets the point started. We introduce the service line in lesson 3 because students might begin to see the value of dropping a short service into the frontcourt.

We do not recommend discussing racket parts or grip. Most students find an approximate Eastern (shake hands) grip the most comfortable for them, and so can be left alone. You can take care of grip problems early and on an individual basis by observing students and quietly correcting them. Most grip problems arise from an exaggerated Western (frying pan) grip, in which the back of the hand points to the sky when the head of the racket is parallel to the floor. To correct the grip, ask students to rotate their grip by a quarter turn either clockwise (right-handed player) or counterclockwise (left-handed player). Correcting individual grips saves students from listening to a lecture they may not need. Likewise, we do not recommend beginning with the underhand serve, which is a difficult skill for many novice players. Allow them to start the rallies by whatever means they find successful so they get to play.

At level I, students can serve any way that feels comfortable to them. Here, students have chosen to use the underarm serve.

LESSON 1

Secondary Level I

Tactical Problem Creating space

Lesson Focus Half-court singles game

Objective Keep the shuttle in play.

GAME 1

Setup Half-court singles, using any serve (figure 17.1)

Goal Keep a rally going as long as possible, using overarm and underarm shots.

Questions

Q: How do you score a point in badminton?

A: Make the shuttle hit the floor on the opponent's side.

Q: How can you stop your opponent from scoring?

A: Keep the shuttle in play.

Q: Is it easier to keep the shuttle in play with overhead or underhand shots?

A: Overhead. (This is the case for most novices.)

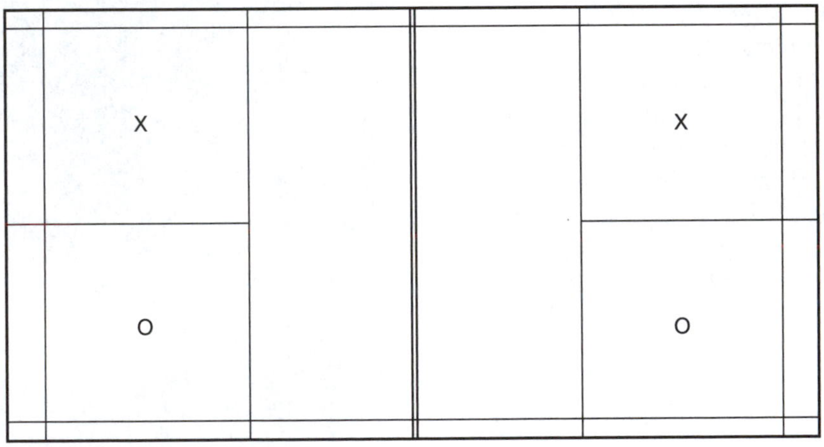

Figure 17.1

PRACTICE TASK

Setup Half-court singles

Goal Keep a rally going as long as possible using only overhead shots.

GAME 2

Setup Half-court singles

Goal Be aware of what spaces can be used on the other side of the net.

Conditions

- Players alternate service (any type).
- Players score 1 point if the shuttle hits the floor on the opponent's side of the court.
- Players score on every service (not only when serving).

LESSON 2

Tactical Problem   Creating space

Lesson Focus   Pushing the opponent back and performing the overhead clear

Objectives

- Understand the value of forcing the opponent back.
- Push the opponent back using the overhead clear (forehand).

GAME 1

Setup   Half-court singles

Goals

- Be aware of what spaces can be used on the other side of the net.
- Understand that it is harder to attack from the back of the court, and so it is useful to push the opponent back.

Conditions

- Players alternate service.
- Players score 1 point if the shuttle hits the floor on the opponent's side of the court.
- Players score on every service (not only when serving).

Questions

Q: Where are the available spaces on the court?

A: In the front and back.

Q: Is it harder for your opponent to attack you from the front or the back?

A: Back.

Q: Why?

A: Because the opponent is farther from the net.

Q: So, is it best to send your opponent to the back or to the front?

A: Back.

Q: Is it easier to send your opponent back by using an overhead or underhand shot?

A: Overhead. (Use the analogy of throwing for distance if necessary to explain this answer.)

EXTENSION

Setup   Half-court singles

Goals

- Understand that more power can be generated from overhead shots.
- Play only overhead shots.
- Push the opponent back.

Condition Players use only overhead shots after the serve.

PRACTICE TASK

Setup Half-court technique practice (cooperative)

Goal Push the opponent back.

Conditions

- Players attempt to maintain a forehand overhead rally.
- Players hand-feed if necessary.

Cues

- Get under the shuttle, using long strides.
- Line up the shuttle with the nonhitting arm.
- Break the elbow.
- Step into the shot.

- Use a throwing action to contact the shuttle with the racket head.
- Snap the wrist and follow through across the body.

GAME 2

Setup Half-court singles

Goal Use a skillful overhead clear to push the opponent back in a game situation.

Conditions

- Players alternate service.
- Players score 1 point if the shuttle hits the floor on the opponent's side of the court.
- Players can score on any service (not only when serving).

LESSON 3

Tactical Problem Creating space

Lesson Focus Pushing the opponent back, performing the backhand overhead clear

Objective Use the backhand when necessary to push the opponent back.

GAME 1

Setup Half-court singles

Goal Maintain a rally and push the opponent back.

Conditions

- Players alternate service.
- Players score 1 point if shuttle hits floor on opponent's side of court.
- Players can score on any service (not only when serving).

Question

Q: How can you push your opponent back if the shuttle does not come to your strong (forehand) side?

A: If possible, lean across and play a forehand anyway. Otherwise, play a backhand.

PRACTICE TASK

Setup   Half-court technique practice (cooperative)

Conditions

- Players maintain a backhand rally.
- Players hand-feed to start if necessary.

Cues

- Move your front foot (on the same side as your hitting hand) toward the shuttle (to turn yourself sideways).

- Keep your elbow high.
- Contact the shuttle at its high point.
- Flick your wrist.

GAME 2

Setup   Half-court singles game; introduce the underarm service.

Goal   Use forehand and backhand overhead clears to push the opponent to the back of the court.

Conditions

- Players alternate service and can score on any serve.
- Each point begins with an underarm serve.
- Introduce the service line and require that players serve beyond it.

LESSON 4

Secondary Level I

Tactical Problem   Creating space

Lesson Focus   Introducing the drop shot

Objective   Use a drop shot to move the opponent forward.

GAME 1

Setup   Half-court singles, underarm serve (if some students still cannot use the underarm serve, allow a second serve by any method)

Goals

- Push the opponent back with overhead clears.
- Be aware of available space at the front of the opponent's court.

Conditions

- Players alternate service and can score on any serve.
- Each point begins with an underarm serve.
- Players must serve beyond the service line.

Questions

Q: Now that you can push your opponent back, where is the space you can attack to win a point?

A: At the front.

Q: How do you attack this front space?

A: Use a drop shot.

EXTENSION

Setup   Half-court singles

Goal   Win points by dropping the shuttle into space in the frontcourt.

PRACTICE TASK

Setup   Half-court technique practice. One player feeds to the back of the court, and the other player hits drop shots back.

Goals

- Land the shuttle as close to the net as possible.
- Land a specific number of shots inside the service line.

Cues

- Disguise your shot by preparing as for an overhead clear.
- Keep a stiff wrist on contact.

GAME 2

Repeat game 1.

LESSON 5

Secondary Level I

Tactical Problem   Defending space

Lesson Focus   Recovery to center court

Objective   Recover to center court between shots, using appropriate footwork.

GAME 1

Setup   Half-court singles

Goals

- Move the opponent.
- Be aware of the need to retain a position at center court.

Questions

Q: Where should you go between shots?

A: Back to the center of the court.

Q: Why?

A: So you can move to either the front or the back of the court for your next shot.

PRACTICE TASK

Setup   Partners practice with one feeder and one hitter. The feeder has two shuttles and feeds first to the back of the hitter's court. The hitter returns and immediately recovers to center court. The feeder feeds the second shuttle to either the front or the back of the hitter's court. The hitter returns and recovers, and then players rotate.

Cues

- Recover immediately after the shot.
- Use long strides to recover.
- Stay on your toes.

GAME 2

Setup   Half- or full-court singles, minitournament

Goals

- Recover to center court between shots.
- Take up a position between the service line and the back alley.

Condition   Each player has a coach to encourage and reinforce movement.

LEVEL II

Level II further develops students' ability to create and defend space by introducing high and low service and underarm clears in the context of the tactical problem at hand. The skills are presented, again through appropriate teacher questioning, as potential solutions to the tactical problems of creating and defending space. Students at level II also can explore solutions to winning a point. Although badminton players can win points by simply moving the opponent about the court until he cannot reach a shot, winning points this way becomes less likely as the opponent's tactical awareness and skill increase. Students seek ways to win points when the opportunity arises, which makes introducing the smash appropriate. Once introduced to the smash, students will see the need to defend against it, another tactical problem to solve. Finally, in level II students encounter the doubles game, which presents added tactical and technical complexities.

Learning the tactical skills necessary to win a point, and how to defend against those tactics, heightens the level of intensity as students practice.

LESSON 6

Tactical Problem   Creating space

Lesson Focus   Starting the point on the attack

Objective   Use the high service to put the opponent on the defensive at the start of a point.

GAME 1

Setup   Half-court singles

Goal   Push the opponent back with service.

Condition   Players alternate service.

Questions

> Q: Where is the best place to serve to in the singles game?
>
> A: To the back of the opponent's court.
>
> Q: Why?
>
> A: Because serving there puts the opponent on the defensive.

PRACTICE TASK

Setup   Half-court technique practice

Goals

- Serve high and to the opponent's backhand side.
- Land a specific number of shots in the back alley.

Condition   Players alternate serving (no rallying).

Cues

- Drop the shuttle.
- Flick your wrist.
- Follow through.
- Land the shuttle as close to the baseline as possible.

Note   Students who have trouble serving often benefit from gripping the racket farther down the handle.

GAME 2

Repeat game 1.

LESSON 7

Tactical Problem   Creating space

Lesson Focus   Underarm shots for maintaining depth

Objective   Use underarm (both forehand and backhand) clears to keep the opponent in the backcourt.

GAME 1

Setup   Half-court singles using correct serving and scoring rules (i.e., players can score only on their own service)

Goal   Be aware that because it's not always possible to play overhead shots to the backcourt, developing the underarm clear is necessary.

Condition   Players use a low serve to the front of the court.

Question

> Q: If the shuttle is low, how can you get it to the back of your opponent's court?
>
> A: Use the wrist in an underarm clear.

PRACTICE TASK

Setup   Half-court partner practice

Goals

- Use the underarm shot to clear the shuttle to the backcourt.
- Land a specific number of shots in the back alley.

Conditions

- One player feeds to the frontcourt while one hits underarm clears to the back of the feeder's court.
- Players alternate feeds to the forehand and backhand.

Cues

- Step to the shuttle (with the opposite foot on the forehand or the same foot on the backhand).
- Snap your wrist to create power.

GAME 2

Repeat game 1.

LESSON 8

Tactical Problem   Winning the point

Lesson Focus   Winning the point with a smash

Objective   Use the smash to win a point.

GAME 1

Setup   Half-court singles

Goals

- Move the opponent.
- Win the point.
- Be aware of the need to attack the weak clear.

Questions

Q: What is the best way to make a shot unreturnable?

A: Hit it hard and straight to the ground—use the smash.

Q: From where can you use a smash most easily?

A: From the front or middle of the court.

Q: What kinds of shots are you looking for from your opponent so you can use the smash?

A: A weak clear or a high drop shot.

PRACTICE TASK

Setup   Half-court partner practice

Goal   Make the shuttle hit the floor as close to the net as possible.

Condition   One partner feeds high serves to midcourt, and the other partner smashes.

Cues

- Prepare as for the clear.
- Contact the shuttle when it is high and in front of you.
- Snap your wrist for power.

GAME 2

Repeat game 1, but as a competitive game.

LESSON 9

Secondary Level II

Tactical Problem   Defending against an attack

Lesson Focus   Returning the smash

Objective   Return the smash positively (i.e., do not provide a second attacking opportunity for the opponent).

GAME 1

Setup   Half-court singles game

Goals

- Win points with a smash if possible.
- Be aware of the need to return the smash without setting up an easy kill for the opponent.

Condition   Each point must start with a high serve.

Question

Q: How can you return a smash without setting up your opponent for another smash?

A: Play a block return or drop shot.

PRACTICE TASK

Setup   Half-court partner practice

Conditions

- One partner feeds a high serve to midcourt, and the other partner smashes.
- Players continue the point and alternate service.

Cues

- Have your feet square and the racket head up to receive a smash (ready position).
- Block the smash, keeping a firm wrist.
- Drop the shuttle into the frontcourt.

GAME 2

Repeat game 1.

LESSON 10

Tactical Problem   Defending space

Lesson Focus   Low service, doubles game

Objective   Prevent an attack against the serve by keeping it low (opponents cannot hit a downward return).

GAME 1

Setup   Full-court doubles

Goals

- Be aware of the potential risk of using the high serve, particularly in doubles play, in which the service box is shorter.
- Be aware of the potential value of a short, low serve.

Condition   Players alternate serving (i.e., change on every point).

Questions

Q: Why is a high serve more risky in doubles than it is in singles?

A: The shorter service box makes a smash off the high serve more likely.

Q: What serve can you use instead?

A: A short and low serve.

Q: What is the danger associated with a short serve?

A: Hitting the net or hitting it too high and setting up an easy smash for your opponent.

PRACTICE TASK

Setup   Half-court partner practice, diagonal

Goal   Land the shuttle just on the other side of the service line, within 2 feet (0.6 meter).

Cues

- Drop the shuttle late to help disguise the serve.
- Keep the elbow (of the serving arm) tucked in.

- Serve from just below waist height to give the shuttle a flat trajectory.
- Use a firm wrist.
- Stroke the shuttle.

GAME 2

Repeat game 1.

LESSON 11

Tactical Problem   Winning the point

Lesson Focus   Attacking the short serve

Objective   Punish a weak, short serve.

GAME 1

Setup   Full-court doubles game

Goal   Be aware of attacking opportunity if the short serve is too high.

Condition   Each point starts with a short serve.

Question

Q: How can you attack a short serve?

A: Get low and hit it straight back overhead with a flick of the wrist. Look for the poor serve that goes too high.

PRACTICE TASK

Setup   Half-court partner practice, singles

Goals

- Attack the serve and put the opponent on the defensive.
- Return the serve flat or downward.

Condition   One partner feeds short serves from the service line, and the other partner attacks the serve.

Cues

- Be in a ready position, with your weight forward and racket up.
- Punch with your arm and flick your wrist.
- Put a downward (if possible) or horizontal trajectory on the return.

GAME 2

Setup   Full-court doubles game

Goal   Attack the short serve to put the opponent on the defensive.

Condition   Each point starts with a short serve.

LEVEL III

Level III further shifts the focus from the half-court singles game to the more tactically complex doubles game. If you have small classes or are teaching high school students, you might prefer full-court to half-court singles. Although still primarily a front-and-back game, full-court singles introduces a greater use of angles in play.

Regardless of the game, students at level III can develop more technically advanced means of winning the point and defending against an attack before exploring the tactical problems presented by the doubles game—specifically, attacking and defending as a pair. Students are guided to solutions involving various formations of play, and then they practice these formations in game situations. The last two lessons of level III are doubles tournament play.

Once students are comfortable with the fundamentals, they can move into playing doubles, which is more tactically complex.

LESSON 12

Secondary Level III

Tactical Problem   Winning the point

Lesson Focus   Attacking drop shot

Objective   Play an effective and fast attacking drop shot.

GAME 1

Setup   Half-court singles

Goal   Be aware of the need to play a drop shot that will reach the floor quickly.

Condition   Players cannot play two consecutive smashes.

Questions

Q: Why is it best not to use two consecutive smashes?

A: The opponent is probably expecting the two smashes.

Q: If playing two smashes is not a good idea, how else can you get the shuttle to the floor quickly?

A: Use the faster, attacking drop shot.

PRACTICE TASK

Setup   Half-court partner practice

Goals

- Achieve a continual downward trajectory of the drop shot.
- Land a specific number of shots inside the service line.

Condition   One partner feeds the serve high to the midcourt, and the other partner plays drop shots into the frontcourt.

Cues

- Prepare as for the smash.
- Contact the shuttle when it is high and in front of you.
- Keep your wrist open and firm.

GAME 2

Repeat game 1.

LESSON 13

Secondary Level III

Tactical Problem   Defending against an attack

Lesson Focus   Returning the attacking drop shot

Objective   Return the drop shot from below net height without giving the opponent an attacking opportunity.

GAME 1

Setup   Half-court singles

Goals

- Execute proficient drop shots.
- Be aware of the need to return the drop shot in an attacking manner.

Condition   No smashes are allowed from behind the service line.

Question

Q: How can you return the drop shot without giving an easy smash to your opponent?

A: Use the underarm clear or touch return.

PRACTICE TASK

Setup   Half-court partner practice for keeping the shuttle low to the net

Goal   Use the touch return to roll the shuttle over the net.

Condition   Both players stay inside the service line and rally.

Cues

- Keep a firm wrist.
- Let the shuttle hit your racket; do not move your racket.

GAME 2

Repeat game 1.

LESSON 14

Tactical Problem   Attacking as a pair

Lesson Focus   Front-and-back offense

Objective   Attack in a front-and-back formation.

GAME 1

Setup   Full-court doubles

Goal   Recognize the most effective attacking formation (front and back).

Condition   Players alternate formations between front and back and side to side.

Questions

Q: What formation (front and back or side to side) gives you the best chance to attack your opponents with a smash, particularly if you are serving?

A: Front and back (figure 17.2).

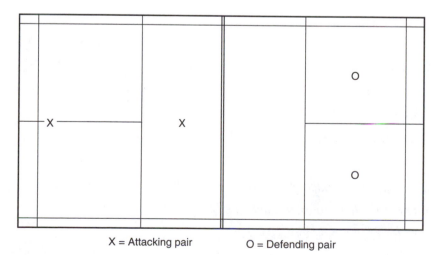

X = Attacking pair   O = Defending pair

Figure 17.2

Q: Why?

A: It gives the best opportunity for making an easy smash at the front of the court, which is the best place to put the point away.

PRACTICE TASK

Setup   Full-court doubles

Goal   Keep the serve low and attack the return.

Conditions

- Players alternate serving on every point.
- Players use low serves and follow them to the net.

Cues

- As server, keep the serve low and follow it to the net with the racket up.
- As partner, cover the middle of the backcourt to get any high, deep returns.

GAME 2

Setup   Competitive doubles game, normal rules

Goal   Attack where possible.

Condition   Use regulation doubles rules.

LESSON 15
Secondary Level III

Tactical Problem   Defending as a pair

Lesson Focus   Side-to-side defense

Objective   Effectively defend against the smash (as a doubles pair).

GAME 1

Setup   Full-court doubles

Goal   Be aware that front-and-back is not an effective formation for defending against the smash.

Conditions

- Every point starts with a high serve.
- Players use a front-and-back formation.

Questions

Q: How can you cover as much of the court as possible if you are being smashed at?

A: Play in a side-to-side formation (figure 17.2).

Q: Why is this formation best for defense?

A: It covers the entire court and gives both players as much time as possible to see the shuttle coming toward them.

PRACTICE TASK

Setup Full-court doubles

Goal Move to a side-to-side formation to receive the smash.

Conditions Players alternate serving and must hit high serves.

Cues

- Serve high and drop back to side to side.
- Be in a ready position to defend against the smash.

GAME 2

Setup Full-court doubles, normal rules

Goal As the defending pair, effectively move to receive the smash whether during a service return or during the point.

Conditions

- Players vary serves.
- Use regulation rules.

LESSON 16

Secondary Level III

Tactical Problem Attacking as a pair

Lesson Focus Reviewing lessons and tournament play to practice attacking as a pair

Objective Attack and communicate.

GAME 1

Setup Full-court doubles play, rotating opponents

Goals

- Effectively attack as a pair.
- Communicate to move each other about the court.
- Move to a front-and-back formation to attack.

Condition Vary serves (high and low).

LESSON 17

Secondary Level III

Tactical Problem Defending as a pair

Lesson Focus Reviewing lessons and tournament play to practice defending as a pair

Objective Effectively defend and communicate.

GAME 1

Setup   Full-court doubles play, rotating opponents

Goals

- Effectively defend as a pair.
- Communicate to move the partner from an attacking (front-and-back) to a defending (side-to-side) formation.
- Cover at the net for the partner pushed back to receive a high serve.

Condition   Players vary serves (high and low).

SUMMARY

If your students complete the three levels of tactical complexity provided in this chapter, they will have progressed from a simple to a complex understanding of badminton. We recommend that you base your instructional units on one level of tactical complexity and use material from other levels to individualize your instruction as necessary.

From an offensive point of view, badminton is about setting oneself up to attack by creating space on the opponent's side of the net and then winning the point in the most effective way possible. You can easily combine these tactical problems in an instructional unit. Once your students learn to solve these tactical problems, they will appreciate the need for defending space on their side of the net and defending against attacks. Presented in this way, the sequencing of instruction is logical and makes sense to students.

Understanding what to do within game situations enables players to select movements and skills to help them solve the tactical problems presented by the game and by the opponent. Some material in this chapter will assist your students in playing other net games, particularly tennis, which from a tactical perspective has much in common with badminton.

Chapter 18

Tennis

Tennis is a game defined by both technical skills and tactics; students need to learn not only how to stroke the ball but also how to play tactically. Playing requires not only physical motor skills but also the cognitive skills of problem solving and decision making. Tactical awareness is every bit as important as technical development. A tactical approach maintains the fun of playing by either modifying the game for "doability" and success or placing players in common game play situations. Players learn as they play, and tactics and techniques all weave together (Hopper, 2003).

Tennis is a popular lifetime activity, and when played on public courts with moderately priced equipment, it is relatively inexpensive. You should focus on enabling your students to experience success and an appreciation for the game. Your challenge is to hook your students into the game through games!

Tennis, like badminton, is an easy game to understand tactically, despite being difficult to play for the novice. We recommend that both games be played 1v1, with players having limited alternating roles of striker and receiver. Two basic tactical conditions guide players: shot selection and court position. The premise behind a tactical approach is that students with tactical skills can play games, and these games can still be interesting, challenging, and even competitive. A first step in your units will be to establish a tennis-like relationship between players and an understanding of the court boundaries.

Similar to chapter 17 on badminton, this chapter focuses primarily on the singles game. Singles is tactically simple and maximizes game play. Consider the playing opportunities of four students who share a court by playing singles on half of it (i.e., play on a long and narrow court). If these four students play doubles on the same court, their opportunities to play are cut in half. We believe that students should learn and play doubles, but we encourage you to start your students with singles. Your teaching challenge will be to modify or arrange games to give your students the opportunity to solve the tactical problems of this net game. The framework of tactical problems, movements, and skills in tennis (table 18.1) can help you

Focus your teaching so that students have a successful learning experience, even if they are having a frustrating time perfecting a skill.

Table 18.1 Tactical Problems, Movements, and Skills in Tennis

Tactical problems	Off-the-ball movements	On-the-ball skills
SCORING (OFFENSE)		

Setting up to attack by creating space on the opponent's side	Read and anticipate	• Ground stroke:
		  o Forehand
		  o Backhand
		  o Crosscourt
		  o Line
		• Lob (offensive):
		  o Forehand
		  o Backhand
		• Serve

Winning the point	Approach shot—footwork	• Approach shot
		• Volley:
		  o Forehand
		  o Backhand
		  o Crosscourt
		  o Line
		• Smash
		• Passing shot
		• Attacking drop shot
		• Serve

Attacking as a pair (doubles)	• Up-and-back formation • Side-to-side offense • Communication	Serve
PREVENTING SCORING (DEFENSE)		

Defending space on your own side of the net	Recovery	• Lob (defensive):
		  o Forehand
		  o Backhand

Defending against an attack		Returning drop shot
Defending as a pair (doubles)	• Up-and-back formation • Side-to-side defense • Communication	Serve

organize the game and provide solutions to tactical problems. Table 18.2 presents the levels of tactical complexity to help you match skills and movements with your students' levels of development.

Students work in pairs during most of the tennis instruction to practice the tactics and skills of the singles game. We also implement a triad formation, advocated in chapter 16 on volleyball, for some practice tasks. In the triad formation you have (a) an initiator to toss or hit balls off the racket; (b) a performer to hit ground strokes, volleys, and so forth; and (c) a retriever to collect tennis balls for repeated trials. Ideally, you would have one court for every four students, but where space is short, you may consider some court options suggested in chapter 17 on badminton. Additional suggestions, related specifically to teaching the novice tennis player, include the following:

- Use badminton courts. We have had success using badminton courts with lower nets, and using these courts allows you to teach tennis indoors.
- Use foam tennis balls. Foam balls help increase tactical understanding and game performance early in a unit because they slow game play.

- Use racquetball rackets. Racquetball rackets help students with lower abilities master difficult techniques because they are shorter and easier to manipulate.
- Use alternatives to a regulation game. As you will read in the following lessons, we integrate 1-point games into teaching. We also use deuce games and no-ad games (4-point games) as alternatives to regulation games.

LEVEL I

At level I, students focus on setting up to attack by creating space on the opposite side of the net, winning the point, and defending space on their side of the net. These tactical problems provide the basics for shaping a tennis game. Creating space is accomplished by being aware of open areas on the court. In a half-court singles game, these spaces are at the back and the front of a long and narrow court (a minicourt). Through questioning, students become aware of these spaces and focus on the ground strokes (forehand and backhand), approach shot, and volley. As players create space by moving their opponents up and down the

Table 18.2 Levels of Tactical Complexity for Tennis

Tactical problems	Level I	Level II	Level III
SCORING (OFFENSE)			
Setting up to attack by creating space on the opponent's side	• Ground stroke: ○ Forehand ○ Backhand • Read and anticipate	• Serve • Ground stroke: ○ Crosscourt ○ Line • Lob (offensive): ○ Forehand ○ Backhand	
Winning the point	• Approach shot—footwork • Volley: ○ Forehand ○ Backhand	• Approach shot • Volley: ○ Crosscourt ○ Line • Smash • Serve	• Passing shot • Attacking drop shot
Attacking as a pair		• Up-and-back formation • Serve	• Side-to-side offense • Communication
PREVENTING SCORING (DEFENSE)			
Defending space on your own side of the net	Recovery	• Lob (defensive): ○ Forehand ○ Backhand	
Defending against an attack			Returning the drop shot
Defending as a pair		• Up-and-back formation • Communication	• Side-to-side defense • Communication • Serve

court, they also see the need to defend space on their side of the court. To teach students to defend space, we introduce the off-the-ball movement of recovery. When implementing level I lessons, you can alternate service and have students use a bounce-hit forehand ground stroke to serve.

Tennis is a difficult game when played with regulation rackets and balls, as it often is in secondary schools. If players cannot control the ball and keep it in play, they won't have a game. With this in mind, some early lessons might need repeating to ensure the development of reliable ground strokes. You need to be able to identify sources of errors and provide corrections, particularly for unreliable ground strokes. Accuracy errors are likely caused by problems in the contact point. Generally, contact for the ground stroke should be made when the ball is about level with the front knee and is falling from waist height to knee height after the bounce. Lack of power might come from having a square stance on contact. The player should step with the opposite foot on the forehand side and the same foot on the backhand side for both ground strokes and volleys.

In level I, tennis players learn to defend their space through the off-the-ball movement of recovery.

LESSON 1

Secondary Level I

Tactical Problem   Setting up to attack by creating space on the opponent's court

Lesson Focus

- Awareness of the court
- Reading and anticipating

Objective   Understand the concept of creating space.

GAME 1

Setup   No-racket game

Goal   Increase court awareness.

Note   You may have your students play either or both of the following no-racket games.

Conditions

- Short-court game (figure 18.1)—short and narrow court, toss-bounce-catch game, underhand toss
- Half-court game (figure 18.2)
  - Long and narrow court, toss-bounce-catch game, underhand toss
  - Extend the game by using rackets.

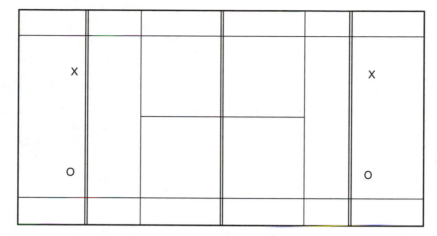

Figure 18.1 Positions for a short-court game of tennis.

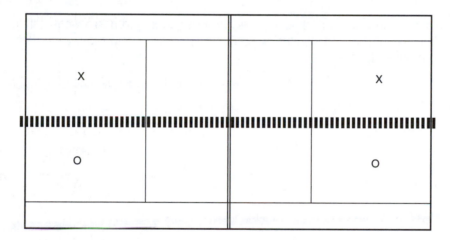

Figure 18.2 Positions for a half-court game of tennis.

Questions

Q: *How do you move your opponent?*

A: *Toss to an open space.*

Q: *When you used a racket, which shot did you use the most?*

A: *Forehand.*

PRACTICE TASK

Setup Forehand ground stroke in triads (figure 18.3)

Goal Perform three of five trials successfully, and rotate.

Conditions

- The tosser tosses or hits the ball from the racket to the hitter, the hitter hits ground strokes, and the retriever retrieves tennis balls.
- Students can say "Bounce, hit," as a cue.
- The hitter should try to hit the ball as it falls.

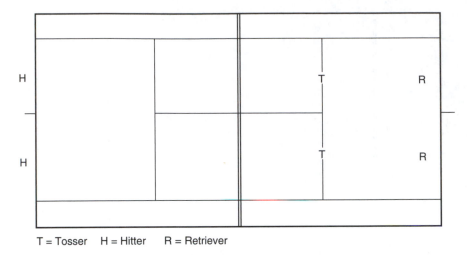

T = Tosser   H = Hitter   R = Retriever

Figure 18.3

Note You can have students practice in pairs and use a long and narrow court if you believe they will experience success. Although using pairs maximizes participation, we advocate working individually with novice players.

Cues

- Keep your side to the net.
- Pull your racket back.
- Step and swing parallel to the ground.
- Follow through.
- Hit to space.

GAME 2

Setup   Half-court singles

Goals

- Be aware of space on the other side of the net.
- Read and anticipate.

Conditions

- Players use a long and narrow court and a bounce-hit serve.
- The player with the ball starts (figure 18.2).

LESSON 2

Tactical Problem   Setting up to attack by creating space on the opponent's court

Lesson Focus

- Awareness of the court
- Reading and anticipating

Objective   Create space using ground strokes.

GAME 1

Setup   Rally, short-court singles

Goal   Keep a rally going for as long as possible using only ground strokes.

Conditions

- Players use a short and narrow court and a bounce-hit serve.
- The player with the ball starts (figure 18.1).

Question

> *Q: What did you do to keep the rally going?*
>
> *A: Hit the ball to each other.*

EXTENSION

Setup   Short-court singles

Goal   Be aware of the space on either side of the net.

Conditions

- Use a short and narrow court.
- Players alternate service, use a bounce-hit serve, and play 1-point games (figure 18.1).

Questions

> *Q: What did you do to win a point?*
>
> *A: Hit to an open space.*
>
> *Q: Into what spaces on your opponent's side of the net can you hit the tennis ball?*
>
> *A: Front and back and side to side.*
>
> *Q: How do you return the ball if it does not come to your forehand side?*
>
> *A: Use the backhand.*

PRACTICE TASK

Setup   Backhand ground stroke in triads (figure 18.3)

Goal   Perform three of five trials successfully, and rotate.

Conditions   The tosser tosses or hits the ball to the hitter, the hitter hits a ground stroke, and the retriever retrieves tennis balls.

Note   You can have students practice in pairs and use a long and narrow court if you believe they will experience success. Pairs maximize participation.

Cues

- Keep your side to the net.
- Pull your racket back.
- Swing parallel to the ground.
- Follow through.

GAME 2

Setup Half-court singles

Goal Be aware of the space on the other side of the net.

Conditions

- Use a long and narrow court.
- Players alternate service, use a bounce-hit serve, play 4-point games, and hit ground strokes only (figure 18.2).

LESSON 3

Tactical Problem Setting up to attack by creating space on the opponent's court

Lesson Focus Understanding the value of forcing the opponent back to the baseline

Objective Push the opponent back with strong ground strokes.

GAME 1

Setup Half-court singles

Goals

- Be aware of the space on the other side of the net.
- Understand that because it is harder to attack from the back of the court, it is useful to push the opponent back to the baseline.

Conditions

- Use a long and narrow court.
- Players alternate service, use a bounce-hit serve, play 4-point games, and use ground strokes only (figure 18.2).

Questions

Q: Is it harder for your opponent to attack from the baseline or at the net?

A: From the baseline.

Q: Is it best to send your opponent to the baseline or to the net?

A: Baseline.

Q: How do you send your opponent back?

A: Play a ground stroke to the baseline.

PRACTICE TASK 1

Setup Ground-stroke mixer in triads (figure 18.3)

Goal Perform five of eight trials successfully, and rotate.

Conditions

- The tosser tosses or hits the ball, mixing forehand and backhand, to the hitter.
- The hitter hits ground strokes, and the retriever retrieves tennis balls.
- Set target areas just inside the baseline for the ball to land in.

Note   You can have students practice in pairs and use a long and narrow court if you think they will experience success. Although using pairs maximizes participation, we advocate working individually with novice players.

PRACTICE TASK 2

Setup   Half-court singles

Goal   Maintain a rally from the baseline by using ground strokes.

Condition   Players cooperate to keep the rally going as long as possible.

GAME 2

Setup   Half-court singles

Goal   Use skillful ground strokes to push the opponent back in a game situation.

Conditions

- Use a long and narrow court.
- Players alternate service, use the bounce-hit serve, play 4-point games, and use ground strokes only.

LESSON 4

Tactical Problem   Winning the point

Lesson Focus   Getting to the net to attack

Objectives

- Practice the approach shot to the net.
- Improve footwork for the approach shot.

GAME 1

Setup   Half-court singles

Goals

- Move the opponent.
- Win the point.
- Be aware of the need to punish short ground strokes.

Conditions

- Players play no-ad score games (4-point games).
- After the serve, players can play the ball before it bounces.

Questions

Q: What did you do when your partner hit a short ground stroke?

A: Moved up to play the ball.

Q: After you move up, is it easier to run back or keep moving toward the net?

A: Keep moving toward the net.

Note You can use either of the following practice tasks.

PRACTICE TASK 1

Setup

- Approach shot practice (figure 18.4)
- Use a half-court or full court.

Goals Perform three of five trials successfully, and rotate.

Conditions

- The tosser feeds a short ground stroke (hits off the racket).
- The hitter executes an approach shot and continues to the net.
- The hitter then returns to the baseline to repeat the practice task.
- Players can practice the task in triads.

Cues

- Adopt a medium to low posture.
- Approach the ball.
- Keep your racket back.

- Swing parallel to the ground and hit the ball in the court.
- Move to the net and get into a ready position (feet set and racket head up).

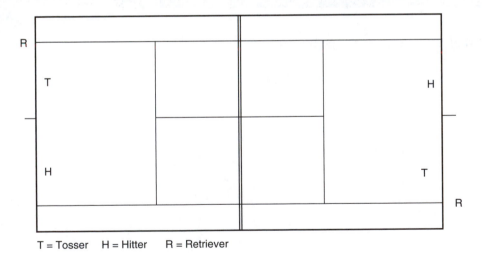

T = Tosser   H = Hitter   R = Retriever

Figure 18.4

PRACTICE TASK 2

Setup Half-court technique practice

Goal Land a specific number of approach shots (e.g., three of five) in the backcourt.

Conditions

- One player feeds short ground strokes.
- One player hits approach shots.
- Players switch roles.

GAME 2

Setup Half-court singles

Goals

- Move the opponent.
- Win the point.
- Be aware of the need to punish weak ground strokes.

Conditions

- Use deuce games.
- Use a long and narrow court.
- One person serves for the entire deuce game.
- After the serve, players can play the ball before it bounces.

LESSON 5

Tactical Problem   Winning the point

Lesson Focus   Winning the point using the volley

Objective   Use a volley to win a point.

GAME 1

Setup Half-court singles

Goals

- Move the opponent.
- Win the point.
- Be aware of the need to punish weak ground strokes.

Conditions

- Use deuce games.
- One person serves for the entire deuce game.
- Use a long and narrow court.
- After the serve, players can play the ball before it bounces.

Questions

Q: What shot would you use if you were moving toward the net?

A: Volley.

Q: What did you do to play the ball before it bounced?

A: Moved closer to the net, to the front of the court.

Note   You can use either of the following practice tasks.

PRACTICE TASK 1

Setup

- Volley technique practice (figure 18.5)
- Use a half-court or full court.

Goals   Perform three of five trials successfully, and rotate.

Conditions

- One player feeds (either with a toss or off the racket).
- One player hits the volley.
- Pairs repeat three times practicing on both the forehand and backhand sides.
- This task can be practiced as a triad.

Cues

- Make yourself light (keep your weight on the balls of your feet).
- Use a short backswing.
- Turn your side to the net.
- Reach forward to hit.
- Recover to a ready position.

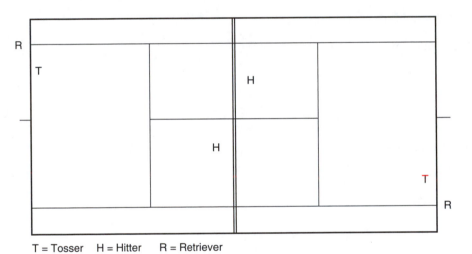

T = Tosser   H = Hitter   R = Retriever

Figure 18.5

PRACTICE TASK 2

Setup   Half-court

Goal   Land a specific number of shots (e.g., three of five) in the backcourt.

Conditions

- One player feeds ground strokes to the frontcourt or net.
- One player hits the volley (backhand and forehand).

GAME 2

Setup   Half-court singles

Goals

- Move the opponent.
- Win the point.
- Be aware of the need to punish weak ground strokes.

Conditions

- Use deuce games.
- One person serves for the entire deuce game.
- Use a long and narrow court.
- After the serve, players can play the ball before it bounces.

LESSON 6

Tactical Problem   Defending space on one's own court

Lesson Focus   Recovering to the center baseline

Objective   Recover to the center baseline between shots.

GAME 1

Setup   Half-court singles

Goals

- Move the opponent.
- Be aware of the need to recover to the center court.

Conditions

- Service alternates.
- Players use the bounce-hit serve.
- Use a long and narrow court.

Question

Q: Where should you go between your shots?

A: Back to the center of the baseline.

PRACTICE TASK

Setup   Full-court singles minitournament

Goal   Recover to the center baseline between shots.

Conditions

- Have one coach per player or court.
- Players use the bounce-hit serve and no-ad scoring (4-point games).
- Players change roles after each game.

GAME 2

Continue the minitournament.

LEVEL II

Level I focuses on the beginning player, and level II is a step up and might be difficult for some students. Level II continues to develop their abilities to create and defend space. You can introduce shots such as the crosscourt or down-the-line ground stroke and the lob. Students should also begin serving. As in all net and wall games, players can win points by moving opponents around the court until they cannot reach the next shot. Nonetheless, this solution reaches its limits as the opponent's tactical awareness and ability improve, so at this level students explore winning a point. After they have practiced the volley, approach shot, and smash, their awareness of the need to defend against these attacks will increase.

The tennis serve is an important skill to hone in order to proactively move opponents around on the court.

LESSON 7

Secondary Level II

Tactical Problem   Setting up to attack by creating space in the opponent's court

Lesson Focus   Starting the point on the attack

Objective   Use the flat service at the start of a point.

GAME 1

Setup   Half-court singles

Goal   Get the ball in the court and push the opponent into the backcourt with service.

Conditions

- Service alternates.
- The game focuses on pushing the opponent back.
- Use a long and narrow court.

Questions

Q: Where does the service have to land?

A: In the service court.

Q: Where is the best place to serve to put your opponent on the defensive?

A: Deep into the service court.

PRACTICE TASK 1

Setup   Toss practice

Goals

- Toss accurately to the racket head.
- Perform five of eight trials successfully.

Conditions

- Players stand with the toe of the nondominant foot on the baseline (left foot forward for right-handers and right foot forward for left-handers).
- Players place the racket butt next to the front foot with the racket extended in front of the body.
- Players toss the ball as for a serve so that it lands on or near the head of the racket on the court.

PRACTICE TASK 2

Setup   Half-court

Goals

- Serve deep and to the opponent's backhand.
- Land a specific number of serves (e.g., three of five) in the back of the service court.

Condition   Service alternates (no rallying).

Cues

- Face the net post.
- Place the racket behind your head.
- Toss up and forward.
- Reach high.
- Swing through.

GAME 2

Repeat game 1 with half-court singles.

Tactical Problem   Setting up to attack by creating space in the opponent's court

Lesson Focus   Variations on the ground stroke

Objective   Use crosscourt and down-the-line ground strokes.

GAME 1

Setup   Full-court singles

Goal   Be aware of and vary ground strokes.

Conditions

- Each server gets two serves.
- Players use ground strokes only.
- The focus is moving the opponent around the court.

Questions

Q: What do you do to move your opponent along the baseline?

A: Vary your ground strokes.

Q: What are the types of ground-stroke placement?

A: Crosscourt or down the line.

PRACTICE TASK 1

Setup   Crosscourt and line practice (figure 18.6)

Goals

- Place ground strokes crosscourt and down the line.
- Play a specific number of strokes crosscourt and down the line.

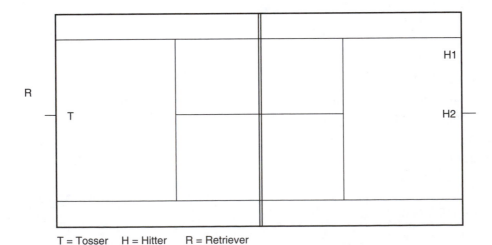

T = Tosser   H = Hitter   R = Retriever

Figure 18.6

Conditions

- One player feeds to the other player's forehand in the corner of the baseline, and the other player hits crosscourt.
- Players switch roles and repeat the task hitting down the line.

Cues

- Step into the shot.
- Follow through to the target.

Note   This task can also be accomplished using half-court singles.

PRACTICE TASK 2

Setup   Crosscourt and line practice (figure 18.6)

Goals

- Use crosscourt and down-the-line placement.
- Play a specific number of ground strokes crosscourt and down the line.

Conditions

- One player feeds to the other player from the corner of the baseline.
- The other player starts in the middle of the court and moves to hit crosscourt.
- Players switch sides of the court and switch roles.
- Players repeat the task, going down the line.

GAME 2

Setup   Full-court singles

Goal   Use crosscourt or down-the-line placement to move the opponent.

Conditions

- Each server gets two serves.
- Players use ground strokes only.
- The focus is moving the opponent around the court.

LESSON 9

Secondary Level II

Tactical Problem   Winning the point

Lesson Focus   Winning the point using an approach shot and volley

Objective   Use the approach shot to volley.

GAME 1

Setup   Half- or full-court singles

Goals

- Move the opponent.
- Win the point.
- Be aware of the need to punish short ground strokes.

Conditions

- Players play no-ad score games.
- After the serve, players can play the ball before it bounces.

Questions

Q: What did you have to do to return a short ground stroke?

A: Move up to play the ball.

Q: After you move up, is it easier to run back or to keep moving toward the net?

A: Keep moving toward the net.

Q: What shot do you use if you keep moving toward the net?

A: The volley.

Q: Where should you place your volley?

A: In an open space or in the corners of the court to move the opponent.

PRACTICE TASK

Setup

- Approach shot to volley practice (figure 18.7)
- Use a half-court or full court.

Goals Perform three of five trials successfully, and rotate.

Conditions

- The tosser feeds two balls (hits off the racket).
- The first ball is a short ground stroke.
- The hitter executes an approach shot and continues to the net for a volley.
- The tosser hits another ground stroke for the hitter to volley.
- This task can be practiced in pairs or triads.

Note This task can be extended to include the forehand and backhand of both the approach shot and the volley.

GAME 2

Repeat game 1 with half- or full-court singles.

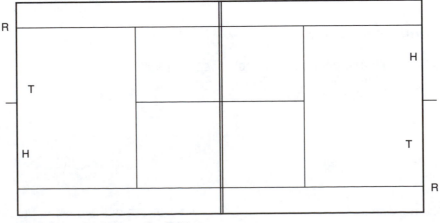

T = Tosser   H = Hitter   R = Retriever

Figure 18.7

Teaching Sport Concepts and Skills

LESSON 10

Tactical Problem   Setting up to attack by creating space in the opponent's court

Lesson Focus   Lob shots for maintaining depth (a logical progression if opponents are now moving to the net more frequently)

Objective   Use the lob (forehand and backhand) as an offensive tactic to keep the opponent back from the net.

GAME 1

Setup   Half- or full-court singles

Goal   Be aware of the need to develop the lob shot.

Conditions

- Use deuce games.
- One person serves for the entire deuce game.
- The focus is on pushing the opponent back.

Question

Q: What do you do to keep the opponent back if you cannot use a ground stroke?

A: Open the face of the racket and use a lob.

PRACTICE TASK

Setup   Half-court partner lob practice (figure 18.8)

Goals

- Clear to the backcourt using the lob.
- Land a specific number of lobs deep to baseline (backcourt).

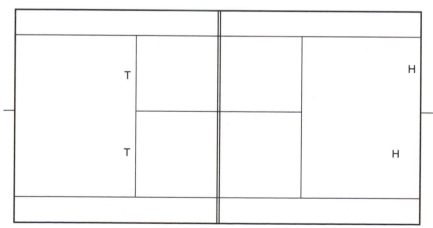

T = Tosser   H = Hitter

Figure 18.8

Conditions

- One player feeds to the backcourt.
- One player hits lobs back to the feeder's court.
- Players switch or alternate forehands, backhands, and lobs.

Cues

- Use a full backswing.
- Open the face of the racket.
- Swing low to high.
- Finish high.

GAME 2

Repeat game 1 with half- or full-court singles.

LESSON 11

Tactical Problem   Winning the point

Lesson Focus   Winning the point using the smash

Objective   Use the smash to win a point.

GAME 1

Setup   Half- or full-court singles

Goals

- Move the opponent.
- Win the point.
- Be aware of the need to punish a weak lob.

Conditions

- Use deuce games.
- After the serve, players can play the ball before it bounces.

Questions

Q: What is the best way to make a shot unreturnable?

A: Hit it hard and straight to the ground—use a smash.

Q: From where on your court can you smash?

A: From the front or middle of the court.

Q: What kind of shot are you looking for from your opponent?

A: A weak lob.

Q: Where should you place your smash?

A: In an open space or in the corners of the court to beat the opponent.

PRACTICE TASK

Setup Half-court partner practice

Goal Make the ball hit the court at an angle and deep.

Condition One partner feeds high ground strokes to midcourt, and the other partner smashes.

Cues

- Prepare as a serve.
- Point to the ball.
- Reach high; hit down.
- Finish the swing after contact.

GAME 2

Setup Repeat game 1 with half- or full-court singles.

Condition Use a competitive no-ad score game.

LESSON 12

Tactical Problem Defending against an attack

Lesson Focus Returning the smash

Objective Return the smash with success (i.e., do not provide a second attacking opportunity for the opponent) using a defensive lob.

GAME 1

Setup Half- or full-court singles

Goals

- Win the point with a volley or smash if possible.
- Be aware of the need to return the smash without setting up an easy winner for the opponent.

Conditions

- Use no-ad score games (4 points).
- One person serves for the entire game.
- The serve must be playable (no-ace rule).

Question

Q: How can you return a volley or smash without setting up your opponent for another smash?

A: Use a defensive lob.

PRACTICE TASK

Setup Half-court partner practice

Goals

- Perform three of five trials successfully.
- Practice both shots (smash and lob).

Conditions

- One player feeds with high ground stroke to midcourt, and the partner smashes.
- The feeding player executes a defensive lob to continue the point.
- One player feeds with a ground stroke, and the partner volleys.
- The feeding player executes a defensive lob to continue the point.

Cues

- Use a short backswing.
- Open the face of the racket.
- Swing low to high.
- Finish high.

GAME 2

Repeat game 1 with half- or full-court singles.

LESSON 13

Tactical Problem   Attacking as a pair

Lesson Focus

- Up-and-back formation
- Communication

Objective   Use an up-and-back formation in doubles.

GAME 1

Setup   Full-court doubles

Goal   Use an up-and-back formation.

Condition   Each player serves 2 points using a flat serve.

Questions

Q: What are the roles and responsibilities of the back player?

A: Serve, serve receive, hit ground strokes, and take all shots the up person does not take.

Q: What are the roles and responsibilities of the up player?

A: Net play and communication.

PRACTICE TASK

Setup   Full-court doubles practice

Goal   Be aware of doubles roles and responsibilities.

Teaching Sport Concepts and Skills

Conditions

- Each person serves two bounce-hit serves.
- Points are played to completion.

GAME 2

Setup   Doubles

Goal   Use an up-and-back formation.

Conditions

- Each player serves a full game using a flat serve.
- Use no-ad scoring (4-point game).

LEVEL III

Level III shifts from a primarily half-court singles game to a more tactically complex doubles game. Students challenge themselves by discovering more advanced ways of winning the point and defending against an attack. The final phase of level III is solving the tactical problems presented by the doubles game (attacking and defending as a pair). Once again, your questions guide students to the solutions they then practice in game situations.

Playing tennis doubles increases the skill challenge.

LESSON 14

Tactical Problem   Winning the point

Lesson Focus   Attacking the short serve

Objective   Punish a weak, short serve.

GAME 1

Setup   Half- or full-court singles

Goal   Be aware of the attacking opportunity if the serve is short.

Conditions

- Each point starts with a short serve.
- Use a deuce game.

Questions

Q: How can you attack a short serve?

A: With a passing shot down the line or a crosscourt shot.

Q: What should you do after attacking a short serve?

A: Move to the net.

PRACTICE TASK

Setup   Half-court partner practice

Goal   Attack the serve and put the opponent on the defensive.

Conditions

- One player feeds short serves from the service line, and the partner attacks the serve.
- Players perform a specific number of successful returns.

Cues

- Hit the serve return like a ground stroke:
  - Move your feet into opposition.
  - Swing low to high.
  - Follow through to where you want the ball to go.

GAME 2

Setup   Half- or full-court singles

Goal   Be aware of the attacking opportunity if the serve is short.

Conditions

- Each point starts with a short serve.
- Use deuce games.

LESSON 15

Secondary Level III

Tactical Problem   Winning the point

Lesson Focus   Attacking drop shot

Objective   Use an effective, fast attacking drop shot.

Teaching Sport Concepts and Skills

GAME 1

Setup   Half- or full-court singles

Goal   Be aware of the need to play a drop shot that reaches the ground quickly.

Conditions

- A player cannot play two consecutive volleys.
- Use deuce games.

Question

Q: What can you do besides the volley to quickly get the tennis ball to the floor?

A: Hit a faster attacking drop shot.

PRACTICE TASK

Setup   Half-court partner practice

Goals

- Perform a fast attacking drop shot.
- Land a specific number of shots inside the service court.

Condition   One player feeds ground strokes to midcourt, and the partner plays drop shots into the frontcourt.

Cues

- Disguise the shot.
- Use an open racket face.
- Swing high to low.

GAME 2

Setup   Half- or full-court singles

Goal   Be aware of the need to play a drop shot that reaches the ground quickly.

Conditions

- A player cannot play two consecutive volleys.
- Use no-ad scoring.

LESSON 16

Secondary Level III

Tactical Problem   Defending against an attack

Lesson Focus   Returning the attacking drop shot

Objective   Return the drop shot without giving an attacking opportunity to the opponent.

GAME 1

Setup   Half- or full-court singles

Goals

- Execute proficient drop shots.
- Be aware of the need to return the drop shot in an attacking manner.

Conditions

- Volleys and smashes are not allowed.
- Use deuce games.

Question

Q: *How can you return the drop shot without giving an easy volley to the opponent?*

A: *With a passing shot on the run, either crosscourt or down the line.*

PRACTICE TASK

Setup   Half- or full-court partner practice

Goal   Use a passing shot to return.

Conditions

- One player feeds drop shots to a partner, who attempts passing shots.
- Players perform four to six trials successfully, and switch roles.

Cues

- Keep the ball low to the net.
- Hit the ball out of the reach of the opponent at the net.

GAME 2

Setup   Half- or full-court singles

Goals

- Execute proficient drop shots.
- Be aware of the need to return the drop shot in an attacking manner.

Conditions

- Volleys and smashes are not allowed.
- Use no-ad scoring.

LESSON 17

Secondary Level III

Tactical Problem   Attacking as a pair

Lesson Focus

- Side-to-side offense
- Communication

Objective   Attack in a side-to-side formation.

GAME 1

Setup   Full-court doubles

Goal   Recognize the most effective attacking formation (both up).

Conditions

- Vary formations among up and back, both up, and both back.
- Use no-ad scoring games.

Questions

Q: Which formation (both up, both back, or up and back) gives you the best chance to attack opponents with a volley or a smash, particularly if you are serving?

A: Both up.

Q: When do you get into a both-up formation?

A: When the back player (in the up-and-back formation) receives a short ball and plays an approach shot.

PRACTICE TASK

Setup   Full-court doubles

Goal   Keep the serve low and attack the return.

Conditions

- Service alternates on every point.
- Servers follow the serve to the net.

Cues

- Keep the serve wide and follow it into the net with the racket up.
- When not serving, set up at the net, protecting the alley.

GAME 2

Setup   Competitive doubles

Goal   Attack where possible (both up).

Condition   Use a regulation game.

LESSON 18

Tactical Problem   Attacking as a pair when serving

Lesson Focus   Setting up a winning volley (the poach)

Objective   Attack in a both-up formation.

GAME 1

Setup   Full-court doubles

Goal   Set up a winning volley.

Conditions

- Use a both-up or up-and-back formation.
- Use no-ad scoring games.

Questions

Q: What type of serve sets up a volley for your partner?

A: A wide, deep serve.

Q: What is the responsibility of the player at the net?

A: To poach to hit a winning volley.

Q: How do you do this?

A: Anticipate, be ready, use footwork, hold the racket up, and volley into the space.

PRACTICE TASK

Setup   Full-court doubles

Goal   Hit a winning volley.

Conditions

- Team A serves to team B for six to eight serves.
- Serves must be wide.
- The net player sets up to poach, and then his or her partner switches sides of the court as the net player moves to intercept the return.

GAME 2

Setup   Competitive doubles

Goal   Attack where possible.

Condition   Use a regulation game.

LESSON 19

Tactical Problem   Defending as a pair against a serve

Lesson Focus   Serve-receive tactics

Objective   Effectively defend against the serve in doubles.

GAME 1

Setup   Full-court doubles

Goal   Focus on serve-receive tactics.

Condition   Each player gets two serves.

Question

> Q: *What are the possible serve-receive tactics in doubles?*
>
> A: *Return the ball to the feet of the advancing server; pass to the net player; lob to the net player; and hit crosscourt, angled toward the server.*

PRACTICE TASK

Setup   Full-court doubles

Goal   Attempt each serve-receive tactic.

Conditions

- Doubles team A alternates serves with doubles team B.
- Teams rotate after six to eight serves.
- Teams do not play points to completion.

GAME 2

Setup   Full-court doubles

Goal   Focus on serve-receive tactics.

SUMMARY

We advocate that you introduce tournament play to challenge your students' tactical awareness and problem solving. You can arrange scoring in tournaments by tactical problems, game forms, or ability groups. We provide three illustrations to guide you. First, if the focus of your unit was to solve the tactical problem of setting up to attack, you may limit tournament play to using ground strokes (i.e., forehand, backhand, crosscourt, down the line). Second, you can choose the game form used throughout the tournament, such as half-court singles, no-ad scoring, or deuce games. Third, students can self-select into ability groups (e.g., rookie, recreation, and all-pro leagues).

Team tennis is another tournament option. Ideally, it involves teams of four to eight players. Each team organizes players to play both singles and doubles matches. Each contest is a set of six games using no-ad scoring. We encourage you to modify team tennis to meet your needs. For example, you might have each team seed itself for singles play so each player plays against the corresponding seed from another team.

This chapter provides a scheme for teaching tennis using a tactical approach. We want you to make these lessons yours! This may mean modifying the content provided. The following are ways you can modify lessons and units:

- *Use court rotations.* If you have limited court space, you can rotate students on and off half-court singles, full-court singles, and doubles games.
- *Use stations.* Stations can provide a great change of pace by focusing on specific skills and movements as well as on tournament play.
- *Let students choose.* Students may choose to focus on either singles or doubles. You can facilitate this choice by mixing singles and doubles practice throughout the unit while still focusing on tactical problems.
- *Use coaches or statisticians.* If you have few courts, you may want to involve students in the roles of coaches or statisticians. Statistics (e.g., of winners and errors) can be helpful when assessing game performance.

Remember, a tactical approach teaches players from a game-based view (Elderton 2002), but you should try to focus on a limited number of tactical problems in your units of instruction. Implement the less-is-more principle!

Chapter 19

Softball

Softball is generally taught in upper elementary through high school. At the secondary level, softball tends to be the last unit of the school year and often serves as more of a recreational activity than a series of instructional lessons. This is perhaps as much because of the nature of the game as the nature of the teacher at the end of a school year. As a game, softball does not lend itself to an instructional setting. The 10v10 game provides few opportunities for students to field or hit and run. Further, the best players tend to dominate key positions (i.e., shortstop, pitcher, first base), with outfield positions filled with four or more players who can't or won't even run to a ball, let alone field it.

The tactical approach promotes small-sided (i.e., 3v3, 4v4) conditioned games that allow students to focus on a specific situation and its required tactics, whether for fielding or batting and running. Not only do small-sided games foster student involvement, but they also highlight what players should do and how to do it. Dividing the class into three or four small-sided games allows you to individualize instruction, because the focus of each game can match the skills of the students participating. Students with less experience can focus on fundamental skills and tactical problems. More experienced students can focus on complex skills and tactical problems that they are likely to encounter as a function of their abilities.

Small-sided games require no more room than the regulation softball or baseball diamond and are best arranged in an open field. We have found the cloverleaf arrangement to be the most efficient for managing three or four small-sided games of softball. First, lay out four playing areas in a cloverleaf shape, with the home plate areas at the center (figure 19.1). Stagger the playing areas to prevent overthrows from endangering players on adjacent fields. The center should include an area (safety zone) large enough for students to safely stand in as they wait their turns to bat. Safety rules are necessary and should define areas where students must stand while others are batting and what batters should do with the bat after they hit the ball.

You can divide students into teams of 6, 8, 10, or 12 for small-sided games of 3v3, 4v4, 5v5, or 6v6 on

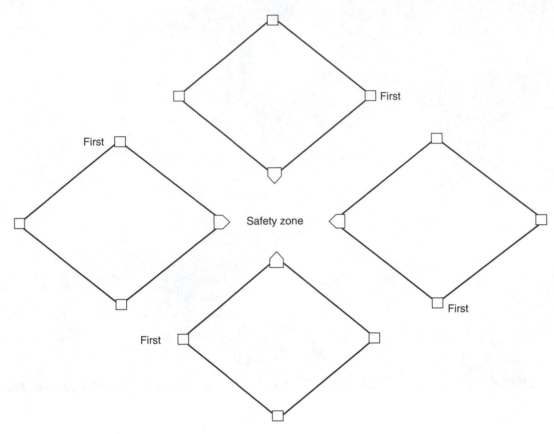

Figure 19.1   The cloverleaf arrangement is efficient for managing multiple games of softball.

each field. We have found it best to assign students to teams and fields for an entire unit, eliminating the need for organizing teams and fields daily. At a minimum, each team and field should have three softballs and one bat. If possible, at least half of the students should have gloves.

We present the tactical problems, situations, movements, and associated skills in softball in table 19.1 and the levels of tactical complexity in table 19.2. The lessons in this chapter serve only as examples and are not intended to encompass every detail of a lesson or every lesson of a unit.

Table 19.1   Tactical Problems and Decisions Related to Scoring and Preventing Scoring in Softball

Tactical problems	Tactical decisions (off-the-ball)	Elements of skill execution (on-the-ball)
SCORING (OFFENSE)		
Game situation: 0-1 out, 0 runners		
Batting	Determining where to hit	• Hitting to the left side of the field • Hitting and running through first
Game situation: 0-1 out, runner on first		
Batting	Determining where to hit	Placing a hit: • Line drive to the outfield • Grounder through the infield
Batting and base running	Anticipating a hit to the left side of the field	• Base running from first to second • Base running from first to third • Rundowns
Game situation: 0-1 out, runner on second		
Batting and base running	Determining (before the pitch) where to hit to advance the runner and get on base	Placing a hit—line drives to center and right fields

Tactical problems	Tactical decisions (off-the-ball)	Elements of skill execution (on-the-ball)
Base running	Determining (before the pitch) when to run	• Running from second to third • Rounding third base • Drawing the throw as a base runner
Game situation: 0-2 outs, 0 runners		
Batting	Determining (before the pitch) where to hit	• Hitting to the left side—outfield • Hitting down the third base line • Placing a hit to the left side of the infield
Batting and base running	Anticipating a run to second	• Hitting and running to first • Rounding first
Game situation: 0-2 outs, runner on first		
Batting	Determining (before the pitch) where to hit	Placing a hit to the right side of the infield to hit behind the runner
Batting and base running	Determining whether to run past or round first base	Running from first to second
Game situation: 0-2 outs, runner on second		
Batting	Determining (before the pitch) where to place the ball	Advancing the runner by hitting to the outfield (line drives)
Batting and base running	• Anticipating a hit to the left side of the infield • Watching the coach	Running from first to third
PREVENTING SCORING (DEFENSE)		
Game situation: 0-1 out, 0 runners		
Fielding	Determining (before the pitch) where to throw	• Fielding and throwing to first • Covering first on a force play
Supporting players	• Determining where to position for backup • Determining the best position for base coverage • Communicating the number of outs	• Defending space by position • Backing up first base
Game situation: 0-1 out, runner on first		

Fielding	• Determining the best position before the pitch
	• Determining where to throw
	• Looking the runner back
		• Outfield:
		  ○ Covering second on a force play:
		    • Shortstop coverage of second
		    • Second-base player coverage of second
		  ○ Outfield play—positioning for a quick throw to the infield or second
		  ○ Throwing to the cutoff
		• Cutting the lead runner (tag play)
		• Setting up the relay
		• Getting the lead runner out
		• Rundowns:
		  ○ Positioning
		  ○ Peeling off

Supporting players	• Determining where to go on backup
	• Determining where to go if runners advance
	• Communicating:
	  ○ Number of outs
	  ○ Where to throw
		• Moving to back up the adjacent outfielder
		• Covering bases on outfield hits:
		  ○ First-base coverage
		  ○ Second-base coverage
		  ○ Third-base coverage
		• Cutoffs by shortstop and second-base player
		• Relays
		• Rundowns:
		  ○ Positioning
		  ○ Peeling off

(continued)

Table 19.1 *(continued)*

Tactical problems	Tactical decisions (off-the-ball)	Elements of skill execution (on-the-ball)
PREVENTING SCORING (DEFENSE) *(continued)*		
Game situation 0-1 out, runner on second		
Fielding	Determining (before the pitch) where to throw	• Looking the runner back • Double play (third to first)
Supporting players	• Determining where to support if the runner advances • Communicating where to throw	• Covering third on a tag play • Sweep tag • Outfielders backing up bases on infield plays
Game situation: 0-2 outs, 0 runners		

Fielding	• Determining (before the pitch) where to throw
	• Communicating:
	  o Number of outs
	  o Where to throw (to make the play)
		Defending space in the outfield:
		• Fielding line drives or fly balls
		• Throwing accurately to second

Supporting players	• Communicating:
	  o Number of outs
	  o Where to throw (to make the play)
	• Determining:
	  o Where to back up
	  o Where and how to cover base(s)
		Moving to back up the adjacent outfielder

Game situation: 0-2 outs, runner on first		
Fielding	• Knowing the situation • Anticipating a double play	Rundowns

Supporting players	• Determining where to go for backup
	• Determining where to go for base coverage
		• Pitcher coverage of first on a ball hit to the first-base player
		• Rundowns:
		  o Backing up
		  o Peeling off as the backup player

Game situation: 0-2 outs, runner on second		
Fielding	• Determining (before the pitch) where to throw • Preparing to look the runner back	Looking the runner back prior to the throw

Supporting players	• Determining where to provide support:
	  o Backup
	  o Base coverage
	• Anticipating an advancing runner
		Moving to back up the bases

RESTARTING PLAY		
Play starts or restarts on every pitch or roll.		

Table 19.2 Levels of Tactical Complexity for Softball

Game situation	Level I	Level II	Level III	Level IV
SCORING (OFFENSE)				
Game situation: 0-1 out, 0 runners (lessons 1, 2, 3)				
Batting	• Determining where to hit • Hitting to the left side of the field • Hitting and running through first			
Game situation: 0-1 out, runner on first				

Batting		• Determining where to hit
		• Placing a hit:
		   ○ Line drive to the outfield
		   ○ Grounder through the infield		

Batting and base running		• Anticipating a hit to the left side of the field • Base running from first to second	Base running from first to third	Rundowns
Game situation: 0-1 out, runner on second				
Batting and base running			• Determining (before the pitch) where to hit to advance the runner and get on base • Placing a hit—line drives to center and right fields	
Base running			• Determining (before the pitch) where to run • Running from second to third • Rounding third	Drawing the throw as a base runner
Game situation: 0-2 outs, 0 runners				
Batting		• Determining (before the pitch) where to hit • Hitting to the left side (outfield) • Hitting down the third base line	Placing a hit to the left side of the infield	
Batting and base running		• Hitting and running to first • Rounding first • Anticipating a run to second		
Game situation: 0-2 outs, runner on first				
Batting			• Determining (before the pitch) where to hit • Placing a hit to the right side of the infield to hit behind the runner	
Batting and base running	Running from first to second		Determining whether to run past or round first	

(continued)

Table 19.2 *(continued)*

Game situation	Level I	Level II	Level III	Level IV
		SCORING (OFFENSE) *(continued)*		
		Game situation: 0-2 outs, runner on second		
Batting			• Determining (before the pitch) where to place the ball • Advancing the runner by hitting to the outfield (line drives)	
Batting and base running			• Anticipating a hit to the left side of the infield • Watching the coach • Running from first to third	
		PREVENTING SCORING (DEFENSE)		
		Game situation: 0-1 out, 0 runners		
Fielding	• Determining (before the pitch) where to throw • Fielding and throwing to first • Covering first on a force play			
Supporting players	• Determining the best position for base coverage • Defending space by position • Determining where to position for backing up • Backing up first • Communicating the number of outs			
		Game situation: 0-1 out, runner on first		

Fielding		• Determining the best position before the pitch
		• Determining where to throw
		• Second-base coverage on a force play
		  ○ Shortstop coverage of second base
		• Second-base player coverage of second
		  ○ Outfield play—Positioning for a quick throw to the infield or second base
		  ○ Throwing to the cutoff
		• Setting up the relay
		• Getting the lead runner out
			• Cutting the lead runner (tag play)
			• Looking the runner back
				Rundowns:
				• Positioning
				• Peeling off

Game situation	Level I	Level II	Level III	Level IV
Supporting play-ers		• Determining where to go on backup • Determining where to go if runners advance • Moving to back up the adjacent outfielder • Base coverage on an outfield hit: ○ First ○ Second ○ Third • Cutoffs by shortstop and second-base player • Relays	Communicating: • Number of outs • Where to throw	Rundowns: • Positioning • Peeling off
Game situation: 0-1 out, runner on second				
Fielding			• Determining (before the pitch) where to throw • Looking the runner back	Double play (third and first base)
Supporting play-ers				• Determining where to support if the runner advances • Communicating where to throw • Covering third on a tag play • Sweep tag • Outfielders backing up bases on infield plays
Game situation: 0-2 outs, 0 runners				
Fielding	• Determining (before the pitch) where to throw • Communicating: ○ Number of outs ○ Where to throw (to make the play) • Defending space in the outfield: ○ Fielding line drives or fly balls ○ Throwing accu-rately to second			
Supporting play-ers	• Determining: ○ Where to back up ○ Where and how to cover base(s) • Moving to back up the adjacent out-fielder			

(continued)

Table 19.2 *(continued)*

Game situation	Level I	Level II	Level III	Level IV
	PREVENTING SCORING (DEFENSE) *(continued)*			
	Game situation 0-2 outs, runner on first			
Fielding				• Knowing the situation • Anticipating a double play • Rundowns

Supporting players				• Determining where to go for backup
				• Determining where to go for base coverage
				• Pitcher coverage of first on a ball hit to the first-base player
				• Rundowns:
				  ○ Backup
				  ○ Peeling off as the backup player

	Game situation: 0-2 outs, runner on second			
Fielding			• Determining (before the pitch) where to throw • Preparing to look the runner back • Looking the runner back prior to the throw	

Supporting players			• Determining where to provide support:
			  ○ Backup
			  ○ Base coverage
			  ○ Moving to back up bases
			• Anticipating advancing runners	

	RESTARTING PLAY			
	Play starts or restarts on every pitch or roll.			

LEVEL I

You can use kickball, T-ball, or softball to introduce the tactics in level I. We have found kickball appropriate for sixth-graders, because many have not developed adequate skills in softball or baseball. This lack of skill development tends to prohibit them from fully exploring many fundamental tactical problems. If you use kickball to present level I in sixth grade, you may want to use T-ball or softball in seventh grade to review this level. Although the lessons for this chapter are mainly for the secondary level, another option is to use lessons from level I to teach kickball in fifth grade and T-ball in sixth grade, and then use some lessons from levels I and II to introduce slow-pitch softball in seventh grade. Do not be afraid to use batting tees at any level. In our college softball classes, many students use batting tees during practices and games.

Tactics at level I focus on situations such as when there no runners on base and a grounder is hit to the infield, or when a runner is on first and a grounder or line drive is hit to the outfield. The tactics for preventing scoring in these situations include defending space by infield position, defending space by outfield position, and defending bases, specifically first and second. The tactics for scoring include getting on base and advancing to the next base, specifically from first to second base.

By the end of the level I, students should know the infield and outfield positions as well as the boundaries and features of the playing area. By solving tactical problems, students learn what to do in infield and outfield positions when there are no runners or a runner is on first, and they learn how to cover first and second base on a force play. Students at level I review catching skills as they field grounders, line drives, and fly balls, and they also review and refine throwing skills.

In level I, students review and refine the offensive skills of kicking (in kickball) or batting as they solve tactical problems related to getting on base when there are no runners. The need to place the ball to the left side of the infield motivates students to work on accuracy and placement. The need to hit and run refines kicking and batting because hitting and running require a fluid motion from the follow-through of the swing to the drive step toward first base. Base running is also a focus of level I, and conditioned games and practices help students understand when to run past and when to round first base as well as how to advance quickly and safely to second base.

Although support play is not the specific focus of any lesson in level I, you can incorporate calling for the ball, signaling the number of outs, and backing up when teaching other elements of game play. As students are ready or as teachable moments arise, you can introduce or reinforce tactical problems through pinpointing critical aspects of a skill, movement, or play. In this chapter we use the term *practice situation* rather than *practice task*. In softball and baseball the

Students in level I review catching skills.

situation (e.g., no outs, a runner on first and one out, runners on first and second, or a ground ball to the shortstop) is the essence of the game, and it prompts players about what to do, whether they are fielders, batters, or base runners.

LESSON 1 🔘

Secondary Level I

Tactical Problem   Defending space by infield position

Lesson Focus   No outs, no runners on base, and a grounder to the left side of the infield

Objectives

- Field grounders from third base and shortstop positions.
- Make an accurate throw to first base.

GAME 1

Setup   No runners on base, no outs

Goals

- Get the runner out at first (defensive team).
- Get to first before the throw (offensive team).

Conditions

- Use 3v3 minimum, 6v6 maximum, and start with no runners on base and no outs.
- The batter (or kicker) must hit (or kick) a ground ball to the left side of the infield (a ground ball is any ball that hits the ground before reaching an infielder, pitcher excluded).
- Players score runs by reaching first base safely.
- Whether safe or out, the runner returns to the dugout area.
- The inning is over after three runs or three outs, whichever comes first.

Questions

Q: What was the goal of the game for the offensive team?

A: Get to first before the throw.

Q: What was the goal of the game for the defensive team?

A: Get the runner out at first.

Q: Today we are focusing on the defensive team's performance. How were you able to get the runner out at first?

A: Move feet to the ball, watch the ball into the glove, catch the ball, and throw it to first. Keep feet moving toward first base.

PRACTICE SITUATION

Setup   Three players are in the field (minimum) playing shortstop, third base, and first base, and three players are hitting (the battery—pitcher, catcher, batter). Extra players serve as pitcher and catcher. From a batting tee (or from a ball rolled from the pitcher's mound), the hitter (or kicker) hits (or kicks) a grounder to the left side of the infield and then runs hard and fast to first. After fielding three balls from each position (third base and shortstop), players rotate to first base or into the battery. The fielding player always calls the ball, and the nonfielding player always backs up the fielding player.

Goals

- Successfully field three balls in a row at third base and at shortstop.
- Throw the batter out five of six times.

Cues

- Move your feet to the ball.
- Watch the ball into your glove.
- Catch and cover.
- Recover to throw.

GAME 2

Repeat game 1.

LESSON 2

Tactical Problems   Defending space by infield position; defending first base

Lesson Focus   No outs, no runners on base, and a grounder to the right infield

Objectives

- Field grounders from second and first base.
- Make an accurate throw to first base.

GAME 1

Setup   No runners on base, no outs

Goals

- Get the runner out at first (defensive team).
- Get to first before the throw (offensive team).

Conditions

- Use 3v3 minimum, 6v6 maximum.
- The hitter (kicker) must hit (kick) a ground ball to the right side of the infield.
- Players score runs by safely reaching first base.
- Whether safe or out, the runner returns to the dugout area.
- The inning is over after three runs or three outs, whichever comes first.

Questions

Q: What was the goal of the game for the offense and for the defense?

A: Get to first ahead of the throw and get the runner out at first.

Q: Today we are focusing on the defensive team's performance. What did you do to get the runner out at first?

A: Moved feet to the ball, watched the ball into the glove, and threw quickly to first.

Q: Were you successful? If not, let's practice.

PRACTICE SITUATION

Setup   Two players are in the field (minimum) at second and first base, a pitcher is on the mound (optional), and three players are hitting (the battery). Extra players serve as catchers. From a ball rolled, pitched, or placed on a tee, the hitter (kicker) hits (kicks) a grounder to the right side of the infield and then runs hard and fast to first. Players field three balls from each position. The task can also focus on the footwork used to cover first base on a force play.

Goals

- Successfully field three balls in a row at second and at first.
- Throw the batter out five of six times.

Cues

- Move your feet to the ball.
- Watch the ball into your glove.
- Catch and cover.
- Recover to throw.

GAME 2

Repeat game 1.

Tactical Problem   Getting on base

Lesson Focus   No runners on base

Objectives

- Hit a grounder to the left side of the infield.
- Run to first as quickly as possible (running through or past the base).

GAME 1

Setup   No runners on base

Goal   Get on first base safely.

Conditions

- Use 4v4 minimum, 5v5 optimum, 6v6 maximum.
- Defensive players play first base and as many other infield positions as possible.
- The hitter (kicker) must hit (kick) a ground ball to the infield and get to first before the throw.
- Players score runs by safely reaching first base.
- Whether safe or out, the runner returns to the dugout area.
- The inning is over after three runs or three outs, whichever comes first.

Questions

Q: To where did you have to hit or kick the ball to get on first base?

A: Along the third base line, on the left side of the infield, close to third.

Q: So, when there are no runners on base, where is the best place on the left side of the infield to hit or kick the ball?

A: Along the third base line.

Q: How did you run to get to first before the throw?

A: Ran fast without looking at the ball and ran through first base.

PRACTICE SITUATION

Setup   Three players are in the field (minimum) at shortstop, third base, and first base, and three players are hitting (the battery). Extra players serve as pitchers and catchers. From a ball rolled or thrown from the pitcher's mound or placed on a batting tee, the batter hits a grounder to the left side of the infield and then runs hard and fast over first base to a cone 20 feet (6 m) past first on the first base line. The batter hits and runs five times, attempting to knock down cones (one cone on the third base line 10 ft, or 3 m, past the base and the other cone just beyond but between third base and the shortstop). After five hits, the batter replaces a defensive player. Defensive players make a play on every ball and attempt to throw the runner out at first (all rules related to backups, calling the ball, and so on, remain in effect).

Note   You may use three or four cones as targets, depending on players' abilities.

Goals

- Angle the bat to hit (or approach to kick) toward the third base line or between third base and the shortstop.
- Run hard and fast through first base.

Cues

- Hit, step, and drive.
- Run hard and through first base.
- Adjust the angle of the bat to hit the ball toward left field.
- Approach (if kicking) or bat (if batting) to send the ball toward left field.

GAME 2

Repeat game 1 and match the final score with the score of the previous game.

LESSON 4

Tactical Problem   Defending space by outfield position

Lesson Focus   Runner on first and a ball hit to the left side of the outfield

Objectives

- Field grounders, line drives, and fly balls in the outfield.
- Back up the adjacent outfielder.
- Make an accurate throw to second base.

GAME 1

Setup   Runner on first

Goals

- Get the runner out at second (defensive team).
- Safely move the runner to second (offensive team).

Conditions

- Use 4v4 minimum, 6v6 maximum.
- Defensive players play left field, left center field, second base, and first base.
- The offensive team must have a runner on first at all times.
- The batter must hit the ball to the left side of the outfield and run to first base.
- Balls hit to the right of second base are considered outs.
- Players score runs by safely reaching second base.
- Whether safe or out, the runner returns to the dugout area.
- The inning is over after three runs or three outs, whichever comes first.

Questions

Q: What was the goal of the game for the offensive team and for the defensive team?

A: Safely move the runner to second, and get the runner out at second.

Q: Today we're focusing on the defense. How were the defensive players, the left fielder and the left center fielder, able to get the ball to second base ahead of the runner?

A: By getting to the ball quickly and throwing to second as quickly as possible.

Q: Why is it important for the outfielders to get the ball to the infield as quickly as possible?

A: To keep runners from advancing or scoring.

Q: What should the nonfielding outfielder do and why?

A: Back up the player fielding the ball and be ready in case the fielder misses the ball to stop it and get it to the infield as quickly as possible.

PRACTICE SITUATION

Setup Four players are on defense (minimum) at left field, left center field, second base, and first base, and four players are on offense—the battery and a base runner. The batter hits a ball from the pitcher or a batting tee to the left side of the outfield and then runs hard and fast to first base. The runner on first advances to second except on a fly ball. After players field three balls from each position (left and left center), they rotate to second base and then to first or into the battery. Fielding players call the ball, and nonfielding players back them up.

Goals

- Successfully field the ball and throw the runner out at second base.
- Perform a proper backup on every play.

Cues

- Move your feet to the ball.
- Watch the ball into your glove.
- Catch and cover over your throwing shoulder.

- Recover and throw quickly.
- Back up to get the appropriate angle, and pretend the fielder isn't there or assume he will miss the ball.

GAME 2

Repeat game 1. The defense scores a bonus run by throwing out a base runner at second base on a throw from an outfielder.

LESSON 5

Secondary Level I

Tactical Problem Defending space by outfield position

Lesson Focus Runner on first and a ball hit to the right side of the outfield

Objectives

- Field grounders, line drives, and fly balls in the outfield.
- Back up the adjacent outfielder.
- Make an accurate throw to second base.

GAME 1

Setup Runner on first

Goals

- Get the runner out at second (defensive team).
- Safely move the runner to second (offensive team).

Conditions

- Use 4v4 minimum, 6v6 maximum.
- Defensive players play right center field, right field, second base, and first base.
- The offensive team must have a runner on first at all times.
- The batter must hit the ball to the right side of the outfield and run to first base.
- Balls hit to the left of second base are considered outs.
- Players score runs by safely reaching second base.
- Whether safe or out, the runner returns to the dugout area.
- The inning is over after three runs or three outs, whichever comes first.

Questions

Q: Today we're focusing on the defense. How were the defensive players, the right fielder and right center fielder, able to get the ball to second base ahead of the runner?

A: By fielding the ball quickly and throwing quickly to second base.

Q: How were you able to quickly catch and throw the ball?

A: By catching the ball over the throwing shoulder and running forward if possible.

Q: What should the nonfielding outfielder do?

A: Back up the player fielding the ball.

Q: What's the best angle to take when backing up the player fielding the ball?

A: Cut behind her so if she misses the ball you'll be in a position to catch it.

PRACTICE SITUATION

Setup   Four players are on defense (minimum) at right field, right center field, second base, and first base, and four players are on offense—the battery and a base runner. The batter hits the ball from the pitcher or from a tee to the right side of the outfield and then runs hard and fast to first base. The runner on first advances to second except on a fly ball. After fielding three balls from each position (right and right center), players rotate to second base and then to first or into the battery. Fielding players call the ball, and nonfielding players offer backup.

Goal   Successfully field the ball and throw the runner out at second base.

Cues

- Move your feet to the ball.
- Watch the ball into your glove.
- Catch and cover over your throwing shoulder.
- Recover and throw quickly.
- Back up to get the appropriate angle, and pretend the fielder isn't there or assume she will miss the ball.

GAME 2

Repeat game 1. The defense scores a bonus run by throwing out the base runner at second base on a throw from an outfielder.

Tactical Problem   Defending bases on a throw from outfield positions

Lesson Focus   Runner on first and a ball hit to the outfield

Objective   Demonstrate proper positioning and footwork when covering second base on a throw from the outfield.

GAME 1

Setup   Runner on first

Goals

- Get the runner out at second (defensive team).
- Safely move the runner to second (offensive team).

Conditions

- Use 5v5 minimum, 6v6 maximum.
- Defensive players play all four outfield positions, second base, and shortstop.
- The offensive team must have a runner on first at all times.
- The batter must hit the ball to the right side of the outfield and run to first base.
- Balls hit to the left of second base are considered outs.
- Players score runs by safely reaching second base.
- Whether safe or out, the runner returns to the dugout area.
- The inning is over after three runs or three outs, whichever comes first.

Questions

Q: When the ball is hit to the left side of the outfield, which infielder covers second?

A: The player at second base.

Q: When the ball is hit to the right side of the outfield, which infielder covers second?

A: The shortstop.

Q: What part of the base should you tag with your foot?

A: The outside edge closest to the person throwing the ball (this may require repositioning).

Q: Why?

A: To keep from interfering with the runner.

PRACTICE SITUATION

Setup   Six players are on defense (minimum) playing left field, left center field, right field, right center field, second base, and shortstop, and six players are on offense—the battery (pitcher, catcher, and batter) and 3 base runners. The batter hits a ball from the pitcher or a tee to the outfield and then runs hard and fast to first base. The runner on first advances to second except on a fly ball. Runners can tag up on fly balls. After catching three balls from the outfielders while playing second base and shortstop, players rotate to the battery. From the battery, players rotate through the outfield positions. Players use the speed of the incoming runner and the position of the incoming throw to adjust their foot positions when covering second base.

Goals

- Keep the runner from advancing to second.
- Cover second as the shortstop or second-base player.
- Cover second using proper footwork and be on the outside edge of the base.

Cues

- Give the thrower a target.
- Position your foot on the edge closest to the incoming throw.
- Use the incoming runner and the incoming throw to adjust your position to cover second base.
- Make catching the ball your first priority.

GAME 2

Setup   Repeat game 1. The defense scores a bonus run by throwing the base runner out at second.

LESSON 7

Tactical Problem   Advancing to second base

Lesson Focus   Runner on first and a ball hit to the outfield

Objectives

- Take off from first base at the appropriate time and run to second base and execute a proper stop.
- Tag up and run to second base on a fly ball to the outfield.

GAME 1

Setup   Runner on first

Goals

- Get the runner out at second (defensive team).
- Safely move the runner to second (offensive team).

Conditions

- Use 5v5 minimum, 6v6 maximum.
- Defensive players play all four outfield positions, second base, and shortstop.
- The offensive team must have a runner on first at all times.
- The batter must hit the ball to the right side of the outfield and run to first base.
- Balls hit to the left of second base are considered outs.
- Players score runs by safely reaching second base.
- Whether safe or out, the runner returns to the dugout area.
- The inning is over after three runs or three outs, whichever comes first.

Questions

Q: As a runner, when should you leave first base?

A: When the batter steps.

Q: How should you stop at second base?

A: Slide, lean back as you approach, and hang onto the base with your foot.

Q: Can the runner on first advance to second on a fly ball to the outfield?

A: Yes, but she must tag up first.

Q: What should the runner do to tag up?

A: Wait until the fielder touches the ball and then run as fast as possible to the next base.

Q: Does she have to run if she is unable to make it to the next base?

A: No. The runner does not have to advance if her team has fewer than two outs.

PRACTICE SITUATION

Setup   Six players are on defense (minimum) at left field, left center field, right field, right center field, second base, and shortstop. Four players are on offense—the battery and a base runner. The batter hits to the outfield and then runs hard and fast to first base. The runner on first advances to second except on a fly ball. Runners can tag up on fly balls. The batter hits and runs to first three times. The base runner runs from first to second three times (the batter should attempt to hit at least one fly ball so the runner can practice tagging up). After running, the base runner should rotate to an infield position and then rotate from an infield position to an outfield position.

Goals

- As the runner, take off when the batter steps.
- As the runner, tag up and take off as soon as any defensive player touches the ball.

Cues

- Be in a ready position.
- Take off (or step off) on the batter's step.
- On a fly ball, go when the ball contacts the glove of any defensive player.
- Run hard and prepare to slide.

GAME 2

Setup   Repeat game 1. The defense scores a bonus run by throwing out the base runner at second base.

LEVEL II

Students who have completed level I or who have previous playing experience, such as on a recreational team, should be ready for level II. Most of the lessons in level II focus on the situation in which there are no outs or one out and a runner on first base. In this situation defenders focus on force plays at second base, including plays from outfield throws and double plays from second to first. Many of these plays require crossover play. In crossover play the shortstop covers second base when the ball is hit to the right side of the infield or outfield. The fielder at second base covers it when balls are hit to the left side of the infield or outfield. We also introduce relays during level II, focusing on when to use a relay, how to perform a relay, and how to line up a relay.

In level II, students also solve the problem of where to hit the ball to get on base or advance the runners. The situation of no outs or one out with a runner on first provides opportunities for students to refine their base running, specifically. They continue to learn how to hit and run to first and advance from first to second quickly and safely.

Players must be able to accurately throw in from the outfield.

LESSON 8

Secondary Level II

Tactical Problem   Getting on base

Lesson Focus   No runners on base and a grounder down the third base line

Objectives

- Hit a ground ball down the third base line.
- Hit and run hard to first base.

GAME 1

Setup   No runners on base

Goals

- Hit the ball to an area of the field that allows you to get on first base.
- On defense, throw the ball to first, ahead of the runner.

Conditions

- Use 4v4 minimum, 5v5 optimum, 6v6 maximum.
- Defensive players play first, second, third, and shortstop.
- The batter must hit a ground ball to the infield and get to first before the throw.
- Players score runs by safely reaching first base.
- Whether safe or out, the runner returns to the dugout area.
- The inning is over after three runs or three outs, whichever comes first.

Questions

Q: When there are no runners on base, where is the best place to hit the ball?

A: To the left side of the infield, down the third base line.

Q: Why?

A: It requires fielders to move to their right creating a longer throw to first, so you are more likely to get on base.

Q: How did you have to run to get to first before the throw?

A: Fast, without looking at the ball.

PRACTICE SITUATION

Setup Place one cone on the left field line and a second cone where the third-base player would stand. Hitting from a tee or pitch, the batter attempts to hit between the cones. The batter gets five attempts and runs to first base following the fifth attempt. The remaining players field at third, shortstop, and first, and others can back up infielders from outfield positions. The remaining players can practice running to first base as the batter hits the first four of the five attempts.

Goals

- Angle the bat to hit toward the third base line or between third and shortstop.
- Hit and run hard.

Cues

- Use a normal to open stance.
- Make contact in the power zone.
- Angle the bat toward the target.
- Follow through to the target.

GAME 2

Setup Repeat game 1. The defensive team scores a bonus run when a fielder at third base or the shortstop throws out the base runner.

LESSON 9

Secondary Level II

Tactical Problems Advancing to the next base (second) and defending bases (second)

Lesson Focus No outs or one out, a runner on first, and a grounder to the left infield

Objectives

- As the base runner, run from first to second base.
- As the fielder at second, cover the base.

GAME 1

Setup   Runner on first and no outs or one out

Goals

- Safely get the runners to first and second (offensive team).
- Turn a double play (defensive team).

Conditions

- Use 3v3 minimum, 6v6 maximum.
- The batter must hit a ground ball to the left side of the infield.
- Players score runs by safely reaching first base.
- Whether safe or out, the runner returns to the dugout area.
- The inning is over after three runs or three outs, whichever comes first.

Questions

Q: Who should cover second base when the shortstop or third-base player fields the ball?

A: The player at second base.

Q: How did the second-base player cover second base when the ball was fielded in front of the base path?

A: Pivoted inside, moved to the inside edge of the base, and then stepped with the left foot (pivoted) to throw to first base.

Q: How did the second-base player cover second base when the ball was fielded behind the base path?

A: Performed an outside crossover, moved to the outside edge of the base, and then crossed her feet on the throw to first.

Q: What if there is a chance that the runner will interfere?

A: The second-base player should use a rocker step, stepping on the base and then pushing away from the base to make the throw.

PRACTICE SITUATION

Setup   The batter hits a ball to the left side of the infield; the play is at second base. The second-base player covers second base. Additional players serve as base runners. The offense should always have a runner on first base. Runners practice proper base running.

Goals

- Use proper footwork when covering second.
- Turn the double play.

Cues

- Adjust to the position of the ball, the incoming throw, and the incoming runner.
- Use the crossover step if the ball is coming from behind the base.
- Use an inside pivot if covering inside the base.
- Use the rocker step if there is no need to cross the base.
- Catch the ball first to get a sure out.

GAME 2

Setup   Repeat game 1. The defensive team scores three bonus runs for every double play turned by the second-base player.

Tactical Problems   Advancing to the next base (second) and defending bases (second)

Lesson Focus   No outs or one out, a runner on first, and a grounder to the right infield

Objectives

- Run from first to second base.
- Cover second from the shortstop position.

GAME 1

Setup   Runner on first, no outs or one out

Goals

- Safely get the runners to first and second (offensive team).
- Turn a double play (defensive team).

Conditions

- Use 3v3 minimum, 6v6 maximum.
- The batter must hit a ground ball to the right side of the infield.
- Players score runs by safely reaching first base.
- Whether safe or out, the runner returns to the dugout area.
- The inning is over after three runs or three outs, whichever comes first.

Questions

Q: Who should cover second base when the first- or second-base player fields the ball?

A: The shortstop.

Q: How did the shortstop cover second base when the ball was fielded in front of the base path (the path from first to second)?

A: Crossed over on the inside, came toward and touched the base while catching the throw, and then used the crossover step to throw to first.

Q: How did the shortstop cover second base when the ball was behind the base path?

A: Used the outside crossover, crossed over and touched the base while catching the throw, and used the crossover step to throw to first.

PRACTICE SITUATION

Setup   The ball is hit to the right side of the infield, and the play is at second base. The shortstop covers second base. Additional players serve as base runners. The offense should always have a runner on first base. Runners practice proper base running.

Goals

- Use proper footwork to cover second.
- Turn the double play.

Cues

- Adjust to the position of the ball, the incoming throw, and the incoming runner.
- Keep your feet moving to first base after the throw.

GAME 2

Setup   Repeat game 1. The defensive team scores three bonus runs for a double play turned by the shortstop.

Tactical Problems   Moving the runner and defending space by outfield positions

Lesson Focus   No outs or one out, a runner on first, and a fly ball to the outfield

Objectives

- As the batter, hit a fly ball to the outfield.
- As a fielder, field a fly ball and throw to second quickly.
- As a base runner, tag up and run from first to second.

GAME 1

Setup   Runner on first, no outs or one out

Goals

- Offensive players:
  - As the batter, hit a long fly ball to an outfield area to help the runner advance to second.
  - As the runner, tag up on the catch and run as quickly as possible to second base.
- Defensive players—Catch the ball on the fly and make the throw to second ahead of the runner tagging up from first.

Conditions

- Use 6v6 minimum.
- Defensive players play all four outfield positions plus shortstop and second base.
- The offensive team starts with a runner on first.
- The batter must hit a ball out of the infield (the ball cannot touch the ground in front of the base path).
- The runner scores by reaching second safely.
- Whether safe or out, the runner returns to the dugout area.
- The inning is over after three runs or three outs, whichever comes first.

Questions

Q: When is the best time to hit a fly ball?

A: When there are no outs or one out and you want to move or score a runner.

Q: How did you have to swing the bat to hit a fly ball?

A: Swing hard and fast, hit through the center of the ball, and follow through.

Q: What is the best way to field a fly ball so you can make a quick throw?

A: Catch the ball over the throwing shoulder.

Q: On a fly ball, when can the runner advance to second?

A: Once a fielder touches the ball.

Q: When should the runner leave the base?

A: As soon as a defensive player touches the ball.

PRACTICE SITUATION

Setup   The batter hits fly balls to the outfield, with a runner on first base. Each batter attempts to hit five fly balls and then rotates. The runner must tag up and run on a fly ball to provide a throwing situation for the outfielders. Batters may have to move up in the infield so they can hit a fly ball to the outfield. Students may also choose to hit fly balls off a tee or throw the ball.

Goal   Reach second base safely after tagging up on a fly ball hit to the outfield.

Cues

- Hitting a fly ball:
  - Swing fast through the center of the ball.
  - Follow through toward the outfield.
- Throwing from the outfield:
  - Catch over the throwing shoulder.
  - Recover and throw immediately.

- Tagging up:
  - Be in a ready position.
  - Listen for the coach to say "Go."
  - Run hard.

GAME 2

Setup   Repeat game 1. The defensive team scores a bonus run for a putout at second base on a throw from an outfielder.

LESSON 12
Secondary Level II

Tactical Problem   Defending bases

Lesson Focus   No outs or one out, a runner on first, and a grounder or line drive to the outfield

Objective   Cover second base properly when the ball is hit to the left side and right side of the outfield.

GAME 1

Setup   Runner on first, no outs or one out

Goal   Cover second base appropriately on a ball hit to the outfield.

Conditions

- Use 6v6 minimum, and have defensive players play all four outfield positions plus shortstop and second base.
- The offensive team starts with a runner on first.
- The batter must hit the ball out of the infield (the ball cannot touch the ground in front of the base path).
- The runner scores by reaching second safely.
- Whether safe or out, the runner returns to the dugout area.
- The inning is over after three runs or three outs, whichever comes first.

Questions

Q: What was the goal of the game?

A: To have the appropriate player cover second base on a hit to the outfield.

Q: Which infield player should cover second base on a hit to the left side of the infield?

A: The second-base player.

Q: Which infield player should cover second base on a hit to the right side of the infield?

A: The shortstop.

Q: Which infield player should cover second base on a hit to center field? Why?

A: The shortstop, because she will be moving for a possible play on the ball.

PRACTICE SITUATION

Setup Use 4v4 to 6v6 with two to four outfielders, a shortstop, and a second-base player. The batter hits or throws three fly balls to each side of the outfield. Extra players run from first to second. Review proper footwork for base coverage on throws from the outfield.

Goals

- As shortstop, cover second on a ball hit to the right side of the outfield.
- As the second-base player, cover second on a ball hit to the left side of the outfield.

Cues

- Cover when the ball is hit to the right (shortstop).
- Cover when the ball is hit to the left (second-base player).

GAME 2

Setup Repeat game 1. The defensive team scores a bonus run for a putout at second base on a throw from an outfielder if the appropriate player is covering second.

LESSON 13

Secondary Level II

Tactical Problem Defending bases

Lesson Focus No outs or one out, a runner on first, and a long ball to the outfield

Objective Use the cutoff to get the ball to the infield from the outfield.

GAME 1

Setup Runner on first, no outs or one out

Goal Use the cutoff to get the ball to the infield from the outfield.

Conditions

- Use 6v6 minimum.
- Defensive players play all four outfield positions plus shortstop and second base.

- The offensive team starts with a runner on first.
- The batter must hit a ball out of the infield (the ball cannot touch the ground in front of the base path).
- The runner scores by getting to second or third safely.
- A runner who reaches third returns to the dugout area.
- The inning is over after three runs or three outs, whichever comes first.

Questions

Q: *When should a shortstop or second-base player move toward the fielding outfielder to cut the ball off?*

A: *When the runners have already advanced and you need to keep them from running to the next base.*

Q: *Which player is the cutoff when the ball is hit to the left?*

A: *The shortstop.*

Q: *Which player is the cutoff when the ball is hit to the right?*

A: *The second-base player.*

Q: *What should the other infielders do while the cutoff is being taken?*

A: *Cover bases (except for the pitcher).*

Let's practice using a cutoff player to keep runners from advancing.

PRACTICE SITUATION

Setup   Use two or three outfielders; a shortstop; and second-, third-, and first-base players. Extra players run from first base. The batter attempts six hits to the outfield. Runners who safely advance to second stay and advance to third on the next hit. Runners must continue running until the cutoff player cuts the throw. Outfielders must throw to the cutoff, who is the only player who can throw a runner out.

Goals

- Do not let runners score.
- Throw to keep the lead runner from advancing.

GAME 2

Setup   Repeat game 1. Defensive players score a bonus run every time they keep a runner from advancing to third base.

LESSON 14

Tactical Problem   Defending bases

Lesson Focus   No outs or one out, a runner on first, and a long ball to the outfield

Objective   Use a relay to get the ball to the infield from the outfield.

GAME 1

Setup   Runner on first, no outs or one out

Goal   Use a relay from the shortstop or second-base player to get runners out at bases.

Conditions

- Use 6v6 minimum.
- Defensive players play all four outfield positions plus shortstop and second base.
- The offensive team starts with a runner on first.
- The batter must hit a ball out of the infield (the ball cannot touch the ground in front of the base path).
- The runner scores by safely getting to second or third.
- A runner who reaches third returns to the dugout area.
- The inning is over after three runs or three outs, whichever comes first.

Questions

Q: *What is the difference between a cutoff and a relay?*

A: *A cutoff is used to stop runners, whereas a relay is used to get the ball in quickly and to possibly make a play at a base.*

Q: *How does the shortstop or second-base player know where to stand to set up the relay?*

A: *Whoever is covering the base (shortstop or second-base player) should tell the relay player to move left or right to help him adjust position.*

Q: *Should you throw the ball to the relay the same way you throw to a cutoff, and why?*

A: *Yes, because if the throw is late, the player might need to just hold the runners.*

Q: *How will the player receiving the throw know whether to cut or relay the ball?*

A: *The player covering the base (or the pitcher) should call, "Cut!"*

PRACTICE SITUATION

Setup   Three players stand about 10 to 15 yards apart. The middle player practices receiving a throw and pivoting to throw to the other player. The end players practice receiving the throw from over their throwing shoulders and throwing quickly and accurately to the pivot player.

Goal   Relay as quickly as possible from one player to another (compete with another group of three).

Cues

- Catch and cover over the throwing shoulder.
- Pivot left on your right foot (if your right side is dominant).
- See the target (glove).
- Transition quickly from a catching to a throwing position.

GAME 2

Setup   Repeat game 1. The defensive team scores a bonus run every time it keeps a runner from advancing to third base.

LEVEL III

Lessons in level III reflect increased tactical complexity. Increasing the tactical complexity of conditioned games motivates players to use more refined skills and tactics. For example, students work on offensive situations that require a batter to place the ball down the right-field line, between infielders, or down the left-field line to get on base and advance runners. Situations with a runner on second provide players opportunities to advance runners into scoring position, practice looking back the runner, and practice covering third base. We provide a few examples of these types of lessons in this section.

It takes knowledge and skill to determine the best place to hit the ball or avoid hitting it, and to follow through by hitting it to that position.

LESSON 15

Secondary Level III

Tactical Problem Advancing to the next base

Lesson Focus No runners and a grounder to the infield

Objectives

- Determine the best place to hit the ball in a given situation.
- Hit and run hard to first.
- Understand when to run through and when to round first base.

GAME 1

Setup No runners on base

Goal Given the situation of no runners on base, the runner advances to as many bases as possible.

Conditions

- Use 4v4 minimum, 5v5 optimum, 6v6 maximum.
- The batter must hit a ground ball.
- Runs are scored for each base safely reached after the initial hit.
- The inning is over after three runs or three outs, whichever comes first.

Questions

Q: How did you run to first when there was absolutely no chance of advancing to second?

A: Ran hard and fast, through or over first base.

Q: How did you run to first when there was a possibility of advancing to second base?

A: Rounded the base and observed the position of the ball (or listened to the coach).

Q: What is the advantage of listening to a coach?

A: You do not have to hesitate before advancing to second, and you know when and where to run without having to watch the ball.

PRACTICE SITUATION

Setup   Three players are in the field (first base, second base, and either third base or shortstop), and three players are batting. One player serves as a coach. The batter hits a grounder to the left side of the infield and then runs hard and fast to first base. The coach tells the runner whether to round through or go to second.

Goal   Do what the coach says.

Cues

- As the coach, let the runner know what to do as soon as possible.
- As the runner, listen to the coach and don't watch the ball.

GAME 2

Setup   Repeat game 1. The coach gets a bonus run for the team for every base runner who advances safely (if the runner gets out at any base, no bonus runs are earned).

LESSON 16

Tactical Problem   Moving the runner

Lesson Focus   No outs or one out, a runner on first, and a grounder behind the runner

Objectives

- Determine the best place to hit the ball.
- Run from first to third.

GAME 1

Setup   Runner on first, no outs or one out

Goals

- As the batter, hit the ball to allow the runner to get to third safely.
- On defense, get the lead runner out.

Conditions

- Use 4v4 minimum, 5v5 optimum, 6v6 maximum.
- Defensive players play first base, second base, shortstop, pitcher, and as many other infield positions as possible.
- Players score runs by safely reaching third base.
- The inning is over after three runs or three outs, whichever comes first.

Questions

Q: Into what area of the field should the batter hit the ball to advance the runner?

A: Behind the runner.

Q: As a right-handed batter, how do you have to position yourself in the batter's box if you want to hit to right field?

A: Angled toward the right side of the field.

Q: At what point in the power zone should you contact the ball if you're attempting to hit down the right-field line?

A: Outside toward the right-field side of the plate, between the plate and the area of the field you want to hit to.

Q: How should you follow through?

A: Follow through toward right field.

PRACTICE SITUATION

Setup The batter hits three balls from a batting tee, attempting to hit down the right-field line. Then the batter hits three pitched balls, attempting to hit down the right-field line. Repeat the drill with the batter attempting to hit the ball between the players covering first and second.

Goals

- Hit balls down the right-field line.
- Hit the ball between the first- and second-base players.

Cues

- Pick a target (before the pitch).
- Angle your body and bat toward the target.
- Follow through toward the target.
- Know where in the power zone to contact the ball before it is pitched.
- Contact the ball in the power zone.

GAME 2

Setup Repeat game 1. The batter scores two bonus runs for hitting a grounder behind the runner and through the right side of the infield.

LESSON 17 🔘 *DVD*   Secondary Level III

Tactical Problem Defending bases

Lesson Focus No outs or one out, a runner on second, and a grounder down the right-field line

Objective Hold the lead runner.

GAME 1

Setup   Runner on second, no outs or one out

Goal   Get the lead runner out.

Conditions

- Use 4v4 minimum, 5v5 optimum, or 6v6 maximum.
- Defensive players play first base, second base, shortstop, pitcher, and as many other infield positions as possible.
- The offensive team must always have a runner at second base.
- The batter must hit a ground ball.
- Players score runs by safely reaching third base.
- A runner who reaches third returns to the dugout area.
- The inning is over after three runs or three outs, whichever comes first.
- The defensive team scores an additional run if it keeps the lead runner from advancing to third base.

Questions

Q: After fielding the ball, what did you do to keep the runner from advancing?

A: Looked the runner back.

Q: Once a throw is made to first, what should the first-base player do if the runner is advancing to third?

A: If the base player has a play, he should step off first and throw to third. If he doesn't have a play, he should get the sure out at first and then put the ball in his throwing hand and move toward third to hold the runner there.

Q: When the runner attempts to advance, what does the third-base player need to do?

A: Cover third base and provide a good target.

Q: How should the third-base player position herself to make a tag on the runner?

A: Straddle the bag.

Q: How should the third-base player tag the runner? Why?

A: Sweep low across the edge of the base closest to the runner, because if the base player sweeps at the runner, the runner may move and avoid the tag.

PRACTICE SITUATION

Setup   The defensive team needs four or five infield players. The offensive team must have a runner on second base. On the hit, the batter must run to third, hesitating if the fielder looks her back, but proceeding to third if the throw is made to first.

Goal   Get the lead runner out at third using a sweep tag.

Cues

- Look the runner back.
- Provide a target at the base (players covering the bases).
- Sweep tag at the base.

GAME 2

Setup   Repeat game 1. The offensive team scores a bonus run when the runner safely advances to third. The defensive team scores two bonus runs for a putout at third and five bonus runs for a double play (first to third).

LESSON 18

Tactical Problems

- Moving the runner
- Advancing to the next base

Lesson Focus   Two outs, a runner on second, and a line drive to the outfield

Objective   Hit a line drive from the left to the middle of the outfield.

GAME 1

Setup   Runner on second, two outs

Goal   Get on base and move the runner to third.

Conditions

- Use 8v8 (you can have fewer players if you place restrictions on where batters can hit).
- The batter can hit the ball anywhere on the playing field.
- A player scores a run by reaching first safely and scores another run if the runner on second reaches third safely.
- A runner who reaches third returns to the dugout area.

Questions

Q: What did the batter do to advance the runner from second to third and to get on base?

A: Hit a line drive from the middle to the left side of the outfield.

Q: Why is this the best place to hit the ball?

A: If the ball makes it to the outfield, the infield still has to make a long throw to get the batter out at first, and the runner still has a chance to advance to third.

Q: Where in the power zone is the best place for batters to contact the ball if they're trying to hit from left to left center?

A: Between the plate and left field or left center field.

Q: How should the batter contact the ball?

A: Swing level, hit through the middle of the ball, and follow through to the target. The batter should know where to hit the ball before the pitch.

Q: What should the base runner do in this situation?

A: Watch to be sure that the ball gets through the infield and that it isn't caught on the fly in the outfield; then go to third (and home if possible).

PRACTICE SITUATION

Setup   From a batting tee or pitch, batters practice hitting (5 to 10 times in a row) line drives over or between infielders on the left side of the field. Base runners practice running from second to third as batters hit line drives.

Goal   Hit line drives between or over infielders and in front of or between outfielders.

Cues

- Know where you want to hit and where you want to make contact.
- Contact in the power zone and swing through toward the target.

GAME 2

Setup   Repeat game 1. Line drives score two bonus runs.

LEVEL IV

Lessons at level IV are for students with extensive experience in softball or baseball. These lessons are structured to provide many competitive experiences to motivate these players. For example, students play the conditioned games against other teams. They can practice against another team or within their team (e.g., intersquad scrimmages).

Situations in level IV should provide opportunities for players to work individually and as a team. More advanced situations include batting and fielding with a runner on second, a runner on third, or even runners on second and third. These situations require more complex tactical play such as positioning for rundowns and backups and defending space as a team. Hitting during these situations requires placing the ball to allow the batter to get on base and score or to advance runners already on base. Students can refine their base running. Sliding and maneuvering to draw a throw can also be incorporated at advanced levels of play.

Placing students in competitive situations helps them learn to think fast about what tactics to use.

LESSON 19

Tactical Problem   Getting on base

Lesson Focus   No runners and a grounder to the left side of the infield

Objective   Hit the ball between the players on the left side of the infield.

GAME 1

Setup   No runners

Goal   Hit grounders between infielders.

Conditions

- Use 4v4 minimum, with defensive players at first, second, third, and shortstop.
- The batter must hit a ground ball.
- Players score runs by safely reaching first base.
- Whether safe or out, the runner returns to the dugout area.
- The offensive team scores an additional run if the grounder goes through the infield.

Questions

Q: *Where in the infield was the best place to hit the ball to get on base?*

A: *To the right side of the infield, down the third base line or between third and shortstop.*

Q: *How should the batter position her body to place the ball?*

A: *In an open stance and slightly toward left field.*

Q: *Where in the power zone should the batter make contact if he is trying to hit through the left side of the infield?*

A: *Out in front, but the contact point and follow-through should be in the direction of the target.*

Q: *How many players were able to consistently hit where they were aiming?*

A: *Most players could not.*

PRACTICE SITUATION

Setup   Put large cones or hoops between infield positions and one on the foul line, behind the base. The batter attempts to hit a cone or hoop with the ball, scoring five bonus runs if successful. Each player should hit five balls from a tee, soft toss, or pitch and run on the fifth trial.

Goal   Place the ball between the players on the left side of the infield.

Cues

- Mentally see (visualize) where you want to hit the ball.
- Contact the ball in the power zone.
- Follow through toward the target.
- Watch the ball contact the bat.

GAME 2

Setup   Repeat game 1. The offensive team scores two bonus runs by hitting the ball between or past the third-base player and shortstop.

LESSON 20

Tactical Problem   Getting on base

Lesson Focus   Runner on first and a grounder to the right side of the infield

Objective   Place the ball between the players on the right side of the infield.

GAME 1

Setup   No runners

Goal   Hit grounders between infielders.

Conditions

- Use 4v4 minimum, with defensive players at first, second, third, and shortstop.
- The batter must hit a ground ball.
- Runners score when they safely reach second.
- Whether safe or out, the runner returns to the dugout area.
- The offensive team scores an additional run if the grounder goes through the infield.

Questions

Q: Where in the infield was the best place to hit the ball to advance the runner to second base?

A: To the right side of the infield, down the first base line, or between first and second.

Q: How should the batter position his body to place the ball?

A: In a closed stance and slightly toward right field.

Q: Where in the power zone should the batter make contact if she is trying to hit through the right side of the infield?

A: Out in front, but the contact point and follow-through should be in the direction of the target.

Q: How many players were able to consistently hit where they were aiming?

A: Most players could not.

PRACTICE SITUATION

Setup   Put large cones or hoops between infield positions and one on the foul line, behind the base. The batter attempts to hit a cone or hoop with the ball, scoring five bonus runs if successful. Each player hits five balls from a tee, soft toss, or pitch and runs on the fifth trial.

Goal   Place the ball between the players on the right side of the infield.

Cues

- Mentally see (visualize) where you want to hit the ball.
- Contact the ball in the power zone.
- Follow through toward the target.
- Watch the ball contact the bat.

GAME 2

Setup   Repeat game 1. The offensive team scores two bonus runs by hitting the ball between or past the first- and second-base players.

Tactical Problem   Defending bases

Lesson Focus   Runner on first and a grounder fielded by the first-base player

Objective   As pitcher, cover first base.

GAME 1

Setup   Runner on first

Goals

- As the batter, get to first ahead of the pitcher.
- On defense, get the ball to the pitcher (covering first) ahead of the runner.

Conditions

- Use 3v3 minimum, with the defense playing first, second, and pitcher.
- The batter must hit a grounder to the right side of the infield.
- Only the pitcher can make the play at first base, unless she fields the ball.
- Players score runs by safely reaching first base.
- Whether safe or out, the runner returns to the dugout area.
- The inning is over after three runs or three outs, whichever comes first.

Questions

Q: What did the pitcher have to do to make the play at first base?

A: Run to first ahead of the runner.

Q: How did the pitcher need to run to avoid colliding with the runner?

A: Parallel along the base path.

Q: Where should fielders throw the ball so that the pitcher has the best opportunity to make the play?

A: Directly over the base.

PRACTICE SITUATION

Setup   Batters hit grounders to the right and run to first base. The pitcher covers first and attempts to make the play ahead of the runner. Each player gets three to five attempts as pitcher. Each player should get at least three attempts to field and throw to first.

Goal   As pitcher, get the runner out at first.

Cues

- Pitcher:
  - Run parallel with the runner.
  - Get to first ahead of the runner.
  - Give a good target.
- Fielder—Time your throw to the base.

GAME 2

Setup   Repeat game 1. The pitcher scores a bonus run for the team for every putout at first base.

Tactical Problem   Defending bases

Lesson Focus   No outs or one out, a runner on second, and a line drive through the middle

Objectives

- Make the double play from third to first.
- Perform a sweep tag and throw.

GAME 1

Setup   Runner at second, no outs or one out

Goals

- On offense, advance the runner by hitting a line drive over or through the middle of the infield.
- On defense, get the lead runner out, hold at second base, or turn a three-to-one double play if the runner tries to advance.

Conditions

- Use 4v4 minimum.
- Defensive players play first, second, third, shortstop, and pitcher.
- The batter must hit a grounder or line drive between the shortstop and second base (place cones behind infield positions to mark the area).
- The batter scores a run by reaching first while the other runner reaches third safely.
- Runners who reach third return to the dugout area.
- The defensive team gets five bonus runs for a three-to-one double play.
- The inning is over after three runs or three outs, whichever comes first.

Questions

Q: When a three-to-one double play occurred, what type of tag did the third-base player use?

A: Sweep tag.

Q: Why is the sweep tag best for a three-to-one double play?

A: It keeps the fielder covering the base out of the way of the runner, and it keeps the runner from knocking the ball out of the fielder's glove.

Q: What's the advantage of a three-to-one double play?

A: It cuts the lead runner and keeps a runner from getting into a scoring position.

PRACTICE SITUATION

Setup   The third-base player practices the three-to-one double play, sweep tag, and throw. A runner is at second. The batter hits or throws the ball toward or over second and runs to first. Infielders attempt to field and throw to third. Each player has at least five opportunities to cover third base and to field and throw to third.

Goals

- Successfully complete the three-to-one double play.
- Use the sweep to tag the runner.

Cues

- Sweep with two hands.
- Sweep and step toward first (play).
- Sweep the ball toward your throwing shoulder (if possible).

GAME 2

Setup Repeat game 1. The defensive team scores five bonus runs for a three-to-one double play.

LESSON 23

Tactical Problems

- Advancing to the next base
- Moving the runner

Lesson Focus No outs or one out, a runner on second, and a grounder or line drive to the right side

Objectives

- As the base runner, serve as a decoy to delay the throw.
- As the player fielding the ball, look the runner back before throwing.

GAME 1

Setup Runner on second, no outs or one out

Goals

- On offense, get on base and move the runner to third.
- On defense, get the batter out and hold the runner at second.

Conditions

- Use 8v8 (you can have fewer players if you place restrictions on where batters can hit).
- The offensive team must have a runner at second.
- The batter must hit to the right side of the field.
- The batter scores a run by getting to first and advancing the runner to third safely.
- Runners who reach third return to the dugout area.
- The inning is over after three runs or three outs, whichever comes first.

Questions

Q: What should the runner on second do to delay the throw to first base?

A: Act like he is going to run.

Q: Where is the best place to hit to move the runner from second to third?

A: Toward the left side of the infield, between the third base line and the shortstop.

Q: Why?

A: It requires a longer throw by the fielder and so the batter is more likely to move the runner and get to first safely.

Q: If the runner gets to third and a throw is made to first, what should the runner at third do?

Teaching Sport Concepts and Skills

A: Lead off toward home. She should run home if the first-base player throws to third but return to third if she can't make it home.

Q: What should the runner on first do if the throw goes to third?

A: Run to second.

Q: What should defenders do to hold runners?

A: Stand next to one of the runners with the ball in the throwing hand and look at the other runner; or call for a time-out.

PRACTICE SITUATION

Setup   Use a minimum of four infielders. The batter hits the ball to the right side of the infield and runs to first. The runner at second attempts to advance to third. After the batter gets to first, the runner on third attempts to lead off to draw a throw. Runners advance depending on throwing or until the defense has the ball under control and has called a time-out.

Goals

- As a base runner, advance to as many bases possible.
- As a fielder, keep runners from advancing past second.

Cues

- Fielders—Have the ball ready to throw as you look the runner back.
- Runners—Fake or take quick steps toward the next base to delay or draw the throw.

GAME 2

Setup   Repeat game 1. The offensive team scores a run for every runner that reaches home safely. The defensive team scores five bonus runs for a three-to-one double play.

LESSON 24

Secondary Level IV

Tactical Problem   Defending bases

Lesson Focus   No outs or one out, a runner on first, and a grounder or line drive to the right side

Objective   Execute a rundown.

GAME 1

Setup   Runner on first, no outs or one out

Goals

- On offense, get on base and move the runner to third.
- On defense, get the batter out and hold the runner at second.

Conditions

- Use 8v8 (you can have fewer players if you place restrictions on where batters can hit).
- The offensive team must have a runner at second.
- The batter must hit to the right side of the field.

- The batter scores a run by getting to first and advancing the runner to third safely.
- Runners who reach third return to the dugout area.
- The inning is over after three runs or three outs, whichever comes first.

Questions

Q: What should you do when the runner is caught between bases?

A: Attempt to run her back to the base she came from.

Q: What should off-the-ball players do during a rundown?

A: Back up to the closest base.

Q: What if someone else is backing up a base?

A: Move in behind him.

Q: Why is support important in a rundown?

A: It keeps runners from advancing and scoring.

PRACTICE SITUATION

Setup   Players are in groups of three with two bases and one runner to play running bases. When the runner is caught between the bases, the base players attempt to tag her or run her back to the other base.

Goals

- Get the runner out.
- If you can't get the runner out, keep him from advancing to the next base.

Cues

- Run the runner back to the original base.
- Have the ball ready to throw while running the runner back.
- Know when to step out (and let a backup player continue the rundown).
- Support, support, support.

GAME 2

Setup   Repeat game 1. The defensive team scores five bonus runs for tagging the runner out while in a rundown.

SUMMARY

This chapter has provided sample lessons for teaching softball tactically. You can extend or refine many of these lessons to create new ones focusing on a variety of off-the-ball movements and on-the-ball skills. The key to creating new lessons is to remember that in each situation (e.g., one out and a runner on first), every offensive and defensive player has a role. As you examine a situation, ask yourself, what off-the-ball movements or on-the-ball skills do players need to adequately perform their roles? Having identified these movements and skills, you can create game and practice conditions to help your students understand what to do and how to do it.

If you find that a particular game is not working, try to identify where the game is breaking down.

Then devise and implement a condition (or rule) that will force students to do what you want them to do. For example, if players are not throwing to second base to cut the lead runner, give the defensive team two additional runs each time it successfully gets the lead runner out. If a game is breaking down because students are unable to perform a particular skill, stop the game and ask students why they think the game is breaking down. Students know when things are not going well and are usually able to identify why. Having identified poorly executed skills as the reason for breakdown, students will be more motivated to practice these skills. Now students know *why* skill practice is necessary. Play ball!

Chapter 20

Cricket

Adrian Turner

Bowling Green State University

This chapter focuses on offensive and defensive tactical principles and skills for striking and fielding that can be developed in modified cricket games and practices. As in other striking and fielding games such as baseball, softball, and rounders, tactical problems in cricket include striking an object and running between safe areas to score, and restricting scoring and getting batters out. In cricket, offensive (batting) principles include scoring runs, avoiding getting out or defending the wicket (staying in), and hitting into space to achieve these offensive goals. Defensive (bowling and fielding) principles include restricting runs scored, getting batters out, and preventing hitting into space to achieve these defensive goals. The simple offensive goals in cricket are to hit the ball into the field so that it eludes the fielders and to not get out. The defense attempts to restrict run scoring and to get batters out.

As with other games, cricket is best taught from a tactical approach by using small-sided games. Spe-cific pedagogical principles are embedded in all of the games and activities in this chapter to maximize learning opportunities. In small groups, students practice offensive (batting) and defensive (bowling and fielding) concepts in modified contexts replicating real game situations. Players equally practice each striking and fielding role. Although cricket is a team game, solo (or pair) activities are used to regularly rotate students through batting, bowling, and fielding roles. Batters of various abilities receive the same number of deliveries in many of the games and practices, so participants equally experience the offensive and defensive components of the game. Most of the lessons in this chapter involve only 6, 7, or 8 players who compete either alone or in pairs. For a class of 24 to 32 students to be active, you will need to set up three or four games simultaneously. At no time in any of these activities does a player sit out—players simply rotate into the next batting, bowling (pitching), or fielding role.

All lessons in this chapter begin with a game form, but some of the associated practices use smaller numbers than are used in the initial game. For example, a lesson on bowling uses a triad practice, but a batting game, hit the gap, involves five students. Other specific practices, such as drive cricket, allow students to develop an offensive tactic and skill under similar conditions to those experienced in the real game. Although the focus in drive cricket is offensive (a batting shot played to a specific ball), most of the game contexts in cricket are reciprocal, and so defensive skills and tactics (catching, picking up, throwing, covering a teammate) are also practiced in these activities. The modified scoring used in the various levels of tactical complexity in this chapter rewards players for their defensive performances (bowling and fielding) in addition to their batting scores. Using small numbers and providing students with multiple opportunities to improve can instill motivation and confidence in players as they experience success in scaled-down situations representing pressures similar to those in the real game of 11 players per side.

Short lessons are a challenge to teaching cricket because of its time-consuming nature. Nevertheless, a conceptual, question-driven approach facilitates players' understanding. In addition, restricting the length (i.e., where the ball bounces) and line (i.e., direction) of the bowler's delivery encourages players to think tactically. In many of the games bowlers are given a numbered target zone (marked by lines, chalk, or spots) in which the ball should bounce. Various types of batting strokes played into specific sectors of the field are learned as responses to different lines and lengths of bowling in various games and practices. In this chapter, all of the concepts and terms used are for right-handed batters and bowlers. For left-handed batters, whenever the chapter references the off-side or leg side, the concepts and terms should be reversed.

Many of the lessons' activities include diagrams. All figures relating to conditioned games use ovals, illustrating a cricket field. Some figures for the practice tasks show rectangles because these practices take place in a specific context.

Following are other issues to consider when teaching cricket:

• *Facilities and equipment.* All of the game's activities can be adapted to specific environments (indoors or outdoors). The dimensions of the playing area (of both modified games and practices) can be varied to suit particular teaching contexts and specific student needs. Inexpensive, lightweight, and safe equipment such as tennis, Nerf, and Wiffle balls can be used in the games to slow the speed of the ball for smaller spaces and novice players. Large cones, chairs, or even trash cans can simulate the wickets. Regulation trainer bats for softball (flat bats) are ideal as modified cricket bats for students at the secondary level. Bats can also be shaped from wood (ideally willow), although these tend to be heavy for younger children. Three cut-off broom handles (28 in., or 71 cm, high and together spanning 9 in., or 23 cm, across) glued onto a piece of wood can be used as a makeshift wicket. Plastic wickets and bats made by Kwik Cricket are also available from physical education retailers around the world. All that is really required for playing cricket is a comparatively flat surface indoors or outdoors and space in which to hit a relatively soft ball.

• *Tactical framework.* Cricket provides players with greater flexibility and many more opportunities for decision making than do other games in the striking and fielding category. A tactical framework and three levels of tactical complexity for teaching cricket are presented in tables 20.1 and 20.2. Several key features of cricket are introduced in the first level of tactical complexity, and these features have major implications for the subsequent tactics and skills learned by the players.

Table 20.1   Tactical Problems, Movements, and Skills in Cricket

Tactical problems	Off-the-ball movements	On-the-ball skills
SCORING AND STAYING IN (OFFENSE)		

Defending the wicket (staying in)	• Batting
	• Judging the line (direction or path) and length (place of bounce) of the ball
	• Moving forward or backward to defend
	• Keeping the ball out (defending a good length)—front foot off side and leg side (forward defense)
	• Keeping the ball out (defending a short ball)—back foot off side and leg side (backward defense)
		• Batting:
		  ○ Grip
		  ○ Stance
		  ○ Backlift
		  ○ Taking guard
		• Defensive strokes:
		  ○ Front foot off side and leg side (forward defense)
		  ○ Back foot off side and leg side (backward defense)

Tactical problems	Off-the-ball movements	On-the-ball skills

Scoring runs	• Moving forward or backward to attack
	• Looking for space—off side and leg side
	• Attacking the half volley or low full toss
	• Attacking the short ball, across the line—leg side (pull shot)
	• Working the short ball, fine-leg side (leg glance or drive)
	• Running between the wickets
	• Communicating (calling)
	• Backing up
		• Attacking strokes:
		  ○ Front foot off side and leg side drive
		  ○ Back foot
		  ○ Across the line—leg side (pull shot)
		  ○ Across the line—off side (cut shot)
		  ○ Down the line (fine, back foot leg glance)
		  ○ Back foot drive
		  ○ Down the line (front foot leg glance)
		  ○ Across the line (sweep or paddle)
		• Turning and changing hands
		• Grounding the bat

PREVENTING SCORING (DEFENSE)		

Getting the batter out	• Bowling:
	  ○ Making the batter play
	  ○ Bowling a straight line and length
	  ○ Attacking the off-stump
	  ○ Moving the ball away
	  ○ Looking for the edge
	  ○ Moving the ball in to the batter
	  ○ Bowling a slower or faster ball
	  ○ Bowling over or around the wicket
	  ○ Bowling from wider on the crease
	• Bowling a spin to tempt the batter (leg breaks, off-breaks)
	• Bowling to a field:
	  ○ Leg side
	  ○ Off side
	• Fielding:
	  ○ Making field placements
	  ○ Working the batter out
	  ○ Attacking the batter
	  ○ Being in a ready position
	  ○ Moving in
	• Being in a ready position
	• Running out the batter:
	  ○ Deciding where to throw
	• Achieving a leg before wicket (LBW)
		• Bowling:
		  ○ Basic action
		  ○ Running up
		• Seam bowling:
		  ○ Leg cutter
		  ○ Off-cutter
		  ○ Yorking the batter
		• Spin:
		  ○ Off-break
		  ○ Leg break
		  ○ Arm ball
		• Fielding
		• Catching:
		  ○ Close-slip catching
		  ○ Long catching
		• Intercepting, picking up, and throwing

Restricting run scoring	• Fielding
	• Defending space in front of the wicket
	• Field placements:
	  ○ Being in a ready position
	  ○ Moving in
	  ○ Saving a single
	  ○ Saving four runs
	• Backing up in the field
	• Defending space behind the wicket
	• Communicating in the field
		• Fielding
		• Ground fielding
		• Using a long barrier
		• Fielding on the move
		• Throwing the ball:
		  ○ Underarm
		  ○ Overarm
		• Wicketkeeper:
		  ○ Stance
		  ○ Position
		  ○ Takes and returns
		  ○ Catching
		• Bowling to a field:
		  ○ Leg side
		  ○ Off side

Umpiring	• Umpire decisions:
	  ○ Out
	  ○ No-ball
	  ○ Bye
	  ○ Wide
	  ○ Six
	  ○ Four	

Table 20.2 Levels of Tactical Complexity for Cricket

Tactical goals and problems	Level I	Level II	Level III
SCORING AND STAYING IN (OFFENSE)			

Defending the wicket (staying in)	• Batting:
	  ○ Grip
	  ○ Stance
	  ○ Backlift
	  ○ Taking guard
	• Judging the line (direction or path) and length (place of bounce) of the ball
	• Moving forward to defend:
	  ○ Keeping the ball out (defending a good length)—front foot off side and leg side (forward defense)
		• Judging the line (direction or path) and length (place of bounce) of the ball
		• Moving backward to defend:
		  ○ Keeping the ball out (defending a short ball)—back foot off side and leg side (backward defense)	

Scoring runs	• Moving forward to attack
	• Looking for space—off side or leg side
	• Attacking the half volley or low full toss
		• Moving backward to attack
		• Looking for space—off side or leg side
		• Attacking the short ball, across the line—leg side (pull shot)
		• Working the short ball, fine-leg side (leg glance or drive)
		• Running between the wickets
		• Communicating (calling)
		• Backing up
			• Moving backward to attack
			• Attacking strokes:
			  ○ Front foot off side and leg side drive
			  ○ Back foot
			  ○ Across the line—leg side (pull shot)
			  ○ Across the line—off side (cut shot)
			  ○ Down the line (fine, back foot leg glance)
			  ○ Back foot drive
			  ○ Down the line (front foot leg glance)
			  ○ Across the line (sweep or paddle)
			• Turning and changing hands
			• Grounding the bat

PREVENTING SCORING (DEFENSE)			

Getting the batter out	• Bowling:
	  ○ Basic action
	  ○ Running up
	  ○ Making the batter play
	  ○ Bowling a straight line and length
	  ○ Attacking the off-stump
	  ○ Moving the ball away
	  ○ Looking for the edge
	• Making field placements
	• Fielding:
	  ○ Being in a ready position
	  ○ Moving in
	• Catching:
	  ○ Close-slip catching
	  ○ Long catching
		• Seam bowling:
		  ○ Leg cutter
		  ○ Off-cutter
		  ○ Yorking the batter
		• Making the batter play:
		  ○ Moving the ball into the batter
		  ○ Bowling a slower or faster ball
		  ○ Bowling over or around the wicket
		• Working the batter out
		• Attacking the batter
		• Running out the batter:
		  ○ Deciding where to throw
		  ○ Intercepting, picking up, and throwing
		• Achieving a leg before wicket (LBW)
			• Bowling a spin to tempt the batter (leg break, off-break, arm ball)
			• Bowling from wider on the crease
			• Bowling to a field:
			  ○ Leg side
			  ○ Off side

Restricting run scoring	• Defending space in front of the wicket
	• Defending space behind the wicket
	• Wicketkeeper:
	  ○ Stance
	  ○ Position
	  ○ Takes and returns
	  ○ Catching
	• Communicating in the field
		• Fielding
		• Ground fielding
		• Long barrier
		• Fielding on the move
		• Throwing the ball:
		  ○ Underarm
		  ○ Overarm
		• Field placement:
		  ○ Being in a ready position
		  ○ Moving in
		  ○ Saving a single
		  ○ Saving four runs
		• Backing up in the field
			Bowling to a field:
			• Leg side
			• Off side

Umpiring		• Umpire decisions:
		  ○ Out
		  ○ No-ball
		  ○ Bye
		  ○ Wide
		  ○ Six
		  ○ Four	

LEVEL I

In the first level of tactical complexity, focus on both defensive (bowling and fielding) and offensive (batting) concepts as you introduce your students to the game. Bowlers develop a basic understanding of a good line and length when attempting to restrict run scoring and get batters out. Batters are taught the importance of defending a good line and length delivery and of attacking a ball that lands close by moving forward to play their shots. At this level students also develop an understanding of defending space behind and in front of the wicket.

Specifically, students need to understand the rules of the game:

- The bowler delivers the ball with a straight arm to the batter. It is illegal for the bowler to throw the ball (called a no-ball, it results in the batting team receiving another delivery and scoring a run). All other defensive players are allowed to throw the ball when fielding.

- The ball is allowed to bounce before it reaches the batter. The bowler can use the bounce to make the ball deviate and thereby make batting more difficult. Doing so helps restrict run scoring and helps get the batter out.

- Fielders can attempt to get one of two players out. In games with two batters, this rule forces fielding players to decide where to throw the ball to execute an out (as in other striking and fielding games).

- The batter is permitted to play the ball through 360 degrees. This range allows for a greater variety of strokes and provides a challenge for field placements. It also allows the defense to get a batter out behind the wicket.

A bowler must deliver the ball with a straight arm.

Although batting and bowling appear to be the more glamorous offensive and defensive activities, explain to your players that they will spend more time defending in the field than in any other activity in the game. To introduce this concept to students, fielding is the focus for the initial lesson at level I.

LESSON 1

Tactical Problem   Defending space in front of the wicket

Lesson Focus   Getting the batter out with effective fielding

Objectives

- Catch the ball.
- Field ground balls consistently.
- Return the ball efficiently to the bowler.

GAME 1

Setup   Nonstop cricket (six to eight players; figure 20.1)

Goal   On defense, get the ball back to the bowler safely.

Conditions

- The bowler tosses the ball underhand to the batter, who stands in front of the wicket.
- The ball must be tossed to where the batter has a chance to hit it.
- If the batter misses the ball and it hits the wicket, he is out (bowled).
- The ball can bounce once before it gets to the batter.
- If the batter hits the ball into the air and it is caught by one of the fielders, the batter is out.
- There is no foul territory, and the ball can be hit anywhere.

When the batter hits the ball, she runs around the cone and returns to her initial batting position to score a run. The batter bats until she is out or for a maximum of six pitches (one over). The fielders must return the ball to the bowler as quickly as possible once they field it. As soon as the bowler has the ball, he may toss it toward the wicket, regardless of whether the batter is there and ready to defend.

Each time a batter is out, a new bowler takes over and the fielders rotate one position clockwise. Each batter counts the runs she scores, and the player with the most runs wins the game.

Questions

Q: What was the goal of your game when you were in the field?

A: To get the batter out.

Q: What did you do when you were fielding?

A: Tried to cover space along with other fielders by spreading out in a semicircle, or horseshoe, around the batter (similar shape to the infield in baseball or softball).

Q: When a batter consistently hits the ball past fielders in a certain area, what should the fielding players do?

A: Move one fielder deeper to cover a hard or high hit (to act as an outfielder does in baseball or softball).

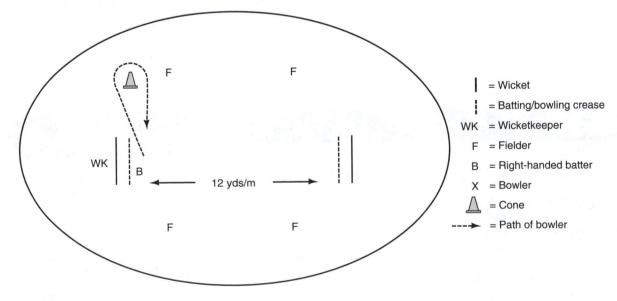

Figure 20.1

Q: So, moving a fielder deeper allows the batter to score a run in the area closer to the wickets?

A. Yes, but only one run rather than two or three.

Q: How can fielders make the batter think they are deeper (farther from the batter) than they really are?

A: As the bowler is about to deliver the ball, they should take three steps toward the batter. The exception is the wicketkeeper (a position similar to a catcher in softball or baseball), who remains crouched behind the wicket.

Q: Where are your hands positioned to be ready to field?

A: At your sides and a little in front (like a gunfighter in the Old West).

Q: When the ball is hit toward you, what are your options?

A: Catch the ball or field the ball (if it cannot be caught) and return it to the bowler.

Q: What position were your hands in to catch a ball coming from high in the air?

A: Either palms turned upward until about at chest level or thumbs together (for higher balls).

Q: How did you field the ball if you were not able to catch it?

A: Moved my feet and body in line with the ball and watched the ball safely roll into both hands.

Q: If the ball bounced awkwardly just in front of you, what did you do to keep from missing it?

A: Crouched low behind the ball.

Q: When you threw the ball back to the bowler, what type of throw did you use?

A: It depended on the distance to the bowler. For short distances an underhand toss worked well, but for longer distances an overarm throw was better.

PRACTICE TASK 1

Setup   Partners use underarm throws to pass the ball high into the air. The receiver moves into position, catches the ball (with either thumbs or little fingers together), and brings it into his body. To extend the practice, have partners throw the ball overhand with a flatter trajectory.

Goal   Catch seven consecutive throws.

Cues   Catching:

- Watch the ball and move into position.
- Form a cup with your hands.
- Relax your arms, elbows away from body, and draw the ball into your body.

PRACTICE TASK 2

Setup   Players are in pairs. Partner 1 rolls the ball underhand to partner 2, who is already moving toward the ball. Partner 2 fields the ball and returns it with a throw. Partner 1 uses an overarm throw to bounce the ball just in front of partner 2. Partner 2 uses a long-barrier technique to safely field the bouncing ball.

Goal   Field and return seven consecutive balls.

Cues   Long barrier:

- Move in line with the ball and field it with little fingers touching and hands pointing down.
- Position the kneeling leg inside the heel of the other leg (to form a sideways barrier at a right angle to the oncoming ball).
- Make the kneeling leg the one opposite your throwing arm (to allow a quick step forward and the throw return in one movement).

GAME 2

Setup   Nonstop cricket

Goal   Fielders will field the ball cleanly and return it to the bowler with speed.

Conditions
- Every catch or fielding assist back to the bowler that results in a batter being out counts as 1 point.
- The player with the most points (not runs) wins.

LESSON 2

Tactical Problems   Restricting run scoring and getting the batter out

Lesson Focus   Bowling straight from a stationary position

Objectives
- Make the ball pitch in line with the wicket or outside the off- (outside) stump.
- Understand the bowling line and length.
- Learn the basic bowling action.

GAME 1

Setup   Nonstop cricket (six to eight players)

Goal   Keep the batter from scoring in the target area through accurate bowling.

Conditions
- The batter scores four runs and does not have to run around the cone to score if she hits the ball between the two cones on the leg side (figure 20.2).
- Only one fielder may stand between the cones.
- If the batter hits the ball anywhere other than between the two cones, she still has to run to score (as in the previous game of nonstop cricket).

Questions

Q: What type of pitch is easy for a batter to hit between the cones?

A: A pitch that arrives at a comfortable height (between thigh and abdomen), either on the fly or after bouncing in imaginary zones 4, 5, or 6 (figure 20.2).

Q: What type of shot will the batter play to this kind of ball?

A: He will pull the ball with a softball-style (horizontal) swing.

Q: What type of pitch is harder for the batter to hit between the cones?

A: A pitch that bounces within 1 to 3 yards of the batter and that comes at a low height (zones 1 and 3 in figure 20.2).

Q: Where does this ball land in relation to the batter and the wicket?

A: The side opposite the batter's legs (the off-side; figure 20.2).

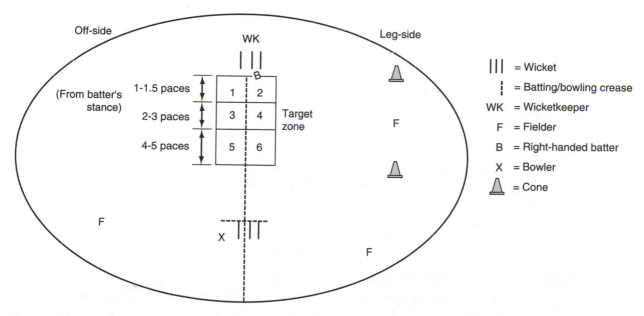

Figure 20.2 Bowling target zones.

Q: So, in this game, what has the bowler learned?

A: To pitch the ball into zones 1 and 3, close to the batter and in line with or outside the batter's off- (outside) stump (wicket) to prevent the ball from being hit (pulled) between the cones. This would be a good line and length.

Notes

- In cricket, three stumps constitute a wicket: the off- (outside), middle, and leg (closest to the batter's legs) stumps (figure 20.2).
- For a left-handed batter, all of the concepts and terms are reversed.
- The positions of the cones in the game also need to be reversed for a left-handed batter.

Now that the bowler knows where to make the ball land, she has to learn the technique of bowling because underarm tossing or throwing is not allowed in cricket.

PRACTICE TASK

Setup   Students are grouped in pairs standing about 12 to 15 yards apart. Each bowler uses an overarm bowling action (keeping the arm straight) to bounce the ball one or two paces in front of the partner. The partner gathers the ball and then bowls the ball back. A set of wickets or a cone can be used to focus the bowler's aim.

Goal   Make the ball land in target zones 1 or 3.

Variation   A batter can be added to play shadow strokes only, deliberately missing the ball and allowing it to hit the wicket or reach the wicketkeeper. (The player who is not bowling can act as wicketkeeper). Ground targets (plastic strips or even bandanas) can also be placed in front of the batter's wicket to represent the target (zones 1 and 3) for the bowler. A triad practice can now include a batter, bowler, and wicketkeeper. Each batter receives six balls (an over) before rotating to the next position. See figure 20.3.

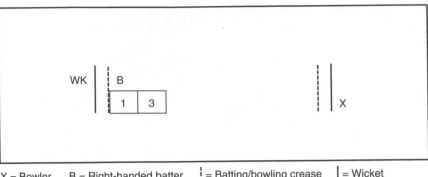

X = Bowler   B = Right-handed batter   ┊ = Batting/bowling crease   │ = Wicket

WK = Wicketkeeper

Figure 20.3   Cricket triad.

Cues

- Bowling:
  - Grip the ball with your fingers (middle and index fingers form a V on the top; the thumb and third finger are underneath).
  - Turn sideways with your arm holding the ball at your side.
  - Make a cross with your arms.
  - Raise your front knee and nonbowling arm as high as possible and look at the wicket (batter) behind your nonbowling arm.
  - Swing your nonbowling arm down past your hip while your bowling arm remains straight, traveling past your head and releasing the ball.
  - Let your bowling arm follow across your body as you step forward.
- Remember:
  - Lift your front leg, bending your knee.
  - Swing your nonbowling arm down behind your body and your bowling arm past your head (like a windmill).
  - Stay sideways as long as possible.
  - The action of the bowling arm is analogous to drawing a number 6.

GAME 2

Setup   Repeat nonstop cricket with bowlers now focusing on the line (accuracy) and length (position of bounce) of each delivery. They should use a cricket bowling action. Force the batter to hit across the line of the ball to score between the cones.

Conditions

- Each time a batter is out (caught or bowled), the bowler earns a wicket.
- The bowler with the most wickets wins the game.

LESSON 3
Secondary Level I

Tactical Problem   Defending the wicket (moving forward using the front foot)

Lesson Focus   Defending a good length ball and pushing to space

Objectives

- Block the ball by coming forward to meet the bounce.
- Practice taking guard and using the correct grip, stance, and backlift.
- Learn when to leave a good ball.

GAME 1

Setup   Students play tip and run. The bowler bowls the ball, aiming at zone 3. After successfully contacting the ball, the batter runs from the batting crease to the bowling crease (figure 20.4).

The ball can be hit anywhere inside the modified boundary (15-yard radius around the batting strip, which is the area between the two wickets). A run is scored when the batter touches the bat over the bowling crease. The batter then walks back to the batting crease, and the bowler and fielders prepare for the same batter's next at bat. The batter can be run out only at the end to which he runs. A run-out is made when the ball is thrown to the bowler and the bowler hits the wicket where she is standing with the ball before the batter gets past the bowling crease. A direct hit by a fielder throwing at the bowler's wicket also runs out the batter. Additionally, the batter can be out if he is bowled (he lets the bowler's pitch hit the wicket) or if a fielder catches the ball on the fly. Each batter faces four to six deliveries (or depending on time, bats until he is out). Each time a batter is out (or his four to six ball innings are over), a different bowler bowls at the new batter. When all players have batted, the player with the most runs wins.

Condition   If the ball rolls outside the 15-yard inner boundary, the run is discounted.

Questions

Q: When you were batting, what were you trying to do?

A: Make contact with the ball and send it to a space inside the inner boundary.

Q: What actions help you to do this?

A: Looking to see where the fielders are positioned before each delivery and then pushing the ball into gaps in the field.

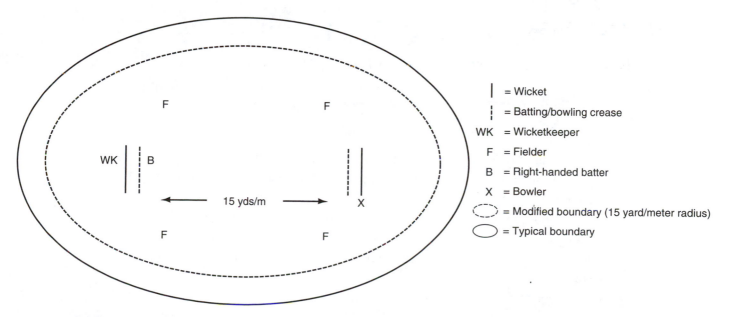

Figure 20.4   Tip and run.

Q: Where do you stand in relation to the wicket?

A: Take guard by lining up with the middle wicket or stump and by marking the batting crease with the bat (or chalk if the ground is hard) so you know where to stand each time.

Q: How far from the wicket do you stand?

A: Straddle the batting crease so you can pick up the bat without hitting the wicket behind you during the backlift (which results in the batter being out).

Q: When the bowler made the ball pitch in zones 1 and 3 and it was likely to hit the wicket, what kind of swing did you use?

A: A vertical swing with a straight bat.

Q: Why did you use this type of swing?

A: Less chance of missing the ball.

Q: When do you pick up the bat?

A: Just as the bowler lifts her front arm.

Q: If the ball lands about two paces in front of you and will hit the wicket if you miss it, what do you do to make sure you contact the ball?

A: Step toward the ball with the front foot.

Q: If the ball is likely to miss the outside (off) wicket, what can you do?

A: Allow it to pass without attempting a shot.

Q: Why would you want to do this?

A: To prevent a slight deflection or edge to the wicketkeeper that would result in an out (caught behind).

Q: By letting the ball pass, aren't you giving up a scoring opportunity?

A: Yes, but the ball is often harder to track when you begin to bat than when you have been batting for a while so you have a chance of hitting the edge, rather than the middle, of the bat.

PRACTICE TASK 1

Setup   Divide the class into pairs, with one bat per pair.

Goal   Help your partner with grip, batting stance, backlift, and taking guard in front of a wicket.

Cues
- Grip:
  - Keep your hands close together toward the top of the handle.
  - Form Vs with the thumb and index finger on each hand that are in line along the handle.
- Stance:
  - Keep your feet shoulder-width apart and parallel with the crease.
  - Flex your knees slightly.
  - Keep your eyes level and watch the bowler's hand at delivery.
- Backlift:
  - Point your front shoulder and elbow to the bowler.
  - Swing the bat straight back above the off-stump with the face of the bat open.
  - Keep your elbows clear of your body.

PRACTICE TASK 2

Setup The practice for the game push in the box includes a batter, bowler, fielder, and wicketkeeper. Each batter receives one over before rotating to the next position. The bowler attempts to deliver the ball into zones 1 and 3. If the bowler has difficulty with accuracy, the bowler can use an underhand toss or dart throw at a closer distance (figure 20.5).

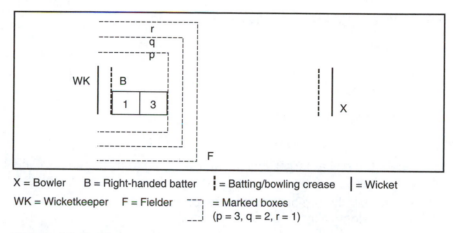

X = Bowler   B = Right-handed batter   ⋮ = Batting/bowling crease   ⎮ = Wicket

WK = Wicketkeeper   F = Fielder   ⌐ ¬ = Marked boxes
                                          ⌙ _ ⌙   (p = 3, q = 2, r = 1)

Figure 20.5 Push in the box.

Goal As the batter, attempt to play the ball with a vertical, straight bat and soft hands.

Conditions

- The batter scores three runs if the ball remains inside box p, two runs if it remains inside box q, and one run if it remains inside box r.
- The batter also scores one run for leaving a ball that is wide of her off-stump.
- If the batter is out, caught, or bowled, four runs are deducted from her score.
- The batter with the most runs wins.

Cues Forward defense stroke:

- Move your head in line with the ball.
- Step with the foot nearer the bowler and bend the same knee.
- Angle the bat vertically down alongside your knee.
- Let the ball hit the bat, and do not follow through.
- Control the bat with the top hand, gripping the bat with the thumb and the first two fingers of the bottom hand.

GAME 2

Setup Tip and run

Goals

- Stay in and avoid getting out (for a greater opportunity to win the game).
- Push the ball to a space inside the inner boundary.

Conditions

- If the ball rolls outside the 15-yard inner boundary, the run is discounted.
- Players score one run for leaving a ball that passes outside the off-stump.
- The player with the most runs wins.
- If the batter is out before the end of his allotted over (six balls), then he is out in this game—no second chances.

LESSON 4

Tactical Problem   Knowing when to attack the ball by moving forward

Lesson Focus   Attacking the half volley or low full toss on the front foot

Objective   Look for space and drive the ball along the ground.

GAME 1

Setup   Second-chance cricket

Goal   Hit the ball into space in the sector.

Conditions

- The bowler bowls the ball at target zones 1 and 2 (trying to make the ball land 1 to 1 1/2 steps from the batter's stance and in line with the wicket or outside the off-stump).
- The batter attempts to hit the ball into the sector (figure 20.6), the only area in which she can score (and so the fielders align to protect this area).
- The batter scores a run each time she hits the ball and runs from the batting crease to the bowling crease.
- The batter scores 4 points and does not have to run if she hits the ball through the field to the outer boundary of the sector.
- The batter can be out by being bowled, caught, or run out at the bowler's wicket.
- Each time a batter is out (or her allotted number of deliveries finishes), a different bowler has a turn to bowl at the new batter.
- Players rotate through the roles of batter, bowler, fielder, and wicketkeeper.
- The player with the most runs after all players have batted wins.

Variation   If the ball does not land in zones 1 and 2 or the batter misses the ball (as long as it does not hit the wicket), he gets a second chance and can hit the ball off a low tee (3-4 in., or 7.6-10 cm). See figure 20.6.

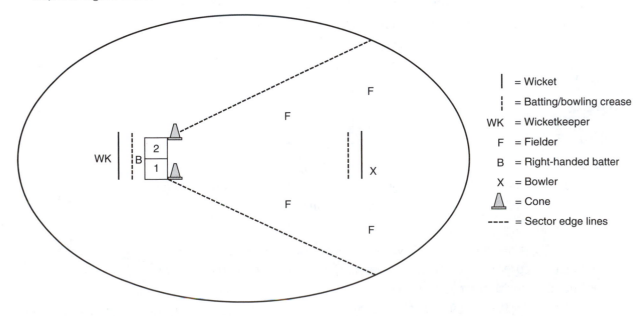

Figure 20.6   Second-chance cricket.

Questions

Q: What type of ball did you hit into the sector?

A: A ball that bounced about a pace away from my batting stance or that could be hit on the fly.

Q: To hit the ball, what did you do with your feet?

A: Stepped the front foot toward where the ball pitched.

Q: What batting techniques helped you hit the ball effectively?

A: Swinging the bat vertically and following straight through.

Q: If the ball pitched in line with or just outside your off-stump (wicket), where did your stroke finish?

A: Pointing where the hit went on the off-side of the wicket.

Q: If the ball pitched on your leg stump, where did your stroke finish?

A: Pointing where the hit went on the leg side of the wicket.

Q: What might cause you to miss the ball?

A: Not watching the ball, swinging too hard, or lifting my head.

Q: When did you lob the ball into the air, giving a fielder an easy catch?

A: When the ball pitched farther away than one big step and bounced up a little higher on the bat.

Q: What stroke could you have played to that ball instead?

A: A forward defensive stroke because the ball was a good-length ball, or a drive by hitting the ball a little harder to try and score runs.

Q: Is it always good to hit the ball along the ground?

A: Generally, yes, but sometimes hitting the ball into the air gets the ball over the fielders and can reach the sector boundary so more runs are scored. The risk of hitting into the air is that the ball can get caught.

PRACTICE TASK

Setup

Drive cricket   The bowler tosses the ball to the batter so that it bounces in zone 1 (figure 20.7). The ball could also be hit off a low tee placed in that zone if the batter is having difficulty hitting. The batter attempts to drive the ball between the cones where the fielders are positioned. If the ball goes past the cones, a run is scored. The batter can double his score by running to the crease where the bowler stands, touching his bat over the bowling crease, and returning to the batter's wicket (this simulates the two runs that would be earned in the real game). Fielders attempt to run out the batter by throwing the ball to the wicketkeeper before the batter returns. The batter decides whether to risk the additional run, and he loses all runs on the shot if he is out. Each batter receives six deliveries and attempts to score as many runs as possible. If a fielder catches a fly ball from the batter, no runs are scored on that shot.

Goals

- Use the off-drive to hit a ball on the off-side.
- Hit the ball into the air or attempt a second run to double your score.

Variation   The bowler tosses the ball into target zone 2 (figure 20.2) and cones are set up on the leg side, or on-side, for an on-drive.

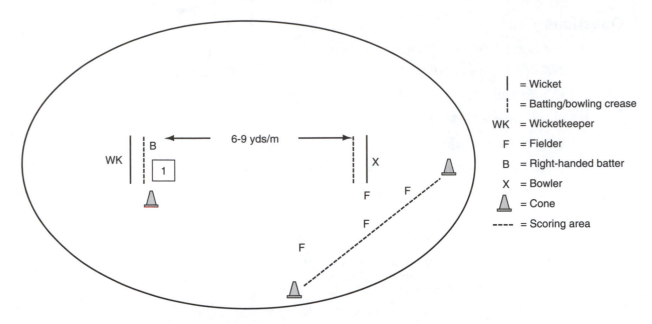

Figure 20.7 Drive cricket (off-drive).

Cues

- Watch the ball.
- Step your front foot toward the ball.
- Use a straight backlift.

- Swing the bat vertically.
- Follow through in the direction of the hit.

GAME 2

Setup   Second-chance cricket

Goal   Use off- and on-drives to score runs.

Conditions

- The batter elects to run or not run (assesses the risk on each shot).
- The second-chance condition may be removed.

LESSON 5

Tactical Problem   Making the batter play

Lesson Focus   Bowling line and length and moving the ball away from the batter

Objectives

- Attack the off-stump.
- Add a run-up to the bowling action.

- Look for the outside edge of the bat.

GAME 1

Setup   Off-side cricket

Goal   As the bowler, aim at zone 3 around the batter's off-stump.

Conditions

- The batter attempts to hit the ball into the off-side (figure 20.8).
- The batter can score only in the off-side, and so fielders protect this area while also helping the bowler get the batter out.
- A ball hit on the leg side of the wicket (figure 20.8) is dead and no runs can be scored.
- Other conditions are similar to those of second-chance cricket, but if the batter misses the ball, there is no second chance in this game.

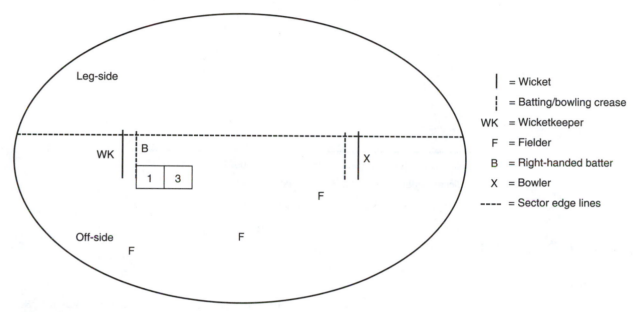

Figure 20.8 Off-side cricket.

Questions

Q: When you are bowling in this game, what are you trying to do?

A: Bowl the batter out or have her shot get caught in the field.

Q: What type of shot will the batter try to play to a ball that lands in zone 1?

A: If the ball lands about a pace in front of the batter's feet, the drive is likely, but if the ball lands farther away, the batter may play a forward defensive stroke.

Q: Why can't the batter let the ball pass by?

A: It's too close to judge whether the ball will hit the wicket, so the batter has to play a shot.

Q: What else can happen here if the batter tries to hit at a ball that is close to but outside the line of the wickets?

A: The ball can be deflected off the outside edge of the bat to the wicketkeeper.

Q: So, is bowling into zone 3 (figure 20.2) and in line with the off-stump an effective place to bowl the ball?

A: Yes, it is a good line and length.

Q: How can you make it even harder for the batter to make good contact with the ball?

A: By bowling a little faster and also by making the ball deviate away from the batter.

Q: What else could you do to tempt the batter into driving the ball on the off-side?

A: Show the batter a big gap in the field by moving a fielder out of the way.

Q: Where could you place the fielder when the ball deflects off the edge?

A: Close to the wicketkeeper in case the ball deflects wide of the wicketkeeper. (The fielder is called a slip; figure 20.9.)

Q: Is there any other time when the batter has difficulty hitting the ball?

A: When the ball lands in line with his toes. (This bowling delivery is called a Yorker.)

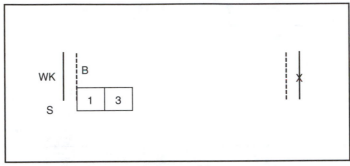

X = Bowler   B = Right-handed batter   ┆ = Batting/bowling crease

WK = Wicketkeeper   S = Slip fielder | = Wicket

Figure 20.9   Looking for the edge.

PRACTICE TASK 1

Setup

- Students line up on the edge of the instructional area and practice running up and bowling a ball that bounces once (in target zone 3).
- Review the overarm bowling position (see cues for lesson 2).
- Students lift the arm they bowl with and stamp the opposite foot (the one they will jump off).
- Students follow this sequence (critical features): Run, jump off the foot opposite the bowling arm, throw both arms in the air, and turn so that the landing foot is perpendicular to the direction of travel (finishing in the overarm bowling position, as practiced in lesson 2).
- Bowlers bowl an imaginary ball.

Goal

- Make four out of six pitches land in target zone 1.
- Work on increasing the delivery speed.

Cues   Bowling from a run-up:

- Run, jump, and land in the overarm bowling position.
- Look where you want the ball to pitch.
- Bowl an imaginary ball by drawing a number 6 with your bowling arm.

PRACTICE TASK 2

Setup   Looking for the edge requires a bowler, batter, wicketkeeper, and slip (figure 20.9).

The bowler aims at target zone 3 around the batter's off-stump. The bowler's front foot must be on or behind the batting crease at the bowler's end as she releases the ball in the bowling action. If the foot is not properly aligned, the bowl is a no-ball and the batter can hit the ball but can only be run out (not caught or bowled). The batter also releases another bowl as a penalty for the bowler's mistake.

Goals

- Bowl the batter out or have the batter caught behind the wicket.
- Bowl a leg cutter (move the ball away from the right-handed batter after it hits the ground).

Conditions

- The batter attempts to hit the ball into the off-side but bats with a softball bat or cricket bat (playing with the edge of the bat facing the bowler).
- Playing with the edge of the bat facing the bowler should facilitate a lot of small deflections resulting in catches to the wicketkeeper and slip.
- Each batter receives six deliveries, and then players rotate.

Cues

- Make sure the seam of the ball is vertical or pointed in the direction of the slip.
- Run your middle finger along the seam, with your index finger placed 1/2 inch (1.3 cm) away.
- Rest the ball between your thumb and third finger.
- As you release the ball, work your index and middle fingers down the inside of the ball (as a right-handed bowler views it when starting with it above the right shoulder) so that your thumb passes under the ball, generating a turn on the ball.

GAME 2

Setup

Off-side cricket   The batter can be out by being bowled, caught, or run out at the bowler's wicket. Each time a batter is out (or her allotted number of deliveries finishes), a different bowler has a turn to bowl at the new batter.

Goal   As the bowler, use pace, good line and length, and the leg cutter to tempt the batter and make the batter play.

Conditions

- The bowler decides whether to attack the batter with one or two slips or place fielders in defensive (run-saving positions) as in figure 20.8.
- The bowler can also place a fielder very deep to save four runs and therefore virtually give the batter one run for a good drive.
- The bowler can change the positions of the fielders anytime during a batter's innings.
- The batter receives another delivery and one run for a no-ball or can score off the no-ball but not be out unless it's by a run-out.

LESSON 6

Tactical Problem   Defending space behind the wicket

Lesson Focus   Wicketkeeper's role

Objectives

- Use the basic wicketkeeper stance and position.
- Learn takes and returns.
- Communicate with the field.

GAME 1

Setup

Stoolball (Know the Game: Indoor Cricket, 1989)   The rules and organization are similar to the previous modified games, with two differences. The ball can be hit anywhere in the field, and there are always two batters (striker and nonstriker) at the respective wickets.

Conditions

- The nonstriker is located at the wicket next to the bowler (figure 20.10).
- After the batter hits the ball, one run is scored when both batters cross and get to the creases or the opposite wickets (i.e., switch places).
- The ways a batter can be out remain the same, but now a run-out can occur at either crease (the wicketkeeper's or bowler's end).
- Only one batter can be out at a time—the one closest to the wicket hit by the fielding team.
- Each batting pair faces 12 pitches (two overs).
- After every six pitches (one over), a different bowler bowls from the wicket at the other end.
- Bowlers aim for zone 3 (they now have a run-up), but the ball often strays off line as bowlers try to bowl faster, making it harder for the wicketkeeper to collect a ball missed by the batter.

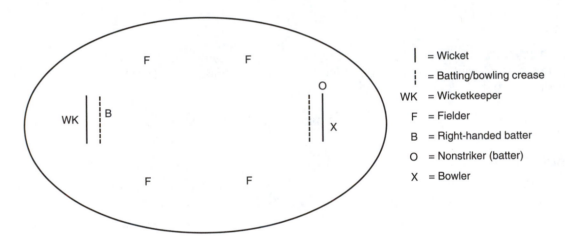

| = Wicket
┆ = Batting/bowling crease
WK = Wicketkeeper
F = Fielder
B = Right-handed batter
O = Nonstriker (batter)
X = Bowler

Figure 20.10   Stoolball.

Questions

Q: When the batter hits the ball into the field, what does the wicketkeeper do?

A: If he is standing back for a faster bowler, he runs to the wicket and stands next to it on the opposite side from where the ball was hit. He lines up with the ball and waits for the fielder's throw to arrive just above the wicket.

Q: If there is the chance the batter will not reach the crease before the throw, what does the wicketkeeper do?

A: Catches the ball and, keeping it in the hands (gloves), touches the ball to (breaks) the wicket.

Q: Anything else?

A: The wicketkeeper appeals, "How's that?" to the umpire standing square of the wicket on the leg side (square leg), and the umpire signals whether the batter is out.

Q: If the bowler is aiming for zone 3, where does the wicketkeeper stand?

A: In line with zone 3 so that if the batter misses the ball or lets it pass, the wicketkeeper can field it.

Q: How far away from the wicket should the wicketkeeper stand?

A: It depends on the speed of the bowler. If the bowler is fast, the wicketkeeper may have trouble reacting to the ball if she stands close to the wicket.

Q: What else could happen that would cause the wicketkeeper a problem?

A: The bowler might bowl the ball into zones 2, 4, or 6 (leg side) (figure 20.2). If the bowler were bowling fast, the wicketkeeper would have to move from a position in line with zone 1 to a position in line with zone 2, and her view would be obstructed by the batter.

Q: Why is this problematic?

A: If the ball gets past the wicketkeeper, even though the batter didn't hit it, she can run (and score a bye), or worse, the ball can go all the way to the boundary and the batters could score four runs (four byes).

Q: So, for a faster bowler, the wicketkeeper stands farther from the wicket, but for a slower bowler, the wicketkeeper stands closer?

A: Yes.

Q: How close should the wicketkeeper stand?

A: Close enough so that when the ball comes through to the wicketkeeper, it has bounced only once. That way, if the batter touches the ball, the wicketkeeper can catch the batter out (the batter is caught behind).

Q: What height is comfortable for catching the ball?

A: Between the knee and waist as the ball begins to drop after having bounced once before reaching the batter.

PRACTICE TASK

Setup

Looking for the edge This task requires a bowler, batter, wicketkeeper, and slip (figure 20.9). The bowler bowls to the batter, varying the line and length between imaginary zones (1 to 3 off side and 2 to 4 leg side).

Goal As the wicketkeeper, take five of six bowling deliveries cleanly (assuming the batter does not make good contact).

Conditions

- The batter uses a softball bat or cricket bat (with the edge of the bat facing the bowler) to generate lots of small deflections and near misses that result in catches to the wicketkeeper.
- Each batter receives six deliveries before players rotate through the other defensive positions.

Cues

Wicketkeeping

- Stand with your feet shoulder-width apart, your weight on the balls of your feet, your knees bent, your hands (gloves) touching the ground, your little fingers together, and your palms open.
- Raise your hands with the ball after it bounces (depending on the height and direction of the bounce, the hands will point to the ground, sky, or side).
- For fast bowlers, slide sideways to take the ball while it is level with your inside hip.

- For slow bowlers, keep your eyes over your hands and slide your feet across the crease in a straight line, with your weight on the foot nearest the wicket, to allow the ball to be brought to wicket for a potential stumping (similar to a run-out in which the batter leaves the batting crease when attempting to hit the ball but misses the ball).
- Watch the ball, not the bat.
- Let the ball come from the bowler—avoid snatching it.

GAME 2

Setup

Stoolball   The player who takes the most catches and is involved in the most run-outs when playing wicketkeeper wins the game.

Condition   Fielders use the wicketkeeper only as the point of return for the throw.

Questions

Q: *Why do fielders usually throw to the wicketkeeper in the real game?*

A: *The wicketkeeper is an expert fielder and has not just bowled a ball like the bowler (who then has to recover to wicket). In the real game the wicketkeeper is the only fielder permitted to wear protective gloves because of the frequency with which she handles the ball.*

Q: *When the ball is hit into the field, what else does the wicketkeeper do once she is in position to receive the throw?*

A: *Tells the fielders if they have time to field the ball or if they should return the ball very quickly to execute a run-out. Usually the wicketkeeper will say, "Time," or "Hit them," referring to her gloves.*

LEVEL II

At level II players learn the importance of using effective defense (ground fielding, catching, field placements) to restrict scoring and get batters out. Bowlers gain a greater understanding of using variations in their deliveries (variations in movement off the pitch, speed, bounce, and angle of delivery) to impair a batter's decisions and to limit the batter's scoring opportunities. Batters learn to judge the line and length of a delivery and to decide whether to move forward or backward to play shots. At this level, lessons emphasize offensive and defensive strokes on the back foot in response to specific variations in bowling deliveries. Batters also learn to communicate when running between the wickets.

In cricket, the batter does not have to run upon contact with the ball (see level II, lesson 8). This condition enables the batter to play shots to defend the stumps rather than to score runs. It also necessitates communication between batters to ensure that they both know whether or not to run.

Batters must learn to judge the line and length of a delivery so they will know how to hit the ball.

Tactical Problem   Running out the batter

Lesson Focus   Ground fielding, deciding where to throw

Objectives

- Move in.
- Pick up and throw.
- Back up the fielder or throw.

GAME 1

Setup   Stoolball

Goal   As a fielder, solve teacher-created scenarios to get the batter out with a run out.

Conditions

- Batters must run upon making contact with the ball.
- Fielders are all close enough to prevent the batters running a single (they're not deep enough in the field to allow a single run).

Questions

Q: When the batter hits the ball into the field and it is not a catch, what do you do?

A: Run the batter out or prevent or restrict scoring.

Q: How do you anticipate where the ball will go?

A: Watch the batter's footwork, backlift, and bat angle to see what type of shot is likely.

Q: What do you do to be quick off the mark?

A: Walk toward the batter as the bowler runs up to bowl, taking short steps and preparing to move in any direction.

Q: Where do you want to return the ball?

A: Usually to the wicketkeeper, but it depends on the position and speed of the batters, the time available to pick up and throw, and the distance to the respective wickets.

Q: What type of throw do you use?

A: It depends on the distance to the wickets—for short distances, an underhand throw; for longer distances, an overarm throw.

PRACTICE TASK 1

Setup   Run-out cricket (figure 20.11)

Goal   As a fielder, run out the batters.

Conditions

- Batters do not hit the ball but avoid being run out.
- The wicketkeeper rolls the ball into the field and calls the name of one of the fielders in that half of the field.

Cricket

- Once the ball is released, both batters run.
- The fielder (F3 at cover point in figure 20.11) attempts a quick pickup and throw to either the wicketkeeper or the bowler in an attempt to run out one of the batters.
- The other fielder (F4 at extra cover) covers her teammate in case of a misfield.
- The other two fielders (F1 at square leg and F2 at midwicket) back up the wicketkeeper and bowler, respectively, in case the ball is overthrown.
- If the ball rolls over the boundary because of a fielder's throw, it results in the one run the batters score plus an additional four runs.
- Each pair of batters begins with six runs and receives six rolls.
- If one of the batters is run out, the batters lose one run from their total.
- If both batters make their ground (get to their respective ends), they score one run.
- The pair with the most runs wins the game.

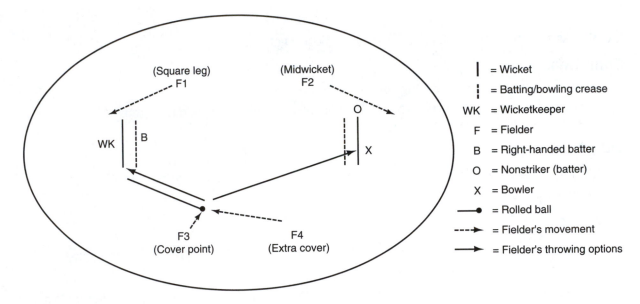

Figure 20.11   Run-out cricket.

Variation   The batter can hit the ball from a tee and call a fielder's name rather than have the wicketkeeper roll the ball.

Cues

- Interception:
  - Move quickly into line and attack the ball.
  - Bend your knees slightly and turn sideways as the ball approaches.
  - Extend your hands to meet ball.
  - Keep your head down and watch the ball roll into your hands.
  - Field the ball in line with your foot on your throwing side, and step with your other foot (two-handed pickup).
  - Use an underarm throw (one-handed pickup).
  - As you approach, point both feet in the direction of the target.
  - Pick up the ball along your foot on your throwing side, step on your other foot, and release.
  - Make sure your arm follows through to the target.

- Overarm throw:
  - Extend your throwing arm behind your body with wrist cocked and arm slightly bent.
  - Step to the target with your lead foot and turn your hips, transferring your body weight.
  - The elbow of your throwing arm comes through first, and your arm finishes on the other side of your body.

PRACTICE TASK 2

Setup   Run-out cricket

Goal   Fielders run out the batters.

Conditions

- Conditions are the same as in run-out cricket except that fielders are positioned on the boundary (figure 20.12).
- Batters must attempt to score two runs (finishing back at their initial positions as striker and nonstriker).
- Fielders back up and cover throws as in practice task 1.

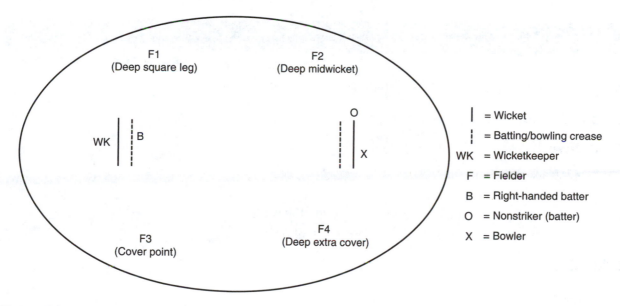

Figure 20.12   Fielders save boundaries.

GAME 2

Setup   Stoolball

Goal   As a fielder, get the batter out in various run-out scenarios.

Conditions

- Batters must run on making contact with the ball.
- The bowler decides which fielders will save a single run and which fielders will be positioned deep on the boundary to prevent four runs (figure 20.13).

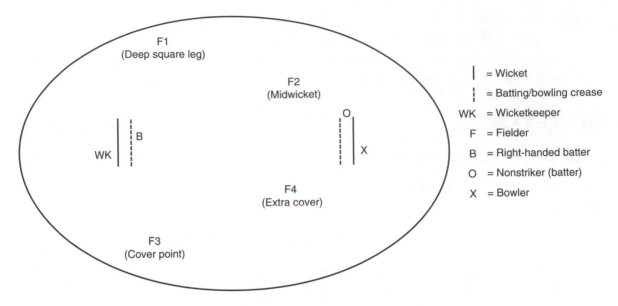

Figure 20.13   The bowler sets the field.

LESSON 8

Tactical Problem   Making the batter play

Lesson Focus   Bowling line and length and moving the ball into the batter

Objectives

- Attack the off-stump.
- Bowl an off-cutter.
- Vary the angle of delivery (over and around the wicket).
- Achieve and understand a leg before wicket (LBW).

GAME 1

Setup

- Pairs cricket
- Assuming that there are four pairs of players (figure 20.14):
    - Pair 1 bats first.
    - Pair 2 fields on the leg side.
    - Pair 3 fields on the off-side.
    - Pair 4 includes the bowler and wicketkeeper (who change roles after one over or six bowls).

Each new over starts from the opposite end wicket from the previous over. The bowler counts the number of balls she has bowled and rotates at the end of her over. If the ball is not delivered so that the batter can play it from a normal batting stance (in his crease), a run is added to the batting pair's total (called a wide) and another ball has to be bowled in that over. The batting players announce the number of runs they scored in their two overs: 10 runs scored plus 2 outs (–6) equals 4 runs total. When all pairs have batted, the pair with the most runs wins.

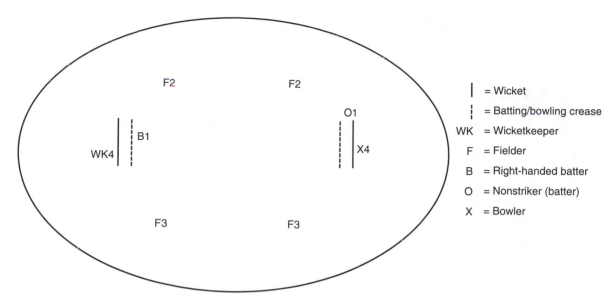

Figure 20.14 Pairs cricket.

Conditions

- Each batting pair faces 12 pitches (two overs).
- Batters score runs as in stoolball.
- Batters decide whether to run based on the chance of being run out.
- When the ball crosses the boundary, four runs are scored and the batters do not have to run.
- When a batter is out (caught, bowled, or run out), three runs are deducted from the batting pair's score.
- Every time there is an out, the batters change ends.
- At the end of two overs, each pair rotates to its next activity.

Questions

Q: What type of shot does the batter try to play to a ball that lands in zone 1?

A: If the ball lands about one pace in front of her feet, the drive is likely, but if it lands a little farther away, she may play a forward defensive stroke.

Q: So, bowling to zone 3 in line with or just outside the batter's off-stump is an effective place to bowl the ball?

A: Yes, it is a good line and length. But the batter can now predict what the ball will do when it hits the ground.

Q: What could make it harder for the batter to make good contact with the ball?

A: Bowling the ball a little faster or slower and making the ball deviate back toward the right-handed batter makes it dangerous for the batter to drive the ball.

Q: Why is doing this problematic for the batter?

A: The ball could hit his wicket by traveling between the batter's front leg and the bat, or the ball could hit the batter on the leg and he could be out because of leg before wicket (LBW).

Q: What does LBW mean?

A: If the batter misses the ball with the bat and the ball hits his body when it would have (in the opinion of the umpire at the bowler's end) hit the batter's wicket, the batter is out (LBW). The bowler also has to appeal ("How's that?") to the umpire.

Q: What else can cause the batter a problem?

A: If the ball bounces higher than expected or quickly comes back into the batter after pitching and hits her bat and body, it can gently lob into the air for a catch on the leg side.

PRACTICE TASK 1

Setup This task calls for a bowler, batter, wicketkeeper, short leg, and slip (figure 20.15).

Goal Bowl for an edge or LBW.

Conditions
- The bowler aims at zone 1 in line with the batter's off-stump. The bowler can bowl "around" or "over" the wicket.
- The batter attempts to play the ball on the front foot but bats with a softball bat or cricket bat (with the edge of the bat facing the bowler) to facilitate a lot of wickets for the bowler, or catches at short leg or slip (figure 20.15).
- Each batter receives six deliveries before players rotate positions.

Cues Off-cutter (moving the ball into the right-handed batter after it hits the ground):
- Make sure the seam of the ball is vertical or pointed in the direction of the short leg.
- Run your index finger along the seam with the middle finger half an inch away.
- Keep your thumb underneath the ball on the seam and rest the ball on your third finger.
- When you release the ball, work your index and middle fingers down the outside of the ball (as a right-handed bowler views it when it is held above the right shoulder) so that your thumb passes over the top of the ball, generating turn on the ball.

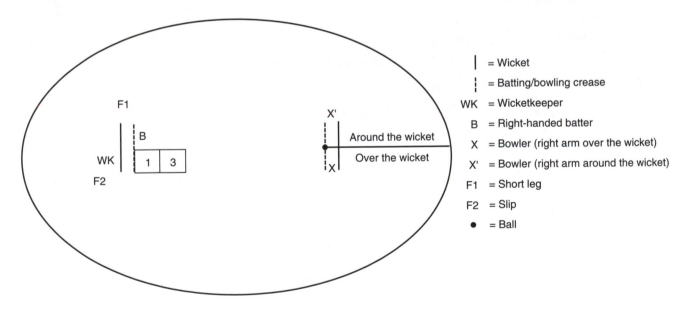

Figure 20.15 Off-cutter attack.

PRACTICE TASK 2

Setup Students repeat practice task 1 with the bowler bowling from where the nonstriker normally stands (on the right of the wicket, or around the wicket).

Goal Bowl a ball that straightens after it bounces.

Conditions

- If the ball does not straighten, it can also find the outside edge of the bat.
- The batter cannot be out LBW to a ball that pitches outside the line of his leg stump.

Note   It is virtually impossible to get an LBW decision by bowling around the wicket because the angle is so difficult for an umpire to judge whether the ball would have really hit the wicket.

Cue   A right-handed bowler (X' in figure 20.15) angles the ball across the right-handed batter and tries to make the ball straighten so that the batter has problems defending the wicket.

GAME 2

Setup   Pairs cricket

Goal   Make the batter play by using change of pace, good line and length, and an off-cutter to tempt the batter.

Conditions

- The bowler decides whether to attack the batter with a leg slip or slip, and whether to place fielders in defensive positions (to save runs).
- The bowler can also decide to attack the batter around the wicket.

LESSON 9

Tactical Problem   Attacking the short-pitched ball (delivery)

Lesson Focus   Moving onto the back foot, looking for space, and playing the ball square of the wicket

Objective   Play the pull shot.

GAME 1

Setup   Pairs cricket

Goal   Move onto the back foot.

Conditions

- Bowlers aim at zones 5 and 6 or farther away from the batter (figure 20.16).
- Bowlers attempt to bowl fast.

Questions

Q: When the ball pitches in zones 5 and 6 or farther away (a long hop), what height does the ball arrive at as you attempt to hit it?

A: Around waist height or higher.

Q: If you step toward this ball, what is likely to happen?

A: It may hit my body rather than the bat.

Q: Where should you first move for this type of delivery?

A: Move backward to hit the ball, which is bouncing high.

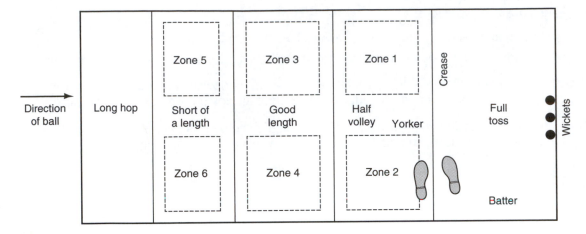

Figure 20.16 Target zones and types of delivery.

PRACTICE TASK

Setup   Hit the gap

Goal   Hit the ball in front of the square on the leg side so that it goes between the target cones to score (figure 20.17).

Conditions

- The bowler makes the ball pitch in zones 5 or 6 or shorter by using a modified overarm throw with minimal arm extension on the backswing.
- The batter receives six balls (one over) and scores four runs every time the ball beats the fielders and passes between the cones (simulating a boundary).
- The batter can be out by being bowled, caught, or LBW.
- If the ball remains inside the scoring arc but does not go past the cones, the batter can score two runs by running to the bowler's crease and returning to the batting crease before the throw is returned to the wicketkeeper.
- The batter elects whether to run and can be run out.
- The player with the most runs wins.

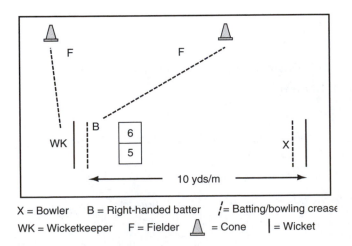

X = Bowler   B = Right-handed batter   ⁞ = Batting/bowling crease
WK = Wicketkeeper   F = Fielder   △ = Cone | = Wicket

Figure 20.17   Hit the gap.

Cues   Pull shot:

- Use a high backlift.
- Keep the head steady.
- Move your back foot back and across toward the batter's off-stump.
- Throw your front foot out to leg side.
- Swing the bat horizontally at full arm's length (chest opens to ball).
- Roll your wrists over the ball on contact.

Variations

- Batters hit the ball from a high tee.
- The bowler tosses the ball on the full so that it arrives at waist height.

GAME 2

Setup   Pairs cricket

Goals

- In pairs, score as many runs as possible.
- As the bowler, make the ball pitch in zones 5 or 6 or shorter.

Conditions

- Batters must hit leg side only; they may not hit the ball on the off-side of the wicket (opposite of the game in figure 20.8).
- If the ball clears the leg-side boundary on a pull shot without bouncing, the batter scores six runs (four runs if the ball bounces before crossing the boundary).
- The pair with the most runs wins.

LESSON 10

Secondary Level II

Tactical Problem   Working the short-pitched delivery

Lesson Focus   Running between the wickets and moving onto the back foot

Objectives   Execute a backward defensive stroke and a back-foot leg glance.

GAME 1

Setup   Pairs cricket

Goal   As the bowler, set the field and make the ball pitch in the front part (closest to the batter) of zones 5 and 6 or the beginning of zones 3 and 4.

Conditions

- The ball can be hit anywhere inside the modified boundary.
- If the ball rolls outside the 16-yard inner boundary, the run is discounted and the batters must return to their original positions (figure 20.18).
- Batters should communicate whether to run a single.
- Bowlers attempt to bowl fast.

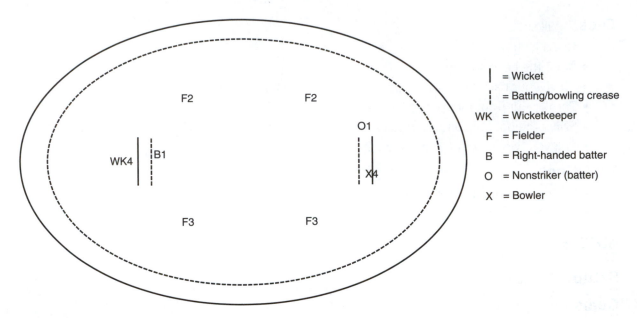

| | = Wicket
|:| = Batting/bowling crease
WK = Wicketkeeper
F = Fielder
B = Right-handed batter
O = Nonstriker (batter)
X = Bowler

Figure 20.18 Pairs cricket with a modified boundary.

Questions

Q: When you were batting, what were you trying to do?

A: Make contact with the ball and send it to a space inside the inner boundary.

Q: What helps you do this?

A: Looking to see where the fielders are positioned before each delivery, and then pushing the ball into gaps in the field.

Q: Who decides when to run?

A: If the ball is hit anywhere in front of the batter's wicket, the batter calls for the run.

Q: What happens when the ball goes behind the wicket?

A: The nonstriker calls for the run because she sees the ball before the batter sees it.

Q: What do you call to indicate your intention to run?

A: "Yes," "No," or "Wait" followed by "Yes" or "No." Nothing else is required.

Q: When you previously played the short-pitched ball using the pull shot, where did the ball bounce?

A: Usually around zones 5 and 6 (short of a length) or even farther away (long hop), and the ball came around waist height or above.

Q: If the ball pitches around the front half of zones 5 and 6 (figure 20.16) or the beginning of zones 3 and 4, what might be a problem with pulling the ball?

A: The ball comes through quickly and may be a little low, and if you miss the ball, it could hit the wicket.

Q: Would you still play the ball with a cross bat?

A: No, a straight bat would provide a better chance of defending the wicket and making good contact with the ball.

Q: If the ball bounces outside your off-stump and is in no danger of hitting the wicket, what else can you do?

A: Allow the ball to pass without playing a stroke.

PRACTICE TASK 1

Setup   Backward defense

Goals

- As the batter, defend the ball on the back foot.
- As the wicketkeeper or fielder, catch the batter out (figure 20.19).

Conditions

- Each batter receives one over before rotating.
- The bowler attempts to pitch the ball into zones 3 and 4 (the part farthest from the batter) from 10 yards away using an overarm throw, making the ball reach the batter off the bounce around thigh height or above.
- The wicketkeeper and the four fielders attempt to catch the batter out.
- No attacking shots can be played by the batter when fielders are close to the bat in front of the wicket (for safety).
- The batter who is out the least wins the practice.

Cues   Backward defense:

- As the ball is thrown, step back toward the wicket with your back foot.
- The front foot follows the back (with the downswing of the bat) and finishes next to the back foot (parallel with the batting crease).
- Keep your front elbow high.
- If you are a right-handed batter, your arms and bat form a P.
- Hold the bat vertically at a slight angle, facing down.
- Let the ball hit the bat and drop down.
- Keep your top hand firm and your bottom hand relaxed on the bat.

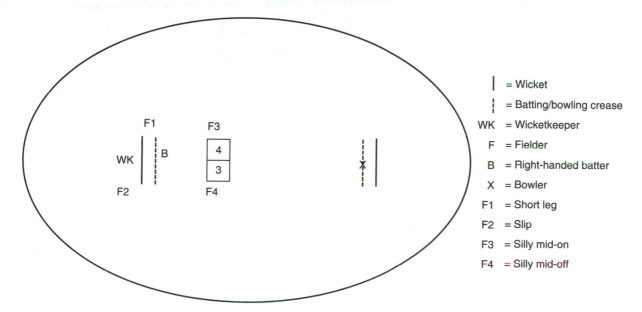

Figure 20.19   Backward defense.

PRACTICE TASK 2

Setup   Back-foot leg glance

Goal   Play a shot to a ball that pitches around the leg stump in zones 4 or 6 by deflecting the ball off the hip toward the fine leg (figure 20.20) using the speed of the bowled ball to generate the power.

Condition   Use the same field set for the backward defense but with the short leg now fielding in a deeper position to save a boundary at the fine leg F1 boundary (shown in figure 20.20).

Cues   Back-foot leg glance:

- Use a similar setup to that for the backward defense.
- Flick the ball off the hip area.
- Angle the bat very slightly toward the fine leg.
- Rotate the wrists after contact to send the ball toward the fine leg.

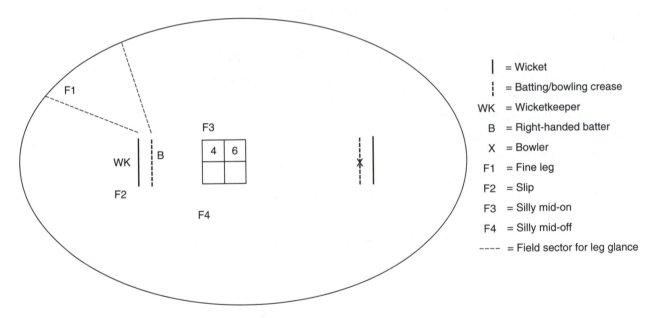

Figure 20.20   Back-foot leg glance.

GAME 2

Setup   Pairs cricket

Goal   As the bowler, set the field and make the ball pitch in the closest part (to the batter) of zones 5 and 6 or the farthest part (from the batter) of zones 3 and 4.

Conditions

- Batters must call for every run.
- The ball can be hit only inside the modified boundary as in game 1 (batters use backward defense) except when the batter uses a back-foot leg glance, in which case the ball can travel in the arc indicated in figure 20.20 and over the outer boundary for four runs.
- The nonstriker should call for any runs in this area.
- The bowler sets the field.

LESSON 11

Tactical Problem   Judging length when batting

Lesson Focus   Moving forward or backward

Objective   Select the appropriate defensive stroke.

GAME 1

Setup   Pairs cricket

Goal   As the bowler, set the field and pitch the ball in any target zone.

Condition   The ball can be hit anywhere.

Questions

Q: When you are batting, what is a major decision regarding your movement at the crease?

A: Deciding whether to move forward to play the ball or to move backward.

Q: If the ball is a half volley (landing in zones 1 and 2), where should you go?

A: Forward to play the ball.

Q: If the ball is short of a length (landing in zones 5 and 6), where should you go?

A: Backward to play the ball.

Q: What about a ball that is a good length (landing in zones 3 and 4)?

A: That's what makes it a good length—you are unsure whether to move forward or backward.

PRACTICE TASK

Setup   Each batter receives two overs before rotating. The bowler delivers the ball to the batter using an overarm throw, varying deliveries to land before or after the bowling decision line (figure 20.21). The batter scores 1 point for each correct decision, playing a vertical (defensive) shot on either the back foot or front foot.

Goal   Decide whether to move forward or backward.

Conditions

- This task calls for a bowler, batter, wicketkeeper, and two fielders (midwicket, extra cover).
- Mark the bowling decision line at the appropriate length (see the dashed line in figure 20.21).
- Mark the batting lines one step behind and one step in front of the batter's crease.
- For any ball that pitches before (shorter than) the dotted line (from the batter's view), the batter steps back past the back-foot line to play the ball.
- For any ball that pitches after the dotted line, the batter steps over the front-foot line to play the ball.

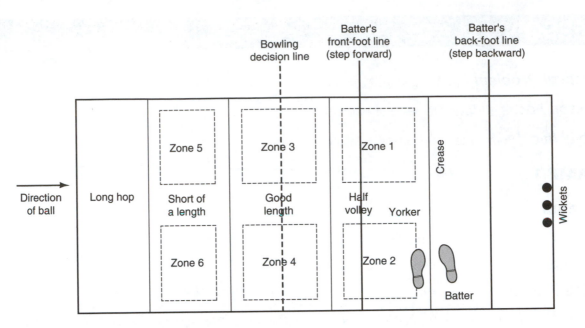

Figure 20.21 Footwork decisions.

GAME 2

Setup   Pairs cricket

Goal   As the bowler, set the field and pitch the ball in any target zone.

Condition   The ball can be hit anywhere.

Questions

> *Q: Unfortunately, the bowling decision line (for the batter) varies from one bowler to the next. Why?*
>
> *A: The speed and subsequent bounce of the ball means that for quicker bowlers the decision line is slightly closer to the batter. The ball bounces higher, so the batter should move onto the back foot. For a slower bowler, the decision line moves slightly away from the batter. The ball tends not to bounce as high, so the batter wants to be on the front foot.*
>
> *Q: So, a ball pitching in the same spot (around zones 3 and 4) could be played on the front foot to a slow bowler and on the back foot to a fast bowler?*
>
> *A: Yes, because the two bowlers are getting a different amount of bounce from the ball hitting the ground.*
>
> *Q: What else can bowlers do to cause problems for the batter?*
>
> *A: They can change the speed of individual deliveries, bowling faster or slower than usual. To make it harder for the batter to time the stroke, the bowler can deliver the ball so that it does not bounce as high as the batter anticipates. The batter could easily play an inappropriate shot to this kind of ball.*

LESSON 12

Tactical Problem   Attacking the batter

Lesson Focus   Working the batter out (making defense offense)

Objectives

- Place the fielders close to the wicket.
- Execute close catching.
- Make correct umpiring decisions and use correct signals.

GAME 1

Setup

Kwik cricket Students are on two teams of six players each (batting and fielding). The batting team starts with no runs. Each batter bats for a maximum of two overs (12 pitches per player), unless he is out. The batter does not have to run every time the ball is hit. When a batter is out (caught, bowled, LBW, or run out), no runs are deducted from the batting team's score and the next batter on the team replaces him. Bowling must be overarm and take place from the same end throughout the game. Each bowler must bowl six legitimate balls in an over (no-balls and wides count as a run and an additional ball for the batting team). At the end of every over, the fielding team rotates clockwise through one position, and the batters change ends.

If a fielding team has fewer than six players, the batting team must provide the fielding team with a wicketkeeper, who subsequently also rotates to other positions in the field but does not bowl. The batting team must provide two impartial umpires (at the bowler's end and square leg) to count the bowler's pitches; to indicate if the batter is caught, LBW, bowled, or run out; to signal wides, byes, and no-balls; and to signal boundaries, awarding four or six runs (figure 20.22). The batting team also records the score on the scoreboard (two scorers). Having faced 12 deliveries (assuming the batter was not out), the batter retires and is replaced by another until the whole team has batted.

Players rotate through batting, umpiring, and scoring duties (see figure 20.23 for a potential setup for kwik cricket). If a team's last two batters are batting and one of the batters is out, the batter who is out may act as a nonstriking partner (runner) until the final batter is either out or has faced two overs. After 12 overs (assuming a team of six batters), or when all the batters are out, the batting team's total is recorded. The fielding team becomes the batting team and attempts to beat the target set by the team that batted first.

Goal Work the batter out.

Condition The bowler places the fielders in positions of her choice but must have at least one player in addition to the wicketkeeper in a close catching position (see figure 20.19 for examples of close catching positions).

Four runs (boundary) Six runs Bye Wide

No ball Out Batter ran a short run Leg bye

Figure 20.22 The umpire's signals.

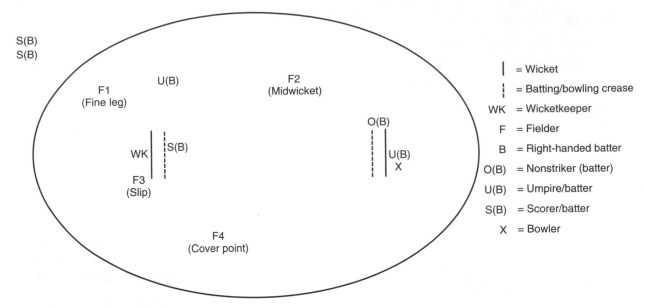

S(B)
S(B)

F1
(Fine leg)

U(B)

F2
(Midwicket)

O(B)

WK S(B)

U(B)
X

F3
(Slip)

F4
(Cover point)

| = Wicket
⋮ = Batting/bowling crease
WK = Wicketkeeper
F = Fielder
B = Right-handed batter
O(B) = Nonstriker (batter)
U(B) = Umpire/batter
S(B) = Scorer/batter
X = Bowler

Figure 20.23 The bowler sets the field.

Questions

Q: When you are bowling, where is your close fielder positioned, and why?

A: At slip because the leg cutter is the delivery of choice.

Q: Is there any other reason?

A: For bowling a full length and because the batter likes to try to drive the ball.

Q: If you are bowling off-cutters, where is the fielder positioned?

A: At leg slip and possibly at regular slip if the ball keeps going straight and doesn't cut back.

Q: When you field at first slip (off side) or are the wicketkeeper, what should you watch?

A: The ball from the time it leaves the bowler's hand.

Q: In all other close catching positions (including leg slip), what does the fielder watch?

A: The bat.

PRACTICE TASK 1

Setup Catch it

Goal Two catchers (6-8 ft, or 1.8-2.4 m, apart) attempt to make the ball land in the opponent's target square (8 by 8 ft, or 2.4 by 2.4 m) using an underhand throw from below knee height (figure 20.24)

Conditions

- Batters score 1 point when the ball hits the ground in the opponent's square.
- Fielders prevent the opponent from scoring by catching the ball before it lands in the square.
- If the ball hits the ground outside the square, the receiving player scores a point.

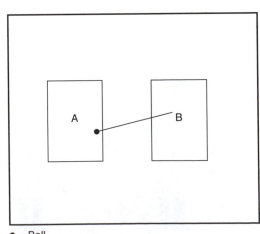

● = Ball

Figure 20.24 Catch it.

Teaching Sport Concepts and Skills

Cues Close catching:

- Position your feet shoulder-width apart.
- Bend your knees and hips.
- Keep your weight primarily on the balls of your feet.
- Keep your elbows slightly bent and not resting on your knees.
- Keep your hands together just below knee height, fingers pointing down.

Variations

- Catchers can vary the height and speed of the underarm throw.
- Reduce or increase the size of the target square.

PRACTICE TASK 2

Setup Repeat practice task 1 of lesson 10 in level II (figure 20.19).

GAME 2

Setup Kwik cricket

Condition For the first four overs, the defense must have two fielders in addition to the wicketkeeper in close catching positions (for safety reasons, fielders should be 8 to 10 yards from the bat if they are in front of the batter).

LEVEL III

Levels I and II emphasize developing batting techniques to help batters stay in (defend the wicket) and use all of the allotted deliveries during their overs. You may advise students that in the real game of cricket, once a batter is out, he does not bat again during his team's innings (usually does not bat for the remainder of the day). Remind batters that avoiding getting out is always a tactical objective, so defending a good length (a delivery from the bowler likely to strike the wicket or find the edge of the bat) is sensible. As defensive (bowling and fielding) tactics and skills develop in the first two levels, batters need greater tactical understanding and associated skills to help them attack the various types of delivery from the bowler.

Level III focuses on a variety of sophisticated offensive batting strokes. Batters increase their offensive stroke armory as more advanced bowling techniques (spin) and associated field placements are introduced. Defensive players recognize the need to bowl to a field and force the batter to hit the ball in a specific area to restrict scoring and to get batters out. Batters no longer surrender their wickets as cheaply as they once did because of the tactical understanding and skills they developed in the first two levels.

Batters have an array of batting strokes that they can employ to make the best offensive plays.

Tactical Problem   Scoring runs

Lesson Focus   Back-foot drive and running between the wickets

Objectives

- Communicate.
- Ground the bat.
- Change hands when turning.

GAME 1

Setup   Circle cricket (six to eight players) played in pairs

Goal   As the batter, score runs by pushing the ball out of the circle and running between the wickets.

Conditions

- All fielders (including the wicketkeeper) must be positioned outside the 13-yard circle (figure 20.25).
- The bowler aims for a good length (target zone 3; figure 20.21).
- Each batting pair receives two overs.
- When the ball is hit outside the circle, the batters can run if they wish.
- Fielders field the ball and throw only at the batter's wicket (not at the bowler's wicket).
- No fielder can enter the circle or run with the ball.
- Batters keep running until the wicket is hit or until four runs have been scored.
- Batters bat until two overs are completed, and then the next pair bats.
- The pair with the most runs wins.

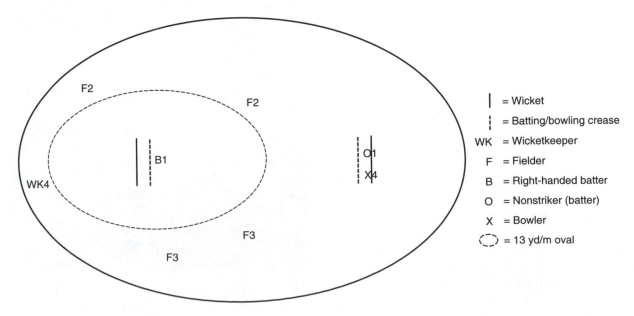

Figure 20.25   Circle cricket.

Teaching Sport Concepts and Skills

Questions

Q: When batting, who decides when to run?

A: If the ball is hit anywhere in front of the batter's wicket, the batter calls for the run.

Q: What happens when the ball goes behind the wicket?

A: The nonstriker calls for the run because she sees the ball before the batter sees it.

Q: What do you call to indicate your intention to run?

A: "Yes," "No," or "Wait" followed by "Yes" or "No." Nothing else is required.

Q: As the bowler releases the ball, what is the nonstriker doing?

A: Moving toward the other wicket (backing up) and continuing to do so as the ball is hit.

Q: If the batter calls "Yes," what is the advantage of backing up?

A: The nonstriker has already gained 2 to 3 yards for the run, reducing the distance to the striking batter's crease.

Q: If the batter calls "No," what does the nonstriker do?

A: Returns to her crease by extending the bat and touching the ground inside the nonstriker's batting (bowling) crease. This is the act of grounding the bat.

Q: Is grounding the bat important regardless of whether the batter attempts a run?

A: Yes, because it reduces the distance to safety (inside the batter's crease) by almost 2 yards at either end (crease). It makes the run shorter and is the reason batters carry their bats.

Q: Does it matter which hand a batter uses to carry the bat?

A: Yes, the batter always wants to see the ball when turning to attempt a second or third run.

Q: So, if a right-handed batter hits the ball into the off-side through extra cover and is looking for a second run, when he turns to call for the second run, the bat should be in which hand?

A: In his left hand. The nonstriker should be turning with the bat in her right hand.

Q: If the ball were hit into the leg side by the same right-handed batter, what would be the hand positions?

A: The players' hands would be reversed so the players could track the ball when turning.

PRACTICE TASK

Setup Students practice the back-foot drive and run in pairs.

Goal Practice the back-foot push and running between the wickets.

Conditions

- Each batting pair receives two overs.
- The bowler aims at target zones 3 and 4 (around or just short of a good length).
- The batter attempts to drive the ball off the back foot into the sector (figure 20.26).
- After successfully contacting the ball, the batters can run as many times as they wish.
- Batters can be caught, bowled, or run out.
- Pairs rotate through batting, fielding, bowling, and wicketkeeping.
- When all pairs have batted, the pair with the most runs wins.

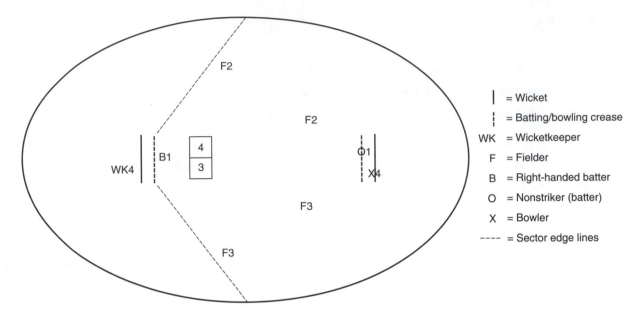

Figure 20.26   Back-foot drive and run.

Cues

- Running and turning:
  - As the nonstriker, back up.
  - Call for each run.
  - Carry the bat in the correct hand.
  - Slide the bat over the crease (ground the bat).
  - Turn low, using the bat as an extension of your hand.
  - Accelerate out of the turn.
- Back-foot drive (extension of the backward defense):
  - Step back toward the wicket with your back foot.
  - The front foot follows the back (with the downswing of bat) and finishes next to the back foot (parallel with the batting crease).
  - Keep your body sideways to the delivery.
  - Have your front elbow high at contact.
  - The bottom hand punches through the ball.
  - Point the blade of the bat in the direction the ball was hit.

GAME 2

Setup   Circle cricket (six to eight players)

Goal   As the batter, score runs by using the back-foot drive and running between the wickets (communicating, grounding the bat, and turning).

Condition   You may allow the wicketkeeper to move to the stumps after the batter contacts the ball.

Note   This game is an excellent review of fielding and intercepting skills.

Tactical Problem   Restricting run scoring by bowling to the leg side and getting the batter out

Lesson Focus   Forcing the batter to play in a designated area and bowling to a leg-side field

Objective   Practice slow bowling (off-break).

GAME 1

Setup   This is a modified version of kanga 8s cricket. Four pairs of players rotate through batting, fielding, bowling, and wicketkeeping as done in pairs cricket. Batters can be bowled, caught, or run out or be out if they hit their own wicket (usually in the backswing with the bat). A pair of batters bats for two overs regardless of the number of times each pair is out. Pairs add run increments to their totals for the following bowling and fielding performances: four runs for a batter who is bowled, two runs for a catch to each fielder and to the bowler who was bowling when the catch was taken, and four runs for a run-out.

Goal   Make the batter play the ball into the leg side to restrict run scoring and to get the batter out.

Conditions

- Batters can score runs only on the leg side (figure 20.27).
- Bowlers may use no more than a three-step run-up.

Questions

Q: Where do most batters like to hit a ball?

A: On the leg side.

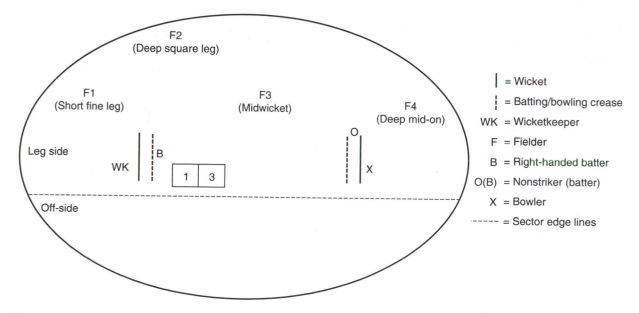

Figure 20.27   Off-break field.

Q: Suppose that when you bowl, you encourage a batter to hit only on the leg side. How does doing that help the defense?

A: You can allocate most of your fielders to this side because you can predict that the batter will hit in that direction.

Q: If you want a batter to hit on the leg side, should you bowl to the leg side?

A: Not exactly, because you still want to get the batter out by bowling at the wicket (otherwise you lose the opportunity to bowl the batter or get an LBW decision).

Q: So, what is your target when you bowl?

A: The off-stump.

Q: Which target zones will you aim at?

A: Zones 1 and 3 (and not 4, 5, or 6 because a ball that is short of a length will easily be pulled by a batter).

Q: If the batter wants to hit on the leg side, what does it mean for the batter's stroke?

A: The batter is hitting across the line of the ball, which means he has a greater chance of mis-hitting or missing the ball completely, particularly when the ball pitches in zones 1 and 3 on a full length.

Q: What else can you do to tempt the batter into hitting on the leg side when the ball pitches in line with the off-stump?

A: Make the ball deviate sharply in the direction of the leg side.

Q: What else can you do to tempt the batter?

A: Bowl the ball fairly slowly; by spinning the ball, you can also cause it to fly into the air unless the batter makes solid contact with the middle of the bat.

PRACTICE TASK 1

Setup   Students practice the off-break in pairs.

Goal   Spin the ball using the offspin.

Conditions

- Partners stand 11 yards apart and throw the ball from in front of their faces (like throwing a dart).
- The ball should land 1 to 2 yards in front of partner, who collects the ball and returns it with a similar action.
- For a right-handed bowler, the ball should hit the ground and spin from left to right.

Cues   Offspin:

- Spread the middle joints of the index and second fingers across the seam.
- Rest the ball against your third finger and your thumb (students with smaller hands may need a modified grip allowing the third finger to help hold the ball).
- Turn your wrist and index finger to generate a clockwise spin on the ball.
- Cock your wrist initially, and then drag your first finger sharply down the side of the ball while your thumb flips up.

PRACTICE TASK 2

Setup   This task calls for a bowler, batter, wicketkeeper, and two leg-side fielders positioned at the bowler's discretion inside the sector (figure 20.28).

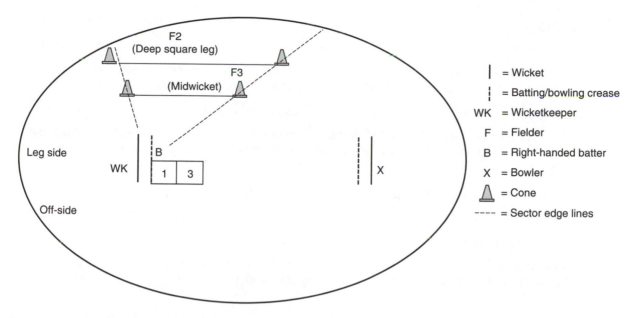

Figure 20.28 Defending the square on the leg side.

Goal Turn the ball using the offspin, forcing batter to play the ball on the leg side across the line.

Conditions

- The bowler aims at target zones 1 and 3 around the batter's off-stump, causing the batter to hit across the line of the ball but with the spin.
- The batter attempts to hit the ball into the sector.
- If the ball goes past the first set of cones, the batter scores one run; if it goes past the next set of cones, she scores two runs; and if it goes past the boundary, she scores four runs.
- Each batter receives six deliveries before players rotate.
- Run increments are awarded for defense as in modified kanga 8s cricket.
- The player with the most runs wins.

Cues

- Vary the speed of delivery.
- Vary your position on the bowling crease (tight to the nonstriker's wicket or wider on the batting crease).
- Bowl a straight ball occasionally with no spin (arm ball).
- Try bowling around the wicket (as with the off-cutter; figure 20.15).

GAME 2

Setup Modified kanga 8s cricket

Goal Make the batter play the ball into the leg side to restrict run scoring and to get the batter out.

Conditions

- Batters can score runs only on the leg side (figure 20.27).
- Bowlers may use no more than a three-step run-up.

Questions

Q: Why is the fielder at short fine leg (in figure 20.27) saving a single run and not on the boundary?

A: The batter may attempt to glance the ball in that direction, but there is little pace on the ball. The fielder could also be positioned at leg slip to attack the batter in this game.

Q: Why is the fielder at deep square leg on the boundary?

A: To prevent a boundary from a pull shot and to cover the fielders at midwicket and short fine leg who are saving the single. A batter may also hit the ball hard and give a catch in the deep near the boundary.

Q: Why is the fielder at midwicket fairly close to the batter?

A: To prevent the batter from pushing the ball into space and scoring a quick single.

Q: Why is the fielder at deep mid-on near the boundary?

A: To prevent a straight, hard hit. A good batter will try to drive an offspinner hard in this direction to minimize the effect of the spin imparted by the bowler.

LESSON 15

Secondary Level III

Tactical Problem   Scoring on the leg side

Lesson Focus   Attacking an off-break bowler, working the ball off the legs, and hitting with the spin square on the leg side

Objective   Play a sweep, paddle, or front-foot leg glance.

GAME 1

Setup   Modified kanga 8s cricket

Goals

- Play the ball into the leg side to score runs.
- Take what the defense offers.

Conditions

- Batters can score runs only on the leg side.
- Batters' scores are doubled if they hit for runs into the target sector on the leg side (figure 20.29).
- Bowlers may use no more than a three-step run-up and must bowl off-breaks pitching in line with the wicket.

Questions

Q: When attacking an off-break bowler, what is your best option?

A: Drive the ball with a vertical bat through the leg side or off-side (on-side only in this game).

Q: What about hitting the ball square, into the space on the leg side, for a single?

A: Pull a ball that is short of a length (pitching in zones 5 and 6).

Q: What kind of ball from an off-break bowler is hard to hit with a cross stroke on the leg side?

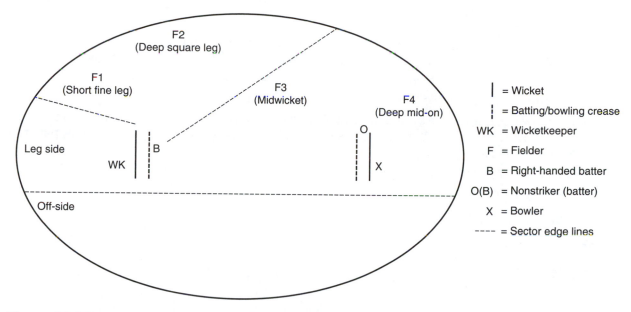

Figure 20.29 Kanga 8s cricket (double the score in the zone).

> *A: A ball that is on a good or full length around the front border of zone 2 (half volley) or is just about a good length (zone 4) and is in line with the leg stump of the wicket. Either ball arrives too low to pull effectively.*
>
> *Q: So, what are your options for hitting the ball into the bonus sector in the game?*
>
> *A: Sweeping or glancing the ball to the leg side.*

PRACTICE TASK 1

Setup   This task call for a bowler, batter, wicketkeeper, and two leg-side fielders positioned at the bowler's discretion inside the sector (figure 20.30).

Goal   As the batter, hit the ball into the sector using a sweep.

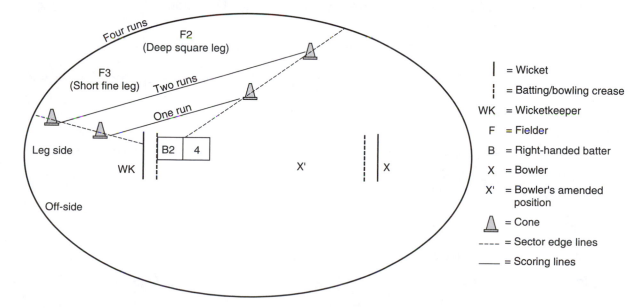

Figure 20.30 Practicing the sweep or leg glance.

Conditions

- The bowler (from position X') throws the ball like a dart from about 11 yards (using the offspin technique) to land on a full length in line with or just outside the batter's leg stump.
- The line of the bowler's throw can vary.
- The batter hits across the line of the ball, but hits with the spin.
- The batter attempts to hit the ball into the sector, and if it goes past the first set of cones, she scores one run; if it goes past the next set of cones, she scores two runs; and if it goes past the boundary, she scores four runs.
- Each batter receives six deliveries before players rotate.
- The player with the most runs wins.

Variation Have the batter hit from a low (4 in., or 10 cm) tee.

Cues

- Sweep shot:
  - Have a high backlift.
  - Hit the ball on the half volley.
  - Step forward with your front leg (bending your knee) to the pitch of the ball.
  - Bend your back leg (the knee can be in contact with the ground).
  - Your legs should cover the line of the ball.
  - Keep your weight forward, head leaning over the ball, watching closely.
  - Make sure the bat is horizontal at impact.
  - Roll your wrists to keep the ball down.
  - The sweep should go roughly square of the wicket.

PRACTICE TASK 2

Setup Repeat task 1 (the sector can be increased to encompass the midwicket area).

Cues Front-foot leg glance:

- Set up as in the forward defensive stroke to the ball on the leg stump.
- Keep your head over the ball.
- Move your front foot to the pitch of the ball.
- Keep your weight on your front foot.
- Keep the bat in front of your front leg—not alongside it as in a forward defense.
- At impact, turn the bat, allowing the ball to run to the fine leg.

Variation

- Have students flick their wrists at the moment of contact to angle the bat face toward the midwicket.
- Remind students that this shot is about timing, not power.

GAME 2

Setup Modified kanga 8s cricket

Goals

- Play the ball into the leg side to score runs.
- Take what the defense offers, using the sweep, paddle, and leg glance.

Conditions

- Batters can score runs only on the leg side (figure 20.29).
- Batters' scores are doubled if they hit the ball for runs into the target sector on the leg side.
- Bowlers may use no more than a three-step run-up and must bowl off-breaks pitching in line with the wicket.
- The pair with the most runs wins.

LESSON 16

Tactical Problem   Restricting run scoring by bowling to an off-side field and getting the batter out

Lesson Focus   Forcing the batter to play in a designated area and bowling to an off-side field

Objective   Use slow bowling and spin (leg break) to get the batter out.

GAME 1

Setup   This game is a modified version of kanga 8s cricket. Four pairs of players rotate through batting, fielding, bowling, and wicketkeeping as in pairs cricket. Batters can be out by being bowled, caught, or run out, or if they hit their own wicket (accidentally with the bat). A pair of batters bats for two overs regardless of the number of times each pair is out. Pairs add run increments to their totals for the following bowling and fielding performances: four runs for a batter who is bowled, two runs per catch to each fielder and to the bowler who was bowling when the catch was taken, and four runs for a run-out.

Goal   Make the batter play the ball into the off-side to restrict run scoring and to get the batter out.

Conditions

- Batters can score runs only on the off-side (figure 20.31).
- Bowlers may use no more than a three-step run-up.

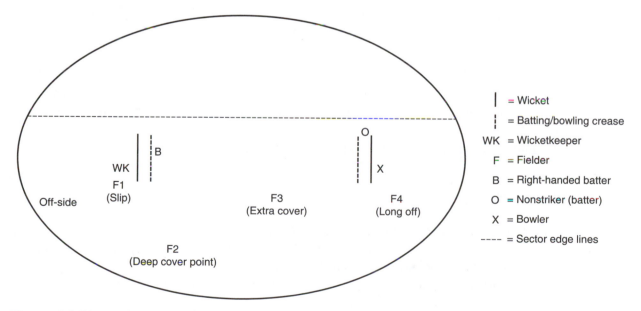

| | = Wicket
┆ = Batting/bowling crease
WK = Wicketkeeper
F = Fielder
B = Right-handed batter
O = Nonstriker (batter)
X = Bowler
---- = Sector edge lines

Figure 20.31   Defending the off-side.

Cricket

Questions

Q: Where do most batters like to hit a ball?

A: On the leg side.

Q: How can you encourage the batter to play the ball on the off-side?

A: Make the ball deviate sharply in the direction of the off-side after it pitches.

Q: How does that deviation help the defense?

A: You can allocate most of your fielders to the off-side because you can predict that the batter will hit in that direction.

Q: If you want a batter to hit on the off-side, should you bowl to the off-side?

A: To some extent, yes, but you still want to get the batter out by bowling at the wicket.

Q: So, what is your target when you bowl?

A: Around the middle and off-stump in target zone 3 so the ball can turn away from the batter toward the off-side after it pitches. (If the ball is really turning, a leg-break bowler may aim at the middle and leg stump and may also take advantage of the bowler's footmarks, from the other end—this happens only in a real game—and sometimes may even try to bowl the batter around her legs.)

Q: What are the two possibilities of getting the batter out in this tactical scenario?

A: The ball finds the edge of the bat for a catch to the wicketkeeper or slip, or the ball does not turn but travels straight after it hits the ground and possibly hits the wicket (an arm ball).

Q: How does hitting on the leg side affect the batter's stroke?

A: The batter is hitting across the line of the ball and against the direction of the spin, which means he has a greater chance of mis-hitting or missing the ball completely.

Q: What else can you do to tempt the batter?

A: Bowl the ball fairly slowly; by spinning the ball, you can cause it to fly into the air for a catch to a fielder on the off-side unless the batter makes excellent contact.

PRACTICE TASK 1

Setup   Students practice the leg break in pairs.

Goal   Spin the ball using leg spin.

Conditions
- Partners stand 11 yards apart and throw the ball underhand.
- The ball should land 1 to 2 yards in front of the partner, who collects and returns it with a similar action.
- For a right-handed bowler, the ball should hit the ground and spin from right to left.

Cues   Leg break:
- Make sure that the middle joints of the index and second fingers are across the seam (not spread).
- Rest the ball against a bent third finger and the thumb.
- As you release the ball, straighten your fingers (most of the work is done by the third finger), turning the ball counterclockwise with a flick of your wrist.
- Turn your wrist from facing in to facing batter as your fingers flick outward.
- Finish with the palm of your hand facing down.

PRACTICE TASK 2

Setup   This task calls for a bowler, batter, wicketkeeper, slip, and two defensive off-side fielders positioned at the bowler's discretion inside the sector (figure 20.32).

Goal   Turn the ball using a leg spin to force the batter to play the ball on the off-side.

Conditions

- The bowler aims at target zone 3 around the batter's off- or middle stump, causing the batter to hit with the spin.
- The batter attempts to hit the ball into the sector.
- If the ball goes past the first set of cones, the batter scores one run; if it runs past the next set of cones, she scores two runs; and if it runs past the boundary, she scores four runs.
- Each batter receives six deliveries before players rotate through the other positions.
- Run increments are awarded for defense as in modified kanga 8s cricket.
- The player with the most runs wins.

Cues   Tactical bowling:

- Vary the speed of delivery.
- Vary your position on the bowling crease (tight to the nonstriker's wicket or wider on the batting crease).
- Bowl a straight ball occasionally with no spin (arm ball).

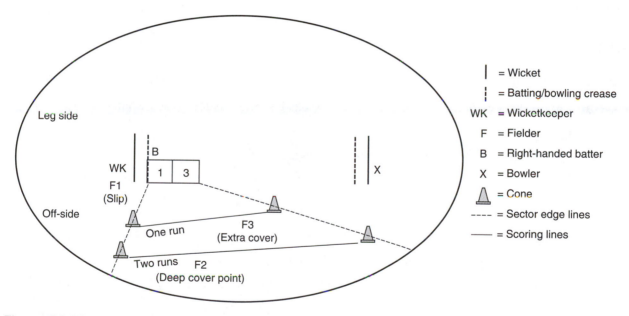

Figure 20.32   Defending the off-side.

GAME 2

Setup   Modified kanga 8s

Goal   Make the batter play the ball into the off-side to restrict run scoring and get the batter out.

Conditions

- Batters can score runs only on the off-side (figure 20.31).
- Bowlers may use no more than a three-step run-up.

Questions

Q: *Why is the fielder at slip (figure 20.31)?*

A: *The batter may attempt to drive the ball, and the leg spin will cause an edge to go to this area.*

Q: *Why is the fielder at deep cover point on the boundary?*

A: *To prevent a boundary from a horizontal bat shot or a square drive from a wide ball bowled on the off-side. This fielder could also cover the player at extra cover, who is saving a single.*

Q: *Why is the fielder at extra cover fairly close?*

A: *To prevent the batter from pushing the ball into space with the spin and scoring a quick single.*

Q: *Why is the fielder at deep long-off?*

A: *To prevent a hard, straight hit. Good batters try to hit a leg spinner hard in this direction to minimize the effects of the spin.*

LESSON 17

Secondary Level III

Tactical Problem   Scoring on the off-side

Lesson Focus   Attacking a leg-break bowler and hitting with the spin square on the off-side

Objective   Play the cut shot.

GAME 1

Setup   Modified kanga 8s cricket

Goal   Take what the defense offers and play the ball into the off-side to score runs.

Conditions

- Batters can score runs only on the off-side (figure 20.33).
- Batters' scores are doubled if they hit a ball for runs into the target sector on the off-side.
- Bowlers may use no more than a three-step run-up and must bowl leg-break pitching on or outside the off-stump.

Questions

Q: *When attacking a leg-break bowler, what is your best option?*

A: *Driving the ball with a vertical bat through the leg side or off-side (in this conditioned game, only the off-side).*

Q: *What about hitting across the line in a real game, in which the leg side is available?*

A: *This hit is very risky—not only are you hitting across the line, but you are also hitting against the spin.*

Q: *Could you hit the ball square of the wicket on the off-side into the space for a single?*

A: *Yes, in two ways: as a square drive to a ball that pitches in zone 1 (very wide outside the off-stump), or by cutting a ball that is short of a length (pitching in zone 5) and well outside the off-stump (figure 20.21).*

Q: *What does a batter need for hitting the ball square of the wicket on the off-side?*

A: *Good footwork to make room to play the shot.*

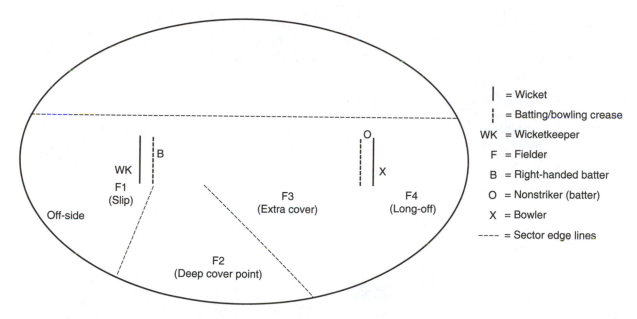

Figure 20.33 Kanga 8s cricket (double the score in the zone).

PRACTICE TASK

Setup   This task calls for a bowler, batter, wicketkeeper, and two off-side fielders positioned at the bowler's discretion inside the sector (figure 20.34).

Goal   Hit the ball into a sector using the cut shot.

Conditions

- Bowler (X') throws the ball underhand or overhand (using leg spin) from about 11 yards to land short of a length in target zone 5 outside the batter's off-stump.
- The batter hits with the spin.
- The line of the bowler's throw can vary from middle to leg stump depending on the amount of spin generated.

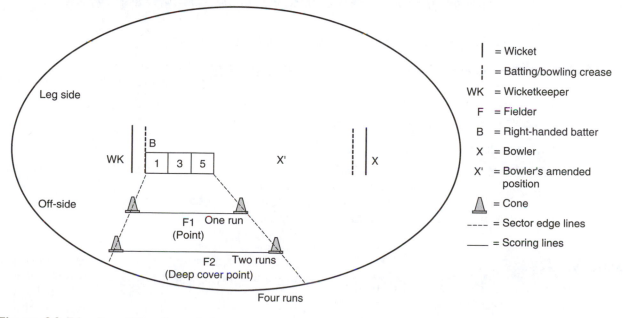

Figure 20.34 Practicing the cut shot.

- The batter attempts to hit the ball into the sector. If the ball goes past the first set of cones, she scores one run; if it runs past the next set of cones, she scores two runs; and if it passes a boundary, she scores four runs. Each batter receives six deliveries before players rotate through the other positions. The player with the most runs wins.

Variation   Have batters hit from a high tee.

Cues   Square cut:

- Have a high backlift.
- Step back and across with your back foot toward the off-stump.
- Get your head in line with the ball.
- Turn your front shoulder toward the direction of the point.
- Fling the bat horizontally (keep hold of it), fully extending your arms and hands at the ball.
- Lean over the ball, not back.

GAME 2

Setup   Modified kanga 8s cricket

Goals

- Play the ball into the off-side to score runs.
- Take what the defense offers using the cut shot.

Conditions

- Batters can score runs only on the off-side (figure 20.33).
- Batters' scores are doubled if they hit the ball for runs into the target sector on the leg side (figure 20.33).
- Bowlers may use no more than a three-step run-up and must bowl leg-break pitching outside the off-stump.
- The pair with the most runs wins.

Questions

Q: When the batter hits the cut shot, what can happen to the ball when less than perfect contact is made?

A: The ball can slice into the air behind the square on the off-side.

Q: What can the defense do to restrict run scoring and potentially get the batter out when this happens?

A: Place a fielder in a catching position wide of slip and almost square with the wicket (a gully fielder) or a little farther away (a backward-point fielder).

Q: How does this fielder affect the batter?

A: The batter must keep her body weight over the ball and hit down or run the risk of being caught in the gully or at the backward point when playing the cut shot and slicing the ball upward. The cut shot is also commonly used against faster bowlers who bowl short and wide of the wicket on the off-side (the ball pitches in target zone 5). See figure 20.21.

SUMMARY

We hope the ideas in this chapter provide the basic tools for teaching cricket from a tactical approach. Students are generally very responsive to learning the concepts of cricket. They understand their responsibilities in offensive and defensive situations and align this understanding with the ability to solve tactical problems using offensive (batting) and defensive (bowling and fielding) skills. The motivation to learn to play cricket seems to be high.

Chapter 21

Golf

Golf is a target game with many unique tactical problems. Approximately one-third of all shots taken during a game of golf require a full swing, a complex skill. The complexity of a full swing increases when the golfer uses drivers and fairway woods. We recommend starting with the putter and working up through irons for short, middle, and long distances and using the driver and fairway woods only with advanced players. In fact, a full swing with a middle iron is all players need off the tee and, in the long run, adds to the novice's success and enjoyment of the game. Encourage novice players to play short, par-3 courses to help them gain confidence, skill, and a tactical understanding of the game.

SAFETY

Safety is a major consideration when teaching golf to a whole class. Arranging students so they are far enough apart yet close enough to monitor is not an easy feat. For easy management and observation of students when indoors, try arranging runners or strips of carpet like the spokes of a wheel (figure 21.1), with putting

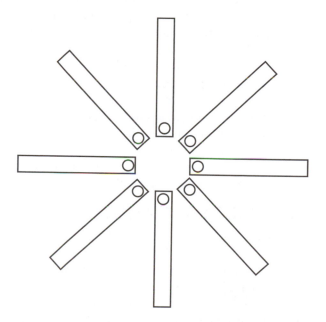

Figure 21.1 Arranging putting cups in a circle with runners radiating outward provides an efficient layout for observing students.

cups at the center. You can use the same arrangement for chipping practice by positioning small pieces of artificial turf or carpet squares about 10 feet (3 m) beyond the end of the runner. This setup allows students to chip onto the green.

Partners are a must when teaching golf. They are useful for providing feedback to their peers and can serve as the primary observers for safety infractions. Select a safety cue such as "Freeze," "Fore," or "No!" When a safety cue is given, everyone should stop and wait for your command to restart activity. Practice this safety cue with your students and periodically yell it out to ensure that students are alert and safety conscious.

Check clubheads after every class, because the constant pounding caused by multiple swings into the floor or ground can cause them to loosen. Also, check the club grips periodically. Grips can become slippery after many uses. Replacing grips is an easy task, and replacement kits are inexpensive. Get to know the owner or manager of a local golf course, who can often provide tips for club repair and may even volunteer services. Local courses are also a good source of scorecards, pencils, tees, and other golf gadgets that you can use in class or as prizes for tournaments, such as the 9-Hole Putt-Putt Golf Classic (just an example).

INSTRUCTION TIPS

We do not advocate teaching the proper grip, the parts of a club, or the history of the game in the beginning. Let students acquire their own grips and intervene only when you observe a dysfunctional grip. Use proper terminology as you demonstrate each swing, referring to the *sweet spot* on the *clubface,* for example. As for the history of the game, assign students the task of finding out how golf got its start. They can ask parents and grandparents about it or look it up in the library or on the Internet. In class, get the clubs into students' hands and let them play. Once they are engaged and having fun, they will want to learn about the game and how to be successful playing it.

TACTICAL REALITY GOLF

To grasp the tactical concepts of golf (learn golf tactically), students need to understand the conditions under which they make each shot. How far the ball is from the hole, obstacles between the ball and the hole, and the lie of the ball are all important aspects of a golf shot. The decisions made before the shot (i.e., preshot decisions) are as important as the shot itself. We rec-

When starting out, use proper terminology as you teach each lesson.

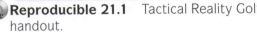

Reproducible 21.1   Tactical Reality Golf handout.

Reproducible 21.1

Tactical Reality Golf

Player 1 _____   Player 2 _____

Instructions

1. Select a partner and have at least one bag of clubs between you.
2. Choose a hole to play (consult the diagrams of golf holes).
3. Begin with a tee shot from a rubber tee using a Wiffle ball and hit remaining shots from turf mats.
4. Let your partner decide how far and in which direction your ball has gone and then tell you where to play your next shot.
5. For each shot, select an appropriate club. The club you select will depend on your distance from the hole and any obstacles in your path (i.e., you might have to hit over a bunker, in which case you will need to get plenty of height).
6. When you reach the green, use your regulation ball and putter and putt the hole out on the artificial green.
7. Record the number of strokes made from tee to green and the number of putts made on the green, and add these two numbers to get your score on the hole.

Maximum Distances Allowed With Each Club

	6-iron—160 yards
Driver—230 yards	7-iron—150 yards
3-wood—210 yards	8-iron—140 yards
3-iron—190 yards	9-iron—130 yards
4-iron—180 yards	Wedge—120 yards
5-iron—170 yards	

Name	1	2	3	4	5	6	7	8	9	Score

From S.A. Mitchell, J.L. Oslin, and L.L. Griffin. 2013. *Teaching sport concepts and skills: A tactical games approach for ages 7 to 18,* third edition (Champaign, IL: Human Kinetics).

ommend using visual aids to help students understand how to use each type of shot within the game of golf (figure 21.2). You can use posters, colored chalk drawings, overheads, and so forth, to illustrate situations on the golf course. Be sure to include bunkers, hazards, trees, and so on, to keep illustrations real. We have often copied diagrams of golf holes from magazines, scorecards, and golf resort promotional materials. If a diagram is too small, enlarge it. Then laminate these diagrams and use them as instructional aids, or let the students pretend to play a few holes in class in the game of tactical reality golf, which can be played outdoors or indoors on mats (see reproducible 21.1).

We present the tactical framework and levels of tactical complexity for golf in tables 21.1 and 21.2. Throughout the chapter, we also describe each level before providing its lesson outlines.

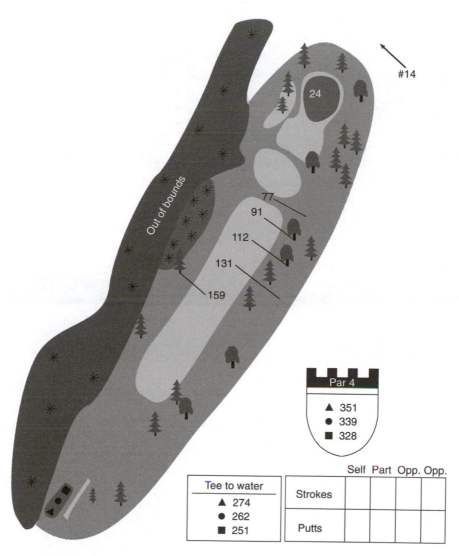

Figure 21.2 Visuals such as this one help students prepare for situations present on the golf course.

Table 21.1 Tactical Problems, Decisions, and Shot Executions in Golf

Tactical problems	Preshot decisions	Shot executions
REDUCING THE NUMBER OF STROKES		

Hitting the ball the proper distance	• Selecting a club
	• Placing the ball
	• Determining the swing length
		• Setup routine
		• Stance
		• Swing plane
		• Putt 1-1, 2-2
		• Swing 6-8, 3-9, 2-10, full with a middle iron
		• Full swing:
		  ○ Long irons
		  ○ Woods
		• Fairway woods
		• Drive from a tee box—tee the ball and swing

Hitting the ball in the intended direction	• Selecting an intermediate target • Reading the green	• Setup • Stance • Putt • Adjusting the setup • Adjusting the swing plane
Hitting out of hazards	• Selecting a club • Placing the ball • Reading the lie	• Sand shot • Deep, dense grass • Swing plane
Uphill, downhill, sidehill, and uneven lies	• Selecting a club • Placing the ball • Reading the angle of the lie	• Stance • Swing plane
Stopping the ball on the green (hitting with spin)	Determining the need for: • Backspin • Left to right • Right to left • Hook • Slice	• Setup • Stance • Swing plane

Table 21.2 Levels of Tactical Complexity for Golf

Tactical problems	Level I	Level II
REDUCING THE NUMBER OF STROKES		

Hitting the ball the proper distance	• Selecting a club
	• Placing the ball
	• Setup routine
	• Stance
	• Determining the swing length
	• Putt 1-1, 2-2
	• Swing 6-8, 3-9, 2-10, full with a middle iron
		• Swing plane
		• Full swing:
		  ○ Long irons
		  ○ Woods
		• Fairway woods
		• Drive from a tee box—tee the ball and swing

Hitting the ball in the intended direction	• Selecting an intermediate target • Reading the green • Setup • Stance • Putt	• Adjusting the setup • Adjusting the swing plane
Hitting out of hazards	• Selecting a club • Placing the ball • Reading the lie	• Sand shot • Deep, dense grass • Swing plane
Uphill, downhill, sidehill, and uneven lies		• Selecting a club • Stance • Ball placement • Reading the angle of the lie • Swing plane

Stopping the ball on the green (hitting with spin)	• Setup
	• Stance
		• Determining the need for:
		  ○ Backspin
		  ○ Left to right
		  ○ Right to left
		  ○ Hook
		  ○ Slice
		• Swing plane

LEVEL I

Level I begins with the putt and ends with a full swing using a middle iron. Lessons focus on club selection, setup, preshot routines, selection of an intermediate target, stance, and swing. Through numerous games and practices, students encounter many problem-solving experiences to help them understand the relationship between the loft of the club and the placement of the ball within the stance.

Many drills require players to observe their partner's swing or the flight characteristics of their partner's ball. Such observations require keen skills that must be taught. Take time to instruct students about how to observe (i.e., using the proper angle, watching one critical element at a time, and viewing multiple trials). Use a marker to stripe the golf balls, because the direction of spin can provide feedback about the swing. By becoming competent observers and evaluators, students can improve their own skills and game performance.

Students work on their putting skills to help them get the golf ball to the hole in fewer strokes.

LESSON 1

Secondary Level I

Tactical Problem   Hitting for proper distance

Lesson Focus   Putt and club selection

Objective   Putt the ball into the hole in the fewest number of strokes.

GAME 1

Setup   Students putt 10 balls at 3 feet (1 m) and 10 balls at 10 feet (3 m), keeping score.

Goal   Putt the ball in the hole in the fewest number of strokes.

Conditions

- See figure 21.1 for equipment setup.
- Ask students to select the club that will best allow them to complete the task.
- Impose a safety rule that students may not raise the clubhead higher than their feet.
- Place balls 3 feet (1 m) and 10 feet (3 m) from a hole on a green (a smooth, flat surface). Use diagrams, posters, overheads, and so on, to give students a mental picture of the green and ball position relative to the hole (figure 21.3 for an example).

Questions

Q: *What stance, grip, and body position helped you get the ball in the hole with one stroke?*

A: *A square and balanced stance, a comfortable grip, and a ready position with head and nose over the ball.*

Q: *How did you swing your club to achieve the goal?*

A: *Smoothly, keeping the blade straight.*

Q: *How was your swing for the 3-foot (1 m) putt different from your swing for the 10-foot (3 m) putt?*

A: *The 3-foot putt swing was shorter than the 10-foot putt swing.*

Q: *Why is it important to know how long your swing should be when you're attempting a 3-foot (1 m) putt?*

A: *So that every time you putt from 3 feet your swing is the same.*

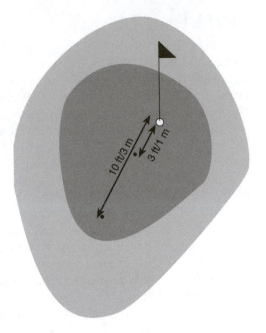

Figure 21.3

PRACTICE TASK

Setup   Students putt between rulers, yardsticks, or measured boards. Each student putts ten 1-1 strokes (1-1 means a 1/2-1 ft, or 0.15-0.3 m, backswing and forward swing), and a partner measures the distances the ball travels on the last five strokes (using a measuring tape). Students switch roles and then repeat the task for 2-2 strokes (2-3 ft, or 0.6-0.9 m, swings) and for 3-3 strokes (3-4 ft, or 0.9-1.2 m, swings). The partner also serves as a coach, repeating cues and giving feedback. Students also calculate the average distance the ball traveled at each stroke length.

Goal   Develop a consistent swing for the 1, 2, and 3 putts.

Cues   Stance and swing:

- Be balanced.
- Have a square blade.
- Use a comfortable grip.
- Have a quiet body.
- Keep your nose over the ball.
- Use a smooth, even stroke.

GAME 2

Repeat game 1.

Conditions

- Students putt balls at 3 feet (1 m), 10 feet (3 m), and 15 feet (4.6 m), keeping score.
- Students compare scores at 3 feet (1 m) and 10 feet (3 m) with their scores from game 1.

LESSON 2

Secondary Level I

Tactical Problem   Hitting the ball in the proper direction

Lesson Focus   Using an intermediate target

Objective   Use an intermediate target to putt the ball into the hole in the fewest number of strokes.

GAME 1

Setup   Students putt five balls each at 10, 15, and 20 feet (3, 4.6, and 6 m), keeping score.

Goal   Get each ball into the hole with one putt.

Conditions

- See figure 21.1 for the equipment setup.
- Ask students to select the club that will best allow them to complete the task.
- Impose a safety rule that students may not raise the clubhead higher than their feet.
- Place balls 8 and 15 feet (2.4 and 4.6 m) from a hole on a green, using an uneven surface (place a rope under the green to change the surface).

Questions

Q: Where did you aim to get the ball in the hole?

A: Right at the hole and at the area or spot between the hole and the ball.

Q: Why use a spot between the hole and the ball?

A: A closer target allows you to be more accurate.

Q: When you use a target between the ball and the hole, we refer to it as an intermediate target. Where is the best place for this intermediate target—closer to the ball or closer to the hole?

A: Don't know.

Let's experiment to find out the best place for your intermediate target.

PRACTICE TASK

Setup   Playing under the conditions from game 1, students use stickers, stars, or small markers to find the best place for an intermediate target when attempting 8-foot (2.4 m) and 15-foot (4.6 m) putts. Have them place their markers between the ball and the hole and then gradually move the marker closer to the hole. When they think they have selected a good place for an intermediate target at 8 feet (2.4 m) and at 15 feet (4.6 m), have them move to another green to try their target placements.

Goal   Determine the best location for an intermediate target when putting.

Cues

- Pick an intermediate target before setting up.
- Once your target is lined up, focus on your swing length.

Questions

Q: What was the goal of the practice task?

A: To find the best place for an intermediate target.

Q: Where did you determine to be the best place for an intermediate target?

A: Fairly close to the ball.

Q: Why is this better than an intermediate target at a farther distance?

A: The closer target is easier to hit, with less chance for error.

GAME 2

Setup   Repeat game 1. Have students keep score and compare their scores with those from the first game.

LESSON 3

Tactical Problems Hitting the ball the proper distance and in the intended direction

Lesson Focus Selecting a club, selecting an intermediate target, and chipping

Objective Select and execute a chip shot from 20 feet (6 m), landing the ball within one short putt of the hole.

GAME 1

Setup Place the ball 3 feet (1 m) off the green on the first cut, and 10 feet (3 m) off the green in the rough.

Goal Hit the ball within 3 feet (1 m) of the hole.

Conditions

- Ask students to select the club that will best allow them to complete the task.
- Impose a safety rule that students may not raise the clubhead higher than their knees.
- Place two balls 20 feet (6 m) from the hole—one 3 feet (1 m) off the green, and the other 10 feet (3 m) off the green. (Use diagrams, posters, overheads, and so on, to give students a mental picture of the green, the surrounding area, and the ball position relative to the hole.)
- Students hit the ball onto the green; then putt out.
- Students record their scores.

Questions

Q: What club did you use for each shot?

A: You can use the 3- to 7-irons for 3 feet (1 m) and the 9-iron or wedge for 10 feet (3 m) because of deep grass.

Q: What stance, grip, and body position worked best for reaching the goal?

A: Open stance, comfortable and choked down, and a ready position with the head over the ball.

Q: What swing was best for reaching the goal from 3 feet (1 m)?

A: Square and smooth, with a follow-through toward the hole.

Q: How were you able to control the direction your ball traveled?

A: By selecting an intermediate target.

PRACTICE TASK

Setup Students chip the ball from between two yardsticks or meter sticks into a target about one-third the distance between the ball and the hole (use a small rope or cord to mark a target). They chip 10 balls each from 3 feet (1 m) and 10 feet (3 m). Then they select a longer distance (between 12 and 20 ft, or 3.7 and 6 m) and adjust their swing and target.

Goal Use appropriate form to chip the ball into a target.

Cues Chipping:

- Use an open stance, with your hands ahead of the blade.
- Keep your weight on your front foot, and follow through with your hands toward the target.
- Keep the club head behind the hands and have a quiet body.

GAME 2

Setup   Repeat game 1 and have students compare their scores with those from game 1.

LESSON 4

Tactical Problems   Hitting the ball the proper distance, in the proper direction, and with the proper trajectory

Lesson Focus   Club selection, pitch shot

Objective   Use a one-quarter (6:00-9:00) and one-half (6:00-12:00) swing with a short iron to pitch the ball over a hazard and land it close to the hole 10 feet (3 m) from that hazard.

GAME 1

Setup   Place balls 30 feet (9 m) and 60 feet (18.3 m) from the hole, with a sand trap between the ball and the hole, and the hole within 10 feet (3 m) of the hazard. Students hit 5 to 10 balls from each distance.

Goals

- Put the ball in the hole in the fewest number of strokes.
- Land the ball within 5 feet (1.5 m) of the hole.

Conditions

- Ask students to select the club that will best allow them to complete the task.
- Impose a safety rule that students may not raise the clubhead higher than their shoulders.
- Place balls at 30 feet (9 m) and 60 feet (18.3 m) from the hole, with a sand trap between the ball and the hole.
- The hole is 10 feet (3 m) on the other side of the trap. (Use diagrams, posters, overheads, and so on, to give students a mental picture of the green, the sand trap, and the ball position relative to the hole.)
- Students record their scores.

Questions

Q: What club was best for reaching the goal? Why?

A: The wedge or 9-iron because it gave more loft and more control.

Q: What stance, grip, and body position worked best for reaching the goal?

A: A square stance; a comfortable, overlapping, and interlocking grip; and a natural, ready position.

Q: The farther you are putting from the hole, the longer your swing should be. How does that concept apply to pitching?

A: The farther you are from the hole, the longer the backswing should be.

Q: Some people use the face of a clock to refer to the distance of a backswing. How could we use the face of the clock to measure the length of backswings?

A: A one-quarter swing is 6:00 to 9:00 and a one-half swing is 6:00 to 12:00.

PRACTICE TASK 1

Setup   Use the situation from game 1 to have students practice one-quarter and one-half swings for pitching the ball onto the green. Use a partner checklist to have them evaluate swing form and length. Each student takes 10 practice swings, and then takes 10 more swings and has a partner evaluate his form. Partners rotate after 20 swings and then move to other distances (30 or 60 ft, or 9 or 18.3 m).

Goals

- Use good form on one-quarter and one-half swings to perform a pitch shot.
- Evaluate your partner's pitch shot.

Questions

Q: Were your setup routines, selections of intermediate targets, and ball placements for the pitch shot similar or different to those you used to chip and putt?

A: The setups and selections of the intermediate target were the same, but the ball placements were different.

Q: Relative to the stance, where was the best place for the ball to be?

A: Don't know.

Let's find out.

PRACTICE TASK 2

Setup   Students use the situation from game 1 to practice ball placement from 30 feet (9 m) or 60 feet (18.3 m). Each student hits two balls placed off the front, middle, and rear of the foot. Partners chart the trajectory of each shot, and then players switch roles and repeat the task.

Questions

Q: How does the placement of the ball in the stance influence its flight?

A: The farther back the ball is, the lower its trajectory will be.

Q: What other factor influences the trajectory of the ball?

A: The loft of the club.

Q: If you want the ball to have a high trajectory, what should you do?

A: Place the ball toward the middle of the stance and select a club with more loft (a 9-iron or wedge).

GAME 2

Setup   Repeat game 1 and have students compare their results with those from game 1.

LESSON 5

Tactical Problems   Hitting the ball the proper distance, in the proper direction, and with the proper trajectory

Lesson Focus   Hitting over a lake and landing on the green

Objective   Use three-quarter and full swings with a short iron to pitch the ball within 15 to 20 feet (4.6 to 6 m) of the hole.

GAME 1

Setup Place balls 90 feet (27 m) and 120 feet (37 m) from the hole, with a lake between the ball and the hole, and the hole within 20 feet (6 m) of the hazard.

Goal Land the ball within 10 to 15 feet (3 to 4.6 m) of the hole.

Conditions

- Ask students to select the club that will best allow them to complete the task.
- Impose a safety rule that students may not raise the clubhead unless their partners give the all clear.
- Students hit 5 to 10 balls from each distance.
- Students record the number of balls that land within 15 feet (4.6 m) of the hole (figure 21.4).

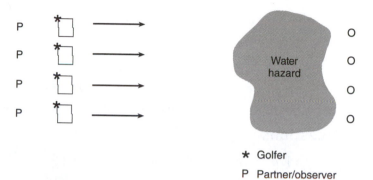

Figure 21.4

Questions

Q: What club was best for these shots?

A: The wedge or 9-iron.

Q: How did your swing differ between the 90-foot (27 m) and 120-foot (37 m) shot?

A: A bigger swing was needed for 120 feet (37 m).

Q: How was this swing similar to the one-quarter or one-half swings?

A: It was the same but longer, with a greater range of motion.

PRACTICE TASK

Setup Use the situation from game 1 to have students practice the three-quarter to full swings for pitching the ball onto the green. Have them use a partner checklist to evaluate swing form and length. Each student takes 10 practice swings and then takes 10 more swings for the partner to evaluate. Partners rotate after 20 swings, and then go to 90 feet (27 m) or 120 feet (37 m).

Goals

- Use good form to perform the three-quarter to full-swing pitch shot.
- Evaluate your partner's swing.

GAME 2

Repeat game 1 and have students compare their scores with those of game 1.

LESSON 6

Tactical Problems Hitting the ball the proper distance and in the proper direction

Lesson Focus Hitting the ball with a low trajectory

Objective Use a three-quarter to full swing with a middle-distance iron to approach the green.

GAME 1

Setup   Set the ball under a tree and 150 feet (46 m) from the hole

Goal   Get the ball onto the green.

Conditions

- Ask students to select the club that will best allow them to complete the task.
- Impose a safety rule that students may not raise the clubhead unless their partners give the all clear.
- Students hit 10 balls and then hit 3 to 5 balls, playing each all the way out. (Use diagrams, posters, overheads, and so on, to give students a mental picture of the green, the surrounding area, and the ball position relative to the hole.)
- Students record the scores of their last 3 to 5 balls.

Questions

Q: Where was the best place to land the ball, and why?

A: Short of the green, letting it roll to avoid a penalty for losing a ball in the woods.

Q: Which club was best for achieving the goal?

A: The middle-distance or long-distance iron, but I had to choke up to keep the ball low.

Q: What swing length was best for achieving the goal?

A: Three-quarter to full swing.

Q: Where was the best ball placement?

A: Forward in the stance to keep the trajectory low.

PRACTICE TASK 1

Setup   Each student takes 10 practice swings, adjusting ball placement (in the stance) to achieve a proper trajectory, and then takes 10 more swings so a partner can evaluate his form. Players rotate after 20 swings. Have the student repeat the task if the partner needs more time to evaluate.

Goals

- Adjust ball placement to get a low trajectory.
- Evaluate your partner's performance of a full swing.

PRACTICE TASK 2

Setup   Use the situation from game 1 and have students practice using a full swing to get out from under a tree and to land the ball in front of the green. Have them use a partner checklist to evaluate swing errors and causes of errors based on the flight of the ball.

Goal   Land the ball in front of the green for a good approach shot.

Cues

- Place the ball and select the club necessary for achieving a low trajectory.
- Use an even, smooth swing.

GAME 2

Repeat game 1 and have students compare their scores with those from game 1.

LESSON 7

Tactical Problems   Hitting ball the proper distance and with the proper trajectory

Lesson Focus   Full swing with a middle iron

Objectives

- Drive the ball from the tee.
- Play five holes of golf on a tactical reality golf course (par-3 holes).

GAME 1

Setup   From a tee box, students hit the ball down the fairway so they can reach the green on a second (approach) shot

Goal   Land a drive within 100 feet (30.5 m) of the green.

Conditions

- Ask students to select the club that will best allow them to complete the task.
- Impose a safety rule that students may not raise the clubhead unless their partners give the all clear.
- Place a tee box 250 feet (76 m) from the hole, with a lake between the ball and the hole, and place the hole 20 feet (6 m) on the other side of the lake. (Use diagrams, posters, overheads, and so on, to give students a mental picture of the green, the surrounding area, and the ball position relative to the hole.)
- Have students record their scores.

Questions

Q: Why do you want to land the drive within 100 feet (30.5 m) and in front of the green?

A: To set up an easy second shot.

Q: Did you change any part of your setup or swing to help you achieve the goal?

A: Used a tee.

Q: How did using the tee help?

A: It made it easier to hit the ball by setting up the ball clear of the grass.

Q: Did you try placing the ball in different places within your stance?

A: No.

Let's practice to determine which ball placement will give you the best distance and trajectory.

PRACTICE TASK 1

Setup   From a tee, all students hit two balls placed off the front, the middle, and the rear of the foot. Partners chart the trajectory and approximate distance of each shot. Players switch roles and repeat the task.

Goal   Determine the best placement for the ball during a drive.

Questions

Q: What was the best ball placement for obtaining the proper distance, direction, and trajectory?

A: In front of the foot.

Q: How high should you tee the ball?

A: There should be approximately the width of an index finger from the ball to the ground.

Q: What is the effect of ball height on the trajectory of the ball?

A: If the ball is too high, the trajectory will be high. If the ball is too low, the trajectory will be low. Let's practice to determine how high the ball should be teed up.

PRACTICE TASK 2

Setup From the tee, students hit balls placed high, medium, and low on the tee (two balls at each height). Partners chart the trajectory and approximate distance of each shot. Players switch roles and repeat the task.

Goal Determine the proper height for teeing the ball.

Questions

Q: How did the height of the ball influence the trajectory?

A: If you tee up the ball too high, you get a high trajectory.

Q: What was the best height?

A: Low to medium for an iron, medium for a driver.

Cues

- Work on your setup and ball placement.
- Swing easy; hit hard.
- Fix your eyes on a spot (on the ball).

GAME 2

Setup Students play three to five holes of tactical reality golf (figure 20.2) and compare their scores with those from game 1.

LESSON 8

Secondary Level I

Tactical Problem Reducing the number of strokes

Lesson Focus Rules and etiquette of golf

Objectives

- Drive the ball from the tee.
- Play five holes of golf on a tactical reality golf course (par-3 holes).

GAME 1

Setup Students play five to nine holes of tactical reality golf.

Goals

- Score par (or better) on every hole.
- Demonstrate a knowledge of proper club selection, shot selection, setup, and swing length.

Conditions

- Students play on tactical reality golf holes (figure 21.2).
- All players must follow the rules or assume the appropriate penalties.
- Players must follow course etiquette.

Questions

After three or four holes

Q: What did you do when your ball went into the woods or other hazard, causing you to lift or pick up your ball?

A: Added a penalty stroke to the score.

Q: Can you describe other instances in which penalty strokes are assessed?

A: Playing the wrong ball, moving the ball while setting up a shot (and so forth).

Q: How did you know whose turn it was?

A: The player with the lowest score on the previous hole went first.

Q: What did you do with your bag on the tees and the green?

A: Left the bag off the tees and green. (You can include other questions about rules and etiquette.)
Let's continue play using official rules and proper etiquette.

LEVEL II

Lessons at level II focus on the full swing with a driver and the fairway woods. Once students have developed consistent swing patterns, they should work on altering their swing planes and club positions to hit a ball left to right or right to left. Once the swing pattern becomes consistent, they can work on uneven lies, uphill and downhill lies, and sidehill lies. Two of the following lessons focus on these irregular lies.

Students must practice their full swing to produce accuracy.

Tactical Problems   Hitting the ball the proper distance and in the proper direction

Lesson Focus   Full swing with a fairway wood; club selection

Objective   Use a fairway wood to hit the ball to the intended target.

GAME 1

Setup   Students play three to five holes of tactical reality golf, par-5 holes.

Goal   Land all shots to allow the easiest approach to the green.

Conditions

- Ask students to select the clubs that will best allow them to complete the task.
- Impose a safety rule that students may not raise the clubhead unless their partners give the all clear.
- Place a tee box 450 yards from the hole, with a lake between the ball and the green, and the green 30 feet (9 m) on the other side of the lake. (Use diagrams, posters, overheads, and so on, to give students a mental picture of the green, the surrounding area, and the ball position relative to the hole.)
- Students record their scores.

Questions

Q: *When you had 200 yards or more to the green after your drive, what club did you select? Why?*

A: *The long iron or wood because the longer club and larger clubhead give a longer distance.*

Q: *What other factors influence club selection?*

A: *The distance the person can hit, the lie of the ball, and the distance to the green.*

Q: *How is hitting with a fairway wood different from hitting a drive from the tee?*

A: *The ball lies lower and is not teed up.*

Q: *What do you think were some of the causes for mis-hitting the ball?*

A: *Setup and stance were not right.*

PRACTICE TASK 1

Setup   In pairs, students practice using a fairway wood (2/3 or 4/5). One partner hits five balls from the forward, middle, and back positions as the other partner charts the direction and trajectory of each ball. Partners then switch roles.

Goal   Determine proper ball placement when hitting with a long iron or fairway wood.

Questions

Q: *What was the best ball placement for hitting with a fairway wood?*

A: *Forward. The exact spot may vary from player to player.*

Q: *How far from your body was the ball?*

A: *(Close, medium, or far away.)*

Q: What distance did you find was best?

A: Not sure.

Let's look at ball placement and the distance the ball is placed from your feet.

PRACTICE TASK 2

Setup   Each student uses a fairway wood (2/3 or 4/5) and hits 15 to 20 balls, placing the ball at various distances from his or her body. A partner provides feedback on the hitting student's form and the flight of the ball. Once the hitting partner believes that he's found the proper distance, the partners switch roles. (Prompt students to use the findings from the problem posed in practice task 1 to place the ball in relation to their stances.)

Goal   Determine proper placement of the ball during a shot with a fairway wood.

GAME 2

Setup   Repeat game 1. Students play three to five holes of tactical reality golf and compare their scores with those from game 1.

LESSON 10

Secondary Level II

Tactical Problems   Hitting the ball the proper distance and in the proper direction

Lesson Focus   Full swing with a driver from the tee box

Objective   Use a driver to hit the ball down the center of the fairway.

GAME 1

Setup   Students play three to five holes of tactical reality golf, par-4 holes.

Goal   Land the drive in a place that will allow the easiest approach to the green.

Conditions

- Ask students to select the club that will best allow them to complete the task.
- Impose a safety rule that students may not raise the clubhead unless their partners give the all clear.
- Place the tee box 300 yards from hole, with a lake between the ball and the hole, and place the green 20 feet (6 m) on the other side of the lake. (Use diagrams, posters, overheads, and so on, to give students a mental picture of the green, the surrounding area, and the ball position relative to the hole.)
- Students record their scores.

Questions

Q: For most holes, where was the best place to land the ball?

A: In the middle of the fairway, with an open shot to the green.

Q: Were you able to hit the ball straight most of the time?

A: (Not many students consistently hit straight.)

Q: How can the flight of the ball help you determine swing errors?

A: If the flight is too low or too high, then perhaps there was not a good placement during the setup; if the ball spins left or right, then perhaps the swing plane was incorrect or the blade was not square at impact.

Q: Let's practice swinging and reading the flight and spin of the ball. If the ball is too high or too low, hooking, or slicing, what should you do?

A: Adjust the swing.

PRACTICE TASK 1

Setup   Students hit Wiffle balls into a curtain or wall or hit real or restricted balls in a cage or outside. As one partner practices her drive, the other partner evaluates her, using a checklist and providing feedback. Partners should rotate after 10 to 20 swings.

Goals

- Improve your full swing.
- Evaluate your partner's full swing.

PRACTICE TASK 2

Setup   Students hit Wiffle balls into a curtain or wall or hit in a cage or outside. As one partner hits 5 to 10 balls, the other partner evaluates the direction and trajectory of the ball and gives feedback.

Goal   Read the trajectory and spin of the ball and use them to provide feedback about your partner's swing performance.

GAME 2

Setup   Repeat game 1; have students play three to five holes of tactical reality golf and compare their scores with those from game 1.

LESSON 11

Secondary Level II

Tactical Problem   Hitting out of hazards

Lesson Focus   Sand shots

Objective   Hit the ball out of a sand trap and land it in the target zone.

GAME 1

Setup   Place the ball in sand, with a hole 30 feet (9 m) from the trap and the ball 10 feet (3 m) from the lip of the trap, or 40 feet (12 m) from the hole.

Goal   Get the ball out of the sand and onto the green in one stroke.

Conditions

- Ask students to select the clubs that will best allow them to complete the task.
- Impose a safety rule that students may not raise the clubhead unless their partners give the all clear.

Teaching Sport Concepts and Skills

- You can use a sandbox or pit to create the sand trap.
- Set up identical lies and have students play against a partner to see who can get the ball out of the trap and into the hole in the fewest number of strokes. (Use diagrams, posters, overheads, and so on, to give students a mental picture of the green, the surrounding area, and the ball position relative to the hole.)
- Students record their scores.

Questions

Q: How were you able to get the ball out of the sand and onto the green?

A: By using a firm, open stance and swinging through the ball.

Q: How did you know how big of a swing you needed to get the ball out of the sand?

A: The swing depended on how deep the ball was lying in the sand.

PRACTICE TASK 1

Setup   Students work with partners to evaluate form and provide feedback. Each student takes 10 practice swings and then switches roles with the partner.

Goals

- Consistently get the ball out of the sand and onto the green in one stroke.
- Evaluate your partner's sand shot.

PRACTICE TASK 2

Setup   Students work with partners and place the ball at different depths in the sand. The partner observes and provides feedback relative to the point of contact in the sand and the swing length required to remove the ball from the sand.

Goal   Identify the point of contact for removing the ball during sand shots.

GAME 2

Setup   Repeat game 1 and have students compare their scores with those from game 1.

LESSON 12

Tactical Problem   Hitting out of hazards

Lesson Focus   Hitting a ball lying deep in dense grass

Objectives

- Select the proper club, setup, and intermediate target.
- Adjust the swing plane to hit down and through the ball.

GAME 1

Setup   Students hit balls out of deep, dense grass about 30 yards from the green.

Goal   Hit the ball out of the grass and to the intended target with one swing.

Conditions

- Ask students to select the clubs that will best allow them to complete the task.
- Impose a safety rule that students may not raise the clubhead unless their partners give the all clear.
- If dense grass is not available, use sand or loose dirt to simulate this shot.
- If possible, place balls 60 to 70 yards from the green.
- Have students alternate hits with a partner.
- Students record their scores and subtract five strokes from their scores every time a ball lands and stays on the green or area designated as the green. (Use diagrams, posters, overheads, and so on, to give students a mental picture of the green, the surrounding area, and the ball position relative to the hole.)

Questions

Q: What did you do to get the ball out of the grass and to your intended target?

A: Hit the ball high and landed it short.

Q: How did you adjust your swing to get the ball out of the high grass?

A: Swung down and through the ball and used a firm grip and a good follow-through.

Q: How many of you were able to consistently land the ball on the green?

A: (Not many.)

Let's practice.

PRACTICE TASK

Setup Use the situation from game 1 and add a hula hoop to provide a target in which to land the ball. With a partner, students take five shots each and then switch. The observing partner should serve as a coach, providing feedback following each shot.

Goal Adjust your swing to get the ball out of dense grass.

Cues

- Select an intermediate target.
- Select a place to land the ball.
- Swing down and through.

GAME 2

Setup Repeat game 1 and have students compare their scores with those from game 1 at the end of class to see if they have improved.

LESSON 13

Secondary Level II

Tactical Problem Hitting downhill and uphill lies

Lesson Focus Setup for downhill and uphill lies

Objective Determine the club, setup, stance, and ball placement for uphill and downhill lies.

GAME 1

Setup   Students compete with partners. Each partner hits five uphill lies and five downhill lies into a target area about 30 feet (9 m) away.

Goal   Land the ball within 10 feet (3 m) of the intended target with one swing.

Conditions

- Ask students to select the clubs that will best allow them to complete the task.
- Impose a safety rule that students may not raise the clubhead unless their partners give the all clear.
- If possible, place the ball 10 to 20 yards from a target if students are using a Wiffle ball.
- Students record their partners' scores, adding one stroke for every shot that misses the target area and subtracting two strokes for every shot that lands in the target area. (Use diagrams, posters, overheads, and so on, to give students a mental picture of the uphill and downhill lies, the surrounding area, and the ball position relative to the hole.)

Questions

Q: How did you adjust your preshot setup to successfully hit uphill and downhill lies?

A: Took a practice swing to determine where to place the ball in the stance and positioned the ball high toward the foot.

Q: How did you adjust your swing to successfully hit uphill and downhill lies?

A: Adjusted the swing length to the degree of the slope and used a choke-up grip (about 3 in., or 7.6 cm, from the top) with shoulders parallel to the slope.

Q: How successful were you at consistently making contact with the ball?

A: (Not many students respond positively.)

Perhaps we should practice.

PRACTICE TASK

Setup   Use partner evaluations, such as checklists, and include an evaluation of the preshot routine. Partners alternate after 10 to 20 shots.

Goals

- Set up properly to allow for good contact.
- Improve the swing used for uphill and downhill lies.

Cues

- Bear weight on your uphill foot.
- Use a practice swing to help with ball placement.
- Swing parallel with the slant of the hill.

GAME 2

Setup   Repeat game 1, or allow students to play two or three holes of tactical reality golf, with each fairway shot played as either an uphill or a downhill lie.

Tactical Problem   Hitting sidehill lies

Lesson Focus   Setup for hitting sidehill lies

Objectives

- Determine the club, setup, stance, and ball placement for sidehill lies.
- Refine the preshot routine.

GAME 1

Setup   In pairs, students take turns hitting 10 sidehill lies (5 sloping away from the target and 5 sloping toward the target) into a target area.

Goal   Land the ball within 10 feet (3 m) of the intended target with one swing.

Conditions

- Students hit the ball from about 30 feet (9 m) away and score one stroke for every shot that misses the target area and subtract two strokes for every shot that lands in the target area.
- Ask students to select the clubs that will best allow them to complete the task.
- Impose a safety rule that students may not raise the clubhead unless their partners give the all clear.
- If possible, place the ball 10 to 20 yards away from the target if students are using a Wiffle ball. (Use diagrams, posters, overheads, and so on, to give students a mental picture of the uphill and downhill lies, the surrounding area, and the ball position relative to the hole.)
- Students record their partners' scores.

Questions

Q: *How did you adjust your preshot setup to successfully hit a sidehill lie?*

A: *Took a practice swing to determine where to place the ball in the stance; selected an intermediate target.*

Q: *How did you adjust your swing to successfully hit sidehill lies?*

A: *Adjusted swing length to the degree of the slope and used a choke-up grip (about 3 in., or 7.6 cm, from the top). Stood closer when the ball was below my feet and shifted my weight toward my heels and insteps.*

PRACTICE TASK

Setup   Use partner evaluations, such as checklists, and include evaluations of the preshot routine. Partners alternate after 10 to 20 shots.

Goals

- Set up properly to allow good contact.
- Improve the swing used for sidehill lies.

Cues

- Use a practice swing to check for proper ball placement.
- Always use a preshot routine.

- Use a closed blade on a downward slope (slopes away from the golfer).
- Use an open blade on an upward slope (slopes toward the golfer).

GAME 2

Setup   Repeat game 1, or allow students to play two or three holes of tactical reality golf, with each fairway shot played as a sidehill lie.

LESSON 15

Tactical Problem   Hitting a ball with spin

Lesson Focus   Hitting a ball with backspin

Objective   Land a pitch shot on a green from 40 to 80 yards.

GAME 1

Setup   Three holes of stroke play with a foursome

Goal   Play three partial holes in as few strokes as possible.

Conditions

- The pin is close to the front edge of the green, and the ball is on the fairway, about 60 yards from the hole.
- Students play three holes, beginning with a short fairway shot.

Questions

Q: What was the best club for the first shot?

A: A 9-iron, pitching wedge, or sand wedge.

Q: Where was the best spot on the green to place the ball?

A: Close to the hole so you could putt once.

Q: How were you able to get the ball to land close to the hole?

A: Used a high trajectory so the ball would stay where it landed.

Q: How successful were you at landing the ball close to the hole and getting it to stay there?

A: Not very.

Let's practice!

PRACTICE TASK

Setup   Students work on varying the loft of the ball in pairs. Each partner uses a 9-iron to hit three balls: one off the target heel, one off the rear heel, and one from the center. The partner observes the ball spin and flight and records observations. Partners then switch and repeat the task. On the second and third rounds, each partner uses a pitching wedge and a sand wedge, respectively.

Goal   Observe the differences in loft and flight caused by different clubs and ball placements.

Cues

- Use a narrower stance.
- Use a forward swing length, 2:00 or 3:00.
- Follow through with your hands toward the target.

Questions

Q: How did the position of the ball influence its trajectory and spin?

A: The farther back in stance the ball is placed, the lower the trajectory is.

Q: How did the type of club influence the trajectory and spin of the ball?

A: The greater the loft is, the higher the trajectory is and the greater the spin is.

GAME 2

Setup Students play two to four par-3 holes of tactical reality golf.

Goal Make as few strokes as possible.

Conditions

- Use visual aids to illustrate the conditions of each par-3 hole.
- Students do not use a tee when hitting from the tee box.

LESSON 16

Secondary Level II

Tactical Problem Hitting a ball with spin

Lesson Focus Modifying the flight pattern of the ball

Objective Determine the elements of the swing that influence the direction in which the ball travels.

GAME 1

Setup Follow the leader

Goal Imitate the flight path of the ball hit by your partner.

Conditions

- In a field or down the length of a gym, partners alternate shots.
- The first partner attempts to hit the ball right to left or left to right, and then the other partner attempts to imitate that shot.
- After 10 shots, partners switch.

Questions

Q: What elements of the swing influenced the direction of the ball?

A: The angle of the clubface at contact, the angle of the swing during the forward swing, and a setup that was not square.

Q: What was the position of the clubface when the ball rotated right (clockwise)? When it rotated left (counterclockwise)?

A: Open. Closed.

Q: What swing plane caused the ball to move left? To move right?

A: Outside-in. Inside-out.

Q: How many of you were successful at imitating your partner's swing?

A: (Not many.)

Let's practice!

PRACTICE TASK

Setup   One partner swings as the other observes and records the flight patterns. The first partner attempts five full swings with an open face and five full swings with a closed face. Partners then switch roles. The first partner attempts five full swings moving the club outside-in (with the clubface staying square) and five full swings moving the club inside-out (again, with the clubface remaining square). Partners switch roles. The first partner combines an outside-in swing with an open clubface for five shots and then with a closed clubface for five shots. Partners switch again. Then the first partner combines an inside-out swing with an open clubface for five shots and then with a closed clubface for five shots. Partners switch roles and repeat the task.

Goal   Intentionally hit hook, slice, and fade shots.

Cues

- Swing normally when the clubface is open or closed.
- Adjust your swing plane only slightly from a normal swing.
- Read the flight of ball for feedback.
- Set up correctly and then let the club do the work.

GAME 2

Setup   Students play two or three holes of tactical reality golf.

Goal   Use the fewest number of strokes possible.

Conditions

- During drive and long fairway shots, partners predetermine their flight patterns.
- Use a one-stroke penalty for flight patterns not matching the predetermined ones, or, if possible, select holes that require certain types of shots to approach the green (e.g., narrow fairways, doglegs, strong breezes).

LESSON 17

Secondary Level II

Lesson Focus   Rules and etiquette

Objective   Play four or five holes of golf, scoring par or better.

GAME 1

Setup   Students play golf on an actual course, or play tactical reality golf, in twosomes, threesomes, or foursomes

Goal   Play four or five holes in as few strokes as possible.

PRACTICE TASK

Setup   Students analyze the four or five holes they just completed and assess (in writing) their game performances (skills such as drives, approach shots, and putting, and game play such as shot selection, performance of the preshot routine, and selection of the intermediate target).

Goal   Assess your golf game to improve your play and lower your score.

GAME 2

Setup   Students play golf on an actual course, or play tactical reality golf, in twosomes, threesomes, or foursomes.

Goal   Play the same four or five holes in fewer strokes.

SUMMARY

There are many videos, books, magazines, and Internet sites on tactical and skill development in golf. You can modify many drills and practice situations found in these resources for your students. Experienced players enjoy working on various aspects of their games, as they realize the value of consistent and accurate shots. Assign students the task of searching for new drills and tips to improve their games so you can help them identify available resources for future reference. In so doing, you not only provide them with golf experience, but also offer them experience with identifying sources for developing personal skill and improving their game performance.

Encourage students to play golf on a regulation course. Give them credit for a family golf outing or for playing a round of golf with friends. Let them know that it's OK to play even if they are not very skilled. After all, most golfers are far from skilled. Teach them that etiquette and courtesy count most on the golf course. As long as they allow faster groups to play through, repair divots, rake traps, and treat the golf course gently, they will be welcome. You may also want to identify three or four local courses that would be best for beginners. Visit these courses yourself to see whether you can get some coupons or other deals (e.g., two games for the price of one, or 18 holes for the price of 9).

Chapter 22

Bowling

Bowling, with its tactical simplicity and potential as a lifelong activity, is an essential component of secondary physical education. Most of the tactics fundamental to bowling apply to almost every other target game, and these tactics embrace a primary concept of movement: accuracy requiring control of both speed and direction. Like golf, bowling requires numerous decisions before rolling the ball, such as determining a starting spot and an intermediate target. These decisions, referred to as preshot decisions, can help even the novice bowler solve tactical problems related to rolling the ball in the intended direction and achieving the desired pin action (table 22.1).

ORGANIZATION OF LANES AND EQUIPMENT

You will want to set up as many lanes as possible to maintain high levels of student engagement. Keep the lane distance shorter rather than longer, because the longer the distance is, the more the ball moves (follows the slight undulation in the gym floor) and the harder it is for students to control the ball. Lanes should end

within 3 to 5 feet (1 to 1.5 m) of a wall to keep balls from rolling into high-traffic areas. Mark the approach with spots, just as with real bowling lanes, and place arrows just ahead of the foul line (figure 22.1). Most gymnasiums can accommodate 10 to 12 lanes. Use 3 or 6 pins rather than 10, because many of the basic tactics can be learned with fewer pins, which require far less time for setup. If you do not have plastic bowling pins, use wooden pins or soda bottles. If you do not have bowling balls especially designed for gymnasium instruction, consider using 8- to 10-inch (20 to 25 cm) playground balls. Because playground balls bounce, students are less likely to loft them; they will want to roll them to avoid the bounce.

To maximize participation, keep groups small. Groups of four are recommended: two players to set up pins and return the ball, one player to bowl, and one player to record the score. The pair setting up pins can provide feedback on performance and etiquette and watch for safety infractions. Two safety rules for the pair resetting the pins are a must: (a) When returning the ball, you must roll it, and (b) when stopping a ball, use your foot (as if trapping a

Table 22.1 Tactical Problems, Decisions, and Skills in Bowling

Tactical problems	Preshot decisions	Skill execution

Rolling the ball in the intended direction	• Selecting a starting point
	• Selecting an intermediate target
	• Adjusting the starting point and the intermediate target according to the remaining pins
		• Consistent setup, grip, and approach
		• Consistent form:
		  ○ Release and follow-through
		  ○ Release point and angle

Attaining proper pin action	Determining: • Speed of the approach • Length of the arm swing • Angle of the entry or contact point • Spin (amount and direction)	Adjusting: • Length of the arm swing • Approach speed • Release point, angle of release, and follow-through
Adjusting the starting point or the intermediate target for lane conditions (or both)	Shadow bowling to determine lane conditions	Adjusting: • Setup position • Starting point • Intermediate target • Approach angle • Approach speed • Spin • Release point • Angle of release • Follow-through
Picking up splits	Determining: • Best place to contact the pin • Start position • Intermediate target for 5-7 and 5-10 splits	Adjusting: • Setup position • Approach angle and the speed of the approach • Release point, angle of release, and follow-through

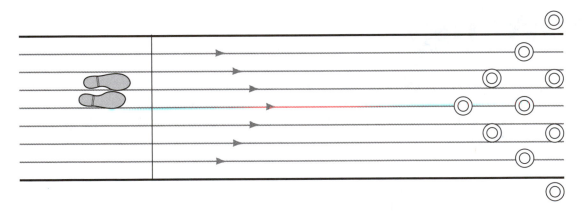

Figure 22.1 Arranging bowling lanes of the appropriate length and adjusting the number of pins to align with your students' skills will improve their success rate.

soccer ball), to avoid being struck in the face by pins that may be flying about.

Get to know the owners or managers of local bowling establishments. They can often provide coupons for free or discounted games and information about equipment and bowling leagues, and they may even volunteer their services. Local bowling proprietors are also a good source of score sheets, pencils, and other bowling paraphernalia. Some proprietors and local bowling associations have portable lanes, pins, balls, and instructional materials, which they lend to schools and nonprofit organizations to promote the sport.

INSTRUCTION TIPS

We do not advocate initially teaching the parts of the ball, pins, or lanes or the history of the game. If using balls with holes, show students where to place their fingers and thumb and let them bowl. Intervene only when you observe a dysfunctional grip or an unsafe approach. Use proper terminology as you present each tactic or skill, referring to the *spots and arrows* on the *lane* or hitting the *pocket* between the *1-3 pins*. As for the history of the game, assign students the task of finding out how bowling got started. They can ask their parents or grandparents about it or look it up on the Internet or in the library. Get the pins set up and the balls in their hands, and let them play. Once students are engaged and having fun, they will want to learn about the game and how to be successful at it.

Establishing an Authentic Context

To grasp the tactical concepts of bowling, students need to understand the situation each time they roll the ball. Where is the best place to stand to win a game or match given the pin setup and pins remaining, lane conditions, and score? The decisions made before the ball is rolled, or the preshot decisions, are as important as the shot itself. We recommend using visual aids to help students understand how to determine the best angle of approach, where to strike the pins, and the effects of various spins and approaches. You can use

posters, colored chalk drawings, overheads, and so forth, to illustrate a situation in an actual bowling alley. Be sure to include gutters, balls of different weights, and lane conditions to illustrate the reality of a bowling alley. We have often copied diagrams of lanes, grips, and approaches from magazines, websites, scorecards, and materials from bowling association tournaments and promotions. If the diagrams are too small, enlarge them. Then laminate these diagrams and use them as instructional aids, or let the students pretend to play a few frames in class. Increasing authenticity may increase transfer to the real context.

The tactical framework and levels of tactical complexity for bowling are presented in tables 22.1 and 22.2. Throughout the chapter, we describe the focus of each level before presenting lesson outlines. Reproducibles 22.1 and 22.2 offer an example of a bowling

Table 22.2 Levels of Tactical Complexity for Bowling

Tactical problems	Level I	Level II	Level III	Level IV
Rolling the ball in the intended direction	• Selecting a starting point • Selecting an intermediate target • Consistent setup, grip, and approach	Adjusting the starting point and the intermediate target according to the remaining pins		Consistent form: • Release and follow-through • Release point and angle
Attaining proper pin action		Determining: • Speed of the approach • Length of the arm swing • Angle of the entry or contact point • Adjusting: • Length of the arm swing • Approach speed • Release point, angle of release, and follow-through	Determining spin (amount and direction)	
Adjusting the starting point or the intermediate target for lane conditions (or both)		Adjusting: • Setup position • Starting point • Intermediate target • Approach angle • Approach speed	Adjusting: • Spin • Release point • Angle of release • Follow-through	Shadow bowling to determine lane conditions
Picking up splits			Determining: • Best place to contact the pin • Start position • Intermediate target for 5-7 and 5-10 splits Adjusting: • Setup position • Approach angle and speed of approach • Release point, angle of release, and follow-through	

Reproducible 22.1

Bowling Score Sheet

Name/Team _____   Lanes _____

League/Tournament _____   Date _____

1	2	3	4	5	6	7	8	9	10

1	2	3	4	5	6	7	8	9	10

1	2	3	4	5	6	7	8	9	10

Total score   _____
New average   _____

From S.A. Mitchell, J.L. Oslin, and L.L. Griffin. 2013. *Teaching sport concepts and skills: A tactical games approach for ages 7 to 18*, third edition (Champaign, IL: Human Kinetics).

Reproducible 22.1   Bowling score sheet.

Reproducible 22.2

Sample Bowling Chart

Name _____   Date _____

Score	Foot Placement (Starting spot)	Lane Markings (Intermediate target)	Pins (Use arrow to show point of contact)

From S.A. Mitchell, J.L. Oslin, and L.L. Griffin. 2013. *Teaching sport concepts and skills: A tactical games approach for ages 7 to 18*, third edition (Champaign, IL: Human Kinetics).

Reproducible 22.2   Sample bowling chart. Chart the starting point, intermediate target, and point at which the ball contacts the pins. This is useful for clarifying tactical concepts, reinforcing preshot decisions, and highlighting the need for consistency.

score sheet and a sample chart highlighting key points and targets for bowlers. These may be reproduced for student use.

LEVEL I

The lessons in level I focus on rolling the ball in the intended direction and should build on the rolling lessons taught in the primary grades. Lesson 1 begins with locating the pocket, so students come to understand where to hit the pins. Lessons 2 and 3 focus on preshot decisions (specifically, determining the starting spot and intermediate target) to help students hit the pocket more consistently. Lesson 4 emphasizes using a consistent setup, approach, and delivery, and it should build on the rolling lessons taught during the primary and intermediate grades. Lesson 5 allows students to put it all together, promoting authentic, gamelike conditions that will prepare them for bowling in a public setting. Depending on the level of your students, you may combine two or more level I lessons or extend some lessons to give students more time to refine their bowling skills and preshot decisions.

A consistent setup, approach, and delivery helps students hit the pocket consistently.

LESSON 1

Tactical Problem   Rolling the ball in the intended direction

Lesson Focus   Locating the pocket

Objective   Identify the pocket as the best place to strike the pins so that they can all be knocked down with one roll of the ball.

GAME 1

Setup   Three pins in the 1, 2, 3 positions

Goal   Determine the best place to strike the three pins to knock them down with one roll.

Conditions

- Groups of two or four play on lanes 30 feet (9 m) long that are marked with spots on the approach and arrows on the lane.
- One or two players set pins while the others bowl.
- Each player takes two consecutive trials to knock down all three pins.
- One player records the number of pins knocked down on each trial and calculates the cumulative score (reproducible 22.1).
- Each player bowls at least four frames. (Remind students of cues from previous rolling lessons, such as bend and send.)

Questions

Q: Where was the best place to strike the three pins to knock them down with one roll?

A: Between the 1 and 3 (if right-handed) or between the 1 and 2 (if left-handed).

Q: Why is the 1-3 (or 1-2 for left-handed bowlers) better than right down the middle?

A: The ball is more likely to knock down all three pins when it approaches from an angle.

Q: What is the area between the 1-3 pins called?

A: The pocket.

PRACTICE TASK

Setup   Students return to the lanes and repeat game 1, using the pocket as the target. They record the score for each ball bowled and compare them with those from game 1.

Goal   Hit the pocket.

Cues

- Bend and send.
- Aim for the 1-3 pocket (right-handed player).
- Aim for the 1-2 pocket (left-handed player).

Tactical Problem   Rolling the ball in the intended direction

Lesson Focus   Determining a starting spot

Objective   Select a starting spot for improving accuracy and consistency in knocking down all the pins with the first ball.

GAME 1

Setup   Three pins in the 1, 2, 3 positions

Goal   Hit the pocket four times in a row.

Conditions

- Groups of two or four play on lanes 30 feet (9 m) long that are marked with spots on the approach and arrows on the lane.
- One or two players set pins while the others bowl.
- Each player takes two consecutive trials to knock down all three pins.
- One player records the number of pins knocked down on each trial and calculates the cumulative score (reproducible 22.1).
- Each player bowls at least four frames.

Questions

Q: *What did you do to consistently hit the pocket?*

A: *Started and stood in the same place, rolled the ball the same way, and aimed.*

Q: *What can you do to be sure that you start in the same place every time?*

A: *Use the spots on the approach lane.*

PRACTICE TASK

Setup   Students try various starting spots to determine which spot allows them to hit the pocket most often. Give them stickers or dry-erase markers to mark their spots. Each student should select a spot and roll three balls and then adjust the spot and roll three more balls. If more adjustment is needed, the student should wait until all other group members have had two attempts at finding their spots. Students then continue until they have found a spot that increases consistency. (Encourage them to select a spot that is to the right of the center, because this location leads to a better angle from which to enter the pocket and will result in better pin action once more pins are added.)

Goal   Find your starting spot.

Cues

- Mark your spot and roll three balls.
- Use the same foot on the starting spot each time you roll.

GAME 2

Setup   Repeat game 1.

Goal   Hit the pocket every time.

Conditions

- Students start from their spots on every trial.
- Students record each other's scores and compare them with those from game 1.

LESSON 3

Tactical Problem Rolling the ball in the intended direction

Lesson Focus Determining an intermediate target

Objective Select an arrow as an intermediate target to improve accuracy and consistency in knocking down all the pins with the first ball.

GAME 1

Setup Three pins in the 1, 2, 3 positions

Goal Determine the best place to aim to knock down all the pins with the first ball.

Conditions

- Groups of two or four play on lanes 30 feet (9 m) long that are marked with spots on the approach and arrows on the lane.
- One or two players set pins while the others bowl.
- Each player takes two consecutive trials to knock down all three pins.
- One player records the number of pins knocked down on each trial and calculates the cumulative score (reproducible 22.1).
- Each player bowls at least four frames.

Questions

Q: Everyone look at this lane and show me (by pointing) where you aim.

A: At the pocket, at the arrows just beyond the foul line, and at the arrows farther down the alley.

Q: Why do you aim at an arrow that is close rather than at the pocket that is far away?

A: A closer target is easier to hit.

Q: What do you call a target between you and the pins?

A: An intermediate target.

PRACTICE TASK

Setup Students try various arrows as intermediate targets to determine which arrow allows them to hit the pocket most consistently. Give them stickers or dry-erase markers for marking their intermediate targets. Each student should select an intermediate target and roll three balls, adjust the intermediate target, and roll three more balls. If more adjustment is needed, the student should wait until all other group members have had two attempts at finding their intermediate targets. Then the students continue until they have found an intermediate target that increases their consistency.

Goal Find your intermediate target.

Cues

- Mark your arrow (intermediate target) and roll three balls.
- Aim and roll the ball over the intermediate target.

GAME 2

Setup Repeat game 1.

Conditions

- Students start from their spots and use their intermediate targets on every trial.
- Students record each other's scores and compare them with those of game 1.

LESSON 4

Tactical Problem Rolling the ball in the intended direction

Lesson Focus Consistent setup, grip, and approach

Objective Determine and use a consistent setup, grip, and approach.

GAME 1

Setup Three pins in the 1, 2, 3 positions

Goal Knock down all three pins four times in a row.

Conditions

- Groups of two or four play on lanes 30 feet (9 m) long that are marked with spots on the approach and arrows on the lane.
- One or two players set pins while the others bowl.
- Each player takes two consecutive trials to knock down all three pins.
- One player records the number of pins knocked down on each trial and calculates the cumulative score (reproducible 22.1).
- Each player bowls at least four frames.

Questions

Q: Besides starting at the same spot and using the same arrow as an intermediate target, what can you do to knock down all three pins four times in a row?

A: Use the same stance, same grip, and same approach.

Q: Let's watch three volunteers as they perform their stance, grip, and approach. What parts of their stance, grip, and approach are the same? What parts are different?

A: Their stance and approach are different. Their grips are all the same.

Q: Notice that they all take a different number of steps, but they end on the foot opposite the one they began on. Why?

A: So they can slide on the last step, which allows them to bend and send the ball low.

Teaching Sport Concepts and Skills

PRACTICE TASK

Setup   Students try various stances and approaches to determine which ones allow them to hit the pocket most consistently. Each student should pick a stance and approach and roll three balls, try a different stance and approach, and then a third stance and approach. Students should select the stance and approach that feels the best and allows them to consistently knock down all three pins.

Goal   Find the stance and approach that is comfortable and results in consistency.

Cues

- Stance—Be still and focused.
- Approach:
  - Be smooth and controlled.
  - Bend and send.

GAME 2

Setup   Repeat game 1.

Conditions

- Students start from their spots, use their intermediate targets, and use a consistent stance and approach on every trial.
- Students record each other's scores and compare them with the scores from game 1.

LESSON 5

Tactical Problem   Rolling the ball in the intended direction

Lesson Focus   Putting it all together, including scoring and etiquette (consistency) and adjusting for lane conditions

Objectives

- Consistently use the same starting point, intermediate target, setup routine, approach, and delivery to knock down all three pins.
- Follow proper bowling etiquette and scoring procedures during a partner or team competition.

GAME 1

Setup   Three pins in the 1, 2, 3 positions

Goal   Knock down all three pins at least 5 out of 10 times.

Conditions

- Groups of two or four play on lanes 30 feet (9 m) long that are marked with spots on the approach and arrows on the lane.
- One or two players set pins while the others bowl.
- Players take turns with opponents on the lanes as in league or tournament play.
- Players also take turns setting up pins and scoring.
- The scorer records the number of pins knocked down on each trial and calculates the cumulative score on a regulation bowling sheet (reproducible 22.1).
- The players on each team total their scores to determine the winner.

Questions   Ask questions after most students have bowled five frames.

Q: How many of you knocked down all three pins in the first five frames?

A: (No students or very few.)

Q: Where does the ball go when you miss?

A: (Left or right.)

Q: If your setup, intermediate target, and form are consistent and you are consistently missing to the right, in which direction should you shift your starting spot (left or right)?

A: To the right, in the direction of the error.

Q: If you are missing the pins sometimes to the left and sometimes to the right, what should you do?

A: Work on using a consistent setup, intermediate target, approach, release, and follow-through.

LEVEL II

Lessons in level II focus on shooting spares, using six pins to teach tactical concepts related to adjusting the starting spot and the intermediate target, as well as ball speed. As level II progresses, students are required to be increasingly accurate. As with lesson 5 of level I, lesson 10 at level II emphasizes putting it all together.

It is important to know how to adjust the starting spot and intermediate target to shoot spares consistently.

LESSON 6

Tactical Problem   Attaining proper pin action

Lesson Focus   Adjusting ball speed

Objectives

- Adjust the speed of the approach and the length of the arm swing to vary the speed of the ball.
- Determine the amount of speed necessary to create sufficient pin action to knock down all six pins on one ball.

GAME 1

Setup   Six pins in the 1 through 6 positions

Goal   Knock down all six pins with one ball four times in a row.

Conditions

- Groups of two or four play on lanes 30 to 40 feet (9 to 12 m) long that are marked with spots on the approach and arrows on the lane.
- One or two players set pins while the others bowl.
- Each player takes two consecutive trials to knock down all three pins.
- One player records the number of pins knocked down on each trial and calculates the cumulative score (reproducible 22.1).
- Each player bowls at least four frames.

Questions

Q: How was bowling at three pins the same as bowling at six pins?

A: Same setup, intermediate target, approach, and release.

Q: How was bowling at three pins different from bowling at six pins?

A: Need more force and more speed to create more pin action.

Q: What kinds of things did you do to increase the speed of the ball?

A: Increased the speed of the approach and the length of the arm swing.

PRACTICE TASK

Setup   Students try adjusting the speed of their approaches and note the difference in pin action that occurs when the ball is rolled slower and faster. After students have had three or four trials, they should try adjusting the length of their backswings. (If cameras are available, have students record the pin action when the backswing is short versus when it is long.) Trying varying approach speeds and backswing lengths, students should establish a consistent approach with sufficient speed to knock down all six pins.

Note   Students may need to adjust their starting points to accommodate the change in ball speed.

Goal   Adjust your approach or backswing length to attain sufficient pin action.

Cues

- Step a bit quicker.
- Match your backswing with your intended speed.

GAME 2

Setup   Repeat game 1.

Condition   Students record their scores and compare them with those from game 1.

LESSON 7   *Secondary Level II*

Tactical Problems   Adjusting the starting spot and the intermediate target

Lesson Focus   Shooting spares

Objective   Determine which spares can be made without adjusting the first ball's starting spot or intermediate target.

GAME 1

Setup   Six pins in the 1 through 6 positions

Goal   Knock down the remaining pins with a second ball.

Conditions

- Groups of two or four play on lanes 30 to 40 feet (9 to 12 m) long that are marked with spots on the approach and arrows on the lane.
- One or two players set the pins while the others bowl.
- Each player is allowed two balls to knock down all six pins.
- One player records the number of pins knocked down on each trial, using a slash (/) in the appropriate place on the score sheet to indicate a spare, adding 10 points to the number of pins knocked down on the next ball, and calculating the cumulative score (reproducible 22.1).
- Strikes are recorded with an X, and 10 points plus the number of pins knocked down on the next two balls are added to the cumulative score.
- Each player bowls at least four frames before the class gathers for questions.

Note   Students who know how to score should help those who do not. Assign worksheets and website research for homework, and recruit assistance from classroom teachers and parents.

Questions

Q: What is it called when you knock all the pins down with one ball? With two balls?

A: Strike. Spare.

Q: How is shooting for a spare different from shooting for a strike?

A: The pins are in a different location, which means you have to use a different starting spot and intermediate target.

Q: Are there any spares in which you do not have to change your starting spot or intermediate target?

A: 1, 2, 3, and 5, plus some combinations such as 1-2 and 1-3.

PRACTICE TASK

Setup   Groups of two or four play on lanes 30 to 40 feet (9 to 12 m) long that are marked with spots on the approach and arrows on the lane. One or two players set up six pins while the others bowl. One player bowls and the other charts (reproducible 22.2) the pins contacted by the first, or strike, ball. Players switch after each has had three attempts. Players then review everyone's charts to determine where the strike ball hit. This in turn gives an indication of how spares can be made depending on where the strike ball hit.

Goal   Determine which pins are the most likely to be contacted by the strike, or the first ball.

Cues   On the chart, put an X through the pins that came in direct contact with the ball.

GAME 2

Setup   1 pin, 2 pin, 3 pin

Goal   Every team member knocks down each pin in order on three consecutive attempts.

Conditions

- If the 1 pin is knocked down, set up the 2 pin, and if the 2 pin is knocked down, set up the 3 pin.
- Repeat for the next bowler.
- If a pin is missed, rotate to the next bowler. That bowler can then resume from where he left off. For example, if a bowler gets the 1 pin and misses the 2 pin, he should start with the 2 pin on his next turn.

LESSON 8

Tactical Problems   Adjusting the starting spot and the intermediate target

Lesson Focus   Shooting spares

Objective   Adjust the starting spot or setup position and the intermediate target to make spares.

GAME 1

Setup   Six pins in the 1 through 6 positions

Goal   Knock down the remaining pins with a second ball.

Conditions

- Groups of two or four play on lanes 30 to 40 feet (9 to 12 m) long that are marked with spots on the approach and arrows on the lane.
- One or two players set pins while the others bowl.
- Each player is allowed two balls to knock down all six pins.
- One player records the number of pins knocked down on each trial, using a slash (/) in the appropriate place on the score sheet to indicate a spare, adding 10 points to the number of pins knocked down on the next ball, and calculating the cumulative score (reproducible 22.1).
- Strikes are recorded with an X, and 10 points plus the number of pins knocked down on the next two balls are added to the cumulative score.
- Each player bowls at least four frames before the class gathers for questions.

Questions

Q: For which spares was it necessary to adjust your starting spot and intermediate target?

A: 2, 3, 4, 6, 2-4, 3-5, 3-6, and so on.

Q: When shooting at the 4 pin, where is the best starting spot?

A: The right side of the lane (when facing the pins).

PRACTICE TASK 1

Setup   Groups of two or four play on lanes 30 to 40 feet (9 to 12 m) long that are marked with spots on the approach and arrows on the lane. One or two players set up 4 pin (6 pin for left-handed bowlers) while the others bowl. One player bowls three consecutive times at the 4 pin, adjusting the starting point or intermediate target, and scores (reproducible 22.1) a pin for every successful attempt. Players switch after each has had three attempts.

Goal   Make the spare three consecutive times.

Cue   Shoot across on corner spares.

PRACTICE TASK 2

Setup   Repeat with the 6 pin (4 pin for left-handed bowlers).

GAME 2

Setup   Repeat game 1.

Condition   Students record their scores and compare them with their scores from game 1.

LESSON 9

Tactical Problems   Adjusting the starting spot and intermediate target

Lesson Focus   Shooting spares

Objectives   Adjust the starting spot or setup position and the intermediate target to make spares.

GAME 1

Setup   Six pins in the 1 through 6 positions

Goal   Knock down all six pins in six consecutive frames.

Conditions

- Groups of two or four play on lanes 30 to 40 feet (9 to 12 m) long that are marked with spots on the approach and arrows on the lane.
- One or two players set pins while the others bowl.
- In the first frame all players get one turn to knock down the 1 pin; in the second frame all players get one turn to knock down the 2 pin; and so on through the sixth frame.

Questions

Q: *What did you need to do to be successful?*

A: *Adjust the starting spots and intermediate targets.*

Q: *Which pins did you hit? Which did you miss?*

A: *(Various answers.)*

Q: *Is there a rule of thumb that could help you adjust?*

A: *If you want the ball to go right, move left—assuming you use the same intermediate target.*

PRACTICE TASK

Setup   Each player bowls five times at all six pins, beginning with the strike ball. On the next ball, the player moves one spot to the right and rolls again, using the same intermediate target. On the third ball, the player moves one more spot to the right and rolls again, using the same intermediate target. On the fourth ball, the player moves one spot left of the strike-ball starting spot and rolls again, using the same intermediate target. On the fifth ball, the player moves one more spot left and rolls again, using the same intermediate target. Another player or partner should chart the point at which the ball contacts the pins, using a small circle and recording the numbers of balls thrown in the sequence (reproducible 22.2). For example, the player writes a 1 in the circle of the first ball thrown and a 2 in the circle of the second ball thrown.

Goal   Recognize that when you move to the right, the ball goes left, and when you move to the left, the ball goes right.

Cue   Change your starting spot and keep the same intermediate target.

GAME 2

Setup   Repeat game 1.

LESSON 10

Tactical Problems   Adjusting the starting spot and intermediate target

Lesson Focus   Shooting spares

Objectives

- Adjust the starting spot or intermediate target to shoot spares.
- Demonstrate appropriate etiquette and rotation, consistent with league or tournament play.

GAME 1

Setup   Six pins in the 1 through 6 positions

Goal   Knock down the remaining pins with the second ball.

Conditions

- Groups of two or four play on lanes 30 to 40 feet (9 to 12 m) long that are marked with spots on the approach and arrows on the lane.

- One or two players set pins while the others bowl.
- Each player is allowed two balls to knock down all six pins.
- One player records the number of pins knocked down on each trial, using a slash (/) in the appropriate place on the score sheet to indicate a spare, adding 10 points to the number of pins knocked down on the next ball, and calculating the cumulative score (reproducible 22.1).
- Strikes are recorded with an X, and 10 points plus the number of pins knocked down on the next two balls are added to the cumulative score.
- Players take turns on lanes with their opponents, as is done in league or tournament play.
- Players bowl and score 10 frames.

Questions

Q: What happens when you get a strike in the 10th frame?

A: You get to bowl two more balls and add the number of pins knocked down to the total score.

Q: What happens when you get a spare in the 10th frame?

A: You get to bowl one more ball and add the number of pins knocked down to the total score.

Q: Besides using the score, how can you analyze your game play?

A: Chart the pins missed on the first and second balls of each frame (reproducible 22.2).

LEVEL III

Lessons in level III use 10 pins to emphasize common spares and the tactics needed to consistently pick up these spares. In lessons 11 through 14, game 1 highlights tactical problems related to adjusting the starting spot and intermediate target. The spares are in groups of three, positioned on the left, center, and right, which should require little to no adjustment when two of the three pins are remaining, and a slight adjustment when one of the three pins is remaining. Lesson 14 highlights the 5-7 and 5-10 splits, two splits that are very doable. Of course, other splits can be included here or covered in additional lessons. The final game is a regulation game that can be set up as a competition with other teams to mimic league play.

Lessons at levels III and IV can be extended to create a Sport Education season. Consistent with the Sport Education model, we suggest awarding points for fair play to teams demonstrating proper etiquette before, during, and after league play. These points can be added to team standings during league play and can level the playing field and temper excessive celebrations that often ensue after strikes. We do not suggest eliminating the celebration, but rather, stressing proper forms of it.

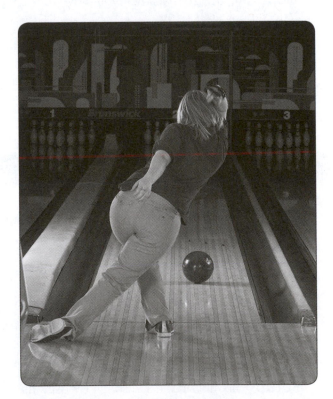

To keep racking up points, students must use the dots and arrows on the lane to adjust their shots and pick up spares.

Tactical Problems   Adjusting the starting spot and intermediate target

Lesson Focus   Shooting spares

Objectives   Adjust the starting spot or intermediate target to successfully shoot the 4-7, 4-8, and 7 pin spares.

GAME 1

Setup   4-7-8 pins

Goal   Knock down the 4-7-8 with one ball.

Conditions

- Three or four students play on lanes 30 to 40 feet (9 to 12 m) long that are marked with spots on the approach and arrows on the lane.
- Set up 4, 7, and 8 pins only.
- Score as though seven pins are knocked down with the first ball.
- One or two players set up pins while the others bowl.
- Allow time for students to bowl three or four frames.

Questions

Q: Point to the spot on which you started.

A: (Students point to spots, most of which are to the right of the center when facing the pins.)

Q: Why is right of center better than left of center?

A: It's a better angle of approach with less chance of the ball going into the gutter.

Q: If only the 4-7 pins were remaining, where would your starting spot and intermediate target be? Where would they be for the 4-8 pins? The 7 pin?

A: Same place.

PRACTICE TASK

Setup   Students take turns shooting at the 4-7 pin spare, four times each, and then at the 4-8 spare, and then at the 7 pin spare. Repeat the task, but alternate lanes as in league play so students can adjust to various lane conditions. Each bowler charts her starting spot and intermediate target, along with the pins remaining (reproducible 22.2).

Goal   Score a spare.

Cues

- Focus on your intermediate target.
- Use feedback to adjust your next shot.

GAME 2

Setup   Regulation bowling game

Goal No missed frames—make a spare or a strike on each frame.

Conditions

- Use league play.
- Students play 3v3, alternate lanes, display proper etiquette, and score on an official score sheet.
- The team with the highest total score wins.

Note Points for fair play can be awarded to teams whose members demonstrate proper etiquette at all times.

LESSON 12

Tactical Problems   Adjusting the starting spot and intermediate target

Lesson Focus   Shooting spares

Objective   Adjust the starting spot or intermediate target to successfully shoot the 5-8, 5-9, and 5 pin spares.

GAME 1

Setup   5-8-9 pins

Goal   Knock down the 5-8-9 with one ball.

Conditions

- Three or four students play on lanes 30 to 40 feet (9 to 12 m) long that are marked with spots on the approach and arrows on the lane.
- Set up 5, 8, and 9 pins only.
- Score as though seven pins were knocked down with the first ball.
- One or two players set up pins while the others bowl.
- Allow time for students to score three or four frames.

Questions

Q: Point to the spot on which you started.

A: (Students point to their individual starting spots.)

Q: How similar is this starting spot to the starting spot on your first ball?

A: Similar. The same.

Q: If only the 5-8 pins were remaining, where would your starting spot and intermediate target be? Where would they be for the 5-9 pins? The 5 pin?

A: Same place. Similar place. Not sure.

PRACTICE TASK

Setup   Students take turns shooting at the 5-8 pin spare, four times each, then at the 5-9 spare, and then at the 5 pin spare. Repeat the task, but alternate lanes as in league play so students can adjust to various lane conditions. Each bowler charts his starting spot and intermediate target, along with the pins remaining (reproducible 22.2).

Goal   Score a spare.

Cues

- Focus on your intermediate target.
- Use feedback to adjust your next shot.

GAME 2

Setup   Regulation bowling game

Goal   No missed frames—make a spare or a strike on each frame.

Conditions

- Use league play.
- Students play 3v3, alternate lanes, display proper etiquette, and score on an official score sheet.
- The team with the highest total score wins.

Note   Points for fair play can be awarded to teams whose members demonstrate proper etiquette at all times.

LESSON 13

Secondary Level III

Tactical Problems   Adjusting the starting spot and intermediate target

Lesson Focus   Shooting spares

Objective   Adjust the starting spot or intermediate target to successfully shoot 6-9, 6-10, and 10 pin spares.

GAME 1

Setup   6-9-10 pins

Goal   Knock down the 6-9-10 with one ball.

Conditions

- Three or four students play on lanes 30 to 40 feet (9 to 12 m) long that are marked with spots on the approach and arrows on the lane.
- Set up the 6, 9, and 10 pins only.
- Score as though seven pins were knocked down with the first ball.
- One or two players set up pins while the other players bowl.
- Allow time for students to score three or four frames.

Questions

Q: Point to the spot on which you started.

A: (Students point to spots, most of which are to the left of the center when facing the pins.)

Q: Why is left of center better than right of center?

A: It is a better angle of approach with less chance of the ball going into the gutter.

Q: If only the 6-9 pins were remaining, where would your starting spot and intermediate target be? Where would they be for the 6-10 pins? The 10 pin?

A: Same place.

PRACTICE TASK

Setup Students take turns shooting at the 6-9 pin spare, four times each, then the 6-10 spare, and then the 10 pin spare. Repeat the task, but alternate lanes as in league play so students can adjust to various lane conditions. Each bowler charts her starting spot and intermediate target, along with the pins remaining (reproducible 22.2).

Goal Score a spare.

Cues

- Focus on your intermediate target.
- Use feedback to adjust your next shot.

GAME 2

Setup Regulation bowling game

Goal No missed frames—make a spare or a strike on each frame.

Conditions

- Use league play.
- Students play 3v3, alternate lanes, display proper etiquette, and score on an official score sheet.
- The team with the highest total score wins.

Note Points for fair play can be awarded to teams whose members demonstrate proper etiquette at all times.

LESSON 14

Secondary Level III

Tactical Problems Adjusting the starting spot and intermediate target

Lesson Focus Shooting spares

Objective Adjust the starting spot or intermediate target to successfully shoot the 5-7 and 5-10 splits.

GAME 1

Setup 5-7 or 5-10 splits

Goal Knock down the split with one ball.

Conditions

- Three or four students play on lanes 30 to 40 feet (9 to 12 m) long that are marked with spots on the approach and arrows on the lane.
- Set up 5-7 pins on one lane and 5-10 pins on an adjacent lane.
- Bowlers alternate lanes.
- Score as though eight pins were knocked down with the first ball.
- One or two players set up pins while the others bowl.
- Allow time for students to score at least four frames.

Questions

Q: *Point to the spot on which you started when shooting for the 5-7 split.*

A: *(Students point to their individual starting spots.)*

Q: *How does this starting spot differ from your starting spot for the 5-10 split?*

A: *(Students may have different answers as to why certain starting points worked best.)*

Q: *Why is it important to have a specific starting spot for each split or spare?*

A: *It increases your chance of knocking down the split or spare.*

PRACTICE TASK

Setup   Students take turns shooting at a 5-7 pin split, four times each, and then at a 5-10 pin split. Repeat the task, but alternate lanes as in league play so students can adjust to various lane conditions. Each bowler charts his starting spot and intermediate target, along with the pins remaining (reproducible 22.2).

Goal   Knock down the 5-7 and 5-10 splits.

Cues

- Focus on your intermediate target.
- Use feedback to adjust your spot on the next shot.

GAME 2

Setup   Regulation bowling game

Goal   Do not miss any frames.

Conditions

- Use league play.
- Students play 3v3, alternate lanes, display proper etiquette, and score on an official score sheet.
- The team with the highest total score wins.

Note   Points for fair play can be awarded to teams whose members demonstrate proper etiquette at all times.

LESSON 15

Secondary Level III

Tactical Problem   Adjusting to lane conditions

Lesson Focus   Using spin and speed to adjust to lane conditions

Objective   Adjust ball spin and speed to align with lane conditions.

GAME 1

Setup   Regulation bowling game

Goal   Knock down all 10 pins on each roll.

Conditions

- Groups of three play on lanes 30 to 40 feet (9 to 12 m) long that are marked with spots on the approach and arrows on the lane.
- One or two players set pins while the others bowl.
- Each player is allowed one ball to knock down all 10 pins.
- Have students alternate lanes, and have one lane designated as the slow lane where bowlers must roll the ball slowly.
- The other lane is designated as the fast lane where bowlers must roll the ball quickly (but with control).
- One player records the number of pins knocked down on each trial.
- Each player charts the point at which the ball contacted the pins (reproducible 22.2).
- Each player bowls at least four frames before the class gathers for questions.

Questions

Q: Where did the ball contact the pins most often when you rolled it slowly?

A: To the left of the center (when facing the pins).

Q: Why would the ball be more likely to roll to the left of the center?

A: The slower the ball is rolling, the more likely it is to break or move with the lane conditions.

Q: Where did the ball contact the pins most often when you rolled it quickly?

A: To the right of the center (when facing the pins).

Q: Why would the ball be more likely to roll to the right of the center?

A: Because it is rolling fast, it is not as affected by lane conditions.

Q: Besides speed, what else can affect how the ball rolls?

A: Spin.

PRACTICE TASK

Setup Students take turns shooting at all 10 pins, twice in a row on one lane and then twice in a row on the other. Students try different speeds and spins and use the feedback from their charts (reproducible 22.2) to determine the most appropriate amounts of spin and speed.

Goals

- Determine the amount of ball speed and spin needed to consistently knock down all 10 pins.
- Determine how to adjust ball speed and spin to achieve the desired results (get strikes, get spares, and adjust to lane conditions).

Cues

- Control the speed of the ball.
- Use feedback to adjust your next shot.

GAME 2

Setup Regulation bowling game

Goal Do not miss any frames.

Conditions

- Use league play.
- Students play 3v3, alternate lanes, display proper etiquette, and score on an official score sheet.
- The team with the highest total score wins.
- League standings from the past five lessons can be used to set up tournament play (level IV).
- Individual standings can be used to calculate handicaps.

Note   Points for fair play can be awarded to teams whose members demonstrate proper etiquette at all times.

LEVEL IV

Lessons at level IV focus on integrating the Sport Education model (Siedentop 1994) and emphasize customary roles, rituals, and sporting behaviors common to bowling. Levels III and IV can be combined, but ought to be extended to last 18 to 20 days. At first, most teachers fear that students will get bored. However, with the careful integration of roles and responsibilities, bowling rituals, scoring, calculating averages and handicaps, league play, and tournament competition, students find multiple ways to engage and are often even motivated to participate in leagues outside of school.

We integrate the tactical approach and Sport Education models into all of our classes so that our physical education majors have firsthand experience with these approaches. For example, lesson 16 focuses on shadow bowling to ensure good preparation before actually bowling. Lesson 17 emphasizes appropriate sporting behavior and allows students to set up their own rules, which they are more likely to uphold than any you may impose. Some lessons may be less active, such as lesson 18, but integrate math skills. You may choose to do this lesson in class, assign it as homework, or work with classroom teachers to integrate it into their lessons.

Lesson 19 provides an example of how you can teach content within a tactical and Sport Education lesson. As in lessons in level III, a problem is posed in the first game, which is followed by questions to guide students to the solution, which is then followed by practice. Practice is followed by league or tournament play. The final lesson integrates bowling festivities, which are often left out of the traditional unit but are very much a part of the bowling league experience.

Proper bowling etiquette should be followed so that everyone in every lane can have a good time.

We offer numerous suggestions for including local bowling proprietors, parents, and administrators. Besides providing an authentic sport experience for the students, Sport Education allows you to promote your program beyond the gymnasium and throughout the community.

Tactical Problems

- Rolling the ball in the intended direction
- Adjusting for lane conditions

Lesson Focus   Shadow bowling

Objective   Use shadow bowling to determine a starting spot and intermediate target on alternate lanes.

GAME 1

Setup   Shadow bowling (no pins)

Goal   Locate and adjust starting spots and intermediate targets for the first ball.

Condition   Students play 3v3, alternate lanes, and bowl without pins.

Questions

Q: *What is the purpose of shadow bowling?*

A: *To warm up, locate and adjust starting spots and intermediate targets, and get used to lane conditions.*

Q: *How did you decide whose turn it was to shadow bowl?*

A: *Stood in line behind the approach, waited for an open lane, and bowled a couple of balls.*

Q: *If you need to throw more shadow balls than most players, what should you do?*

A: *Take more turns, but wait until the end when fewer players are shadow bowling.*

Extensions

- League meeting: Have students elect a secretary (or two) to assist with scheduling and with calculating averages, handicaps, and final standings.
- Team meeting: Have students elect a team captain. Using individual averages from league play, the team captain determines a team lineup and enters it on the score sheet. Besides team captain, roles can include a statistician (to calculate individual averages and handicaps) and a technical support person (to troubleshoot automated scoring machines or to set up a team website).
- Tournament play: For the first round in tournament play, have students play 3v3, alternate lanes, and use an official score sheet or technological device (e.g., various apps available on devices such as an iPod or iPad).

LESSON 17

Secondary Level IV

Tactical Problem   Adjusting for lane conditions

Lesson Focus   Appropriate sporting behavior

Objective   Demonstrate proper etiquette, decorum, and fair play before, during, and after league play.

GAME 1

Setup Shadow bowling (no pins)

Goal Locate and adjust starting spots and intermediate targets for the first ball.

Condition Students play 3v3, alternate lanes, and bowl without pins.

Extensions

- League meeting: Students determine the rules of etiquette necessary to allow all bowlers to participate in a fair and respectful environment. Each team should contribute one or two possible rules of etiquette. Limit the number of rules to five, and post them for all to see.
- Tournament play: In the second round of tournament play, students play 3v3, alternate lanes, and use official scoring. Teams following all rules of etiquette before, during, and after league play score 1 point for fair play.

Goal Always follow the rules of etiquette.

LESSON 18

Lesson Focus Calculating averages and handicaps

Objective Demonstrate how to calculate individual averages and handicaps and use handicaps to establish fair competition between teams.

GAME 1

Setup Regulation bowling game

Goal Bowl head-to-head against another bowler.

Condition Students select an opponent and bowl five frames of regulation play.

Questions

Q: How many of you were within 10 pins of your opponent's score? How many were more than 10 pins from your opponent's score?

A: (A few, or many.)

Q: When bowling against an opponent who has more (or less) experience, what can you do to set up a fair competition?

A: Spot the less-experienced bowler some pins. Use a handicap.

Q: What do you need to know to calculate a handicap?

A: Individual averages.

PRACTICE TASK

Setup Students work with team captains and a league secretary to calculate their averages and handicaps. Teams work together to calculate the team handicap and the handicap for the next tournament game. An average is the total score divided by the number of games bowled. Individual handicaps are calculated based on 80% to 100% of a 200-point scale, but 100% is used most often and is easiest to calculate (200 − individual average = individual handicap). Individual or team handicaps can be used in league or tournament play. The number of games needed to establish an average can be determined during a league meeting, with recommendations from you and the league secretary.

Goal Calculate individual averages and handicaps and team handicaps for league and tournament play.

Cue 200 − your average = your handicap

GAME 2

Setup In the third round of tournament, students play 3v3, alternate lanes, and use official score sheets.

Goal Calculate a new average and handicap after the tournament.

LESSON 19

Tactical Problem Rolling the ball in the intended direction

Lesson Focus Release point and angle

Objective Demonstrate a proper release point at the very bottom of the downswing (not beyond the toe) and a release angle that is low and extended out (rather than up).

GAME 1

Setup Regulation bowling game

Goal Achieve a smooth, consistent release.

Conditions

- Teams of three or four bowl five frames on their home lanes.
- Bowlers use stickers to mark where their balls land on the lane and score and chart the results.
- At the end of five frames, each player notes her pattern to check for consistency or lack of consistency.

Questions

Q: *Were you able to demonstrate a consistent release—that is, were you able to release the ball at just about the same place (or along the same line) on the lane every single time?*

A: *Sometimes, but not consistently.*

Q: *Why is it important to have a consistent release?*

A: *To control speed, keep the ball from bouncing, and increase overall control.*

PRACTICE TASK

Setup Use shadow bowling so students can focus on the release and not the pins. Emphasize the acceleration of the hand at the bottom of the downswing that should begin about 12 inches (30 cm) before the release. This acceleration requires precise timing, so encourage students to focus on the

Teaching Sport Concepts and Skills

rhythm of their swings. The hand motion is similar to that for accelerating a golf club through the ball. The release angle (or loft) should be outward, as a natural extension of the release point. After about 10 to 15 rolls per player on the home lane, have players alternate lanes and roll 10 to 15 more times. Set up pins on the last three or four rolls.

Goal   Accelerate through the bottom of the release and consistently land the ball on the same spot.

Cues

- Bend and send as low as possible.
- Keep your shoulders square.
- Do not tilt your shoulder beyond your knee (on the release).

GAME 2

Setup   In the fourth round of the tournament, students play 3v3, alternate lanes, and use an official score sheet.

Goals

- Achieve a consistent release point and angle.
- Get more strikes and have fewer open frames.

LESSON 20

Secondary Level IV

Lesson Focus   Bowling festivities—end-of-the-year league banquet

Objective   Organize and participate in a league banquet following league and tournament play.

GAME 1

Setup   10 pins

Goal   Determine league and tournament standings.

Conditions   Use a regulation game with 3v3, alternating lanes, and official scoring.

Note   This lesson could be a field trip to a local bowling establishment.

Extension: Bowling Banquet   Have students and parents arrange for refreshments at a bowling banquet (e.g., juice and cookies). Consider asking the principal or a member of the school board to hand out awards. Allow students to organize as much of the banquet as possible. Involve the proprietor of a local bowling establishment, members of local bowling associations, and parents or grandparents with league experience. Consider alternatives for awards, such as having the winning teams sign a bowling pin that is displayed in the school trophy case, or adding the winning team's name to a (donated) bowling trophy. Post team pictures on the school website or on the website of the physical education department.

SUMMARY

This chapter provides four levels of lessons. At the first level, we recommend using only three pins so students can establish consistent form and make essential preshot decisions. The recommended number of pins increases to six in level II. Using six pins keeps the context efficient while allowing students to focus on adjusting their starting spots and intermediate targets so they can gain sufficient control to consistently knock down spares. The emphasis on adjusting starting spots and intermediate targets to knock down spares continues in level III, with students shooting at all 10 pins. Level IV illustrates the integration of the Sport Education model with the tactical approach. For more ideas and examples of the Sport Education model, we recommend the book *A Complete Guide to Sport Education* (Siedentop, Hastie & van der Mars 2011).

Lessons at all levels also include a progression for score keeping that begins with calculating cumulative scores at level I and moves to adding spares and strikes at level II. Encourage students to share scoring responsibilities so everyone can learn how to score. Although bowling scores are automated, there are often errors and miscalculations that an educated bowler can catch. Calculating bowling scores, averages, and team and individual handicaps can be used to integrate physical education content into the classroom as well as mathematics content into physical education (Pritchard & McCollum 2008).).

We encourage establishing and maintaining an authentic context throughout all four levels. This includes etiquette, safety, and fair play before, during, and after bowling. Both the tactical approach and Sport Education models provide a framework for teaching appropriate sporting behavior. Etiquette, safety, and fair play must be addressed directly and include measures of accountability, such as points for fair play. Providing an authentic context is also important for fostering the transfer of bowling tactics, skills, and positive sporting behavior to public venues, where bowling can be played for a lifetime.

Final Thoughts

Here we share our collective thoughts about tactical games teaching and its curriculum potential. These thoughts accumulated during the writing of this book and our previous books and during the 25 years in which we individually and collaboratively applied our learning.

- *Collaboration makes life much easier.* In chapter 4, we suggest finding company when getting started with tactical games teaching. Collaboration is critical for sharing ideas, goals, materials, and frustrations. We learned the value of collaboration through sharing our work since 1992, and the ability to bounce ideas around has no doubt helped us develop our own understanding of tactical games. The international community of scholars interested in tactical games teaching has also recognized the importance of collaboration by hosting regular conferences on Teaching Games for Understanding. Conferences have been held in New Hampshire, USA (2001); Melbourne, Australia (2003); Hong Kong (2005); Vancouver, Canada (2008); and Loughborough, England (2012).

- *The name of this approach to teaching does not matter.* The original conception of tactical games teaching was developed by David Bunker and Rod Thorpe at Loughborough University in England. They called it Teaching Games for Understanding (TGfU) and presented it as a model for teaching decision making in secondary physical education. Since the early 1980s, the model has been viewed in various ways, and a number of names have emerged. We initially saw it as a tactical approach to games teaching, hence our use of the term *tactical games approach.* We later recognized the value of using a tactical games approach in elementary and secondary physical education, and hopefully developed the potential for doing so. We also saw the tactical approach as a way of organizing games content within the curriculum—we saw it as a curriculum model, and hence our use of the term *tactical games model.* Other names include *game sense* and *games-centered games.* Regardless of nomenclature, scholars and practitioners interested in authentic approaches to games teaching within physical education have collaborated to develop a model that places the learner in problem-solving situations in which decision making is of critical importance

and skill development occurs in context. Therefore, the name does not matter as much as the concept.

- *Using this approach isn't rocket science.* Some teachers and many preservice teachers like to over-complicate things! We have often witnessed our own preservice teachers develop complex game conditions and modifications, use numerous and sometimes unnecessary questions, and then wonder why their students switched off or did not get it. As a middle school student once said, "So, we play a game, figure out what we need to do, practice it, then play again to see if we can do it. Right?" Right!

- *Using this approach doesn't require a games expert.* One school of thought is that you have to be a games expert to experience success with tactical games teaching. This view is one reason tactical games approaches have been slow to take hold in elementary and secondary physical education. When told that expertise is needed, the nonexpert tends to avoid the challenge of tactical teaching and stick with traditional skill-based teaching as a safer option. Remember the principle of transfer, which we have argued applies to you as a teacher just as much as it applies to your students. Having expertise in a broad range of games would no doubt comfort you in taking a new approach to games teaching, but not having expertise should not discourage you. In saying this, we also recognize that good physical educators come from specific backgrounds such as aquatics, gymnastics, dance, and track and field. If your range of expertise is narrow and you do not have extensive games knowledge, be prepared to learn one game from each tactical category and apply the principles of instruction for that game across others within the category. Reread chapter 2 to reassure yourself of your ability to transfer understanding. In fact, one might argue that being an expert hurts you because you have developed strong beliefs about how a game should be taught. The key to tactical games teaching is to understand the model. Further, perhaps your comfort level is as much a result of what you value as what you know. If you value the game (and the problem-solving challenges it brings) as the essence of teaching, then tactical games teaching is more likely to make sense. However, if your focus remains on discrete skills, you will have more difficulty getting it.

- *All students can play games.* We modify games so that students believe that they can indeed play a game with some success. Beginning with the game counters the old argument that students must learn the skills before they can play the game. When we hear this argument, the proponent is inevitably referring to the full game. If we were to stick faithfully to the opinion that students must learn the skills before they can play the game, then some students would never play. Consider tennis and volleyball, perhaps the two most difficult games to learn in terms of their skill requirements. Unless the ball can be kept in play and sent in the necessary direction, a game cannot be played. It is no wonder that when novices play volleyball and tennis, points rarely last more than one or two hits. However, by appropriately modifying equipment, playing areas, and team sizes (in the case of volleyball), these games, and indeed all games, can be playable by students of all ability levels. Making the game playable is critical from a motivational standpoint because repeated failure only discourages students. Once the game is playable, skill development and refinement can continue.

- *It's not just about playing the game.* One of the greatest misconceptions about the tactical games model is that students "just play a game." It is not just "play," which would be spontaneous; rather, it is the game (and its required tactics and skills) that establishes the learning activities for each lesson or unit. The learning activities include games, questions, and practice tasks. All of these help students solve the various tactical problems of games and thus improve their decision-making skills. In sum, the initial modified game sets the problem, the skill focus provides solutions to the problem, and the closing game applies the solutions to their game context.

- **Competition *is not a bad word.*** When we teach games, competition becomes a natural part of the instructional context. Rather than avoid competition, we address issues that arise from heated competitions and student perceptions about sporting behavior acquired from popular media. Rather than waiting until tempers flare or trash talking begins, integrate content related to teamwork and appropriate social behavior before, during, and following competitive events. Address other social issues such as equity, the inclusion of all players, and the values of lifelong participation. Sport can build character, but only when we deliberately emphasize appropriate sporting behavior.

- *Students respond when they are empowered.* Tactical games teaching places students at the center of the learning environment by making them responsible for running games and asking them to find solutions to problems posed by game situations. These responsibilities empower them to guide their learning, and in our experience students respond well when we require input from them. Empowering students also involves relinquishing some control, which may feel uncomfortable. Again, we have found that our students are able to assume responsibilities that are presented to them in a structured fashion.

- *Teaching and coaching have much in common.* You may well be a skilled tactical games teacher but do not know it. This is particularly true if you coach. The game play emphasized in tactical games teaching lends itself to commonly used coaching strategies in which game play is frozen and situational responses are critiqued, reconstructed, and rehearsed to improve problem solving within the game. These behaviors make teaching and coaching interchangeable in games teaching. As a teacher in one of our early workshops said, "I do this all the time when I coach. I just never thought about doing it in a physical education class."

That you may unknowingly already be a skilled tactical games teacher is an encouraging note on which to close. Take what you already know, apply it as broadly as you can, and supplement it with available resources (including this book), and you will experience success in a motivational and engaging approach to the games curriculum. Good luck!

References and Resources

Almond, L. 1986. Reflecting on themes: A games classification. In *Rethinking games teaching,* eds. R. Thorpe, D. Bunker, and L. Almond, 71-72. Loughborough, England: University of Technology.

Armour, K.M., and M. Yelling. 2007. Effective professional development for physical education teachers: The role of informal, collaborative learning. *Journal of Teaching in Physical Education* 26: 177-200.

Australian Cricket Board. 2002. *Coaching youth cricket.* Champaign, IL: Human Kinetics.

Beard, C.H. 1993. Transfer of computer skills from introductory computer courses. *Journal of Research in Computing in Education* 25: 413-430.

Benson, N.J. 1970. Training and transfer-of-learning effects in disabled and normal readers: Evidence of specific deficits. *Journal of Experimental Child Psychology* 64: 343-366.

Berkowitz, R.J. 1996. A practitioner's journey from skill to tactics. *Journal of Physical Education, Recreation and Dance* 67 (4): 44-45.

Berman, R. 1994. Learners' transfer of writing skills between languages. *TESL Canada Journal* 12: 29-46.

Black, P., C. Harrison, C. Lee, B. Marshall, B, and D. Wiliam. 2004. Working inside the black box: Assessment for learning in the classroom. *Phi Delta Kappan* 86 (1): 9-21.

Blythe, T. 1997. *The teaching for understanding guide.* San Francisco, CA: Jossey-Bass.

Booth, K. 1983. An introduction to netball. *Bulletin of Physical Education* 19 (1): 27-31.

Bowling Index. 1995. *Instruction: Tips from Bob Strickland.* Retrieved January 19, 2005, from www.bowlingindex.com/instruction/instruction.htm.

Brooker, R., D. Kirk, S. Braikua, and A. Bransgrove. 2001. Implementing a game sense approach to teaching junior high basketball in a naturalistic setting. *European Physical Education Review* 6 (1): 7-26.

Bunker, D., and R. Thorpe. 1982. A model for the teaching of games in secondary schools. *Bulletin of Physical Education* 18 (1): 5-8.

Bunker, D., and R. Thorpe. 1986. Is there a need to reflect on our games teaching? In *Rethinking games teaching,* eds. R. Thorpe, D. Bunker, and L. Almond, 25-34. Loughborough, England: University of Technology.

Burrows, L. 1986. A teacher's reactions. In *Rethinking games teaching,* eds. R. Thorpe, D. Bunker, and L. Almond, 45-52. Loughborough, England: University of Technology.

Butler, J. 1993. Teacher change in sport education. *Dissertation Abstracts International,* 54 (02A).

Clement, J. 1993. Using bridging analogies and anchoring intuitions to deal with students' perceptions in physics. *Journal of Research in Science Teaching* 30: 1241-1257.

Cohen, E.G. 1994. Restructuring in the classroom: Conditions for productive small groups. *Review of Educational Research* 64: 1-35.

Cohen, S.A. 1987. Instructional alignment: Searching for the magic bullet. *Educational Researcher* 16(8): 16-20.

Collier, C. 2005. Integrating tactical games and sport education models. In *Teaching Games for Understanding: Theory, research and practice,* eds. L. Griffin and J. Butler. Champaign, IL: Human Kinetics.

Dan Ota, K., and J.N. Vickers. 1998. The effects of variable practice on the retention and transfer of two volleyball skills in male club-level athletes. *Journal of Sport and Exercise Psychology, NASPSA Abstracts* Suppl. no. 20: S121.

Den Duyn, N. 1997. *Game sense: Developing thinking players.* Belconnen, Australia: Australian Sports Commission.

Dodds, P., L.L. Griffin, and J.H. Placek. 2001. A selected review of the literature on development of learners' domain-specific knowledge. *Journal of Teaching in Physical Education* 20: 301-313.

Doolittle, S. 1983. Reflecting on an innovation. *Bulletin of Physical Education* 19(1): 36-38.

Doolittle, S., and K. Girard. 1991. A dynamic approach to teaching games in elementary PE. *Journal of Physical Education, Recreation and Dance* 62(4): 57-62.

Dyson, B. 2005. Integrating cooperative learning and tactical games models: Focusing on social interactions and decision-making. In *Teaching Games for Understanding: Theory, research and practice,* eds. L.L. Griffin and J.I. Butler. Champaign, IL: Human Kinetics.

Dyson, B., and M. O'Sullivan. 1998. Innovation in two alternative elementary school programs: Why it works. *Research Quarterly for Exercise and Sport* 69: 242-253.

Ellis, M. 1986. Making and shaping games. In *Rethinking games teaching,* eds. R. Thorpe, D. Bunker, and L. Almond, 61-65. Loughborough, England: University of Technology.

Fonske, H. 2007. *Teaching cues for sport skills for secondary school students,* 4th ed. San Francisco: Benjamin Cummings.

French, K.E., and S.L. McPherson. 2003. Development of expertise. In *Developmental sport and exercise psychology: A lifespan perspective,* eds. M. Weiss and L. Bunker, 403-424. Champaign, IL: Human Kinetics.

French, K.E., and J.R. Thomas. 1987. The relation of knowledge development to children's basketball performance. *Journal of Sport Psychology* 9: 15-32.French, K., P. Werner, J. Rink, K. Taylor, and K. Hussey. 1996. The effects of a 3-week unit of tactical, skill, or combined tactical and skill instruction on badminton performance of ninth-grade students. *Journal of Teaching in Physical Education* 15: 418-438.

Friedman, T. 2008. *Hot, flat, and crowded: Why we need a green revolution and how it can renew America.* New York: Farrar, Strauss and Giroux.

Fullan, M.G. 1991. *The new meaning of educational change,* 2nd ed. New York: Teachers College Press.

Fullan, M. 2001. *The new meaning of educational change,* 3rd ed. Columbia, NY: Teachers College Press.

Gentile, A. 1972. A working model of skill acquisition with application to teaching. *Quest,* 17, 3-23.

Graham, G., Holt/Hale, S., and Parker, M. 2013. *Children moving: A reflective approach to teaching physical education,* 9th ed. New York: Mcgraw-Hill.

Grehaigne, J-F, P. Godbout, and D. Bouthier. 1997. Performance in team sports. *Journal of Teaching in Physical Education* 16: 500-516.

Grehaigne, J-F, J-F Richard, and L.L. Griffin. 2005. *Teaching and learning team sports and games.* New York: Routledge Falmer.

Griffin, L. 1994. Designing drills to make practice more perfect. *Strategies* 8(3): 19-22.

Griffin, L. 1996. Improving games playing: Teaching net/wall games for understanding. *Journal of Physical Education, Recreation and Dance* 67(3): 34-37.

Griffin, L., P. Dodds, and I. Rovegno. 1996. Pedagogical content knowledge for teachers: Integrate everything you know to help students learn. *Journal of Physical Education, Recreation and Dance* 67(9): 58-61.

Griffin, L., J. Oslin, and S. Mitchell. 1995. Two instructional approaches to teaching net games. *Research Quarterly for Exercise and Sport.* Suppl. no. 66(1): 65-66.

Griffin, L., and J.H. Placek. 2001. The understanding and development of learners' domain-specific knowledge [Monograph]. *Journal of Teaching in Physical Education* 20: 299-419.

Griffin, L.L., P. Dodds, and A. James. 1999. *Game performance assessment in 5th/6th grade tactical badminton curriculum unit.* Paper presented at the annual meeting of the Association Internationale des Ecoles Superieures d'Education Physique, World Sport Science Congress, Besancon, France.

Griffin, L.L., S.A. Mitchell, and J.L. Oslin. 1997. *Teaching sport concepts and skills: A tactical games approach.* Champaign, IL: Human Kinetics.

Griffin, L.L., and J.L. Oslin, 1990. Got a minute: A quick and easy strategy for knowledge testing in physical education. *Strategies: A Journal for Physical and Sport Educators* 4(2): 6-7, 23.

Griffin, L.L., and D. Sheehy. 2004. Using a tactical games model to teach problem solving in physical education. In *Critical inquiry and problem solving in physical education: Working with students in schools,* eds. J. Wright, D. MacDonald, and L. Burrows. London: Routledge.

Grossman, P. 1990. *The making of a teacher: Teacher knowledge and teacher education.* New York: Teacher College Press, Teachers College, Columbia University.

Gubacs, K. 1999. Action research on a tactical approach to teaching a preservice tennis class. *Research Quarterly for Exercise and Sport* 70(1), Suppl., 82.

Gubacs, K. 2000. Action research on a tactical approach to teaching a preservice tennis class. *Dissertation Abstracts International, 61*(07), (UMI Number 9978503).

Gubacs, K., M.P. Carney, L.L. Griffin, and S. Supaporn, S. 1998. "Orderly chaos": Future teacher educators' learning experiences implementing a tactical approach to games teaching. *Research Quarterly for Exercise and Sport,* 69, Suppl., A-92.

Gubacs-Collins, K. 2007. Reflective pedagogy through action research: Implementing a tactical approach to teaching games in PETE. *Physical Education and Sport Pedagogy* 12(2): 105-126.

Hall, G., and S.M. Hord. 2001. *Implementing change: Patterns, principles, and potholes.* Needham Heights, MA: Allyn & Bacon.

Harvey, L., and J. Anderson. 1996. Transfer of declarative knowledge in complex information-processing domains. *Human-Computer Interaction* 11: 69-96.

Hellison, D. 1996. Teaching personal and social responsibility in physical education. In *Student learning in physical education: Applying research to enhance,* eds. S.J. Silverman and C.D. Ennis, 269-286. Champaign, IL: Human Kinetics.

Holt, N.L., W.B Strean, and E.G. Bengoechea. 2002. Expanding the teaching games for understanding model: New avenues for future research and practice. *Journal of Teaching in Physical Education* 21: 162-176.

Hopper, T.F. 2003. Four Rs for tactical awareness: Applying game performance assessment in net/wall games. *Teaching Elementary Physical Education, 14*(2), 16-21.

Hopper, T. 2003. Teaching Games for Understanding: The importance of student emphasis over content emphasis. *Journal of Physical Education, Recreation and Dance* 73(7): 44-48.

Hopple, C. 1995. *Teaching for outcomes in elementary physical education: A guide for curriculum and assessment.* Champaign, IL: Human Kinetics.

Howarth, K., and J. Walkuski. 2003. Teaching tactical concepts with preservice teachers. In *Teaching games for understanding in physical education and sport: An international perspective,* eds. J. Butler, L. Griffin, B, Lombardo and R. Nastasi. Oxon Hill, MD: AAHPERD.

James, A., L.L. Griffin, and T. France. 2000. Students', teachers', parents', and a principal's perceptions of assessment in elementary physical education. *Research Quarterly for Exercise and Sport,* Suppl. no. 71: 73.

Johnson, D.W., and R.T Johnson. 1989. *Cooperation and competition: Theory and research.* Edina, MN: Interaction Book.

Joyce, B., and B. Showers. 1995. *Student achievement through staff development.* White Plains, NY: Longman.

Kessel, J. 2008. *The uniqueness of volleyball.* From http://assets. usoc.org/assets/documents/attached_file/filename/16138/ The_Uniqueness_of_Volleyball_6.01.08.pdf.

Kirk, D. 2005. Future prospects for Teaching Games for Understanding. In *Teaching Games for Understanding: Theory, research and practice,* eds. L. Griffin and J. Butler. Champaign, IL: Human Kinetics.

Know the Game: Indoor Cricket. 1989. London: A and C Black Limited.

Lave, L., and E. Wenger. 1991. *Situated learning: Legitimate peripheral participation.* Cambridge, England: UL.

Light, R. 2003. Preservice teachers' responses to TGfU in an Australian University: "No room for heroes." In *Teaching games for understanding in physical education and sport: An international perspective,* eds. J. Butler, L. Griffin, B, Lombardo, and R. Nastasi. Oxon Hill, MD: AAHPERD.

Lortie, D.C. 1975. *Schoolteacher: A sociological study.* Chicago: University of Chicago Press.

Magill, R.A. 1993. *Motor learning: Concepts and applications.* Madison, WI: Brown and Benchmark.

Martin, R.J. 2004. *An investigation of tactical transfer in invasion games.* Poster presented at the annual convention of the American Alliance for Health, Physical Education, Recreation and Dance, New Orleans, LA.

McAloon, N.M. 1994. Connections (from the teacher's desk). *Journal of Reading* 37: 698-699.

McNeill, M.C., J.M. Fry, S.C. Wright, W.K.C. Tan, K.S.S. Tan, and S.G. Schempp. 2004. In the local context: Singaporean challenges to teaching games on practicum. *Sport, Education and Society* 9(1): 3-32.

McPherson, S.L. 1994. The development of sport expertise: Mapping the tactical domain. *Quest* 46: 223-240.

McPherson, S.L. 1995. *Expertise in women's collegiate tennis: Development of knowledge and skill.* Paper presented at the annual conference of the North American Society for the Psychology of Sport and Physical Activity, Monterey, CA.

Melograno, V. 1996. *Designing the physical education curriculum,* 3rd ed. Champaign, IL: Human Kinetics.

Metzler, M.W. 2011. *Instructional models for physical education, 3rd ed.* Boston: Allyn & Bacon.

Mitchell, S.A., L.L. Griffin, and J.L. Oslin. 1994. Tactical awareness as a developmentally appropriate focus for the teaching of games in elementary and secondary physical education. *The Physical Educator* 51(1): 21-28.

Mitchell, S.A., and J.L. Oslin. 1999a. *Assessment series K-12 physical education series: Assessment in games teaching.* Reston, VA: National Association for Sport and Physical Education.

Mitchell, S.A., and J.L. Oslin. 1999b. An investigation of tactical understanding in net games. *European Journal of Physical Education* 4: 162-172.

Mitchell, S.A., J.L. Oslin, and L. Griffin. 1995. The effects of two instructional approaches on game performance. *Pedagogy in Practice: Teaching and Coaching in Physical Education and Sport* 1: 36-48.

Mitchell, S.A., J.L. Oslin, and L.L. Griffin. 2003. *Sport foundations for elementary physical education: A tactical games approach.* Champaign, IL: Human Kinetics.

Mohnsen, B. 1997. *Teaching middle school physical education: A blueprint for developing an exemplary program.* Champaign, IL: Human Kinetics.

National Association for Sport and Physical Education. 2004. *Moving into the future: National standards for physical education.* Reston, VA: National Association for Sport and Physical Education.

Nevitt, M., I. Rovegno, and M. Babiarz. 2001. Fourth-grade children's knowledge of cutting, passing and tactics in invasion games after a 12-lesson unit of instruction. *Journal of Teaching in Physical Education* 20: 389-401.

Nisbett, R.E., and L. Ross. 1980. *Human inference: Strategies and shortcomings in social judgment.* Englewood Cliffs, NJ: Prentice Hall.

Oslin, J. 2005. The role of assessment in teaching games for understanding. In *Teaching Games for Understanding: Theory, research and practice,* eds. L. Griffin and J. Butler, 125-135. Champaign, IL: Human Kinetics.

Oslin, J., C. Collier, and S. Mitchell. 2001. Living the curriculum. *Journal of Physical Education, Recreation, and Dance* 7 (5): 47-51.

Oslin, J., and S. Mitchell. 2006. Game-centered approaches to teaching physical education. In *The handbook of physical education,* eds. D. Kirk, D. Macdonald, and M. O'Sullivan. Sage: London.

Oslin, J.L., S.A. Mitchell, and L.L. Griffin. 1998. The Game Performance Assessment Instrument (GPAI): Development and preliminary validation. *Journal of Teaching in Physical Education* 17: 231-243.Pajares, M.F. 1992. Teachers' beliefs and educational research: Cleaning up a messy construct. *Research of Educational Review* 62: 307-332.

Peterman, F.P. 1991. *An experienced teacher's emerging constructivist beliefs about teaching and learning.* Paper presented at the annual meeting of the American Educational Research Association, Chicago, IL.

Pigott, B. 1982. A psychological basis for new trends in games teaching. *Bulletin of Physical Education* 18(1): 17-22.

Pritchard, T., and McCollum, S. 2008. Bowling for a lifetime using sport education. *Journal of Physical Education, Recreation and Dance,* 79(3): 17-23.

RFU (2012). *Tag Rugby.* From www.rfu.com/TheGame/FormsOfRugby/Tag.

Rokeach, M. 1968. *Beliefs, attitudes, and values: A theory of organizational change.* San Francisco: Jossey-Bass.

Rovegno, I., and D. Bandhauer. 1997a. Norms of the school culture that facilitated teacher adoption and learning of a constructivist approach to physical education. *Journal of Teaching in Physical Education* 22: 473-511.

Rovegno, I., and D. Bandhauer. 1997b. Psychological dispositions that facilitated and sustained the development of knowledge of a constructivist approach to physical education. *Journal of Teaching in Physical Education* 16: 136-154.

Shulman, L. 1986. Those who understand: Knowledge growth in teaching. *Educational Researcher* 15(2): 4-14.

Siedentop, D., P. Hastie, and H. van der Mars. 2011. *Complete guide to Sport Education,* 2nd ed. Champaign, IL: Human Kinetics.

Siedentop, D., Herkowitz, J., and Rink, J. 1984. *Elementary physical education methods.* Englewood Cliffs, NJ: Prentice Hall.

Siedentop, D., and D. Tannehill. 2000. *Developing teaching skills in physical education,* 4th ed. Mountain View, CA: Mayfield.

Singer, R.N., C. DeFrancesco, and L.E. Randall. 1989. Effectiveness of a global learning strategy practiced in different contexts on primary and transfer self-paced motor tasks. *Journal of Sport and Exercise Psychology* 11: 290-303.

Slavin, R.E. 1996. Research on cooperative learning and achievement: What we know, what we need to know. *Contemporary Educational Psychology,* 21: 43-69.

Spackman, L. 1983. Invasion games: An instructional strategy. *British Journal of Physical Education* 14(4): 98-99.

Sparkes, A. 1990. *Curriculum change and physical education: Towards a micropolitical understanding.* Geelong, Australia: Deakin University.

Stallings, J.A. 1989. *School achievement effects and staff development: What are critical factors?* Paper presented at the annual meeting of the American Educational Research Association, San Francisco.

Stevens, P., and C. Collier. 2001. Shooting hoops: WallTar as an alternative. *Teaching Elementary Physical Education* 12(1): 17-19.

Sullivan, E. and Swabey, K. 2003. Comparing assessment of preservice teaching practices using traditional and TGFU instructional models: Data from Australia and the United States. In *Teaching games for understanding in physical education and sport: An international perspective,* eds. J. Butler, L. Griffin, B. Lombardo, and R. Nastasi. Oxon Hill, MD: AAHPERD.

Thorpe, R., D. Bunker, and L. Almond. 1986. A change in focus for the teaching of games. In *Sport pedagogy: The 1984 Olympic Scientific Congress proceedings,* vol. 6, eds. M. Piéron and G. Graham, 163-169. Champaign, IL: Human Kinetics.

Toh, K., and B. Woolnough. 1994. Science process skills: Are they generalisable? *Research in Science and Technological Education* 12: 31-42.

Tucker, G.R. 1996. Some thoughts concerning innovative language education programmes. *Journal of Multilingual and Multicultural Development* 17: 315-320.

Turner, A., and T. Martinek. 1992. A comparative analysis of two models for teaching games (technique approach and game-centered [tactical focus] approach). *International Journal of Physical Education* 29(4): 15-31.

Veal, M.L. 1993. The role of assessment and evaluation in secondary physical education: A pedagogical view. In *Critical crossroads: Middle and secondary school physical education,* ed. J.R. Rink, 93-99. Reston, VA: National Association for Sport and Physical Education.

Wandersee, J., J. Mintzes, and J. Novak. 1994. *Handbook of research on science teaching.* New York: Macmillan.

Werner, P., and L. Almond. 1990. Models of games education. *Journal of Physical Education, Recreation, and Dance* 61(4): 23-27.

Wrisberg, C.A., and Z. Liu. 1991. The effect of contextual variety on the practice, retention, and transfer of an applied motor skill. *Research Quarterly for Exercise and Sport* 62: 406-412.

Zessoules, T., and H. Gardner. 1991. Authentic assessment: Beyond the buzzword and into the classroom. In *Expanding student assessment,* ed. V. Perrone, 47-71. Alexandria, VA: Association for Supervision and Curriculum Development.

About the Authors

Steve Mitchell, PhD, is a professor of physical education teacher education at Kent State University. He received his undergraduate and master's degrees from Loughborough University, England, where the tactical approach was developed. He earned a PhD in teaching and curriculum at Syracuse University. An avid soccer player and licensed coach, he has employed a tactical approach in teaching and coaching at the elementary, middle school, high school, and college levels since 1982.

Mitchell is a member of the American Alliance for Health, Physical Education, Recreation and Dance (AAHPERD); the Ohio Association for Health, Physical Education, Recreation and Dance (OAHPERD); and the National Association for Sport and Physical Education (NASPE).

He resides in Kent, Ohio. In his free time he enjoys soccer, tennis, golf, swimming, kayaking, cycling, and skiing when his aching knees allow.

Judy Oslin, PhD, is professor emeritus at Kent State University. She received her undergraduate and master's degrees from Kent State and earned a PhD in sport pedagogy at Ohio State University. Oslin has more than 35 years of experience as a physical educator and teacher educator. She has used the tactical approach with elementary, middle school, high school, and university students.

Oslin has also presented numerous papers and workshops focusing on implementation of the tactical approach and the Game Performance Assessment Instrument at the international, national, regional, state, and local levels. She continues to work with teachers locally, nationally, and internationally to improve the quality of curriculum and assessment. Oslin is a member of numerous professional organizations, including AAHPERD, National Association for Physical Education in Higher Education (NAPEHE), the American Educational Research Association (AERA), and the National Association for Girls and Women in Sport (NAGWS).

Judy resides in Kent, Ohio, and enjoys traveling and participating in numerous outdoor activities.

Linda Griffin, PhD, is a professor and associate dean for academic affairs in the School of Education at the University of Massachusetts at Amherst. She earned her bachelor's degree from Black Hills State University, her master's degree from Ithaca College, and her PhD from Ohio State University. She has more than 35 years of experience as a physical educator and teacher educator. Her research and scholarly interest for over 20 years have focused on the teaching and learning of sport-related games through a games-centered approach grounded in constructivist learning. Throughout the United States and abroad, Linda has presented numerous papers and workshops focused on the tactical approach.

Griffin served on the planning committee for the first Teaching Games for Understanding Conference in New Hampshire in 2001. She is a member of AAHPERD, NASPE, NAGWS, and AERA. Griffin has also served as chair for the Curriculum and Instruction Academy, president of the Research Consortium, and a reviewer for various professional journals, including *Journal of Teaching in Physical Education* and *Research Quarterly*.

Linda stays active by biking, walking, kayaking, and practicing yoga. She enjoys the sound of the ocean and listening to books on long walks with her dogs, Finnigan and Devon. She lives in Holyoke, Massachusetts.

DVD-ROM
User Instructions

The PDFs on this DVD-ROM can be accessed using only a DVD-ROM drive in a computer (not a DVD player on a television). To access the PDF, follow these instructions:

Microsoft Windows

1. Place DVD in the DVD-ROM drive of your computer.
2. Double-click on the My Computer icon from your desktop.
3. Right-click on the DVD-ROM drive and select the Open option from the pop-up menu.
4. Double-click on the Documents and Resources folder.
5. Select the PDF file that you want to view or print.

Macintosh

1. Place DVD in the DVD-ROM drive of your computer.
2. Double-click the DVD icon on your desktop.
3. Double-click on the Documents and Resources folder.
4. Select the PDF file that you want to view or print.

Note: You must have Adobe Acrobat Reader to view the PDF files.